Savarkar

ADVANCE PRAISE FOR THE BOOK

'In the concluding volume of his path-breaking biography, Vikram Sampath shows us the world-shaping events culminating in the independence and partition of India through Savarkar's eyes. The perspective is both novel and sobering, and the picture he presents of Savarkar picking his way through the debris of history a vivid and compelling one'—**Faisal Devji**, professor of Indian history, University of Oxford

'The mere mention of Vinayak Damodar Savarkar raises blood pressures, even today. To be better informed about the man, his times and his legacy, there is only one biographer one can think of. That happens to be Vikram Sampath. The quality of writing and research in the first volume made every reader wait expectantly for the second. As careful and meticulous as in the first, Vikram doesn't disappoint with this concluding volume'—**Bibek Debroy**, eminent economist, scholar and translator

'Vikram Sampath's *Savarkar* is a major achievement. Rooted in wide-ranging research, but also very easy to read, it brings to life the world and the ideas of a revolutionary Hindu who did much to shape modern India'—**Francis Robinson**, professor of the history of South Asia, Royal Holloway, University of London

'Vikram Sampath has now completed his monumental biography of Vinayak Damodar Savarkar. His mastery over the sources, his painstaking effort to bring balance to the narrative and the extent of his coverage of the praise and the criticism of Savarkar by other people make this one of the best biographies of any of the political giants of the first generation of freedom fighters. Given that Savarkar has been excommunicated from India's history for his alleged involvement in the assassination of Mahatma Gandhi, I particularly commend his chapter on the Gandhi assassination story. Of the many accounts I have read over the years, this is the most thorough. Whatever your political views, read this book as a fine piece of historical writing'—**Meghnad Desai**, eminent author and columnist, professor emeritus at the London School of Economics

'Savarkar is an extremely controversial figure whose legacy is considered troubled by many but inspiring by many others. This makes him an appropriate subject for deeper study. Vikram Sampath has already written one highly readable book on him and this is his second volume. By examining Savarkar's own writings and actions as well as those of his contemporaries and by admirable archival research, Sampath succeeds in presenting Savarkar in all his contradictions. Sympathetic but not apologetic, this is a work of considerable scholarship, something difficult to achieve in India as far as writing about public personalities is concerned. My endorsement of Sampath's fine book is as a student of Indian political history and not as someone still in active politics who believes that Savarkar is a profoundly divisive figure and the very opposite of what Mahatma Gandhi lived for—and ultimately killed for as well.' **Jairam Ramesh**, former union minister and author

'The two-volume series titled *Savarkar: Echoes from a Forgotten Past* on the life of Veer Savarkar is a valuable addition by Vikram Sampath to existing literature. It documents the contributions of one of the greatest heroes of India's struggle for Independence. Savarkar's life is an epitome of the extent to which a man's will can determine his life. Despite enduring unconscionable sufferings at the hands of the colonial masters his zeal to fight for the independence of his motherland did not get hindered. His contributions in shaping the India of today are cross-sectoral. From social issues to cultural, Savarkar's imprints are omni-present. I congratulate Vikram on having documented the various aspects of Savarkar's life as a political activist, thinker, and an orator while also touching on the lesser-known aspects of being a poet, writer, and playwright. I am sanguine that this work will go a long way in introducing Indians to the much-forgotten hero of India's struggle for Independence'—**Ram Madhav**, former national general secretary of BJP, member of National Executive Committee, RSS

'This is a fitting sequel to what I consider the best biography ever written by an Indian writer. This volume by Vikram brings alive the complex story of Savarkar after Kala Pani—his transformation from fiery revolutionary to social worker, his role in creating a modern political consciousness among Hindus—and provides the background to debates that continue in 21st century India'—**Sanjeev Sanyal**, writer and economist

'Vikram Sampath's two-volume series, *Savarkar,* is not limited to providing mere biographical details of the life of Savarkar but offers historical context through providing detailed descriptions of historical events of that era. Thus, *Savarkar* makes dual contribution to Indian history. The author staggers Savarkar's biography with details of sinister British rule in India, which incidentally gave rise to powerful nationalist leaders of multiple stripes during the early phase of the Indian independence movement.

'*Savarkar* fulfills the long overdue need for an authentic historical biography of the brave son of India. The book examines the life of Savarkar closely, while also providing lesser-known details, which help dispel the many mythical accounts surrounding Savarkar's life. As a corollary, this series also supplements our existing patchwork of knowledge on the history of Indian independence.

'The series is a historiographical work, while simultaneously serving as a biographical book on one of the most misunderstood nationalists of India. This series brings forward for the first time an authoritative examination of documents (letters, speeches, official communication, newspaper reports) as well as numerous never-before-studied documents.

'The first volume begins rightfully with the birth of Savarkar along with the events of his childhood and young-adult life, which are captured in the first few chapters interspersed with thought-provoking details of the political circumstances of India. Through the depiction of successive struggles of young Savarkar in plague-affected western India between 1899–1900, the author realistically demonstrates the struggles of average Indians under British rule. With Savarkar's move to Nasik from 1900 onwards, his nationalist activities gained momentum as he founded Mitramela (also its affiliate Rashtrabhaktasamaja). Savarkar's activities and entanglements with national movement here increasingly pitted him against the British authorities, and at times brought him in opposition to established national leaders, including Tilak. Crucial is Savarkar's decision to champion the celebration of Shivaji Utsav as national mela during this early phase. Savarkar's brilliant speeches inspired numerous young nationalist leaders, while the British government used these speeches to prosecute him on charges of sedition many years later. Of utmost interest are the chapters discussing the life of Savarkar in London (including his short stint in Paris) followed by his imprisonment in Andamans and later in India.

'Dr. Sampath's organization and rich prose brings history to life with amazing clarity.

It makes the most valuable and original contribution to historical scholarship on Indian independence movement. *Savarkar* makes important "modifications" to the hitherto established views on the independence movement giving a fresh and critical analysis of the events.

'Sampath's study infuses India's independence movement with the necessary complexity, which remained simplistic for far too long due to missing information. Dr. Sampath offers a consciously alternative narrative of India's independence that is representative of her numerous trials and tribulations. *Savarkar* captures the formative period of India's independence movement, which was the true crucible of India. Emerging under alien rule, India endured the most arduous journey, which was only partially recollected in the simplistic narrative preserved in India's history books. *Savarkar* successfully fills this lacuna by bringing forward the dimensions that missed critical evaluation. The book offers an alternative narrative to the prevailing colonial and western recollections of the Indian Independence movement, thus providing a new lens to examine Indian history.

'*Savarkar* is a necessary reading for every student of Indian history. I also strongly suggest this book for anyone interested in learning about India'—**Lavanya Vemsani**, professor, Shawnee State University; president, Ohio Academy of History; editor-in-chief, *International Journal of Indic Religions*

'Vikram Sampath's volume 2 on the life of Veer Savarkar is a meticulously researched work, which is exhaustive in chronicling his life experiences, and is a fitting tribute to celebrate the role he played in India's independence movement. This work also provides an outstanding context for Indian politics during 1924 when he was released from prison to 1964 when he passed away. The assassination of Mahatma Gandhi in 1948 and the subsequent accusations on Savarkar are examined through an objective lens and respect for the period's context. Savarkar was a great patriot and one of the first leaders of our freedom movement—this is even acknowledged by Gandhi. He is yet to get his due recognition for his service to a nation still recovering from its colonial PTSD. Hopefully, readers will be better equipped to judge him on the facts presented in this volume and give Savarkar his due recognition for his great service to India'—**T. V. Mohandas Pai**, chairman, Aarin Capital

Savarkar

A CONTESTED LEGACY

1924-1966

VIKRAM SAMPATH

PENGUIN
VIKING
An imprint of Penguin Random House

VIKING

USA | Canada | UK | Ireland | Australia
New Zealand | India | South Africa | China | Singapore

Viking is part of the Penguin Random House group of companies
whose addresses can be found at global.penguinrandomhouse.com

Published by Penguin Random House India Pvt. Ltd
4th Floor, Capital Tower 1, MG Road,
Gurugram 122 002, Haryana, India

First published in Viking by Penguin Random House India 2021

Copyright © Vikram Sampath 2021

13

The views and opinions expressed in this book are the author's own and the
facts are as reported by him which have been verified to the extent possible,
and the publishers are not in any way liable for the same.

ISBN 9780670090310

Typeset in Adobe Caslon Pro by Manipal Technologies Limited, Manipal
Printed at Thomson Press India Ltd, New Delhi

www.penguin.co.in

Dedicated to my beloved Amma, my mother, who, though not around in flesh and blood, continues to be my perennial guiding spirit in everything that I do.

Contents

Acknowledgements

This biographical series has been the result of several years of painstaking research, wading through an ocean of extant documents. Several people assisted in the course of this rewarding journey and to all of them I express my sincere thanks.

I owe my heartfelt gratitude to Ranjit Vikram Savarkar, chairman of the Swatantryaveer Savarkar Rashtriya Smarak in Mumbai. As the grandnephew of Vinayak Damodar Savarkar, he has a legacy to carry forward and he, the Smarak and its affable members have been doing just that, with great aplomb. Savarkar has been a great sounding board on this project and a ready reckoner, each time I was stuck with a paucity of research material. Notably, not once did he insist on the narrative that the books need to take or object to the many critical references to Savarkar that I have made in the volumes. His colleague at the Smarak, Manjari Marathe, too has been a great source of support all through the project and I owe her my thanks. Savarkar's assiduous and sincere team of silent workers, in particular Dhananjay Balkrishna Shinde, deserve my utmost gratitude for making documents and photographs available to me at short notice.

I am deeply honoured and obliged to the Nehru Memorial Museum and Library (NMML), New Delhi, for offering me a prestigious senior research fellowship for the years 2018–20, to facilitate this research. Shakti Sinha, former director of the NMML, has been an inspiring presence in the course of this work. My special thanks to Narendra Shukla—head, research and publications division, NMML—for his immense support.

The Indic Academy and Hari Kiran Vadlamani have been pioneering a renaissance and resurgence of a new cultural and historical narrative of India. I am extremely thankful to them for reposing faith in me and funding my research in the United Kingdom.

I am extremely grateful to Subodh Naik in Mumbai, a passionate fan of Savarkar whose zeal that this story deserved to be told and told interestingly, propelled me through several phases of self-doubt through both the volumes. I am equally grateful to another passionate researcher and author on Savarkar in Pune, Akshay Jog, who selflessly shared several documents and photographs from his collection for ready reference. The passion with which gentlemen like them have kept the spirit of Savarkar alive, despite all the calumny, is truly heartwarming.

I am also grateful to several others who stepped in at the right time to assist me in this journey: my friends Akil Bakhshi, Pratibha Chopra and Kanad Mandke for their critical review and invaluable feedback on several chapters of the book; to Shefali Vaidya for assisting me in translating some Marathi works; Samir Inamdar (son of lawyer P.L. Inamdar in the Gandhi Murder Trial case) for sharing valuable documents from his father's collection; Abhijit M. Patwardhan, associate professor in the USA, for sharing several valuable nuggets, Rohit Sharma for helping in translation and sources and Lord Meghnad Desai for assiduously going through all the chapters and sending back his feedback at lightning speed, faster than my PhD supervisor ever did! I am grateful to all the individuals who shared their angst-ridden stories on the 1948 anti-Brahmin genocide in Maharashtra, responding to my social media query on the subject. The outpouring seemed like a catharsis for many of them and left me deeply touched. In particular, I wish to place on record my thanks to Gopal Waman Kulkarni, aged eighty-nine, who was kind enough to give me a detailed interview on the subject, and Vivek and Bindu for facilitating this.

Several institutions where I researched for the two volumes have been kind and forthcoming with their support. My sincere thanks to them all (in no particular order) and their staff: The Nehru Memorial Museum and Library (NMML), New Delhi; the Swatantryaveer Savarkar Rashtriya Smarak, Mumbai; National Archives of India, New Delhi; Maharashtra State Archives, Mumbai; the Deputy Inspector General's Office, Mumbai; British Library, London; Bombay High Court; National Archives of the United Kingdom, Kew; Bow Street Court Records, London; the Cellular Jail, Port Blair; the Kesari Wada–Tilak Trust, Pune; and the Savarkar Memorial, Nashik.

My sincere thanks to the eminent professors, authors and scholars who consented to review the work prior to its publication: Prof. Francis Robinson, Prof. Faisal Devji, Prof. Lavanya Vemsani, Lord Meghnad Desai, Bibek Debroy, Ram Madhav, Jairam Ramesh, Sanjeev Sanyal and T.V. Mohandas Pai.

During the early phase of this sojourn, my mother Nagamani Sampath was the one I often consulted on structuring the work. Being daunted by the gigantic nature of the subject, I had confided in her my diffidence in carrying this forward and on many occasions wanted to drop the project altogether given its complexity. 'While climbing Mount Everest, do not look or think about the peak. Take small, baby steps and soon you will see yourself at the top'—these wise words from her have been my guiding talisman. She was to be my 'research assistant' in this project, but destiny sadly seemed to have had other plans and I lost her midway. As I struggled to cope with this loss, if there is someone I owe my total gratitude and love, it is my father Sampath Srinivasan who lovingly tended me back to action, as also my aunt Roopa Madhusudan for her support.

I am very thankful to my publishers Penguin Random House India and Meru Gokhale for reposing faith in me and this work. I owe my sincere thanks my friend and editor Premanka Goswami for diligently editing this work and planning the entire production schedule, as also to the entire team—Preeti Chaturvedi, Shantanu Ray Chaudhuri, Shiny Das, Sameer Mahale and Vijesh Kumar among several others.

Most importantly, I am grateful to the Divine, without whose grace, not a single word could have been written.

Prologue

Since the time the first volume *Savarkar: Echoes from a Forgotten Past*, was released in August 2019 the amount of love and affection that I have received from readers, within and outside India, has been most heartwarming. Being accosted for 'selfies' or being recognized and appreciated as the biographer of Savarkar in public places by complete strangers was deeply humbling and made all the efforts seem so worthwhile. My lectures on him in various cities drew large crowds; the book went into multiple translations and reprints in no time and my publishers were happy! But all this went on to show the genuine hunger that people had in them to know more about this hotly contested character of the past and something that they had been denied in all these decades after independence. Hence, despite attempts made by some bookstores to not even stock the book, given they did not agree with the ideology of the protagonist, or some leading media houses to block out any reviews or mentions of the book (so much for their self-alleged 'liberalism'!), it managed to reach far and wide, through online channels, social media and sheer word of mouth. I have been constantly badgered with questions about when the second volume would be out. The Covid-19 pandemic and the lockdown in 2020 slowed down everyone's lives and so did the pace of my research work and field trips, with travel being impaired. My sincere apologies to all the readers who have had to wait so patiently for so long for this volume to be out and I do hope they feel that the wait was worth the while after reading this book.

This volume carries forward the story of Savarkar from the time he was released conditionally from jail in 1924 and captures the tumultuous decades of his life thereafter—the wide-ranging social reforms that he undertook in Ratnagiri under house arrest; his entry into active politics as the President of the All-India Hindu Mahasabha in 1937; the stormy years that led to freedom and Partition of India; the assassination of Gandhi and Savarkar's implication in it; his eventual acquittal and release; the final years of his life culminating in his sacrificing his own life in 1966.

The picture that emerges of the man through the perusal of original statements, archival documents and extant papers in several languages is markedly different from what we are normally led to believe of him in popular discourse. The clear stances that he took on the total eradication of the caste system, unification of Hindu society and putting the theories of human equality and justice into practice in the social laboratory of Ratnagiri—most often earning the ire of the orthodoxy, runs contrary to the belief that proponents of Hindutva have always been perpetuators of upper caste hegemony. After his final release in 1937—27 years after being first arrested in London in 1910, the Congress was waiting to take him under its wings. Had he consented, Savarkar might well have managed to ascend to positions of prominence within that party or been in government since the time provincial ministries got sworn in from 1937. But he chose to lead a hitherto decrepit party like the Hindu Mahasabha that was more like a broad social coalition with several leaders having dual membership with the larger Congress umbrella, and give it a definitive programme and plan of action. He firmly believed that the Hindu community needed a strong political voice and that the Congress, having gone way too far in its agenda of Muslim appeasement, had grievously wronged the Hindus. The Mahasabha came into a competitive contention with both the Congress and the Muslim League in India's electoral politics in no time. It slowly also began to be invited to the high table of negotiations by the viceroy, where hitherto it was only the Congress and the Muslim League that were called upon as being true representative voices of the people of India.

The virulence of what could be perceived as his anti-Muslim rhetoric during his years as the head of the Mahasabha and thereafter would need to be seen in the context of the times where the vivisection of the country on communal lines was being vociferously demanded and pushed through by the leaders of that community. However, the promised land of 'Hindu Rashtra' that was conceptualized by Savarkar and the 'Constitution of Free Hindusthan' that the Mahasabha came up with in 1945 envisioned a truly secular India where no individual was to be discriminated on the basis of religion, caste, gender and community. Nowhere in these speeches or documents are there threats or allusions to second-class citizenship to any community. What is an unambiguous ask of every citizen is unalloyed

allegiance, sans any extraterritorial loyalties, towards the Indian nation
state, to be eligible for any privileges and rights of citizenship.

Yet, Savarkar perhaps failed as a leader in these difficult times that the
country was going through. He failed in his attempts to create a coalition
of like-minded parties who did not see eye to eye either with the Congress
or the Muslim League. But more tragically, he failed in creating consensus
even within his own party. Factional feuds and individual–centric coteries
within the Mahasabha spoilt whatever chances that the party which had
just been galvanized into electoral success could hope for. Policy flip-flops
and an inability to take decisions at crucial times, such as the call for Direct
Action that could pressurize the British to commit to their promise of
freedom, demoralized the rank and file of his party and several ardent
followers. His party came a cropper in the 1946 elections and was soon to
disintegrate into political irrelevance.

The biggest challenge that Savarkar perhaps faced in his life was his
implication in the murder of his lifelong political and ideological opponent,
Gandhi, in 1948. The implication had been based on a police approver's
confessional statements and as the prosecution was to discover in the
course of the year-long trial, the 'evidence' did not quite add up. Savarkar
was the only accused to be honourably acquitted. Despite a legal clearance,
the moral albatross hung on him and the dark shadow of the assassination
continues to cloud his legacy till date. The Jeevan Lal Kapur Commission
that reopened the debate around the murder, after Savarkar's passing away
in 1966, did more harm to his legacy posthumously.

Hence, even more than five decades after his death, Savarkar intrudes
contemporary political debates like a few characters of our recent past have.
Conferment of the country's highest civilian honour, the Bharat Ratna, still
becomes the topic of intense contention, necessitating its inclusion even in
the election manifestos of political parties. From being called a cowardly
stooge who wrote groveling apologies, a casteist and Islamophobic bigot
who allegedly pioneered the two-nation theory, a British-collaborator who
drew pension from the government to personal slurs of a megalomaniac
who penned his own biography in a pseudonym and someone who justified
rapes—the basket of toxic allegations is mind bogglingly wide-ranging.
The demonization is so absolutist in nature that there hardly seems to be
any trace of positive virtue that his opponents can find in him.

These two volumes however are in no way an apology for Savarkar.
They do not take on themselves the lofty goal of correcting historical

wrongs done to a national figure. If these do happen, they would be purely coincidental and not intended to be so. Stripping off any personal biases, the records must be allowed to speak for themselves. This, to me is more a historian's burden and a duty—to illuminate the extant records and on the basis of that let the discerning reader make up her own mind. While all the above-stated allegations have been dealt with in this two-volume biography, the intent is not for me to become Savarkar's mouthpiece or his lawyer, as I am sure he deserves better. As a historian committed to my profession of an unending quest for the truth, bringing to light the evidences and documents in a conscientious manner is what I have honestly tried to attempt. The jury is of course out there to decide if I have succeeded in what truly seemed like a herculean task.

What is noteworthy is that unlike in the past decades, there is at least space for a debate and discussion around Savarkar to happen in our public realm now. The *persona-non-grata* that he had become and the heavy price that anyone invoking his name with any modicum of positivity had to bear, are luckily not as pronounced. The idea of these two volumes is not to create an army of Savarkar fans who have an answer to every allegation hurled against him by any loony or vested quarter. I myself disagree vastly with several of his stances and I am deeply critical of his actions at various stages of his life, as seen from the happy comfort of a retrospective review. One may hate or love him as much as one might want. But then to blackout even a discussion and debate around him, based on facts and documents, rather than rhetoric and politics (as has been the case till now) is deeply prejudicial to the tenets of liberalism and democracy, where every opposing view needs to find a platform. In his own life, Savarkar welcomed those who were opposed to his ideas and even kept a record of critical assessments of him by the press or his contemporaries. It is in that very spirit of true liberalism that these two volumes have been approached by me and I hope it is the same with the readers as well, even as I heave a huge sigh of relief and satisfaction at being able to finally 'exorcise' the ghost of a man who has consumed my thoughts and work for almost five years now!

Bangalore, March 2021.   **VIKRAM SAMPATH**

1

Rising from the Ashes

Yerawada Jail, Poona, 1924

Close to fourteen years had elapsed since the time Vinayak (*hereinafter referred to by his surname, 'Savarkar'*) was shut behind bars in the Bow Street prison of London in March 1910. Facing multiple trials, being shifted across continents, and suffering the most inhuman tortures in the Cellular Jail for over a decade, prison life had almost become a part of Savarkar's existence. In the Royal Amnesty of 1920, a petition was signed by close to 75,000 citizens urging the release of political prisoners lodged in various prisons and many of them had been released. However, the Savarkar brothers had remained confined at Cellular Jail. In 1921, Savarkar was shifted to the district jail in Ratnagiri while his elder brother Babarao was moved to the Bijapur prison. While Babarao was released in September 1922 due to seriously failing health, Savarkar was shifted to Poona's Yerawada Jail in 1923.

On the morning of 6 January 1924, Savarkar was summoned to the office of the Superintendent of Poona's Yerawada Jail, where he had been lodged for a year now. When told that he was to be released, Savarkar could barely trust what he heard. He had received several such false alarms of his imminent release in Port Blair too. Was this yet another cruel joke that destiny was playing on him, he wondered. It was only when he saw the letter of Alexander Montgomerie, Secretary to the Home Department in Bombay, authorizing his release that reality finally hit him.

Just two days before, on 4 January 1924, his brother Narayanrao had received an official letter from Montgomerie that he could come and take his sibling home. But given the short notice, the family could not reach on time to receive Savarkar while he was being released. The government did not want to publicize the release or give the Savarkar brothers time since they feared that it could lead to social disturbances.[1] Montgomerie noted in his letter: 'In exercise of the power conferred by Section 401 of the Code of Criminal Procedure, 1898, the Governor-in-Council hereby remits conditionally the unexpired portion of the sentences of transportation for life passed upon Vinayak Damodar Savarkar.'[2]

Savarkar was being released conditionally. For a five-year term, it was stipulated that:

1) The said Vinayak Damodar Savarkar will reside within the territories administered by the Governor of Bombay in Council and within the Ratnagiri District within the said territories, and will not go beyond the limits of that district without the permission of Government or in case of urgency, of the District Magistrate.

2) He will not engage publicly or privately in any manner of political activities without the consent of Government for a period of five years, such restriction being renewable at the discretion of Government at the expiry of the said term.[3]

Savarkar clearly understood the repercussions of his failure to adhere to the above conditions of his release. As he noted: 'Should I fail to fulfill those conditions or any portion of them . . . I may be arrested by any police officer without warrant, and remanded to undergo the unexpired portion of my original sentences.'[4] If he committed offences that would warrant his remand, he would have to serve yet another term of imprisonment for at least twenty-five years!

As part of the deal, Savarkar signed a declaration that went completely contrary to his conviction. Yet, he signed it because he believed he was of more use to the country being outside rather than inside the jail. This declaration was released to the press to discredit him. This stated:[5]

I hereby acknowledge that I had a fair trial and just sentence, I heartily abhor methods of violence resorted to in days gone by, and I feel myself duty bound to uphold Law and the constitution to the best of my powers and am willing to make the Reform[6] a success in so far as I may be allowed to do so in future.

Regarding the way this declaration was signed by him, Savarkar writes in his memoirs, *My Transportation for Life*:

In a moment the Superintendent took out a sheet of paper and wrote
on it the conditions of acceptance, which I had been proposing all these
years, and along with it he handed over to me a written statement that
he had received from the Government. I read them both. Referring to
my letter in the 'Echo from the Andamans' written in 1920 [see pp. 88–89
of that book], I told him that I was willing to make a statement on
that line, and that the statement from Government had to be modified
accordingly. I was told by the Superintendent to draft such a statement.
He warned me not to introduce any radical changes in it, but just a few as
would make the course smooth for my release. He expressed a wish that
on no account should I let this rare opportunity slip from my hands. I
drew up my statement. I had added some sentences to clarify the original
statement. The Superintendent, having found it too lengthy, abbreviated it.
The words that I had introduced in my statement and the meaning
thereof I have given in the book 'Echo from the Andamans' at pages 88
to 93. The Superintendent assured me that they would be interpreted
exactly in the sense I had used them. So I agreed to the omission of a few
sentences I had inserted in my statement. The statement was dispatched
to the proper authorities and I returned to my room in that prison.[7]

The extract of the letter that Savarkar refers to here in his book *Echo
from the Andamans*, written to his younger brother Narayanrao on 6 July
1920, shows Savarkar touching upon his own resolve to work through
constitutional means and also about the demand by the government to
make political prisoners claim that they were given a fair trial before they
were released:

We believe in an universal state embracing all mankind and wherein all
men and women would be citizens working for and enjoying equally the
fruits of this earth and this sun, this land and this light, which constitute
the real Motherland and the Fatherland of man. All other divisions
and distinctions are artificial though indispensable . . . With this end in
view I am willing to work now. And therefore I rejoiced to hear that the
Government have changed their angle of vision and meant to make it
possible for India to advance constitutionally on the path to Freedom and
strength and fullness of life. I am sure that many a revolutionist would
like me cry halt under such circumstances and try to meet England under
an honourable truce, even in a halfway house as the reformed Council

Halls promised to be, and work there before a further march on to progress be sounded . . . We were revolutionists under necessity and not by choice. We felt that the best interests of India as well as of England demanded that her ideals be progressively and peacefully realized by mutual help and co-operation. And if that be possible even now I shall take the first opportunity to resort to peaceful means and rush in the first constitutional breach effected by revolution or otherwise, however narrow it be and try to widen it so as to enable the forces of evolution to flow in an uninterrupted procession . . . Such were my views when I was working in the revolutionary camp. And such are my views after 12 long years of being pent up within the four walls of a solitary cell . . . Speaking relatively to barbarian times it is true that I had a fair trial and a just sentence and the Government is at liberty to derive whatever satisfaction they can from the compliment that they give a fairer trial and a juster sentence to their captives than the cannibals used to do. But it should not be forgotten that if in olden days the rulers flayed their rebels alive then the rebels too when they got the upper hand flayed alive the rulers as well. And if the British people treated me or other rebels more justly i.e. less barbarously then they may rest assured that they too would be as leniently treated by the Indian rebels if ever the tables are turned?[8]

However, quite conscious of the coup that they effected through such a declaration from him, Montgomerie wrote in a celebratory tone to the Home Department of the Government of India on 15 January 1924 that 'any tendency to make political use' of his release due to the stringent conditions were totally blunted 'by his full acknowledgement of the justice of trial and sentence'. Montgomerie submitted in a matter-of-fact manner that 'this letter has aroused some anger in extremist circles and has been described by some papers as a "shocking admission"'.[9] There seemed to be a sense of quiet triumph that they had finally managed to pin down their most notorious enemy and humiliated him in the eyes of his comrades.

In an attempt to warn people and make them keep Savarkar at a safe distance from themselves, the *Times of India* carried a curious piece on 7 January 1924 that said: 'At Ratnagiri, Savarkar will have a predecessor of a very different stamp . . . King Thibaw.'[10] The unnecessary reference here was to Thibaw Min, the last king of the Konbaung dynasty of Burma who was deported to Ratnagiri after the defeat of the Burmese forces in the Third Anglo-Burmese War of 1885. A recluse after his defeat, Thibaw died a sad and dejected man in December 1916. Invoking his name in the context of Savarkar's release as his 'predecessor' was an overt allusion on how those vanquished by the British would be condemned to die in exile and isolation.

~

Even as the news of Savarkar's release spread in the jail, the other political prisoners exulted and congratulated him. He was feted for suffering agonies like Lord Rama who spent fourteen years in the forest. To this, Savarkar replied: 'Even though we are celebrating, there is immense sadness in my heart. This fact must enter our minds firmly that Lord Rama surely did suffer his life in the jungles for long; but in my case when "that" will be achieved, only then my *vanvaas* (exile in the forest) would end in the real sense. If God is sufficiently kind, I am sure we would achieve that too!'[11] The reference here was to the complete liberation of India. Savarkar spoke in riddles and unfinished sentences, as he knew that every word that he spoke or wrote was under close scrutiny by the British. They just needed an excuse to charge him guilty of another offence and put him behind bars.

Such was Savarkar's pitiable condition at the time of his release that he did not even have civilian clothes to change into while getting out of the prison. A sympathetic jail employee, Mhatre, was moved by his condition and offered his used clothes to Savarkar. They were ill-fitting but that was all the luxury that a 'criminal' who had waged war against the state and suffered incarceration for fourteen years could afford.

The large iron gates of the prison creaked open. Savarkar struggled to keep his eyes open and catch the bright sunlight—he had not been used to it for so long. Only his friend Dr R.M. Bhat was waiting for him outside the prison to receive him. It was an emotional reunion.

They proceeded to Bhat's house where, thanks to the efforts of one Shankarrao Deo (popularly referred to as the Lokamanya Tilak of Khandesh) who had got handbills printed announcing Savarkar's release, nearly 200 people had gathered to welcome their hero.

The same noon, the family left for Bombay and reached Narayanrao's house in Girgaon. A celebratory feast was prepared by Savarkar's wife Yamunabai and Narayanrao's wife Shanta, which included Savarkar's favourite sweet dish *gavachi kheer* or broken-wheat porridge. It had been ages since he had eaten something tasty and edible. Overwhelmed by emotion, Savarkar gifted his wife and Shanta three silver coins—his prized earnings at the Cellular Jail.

The following day, Savarkar was to proceed to Ratnagiri by boat. Since they missed the morning boat, they took the one at night and reached Ratnagiri in the early hours of the morning of 8 January. Narayanrao had sent a telegram to his friend and editor of Ratnagiri's *Balwant* newspaper, Gajananrao Patwardhan, about his brother's arrival. Patwardhan had a huge music band organized to welcome Savarkar to Ratnagiri. People thronged to catch a glimpse of the man whose heroic tales preceded him. Patwardhan offered his house, known as '*Nau Patwardhanaanche ghar*' or the house of the nine Patwardhans, for Savarkar to stay at. Savarkar stayed here for a while and then moved to the house of Balasaheb Kher. Most part of his stay in Ratnagiri was at the house of Uddhav Vaidya.[12]

The same day, Sadashiv Rajaram Ranade from the neighbouring village of Makhajan came to meet Savarkar. He recollected his impressions about him in the spring 1925 edition of the journal *Mauj* thus:

> He was of short stature, but well-maintained and of fair complexion. He had an immaculate set of teeth and his eyes glittered while he spoke. His manner of speaking was affectionate and captivating. He enquired such minute and seemingly innocuous details about everyone he met, which made us wonder if this was the great national hero and patriot who had such attention for small detail. Most people who heard him speak would end up getting mesmerized and become his followers.[13]

On their conviction, the ancestral property of the Savarkars—Babarao and Vinayak—was acquired by the government in 1907. The property of Savarkar's father-in-law, Bhausaheb Chiplunkar, too was confiscated in 1911. The same year the Bombay University had withdrawn Savarkar's BA degree. The Gray's Inn in London had not called him to the bar despite his completion of his law degree. So technically, Savarkar had just a matriculation certificate despite all his qualifications. Ratnagiri being a small town, far away from the industrial towns of Maharashtra, made it next to impossible to find suitable job opportunities. All his books were banned and therefore, the royalty from these titles too was not accrued. Babarao's health had been ruinously affected due to the travails at Cellular Jail and he frequently had terrible bouts of migraine. In such a scenario, Narayanrao was the only breadwinner of the family with his small medical dispensary that helped him earn a meagre monthly income. His wife, his two brothers and sister-in-law depended on this for their livelihood. Having been held in the bombing case in Ahmedabad, Narayanrao too was under constant police surveillance. He was arrested in the Lord Minto bombing case but later released for lack of evidence. Thereafter he had been sentenced to six months' imprisonment in the Nasik Conspiracy case. Patients coming from his dispensary would randomly be questioned by the lurking policemen and hence, to avoid this discomfort and embarrassment, many people avoided going to him. The financial crisis that the Savarkar family faced was acute and for a while it seemed to them that prison life was perhaps better, where they did not have to worry about their meal, however bad it might have been.

It was a stigma and also a danger to even bear the surname Savarkar, as that automatically aroused government suspicions. This is substantiated by several anecdotes. A writer, playwright and novelist, P.B. Bhave, who later became a leader of the Hindu Mahasabha, notes in his autobiography that one of his relatives, Godubai, had been widowed, but she managed to graduate from the Karve Institute. Bhave's maternal grandfather, Haribhau, advised her that it would be far prudent to keep her maiden surname of Tamhankar and not retain the surname of her husband, which was Savarkar. Being called 'Godubai Savarkar' would severely jeopardize her chances of securing a teacher's job in any government school and unnecessary questions would have to be faced, though their family had no connection with Savarkar's.[14]

Years after India's independence, Shreeram Bhikaji Velankar, an eminent official of the Indian Postal Service, was waiting for his flight in the New Delhi airport when a gentleman approached him and enquired if he was Mr Velankar. A flummoxed Velankar replied in the affirmative. The other gentleman told him that despite Velankar having topped the Indian Civil Service, he had been allotted the postal cadre and not the top administrative cadre. The reason was that as a child Velankar used to visit Savarkar's evening storytelling sessions for children. When this fact was revealed during police background checks, it was enough to make the government suspicious of his motives and hence he was given a lower cadre. The man revealing this to Velankar was his chief examiner, who also happened to be the principal at Fergusson College, Poona, who had rusticated Savarkar for participation in the bonfire of 1905—Sir Raghunath Purushottam Paranjpe or Wrangler Paranjpe.[15]

With absolutely no source of income and the immense social stigma, the Savarkars were in as bad a condition as they were when they left Bhagur for Nasik after the death of their father Damodar. The question of the financial crisis of the Savarkars echoed in the Bombay Legislative Council too in February 1924 with members such as R.G. Pradhan, W.S. Mukadam and S.S. Dev questioning the government if there were any rehabilitation plans in place for them.[16] The reply was in the negative.

It was then left to the editor of the *Kesari*, Narasimha Chintaman Kelkar, to announce a 'Savarkar Brothers Purse Fund' on 22 January 1924, with a committee overlooking the contributions that people could make for the cause of the Savarkars. Interestingly, in an article dated 24 April 1924, the moderate newspaper *Indu Prakash*, started by Justice Mahadev Govind Ranade, strongly condemned the move. It held Savarkar's revolutionary path to be completely wrong. Alongside, it said that the conditions he had accepted to effect his release made him doubly guilty and undeserving of any sympathy. It accused him of surrender and begging for mercy and held that 'if donations started coming in to such people, then virtues like courage and patriotism seem to be unnecessary in today's India'.[17]

On 10 May 1924, a public event was organized at Chiplun where Savarkar was felicitated and offered Rs 101 as a token of appreciation for his revolutionary efforts. In his acceptance speech, among other things, Savarkar mentioned that he wished more brave hearts fought like him so that his role was automatically forgotten by people.[18] The police, who had kept a close watch on his public utterances and activities, immediately brought this to the attention of Montgomerie. They opined that this was an open call to violence and inciting more people to take up the cause that he did, of revolution. It hence breached the conditions of his release and that he needed to be castigated. It was thus an extremely difficult tightrope walk for Savarkar. Every word he wrote or spoke in public were subject to the strictest strictures and surveillance.

Montgomerie however ruled that, 'We can hardly say he [Savarkar] has engaged in political activity. We ought to give him a fair chance . . . [and avoid] the harassment of being watched or reported on. We shall hear soon enough, if he does anything that might be filed.'[19]

~

Around this time, Ratnagiri was afflicted with the plague epidemic. Savarkar sent his wife Yamunabai and Babarao to leave for Nasik till the scourge of plague subsided. For his own movement out of Ratnagiri, on 27 May 1924, he sent a letter to the Government of Bombay seeking their permission. He mentioned that though he had inoculated himself, it was always safer to stay away from areas that were in the grip of the epidemic. Normally, political detainees would correspond with the local district administration for such matters. But in Savarkar's case, all communication had to be sent to the government in Bombay. They in turn would seek several fact checks from the local administration and only then a decision would be communicated. It was only after the local administration confirmed on 9 June that Savarkar was indeed staying in a plague-infected area that Montgomerie passed an order on 10 June that permission might be granted to Savarkar to leave for Nasik, but only for a period of three months. This was communicated to Savarkar on 14 June 1924 and he finally proceeded to Nasik on 1 July.[20] Sadashiv Ranade of Makhajan accompanied him.

On the way, Savarkar visited Kolhapur. From there he travelled by train and was welcomed at Miraj, Satara, Poona and Kalyan before alighting at Deolali station. Nearly 400 to 500 people had gathered at the station to welcome him. Several youths climbed onto treetops to catch a glimpse of the brave heart from their region who had weathered the storm of the Cellular Jail and returned alive. A stream of memories flooded Savarkar's mind. With these ghosts of the past haunting him, Savarkar became very emotional while getting down from the train. Several prominent people received him at Deolali, but a grand reception awaited the popular son of the region in the town of Nasik. He had left the town in fetters decades ago and was now entering the town as a hero, in a mile-long procession from the town gate. Crowds thronged everywhere to catch a glimpse; women and children showered him with flower petals as he drove by.

When he rose to speak at Nasik in a public reception ceremony at the end of the procession, Savarkar was choked with emotion and could barely say anything for a few minutes. A powerful and fiery orator like him fell short of words. However, composing himself, he told the large gathering that a wounded soldier stood before them all. He could recognize a few people in the audience and said his life was an open book and all his past activities were known to everyone in the crowd. Whether they judged them as good or bad was their discretion. He confessed that while in Andaman he had lost hope of seeing his hometown again. But with the grace of the Almighty, destiny had taken a turn for the better. Yet he could not speak his mind out freely to all of them as he was under severe strictures.

Though many areas of work were shut for him, he said that there were 'still few fields open where I can work unhampered, such as organizing the Hindu society, writing of scientific and literary works and so on. But even if I cannot work in these fields too, I will be ever ready to massage the feet of the youth who are exhausted in the service of the motherland.'[21]

The *Bombay Chronicle* reported this reception accorded to Savarkar in Nasik:

Barrister Savarkar arrived at Nasik yesterday. The grandest reception Nasik ever gave was accorded to him. The streets could hardly contain the crowds that poured in to see their long lost citizen. The procession extending over a mile was lined by rows of people of both the sexes. Ladies showered flowers on the returning patriot, almost at every step.[22]

He then went to the house of his parents-in-law where his mother-in-law welcomed him warmly in a traditional *arati*.

To visit different parts of the Nasik district, Savarkar required to take the government's permission, which he duly received on 11 July 1924 from the district collector of Nasik.[23]

In Savarkar's honour, a play titled *Rajsanyas*, written by a doyen of Marathi literature, Ram Ganesh Gadkari (also known as the *Bhasha Prabhu* of the Marathi language), was staged on 18 July by a local theatre group called Govindagraj Natak Mandal. The venue was the same Vijayanand Theatre where Anant Laxman Kanhere had assassinated the district collector of Nasik, A.M.T. Jackson, fourteen years ago and for which the Savarkars were caught and tried. The play was about Shivaji's son Sambhaji Maharaj, who had been captured by Aurangzeb and executed when he refused to convert to Islam. During the interval, Vishwanathrao Kelkar, Tilak's son-in-law, requested Savarkar to come on stage, garlanded him and asked him to say a few words. Savarkar once again recalled that he had never dreamt of being able to see a play in the theatre while he was undergoing the worst of tortures in Port Blair. He commended the theatre group and remarked that historical plays were the need of the hour as they helped instill a sense of pride and awareness among the audience. He also paid his tribute to Sambhaji who chose to sacrifice his life over converting to another faith and said this was the true hallmark of a brave martyr.

In an interview given during this time to a Nasik newspaper, *Swatantrya* (different from the one from Nagpur), edited by Janardhan Balakrishna Marathe,

Savarkar outlined the philosophy and path of work that he would chalk out for himself. He candidly said that working for the eradication of untouchability was topmost on his agenda. He supported movements of so-called untouchables to enter temples or use public utilities such as wells and ponds. Savarkar admitted that there was bound to be resistance to any change and reformers must brace themselves for all kinds of social boycotts, insults and even violence that will be heaped over them by the orthodox. According to Savarkar, satyagraha was the most effective weapon to solve issues amongst ourselves. *Shuddhi* or reconversion to the Hindu faith of those who had been forcibly or through allurements drawn away was to be another of his work areas. He acknowledged the laudable work done by Swami Shraddhanand of the Arya Samaj in this matter. In the context of the communal riots across the country, Savarkar stressed on the need for Hindu unity and volunteer camps.[24]

Notably, at a Shivaji Jayanti function in Nasik in 1924, Veer Wamanrao Joshi, the famous Marathi journalist and playwright, gave Savarkar the honorific of '*Swatantrya Veer*' or 'The Valorous Soldier of Freedom'. Another renowned Marathi poet Vaishampayan also often referred to Savarkar by this title. This prefix was to remain with him all his life, as he was popularly called 'Swatantrya Veer' Savarkar.

Following permission from the government on 11 July 1924, he visited his birthplace Bhagur and then Yeola and Trimbak. At Yeola, on 29 July, Savarkar gave a speech on the upliftment of untouchables. By coming forward to embrace them, the other castes were doing the untouchables no favour, he contended. We are instead obliging ourselves. He reeled out statistics that the Hindu population in Asia was about 60 crore before the advent of the First World War. This had fallen to less than half and stood at 22 crore. Of these nearly 7 crore belonged to castes considered untouchables. If they get frustrated, and naturally so, and leave the Hindu fold, it would shrink the community further, he warned. The only way to strengthen and consolidate Hindu society was to break the shackles that prevented it from unifying.[25]

At Bhagur the villagers welcomed him with great pomp and enthusiasm. It was a nostalgic and emotional moment for Savarkar to visit the temple of Khandoba that now housed his family goddess, the Ashtabhuja Bhawani, and participating in public dinners organized in his honour in his hometown. Addressing a gathering at Bhagur on 14 August 1924, Savarkar brought the issue of caste differences that plagued Hindu society. He said:

Howsoever we may fight with each other, our religion and our God are one. Today is the full moon and the festival of *raksha bandhan*. The purpose behind this festival is that people should come together. Untouchability is an insult to humanity but it is practiced by many castes. In Maharashtra, Mahars do not touch Mangs, while Mangs consider Dombs as untouchables. We must forget all these differences and remember that finally we are all Hindus. That is the only common denominator.[26]

He ended his speech to a thunderous applause by saying, 'When I die, I want Hindus from all caste—a Mahar, a Maratha, a Brahmin and a Mang—to shoulder my dead body.'[27] He then bought *chivda* or beaten rice worth five rupees and shared it amongst all present. Leading by example, he invited a so-called untouchable, Kashinath Bhikaji Jadhav Ozarkar, and tied the sacred thread of *raksha bandhan* on his wrist and hugged him. This greatly inspired everyone in the audience and eventually all the residents of Bhagur tied raksha bandhans on one another's irrespective of their castes.

Savarkar spoke at several public occasions and during the Krishna Janmashtami and Ganeshotsav festivals. Everywhere the common theme was an emphasis on Hindu unity, an abolition of caste and untouchability and the need for shuddhi or reconverting those who had been coerced or lured into leaving the Hindu fold. While addressing a women's gathering, he emphasized on the need to make women 'physically strong, mentally alert and politically aware'.

On the occasion of the birth anniversary of Tilak on 23 July, one of Savarkar's poems, 'Saptarshi', which he had penned while in prison, was published by one P.V. Nagpurkar. It had 257 stanzas and is full of philosophical ruminations on life and its meaning. Gazing at the stars at night, Savarkar often penned these poems from his cell in Port Blair. Many verses of the poem were inscribed by him on the cell walls with his nails when he was denied pen and paper. He had committed these to memory, and later put them all down. Another book, *Echo from Andamans*, a collection of the letters that he wrote to Narayanrao from the Cellular Jail, was also published by Vishwanathrao Kelkar of Nagpur.

At another public speech in Nasik on 6 September 1924, Savarkar addressed a group of untouchables at the Ram Mandir that was meant exclusively for the so-called untouchables:

I do not call you as 'untouchable' but call you by your castes such as Mahar, Mang, Dhor, etc. because we are all equals. Just now, one Mahar said to me, 'Oh! I am not a Bhangi!' What he meant was that he was superior to a Bhangi. When I visited Bhagur, I attended a function of Mahars. I drank the milk given to me by a Mahar. But when I asked him to give a cup of milk to a Bhangi who was present, he was hesitant. And thus we all, not just the people of high castes, feel that some others are inferior to us. We must reject that notion.[28]

In all his writings, Savarkar revealed his contention and strong belief that while the upper castes were certainly guilty of exploiting those below them in the caste pyramid, and worse, treating a few as untouchables, the process of discrimination ran all the way down the hierarchy. Even among the so-called lower castes and untouchable communities, there were 'high' and 'low' sub-castes, and intermingling, inter-dining or contact with each other was sorely frowned upon. Hence Savarkar's prescription was not to merely target the upper castes but remove this abhorrent practice from the entire Hindu society, top to bottom.

Despite all the opposition to the fund that had been proposed to support Savarkar financially, a sum of Rs 12,757 was collected from the people of Maharashtra and Rs 210 from abroad—all within a span of four-and-a-half months.[29] This gave a much-needed means of sustenance for the beleaguered Savarkar family. The purse was presented to him in a public function in Nasik on 28 August 1924. The event was to be held at the Brahmanand Theatre, but at the last minute the owner of the theatre buckled under government pressure and refused to let the venue for this purpose. So it was hastily shifted to the Kalaram Mandir in the town. Balakrishna Shivram Moonje (1872–48), a staunch Tilakite and a Hindu Mahasabha leader, was present at the event presided over by N.C. Kelkar, who praised Savarkar's bravery and sacrifices for the cause of the motherland. 'Savarkar's patriotism is not merely emotional,' he said, 'it is translated into action. This purse is being presented to him as a protest against the barriers erected around him by the government.'[30] The Shankaracharya, Dr Kurtkoti, the religious head of the Karwir Peeth, a dissident Maharashtra branch of the Sringeri Mutt, sent his blessings and a shawl to Savarkar on this occasion. A silver casket containing Rs 11,989 in cash and a copy of Tilak's *Gita Rahasya* was presented to him. In his acceptance speech Savarkar said: 'How could I ever imagine that fetters would one day become flowers! The youth should not merely sing my praises, but they should try to exceed me in valour. I am accepting this purse not as a reward for the earlier service rendered without your consent, but as an advance gift by way of encouragement of further national service.'[31]

The British government meanwhile had kept a close track of all of Savarkar's activities during this time. The collector of Nasik sent in a weekly report on 28 July 1924 to the Bombay government about Savarkar's activities. The report mentioned his visit to Yeola, a town that had emerged as the hotbed for anti-British activities, along with K.B. Mahabal. It detailed the enthusiasm with which Savarkar was received in all such public meetings. It also highlighted that despite Savarkar sticking to social issues, the people attending such meetings knew that he had been a hot-headed revolutionary. It also spoke about a Marathi play *Swarajya Toran* that Savarkar watched in Nasik, whose narrative advocated ideas of an independent flag and violence for political ends. These were alarming to say the least, the report opined.[32]

~

Meanwhile, Savarkar's supporters in the Legislative Council continued to make a passionate plea for the restoration of his complete liberty. They drafted a resolution that read as follows: 'This House recommends to the Government that the conditions on Mr. V.D. Savarkar at the time of his release be withdrawn and he be restored to his liberty.'[33] Moving the resolution on 31 July 1924, Dr M.B. Velkar brought attention to the fact that Savarkar had supported 'Responsive Cooperation' with the government in the wake of the 1919 Reforms. After a lot of debate in the House where members A.N. Surve, H.B. Shivadasani, Khurshed Framji Nariman and others participated, the motion was put to vote, but was defeated by 37–51.[34]

The government continued to keep a close watch on Savarkar's movements in Nasik district. On 22 August 1924, he received a letter from Montgomerie that according to the enquiries he had made of the collector of Ratnagiri, the plague seemed to be subsiding and hence Savarkar must strictly adhere to the three-month deadline of 'the original date of return to Ratnagiri, namely 14 September 1924'.[35] But since in reality the scare of plague continued he was allowed to stay on in Nasik till the end of October 1924.[36]

During this stay in Nasik, Savarkar also met his old comrade from the London days, Pandurang Mahadev Bapat or 'Senapati' Bapat, on 16 October 1924.[37] Bapat had been arrested a year ago for spearheading the Mulshi Satyagraha in April 1921 protesting the construction of a hydroelectric project that was a joint collaboration of the Tatas and the British government, as it involved a coerced usurpation of arable lands of the farmers. Mahatma Gandhi, who had hitherto supported the cause, dissolved the Mulshi Satyagraha Guidance Committee, stating that the leader (Bapat) was a former revolutionary who did not believe in the tenets of non-violence and hence there was no reason why he needed to support the movement.[38] This could have been the main topic of discussion between the two friends when they met at Nasik. Shortly afterwards, on 12 November 1924, Bapat launched his own style of satyagraha that blended both Gandhian and violent means, a call to action with arms. Bapat and his associates attacked a train that carried workers of the Mulshi Dam project at Paund near Poona.[39] After the attack, in a Gandhian manner, Bapat surrendered to the police. The British intelligence that had kept a track of Savarkar's activities pounced to correlate Bapat's actions to his meeting with his former comrade in Nasik

~

On his way back to Ratnagiri in November 1924, Savarkar stopped over at Bombay. In a public reception in Dadar where the local Congress committee too participated, Savarkar said, 'Muslims participate in the Khilafat movement and Ulema conferences, even while remaining in the Congress; Hindus don't blame them. Similarly, Hindus belonging to the Congress have a right to participate in Hindu unification movements.'[40] On 15 November 1924. Dr M.B. Velkar organized a get-together at his home in Savarkar's honour. In his short speech he said, 'When I think that people have forgotten gallant men like Tanhaji, I feel embarrassed in accepting honours for my insignificant valour.'[41] He further added: 'Only the people who agree with my opinions have gathered here today. But I will be equally pleased to meet people who do not agree with me. It is essential to know the opinions of others who are both for and against one's own opinions.'[42] Savarkar kept an open mind about anyone who held a dissenting viewpoint. It is said that he regularly read criticism against him written in various newspapers, from 1924 till the end in 1966.[43]

He in fact systematically preserved such paper cuttings with his annotated comments.[44]

Two days later, on 17 November 1924, speaking to the students of the National Medical College, Savarkar told them that progress in the world was due to men of genius who had made discoveries and accomplished great deeds. This was true of all fields—political, social, scientific or economic. Unless great men were born in India, it would be tough for the country to re-emerge from its current degenerate condition. He motivated the students to aim for excellence and not settle for mediocrity. He told them that they were at that stage in their lives when doing daring acts comes naturally to a person and hence they should become physically fit and also strive to achieve something extraordinary. No one knows when they would be called upon to serve the motherland and fight for it as a soldier and hence preparedness on that front was necessary. He advised the management to organize physical fitness, fighting with sticks and military drills. He reiterated to the young crowd that all over the world it was men of genius who had made discoveries and made their countries proud, and unless India too produced such great men, it would be tough for her to come out of her present situation.

Reporting his speech at the college, the *Bombay Chronicle* dated 19 November 1924 wrote: 'The speaker would go to the length of addressing the young men to be rash, to strive to achieve something extraordinary, to outgrow the narrow limits of their nature. It was the men of extraordinary daring and rashness of character, who had contributed to the sum total of world's progress, whether political, social, literary or scientific.'[45]

Just this little excerpt was enough to cause a flutter in government circles. Wilson, the police commissioner of Bombay, sent a secret note to the Home Department along with the newspaper cutting that covered the event, recommending that the district magistrate of Ratnagiri probe the matter and seek an explanation from Savarkar over the text of his lecture:

> We see Savarkar here in his old familiar surroundings of 1907, ploughing the same furrow and sowing rather adroitly the seeds of his pernicious doctrines. It is up to him to play the game and not to allow himself to be exploited or tempted into laying round the terms of his bond . . . After the almost open incitement to violence, he passes on to his usual social reform propaganda. If accused of making a political speech, he would, no doubt explain that he was merely urging the youth of the country to be

self-sacrificing and rash in the cause of social reform. He has violated the condition of his release.[46]

Montgomerie then opined:

Mr Wilson may be told that in the opinion of the Government, Savarkar actually has not broken the conditions of his release, though he is getting very near to the margin and must, therefore, be carefully reported. Beyond calling India a fallen and downtrodden country, I doubt, if there is a phrase, which in itself is objectionable. That Savarkar intends to and did convey animosity to the Government, there is not the slightest doubt. But it would be exceedingly difficult to prove that in any one sentence, he had broken the conditions of his release. The incident only proves, he accepts the letter for his own safety, but never respects the spirit [of conditions of release].[47]

This was the recurrent feature of much of Savarkar's life in captivity in Ratnagiri where every sentence and word that he uttered were dissected and analyzed by several government departments keen to put the onus on him and rescind his release. The distrust with which the British government viewed him becomes amply clear in several of these official secret reports.

~

While in Bombay, Gandhi's close associate, Maulana Shaukat Ali of the Khilafat fame, called on him. The meeting was reported in detail in special issues of *Lokamanya* and the *Mahratta* dated 25 February 1925. The animated discussion that the duo had presents a fascinating picture of the mood of the nation and its religious leadership at that time. Hence it is reproduced here exactly as it transpired:[48]

Shaukat Ali: I hope you received the message that I sent across to you earlier?

Savarkar: Yes, indeed. And for the cause of Hindu–Muslim unity, I have set aside the issue that you consider contentious—that of Hindu sangathan [unity].

SA: Oh that's wonderful news! We have striven so hard to attain Hindu–Muslim unity. In the wake of that, this sangathan campaign unnecessarily vitiates the atmosphere. The Muslim community automatically asks leaders like me that if the Hindus are going to unify, so are we. Hence for the sake of swaraj and for the cause of our helpless nation, it is best if all Hindus count themselves only as Indians and forget these religious differences. It always pained me that a patriot like you who has suffered so much for the cause of the nation's freedom is unnecessarily getting embroiled in all these communal issues. Now that you say you have eschewed it, it is a big relief for me!

S: What you say is absolutely true, Maulana Sahab. However, I have not publicized my announcement to abandon the sangathan movement only in anticipation of a single commitment from you.

SA: And what is that?

S: I wish to know from you when you plan to abandon the Khilafat movement and All-Ulema movement? Once I know that, I will immediately give up my movement too.

SA (*angrily*): How is that possible? Be practical and think coolly. A foreign force has occupied us and is hell-bent on ruining both our communities. In such a scenario, instead of uniting, if you organize these sangathan movements, how can we face the external challenge? And do please remember that all through history, you Hindus have always been defeated by Muslim forces. So let us not create false equivalences here. Joining hands with the Muslims is the only way out for Hindus if they wish freedom.

S: This conversation is going nowhere. I am not permitted to dabble in politics. Hence I will not get into political discourses. Just suffice it to say that even before you and people like you began public careers, several of my comrades and I were neck-deep into revolutions and political life. Hence lessons to us on politics might be unnecessary. Secondly, regarding history, you must know that Arabia might have had a thousand-year history, but not Hindustan. And each time, we have been beaten, we have given it back with interest. From Attock to Rameswaram it was the

Marathas who held sway over India, snatching from the Mughals. Hence let us not get into all these polemics. Just answer the limited question that I have asked about when you plan to abandon Khilafat and Ulema movements.

SA: Look, we never conducted the Khilafat in secrecy. Hindus have nothing to fear from it as it is being led by a Hindu after all [Gandhi].

S: Possible. If Khilafat is not supposed to be dangerous because it is led by a Hindu, why should Hindu sangathan which is also led by a Hindu become dangerous? You are saying that the Hindus need to trust the Khilafat only because it has a Hindu leadership and the movement on the other hand is not trustworthy only because it has not got a Muslim to lead it. I ask you that when for the sake of communal unity and for the country the Hindus disregarded their apprehensions and lent their support to the Khilafat in their thousands, why can we not find even a handful of Muslims who, for the sake of the same unity and nation, support a Hindu sangathan movement too? In fact in gratitude towards the Hindus for standing with them, shoulder to shoulder, for a cause that is dear to them, the Muslims too must reciprocate and lend their support to Hindu unity. Where has there been any secrecy in sangathan, just as you claim there is none in Khilafat? It is no secret society. Instead of looking into the surreptitious nature of the Aga Khan mission or Hasan Nizami mission, why do you advise Hindus? Whatever happened in Malabar, Gulbarga, Kohat . . .

SA (*interrupting*): What happened in Kohat? Hindus have not complained, please ask Gandhi.

S: Let us not bring Gandhi into this. He has given several statements, which are quite economical with the truth even in the past. During the Malabar riots he did mention that just one Hindu was converted forcibly. The facts staring us in the face say otherwise. Hence I will not take into account his statements at all. I think we are going around in circles. Kindly answer me whether for the sake of the country and its unity you will completely eschew divisive movements like Khilafat and those that forcibly convert Hindus. The very next moment I pledge to wind up the sangathan and will prevail upon all my colleagues to do the same.

SA: But preaching our religion to Hindus is an integral part of our faith. Just this morning I met a young man who told me that last night he had a dream where God Almighty appeared and advised him to save himself by becoming a Muslim. I immediately directed him to the nearest mosque so that he could convert. Now this is no coercion; people are taking up the true faith out of their own enlightenment.

S: Okay, let me agree with you for a moment. Likewise, tomorrow if a Muslim young man comes to me and narrates his dream where he was guided to become a Hindu, why can I not use shuddhi to make him one? After all that is what is shuddhi, there is no coercion here too, it is completely voluntary.

SA (*angrily*): Fine, you carry on with your shuddhi, and we will with our *tabligh* [conversion]. Let's see who wins. We are one unit; we do not have the scourge of castes and untouchability or regional differences like your community.

S: No provincial differences? It was by taking advantage of the differences between Durrani and Mughal Muslims, southern and northern Muslims and Sheikh and Sayyid Muslims that the Marathas overthrew the Mughal Empire. Shia–Sunni riots are a hundred times more violent and prevalent than Shaiva–Vaishnava ones that do not happen. The Sunnis recently killed an Ahmadi Muslim in Kabul by stoning him. The Bahavis think all other denominations of Muslims are worthy only of being killed or condemned to hellfire. Speaking of untouchability, I know of several Bhangi Muslims who are not allowed to touch the water of other Muslims or offer prayers in mosques with their co-religionists. In Travancore, a riot recently occurred between touchable and untouchable Christians. Maulana Sahab, the hearths of all houses are made of the same brick! I am a little aware of Muslim theology, history and literature. Hence I can confidently make these assertions to you. If you say that you are a united force of 7 crore Muslims, how did the Hindu Marathas overthrow you? How did the British manage to take over India?

SA: It is this arrogance of you Maharashtrians that comes in the way of any logical explanation by me for the larger picture of the country. You Marathas do not consider this country as yours or as one, else, for the sake of its unity you would have accepted my suggestion of abandoning these divisive and communal movements just as other provinces have so readily done.

S: I think you are unnecessarily blaming Maharashtrians. The battle of Shivaji was not just for the Marathas, but for the whole Bharatvarsha. From the last two decades and more, the flag of struggle that we have unfurled is also for the country. Have Ranade, Gokhale or Tilak fought only for Maharashtra? All the major political and revolutionary movements in the country in the last fifty years have come from this soil. Bengal was partitioned. But did Maharashtra not stand in strong protest and suffer that as though she herself had been vivisected? We protested and grieved with Punjab when the tragedy of Jallianwala Bagh happened. These are no favours that we have done; it is our sacred duty to stand with all our brethren and countrymen wherever and whenever they are in peril. Hence it is utterly ungrateful of you to not acknowledge this and rather make such atrocious allegations against Maharashtra. Secondly, you said that you are all the leaders of the united Muslim community and that the community does nothing without your orders. So did the riots in Malabar, Kohat, Delhi, Gulbarga—all of which were accompanied by the desecration of our temples and the piteous rape of our women—too happen under your instructions? If not, how can you claim that you represent that community or that they listen to you?

SA: We were jailed then and in our absence, the Muslim community became disillusioned, directionless and impatient.

S: But you were out of jail when the riots in Kohat, Delhi and Gulbarga happened. When such heinous and barbaric crimes are meted on us Hindus, how can we trust that your words and advice will assuage the rioters and they will give up the violence? Tomorrow, if and when you or I die, what would happen to the interactions between the two communities? Our organization is not against you or anybody else. It is only for self-defence and protection against any kind of atrocity that we might face now or in future. As long as the Hindu sangathan movement is not violent, aggressive, usurping of your rights, property or life and as long as it stands for truth and self-protection, why should anyone have a grouse with it? As long as all these communal movements and missions of Aga Khan, Hasan Nizami or Khilafat carry on; as along as thousands of Hindus are forcibly coerced and converted; as long as Urdu newspapers openly proclaim the agenda to mass-convert Hindus in the next 5–10 years, advising Hindus to give up any attempts to organize and protect themselves for the sake of some mirage that you call national unity is utter hypocrisy.

SA: But you do realize that you polarize the minds of Muslims with your activities. Muslims have been converting Hindus for such a long time. It is not a new thing that has come up now. It is your shuddhi that is a new phenomenon that sows seeds of discord amidst tranquil society. Isn't it blatantly anti-Muslim?

S: But whose fault is this, Maulana Sahab? If a religion as tolerant and peace-loving as Hinduism—that never proselytized anyone forcibly and even forgave or forgot the coercive and violent attempts made on its faith—has to today take the help of shuddhi, where should the blame lie? On the victim or the aggressor? Till date we trusted people and kept the doors of our houses open. Thieves from across the world came in and looted our possessions. Today we have gathered some sense, become alert and have decided to keep our doors locked. And if the same dacoits come and tell us, 'We have been looting for so long, putting a lock on your doors is being unfair to us and this will spoil relationships between us', what are we to reply? Such a lethal unity is best broken in my view. Secondly, Christian, Parsi, Jew and other communities too have their sangathans and unions. Why doesn't that pinch the Muslim psyche as much? Isn't it logical to assume that Hindu sangathan harms some selfish political and religious interests of the Muslim leadership? Hence I asked you so many times about when you will abandon your movements and till now you have evaded a direct reply.

SA (angrily): We will not leave it. There is nothing anti-Hindu in it.

S: Good, then we too will not leave our movement. Our movement is not only not anti-Muslim, it has no angst against any community—Christian, Jew, Parsi or whoever else. Our movement believes that you have every right to organize yourself as a community. Just stop being aggressive predators. We have no such intentions and want to peacefully coexist with you in this country, which belongs to all of us. Just as Islam and Christianity proselytize a faith that they dearly believe to be the only true word, we Hindus too have a right to propagate a faith that we have come to believe for thousands of years and for generations—and that too not with a knife held to someone's throat. We are organizing ourselves only to protect our community from any aggression. Self-protection is the natural right of any society. With no concern for religions, and believing in universal humanity, our movement believes in holding hands with everyone on the basis of One God, One Church, One Language, One prayer and the sanctity of our motherland.

With this, the heated discussion between the two ended inconclusively.

~

Savarkar met Montgomerie while he was in Bombay in November 1924. In a letter to the government dated 19 November 1924, he urged for a change in residence given the lack of opportunities that Ratnagiri town offered him to resurrect his life and the spectre of plague that still loomed large. He had come down with severe fever and there were no facilities for inoculation in the town. He wondered if the government would consider shifting him under the same conditions to Satara, Nagar or Belgaum.

A month later, on 29 December 1924, Savarkar received a reply that stated the reluctance of the government to effect any changes in this decision. 'As you are not restricted to Ratnagiri town, you are at liberty to select any other place in the Ratnagiri District,' noted J.A. Shilidy, the deputy secretary to the Home Department of the Bombay government.[49] One of the reasons for the government's reluctance was the association they made between Bapat and Savarkar, and the former's violent satyagraha at Mulshi after meeting his former colleague.[50]

With no options left, Savarkar moved to Shirgaon village on the outskirts of Ratnagiri. An admirer and associate, Vishnupant Damle, who was in Shirgaon, helped him settle down. His son Gajanan Damle was to become Savarkar's personal assistant for the next twenty-three years, with meagre salary and no expectations.[51] Given the precarious situation with regards to the epidemic, Savarkar sent his pregnant wife Yamuna to Satara to her sister's place before moving alone to Shirgaon.[52]

Montgomerie had suggested that Savarkar write to the Bombay High Court seeking permission to practise there. Accordingly, on 25 January 1925, he sent in his application:

> I have the honour to say that I am desirous to be allowed as an advocate of this High Court and intend to practice in the capacity of a Barrister. I was the member of the Gray's Inn, London and passed the necessary examination in 1909. But before I could actually be called to the Bar, complaints as to my political activities were filed against me by the Indian Police before the Honourable Benchers of the Inn. Consequently, a sort of informal trial was conducted against me calling upon me to explain my position and failing to get satisfied with my political views and feeling the evidence before them did not justify striking my name altogether from the list of those due to be called the Benchers decided not to call me to the Bar then and there but yet allow my name to continue on the roll of the Inn, obviously with a view to take up the question of calling me to the Bar if they found me no longer engaged in any objectionable political activities.
>
> But a few months after that I was arrested and financial difficulties forced me to resign the membership of the Inn and to claim deposit back. Soon after I was convicted under Section 121 and 302 Indian Penal Code and was sentenced to two terms of transportation for life in December 1909. But after having put in some 14 years of my sentence, the Government was pleased to remit the remaining transportation of it on the condition of my taking no part in politics and I was released in January 1924. Since then I have observed the condition under which I was released as best as I could.
>
> I venture to hope and pray in virtue of the special powers vested in the Honourable Chief Justice and Judges of this High Court under which, they can, in their discretion decide special cases as mine. The Honourable Chief Justice and Judges will be pleased to consider my case favourably . . .[53]

The rules of the high court stated that any person applying to be admitted as an advocate of a high court in British India shall produce satisfactory proof that he has been called to the Bar of England, Ireland or Scotland; that he has read in the chambers of a practising European barrister of more than ten years' standing for at least one year and he is of good character and ability.[54]

Almost three months later, on 17 April 1925, Savarkar received a response from the Bombay High Court where he was told tersely that, 'the Lordships have rejected your said petition'.[55] All doors of resurrecting his career or earning his livelihood were thus banged shut on him. The worry of how he would maintain himself and his family in the absence of any resurrection loomed large. At around the same time, his responsibilities too increased with the birth of a child. Yamunabai gave birth to their daughter on 7 January 1925. She was named Prabhat. Savarkar was denied permission to go to Satara for his daughter's naming ceremony.[56] What should have been an occasion of great joy to the couple that had suffered so much became one of worry in the face of Savarkar's shattered career.

Just like Savarkar's personal life and career, the country too was in the doldrums in the aftermath of the failure of the Khilafat agitation with communal riots, year after year, threatening to strike at the very vitals of the nation.

Hindu–Muslim situation in India at the time of Savarkar's release

One of the terrible fallouts of the failure of the Khilafat movement's stated objectives was the murderous Moplah genocides in Malabar that have been discussed earlier. The *Times of India* reporting widely on these atrocities said:

> The rebels . . . captured beautiful Hindu women, forcibly converted them, pierced holes in their ears in the typical Mopla fashion, dressed them as Mopla women and utilized them as their temporary partners of life. Hindu women were threatened, molested and compelled to run half-naked for shelter to forests abounding in wild animals. Respectable Hindu gentlemen were forcibly converted and the circumcision ceremony performed with the help of certain Musliars and Thangals.[57]

Despite all these reports of atrocities, neither Shaukat Ali, as was evident in his combative conversation with Savarkar, nor Gandhi, the original progenitor of the Khilafat movement, was awake or responsive to the irrevocable perils that such communal mobilization in politics had caused.

While conflicts between the two communities had ample precedent earlier, the intensity and the extent of mobilization of the respective communities and the resultant incidents of mob violence were possibly never at the peak that they were in the 1920s. In his letter dated 22 April 1926 to Viceroy Lord Irwin, Sir Henry Wheeler, the Governor of Bihar and Orissa, summed up this tinderbox situation that much of India found itself in during this time. 'In the old days,' explained Wheeler, 'we used to be on the lookout for riots at the Muharram or Bakr Id [festival times], but not otherwise; nowadays they occur over anything . . .'[58] The deep polarization that the 1920s created culminated in the eventual painful partition of the country. No doubt, the 1920s were seen as a 'watershed in communal relations in India'.[59] As another scholar, Wilfred Smith, notes: 'From this period communalism has been a serious and all-pervading vitiation of Indian affairs, and increasingly so.'[60]

May 1923 saw dreadful communal conflagrations in Calcutta when an Arya Samaj procession playing music passed in front of a mosque. Riots continued for months, culminating in large-scale violence in July 1923 during the Bakr Id festival.[61] By July 1923, Viceory Lord Reading bemoaned in his letter to the Secretary of State for India that 'the difficulty at present is to keep the Mahomedan and the Hindu from each other's throats . . .'[62]

In September 1923, Multan erupted in communal clashes during the Muharram procession of the Shia Muslims. This marked the beginning of a series of tumultuous events in the north-west frontier provinces for several years to come. Down south, communal riots broke out in the Nizam's domain in the town of Gulbarga in 1924. Nearly fifteen Hindu temples were attacked, idols broken and the famous Sharana Vishweshwara temple plundered and attempted to be set on fire. Police firing resulted in many deaths. On 14 August 1924 more than fifty Hindu temples in and around the town were completely desecrated.[63]

But the most tragic consequences of the animosity between the two major communities was felt in Kohat in the North-West Frontier Province (NWFP). The incitement came in the form of a provocative poem in a booklet that was deeply hurtful of Muslim sentiments. Following this, riots broke out on 9 and 10 September 1924. Around 155 people were killed and wounded, Rs 9 lakh worth of property destroyed, and large-scale arson and looting continued.[64] Almost all the Hindus of Kohat (numbering over 20,000)[65] had to flee and became refugees in Rawalpindi for several months.[66] Gandhi, who had been released from jail, made a joint enquiry with Shaukat Ali and observed:[67]

The Muslim fury knew no bounds. Destruction of life and property, in which the Constabulary freely partook, which was witnessed by the officials and which they could have prevented, was general. Had not the Hindus been withdrawn from their places and taken to the Cantonment, not many would have lived . . . even some Khilafat volunteers, whose duty it was to protect the Hindus, and regard them as their own kith and kin, neglected their duty, and not only joined in the loot but also took part in the previous incitement.

Following the Kohat riots, Viceroy Reading was informed by Secretary of State Olivier that, 'the Government of India is accused of having been culpably negligent in preventing or not dealing with these disturbances . . . [and] some explanation seems to be required of the manner in which things were allowed to take their course at Kohat.'[68]

Several rounds of negotiations were held at the government's behest. It also advanced interest-free loans in some cases, amounting to almost Rs 5 lakh to enable the Hindu refugees to get back to Kohat and restart their businesses. Gandhi intended to visit Kohat in November 1924 to assuage the communal feelings and bring the two communities together. But so charged was the atmosphere, and the negotiations that the government was undertaking hung so precariously, that they did not wish any disturbance. In a telegraphic reply to Gandhi dated 27 October 1924, the viceroy's office denied him permission from visiting Kohat as 'feelings are raw and any cause may again arouse irritation in recent wounds'. They felt that inevitably 'excitement may be aroused' by his visit and cause a setback to the negotiations.[69]

Several months later, when Gandhi requested the government's permission to visit Kohat in March 1925, the viceroy's office was yet again informed by the NWFP government that this would have disastrous consequences. The telegram states:

Proposed visit of Gandhi and his party to Kohat, in my opinion, can do no good and may do indefinite harm. Hindus and Khilafat Muhammadan party visited Gandhi and party at Rawalpindi from 4th to 6th February. Muslim Working Committee refused to attend. Gandhi conducted enquiry into responsibility for riots which revived tension between parties and for a time jeopardized settlement . . . I am reliably informed that Gandhi dissuade [sic] Hindus from returning to Kohat and offered them permanent asylum in India, but majority told him frankly that they had no wish to learn spinning in India and intended to return to Kohat. Object of Rawalpindi visit seems to have been to break up our settlement and make a fresh one for which Gandhi's party could claim credit. Attempt has failed as most of the Hindus are undoubtedly preparing to return. They are bringing timber for houses in Peshawar and applying for loans . . . having failed to break up our settlement, Gandhi now apparently intends to try and get credit for practical accomplishment of it. I do not see what object he can have in wishing to visit Kohat now. Settlement is in fair way of being carried out and even if Gandhi's object is to assist, it his visit to Kohat will cause great excitement and is much more likely to have opposite effect. Reilly has consulted Kohat leaders privately and reports that Mussalmans object to visit . . . Divan Anant Ram says visit is undesirable; other Hindus except Punjab party of Bhagat Ram, are of same opinion. So far as local considerations go I am strongly opposed to grant permission.[70]

The much-touted Hindu–Muslim unity drive that Gandhi had attempted during the Khilafat times obviously lay in tatters, with members of both communities being quite suspicious of his intentions or his efficacy in controlling the alarming situation.

Communal riots rocked other parts of India too: Delhi and Nagpur in July 1924, in August–September in Lahore, Lucknow, Moradabad, Bhagalpur and Nagpur; in September–October at Lucknow, Shahjahanpur, Kakinada and Allahabad.[71]

A deeply pained Gandhi decided to go on a fast of twenty-one days commencing 17 September 1924. Stating his reasons for the same he said:[72]

The fact that Hindus and Mussalmans, who were only two years ago apparently working together as friends, are now fighting like cats and dogs in some places, shows conclusively that the non-cooperation they offered was not non-violent. I saw the symptoms in Bombay, Chauri Chaura and in a host of minor cases. I did penance then. It had its effects *protanto*. But this Hindu-Muslim tension was unthinkable. It became unbearable on hearing of the Kohat tragedy . . . Had I not been instrumental in bringing into being the vast energy of the people? I must find remedy if the energy proved self-destructive . . . I must do penance. It is a warning to the Hindus and Mussalmans who have professed to love me. If they have loved me truly and if I have been deserving of their love, they will do penance with me for the grave sin of denying God in their lives. The penance of Hindus and Mussalmans is not fasting but retracting their steps. It is true penance for a Mussalman to harbor no ill-will for his Hindu brother and equally true penance for a Hindu to harbor none for his Mussalman brother.

Alarmed Congressmen and well-wishers invited over 200 all-India leaders of all parties and communities for a unity conference in Delhi to find a solution to the communal problems and also save Gandhi's life in the wake of his prolonged fast. More than 300 people attended the conference in Delhi that was presided over by Motilal Nehru. Several resolutions on peace and amity were passed, which, as Dr Ambedkar mentions, were 'pious' and 'were broken as soon as they were announced'.[73]

The reasons for Ambedkar's assessment seem twofold. Discussions in the conferences held in Delhi and later focused on the fault lines that existed between the two communities—cow slaughter, music before mosques, conversions and reconversions, etc. However, the core issue of representation of the communities in legislatures was never addressed head-on. Secondly, despite the enormous goodwill, anxiety and moral coercion that Gandhi's fast produced among people, it had little tangible impact. As historian R.C. Majumdar notes:

How far Gandhi's fast had any salutary effect on the communal relations may be judged by the fact that four days after Gandhi began his fast there was a serious communal riot at Shahjahanpur in which the military had to intervene and 9 were killed and about 100 injured. On October 8 when Gandhi broke his fast, there were serious communal riots at Allahabad, Kanchrapara near Calcutta and at Sagar and Jubbulpore in C.P.[74]

The situation only worsened in 1925 and 1926. No less than sixteen communal riots occurred in 1925, the most terrible being those at Delhi, Aligarh, Arvi (Central Provinces) and Sholapur. On 2 April 1926, deadly riots erupted again in Calcutta. They went on over three waves leaving hundreds killed and injured. Riots rocked interiors of Bengal, Rawalpindi, Allahabad and about five riots occurred in Delhi alone. Curiously, after his fast produced no impact on the ground, Gandhi kept himself aloof from the communal question right from January 1925.[75]

Between 1922 and 1927, approximately 450 lives were lost and 5000 persons injured in communal clashes.[76] Almost every province seemed to have been affected by the virus. The storm spread easily and widely from one place to another, bringing in its wake enormous loss of life and property. As a government-appointed Statutory Committee observed in 1928:

> Every year since 1923 has witnessed communal rioting on an extensive, and in fact, on an increasing scale which has as yet shown no sign of abating. The attached list, which excludes minor occurrences, records no less than 112 communal riots within the last 5 years, of which 31 have occurred during 1927.[77]

Savarkar was observing with deep concern the horrendous flames that had engulfed the nation, threatening to subsume the entire country in its wake. He was particularly concerned about the lives and property of the Hindus in those provinces where they were in a minority and hence vulnerable to attacks. On the Hindus in the Sindh area, he wrote a series of three articles in the periodical *Swatantrya* on 16, 19 and 23 March 1924, under a pseudonym of '*TaLamaLanara Aatma*' (A Troubled Soul) since writing in his own name would have attracted government ire and censure.[78] These were titled '*Kaay Ajoonahi Nijalaat?*' (Are You Still in Deep Slumber?)

> A letter I received from a Hindu leader in Sindh makes it clear that the condition of Hindus in Sindh is worrisome. There is a caste called Sanyogi in Sindh who were converted by force centuries ago, but they have retained their Hindu roots and customs. They want to become Hindu again, but their Hindu caste panchayats are not willing to accept them back. The organizations that want [sic] to get these people back into Hinduism face a stiff resistance from the Muslim organizations of Sindh, who are saying that such efforts will go against 'Hindu Muslim unity' in the region. But the unity that tells only Hindus that they shouldn't propagate their religion even by talking about it, but we are free to spread our religion using force, you should not do '*shuddhikaran*' but we will do '*bhrashtikaran*', is not unity. It is a division that must be fought.
>
> The threat to Hindus in Sindh is not so much from Islamic fundamentalists as it is from the naïveté and denial of the Hindus to recognize the danger of conversions. The Khilafat movement that is spreading in the country in the last three years is only fanning this.

Muslims are emboldened and Hindus are turning a blind eye to the dangers of Islamic conversions. This is not Khilafat, this is an *aafat*.[79]

I want to tell our Muslim brethren that you are Hindus by blood and race, and you are dearer to us than the Muslims of the world, but if you feel that you are dearer to the Islamic countries like Turkey than to the 'Hindu Kafirs', do understand that this delusion will end in your downfall.[80]

On 1 March 1925, a sarcastic article by Savarkar was published in the *Mahratta* titled 'The Suffering Moslems of Kohat'. The government took strong objections to the article and sent a show-cause notice to him on 28 March 1925. Savarkar replied on 6 April 1925 saying that his article was non-political, and therefore he had every right to write it. It was based on government data, he claimed, and asked the government to provide any new data that it might have so that he could correct his article. He said in his reply:

By writing this article I have not broken any promise not to take part in politics. The word Swaraj is used in the context of what one thinks of Swaraj and Khilafat. I have not expressed my opinion. My article is purely on social and religious issues. As for the views on Muslims, these are based on quotations from the Koran. I would refer to the fourth chapter of the Koran in support of my arguments. I have thus not breached any conditions of my internment.[81]

However, the government was far from satisfied with his explanations. In their reply dated 6 May 1925, they admonished him that it should have been obvious that an article of that nature 'was bound to inflame the feelings and increase the tension between Hindus and Muhammadans'. This, the government said, was contrary to Savarkar's undertaking 'not to engage in any manner in political activities without the consent of the Government'. They issued a strict warning not to repeat the act as this might 'necessitate a reconsideration' of his release.[82]

Hindu Sangathan Movements and the All-India Hindu Mahasabha

The nineteenth century in India was a period of 'cultural adjustments' that led to the emergence of new forms of group consciousness.[83] This in turn gave rise to political and semi-political movements in the twentieth century. Hindu religion, sentiments and traditions too were reinterpreted, especially in the provinces of Bengal, Punjab and Maharashtra. These varying regional expressions that were drawn from local culture and experience coalesced in the twentieth century into a larger pan-India Hindu consciousness. Throughout the nineteenth century, Hindu Sabhas sprang up in several cities and towns across India. They had short shelf lives and a wide range of goals from radical social reforms such as widow remarriage on the one hand to defending orthodoxy and tradition on the other.

An early precursor of the Hindu Mahasabha was the Bharat Dharma Mahamandal founded by Pandit Din Dayalu in 1887 along with other orthodox leaders from Punjab and the United Provinces. Akin to the Indian National Congress, the Mahamandal too held annual meetings with much fanfare and religious rituals. Resolutions were read and passed. Prominent Hindu leaders such as Pandit Madan Mohan Malaviya (1861–1946) and the maharaja of Darbhanga lent their support to the Mahamandal, as they would later support the Hindu Mahasabha. The Mahamandal however slowly faded away in the early years of the twentieth century.

The accentuated need for a Hindu organization was felt in the wake of conversions that the community faced from proselytizing religions unlike itself. In 1871, for the first time, the British government attempted a census, gathering data for the whole of India, including British presidencies and princely states. The *Memorandum on the Census of British India of 1871-72* was written by the British civil servant, Henry Waterfield, who had served for nearly forty-four years in the India Office. Waterfield notes that the data coming from the princely states was only 'fairly accurate' and that the numbers were 'mostly estimates'. Hence this census represented British India more than the native states. For the first time people began to notice, quantifiably, the numbers of communities and castes. As per the *Memorandum*, around 140.5 million Hindus (and Sikhs) constituted 73.7 per cent of India's population and 40.75 million Muslims made up for approximately 21.5 per cent. The 'Others' (9.25 million) who comprised Buddhists, Jains, Christians, Parsis, Brahmos and the 'hill people' of indeterminate religion made up the remaining less than 5 per cent.[84] In Punjab, the Muslims formed the larger half, almost 53 per cent of the population, while the number stood at 32.3 per cent and 26.75 per cent in Bengal and Assam respectively.[85] Of the 20.5 million Muslims in Bengal and Assam that formed the larger moiety of Muslim population in British

India, 17.5 million were to be found in East Bengal and the adjoining districts of Sylhet and Cachar. Here they amounted to 49 per cent of the total population. In some districts here, their number had risen to even above 80 per cent of the population.[86] The *Memorandum* itself attributed the rising numbers of Muslims to 'conversion of the lower orders from the old Hindoo religion under which they held the position of out-castes'.[87]

The all-India census of 1871 giving the numbers, particularly of the Muslim populations, in Punjab and Bengal created a scare. This is reflected in the writings of several prominent leaders from these regions. Through his paper *Punjabi*, Rai Bahadur Lal Chand, an eminent judge of the Punjab High Court, and Lala Lajpat Rai in the *Hindustan Review* repeatedly urged the need for a regular Hindu political or semi-political conference being organized to take stock of the concerns of the community. In Bengal, Lt. Col. U.N. Mukherjee, in his book *A Dying Race*, concluded:

> We Hindus are most ridiculously, most contemptibly ignorant, we have no idea about what is going on around us. Others are not quite so ignorant . . . How do the two communities stand? The Mohammedans have a future and they believe in it. We Hindus have no conception of it. Time is with them . . . time is against us. At the end of the years, they count their gains, we calculate our losses. They are growing in number, growing in strength, growing in wealth, growing in solidarity . . . we are crumbling to pieces. They look forward to a united Mohammedan world . . . we are awaiting our extinction.[88]

While organizations such as the Brahmo Samaj or Prarthana Samaj advocated radical social reforms in Hindu society that even meant dismantling several tenets of the faith including rituals and idol worship, there were counter-reformation movements too that were based on the premise of a reassertion of ancient Indian culture and heritage. The work of Swami Vivekananda and the Arya Samaj of Swami Dayanand Saraswati falls under the latter category. The Arya Samaj with its 'Back to the Vedas' call was certainly not a proponent of Hindu nationalism. In fact, its leadership in Punjab asked its members to declare themselves as 'Aryas' and not Hindus in the 1891 census. But its ideological features made it the early crucibles for Hindu nationalism and for the birth of organizations such as the Hindu Mahasabha. Savarkar in fact writes: 'The Hindu Mahasabha itself is in fact but an enlarged and more comprehensive edition of the Arya Samaj.

The honour of being the first apostle of Hindu Sanghatna in modern days must ever rest with Swami Dayanand Saraswati . . .'[89]

Several other factors contributed to the need for this Hindu *sangathan* or unity movement. These included the Land Alienation Act of 1901 in Punjab, the Partition of Bengal in 1905, the formation of the Muslim League in 1906 and the Morley–Minto Reforms or the India Act of 1909. The Land Alienation Act that was promulgated in Punjab in 1901 prohibited the upper class from buying land from the lower class. The Act categorized the 'upper class' to include Hindus who were engaged in trade and industry while the 'lower class' was to include largely the Jat Hindus, some other agricultural castes and all Muslims. It did not take into account the financial well-being that several Muslims too enjoyed and that they could not be homogenized into one block as 'lower class'. Consequently, if any poor Hindu wanted to sell his land off, he had no option to sell it to a rich Hindu. As a result of this Act, within ten years of its enactment, Muslims began gaining control over large tracts of land in Punjab. While this might not have been a problem per se, the Reforms of 1909 granted voting rights based on property owned. This helped the Muslims to garner large number of seats and even a majority at times in the legislature despite the fact that they were in a minority. When the Hindus of Punjab urged the Congress to take up their cause against this injustice, it was met with indifference. They finally decided to fight for their rights themselves.

The Morley–Minto Reforms, officially known as the India Act of 1909, sowed the seeds of separation and suspicion between the Hindu and Muslim communities. Separate electorates for Muslims and some seats for them in the joint electorates were given. Additionally, discriminatory provisions for eligibility to vote were a glaring bias. Thrice the amount of tax paid and seven extra years after one's degree were the eligibility criteria for a Hindu to vote vis-à-vis a Muslim. These measures and the Land Alienation Act created a disproportionately larger voter base among the Muslim community. And when one added dwindling numerical strength due to forced or voluntary conversions, as also bolstered by the numbers of the 1871 census, the alarm bells began ticking for the Hindu leadership.

A Hindu Sabha came up in 1909 in Punjab.[90] Its first conference was held in Lahore with Sir Pratul Chandra Chatterjee, a retired judge of the Punjab High Court, as president. Rai Bahadur Lal Chand was the chairman of the Reception Committee. The conference was attended by eminent Hindu leaders of Punjab such as Lala Lajpat Rai, Lala Hans Raj and others. It was noted that for the first time Sanatanis, Arya Samajists, Sikhs, Brahmo Samajists and members of other denominations within the larger Hindu umbrella shared a common platform at Lahore.[91] It called for Hindu-centred political action and bitterly criticized the Congress for failing to protect Hindu interests. That very year Hindu Sabhas came up in Bengal and the United Provinces.

The second conference of the Punjab Hindu Sabha was held at Multan in 1910, interestingly under a Sikh guru, Baba Gurubaksh Singh Bedi. In subsequent meetings and conferences held in Allahabad, Amritsar, Delhi, Ambala and Ferozepur between 1911 and 1914 the leaders kept mooting the idea of a pan-India Hindu organization.

Finally, this national organization to represent Hindus and their interests took shape in 1915. It was named the 'Sarwadeshak Hindu Sabha' (later All-India Hindu Mahasabha in 1920) and met at Hardwar during the Kumbh Mela under the leadership of Maharaja Manindrachandra Nandi of Kasim Bazaar. Several important personalities such as Pandit Madan Mohan Malaviya, Swami Shradhhanand and Sir Tej Bahadur Sapru attended the conference. The goals of the new organization were:[92]

1. To promote greater union and solidarity amongst all sections of Hindu community and to unite them as closely as parts of one organic whole.
2. To promote education among members of the Hindu community.
3. To ameliorate and improve the condition of all classes of the Hindu community.
4. To protect and promote Hindu interests wherever and whenever it may be necessary.
5. To promote good feelings between the Hindus and other communities in India and to act in a friendly way with them and in loyal co-operation with the government.
6. Generally to take steps for promoting religious, moral, social, educational and political interests of the community.

The Hindu Mahasabha was deeply critical of the Lucknow Pact of 1916 between the Congress and the Muslim League that agreed on separate communal electorates and also a larger share of seats for Muslims in provincial legislative councils than their numbers warranted. In its 1920 convention at Hardwar, the Hindu Mahasabha altered Clause 5 of its objective—from 'in loyal co-operation with the Government' to 'with a view to evolving a limited and self-governing Indian nation'. The new constitution also formally added 'low castes' to its definition of members.[93] In the wake of the Khilafat agitation and the Moplah carnage of Malabar, the Hindu Mahasabha resolved that reconversion or shuddhi of those who had deserted the faith was the only way to restore the confidence of the community.

Subsequently, a major programme of shuddhi (literally meaning purification) and *sangathan* (organization and unity) was launched with the blessing of the Shankaracharya, Dr Kurtkoti, by Hindu Mahasabha leaders such as Swami Shraddhanand, Dr B.S. Moonje, Bhai Parmanand and Lala Lajpat Rai. A Sanskrit scholar, Dr Kurtkoti, shared the ideology of the Hindu Mahasabha and acceded to the requests of the *Mahratta* that religious pontiffs must step up to guide Hindu society and cleanse its evils. According to Dr Kurtkoti, '*Shuddhi* would imply cleansing oneself of all the mental, moral and spiritual inertia. Let us turn our attention to those that we have repulsed, let us reclaim them first.'[94] As a religious authority, he gave a decree that Hindus were theologically free to reconvert members who had left their fold involuntarily due to threats, allurements and coercion. Dr Kurtkoti supported the indissoluble bond between politics and religion and showed that he was prepared to defend Hinduism by assuming an active spiritual authority in politics.[95]

The advocates of the Hindu Mahasabha and the shuddhi movements argued that the shuddhi movement was ancient in origin and not restricted to converted Hindus but extended to peoples of all faiths and religion who desired to embrace Hinduism. Siddheshwar Shastri Chitrav, one of the leading figures in the Hindu Mahasabha, was an active proponent of shuddhi trying to locate its theological legitimacy in scriptural and historical records. Before the Hindu Mahasabha started the shuddhi movement in Poona in 1923, Gajanan Bhaskar Vaidya from Bombay had already established the Hindu Missionary Society around 1917 and started the work of shuddhi. He performed more than 100 *shuddhikaran* or reconversion ceremonies between 1917 and 1924 and his work was also appreciated by Lokmanya Tilak.[96]

The shuddhi movement surprised many orthodox Hindus who were sceptical and also opposed to it, as was witnessed by Savarkar even in the Cellular Jail when he undertook such measures of reconversion. Dr Kurtkoti however supported the enduring bond between politics and religion and showed that he was prepared to defend Hinduism by assuming the role of an active spiritual authority in politics.[97]

It is noteworthy that many of their members were simultaneously members of the Congress as well. With the growing fire of communal riots flaring across the country in the 1920s, when they tried to mobilize the Congress to denounce the riots and assuage the feelings of Hindus, this met with a cold response from the leadership. This slowly led to disenchantment and disassociation of Hindu Mahasabha members from the Congress movement. The leaders from Maharashtra who were avowed Tilak supporters disagreed with Gandhi's total non-violence approach as well. These included N.C. Kelkar, Karandikar, Baptista, B.S. Moonje, Babasaheb Khaparde, Gangadharrao Deshpande and Shivrampant Paranjpe.

The non-Brahmin movement in Maharashtra was spearheaded by the ideals of Jyotiba Phule and his Satyashodhak movement in the latter half of the nineteenth century. It challenged Brahminical hegemony in all aspects of life. However, by the second and third decades of the twentieth century, some of the factions within the larger non-Brahmin movement in Maharashtra began projecting and hailing Kshatriya consciousness as a counter against Brahminism. This indirectly helped in nurturing and consolidating a larger, unified Hindu consciousness. Marathas began asserting their Kshatriya status with books being written on their heroic Kshatriya lineage. For instance, Vasudeorao Birze wrote a book in 1912 titled *Kshatriya Ani Tyanche Astitva* (Kshatriya and Their Origins) and Kashinath Bapuji Deshmukh authored two volumes, entitled *Kshatriya Marathyancha Prachin va Arvachin Itihas* (The Hoary Past of the Kshatriya Marathas).[98] This assertion of identity was to counter the Brahmin claims that everyone who was a non-Brahmin was a Shudra by their varna. So, the consolidation of the non-Brahmin communities was in fact an assertion of their varna identity (as Kshatriya) in preference to being called 'low caste'. But the unintended consequences of this consolidation gave a wide social base and space for Hindu nationalism to evolve.

Delinking and underemphasizing Brahminism from Hinduism was seen by the Hindu nationalist leaders as an effective way to enhance the social base and integrate the Hindus, overcoming caste barriers. This was also the idea behind Savarkar's conception of Hindutva that was beyond caste and even beyond pan-Indic faiths.

The communal riots of the 1920s intensified the fears and insecurities of Hindus. The manner in which the entire Hindu community was

thrown out as refugees in Kohat was a grim reminder of the tinderbox
that the society had become. Closer home, in Maharashtra, with riots in
Nagpur, Solapur, and neighbouring Gulbarga in the Nizam's state made
the Hindus realize that their being disorganized was what was leading to
their vulnerability to attacks.

Savarkar's letters in *Lokmanya* under the pen-name *Hutatma*
(literally meaning martyr) echoes this sentiment, 'The Hindus in Kohat
and Gulbarga were unprepared and disorganized and therefore were
not capable of meeting the Muslim threat, while the Hindus in Nagpur
were organized, united and ready and therefore succeeded . . . The point
which Hindus should keep in mind is the relationship between peace and
strength . . .'[99]

This 'strength' of organization came to the fore when disturbances
broke out in Nagpur's Dindi in September–October 1923 during the
occasion of Ganeshotsav. The usual issue of procession and playing of
music in front of mosques led to tension between Hindus and Muslims.
Heeding Muslim objections, the police and the city magistrate curtailed the
rights of the procession. The Hindu community that had by now become
conscious and organized decided not to take this lying down. They began
a satyagraha (agitation) against this decision from 31 October 1923 and
carried it on till 11 November. Many young and old leaders participated
in the satyagraha. Among them were N.B. Khare, L.B. Paranjpe,
Dr Keshavrao Baliram Hedgewar, Gopalrao Ogale, Jaikrishanabha Upadhye
and others. They were arrested by the police but the movement continued
gaining momentum. On 11 November when one of the leaders Raje
Laxmanrao Bhonsle participated in the satyagraha nearly 40,000 Hindus
gathered to hear him and lend their support.[100] Realizing the popular
support that the movement was gaining, the police and the Muslims finally
gave in and assured the Hindus that they would not object to the Hindus'
procession. To celebrate the victory of the Dindi satyagraha, a sabha was
held at night with Dr Hedgewar presiding over it. The establishment of
the Nagpur Hindu Sabha under the leadership of Raje Laxmanrao Bhonsle
was announced. Dr B.S. Moonje was chosen as the vice-president and Dr
Hedgewar as its secretary.

All these momentous developments in Maharashtra politics coincided
with the release of Babarao Savarkar from prison. Despite his failing
health, Babarao decided to take an active part in the activities of the Hindu
Mahasabha. He formed a separate 'Tarun Hindu Sabha' in 1923–24 to

enlist the support of young Hindus and consolidate them politically. People in the age group of sixteen to forty were eligible to be members and it was open to Santanis, Arya Samajis, Jains, Buddhists, Sikhs and Lingayats. Apart from celebration of festivals and weekly intellectual meets, the Sabha was aimed at protecting Hindus and their women from non-Hindu attacks, stop conversion attempts, promote shuddhi, train youngsters in wielding the lathi in self-defence, and create a political awareness and consciousness among the Hindu youth.[101]

Babarao travelled extensively to start branches of the Sabha and managed to establish nearly twenty-five to thirty branches with some 500 youths under its banner. Like the Abhinav Bharat,[102] members of the Tarun Hindu Sabha were involved in physical exercise and gymnastics, in addition to shuddhi and attempts towards abolition of the caste system.

Towards end-1924, Babarao arrived in Nagpur to create support for the Tarun Hindu Sabha. He stayed at the residence of his advocate friend and distant relative Vishwanathrao Kelkar. Through Kelkar, he was introduced to the young, spirited physician, Dr Keshav Baliram Hedgewar, who was one of the heroes of the Dindi satyagraha. Hedgewar had earlier been a member of the revolutionary Anushilan Samiti as a student in Calcutta's National Medical College. Instead of pursuing medical practice, he had submitted himself to the cause of the nation. In 1919, he had begun an organization of youngsters known as National Union and later worked with the Hindu Mahasabha in Nagpur. Over several hours of discussions with Babarao, they decided that there was no point having multiple organizations serving the same cause of Hindu unity. The 1924 Hindu Mahasabha Convention had in fact put forward a suggestion of starting a 'Hindu Swayamsevak Sanghatana' or Volunteer Corps of youngsters and this responsibility had been entrusted to Dr B.S. Moonje and Babarao Savarkar.[103]

Hedgewar seemed like the right man to take up this task. He was fired with the imagination of having a united, well-oiled pan-Indian volunteer organization for and of the Hindus. Along with Babarao and other leaders such as Dr B.S. Moonje, Dr L.V. Paranjpe, Bhauji Karve, Anna Sohoni, Cholkar, Vishwanath Kelkar and Dr Tholkar, Hedgewar started the Rashtriya Swayamsevak Sangh (RSS) on 27 September 1925, on the auspicious day of Vijayadashami. All these men broadly opined that Hindu–Muslim unity was a mirage and 'Hindutva' is the only nationalist creed.

A shakha or branch of Hindu teenagers and youngsters congregated in the ruins of Salubai Mohite Wada in Nagpur's Mahal area. Babarao was present on this momentous occasion. He was thus among the founding members of the RSS. Hedgewar had immense respect for Babarao. It is said that he asked the latter to design the *bhagwa* or saffron flag and the pledge of the fledgling organization. Babarao also merged his Tarun Hindu Sabha with the RSS. The pledge had the words 'Hindu Rashtra' or Hindu Nation used possibly for the first time in Indian polity.

The swayamsevaks or volunteers were entrusted with the responsibility of protecting Hindus, especially during religious processions or during riots. On 18 February 1926, the first shakha of the RSS was started at Wardha. Dr Hedgewar was formally chosen as the head of the Sangh in December 1926. He used all his organizational skills to slowly build it up in these formative years. With Hedgewar's close association with the Savarkars, branches came up in western and coastal Maharashtra, while Bhai Paramanand and other Hindu Mahasabha leaders helped the RSS get a foothold in the north. Given its close umbilical ties with the Hindu Mahasabha, the RSS was seen to be a youth wing of the Hindu Mahasabha. But as later years were to witness, it slowly sought to distance itself from the Hindu Mahasabha.

The Hindu Mahasabha was not restricted to merely sociocultural and religious issues but also expressed itself in the politics of the nation through parties like the Swarajya Party, Responsivist Party and the Lokshahi Swarajya Party. The rift within the Congress after the Khilafat movement and the abrupt calling off of the *Non-cooperation* movement by Gandhi led to the establishment of the Swarajya Party on 1 January 1923 under the leadership of Chittaranjan Das. Other important members of the party included Motilal Nehru, N.C. Kelkar, Dr B.S. Moonje, Bapuji Aney and others. They decided to actively participate in the electoral process that was kick-started with the 1919 reforms and secure a voice for Indians in the legislative councils. The Maharashtra unit of the Swarajya Party was established under M.R. Jayakar. In the elections that were held to the Central Legislative Council and the provincial councils in 1923, the party won a handsome twenty-three seats out of the twenty-eight that it had fielded candidates for. The victorious candidates included M.R. Jayakar, Barrister K.F. Nariman and Annasaheb Bhopatkar. N.C. Kelkar was elected to the Central Legislative Council. In the Central Provinces and Berar, out of a total of seventy members, forty-one from the Swarajya Party were elected. These included Dr B.S. Moonje, N.B. Khare, S.B. Tambe, Babasaheb Khaparde and others.

With the release of Gandhi from prison in February 1924 and his continued insistence on non-participation in elections and opposition to council entry, the differences only widened. The communal riots that rocked the country and the feeble response of the Congress leadership furthered the schisms. Despite Gandhi's epic fast of twenty-one days following the riots, the staunch Hindus within the Congress, who also owed allegiance to the larger Hindu sangathan movement either through the Hindu Mahasabha or through the Swarajya Party and its allies, began to feel increasingly disillusioned about what they perceived as Congress indifference to Hindu causes and interests. Increasingly, they began to use the platform of Hindu Mahasabha to express their views. Till 1934, members of the Hindu Mahasabha and the Congress shared common platforms, had common leaders, and their meetings too were held in the same *pandal* most often. But with time, the divorce between the two ideologies became imminent.

The leadership of the Hindu Mahasabha rested in the 1920s with people like N.C. Kelkar (he was the president twice in 1925 and 1929) and Dr B.S. Moonje (1927–33). In his presidential address at the Dacca Provincial Hindu Conference on 27 August 1929, N.C. Kelkar emphasized that Hindus had only India wherein they could organize and reinforce Hindu religion and culture.[104] He stated that in this respect the Hindus did not have the advantage 'which the Mohamedans and more so the Christians enjoyed, as there was hardly any country in the world where there were no Christians. The Mohamedans could look beyond the Indian frontier and see as far as Constantinople, to get at least inspiration if not material help . . . But as regards Hinduism . . . where in the whole wide world was there an inch of space which the poor un-befriended and threatened Hindu could call his own outside Hindustan?' The only hope, therefore, of this beleaguered community, according to Kelkar, lay in strongly fortifying itself and cementing ties among its many factions and castes. He stressed the need for an internal organization and strengthening of Hindu society, from top to bottom, for its self-defence. He also called for progressiveness within the Hindus to effect rational reforms needed to achieve this goal. He came down heavily against those opposed to reforms and the changes to modernism within Hindu society:

The Benaras Pandit and the Malabar Brahman must be taught that they are living in a new age, and must come out in the open field and full daylight, leaving their cells behind them . . . The present caste system must be so diluted or tempered as hardly to be felt for practical purposes. And there must be a bold open preaching in favour of the annihilation of the sub-divisions within the four castes.[105]

Kelkar also wanted to make Hindus aware of their rights and prevent any injustice that might be done to them in the course of realization of political self-government in India. And for this, the Hindu Mahasabha was to be their political voice.[106] Both Kelkar and M.R. Jayakar pointed out the difference between conversion by Hindus and conversion of Hindus. According to them, in the former case, conversion was always a voluntary one and a matter of actual change of faith, while in the latter, conversions were often involuntary and brought about by force or fraud.[107]

Issues related to Hindu women, be it child marriage, polygamy, condition of widows, dowry, female illiteracy and other social evils and their eradication formed a major part of the Mahasabha's agenda for deliberations, as also militarization and self-defence especially to protect the women of the fold from being abducted and violated by the 'other'. Possibly for the first time on a public platform, it was the Hindu Mahasabha's conference in Banaras in August 1923 that strongly criticized the marriage of minor Hindu girls as a social evil.[108] Kelkar championed equal rights to women in the inheritance of ancestral or self-acquired property.

In April 1927, in its annual conference held in Patna, Dr B.S. Moonje took over as the president of the Hindu Mahasabha. He was one of its most militant leaders so far and under him the Mahasabha developed explicit political objectives. He travelled extensively throughout the country addressing Hindu gatherings and conferences, meeting students, visiting areas of communal tension and inspecting places of potential disturbance. The constant theme was the urgent need for Hindus to bargain from a position of strength and, if necessary, defend their interest through force. For this he encouraged military preparedness and physical strength through the formation of a Rifle Association and a Flying Club in Nagpur.

It was this Hindu consciousness in the wake of the communal riots after the Khilafat and the non-cooperation movements that Savarkar utilized as a crucible in Ratnagiri for his experiments on social reforms and the Hindutva philosophy that he had conceived in prison. The Ratnagiri Hindu Sabha was to become his new social laboratory.

2

Caste in Stone

Ratnagiri, 1924

Within a fortnight of Savarkar's arrival in Ratnagiri, a Hindu Sabha was started there on 23 January 1924. The meeting was attended by Babarao, Advocate Bhaskar Nanal, Mahadev Sahasrabuddhe, Vishnu Patwardhan, Purushottam Bhikaji Joshi, Gajanan Patwardhan, Hari Gandhi, Narayan Jog, Prahlad Joshi and Mahadev Patwardhan. Savarkar himself did not attend the meeting, but he was aware of it and had given it his tacit support.

The Sabha drafted for itself the following objectives, which had a clear stamp of Savarkar:[1]

1. To establish and maintain maximum co-operation with Hindu Sabhas and organizations working for the Hindu cause across India.
2. To create bonds of harmony and unity among different castes within Hindu society.
3. To commemorate the memory of martyrs who had laid down their lives for the cause of the Hindu nation.
4. To promote the use of home-made or swadeshi goods.
5. To impart physical education to Hindu society through gymnasiums and other means.
6. To eradicate untouchability completely from the Hindu society and strive to the maximum towards this objective.
7. To propagate shuddhi into Hindu religion for those desirous of coming back into the fold.
8. To work as a genuine and powerful opponent against all forces that hamper the safety, security and material possessions of Hindu society, wherever they arise.

The definition of a Hindu was once again discussed in this inaugural meeting of the Ratnagiri Hindu Sabha and they decided to use the terminology that Savarkar had provided in his thesis on Hindutva in 1923 while in prison:

Aasindhu Sindhu paryanta yasya Bharata bhumika
Pitrabhu punyabhushchaiva sa vai Hinduriti smritah.

(The one who considers this vast stretch of land called Bharat,
from the Sindhu [the Indus] to the Sindhu [the sea] as the land of
one's ancestors and holy land, he is the one who will be termed and
remembered as a Hindu.)

An annual membership fee of 4 annas was stipulated for the Sabha, though those who did not have the means to pay but had a zeal for the cause and believed in it were exempt. The people of Ratnagiri were urged to contribute whatever small amounts they could to the Sabha on occasions of festivals or marriages and auspicious occasions in their households.[2] Gymnasiums and theatre companies such as Shri Shahu Nagarwasi Company and Lalit Prabha Sangeet Mandali voluntarily donated half of their incomes to the Ratnagiri Hindu Sabha in its fledgling years.[3]

Advocate Babarao Nanal (BA, LLB and Member of Legislative Council) was elected president of the Sabha and G.V. Patwardhan its secretary. It was further decided that a member of the Sabha would represent it in the annual national conference of the All-India Hindu Mahasabha to be held at Allahabad. As editor of the *Balwant* newspaper, it was Patwardhan's additional responsibility to popularize the Sabha and draw more members to it. All members were encouraged to read the following books: Savarkar's *Hindutva, Shuddhi* and *Asprushyata Nivaaran* (Eradication of Untouchability) published by the Pradnya Pathashala of Wai. The Pathashala was started in 1916 under the guidance of spiritual guru Swami Kevalananda Saraswati (earlier known as Narayan Shastri Marathe). He was a close associate of Tilak and his ashram was also a safe hideout for revolutionaries. He had established a school that propagated patriotic sentiments and nationalism, which had been forcibly shut down by the British in 1908. The reason that these books were prescribed as reading material was to convince the members of the theological sanction from Hindu scriptures for shuddhi and also for delegitimizing untouchability from a scriptural standpoint. Savarkar was a rationalist but he never forced anyone to accept his viewpoint. He always preferred to lay the facts bare for everyone to discern. At the same time, he openly invited dissenting opinions and was ready to discuss and debate them without any prejudice. He knew that subjects such as shuddhi or eradication of untouchability were sensitive ones for orthodox Hindus. Hence a forcible imposition of these beliefs would lead to social tensions and ferment. Rather a nuanced, considered discussion and change of heart was his approach to solving these centuries-old societal problems.

After the formation of the Ratnagiri Hindu Sabha, Savarkar began his crusade regarding social reforms on 16 February 1924 through a visit to the neighbouring village of Makhajan. This was organized at the behest of Sadashiv Rajaram Ranade. Accompanying Savarkar was a former Abhinav Bharat member and the maternal uncle of Narayanrao's wife Shanta—Vishwanathrao Kelkar. Kelkar was also the editor of the periodical *Swatantrya* that he had started from Nagpur, along with Dr Keshavrao Baliram Hedgewar. There are no references to any speeches that Savarkar made at Makhajan, since he was just out of jail and the police was keeping a close watch on his movements and utterances. He met groups of people in private and articulated his ideas on the 'Seven shackles of Hindu society': *Vedokta bandi* (denial of access to Vedic literature to non-Brahmins), *Vyavasaya bandi* (choice of profession by merit and not heredity), *Sparsha bandi* (untouchability), *Samudra bandi* (barring crossing the seas fearing loss of caste), *Shuddhi bandi* (denial of reconversions to Hinduism), *Roti bandi* (denouncement of inter-caste dining) and *Beti bandi* (denial of inter-caste marriage).[4]

It was in the 26 February 1924 issue of *Swatantrya* that Savarkar decided to begin his career as a columnist—albeit with various pseudonyms. His first article was named after his epic poem '*Sagara Prana TaLamaLala*' (My Soul Is in Torment, O! Ocean!) that he composed in 1909 in Brighton, sitting by the sea and being surcharged with emotion after the execution of his friend Madan Lal Dhingra. Apart from the poem, it had a list of all the brave hearts and revolutionaries who had either sacrificed their lives for the nation or were still exercising their might in exile in different countries.

On 13 April, he wrote another article titled '*Nepal aaNi Hindu Sangathan*'. Most of the Hindu Mahasabha ideologues and, particularly Savarkar, had this great fascination for Nepal, which was the world's only Hindu kingdom. In this article, Savarkar rued that while Afghanistan too had once been a part of the Hindu civilization, two centuries of Islamization had made it hostile to India. But while the dome of the Kashi Vishwanath temple in Benares had been desecrated during the reign of Aurangzeb, that of Pashupatinath was still intact in Nepal and narrating the tale of Hindu pride. It was truly the ideal to aspire for, and for India to have close and friendly ties with.[5]

~

Ratnagiri—The Laboratory of Savarkar's Social Reforms

Around this time, Savarkar embarked on his mammoth mission of reuniting and cleansing Hindu society—at least in Ratnagiri. Among his close associates in this movement were legal luminaries such as Advocate Nanal and Rao Bahadur Parulekar, editor of the *Satyashodhak*, Dattopant Limaye, Gajananrao Patwardhan, Rao Saheb Ranade, Dr B.N. Savant, Kashinathpant Parulekar, G.D. Lubri, R.V. Chiplunkar, Vishnupant Damle, Wamanrao Chavan, Bhalachandra Patkar, Achutrao Malushte, Narayanrao Khatu, Hari Gandhi, Dattatreya Savant, Atma Ram Rao Salvi, Keruji Mahar, Palukaka Joshi and several others.

The entire crusade of social reforms that Savarkar undertook while in Ratnagiri rested on four pillars of activity: Persuade the orthodox and sceptics through clear logical arguments; talk about the high and low castes prevalent even among the so-called untouchables and call for their complete eradication; expose the myth of a homogeneous society among Muslims and Christians by enumerating the untouchability that existed among them too (and hence establishing that conversion was no panacea for untouchability); and finally, lead by example through simple, practical steps that led to social harmony, removal of caste barriers, and unity of Hindu society.

On 17 April 1924, Savarkar strategically chose the Vitthal temple in the village of Parashuram to launch his experiments with social reforms. The temple was important for multiple reasons. It was considered the most sacred spot for the Chitpawan Brahmins. It was the place of inspiration for Peshwa Baji Rao I and his spiritual teacher Brahmendra Swami had established this temple. Savarkar's first major speech after being released was at such a spiritually and politically prominent place. The topic he chose to speak on was '*ShuddhikaraN aaNi Asprushyoddhar*' (Shuddhi movement and uplift of untouchables). This invited a barrage of criticism from orthodox Hindus, but Savarkar was determined to not let himself be affected by their denunciation.

Savarkar's first obstacle was creating mass awareness. During the Ganeshotsav of 1925, he organized lectures and public discussions, and published articles on how untouchability was unjust and harmful to Hindu society. He admitted that while people might be convinced with some of his arguments in principle, implementing them practically was tough, given the long-term social conditioning that one was born with. But undaunted by this, Savarkar went to the locality where the untouchable Mahar community lived, much to the horror of the orthodox Hindus of Ratnagiri. It was impossible for the Mahars to come to town and sing devotional songs. Hence, he decided to enter their locality, the Maharwada, to sing and dance with them. They were sceptical, hesitant and scared of this upper-caste Brahmin coming to their locality, and felt uneasy in his presence. The women or children of the house would peep from their windows and tell Savarkar that the master is not at home and he must come later. It took a lot of effort and convincing on Savarkar's part to make them come out of their homes, sit in the forecourt on the same mat and sing devotional songs with Savarkar and his associates.

His own colleagues accompanied him grudgingly. After these visits to the localities of untouchables, they often went home and took a purification bath. The situation was so bad that it was considered that even the shadow of a Mahar was enough to pollute a high-caste Hindu and the latter often took a bath with his clothes on to purify the garment too. Even uttering the word 'Mahar' was considered anathema and caused pollution to one's caste. In a society ridden with such complex prejudices that had come down through centuries, one can imagine the backlash and the difficulties that Savarkar might have faced while trying to dislodge this edifice. Upper-caste Hindus threatened him and his colleagues with social boycott. Yet the members of the Ratnagiri Hindu Sabha remained undeterred. They kept visiting the ghettos of the untouchable communities, cleaned their premises, planted the sacred tulsi or basil plants, sang devotional songs with them, distributed soaps and urged them to bathe and remain clean and even offered to wash their clothes. Slowly the untouchable community started reposing their faith and gave up their inhibitions. But this was just the preliminary step in the struggle. The next step was to bring the untouchables into town to participate in public functions with the upper castes.

This was fraught with numerous challenges and dangers. The untouchables such as the Chamars and Mahars were themselves not too keen, and even those who were, were deeply scared of the wrath of the upper castes. With great difficulty and sometimes by even paying them some money, they would invite some of them to sit with reformers and sing songs openly in the town. While walking along the streets, Savarkar would deliberately put his hand around the shoulder of an untouchable or take something from his hand or give him something. Such activities were viewed with utter shock and disbelief. Slowly, as time progressed, people began allowing some of these members of the untouchable communities into the town, to participate in religious festivals or even purchase goods at their shops. Unlike earlier times when the purchased item would be thrown in a bag kept far away, they began to hand these over in a more civil manner.

During the Ganeshotsav in Ratnagiri in 1925, a special idol named the 'untouchables' Ganapati' was set up and many Brahmins went there to receive their blessings and offer greetings. One Shivu of the Bhangi community undertook the worship of the Ganesh idol. More than 5000 people took part in the festivities. This was indeed a revolutionary act for a community steeped in tradition.

In 1925, the Ratnagiri Hindu Sabha undertook the most challenging work of admitting children of untouchables to schools along with other children. This was to strike at the very root of the system by encouraging behavioural changes from childhood. Hitherto, children of untouchables could not sit in the same classrooms as the rest of society. They squatted outside the rooms and heard the lectures, beyond the walls and sight of upper-caste children. The teachers never touched their notebooks or slates. Even when they wanted to punish one of them, they would throw a stick at them rather than go near and beat them up. There was not a single school in the towns of Ratnagiri or Malwan where children were taught together. A half-hearted government circular of 1923 urged schools to intermix children of all castes. But given the societal taboos that remained a circular merely on paper.

Hence, starting 1925, Savarkar decided to tackle this problem head-on. In Dapoli, Khed, Chiplun, Devarukh, Sangameshwar, Kharepatan and other places, he conducted a series of lectures, public debates and tours to

convince and urge people to let children study together. In public meetings
he exposed the hypocrisy of his opponents:

> Can you prevent Christian children from attending public schools?
> No! You dare not, since you know the consequences. The British
> Government will reply with bullets. You insult the untouchables because
> they are ignorant and helpless. But you yield to the unjust demands of the
> Muslims because they are aggressive. When a Mahar becomes a Muslim
> or a Christian convert, you treat him as your equal. But as a Mahar, he
> will not receive the same treatment.[6]

In the town of Ratnagiri, he pursued this crusade painstakingly, in school
after school. Interestingly, the non-Brahmin communities such as the
Marathas, Kulavadis, Bhandaris and others were more resistant to change
than the Brahmins.

When the chairman of the School Board passed a resolution to allow
children to study together, Savarkar faced severe opposition from all
communities throughout the district. Brahmins, Marathas, Khots, Savkars,
Patils and all communities protested to get the decision cancelled.[7] There
were strikes, skirmishes, violent agitations, riots and even sabotage in
Kotavade, Fonda, Kanakavali, Shiposhi, Kandalgaon, Adivare and other
villages against Savarkar's moves. This naturally terrified the School Board.
In 1929, the District Board passed a resolution that mixing of children
in schools was not compulsory. But Savarkar refused to give up. On one
hand, he wanted to bring about a change of heart among the people, and
on the other, he wanted to take this struggle to the higher authorities and
even the legislative council.

While Savarkar and his colleagues were labouring so hard for the
cause of the children of the untouchables, their own parents were fearful
or hesitant to participate wholeheartedly. The Hindu Sabha members
paid the parents to send their children to school, provided textbooks,
notebooks, pencils and slates to urge them to go. Despite that, they
were reluctant. They kept making excuses. During the rainy season, they
would tell Savarkar that he must provide umbrellas first and only then
they would send their children to school. But even when that was done,
there was dereliction. Finally, after seven long years of relentless struggle
and several thousand rupees spent on this cause by the Hindu Sabha from
the fund that was collected slowly, Savarkar's efforts began to yield fruits.

Children began to be taught together in a few schools. The movement then slowly spread to others by word of mouth. Savarkar writes about how important this intermixing at the level of children was:

> High caste children come in contact with children from untouchable families at a very young age and this was very important. On the one hand, education helps to uplift the untouchable children. On the other hand, this early contact makes upper caste children realize that these untouchables whom their families despise, are just like them. Some of them can be as clever or even better than them. This removes all arrogance of superiority of birth. When this evil practice is uprooted from their minds at a very early age, it has a positive impact throughout their life. Hence we recommend every reformer to study our work and methodology that we adopted in these seven years.[8]

Savarkar wrote several letters to those in positions of power on this matter and brought to their notice the names of schools that still continued with the abhorrent practice of discriminating children based on caste. He also made efforts to get untouchables employment in government. On behalf of the Ratnagiri Hindu Sabha, he made a presentation to British officer Mr Lamington, ICS, who had the special responsibility of looking after the interests of repressed classes in Bombay Presidency. Savarkar told him in an appeal in 1932:

> Once the children are educated together, they will not accept the caste hierarchy in later life. They will not feel the need to observe caste divisions. Therefore the Government Regulations of 1923 should be strictly enforced. In addition, the Government must abandon the title of 'Special Schools for Low-Caste Children'. This very title creates a feeling of inferiority among children attending the school.[9]

An incident that underscores how important this was in Savarkar's mind occurred in 1932. A visitor came to him with a plea to invite him to his village. Savarkar immediately asked him if there was a school in the village, whether untouchables were allowed to attend them and, if so, whether the children sit together and study. The visitor was flummoxed. He sheepishly answered that they sat separately. Savarkar politely told him with folded hands: 'Give my regards to the villagers. I have only one request to them.

At least in the sacred house of Goddess Saraswati, the goddess of learning, they should not follow any discrimination. Once they accept this small request of mine, I will set aside all other work and readily come to your village.'[10]

The district magistrate was to himself attest the beneficial results of Savarkar's efforts: 'It is the good result of Mr. Savarkar's lectures that the untouchable boys have been allowed to sit mixed and get their education without any invidious distinction being made in their case.'[11]

In 1928, when an untouchable teacher was transferred to a school that was attended largely by upper-caste children, all hell broke loose. The orthodox Hindus tried every means to get this order rescinded. Savarkar prevailed upon the School Board not to succumb to such pressures. The Board finally threatened the opponents that it would shut the school down if such demands were made. This finally made them see sense and wind up their meaningless agitation.

From 1927 onwards, Savarkar made another daring attempt. On the occasions of Hindu festivals such as Dussehra or Makar Sankranti, Hindu Sabha representatives belonging to the untouchable communities such as Mahars, Chamars or Bhangis would accost the upper castes with their wishes: 'We greet you on behalf of the Ratnagiri Hindu Sabha by offering you the *sona* leaves.[12] Please allow us to at least come as far as you allow non-Hindus in your homes. Is it not an insult to regard the untouchables, who follow the same religion as you do, as being inferior to the non-Hindus?' Many would be moved by this and Savarkar and his untouchable associates would be welcomed into homes. They would exchange the sona leaves symbolizing camaraderie, distribute sweets and shout, 'Long live Hindu dharma.' Savarkar recounts that many people also shouted and abused them, throwing them away from their doorsteps with vile curses. But the group never gave up. They kept persisting in their attempts and played on the humanity of the oppressors. Gradually the resistance petered out. By 1930, despite the fact that names of people who exchanged the leaves with other castes and untouchables started getting published in newspapers, more than 90 per cent of households in Ratnagiri welcomed Savarkar's team.

Savarkar then shifted his attention to another important demographic—women. Most often women hardly had any say in determining such matters. Here too, the women's wing that included Savarkar's wife Yamunabai sat with other women, convinced them and urged them to mix with women of other castes. The attempt began in 1925. Only five women (which included Yamunabai) of the upper castes were willing to participate. Untouchable women who were hesitant had to be induced through incessant pleas to give up their reluctance and meet the upper caste women. With time, hundreds of women began mixing with each other freely, and without any prejudices.

Even in places of public entertainment such as theatres and cinemas, untouchables were seated separately. When some of Savarkar's plays were staged in Ratnagiri, he gave free passes to untouchables to occupy prominent front seats. This caused a lot of unease. The local magistrate too intervened and wondered if this would create a law-and-order situation. Savarkar assured him that it would be his responsibility to maintain amity. Finally, after long arguments with the audiences who had gathered to watch the play, everyone reconciled and sat together to enjoy the show.

Owners of public carriages and carts refused to seat untouchables, though they had no problems with non-Hindus. The Hindu Sabha actively campaigned with the drivers of these carriages and urged them to seat everyone without any discrimination. They even paid for the journeys of untouchables. Mock journeys were organized just to display to the rest of society that an untouchable was happily travelling around town in a public carriage! Yet again, after immense resistance, slowly this fortress too was breached by Savarkar.

In 1925, on the occasion of Hanuman Jayanti, a new temple was built by the Guravas in Shirgaon. Their community leader Mahadev Laxman requested Savarkar to inaugurate the temple after its consecration. Savarkar pleaded that the untouchable Mahars and Mangs too be allowed to circumambulate the temple. Laxman grudgingly agreed. The temple was thus thrown open to all castes. Cutting across caste barriers, women performed the ritual of offering each other *Haldi-Kumkum* or turmeric and vermillion, as symbols of auspiciousness. It was on this occasion that the famous song composed by Savarkar '*Tumhi amhi sakal Hindu bandhu bandhu*' (All of us Hindus are brethren) was sung. The importance of this act of letting all castes participate in the worship lies in the breaking of one of the seven shackles of Sparsha bandi where the application of turmeric and vermilion on the forehead meant touching a woman from the lower caste.[13]

On 16 June 1925 when Congress leader Chittaranjan Das died, a memorial service was to be held at the Vitthal temple of Ratnagiri.

Savarkar insisted that untouchables too must be allowed to participate in this memorial service. The organizers agreed and Mahar, Chamar and other castes joined this meeting.[14]

In Shirgaon, a Satyanarayan pooja was performed in the house of a Chamar. Savarkar and his associate Vishnupant Damle accepted the holy offering or prasad from the hands of the untouchable, thereby breaking the traditional Roti bandi, which forbade upper castes from dining with untouchables.[15] At another Satyanarayan puja organized on 29 May 1927 by the non-Brahmin communities of Kunbi and Bhandari castes, Savarkar made a passionate plea to let his untouchable friends participate in the event too. Those who were sitting outside the house were finally allowed to come in and participate in the ceremonies.[16] This was breaking the hierarchies among the lower castes themselves. Similarly, in 1928, be it during the Gokulashtami celebrations in August or in a circus show in Ratnagiri, Savarkar used all opportunities to integrate the untouchable community with the rest of society.[17]

To dismantle the proprietary rights that Brahmins held over traditional Vedic knowledge, making it inaccessible to other castes (Vedokta bandi), Savarkar freely taught the sacred Gayatri mantra to everyone. In May 1929, he organized a function in Ratnagiri to declare that anyone who called himself a Hindu had the right to conduct Vedic ceremonies as the Vedas belonged to all castes, and also to wear the sacred thread. He distributed sacred threads to several untouchables of the Mahar and Chamar castes and told them, 'Take these holy threads and stop bickering.' The thread was a symbol of a huge division between the Brahmin and the non-Brahmin castes. This simple act of Savarkar brought down a big bastion of Brahminism and caste discrimination, making it an extremely emotional moment for the untouchables who had all along been despised.

One could well argue as to why someone like Savarkar who stood for dismantling the caste system would perpetuate the practice of wearing the sacred thread that was perceived as a symbol of caste oppression for many in the country. There could be two approaches to remove a symbol or icon that is seen as being discriminatory—be a nihilist and break it completely for everyone or universalize and co-opt its acceptance by all and thereby render the discrimination infructuous. Savarkar chose the latter path rather than advocate the violent methods of storming people's homes and cutting off their sacred threads, as was adopted by social reformers in some parts of the country. His approach was to also take into account the religious sanctity, sentiments and the respect that people accorded to the wearing of the sacred thread.

So overwhelmed were the untouchables by Savarkar's gestures that they invited him to preside over The Untouchables Conference in Malvan in 1928. Everyone sang Vedic hymns in unison. Savarkar distributed sacred threads to everyone amidst a thunderous applause. He said:

> A battle royal has been raging for the last seven generations over the right of studying the Vedas. Here is the sacred thread. Take them. When non-Hindus are reading the Vedas, why should not the Hindu Mahars read them? The feud over this problem was useless. Lets us expiate the sins we committed. We are all responsible for our political subjugation. That is now the past. At least now let us declare an oath that we shall rectify our past blunders and win back our wealth and glory. The people who regard untouchability, which has been a disgrace to humanity, as a part of their religion, are really the fallen people.[18]

Savarkar's passionate speech moved one among the leaders of the untouchables, Sergeant Ghatge, who got up and declared, 'Now, who says that Mahars should convert and become Muslims? We Mahars and Chamars love the Hindu Dharma and will never abandon it. The Brahmins might convert to Islam, but we will not!'[19] This gesture of acceptance and inclusion that Savarkar experimented had achieved the results that he had hoped for.

After the conference at Malvan, Pandurang Nathuji Rajbhoj, a prominent leader of the depressed classes from Poona, observed:

> I was really sceptical of the Savarkarian movement at the beginning. My contact and discussions with Barrister Savarkar and my personal observation have thoroughly convinced me of its far-reaching effect. I am extremely rejoiced to declare that this famous leader of the political revolutionaries is also an out and out social revolutionist![20]

In 1930, one of the lowest among the untouchable class, the scavenger community of Bhangis, approached Savarkar with their grouse that given their supposed lowly status no Brahmin or even Mahar priest officiated in their marriages. Savarkar immediately summoned two of his Brahmin followers, taught them the rituals necessary to officiate a Vedic wedding ceremony and they conducted the marriages of the Bhangis.[21] It was again an attempt to open the timeless treasure of Vedic knowledge, which was truly for all of humanity and not for one community or caste alone. In the process, Savarkar helped build bridges within Hindu society and strengthen it.

It was a strange practice that caste Hindus were comfortable with hiring Muslim bandsmen for their religious or family celebrations, but abhorred untouchable Hindus. So, Savarkar decided to create a 'Hindu music band' comprised only of the untouchables. This also gave them a definite source of income. His singing group that sang devotional songs at religious events also became a huge hit among the masses.[22] They met regularly at the Vitthal temple to practise there. It was symbolic of temple entry as well as community worship. By 1929, his group was regularly invited to sing devotional songs at festivals such as Ganeshotsav and Krishna Janmashtami. There were obviously conservatives who opposed these moves, but Savarkar remained unmoved by societal pressures. He had a clear vision of what he wanted to achieve and how to get there as well.

~

Around this time, the country found its great champion for the cause of the depressed classes, Bhimrao Ramji Ambedkar (1891–1956). Born in a family of Mahars, Ambedkar suffered the same scourge of untouchability and social humiliation in his early life. But being supremely gifted, he overcame all these limitations that society imposed on him and went on to earn doctorates in economics from both Columbia University and the London School of Economics. He served as a professor in the Sydenham College of Commerce and Economics in Bombay by 1918. During the discussions around the Government of India Act of 1919, Ambedkar was an active votary of separate electorates and reservations for untouchables.[23] Despite his personal advancement as a scholar and a practising lawyer in the Bombay High Court, his heart ached for members of his community who still faced the same discrimination and could not achieve the upward mobility that he had managed to by his sheer hard work and genius. He formed a Bahishkrit Hitakarini Sabha (Untouchables' Welfare Organization) for the cause of socio-economic and education amelioration of untouchables. In 1927, he burst forth with active movements that mobilized untouchables in mass struggles.

In 1923, Rao Bahadur C.K. Bole had moved and got passed a resolution in the Bombay Legislative Council, as its member, that untouchables should have access to drinking water from common wells, ponds and lakes. The oppressive social discrimination had hitherto barred so many castes from even drinking water from common sources. But just like the resolutions on combined educational classes for all castes, this too remained a law on paper and was never put in practice. On 5 January 1924, the municipal corporation of the town of Mahad declared that the Chavdar Tale or lake was now open to all castes including untouchables. But given the intense social taboos and pressure, even untouchables were scared to break the centuries-old custom. During the conference of the Bahishkrit Hitakarini Sabha held in Kulaba district (now Raigad district), Ambedkar decided to make Mahad the starting point for his agitation and also the implementation of the government resolution.

On 20 March 1927, Ambedkar and his followers took out a procession to Chavdar Tale. This agitation came to be known as the 'Mahad Satyagraha' and was a decisive moment in the struggle against untouchability. Ambedkar drank water from the lake to assert the right of the untouchables to public utilities. This led to a huge uproar from the other castes. Rumours were rife that the untouchables were also planning to enter the town's Vireshwar temple. This led to a massive retaliation from the upper castes, with an almost riotous situation of armed conflict. A day after Ambedkar's defiance, on 21 March 1927, orthodox Hindus (also known as Sanatanis) conducted a purification ritual of the Chavdar lake. They unilaterally revoked the resolution of the legislative council, which had given access of the lake water to the untouchables.[24]

Ambedkar began yet another agitation against this and enrolled people to the movement. Other social organizations were varied in their support. From the non-Brahmin group, Keshavrao Jedhe and Dinkarrao Javalkar rendered support. The appeals to the Marathas and non-Marathas to support the Mahar and Mangs in this agitation were however not well received. This was yet another instance of what Savarkar kept mentioning about the hierarchies even among the non-Brahmin and untouchable communities, leading to an overall lack of social cohesion. Among the Sanatanis, only Bapurao Joshi of the Hindu Mahasabha expressed his support to the cause.[25]

Savarkar provided unconditional support to Ambedkar's Mahad Satyagraha. He stated: 'Untouchability must be condemned and abolished not only as the need of the hour but also as the command of true religion; not only as a policy or as an act of expediency but also as a matter of justice, not only as a matter of obligation but also as a service to humanity.' He declared that the pious and bounden duty of every Hindu was to restore full human rights to their co-religionists.[26]

On 7 September 1927, writing in the *Shraddhanand* weekly in an article titled 'A Warning to Our Untouchable Brothers', Savarkar said that Hindus should accept and support the right of untouchables to take water from the Chavdar Tale in Mahad. In the same article he appealed to the untouchables: 'Don't threaten to leave Hinduism if the so-called upper-caste Hindus oppose your just demand. The Hindu religion is not an exclusive preserve of upper castes alone. It belongs to you as much as it belongs to them'.[27] He further added in this article:

> If, on account of the high caste Hindus obstructing the legitimate rights of our untouchable brothers, the latter then resort to Satyagraha, how can we blame them in any way? Of course, we would prefer that such disputes are settled peacefully with negotiations rather than confrontations. I can say from my own experience that it is possible to convince the high caste people that the untouchability in public places and facilities such as drinking water is wrong and that it can be removed by appealing to them in the name of brotherly love. However, we are also aware of the fact that, if in some cases, the problem is not solved, the untouchables will have to resort to civil disobedience. This is not and should not be a norm but may regrettably become inevitable.
>
> We have been preaching that in public places such as schools, public tanks, water taps, municipalities, district councils and gatherings, we must allow the untouchables access, not only less or perhaps more than what Muslims have. It is their legitimate right. Therefore, we do not blame Dr. Ambedkar in any way for his movement for the right of untouchables to take water form public tanks.
>
> Muslims are allowed to take water from the same tank and wash their utensils and yet our untouchable brothers are forbidden to take water from it even in days of scarcity of water. Not only that, when they tried to exercise their legal rights to take water, they were beaten up. We cannot believe that this beating took place because of the rumours that they were about to enter Hindu temples.[28]

Another discriminatory issue was that of temple entry to untouchables. Temples were not merely centres of worship but also served as important focal points for social, religious and political interactions among different communities. Barring temple entry to untouchables forbade their participation in these vital activities and thereby disrupted feelings of brotherhood, unity and oneness. Savarkar kept labouring for the cause of temple entry, at least up to the sanctum for untouchables. But while his other experiments succeeded, this was one prickly issue that the Sanatanis were obdurate and unrelenting about.

Numerous movements for temple entry occurred during this time across the Bombay Presidency. In 1925, when the untouchables attempted entry into the ancient Amba Devi temple in Amravati, the orthodox trustees of the temple summarily rejected it. On 21 July 1927, a gathering under the leadership of Dadasaheb Khaparde, a senior Hindu Mahasabha leader threatened a satyagraha or agitation if untouchables were not allowed entry within fifteen days. This was summarily rejected by the trustees. A movement was launched and a month's notice was given. But none of these yielded any results. Finally, the frustrated untouchables gave up and declared their intention to leave the Hindu fold and convert.

A similar movement was organized for entry into the Parvati temple in Pune by Annasaheb Bhopatkar of the Hindu Mahasabha on 27 August 1929. Like at Amravati, this proposal too was rejected by the temple board. When all negotiations failed, on 13 October 1929, nearly 100–150 people began a mass agitation that involved defying the ban and entering the temple by force. Activists such as Pandurang Nathuji Rajbhoj, Vinayakrao Bhuskute, Shivram Janba Kamble and Brahmin leaders such as Kakasaheb Gadgil, S.M. Joshi and others, began trekking the hill atop which the temple was located. Stones were pelted at them from within the temple and several people including Rajbhoj and Gadgil were badly injured. Gandhi meanwhile gave a call to the agitators to postpone their movement. But they were adamant and were willing to give a buffer of a mere fortnight. Savarkar and Ambedkar expressed their support and urged the agitators to carry on with their movement. The Sanatanis mocked the movement by advising the untouchables to press their demands in a slow and steady manner and assured them that by the end of 200 years, their demand would surely be met.[29] However none of this deterred the agitators. Finally, the temple trust relented and with the active intervention of Rajbhoj, the untouchables were allowed entry up to a certain point inside the temple.

In Ratnagiri, which was all that Savarkar was confined to, the Vitthal temple became the focal point of his temple entry movement. People of all castes had already congregated in the precincts in 1925 to mourn the death of C.R. Das. But in November 1929, Savarkar called for a total and unconditional entry to the temple. Given the passions that this sensitive issue ignited in the rest of the Bombay Presidency, the city magistrate too was present to observe the proceedings of a public meeting that Savarkar had called for. In his fiery speech, Savarkar laid out all his arguments in favour of a total eradication of untouchability and an entry into the temple. At the end of it, he asked his audience if anyone had objections to raise. There was pin-drop silence and none objected. Thus, in a peaceful, non-agitation mode, hundreds of untouchables entered the temple of Vitthal. With every step that they took, the centuries-old social evil was given a small death blow. Singing songs of their Lord, the untouchables entered the temple, in what was a deeply emotional moment. Tears streamed out of the eyes of many. Savarkar composed a special poem in Marathi for this occasion that was sung by all once they entered the temple. 'Mala Devaache Darshan Gheudya' or 'Allow Me to See My God' was a heart-rending angst of the untouchable that found its articulation through Savarkar's pen:

> To see my God in his temple
> Allow me, I beseech.
> Let my eyes have their fill of Him
> Please, O please.
> Defiled my hands are
> Cleaning your filth night and day.
> To cleanse them in the pure heart
> Allow me, I pray.
> I am but the body, He its life,
> I am the thirst only He can sate.
> I am the Wretched, He the Compassionate,
> Oh let me fall at His feet, prostate.
> I am his devotee, He my Lord,
> I am a Hindu, He my Hindu God.
> O Fellow Hindu Brothers,
> Bar not, beg I, my way to my God![30]

After the emotional entry to the temple, there was the joy of having the *darshan* of the Lord and an unshackling of fetters:[31]

> The impurity of centuries is gone
> Scripture-born stamp is finally torn
> The age-old struggle has ended
> The net of the enemies lies shredded
> The slave of ages hoary,
> Is now our brother in glory!

The same year, in September 1929, Ambedkar was visiting Ratnagiri in connection with a case at the district sessions sourt. Savarkar extended an invitation to him, along with signatures from several citizens for an address from the Vitthal temple, the principal laboratory of Savarkar's efforts. Ambedkar agreed. However, as luck would have it, he received a telegram that necessitated his urgent presence in Bombay and he had to abort his Ratnagiri tour. The town hence missed an opportunity to witness the two social revolutionaries on the same stage and hear them speak.

Savarkar tried to influence the upper-caste Hindus beyond Ratnagiri, where he was restricted. He decided to write an open letter of appeal to the citizens of Nasik, the town of his childhood and growing-up years, to allow untouchables into the famous Lord Rama temple there. In his letter dated 13 March 1931, he said:[32]

> I was brought up in Nasik. Citizens of Nasik had given me great deal of affection as a child. I wish to influence them with the same affection. I have been struggling for the benefit of our Hindu society for the last thirty years and have learned from experience what is good for our society. I am therefore appealing to the people of Nasik to kindly allow untouchables into the temple of Lord Rama. I can guarantee that this will strengthen our society enormously and there is not the slightest harm in it. The demand of the untouchables is perfectly just. They have now come to a decision to carry out a satyagraha for that demand. But this is an inevitable result arising from our own obstinacy to not concede to their legitimate demands. They have waited for sixty to seventy generations now for their rights. How much longer should they wait? It is really up to us now to make way for their entry into the temple. I therefore appeal to all of you that you welcome them with folded hands, and open arms and

ask for their forgiveness for the past deeds and experience the tremendous
sensation that this will create. Let us all say *'Hindu Dharma ki Jai*!
Victory and Glory to our Hindu Dharma!' That will crush the designs
of foreigners who have been looking forward to converting our people,
these very untouchables, to their faiths. Our Lord Rama opened his own
palace to Vibhishan and others though they were born in the family of
Ravana, but they had repented and surrendered to Rama. I sincerely pray
that the same Rama will give you all the good sense to open the doors of
his temple to our brothers and sisters of the untouchable communities.

The letter was sent to Nasik through Bhaurao Gaikwad who had come
to meet Savarkar in Ratnagiri. The letter was published in all the leading
newspapers of Nasik on 16 March. From 15 March itself, the untouchables
had gathered in processions to seek entry into the Rama temple. Despite
Savarkar's passionate plea, they were all beaten up by upper-caste Hindus
who prevented their entry. A local newspaper *Kohinoor* cited this event
and called it a 'Mess created by Savarkar'.[33] The stranglehold of fossilized
traditions was too strong to make any impact, even if it came from someone
they deeply admired and adored.

Numerous such agitations for temple entry marked the late 1920s and
early 1930s where the suppressed communities asserted their rights to
enter places of worship or use common public utilities. Every organization,
be it the Congress or the All-India Hindu Mahasabha, held ambiguous
views on these issues. Many Sanatanis within these bodies were not in
favour of upsetting the status quo and creating social ferment. Within the
Hindu Mahasabha too, Sanatanis like Bhaskar Balwant Bhopatkar were
totally against temple entry for untouchables. Many close associates of
Savarkar such as Vishwas Dawre and Damodar Chandatre, who otherwise
supported his extremist or revolutionary ideas, were reluctant to support
him on the issue of social reforms and his daring measures for the uplift
of untouchables. While Savarkar was in complete favour of temple entry
to untouchables, other Hindu Mahasabha leaders including N.C. Kelkar
and Bhaskar Balwant Bhopatkar only lent vocal support and not active
participation. Hence the issue was complex and there was no homogeneous
support or opposition from any of the social and political leaders of the
time to these vexed matters.

But this dichotomy was particularly peculiar when it came to a body
like the Hindu Mahasabha. On one hand it spoke so much about shuddhi

and sangathan to unite and strengthen Hindu society, and on the other, any attempts to dismantle the Varna system or eradicate untouchability—all of which were detrimental to the unity of Hindu society—were met with varying degrees of response and was, by and large, lukewarm. The Swarajists who represented the Hindu Mahasabha ideology in the legislative council opposed many legislative measures that could have ushered in social reforms. Instances of these are their staunch opposition to the Khoti Abolition Bill and the scrapping of the Joshi Vatan and Kulkarni Vatan Bills. Between 1921 and 1929, council members such as A. N. Surve and C.K. Bole raised the complaints of the agricultural classes (*kulas*) against the oppression of the landlords (*khotis*) in the Ratnagiri and Kulaba districts of Konkan. Many khots were from the upper castes and belonged to the Swaraj Party and the Congress. Since their interests were being hurt, they managed to lobby with the government to scrap such attempts. Similarly, the bills that sought to strip off the hereditary special privileges to village priests (Joshis) and accountants (Kulkarnis) were opposed by the Swaraj Party and Hindu Mahasabha leaders, given the obvious conflicts of interest. Though in this case, despite their opposition, the bills that stripped the Joshis and Kulkarnis of money and *jagirs* (lands) merely on the basis of their heredity were eventually introduced and passed in the legislative council. But the stand taken by the Hindu Mahasabha on such crucial reforms impacted its image badly.

Savarkar was perhaps among the few exceptions who walked the talk when it came to his conviction on this matter. But that was not enough to create a mass acceptance of the Hindu Mahasabha as a pan-Hindu body and it was still seen as a caucus of privileged upper-caste Hindus who offered mere lip service to social reforms. Where the Hindu Mahasabha managed to capture the imagination and support of Hindus was by entering the space of being champions for the community in the wake of deteriorating relations with Muslims. Hence, despite communities within the Hindu fold being opposed to it over its stand on issues of social reforms, the Hindu Mahasabha managed to appropriate the position of being a champion for the community's interests, vis-à-vis the Muslim organizations or the Congress that had an ambivalent stand.

The high point of Savarkar's social reform movement in Ratnagiri came in 1931. Given the various agitations centring around temple entry, Savarkar envisioned a pan-Hindu temple that was open to prayer by all castes and creeds without any discrimination. With this in mind, he approached the wealthy businessman Bhagoji Baloji Keer, who was famous for several temples that he had built. Keer was a great admirer of Savarkar and immediately agreed to fund the project at a cost of Rs 2.5 lakh. On 10 March 1929, the Shankaracharya, Dr Kurtkoti, laid the foundation stone (*bhoomipoojan*) of the proposed temple. Savarkar's dreams were realized on 22 February 1931 when the magnificent temple, which he named 'Patit Pavan Mandir' (literally meaning the Saviour of the Downtrodden), was inaugurated in Ratnagiri with much fanfare. Enumerating the reasons for the temple, Savarkar writes:

> We realized that there were bound to be many difficulties in opening up long standing temples to untouchables. The diehards could raise legal objections. Some priests could argue that the temples were private property and they had the right to refuse entry to untouchables. We therefore decided to build a new temple where Hindus of all castes, including untouchables, would be permitted. And once Hindus get used to the idea of worshipping and praying together, they would not feel it necessary to go to the old temples where untouchables were not allowed . . . thousands of men and women of all castes, including the untouchables, have come together in this temple, taking part in many functions, praying together, celebrating together, singing together without slightest notion of their castes. The well, the gardens, the premises are open to ALL Hindus.[34]

Several scholars and pundits graced the inauguration. Many Brahmin priests from Nasik and Kashi refused to do the *prana pratishtha* or consecration of the idol in the Vedic traditions, given the intent of the temple. But Savarkar was unrelenting. He convinced Ganesh Shastri Modak, a disciple of Vinayak Maharaj Masurkar, the head of a Vaishnava ashram in Satara district's Masur, to conduct the rituals, with Bhagoji leading the puja. Mahars read the sacred Gita, a scavenger officiated as the temple's priest to whom Brahmins put garlands and bowed down to. It was truly an epic moment in the history of Indian social reforms and dismantling of the inhuman practice of untouchability and caste barriers. However, it turned several orthodox Hindus and Sanatanis against Savarkar.

~

Another major initiative that Savarkar undertook was the initiation of inter-caste dining or *sahabhojan*. At the time when he began this movement, people of a caste who belonged to different sub-castes within that same caste also refused to eat together. For instance, despite being Brahmins, the Deshasthas and Chitpawans would not dine together. Mahars refused to eat with the Bhangis, and the Bhangis in turn with the Dhors. Unlike the usual practice to blame the Brahmins or upper castes alone for the scourge of untouchability, Savarkar understood that the malaise ran deep. Time and time again, Savarkar emphasized this aspect of the highs and lows even among the so-called lower castes and untouchables in his speeches and writings and the imperative to get rid of all these divisions within Hindu society equally. A Mahar priest would never officiate a Bhangi wedding or a Mahar would never accept tea or water from a Dhor, Chamar, Maang, Matang or Bhangi who were considered lower in caste status than him.

Once, during a public speech on 28 March 1934, a Mahar brought a cup of tea to Savarkar with the intention to test him and was flummoxed when the latter readily drank it. He immediately told the Mahar: 'You put me to test, right? Now will you accept the same tea served by this Maang or Matang here? Please don't make such a show again. Untouchability is not being observed by Brahmins alone. Untouchables do the same. We are all equally guilty of this offence.'[35]

Writing further on these deep-rooted divisions among castes in the *Kirloskar Magazine*, January–February 1935 issue, Savarkar postulated:

> But it is not just the high castes who persecute untouchables. Persons of one group of untouchables persecute persons of another group of untouchables whom they consider as their inferior or as 'their untouchables' with just the same vigour. Consider a hot summer's day. A Mahar is thirsty, on a village well there are crows and dogs drinking water, but he is forbidden to drink water from that well. He becomes furious and curses the Brahmins and Marathas who will hound him out. When he says they are demons, he does tell the truth. But if a Bhangi was to take water from a well in a Maharwada, the Mahars would also hound the Bhangi with equal wrath. Then the Mahars become Brahmins to that Bhangi. Recently, there was a Satyagraha by Mahars who wanted to enter the Rama Mandir of Nasik. They were badly beaten up by Brahmins and Vaishyas. True, that was terribly unjust. But it should not be forgotten that if a Bhangi were to enter a Mariaii temple of the Mahars, they too would have thrashed that Bhangi just as badly.[36]

In such a deeply fractured social order, expecting people to sit down and share their meals with untouchables was both unimaginable and also considered blasphemous. There were reports of how even Mahar beggars would rather die of hunger than accept food served at Savarkar's inter-caste dining only because castes lower than them were also part of the congregation.[37] But Savarkar with his perseverance slowly managed to convince people. The first such inter-dining programme took place in 1930. About this event, the *Times of India* dated 9 December 1930 wrote:

> This all-caste dinner was organized in a unique manner—a manner that has given deep offence to Nationalist Congressmen, who are mostly believers along with Mr. Gandhi in four watertight castes by birth. For, at Ratnagiri, some enthusiastic reformers, who regarded caste system as the bane of Hinduism, held an all-caste dinner, which was attended by Brahmins, Banias, Chambhars, Mahars and Bhangis . . . what is still more interesting, the spirit of this splendid essay in practical reform, Mr. V.D. Savarkar, delivered a speech in which he flung into the teeth of orthodoxy . . . 'From today, I shall not believe in highness or lowness of caste. I shall not oppose the intermarriage between the highest and lowest castes. I shall eat with any Hindu irrespective of caste. I shall not believe in caste by birth or by profession and henceforth, I shall call myself a Hindu only—not Brahmin, Vaishya, etc.[38]

On the third day of the inauguration of the Patit Pavan Mandir, he organized inter-dining in the temple complex. He preached on this occasion: 'Eat with anybody. Eat anything that is medically fit and clean. That does not deprive you of your religion. Remember, the root of religion is not the dish or the stomach, but the heart, soul and the blood!'[39] But interestingly, several of his closest associates and supporters including the Shankaracharya, Dr Kurtkoti, religious figures such as Masurkar Maharaj, Pachalegaonkar Maharaj, Chowde Maharaj and even Sheth Bhagoji Keer, who bore the expenses of the temple, refused to join. Savarkar was a liberal who was extremely accommodative of differing opinions and never forced his ideas over others. When he heard about their reservations on the inter-dining plan, he said: 'I respect the wishes of those who do not wish to join in. They can have their dinners separately according to the tradition. I do not insist that they must join in. However those who wish to eat together should also be free to do so.'[40] He held the same view all along that any societal change must come from within the society and with a genuine change of heart. Forcing people to do something against their wishes creates ill will and ruptures in society. Even in an article of December 1936, he said: 'We want to abolish the caste system and propagate dining together. But, we do not insist that everyone must take part in such communal dinners. Those who do not want to join in must not regard others as sinners or behaving unethically. That is all!'[41]

His inter-dining project was truly pushing the envelope a bit too much in its initial days, especially in a caste-ridden, orthodox society. Conservatives and sanatanis were livid and made declarations that if the Peshwas had been around, Savarkar would have been trampled under the foot of an elephant as a punishment for such blasphemy. To these barbs hurled against him, Savarkar wrote:

> We, the reformers, have realized that unless we eradicate the division by castes, the Hindu society cannot make progress. We do not feel that by propagating our views on the subject we are hurting religious feelings of anyone. We say to our opponents, if you feel that our opinions are wrong, you put forward your arguments. We do not object to that. On the contrary, we say that, just as the reformers have the right to propose social reforms, the society, reluctant to reform, also has the right to boycott the reformers.[42]

In an article, Savarkar mentions how his crusade for social reforms led to his boycott. Even those who deeply revered him for his revolutionary work and patriotism were uncomfortable on sensitive issues such as inter-dining. He narrates in the article how many of these people would invite Savarkar to their family celebrations and marriage parties. Out of immense respect for him, they would have a special seat with decoration and dishes served in silver vessels and so on. But Savarkar would approach the host and tell them candidly:

> Listen, I do not want to cause any embarrassment to you. It is well known that I propagate and do take part in dining with the Mahars. It is not right that my eating at your place should lead to spoiling the atmosphere at your festivities, as many of your guests may not like to dine with me. So, I suggest a compromise. In accordance with the tradition, you would provide dinner to the Mahars and other untouchables outside the

compound. I would also sit in their company. Then there would be no ill feeling of any kind.

This statement would baffle and also melt the hearts of even his opponents. They would then insist on him joining the main party.[43]

Extending this idea of inter-caste dining, on 1 May 1933, Savarkar got an All-Hindu cafe (Akhil Hindu Upaharagruha) opened in Ratnagiri. He writes about the need for such a cafe:

When I first came to Ratnagiri in 1924, the restaurant owners would serve tea to untouchables only by pouring into their own cups or coconut shells from a distance. However, Muslims were welcome and allowed to sit inside and were served tea normally. We therefore established a restaurant that would be open to ALL Hindus. In this place, it was the usual practice to publish names of those who take food, tea and snacks. Despite this publicity, Hindus of ALL castes openly used this restaurant for their regular meals. No one was made outcast for eating in this place. This happened on 1 May 1933. It must be emphasized that tea and food was [were] served by untouchables. Once again, we have to remember that such a café was unique in the whole of India at that time. It was not possible to run such a café even in urbanized Mumbai.[44]

It was not as if those who dined at the cafe were openly accepted in society. N.C. Kelkar drank tea in this cafe on 15 May 1933 for which he was severely criticized by orthodox Hindus. Savarkar's biographer Dhananjay Keer too faced social ostracism for drinking tea at this cafe.[45] Almost always, the cafe ran on losses and Savarkar made up the deficit from his own pocket, despite the paltry income that he got. In March 1934, when Savarkar went to Khed to deliver a lecture on the need to break the caste barriers, followed by a public reception, attendees refused to drink water with him![46]

But Savarkar was never miffed with people, including his supporters, who differed with him, especially on touchy matters such as inter-dining. In a December 1936 article, he writes:

Among the people who boycott our programmes for dining together, there are many conservatives who sincerely believe that it is a sin to dine together with people of all castes. They naturally feel hurt by such reforms. They do not want to keep any contact with the reformers. That is but natural, due to centuries of social conditioning. We should not be angry with them. We must never ever hate them. We should gladly suffer their boycott and persecution till they voluntarily change their minds, as long as they adopt legal and peaceful means of protesting against us. We must disregard their opposition and simply carry on with our reforms. We require dynamism and movement for the good of the society. But we also require stability and restraint to some extent. A train needs an engine as a driving force. But it also needs brakes. Our Hindu society has shown remarkable capacity for both survival and revival under enormous threats from outside. There is a danger that the reformers may get carried away. They therefore need a control, some exercise of restraint. To what extent and proportion are they necessary is a matter of judgment. We need to understand that reforms and restraints are complementary. It is therefore vital that we try to convince the conservatives of our point of view, try to persuade them and try to convert them. That is essential for the nation's good.[47]

After the initiation of inter-dining in 1930, Savarkar used numerous occasions—be they family ceremonies or religious festivals—to propagate and popularize the concept. At times he would even put this as a precondition for his participation in events or staging of his plays. In March 1936, when the renowned Marathi theatre artist Bal Gandharva, a great admirer of Savarkar, insisted that he attend a play, Savarkar agreed to come if an inter-dining was organized after the staging. Bal Gandharva readily agreed and the play was followed by *sahabhojan*.[48] That same year, during Ganeshotsav on 26–27 August, inter-dining was organized, in which Prabodhankar, the father of Shiv Sena founder Bal Saheb Thackeray, too participated.[49] On 11 September 1935, a Bhangi woman came to the Patit Pavan temple, sat in the company of upper-caste women and was served food. This news was published in several newspapers along with the names of the participants, but no one seemed to bother much about their names being made public.

Despite this eventual success, among all his reform movements, the inter-dining seemed to face the maximum resistance from society. It was difficult to hire halls for conducting the dinners or even get a cook.[50] Conservative Hindus began treating those who participated in Savarkar's inter-dining programmes as outcastes. They refused to marry into the households of such people and boycotted them socially.[51] Even if a person who participated in inter-dining was of their own caste, he/she was refused entry into houses or disallowed from drawing water from the other's wells.[52] Priests refused to officiate in marriages or sacred thread ceremonies of inter-dining participants.[53] One can imagine the amount of mental trauma that anybody participating in such activities faced on a daily basis. Many of them could not take it any more and rushed back to their religious heads to purify themselves and eschew the idea.

But none of this deterred Savarkar. He was resolute in his mission. The perseverance paid off. In due course, the movement spread all over Maharashtra and other parts of India too—Poona, Bombay, Vasai, Sangli, Kalyan, Kolhapur, Karhad, Savantvadi, Amravati, Shahabad, Indore, Karachi and Rajputana. Many eminent people lent their names and support to his mission. They included Keshavrao Jedhe, Parsi leader K.F. Nariman, theatre superstar Bal Gandharva, the maharaja of Aundh State, social reformer Maharshi Annasaheb Karve (or Dhondo Keshav Karve), novelist V.S. Khandekar, social worker and Congressman 'Kakasaheb' Narhar Vishnu Gadgil, writer, educationist, orator and poet 'Acharya' Prahlad Keshav Atre and others. The inclusion of such 'celebrities' normalized inter-dining and the fierce opposition that it faced in its initial years, gradually seemed to taper down.

In course of time, the Patit Pavan Mandir became the venue for several conferences that brought together people of all castes. In end-February 1931, the Depressed Classes Mission led by V.R. Shinde held its sixth annual session at the temple and requested Savarkar to preside. The members concurred that if the successful social experiments conducted by Savarkar in Ratnagiri could be replicated across India, untouchability and caste barriers would be a thing of the past. The Ratnagiri District Somavanshiya Mahar Conference too was held in the temple on 26 April 1931. Hundreds of Mahars from all over Bombay Presidency participated and Savarkar presided over the conference. His work and speeches on these occasions brought in praise from Ambedkar in his newsletter *Janata* dated 11 May 1931. Savarkar lent his support to Ambedkar's famous Nasik Satyagraha that began on 2 March 1930 to gain entry for the untouchables into the Kala Ram temple. Savarkar issued a statement that had he not been under the restrictions imposed on him by the government to not leave Ratnagiri or participate in political activities, he would have been among the first to participate and court arrest in the Nasik Satyagraha.[54]

In 1933, Savarkar and his associates decided to celebrate 22 February as 'Death of Untouchability' day. Over a decade of strenuous efforts accompanied by logical reasoning and convincing all communities had brought Hindus of all castes in Ratnagiri together. An effigy of untouchability was also burnt with the consent of all Hindus to send a symbolic message of its losing influence in Ratnagiri.

A noted Brahmo Samaj practitioner and social worker who had been working relentlessly for the eradication of untouchability since 1908, 'Karmaveer' Maharshi Vitthal Ramji Shinde, was present at this momentous occasion of the burning of the effigy of this social evil. Speaking at the ceremony, he said:

I have observed closely the change in the mental outlook of people in Ratnagiri and I can say without any doubt that this social revolution is unparalleled. I have been a social reformer all my life. I know how difficult and tedious the work is. At times, I have myself felt utterly frustrated. And yet, within a short period of seven years, by Savarkar's movement, thousands in Ratnagiri have abandoned untouchability, thus striking at the very heart of caste barrier. You are all mixing freely even with the Bhangis, eating with them, worshipping with them. I have noticed all these changes. This is even more incredible as Ratnagiri was said to be a hotbed of traditional conservatives. Besides, this town has no railway station, no telephones. It is so isolated. I am so glad to say that I am alive to witness this day.

I do not want to be a bard of anyone, but I am lost for words for the incredible social reform carried out by Veer Savarkar. I know that thousands of youths trust him without a second thought. But I say that fearless Veer Savarkar is the youngest of you all. In a way, we must thank the British that he was interned in Ratnagiri, because that gave him an opportunity to carry out these reforms. I am so pleased with what Savarkar has achieved that I pray to the Lord that He should give the remainder of my life to Savarkar so that he will fulfill my ambitions and aspirations. Mr. Rajbhoj and I have decided to ask the British Government that Savarkar should be given freedom to move in the country at least for doing social work. I am sure you will all agree with us on this proposal.[55]

The renowned Gandhian who was hailed as the 'Gandhi of Konkan', Sitarampant Patwardhan[56] or Appasaheb Patwardhan, wrote an article in the *Satyashodhak* on 30 May 1925 praising Savarkar's efforts at untouchability eradication. He said:

Till a few years back, the movement regarding untouchability eradication was confined to merely talking about it in intellectual gatherings and writing articles lampooning the scourge. But when Mr Savarkar came to Ratnagiri, he dared to talk openly about this at a 'Shivaji Jayanti' and also act on his words. He advised me to work dedicatedly towards the eradication of untouchability. Mr Savarkar is solely responsible for translating the idea into an organized and practical form.[57]

As a man of action and not mere preaching, Savarkar constantly urged his followers to demonstrate their resolve tangibly. In continuation of the lecture series (*Vyakhyanamala*) that Justice Ranade had begun in Poona, similar series were routinely organized in various parts of Maharashtra and covered sociocultural and political themes. At one such lecture series in Ratnagiri in May 1932, Savarkar said at the valedictory that Vyakhyanamalas were necessary in the times of Ranade and Chiplunkar, but what was the need of the hour was *Kriyamalas*—or action, not mere talk. The awakening needed to be transformed into actions in order to see tangible results.[58]

On his decade-long struggle with his associates to usher in social reforms in the town, Savarkar writes:

In Ratnagiri, almost every Hindu had taken part in inter-caste dining or had taken food with those who did. In other words, inter-caste dining is no longer considered an objectionable deed. Within a period of ten years (1924 to 1934), we removed not only the shackles of untouchability but also of inter-caste dining. This social revolution is indeed praiseworthy. However, we must remember that it was like saying 'It is better to make progress at the speed of a tortoise than no progress at all!' Look at what other people have achieved in the last ten years. Russia progressed at the speed of an aeroplane, and we congratulate ourselves that we can walk without the support of a baby-walker. Still when we were almost dead, at least we have now started to walk, that is progress. We need to make this progress thousand fold.[59]

For Savarkar the eradication of these social evils was as important as political freedom of India. He made this point clear in several of his writings and public speeches. Three such are quoted below:

Though I said it a hundred times before, I say it again so that no one should have any doubts about the reality that for the progress of the Hindu nation, we need both political and social reforms. Consider politics as a sword and social reforms as a shield. Both are complementary to each other. One is ineffective without the other.[60]

Some may feel that social reforms are much less important than gaining of political power. But they are closely related to each other. It is therefore essential to pay attention to social reforms too. It is no good assuming that social reforms will take place with the passage of time. Sometimes that may appear to be the case. However, those changes took place because someone in the past made efforts for them. Therefore, we must make persistent efforts for the changes that we wish to see in future.[61]

The abolition of the caste system is far more important than the mere thinking of political movements. It is true that many social reforms cannot be pursued with vigour without political independence, but a start has to be made for those social reforms, which would enable us to sustain our freedom after independence.[62]

Around the time when the Patit Pavan temple at Ratnagiri's fort locality was thrown open to all castes, Savarkar was desirous of having Ambedkar preside over such a momentous event. However, due to prior commitments, Ambedkar could not make it. He sent Savarkar his apologies and also a message:

I take this opportunity of conveying to you my appreciation of the work you are doing in the field of social reform. If the untouchables are to be a part and parcel of the Hindu society, then it is not enough to remove untouchability; for that matter you must destroy *chaturvarnya*.[63] I am glad that you are among the very few who have realized this.[64]

A few years later, on 13 November 1935, Savarkar again extended an invitation to Ambedkar to visit Ratnagiri:

You say that you do not need mere sympathy but show me something concrete that you can achieve. Your demand is perfectly justifiable and understandable. For the last five to six years, I have been asking my followers for specific programmes of action. We have managed to break the shackles of the caste system in Ratnagiri and also in Malvan. What succeeds in one place can also succeed elsewhere because human beings and the pattern of their behavior are same all over. Come and see for yourself what we have achieved.

One of the major obstacles to breaking the barriers of the caste system is the barrier to inter-caste dining. One who breaks the taboo of inter-caste barrier also breaks the shackles of untouchability. What remains is the barrier of inter-caste marriages. But this is up to individual brides and bridegrooms. As long as inter-caste marriages are acceptable and not regarded as anti-religion or such couples are not treated as outcastes, then it would be the end of that matter. I propose the following:

1. Please come to Ratnagiri after a fortnight, and give me, if you can, one week's notice.

2. We propose to arrange a huge inter-caste dining ceremony of about one thousand people that includes Brahmins, Marathas, Vaishyas, Shimpis, Kulavadis, as well as Mahars, Chamars, and Bhangis. People will include all layers of society from well-respected citizens to workers and cleaners. Such ceremonies are not new. In the past, untouchable leaders such as Shri Rajbhoj and Shri Patitpavan Das have witnessed such inter-caste dinings.

3. If you like, we can also arrange an inter-caste dining of ladies. They would include old and young and ladies from well-to-do families to working women. They would also be from all castes—Brahmins, Khatris, Vaishyas, as well as Mahars, Chamars and Bhangis.

4. It is a condition that names of everyone who takes food in such functions would be published in newspapers. Only those who accept this condition will take part.

5. It is the usual practice that religious discourse is delivered by a preacher from one of the castes regarded as very low. You will observe that at the end of the session, the attendees, irrespective of their castes, would bow to that preacher. Recently, Mr. Kajrolkar was honoured in this manner.

6. If you agree, we would like to arrange a lecture by you.

7. Our functions will take place at the Patit Pavan Mandir, which is owned by Seth Bhagoji Keer. There is therefore no legal obstruction whatsoever. Only those who are prepared to participate in inter-caste dining will attend.

8. One important point. So far we organized about 150 inter-caste dinings. The names of the participants have been regularly made public. And yet, no one has been treated as outcaste by his or her people. It has become a matter of personal choice. You will notice the evidence of this change in peoples' attitudes.

We are not saying that by what we have done, we have solved the national problem. But it is a good indication of what can be achieved. We have shown that even the tradition of six thousand years can be broken, as we have done, within six years. And our success in Ratnagiri and Malvan can be repeated elsewhere. You can be sure of that. And it is for this reason, that we are inviting you to Ratnagiri.[65]

In the same letter, Savarkar also brought to Ambedkar's notice his constant theme of the divisions among untouchables too and how those must be eschewed completely if the caste system had to be dismantled. He wrote:

The responsibility for abolishing untouchability and the division created by the caste system lies not only on the shoulders of the high castes. Untouchability and caste division is strongly observed by untouchables too. From the highest (Brahmins) to the lowest (Bhangis) all have committed the same sin. Both must show that they have changed their minds. Both together must absolve this sin. Fault lies with both, question is of degree. One can say that the rigours of the caste system have been broken only if it can be proven that Mahars share food with Brahmins and Marathas but Mahars also share food with Bhangis. I am sure you too have experienced that Mahars are not free from caste prejudice and cannot therefore demand proof of changed mentality only from high castes.[66]

For reasons best known to him, Ambedkar could not oblige this request as well, though he always held Savarkar's social reforms project in great esteem. Strangely, despite hailing from the same state and working for similar causes, these two leaders never met during Savarkar's stay in Ratnagiri. Ambedkar's unwillingness to share stage with Savarkar is inexplicable.

However, Ambedkar's praise of Savarkar on the social reforms front seemed to stem from his strong disagreement on this issue with the other major player in the field of social reforms in India during this time—

Gandhi. Their ideological differences on this matter were legendary. Quoting Gandhi from his Gujarati journal *Navajivan* of 1921–22, Ambedkar wrote about the quintessence of Gandhi's beliefs when it came to the caste system:

Says Mr. Gandhi:

'I believe that if Hindu society has been able to stand, it is because it is founded on the caste system. The seeds of swaraj are to be found in the caste system. Different castes are like different sections of military division. Each division is working for the good of the whole. A community, which can create the caste system must be said to possess unique power of organization. Caste has a ready-made means for spreading primary education. Every caste can take the responsibility for the education of the children of the caste. Caste has a political basis. It can work as an electorate for a representative body. Caste can perform judicial functions by electing persons to act as judges to decide disputes among members of the same caste. With castes it is easy to raise a defence force by requiring each caste to raise a brigade. I believe that inter-dining or intermarriage are not necessary for promoting national unity. That dining together creates friendship is contrary to experience. If this was true, there would have been no war in Europe . . . taking food is as dirty an act as answering the call of nature. The only difference is that after answering call of nature we get peace, while after eating food we get discomfort. Just as we perform the act of answering the call of nature in seclusion, so also the act of taking food must be done in seclusion. In India children of brothers do not intermarry. Do they cease to love because they do not intermarry? Among the Vaishnavas, many women are so orthodox that they will not eat with the members of the family nor will they drink water from a common water pot. Have they no love? The caste system cannot be said to be bad because it does not allow inter-dining or intermarriage between different castes. Caste is another name for control. Caste puts a limit on enjoyment. Caste does not allow a person to transgress caste limits in pursuit of his enjoyment. That is the meaning of such caste restrictions as inter-dining and intermarriage. To destroy caste system and adopt Western European social system means that Hindus must give up the principle of hereditary occupation, which is the soul of the caste system. Hereditary principle is an eternal principle. To change it is to create disorder. I have no use for a Brahmin if I cannot call him a Brahmin for my life. It will be a chaos if every day a Brahmin is to be changed into a Shudra and a Shudra is to be changed into a Brahmin. The caste system is a natural order of society. In India, it has been given a religious coating. Other countries not having understood the utility of the caste system it existed only in a loose condition and consequently those countries have not derived from caste system the same degree of advantage, which India has derived. These being my views, I am opposed to all those who are out to destroy the caste system.'[67]

The stand of the Mahatma justifying the caste system and its merits went completely tangential to Ambedkar's philosophy and also the writings of Savarkar during the same period. While one must give the benefit of doubt to any political leader whose thoughts and philosophy change with time, preferably evolving for the better, Gandhi went a step back in 1925 by expressing his deep faith in the varna system but interpreting it in his own creative manner. In Gandhi's justification for the varna, it is a cloak for the same caste system that he found appealing earlier. Ambedkar quotes Gandhi's writings dated 3 February 1925:

I gave support to caste because it stands for restraint. But at present, caste does not mean restraint, it means limitations. Restraint is glorious and it helps to achieve freedom. But limitation is like chain. It binds. There is nothing commendable in castes as they exist today. They are contrary to the tenets of the shastras. The number of castes is infinite and there is a bar against intermarriage. This is not a condition of elevation. It is a state of fall . . . the best remedy is that small castes should fuse themselves into one big caste. There should be four such big castes so that we may reproduce the old system of four varnas . . . I believe that the divisions into varna is based on birth. There is nothing in the varna system, which stands in the way of the Shudra acquiring learning or studying military art of offence or defence. Contra, it is open to a Kshatriya to serve. The varna system is not bar to him. What the varna system enjoins is that a Shudra will not make learning a way of earning a living. Nor will a Kshatriya adopt service as a way of earning a living. Similarly a Brahmin may learn the art of war or trade . . . but he must not make them a way of earning his living . . . the varna system is connected with the way of earning a living. There is no harm if a person belonging to one varna acquires the knowledge or science and art specialized in by persons belonging to other varnas. But as far as the way of earning his living is concerned he must follow the occupation of the varna to which he belongs which means he must follow the hereditary profession of his forefathers. The object of the varna system is to prevent competition and class struggle and class war. I believe in the varna system because it fixes the duties and occupations of persons. Varna means the determination of a man's occupation before he is born. In the varna system no man has any liberty to choose his occupation. His occupation is determined for him by heredity.[68]

Gandhi held on to this for several years. When a deputation of untouchables came to meet him on 15 December 1932, among other things, he said candidly: 'I do believe in the four varnas . . . All occupations should be hereditary. Millions of people are not going to become Prime Ministers and Viceroys.'[69] This to an Ambedkar or Savarkar would be construed as being antithetical to the fundamental concept of democracy where anyone, irrespective of their dynastic heritage, could actually aspire to become a prime minister or a viceroy!

Writing about the same four varna system around the same time, Savarkar had said:

Refer to Lord Krishna's declaration in the Gita: 'Chaturvarnyam maya srushtam' or 'It is I who have created the four varnas'. Another meaning of the word 'varna' is colour. Evidently, different human beings have different qualities and virtues. All that Krishna is saying is I create human beings who are different in nature, character, virtues and values—yet, good or bad, they are all my creation alone. Nowhere in this declaration does he state that I also make those virtues hereditary for the person's successive generations! When Lokamanya Tilak created a Board of Trustees for the Kesari newspaper, does that mean those trustees were to hold that position for heredity? When such a truism cannot exist for a simple newspaper, can it be true for human existence? The belief is that 'Janmana jaayate Shudraha' or we are all shudras at birth. As life progresses, we attain qualities, education, and virtues to graduate to various levels of consciousness and thinking—that is the fundamental concept behind the four varna system. If these varnas were indeed the bedrock of our civilization and if we believe in the verse that states that there can be no further categories, how is it that we have defied this maxim and created a fifth class of untouchables? . . . Thus those who have already destroyed the *chaturvarna* system by creating the fifth *varna* of untouchables are crying foul about the collapse of Sanatan Dharma if the practice is abolished. What can be more ironical?[70]

Savarkar's declaration during the inauguration of the inter-dining programme in 1930 that he does not wish to be identified as a Brahmin or Vaishya but as a Hindu alone was essentially a call for complete dismemberment of the varna system. He understood that the seeds of the caste system were in the varna concept. One could not eradicate caste without eradicating varna. Gandhi's idealistic prescription was hence not in harmony with ground realities of how varna translated into the caste system. The fundamental philosophical and political differences in the approach to social reforms among all the main protagonists of the time becomes clear here.

On his part, Ambedkar was appalled by Gandhi's initial justification of the caste system and later denouncing it to justify the varna system. He believed that the varna system was the parent of the idea of the caste system. 'If the idea of caste is a pernicious idea,' he argued, 'it is entirely because of the viciousness of the ideas of varna. Both are evil ideas and it matters very little whether one believes in varna or in caste.'[71] 'The outcaste,' said Ambedkar, 'is a bye-product [sic] of the caste system. There will be outcastes as long as there are castes. Nothing can emancipate the outcaste except the destruction of the caste system. Nothing can help to save Hindus and ensure their survival in the coming struggle except the purging of the Hindu faith of this odious and vicious dogma.'[72]

He goes on to elaborate:[73]

The varna system of the Bhagvat Gita has at least two merits. It does not say that it is based on birth. Indeed it makes a special point that each man's varna is fixed according to his innate qualities. It does not say that the occupation of the son shall be that of the father. It says that the profession of a person shall be according to his innate qualities, the profession of the father according to the father's innate quality and that of the son according to the son's innate qualities. But Mr. Gandhi has given a new interpretation of the varna system. He has changed it out of recognition. Under the old orthodox interpretation caste connoted hereditary occupation but varna did not. Mr. Gandhi by his own whim has given a new connotation to varna. With Mr. Gandhi, varna is determined by birth and the profession of a varna is determined by the principle of heredity so that varna is merely another name for caste. That Mr. Gandhi changed from caste to varna does not indicate the growth of any new revolutionary ideology. The genius of Mr. Gandhi is elfish, always and throughout. He has the precocity of an elf with no little of its outward guise. Like an elf he can never grow up and grow out of the caste ideology.

Explaining the intertwining of the varna and caste systems, Ambedkar maintained:

Chaturvarnya is based on worth. How are you going to compel people who have acquired a higher status based on birth, without reference to their worth, to vacate that status? How are you going to compel people to recognize the status due to a man, in accordance with his worth, who is occupying a lower status based on his birth? For this, you must first break up the Caste System, in order to be able to establish the Chaturvarnya system. How are you going to reduce the four thousand castes, based on birth, to the four Varnas, based on worth? This is the first difficulty that the protagonists of the Chaturvarnya must grapple with. Modern science has shown that the lumping together of individuals into a few sharply-marked-off classes is a superficial view of man, not worthy of serious consideration. Consequently, the utilization of the qualities of individuals is incompatible with their stratification by classes, since the qualities of individuals are so variable. Chaturvarnya must fail for the very reason for which Plato's Republic must fail—namely, that it is not possible to pigeonhole men, according as they belong to one class or the other. That it is impossible to accurately classify people into four definite classes is proved by the fact that the original four classes have now become four thousand castes.[74]

Gandhi's response to Ambedkar's critique was revealing of his beliefs:

I do not believe the caste system, even as distinguished from varnashrama, to be an 'odious and vicious dogma'. It has its limitations and its defects, but there is nothing sinful about it, as there is about untouchability, and, if it is a bye-product of the caste system it is only in the same sense that an ugly growth is of a body, or weeds of a crop. It is as wrong to destroy caste because of the outcastes as it would be to destroy a body because of an ugly growth in it, or a crop because of the weeds. The outcasteness, in the sense we understand it, has, therefore, to be destroyed altogether. It is an excess to be removed, if the whole system is not to perish. Untouchability is the product, therefore, not of the caste system, but of the distinction of high and low that has crept into Hinduism and is corroding it. The attack on untouchability is thus an attack upon this 'high-and-low'ness. The moment untouchability goes, the caste system itself will be purified, that is to say, according to my dream, it will resolve itself into the true varnadharma, the four divisions of society, each complementary of the other and none inferior or superior to any other, each as necessary for the whole body of Hinduism as any other.[75]

Ambedkar's anger was further roused when as the president of a conference of untouchables, Gandhi made the following statements:

I do not want to attain *moksha* (liberation) . . . but if I have to be reborn, I should be reborn as an untouchable, so that I may share their sorrows, sufferings and the affronts leveled at them, in order that I may endeavor to free myself and them from that miserable condition. I therefore prayed that if I should be born again, I should do so not as a Brahmin, Kshatriya, Vaishya or Shudra, but as an Atishudra. I love scavenging. In my Ashram, an eighteen years old Brahmin lad is doing the scavenger's work in order to teach the Ashram scavenger cleanliness. The lad is no reformer. He was born and bred in orthodoxy. But he felt that his accomplishments were incomplete until he had become also a perfect sweeper, and that if he wanted the Ashram sweeper to do his work well, he must do it himself and set an example. You should realize that you are cleaning Hindu society.[76]

The above construct was to Ambedkar an unwanted attempt to romanticize the idea of both poverty as well as untouchability. Instead of giving a call to abolish the practice, the prayer to be born as one of the untouchables to suffer their plight did not appeal to Ambedkar's rational and practical mind. In his scathing criticism of this warped idea, Ambedkar wrote:

What is the use of telling the scavenger that even a Brahmin is prepared to do scavenging when it is clear that according to Hindu shastras and

Hindu notions even if a Brahmin did scavenging, he would never be subjected to the disabilities of one who is born scavenger? For in India, a man is not a scavenger because of his work. He is a scavenger because of his birth, irrespective of the questions whether he does scavenging or not. If Gandhism preached that scavenging is a noble profession with the object of inducing those who refuse to engage in it, one could understand it. But why appeal to the scavenger's pride and vanity in order to induce him and him only to keep in to scavenging by telling him that scavenging is a noble profession and that he should not be ashamed of it? To preach that poverty is good for the Shudra and for none else, to preach that scavenging is good for the untouchables and for none else and to make them accept these onerous impositions as voluntary purposes of life, by appeal to their failings is an outrage and a cruel joke on the helpless classes which none but Mr. Gandhi can perpetuate with equanimity and impunity. In this connection, one is reminded of the words of Voltaire who in repudiation of an 'ism' very much like Gandhism said: 'Oh! Mockery to say to people that the suffering of some brings joy to others and works good to the whole! What solace is to a dying man to know that from his decaying body a thousand worms will come into life?' Criticism apart, this is the technique of Gandhism: to make wrongs done appear to the very victim as though they were his privileges. If there is an 'ism' which has made full use of religion as an opium to lull people into false beliefs and false security, it is Gandhism. Following Shakespeare, one can well say: Plausibility! Ingenuity! Thy name is Gandhism![77]

The scope of Gandhi's anti-untouchability plan too was limited, according to Ambedkar. Unlike Savarkar's explicit assertion that the concepts of purity and pollution in terms of Sparsha bandi or Roti bandi had to be uprooted, Ambedkar opined that Gandhi's programme did not state that a Hindu should not bathe after touching an untouchable. Hence it could not lead to any tangible means of social assimilation for the untouchable community. Gandhi had also categorically stated his opposition to the concepts of inter-dining and intermarriage between untouchables and other Hindus in his paradigm of amelioration. Unless the experiments that Savarkar conducted in Ratnagiri, of bringing the untouchables into the mainstream and intermixing them in various spheres of life, were implemented, mere changing of nomenclatures could hardly count as reform. Also, as Savarkar constantly harped on the hierarchies within the lower castes too that had to be broken, the Gandhian model did not consider these nuances. Elaborating on this, Ambedkar states:

> Mr. Gandhi's anti-untouchability means that the untouchables will be classified as Shudras, instead of being classified as Ati-Shudras.[78] There is nothing more in it. Mr. Gandhi has not considered the question whether the old Shudras will accept the new Shudras into their fold. If they don't, then the removal of untouchability is a senseless proposition for it will still keep the untouchables as a separate social category. Mr. Gandhi probably knows that the abolition of untouchability will not bring about the assimilation of the untouchables by the Shudras. That seems to be the reason why Mr. Gandhi himself has given a new and a different name to the Untouchables. The new name registers by anticipation what is likely to be the fact. By calling the untouchables Harijans, Mr. Gandhi has killed two birds with one stone. He has shown that assimilation of the untouchables by the Shudras is not possible. He has also by his new name counteracted assimilation and made it impossible.[79]

Again, the Gandhian model did not call for combined education efforts of the kind that Savarkar implemented in Ratnagiri. He merely stated that it was perfectly right for any varna to acquire skills of any other varna. But these could not be used for earning a livelihood. So an untouchable could study medicine or warfare, but he could not become a doctor or a soldier to earn his living. He had to follow the hereditary profession of his ancestors. The untouchables would then have been as per Ambedkar 'eternal scavengers' even if they studied law, medicine or any other subject. Gandhism, for him, was another form of Sanatanism—the old, militantly orthodox Hinduism. Hence, he concluded, 'Gandhism which compels an educated untouchable to do scavenging is nothing short of cruelty. The grace in Gandhism is a curse in its worst form. The virtue of the anti-untouchability plank in Gandhism is quite illusory. There is no substance in it.'[80]

In contrast, Savarkar's practical model of anti-untouchability, in gradual phases, is best explained in his own words.

> The present tradition of Untouchability among Hindus is unjust and suicidal . . . It is a hideous crime to regard the 70 million untouchable people as worse than animals. It is contempt not only of the whole

humanity but also of the sanctity of our inner soul. Some may argue that I am advocating abandonment of untouchability because such action is beneficial to the Hindu society. I must state quite clearly that even if untouchability was proved to be beneficial to the Hindu society, I would have just as vigorously preached for its abandonment. When I refuse to touch someone because he was born in a particular community, but play with cats and dogs, I commit an offence against humanity, because I consider fellow human beings as less than animals. When we consider any aspect of our religion, it is impossible to justify this inhuman tradition. What benefits the abandonment has, is a secondary consideration. Abolishing untouchability is true religion.

On many occasions it is difficult to grasp the true meaning of religious principles. It may also be difficult to understand some abstract concepts. We therefore have to preach in a different tone. We therefore say 'Pray to God for your prosperity, for gaining children, health, wealth, and other earthly pleasures'. Similarly, if people have not been enlightened enough to consider that Untouchability should be rejected, we have to preach that at least on some occasions one need not and should not observe Untouchability, and this is according to our religious scriptures. Indeed there are examples in the past where Untouchability had not been observed by our forefathers, at least under certain circumstances.

Children do not understand the benefits of education. So, we say to them, 'If you go to school, I will give you sweets'. The reasoning behind this is that once the children start going to school, they will develop an interest in learning and slowly they will attend schools to learn rather than for sweets. Similarly we have to convince large number of people about the undesirability of Untouchability. Our true religion is lost and people consider suicidal traditions like Untouchability as religion. We therefore have to say, 'Time is running out. We cannot wait till you are fully convinced that Untouchability is inhuman. Therefore we ask you to abandon it because it is suicidal for the Hindu nation'. That is vital and it is our duty.

While doing this duty we have to explain that many Untouchables are being tempted to accept Islam and thereby we lose our numerical as well as intellectual strength. Even if we assume, for the sake of argument, that Untouchability is sanctioned by our scriptures, we have to point out that the same scriptures also state that under certain circumstances this practice need not be observed. For example, it is stated that when faced with a national calamity, no one should be considered as Untouchable (*Rashtra Viplave Sprushya-Aspurshya na Vidyate*).

Many people accept this argument and are prepared not to observe Untouchability, at least on some occasions. And once they do that and as a result come in contact with Untouchables, they realize the prejudices against Untouchability that they harboured for centuries. They realize how unjust and unjustifiable the tradition has been and later they reject the practice as being against humanity for all times. They even start calling them 'former untouchables'. That has been my experience, which includes people from all walks of life, from learned but strongly traditionalist priests to illiterate farmers.

Why am I saying all this? Readers may feel that I am preaching abandonment of Untouchability for exceptional circumstances only. I have explained why I have to do that. That is only a tactic to get the people moving forward. I wish to emphasize that Untouchability is unjust and suicidal, and for the sake of humanity, it has to be abolished. That is the main reason behind my movement. Other reasons are secondary and accidental.'[81]

Despite their convergence of views on matters of eradication of caste and untouchability, Savarkar and Ambedkar differed on issues related to Hindu religion. In 1935, Ambedkar made public statements about renouncing Hinduism and that while he might have been born as a Hindu, he had no obligation to die as one. Ambedkar had at that time not specifically decided to adopt Buddhism. Savarkar wrote a long article with his views on the matter, in *Nirbhid* dated 3 November 1935. He questioned Ambedkar's intent of leaving Hinduism citing the lack of rationalism in its practices and countered it by saying that any 'ism' or organized religion by its very nature had irrational practices within it. The words of Prophet Muhammad or every word of holy books such as the Quran and the Bible being the word of God, or the idea of immaculate conception of Jesus—were to Savarkar as much irrational as numerous superstitions of Hinduism. He urged Ambedkar to use his intellect and influence to rather stay within the religion and help reform it through rational and positive measures. If untouchability was what was spurring him to take this step, Savarkar urged Ambedkar to be patient for about ten years thence, when the scourge could be completely eradicated if they worked jointly on several measures. He exuded confidence that even if Ambedkar did convert to some other religion, his future generations and followers would realize the folly and reconvert to Hinduism—given that the doors of shuddhi were now open to them all.[82]

The following year when Ambedkar declared that untouchability among Hindus would remain even after a hundred years, Savarkar countered it:

> Even if we assume that Ambedkar is right, by the same token the divisions within untouchables too will remain after 100 years. Mahars of Maharashtra will not intermarry or dine with Chamars of Maharashtra, or Dheds of Gujrat or other untouchables of Bihar and Bengal. Moreover untouchability will also not vanish by embracing Islam.[83]

Savarkar constantly wrote against the false notion of a homogeneous society of Muslims and Christians, making those faiths attractive for lower-caste Hindus to convert into. He elaborated on the caste divisions of highs and lows that existed among Muslims and Christians of India too. He spoke about how in the princely state of Travancore and other parts of south India, there was division among high-caste Christians and untouchable Christians. 'The former,' he said, 'do not allow the latter into their churches. The untouchable Christians in Travancore have asked for separate representation in the legislative assembly. Has not Dr Ambedkar heard about it?'[84] He argued that Buddhism too was not free from the scourge.

> Even today many people, historians and propagandists are under the illusion that Indian Buddhists did not observe untouchability and that under the rule of Buddhist kings, there were no untouchables. But this is a fallacy . . . killing of animals became a capital offence. And these castes that had no choice but to kill, their lives became intolerable . . . Suffice to quote from the descriptions of the contemporary Chinese travellers: 'Those castes (like Chandals) which did not stop killing animals no matter what punishments were meted out to them, were driven out of their villages. They were treated like lepers and had to live outside the village boundaries. If for any reason, like the market day, they needed to come into the villages they had to walk with a stick with a bell or beat drums to announce their arrival so that the villagers could keep away and be not polluted by them.' Those untouchables who are preaching that

there is no untouchability in Buddhism and want to give unwarranted importance to Buddhism should realize that it was Buddhism that enforced untouchability more rigorously than ever before. That is a historical fact.[85]

The preceding elaborate quotations of these national heroes become necessary to understand where they ideologically stood on matters such as caste that were quintessential to Indian existence and also her problems. More of these contesting 'Ideas of India' will be seen in the chapters to come. But while in the 1920s and early 1930s, these competing notions on matters of nationalism, means of attainment of freedom, social reforms and communal harmony might have been more of philosophical debates between various protagonists, in the decades to come, they were to determine the trajectory of independent India and the bloodbath amidst which it was to be born.

3

Communal Cauldron

Delhi, December 1926

It was a cold winter afternoon in Delhi on 23 December 1926. Swami Shraddhanand, the leader of the Arya Samaj, was in his Naya Bazar residence in Delhi. After a whirlwind campaign of shuddhi activities that he had undertaken, he was exhausted. He was also convalescing after an attack of bronchial pneumonia. It was close to 4 p.m. when a Muslim man knocked at the doors and insisted on meeting Swamiji. The attendant, Dharam Singh, tried explaining that Swamiji was unwell and was resting. But the man was persistent and said he had pressing religious matters to discuss, and also that it would not take too long. Hearing the altercation from inside, Swamiji asked his attendant to let the man in. He was led inside. When the attendant went to get him a glass of water, the visitor, Abdul Rashid, whipped out his revolver and fired two rounds at the seventy-year-old seer point blank. The secretary Dharam Pal and others came running, overpowered the assassin and held him till the police was called. But Swamiji was dead by then.

The assassination sent shock waves across the country, as Swamiji was a deeply respected seer who had done yeoman service for the causes of Hindu unity and shuddhi. Coincidentally, the All-India Congress Committee (AICC) meeting was under way in Gauhati and Gandhi was to address the gathering on 24 December 1926. In a strange rationalization of a crime so heinous, Gandhi shocked his audiences with his audacious remarks:

From Swami Shraddhanand's point of view what has happened may be called a blessed event. He had been ill. I had not been aware of it, but a friend told me that it would be a miracle if Swamiji survived . . . you see, he (Shraddhanand) was a brave man . . . he had no fear of death for he had faith in God . . . there is nothing to be wondered at that he was killed . . . Today it is a Mussalman who has murdered a Hindu. We should not be surprised if a Hindu killed a Mussalman. God forbid that this should happen but what else can one expect when we cannot control our tongue or our pen? I must, however, say that if any Hindu imitated this act he would only bring disgrace to Hinduism . . . Let us pray to God that we may understand the real meaning of this assassination . . . Let the Hindus remain peaceful and refrain from seeking revenge for this murder. Let them not think that the two communities are now enemies of each other and that unity is no longer possible. If they do, they will be committing a crime and bringing disgrace upon their religions.[1]

Gandhi's repeated reference to Abdul Rashid as a 'dear brother' caused a lot of consternation among an already agitated crowd. In an attempt to clarify this, he spoke again on 26 December, which did not make matters any better.

Brother Abdul Rashid was shown in. I purposely call him brother, and if we are true Hindus you will understand why I call him so. Swamiji asked his servant to admit Abdul Rashid, because God had willed to show there through the greatness of Swamiji and the glory of Hinduism . . . The murder has been possible because the two communities look upon each other with feelings of hatred and enmity . . . Let every Mussalman also understand that Swami Shraddhanandji was no enemy of Islam, that his was a pure and unsullied life, and that he has left for us all the lesson of peace written in his blood . . .

You will all be accepting this resolution standing while, at this moment perhaps, there are Hindu-Muslim disturbances going on in Delhi. But I tell you that, if every one of you understands and lays to his heart the lesson that Swami Shraddhanandji has left for us, it is again possible to win swaraj in no time. I am a mad man, you will say, accustomed to giving rash promises. Well, I tell you I am not mad, I am still as much in earnest about my programme as I was in 1920, but those who made pledges in 1920 broke them and made swaraj impossible then. We are all children of the same Father—whom the Hindu and the Mussalman and the Christian know by different names . . .

Now you will, perhaps, understand why I have called Abdul Rashid a brother, and I repeat it, I do not even regard him as guilty of Swami's murder. Guilty, indeed, are all those who excited feelings of hatred against one another. For us Hindus, the Gita enjoins on us the lesson of equality; we are to cherish the same feelings towards a learned Brahmin as towards a Chandal, a dog, a cow and an elephant. This is no occasion for mourning or tears; it is an occasion that should burn in our hearts the lesson of bravery. Bravery is not the exclusive quality of the Kshatriyas. It may be their special privilege. But, in our battle for swaraj, bravery is essential as much for the Brahmin and the Vaisya and the Sudra as for the Kshatriya. Let us not therefore shed tears of sorrow, but chasten our hearts and steel them with some of the fire and faith that were Shraddhanandji's.[2]

In a *Young India* essay dated 30 December 1926, Gandhi further elaborated:

I wish to plead for Abdul Rashid. I do not know who he is. It does not matter to me what prompted the deed. The fault is ours. The newspaper man has become a walking plague. He spreads the contagion of lies and calumnies. He exhausts the foul vocabulary of his dialect, and injects his virus into the unsuspecting, and often receptive minds of his readers. Leaders 'intoxicated with the exuberance of their own language' have not known to put a curb upon their tongues or pens. Secret and insidious propaganda has done its dark and horrible work, unchecked and unabashed. It is, therefore, we the educated and the semi-educated class that are responsible for the hot fever, which possessed Abdul Rashid. It is unnecessary to discriminate and apportion the blame between the rival parties. Where both are to blame, who can arbitrate with golden scales and fix the exact ratio of blame? It is no part of self-defence to tell lies or exaggerate . . . Swamiji was great enough to warrant the hope that his blood may wash us of our guilt, cleanse our hearts and cement these two mighty divisions of the human family.[3]

Along with the shock of the murder, Savarkar was disgusted by Gandhi's rationalization of it and the absence of an unequivocal condemnation. In a sharp riposte to these utterances of Gandhi, Savarkar wrote an essay titled 'Gandhiji and the Innocent Hindu' on 10 February 1927.[4] Condemning the addressing mode of 'brother' for a violent assassin, Savarkar said that it was alarming that the Hindu community had quietly decided to follow Gandhi's dictates. 'All the world is after all a stage and every man an actor. So one has to live up to the role that one has donned. Given that he has donned the role of a Mahatma, a great soul, he has to buttress it with such classic dialogues. He is not a man of common abilities, like a Shivaji or a Ramdas, but a great Mahatma!' With this sarcastic take, while he rationalized the need for Gandhi to take such irrational, moral high grounds even on a matter as heinous as murder, he wondered why the Hindus had to blindly follow all his edicts. Why did Gandhi, who was so eager to call Abdul Rashid a 'dear brother', not address the eighteen-year-old Bengali revolutionary Gopinath Saha too as a brother, he questioned. On 12 January 1924, Saha had attempted to murder Charles Tegart, the then head of the Detective Department of Calcutta Police. His attempt failed and he erroneously ended up killing a European civilian, Ernest Day, whom we mistook for Tegart. Saha was arrested and hanged in March 1924. 'When C.R. Das had tried to express some sympathy for this young man, Gandhi had leapt at him with ferocity that such violent acts could not be condoned. Could Gopinath have been a "dear brother" too?' asked Savarkar.

Answering his own question, Savarkar said, 'Oh! Innocent Hindus! Why do we even ask such a query of the Mahatma? Gopinath was a Hindu and a dastardly assassin. Does supporting a Hindu assassin befit the status of a great Mahatma? Certainly not! So it was but natural for him to reprimand C.R. Das for taking a lead on expressing love for a Hindu. How dare he, after all!' Gopinath, according to Savarkar, had made another cardinal mistake, in addition to having been unfortunately a Hindu—he had not murdered a Hindu saint. 'To take the side of an assassin, a Hindu at that, and of a British to moot, is blasphemy not just for a "Deshbandu" C.R. Das, but for the veritable Mahatma ji too. From the Indian Penal Code to Special Ordinance Acts and all our religious scriptures, which tenet can support such a sacrilege? But how will these foolish Hindus ever understand such lofty principles!'

Savarkar further postulated that Gandhi's calling the Muslims his own blood relatives in the context of this assassination was also true and correct. Most of them, being converts, had Hindu blood in them after all. Moreover Muslims being human beings like the Hindus, the same human blood flowed in all of us. But then just last year when a young revolutionary Hindu had asked Gandhi in *Young India* whether we had the blood of brave warriors like Shivaji and Rana Pratap running in our veins, Gandhi had totally denounced the idea. Savarkar said that Gandhi had then remarked that 'this was impossible. There are so many castes among Hindus. Hence the blood of a Rajput or Maratha cannot be the same as a Brahmin or a Bania.' Poking fun at Gandhi, Savarkar wrote:

> It is after all quite understandable. To declare that I share the blood of warriors like Shivaji, Rana Pratap, Guru Gobind Singh is such a pedestrian thought and where is the elevation to a 'Mahatma' status in such loose talk? But it is the hallmark of a saintly Mahatma to say the blood that shed the 'Hindu blood', that too of a saint, is that of my own sibling . . . how do we ordinary mortals know the ways of Mahatmas? Else, we could find some rationale as to why a great soul who advises us not to pick up arms against a person who has raped our sisters as that is not ahimsa (non-violence), had no qualms recruiting Indians into the British army to kill Germans (in the First World War). But we are thick-headed commoners, and Hindus at that; how are we to understand all these esoteric matters. We just need to keep shut and follow the diktats.[5]

Equally critical of Gandhi's stand was B.R. Ambedkar. He mentioned that it did not matter whether the number of prominent Hindus killed by fanatics among the Muslims was large or small. What mattered more was 'the attitude of those who count, towards these murderers'. The murderers of course received the penalty under the law, as they rightly deserved. But Ambedkar was upset that influential figures in the Congress or among the Muslims 'never condemned these criminals'. He drew the attention to a *Times of India* article dated 30 November 1927 that brought to light a dangerous trend:

> It is reported that for earning merit for the soul of Abdul Rashid, the murderer of Swami Shradhanand, in the next world, the students and professors of the famous theological college at Deoband finished five complete recitations of the Koran and had planned to finish daily a lakh and a quarter recitations of Koranic verses. Their prayer was 'God Almighty may give the *marhoom* (martyr i.e. Rashid) a place in the "*ala-e-illeeyeen*" (the summit of the seventh heaven)'.[6]

Training his guns on Gandhi, Ambedkar lamented:

What is not understandable is the attitude of Mr. Gandhi. Mr. Gandhi has been very punctilious in the manner of condemning any and every act of violence and has forced the Congress, much against its will, to condemn it. But Mr. Gandhi has never protested against such murders. Not only have the Musalmans not condemned these outrages, but even Mr. Gandhi has never called upon the leading Muslims to condemn them. He has kept silent over them. Such an attitude can be explained only on the ground that Mr. Gandhi was anxious to preserve Hindu-Moslem unity and did not mind the murder of a few Hindus, if it could be achieved by sacrificing their lives.[7]

He also quoted Swami Shraddhanand's anguish that he expressed in his weekly, the *Liberator*. Writing in it on 30 September 1926, Swamiji had said the task of removal of untouchability was the duty of Hindus and an internal matter of Hindu society. The Muslim and Christian Congressmen openly revolted against Gandhi's dictum at Vaikom and other places. 'Even such an unbiased leader as Mr. Yakub Hassan,' said Swamiji, 'presiding over a meeting called to present an address to me at Madras, openly enjoined upon Musslamans the duty of converting all the untouchables in India to Islam.'[8] Ambedkar lamented that Gandhi said nothing by way of remonstrance to these openly provocative acts by his own leaders or allies. Even during the bonfire of foreign clothes, which was assiduously followed by Hindu leaders from the Congress, the Khilafat leaders got permission from Gandhi to 'send all foreign cloth for the use of the Turkish brethren'.[9]

The 1920s were also vitiated by the publication of books and pamphlets that were deeply offensive of Prophet Muhammad. The first of these was the book *Vichitra Jivan* (Weird Life) by Pandit Kalicharan Sharma, published by the author in Agra in November 1923. Another publication that caused huge consternation was *Rangila Rasul* (The Colourful Prophet) by Pandit Chamupati, a pamphlet published by Rajpal in Lahore in May 1924. Rajpal was later murdered by Ilamdin on 6 April 1929 while he was sitting in his shop.[10] The last in this series was '*Sair-i-Dozakh*' by Devi Sharan Sharma, an essay published in the monthly *Risala-i-Vartman* in Amritsar in May 1927. *Rangila Rasul*, for instance, sketched the personal life of the Prophet, especially with regard to his domestic life and multiple wives. These led to riots and violence; cases were filed against the authors and distributors that stretched on for several years. That many of the writers, publishers or distributors were directly or remotely linked with the Arya Samaj made matters worse for the communal situation in the country. If shuddhi was the main area of grouse, these publications added fuel to the communal fire.

The assassination of Swami Shraddhanand was an unfortunate milestone in the deteriorating communal situation of the 1920s. He had been engaged in an active shuddhi programme across northern India. Like Savarkar, he too was committed to the cause of the uplift of the untouchables. Apart from the fears he had about the intent of the Khilafat protagonists, he was also getting impatient about the Congress, with whom he was working, putting the issues of untouchability eradication on the back burner. He even put this on record in a letter dated 23 May 1922 to the then General Secretary of the Congress, Vithalbhai Patel: 'There was a time . . . when Mahatmaji put the question of untouchability in the forefront of the Congress programme. I find now that the question of raising the depressed classes has been relegated to an obscure corner.'[11]

In early 1923, he embarked on a shuddhi mission in western United Provinces. The Malkanas were Rajputs who were scattered across various parts of Mathura, Agra, Etah, Mainpuri and other areas. Though their customs were largely Hindu, long centuries of Muslim influence made them adopt Muslim practices and declare themselves as Muslims in census and surveys. Swami Shraddhanand joined forces with several social groups that were working for the shuddhi of the Malkanas. On their part, the Muslims mobilized themselves against the reclamations from their ranks. The largest such 'anti-shuddhi' movement undertaken was the formation of the Jamiat-ul-Ulema in 1919. It brought together several Muslim clerics or ulemas, even during the peak of the Khilafat movement, to pass religious diktats or fatwas in favour or against different political and social movements of the time. They decided to collect funds and combat the efforts of Shraddhanand with regard to the Malkana shuddhi movement. The backlash of the shuddhi movement was what ultimately led to the assassination of Swami Shraddhanand.

Savarkar was aware of the perils and repercussions of the shuddhi movement. He had faced them in the Cellular Jail too when he made attempts to reconvert the prisoners who had been lured into Islam by the Pathan jamadars in lieu of less harsher tortures.[12] As a tribute to the man who was martyred for the Hindu cause, Savarkar's brother Narayanrao decided to start a weekly titled *Shraddhanand* from Bombay, beginning 10 January 1927. Savarkar contributed several articles to this weekly under pen-names. It was envisaged to be a mouthpiece for Hindu sangathan and shuddhi movements. Savarkar and the Hindu Mahasabha also started a fund called 'The Swami Shraddhanand Fund' to carry forward Swamiji's mission of shuddhi.

In the very inaugural issue, in a stinging editorial titled 'Murder of Swami Shraddhanand and Gandhiji's impartial partiality'[13] Savarkar strongly denounced the ambivalent stand taken by Gandhi and his attempts to blame the Hindu community for it. Savarkar argued that Abdul Rashid had himself confessed that the motives behind the gruesome crime were apprehensions that Islam was in danger because of the shuddhi movements and to avenge the Malkana Rajput agitation that Swamiji had launched. Yet to apportion the blame on both communities equally or to chide the Hindus for everything in order to create false equivalences was becoming a hallmark of the Mahatma, Savarkar opined.

Dissecting the *Young India* article of 30 December 1926 by Gandhi, Savarkar mentioned that his declarations fell way below the standards of truth and honesty that the man had set for himself and his followers. Even if one were to metaphorically assume that the newspapers had indeed been spreading hatred, as Gandhi claimed in his article, how does that apportion an equal measure of blame on the Hindus, he asked. What would the Mahatma have to say about the countless documented atrocities, the mass conversions and rapes in Malabar committed by the Moplahs and testified by so many in courts of law? Whose handiwork was behind these—the Hindus again? He accused Gandhi of taking the side, in one of his articles, of a lone Muslim witness who had claimed that the Moplahs were hardly responsible for the genocide. So, was one to assume the *Young India* and its esteemed editor too were guilty of being a 'walking plague' that fanned communal passions, he wondered. Was Gandhi not guilty of addressing even those brute Moplah rioters as 'brave', though here he seemed to whitewash Abdul Rashid's crime by claiming that he was ignorant and hot-headed. Savarkar wanted Gandhi to make an assessment of the riots that had rocked India after Malabar—Gulbarga, Kohat, Delhi, Panipat, Calcutta, East Bengal, Sindh and several low-intensity clashes all round the year in some place or the other—and analyze which community began the skirmish in each case and who perpetrated the crimes. Could Gandhi list cases of rapes of Muslim women by Hindu mobs, or was it the other way round, he challenged. Were there assassinations of any leaders of the Muslim community by Hindus, while the converse had numerous examples of martyrs for the shuddhi cause beyond Shraddhanand? On the other hand, innumerable Hindu leaders had courted jail and hardships for a cause alien to them—that of establishing a caliphate in Turkey. Yet, the Mahatma insists that the responsibility of spreading venom is equal for both communities, said Savarkar in exasperation.

What astonished Savarkar was that the man making these claims was not someone unaware of ground realities or the recent history of clashes. Yet, his taking a stand like this, just to prove his own greatness, was according to Savarkar not only foolishness and cowardice but also a crime against one's community. He opined that it was this 'impartial partiality' that had the potential of destroying the whole nation that was the real 'walking plague'. When reports had been pouring in about how Abdul Rashid's photographs were being circulated in several places as a 'Ghazi' or martyr for a religious cause and his act was being eulogized, did the Mahatma's statement that it was just an individual act of foolhardiness cut any ice, questioned Savarkar.

Concluding his piece, Savarkar rationalized that if the diagnosis of a disease was done wrongly, the medication and the subsequent side effects were bound to have detrimental effects. It was the same with Gandhi's assessment of the fundamental reasons behind Hindu–Muslim conflicts in India. A candid and honest identification of the fanaticism in certain sections of the Muslim community and the manner in which that impinges on other faiths, especially the Hindus, and unequivocal condemnation and steps to eradicate it were Savarkar's prescriptions for this malaise. Not constructing false equivalences and balancing acts of blaming both communities in equal measure as Gandhi had done.

Gandhi had maintained his characteristic ambivalence even during the murder of Rajpal, the publisher of the controversial *Rangila Rasool*. This had riled many nationalist leaders including B.R. Ambedkar.

Savarkar was obviously more scathing. More so, since the murderer of Rajpal, Ilamdin, was hailed in his community as a Ghazi or martyr. But when Rajpal was praised as a *Dharamveer* (Religious Hero) as he allegedly published the controversial pamphlet in protest against a Muslim slogan—'*Kishan teri Gita jalani padegi*' (Krishna, we will need to burn your Gita), Gandhi was upset about it. Writing in this piece dated 30 November 1929, Savarkar said:

But while the two lakh Muslim Ghazis were making a martyr out of Illamuddin, how has all that noise not cracked out Mahatma Gandhi's meditative pose even a bit? If it is unbreakable, then when Rajpal's body was taken out in a procession and people were shouting 'Dharamveer (Religious Hero) Rajpal ki Jay' this memorial came out lashing and like the bellows of the blacksmith forged ahead to bite the procession like a snake. Rajpal's body was not being released, but the Hindus undeterred by the lathi charge of the Police got hold of the body. The whole of the Hindu Lahore was showering flowers on Rajpal's body and shouting 'Rajpal ki Jay', the Muslims imitated the same and called Illamuddin 'Ghazi'. Out of these both shouts, actually Illamuddin was a murderer and he had actually stabbed and killed, seeing this any non-violent person should have felt disgust towards this procession; but no! Mahatma Gandhi did not feel any disgust towards it. He did not accuse the Muslims of anything or write a single word against them other than calling him a Ghazi; but when Rajpal was given the title Dharamveer (Religious Hero), his meditation and peace was shattered so much so that he could angrily abuse the Hindus.

He said, the readers of Maharashtra may not know this but I will tell you a story that may hurt the Hindus of Punjab—Gandhiji angrily said, Rajpal is just a bookseller. He printed a book that would hurt the Muslim mentality. That is why he was killed, what great religious bravery did he show in that? The books he had printed were all sold out, that means he suffered no loss, then what selfless act did he do? . . .

As Rajpal's book was being sold, even if he was dying for his religion, you should not call him a Martyr. Then when all of Gandhiji's books are sold and especially the 'Young India' is running on subscriptions then why should we call him Mahatma? The shameless comment of Rajpal died due to his business, tomorrow will go ahead and say that Tilak also was imprisoned, punished due to his business—of *Kesari* Newspaper—then why call him Lokmanya?[14]

Around the same time (in 1926), Savarkar also wrote a Marathi novel *Mala Kaay Tyaache* (What Do I Care?). It graphically described the atrocities committed against the Hindus, their women, the defilement of temples and towns in Malabar by the Moplahs. Being a prolific writer, he wrote several books, plays and articles during this period when he was busy with his shuddhi and untouchability eradication movements. For *Shraddhanand*, he contributed nearly four or five articles every week. They were later compiled in the form of different books titled *Garma Garam Chivda*,

Gandhi Gondhal and so on. Elaborating the travails of his life at the Cellular Jail, he wrote the book *Maajhi Janmathep* (My Transportation for Life). The first half of it was published in the *Kesari* in 1925 and the latter half in *Shraddhanand*. The creative poetry that he hitherto wrote certainly dwindled. Even his poems, such as '*Akhil Hindu Vijay Dhwaja Ha*' (The Pan-India Hindu Flag) or '*Tumhi Amhi Sakal Hindu Bandhu Bandhu*' (You and I Are Hindu Brethren) dealt with political or social themes.

His writings were sharply worded and many of them highly sarcastic, where he seemed to enjoy poking fun at the double standards, hypocrisies and blatant appeasement by the Congress and its leaders, especially Gandhi. In an article published on 18 April 1926 in the *Mahratta*, Savarkar stung Motilal Nehru with his sarcastic wit when the former made a speech alleging that the Hindu Mahasabha and the Muslim League were two sides of the same coin. Savarkar wrote: 'To be the icon of perfect Hindu-Muslim unity, Motilal Nehru should change his name to Motimiya, grow a beard on half his face and wear an outfit that has a Hindu Dhoti on one leg and Islamic Lungi on the other, so he looks like a living proof of Hindu-Muslim syncretism.'[15]

Savarkar wrote three plays between 1927 and 1933: *Sangeet Ushap* published in 1927, *Sangeet Sanyasta Khadga* in 1931 and *Sangeet Uttar Kriya* in 1933. *Ushap* dealt with untouchability and also how the scourge had left millions of Hindus of depressed classes open to the machinations of conversions. It tried to educate the Hindus, who were opposing his movements to eradicate untouchability, about the dangers that such conversions could pose to their own fold. This was done through a few Muslim characters in the play.

For instance, in Act II, Scene 3, one of the characters, Ibrahim, says:

It has been four years since I became a Muslim, but I swear on the Almighty that my tongue knows not a single verse of the Koran. The kind of Urdu they speak, I hardly know how to. I am a born Hindu, my mind thinks like a Hindu's, but till the time I was a Hindu, right from the Brahmins to the Shudras, and even the Mahars, I was condemned and thrown away as a lowly born. There was almost a fierce competition among all their castes about who can oppress us better than the other. Hence in frustration I decided to eschew this religion and adopt Islam. My sister tried her best to dissuade me. But the irony of ironies—our Subedar, Bangash Khan's eyes fell on my sister! He eventually managed to convert her first and I became the Muslim brother-in-law later. Not just this, I was also the commander of some fifty odd sepoys. Such respect I now commanded, while I was hitherto used to only social disgrace. Almost with a vengeance, any Hindu beauty who caught my eyes, I would inform or hand her over to my brother-in-law. This enhanced my prestige further in his eyes.[16]

But as a complete contrast to the fanatic Bangash Khan or Ibrahim, a Muslim mullah is made to appear as the voice of sanity in the play. Making an appearance in Act IV, Scene 3, he advises the subedar and Ibrahim:

Pardon me, but as a true devotee of Allah, I disagree with the politics being done here. Propagating Islam this way is totally against the tenets of our holy Koran and disgraces it. My Koran teaches me tolerance and acceptance and asks me to propagate it through love and brotherhood. But when politics enters the scene, the means are replaced by the sword and through coercion. This does not comply with the words of the Almighty.[17]

But the government that had kept a strict vigil on Savarkar's movements was not in the least amused. In an undated letter written to him, he was informed:

The Governor-General in Council considers that Mr. Savarkar was very ill-advised in publishing this play at a time when Hindu-Moslem feelings are hypersensitive. The book is certainly not a publication that one would expect from a party who is at large through the clemency of Government and under the express condition that he would not engage in political activities, which Mr. Savarkar was informed in Government letter No. 724/3266, dated the 6th May 1925, a copy of which was forwarded to you. The book included attempts to influence feelings and arouse communal tension. The Governor-in-Council therefore considers that Mr. Savarkar should be asked to withdraw the book from publication.[18]

In his reply to the secretary to the Government of Bombay's Home Department, dated 6 June 1927, Savarkar wrote:

Sir,

I beg to inform you that the District Magistrate of Ratnagiri read out a letter to me the other day whereby I was given to understand that the Government of Bombay wished me to withdraw the publication of the play USHAP as they felt it was unwise to publish it at a time when Hindu-Moslem relations were very much strained. The Government have already informed that thereupon I agreed to withdraw books from sale. I also ordered as soon as possible, my sole agents at Bombay to stop any further sale and to cease advertising it in 'Shraddhanand' and other papers as before. These instructions have already been carried out by them.

Having already done all that the Government wished me to do in the letter I now take leave to point out to the Government that the play cannot for the following reasons be suspected of causing or aiming to cause any serious tension between Hindus and Moslems for:

a. It is chiefly concerned with the removal of untouchability alone. The Mohamedan characters are all secondary personages.

b. Even then great care is taken in dealing with them so as never to attribute any undignified character to their community as such nor to represent only the ugly side of their society. Just as the better mentality of the present-day Brahmin is represented (e.g. Purushottam Shastri's character) along with the meaner (e.g. Naren Bhat), so also the noble element in the Mohamedan community is eloquently brought out in some characters notably the Mulla (Act IV, third scene) who holds up the best human ideals as consistent with the teachings of true Islam and condemns forcible conversions and other outrageous crimes of fanaticism.

c. As to the story of a Hindu girl being pursued by Moslem bad character and forcible conversions of the Hindus—well, from the days of Allauddin to Aurangzeb, history bears testimony to its truth and the play too is merely historical. And even if today is taken into consideration, the courts of Bengal and the public everywhere are busy dealing with such incidents to such an extent that the two communities have got used to them as occurrences of daily life and are therefore not likely to get shocked by witnessing a stray incident staged in a secondary drama like the USHAP.

d. But above all, the fact that conclusively proves that the drama is least likely to inflame any ill-feeling is that several plays and novels whose main theme had been the upselling of the Moslem kingdom and fights and wars that took place between the two communities in Maratha history and in which we use language far bitter than USHAP ever does—are being read and staged daily for the last 20 years and more and yet they (e.g. *Panipatcha Mokabla*, novel of Mr. Hari Narayan Apte, *Shiva Sambhava* and several other books)— have never caused nor are even suspected of being likely to cause any serious ill-feeling between these communities.

In view of these facts, I cannot but feel that this historical play USHAP would have also passed off unnoticed, just as plays spirited [sic] than it have ever been, but for the fact of it being written by me.

On all these grounds, I submit that the government shall reconsider their decision and allow me to re-continue the sale. The play, I honestly feel, is not likely to cause any public tension and does not deserve any undue importance or notice at the hand of the Government. But, if in spite of this pleading and request, the Government sticks to their former decision, then I too will stick to my former undertaking and will not reopen the sale of the book. Of course it will spell financial ruin but then I must, grudgingly or not, but bear it. For it is my earnest desire not to give any reasonable cause for any misunderstanding to rise in the mind of the Government and therefore I, in spite of my opinion to the contrary will withdraw all copies from the market of myself and wait till communal tension gets relaxed and the Government allows me and that you will kindly acquaint His Excellency, the Governor with the contents of this letter as soon as it is received and to resume the sale.[19]

But the government stuck to its stand and Savarkar had to withdraw the book from sales.

The other two plays did not face such a plight. *Sanyastha Khadga* attempted to show the perils of the philosophy of non-violence (as propounded by Gandhi) to society. It became quite a rage among audiences. It failed to leave even Congressmen unmoved. It is said that during a staging of it in Nagpur, Congressman N.B. Khare, who was for sometime the chief minister of the Central Provinces and Berar, was so overwhelmed that he stood up in the middle of the play and exclaimed: 'A great man who can speak this language is wanted today in Indian politics.'[20] The play *Uttar Kriya* dealt with the aftermath of the defeat of the Marathas in the Battle of Panipat and how the defeat was eventually avenged.

One must bear in mind that the effusion of Savarkar's literary output was possible despite the immense strictures and surveillance that the British had imposed on him. The copious documents exchanged between him and the government make it amply clear that his every movement was being closely watched and that he needed to take their permission for everything. When he wrote to the government on 19 July 1926 seeking permission to visit Nasik and Bombay, he was denied permission for Nasik but allowed to reside in 'Bandra for a period not exceeding fourteen days, the period to count from the date of your arrival there'. During his stay in Bombay in Narayanrao's house, he was supposed to not 'engage in any public movement, lectures or agitations'.[21] This was the second time that he was allowed to leave Ratnagiri after being allowed to go to Nasik in 1924 following the outbreak of plague in Ratnagiri.

Savarkar was told specifically what he was allowed to do and what he was not. He could, for instance, 'attend any places of amusement, cinemas and the like', provided he did not attend any 'political gathering, public or private' and that his 'presence at any theatre or other places of amusement is entirely private and not made the occasion of any demonstration', and that he promptly 'returns at night within such home, if any as the Commissioner of Police may specify to the place' where he was staying in Bandra. Savarkar was to inform in advance the list of all the places that he intended to visit, to the commissioner of police, and abide by the same to the fullest.[22]

The government even went to the extent of fixing the time when he could leave or return home. During his Bombay stay, for instance, he was informed that 'the Commissioner of Police has decided that you should return by 1.30 A.M. to your residence at Khar Road, Bandra, whenever you have an occasion to attend theatrical performances in Bombay'.[23]

In an earlier telegram dated 26 April 1926, Savarkar had also sought the permission of the government to stand as a candidate in the forthcoming elections to the Bombay Legislative Council. But since this would invariably mean a 'relaxation of the conditions' of his release as a 'necessary corollary to the grant of permission to stand for the election to the Council' the request was denied.[24] Similarly his request to visit Delhi for two days to preside over the All-India Depressed Classes Conference that was to be held on 6 November 1927 was summarily rejected.[25]

Braving these strictures, Savarkar continued his shuddhi and sangathan work, as also his movement for uplift of untouchables—all the while positing himself as a strong intellectual opponent and critic of Gandhi. In the 20 January 1927 edition of *Young India*, a letter from a reader that was titled 'A candid critic' was published. It was truly candid in its estimation and denunciation of Gandhi's stand on the assassination of Shraddhanand. 'Do you feel Mahatmaji,' asked the critic, 'that the murder of Swamiji was an inhuman, barbarous and cruel act of a Muslim ruffian and that the entire Muslim community should be ashamed of it? Why do you refuse to characterize it as such? Instead of condemning the deed and the doer, and those who are responsible for this act (those who describe Hindu leaders as Kafirs—the hot Muslim propagandists and the mad Muslim priests), you have begun to defend the murderer and hold an apology for the community. You never defended Dyer. Is not a European a brother too?'[26] The critic was too direct in his questioning. Challenging the fundamental premise of Gandhi on the peacefulness of religions, he asked:

> You say further, Islam means peace. Is this truth? Islam as taught by the Koran and practised by Muslims ever since its birth never meant peace. What makes you write a thing so patently wrong? Buddhism, Christianity, Hinduism of course teach peace, but not Islam. May I know what makes you think and write like this? You never minced matters when condemning the wrongs of the Government, you never minced matters when you condemned Arya Samaj, why fear to condemn Muslims for even proved wrongs? I am sure if such a black act had been committed by a Hindu against a Muslim leader (which Heaven forbid!), you would have condemned the murderer and the community in unsparing terms. You would have asked Hindus to repent in sack-cloth and ashes, to offer fasts, hold hartal, raise memorial to the departed Muslim and many other things. Why do you accord preferential treatment to your 'blood brothers' the Muslims?[27]

In an equally candid manner, Gandhi replied to this reader. He absolved himself of any suppression of truth with regard to Swamiji's murder. He also said that he 'felt pity for the murderer even as I felt for General Dyer'. He also reminded his critic that this was the reason why he even 'refused to be party to any agitation for the prosecution of General Dyer'. Even as he confessed that he held 'the maulvis and all those who have indulged in exciting hatred against Swamiji to be responsible' for his murder, he reiterated his belief in Islam being a religion of peace 'in the same sense as

Christianity, Buddhism and Hinduism are. No doubt there are differences in degree, but the object of these religions is peace.' He added that 'passages can be quoted from the Koran to be contrary' to this belief of his, but countered it by saying 'so is it possible to quote passages from the Vedas to the contrary'. He brought in the treatment of untouchables, which was not the burden of the Vedas anyway. Hence, he justified by saying 'let not the pot call the kettle black'. Conceding that 'the followers of Islam are too free with the sword', Gandhi hastened to add that Islam or Christianity were 'religions of but yesterday' and therefore 'yet in the course of being interpreted'. He rejected the claims of maulvis or Christian clergies of delivering the final word or interpretation of these faiths. 'Bluster,' he said, 'is no religion nor is vast learning stored in capacious brains. The seat of religion is in the heart. We Hindus, Christians, Mussalmans and others have to write the interpretation of our respective faiths with our own crimson blood and not otherwise.'[28]

This was too controversial a reply for Savarkar to let pass without a contestation. In an article titled 'Which religion is peace-loving?', dated 27 January 1927, he took the matter head-on.[29] When Islam as a political force conquered Syria, the local Christians underwent immense genocides and had to abandon their homes and homeland, said Savarkar. It was India that gave these persecuted Syrian Christians shelter in its southern provinces. Moving further in history, Savarkar argued that the same fate befell the entire region of Persia, and the victims held their sacred fires and *Zend Avesta* close to their heart and sought shelter in this very land of the Hindus. They were still in India as Parsis. From the time of the Islamic conquest of India and the attack on the Somnath Temple in Gujarat, it was a story bloodied with the sacrifices of a million Hindu martyrs, said Savarkar. Questioning the fundamental antithesis of Semitic faiths which offer no hope of life, liberty of freedom of religion to those who are not followers of the same faith, Savarkar thundered at Gandhi for making an utterly false equivalence. The history of Islamic rule in India, according to Savarkar, was personified by the barbarities of Muhammad Ghazni, Muhammad Ghori, Muhammad-bin-Tughlak, Aurangzeb and Tipu Sultan. Savarkar added that there was no point getting into these long-buried tales. But if one has to solve a contemporary problem, one has to go to the root of it, address it and not window-dress from the outside even as the volcano keeps building within and readies to erupt. If the Mahatma was serious about curing the disease, he must swallow the bitter pill of doing a truthful diagnosis of the problem, said Savarkar. In his own candid manner, he wrote:

> The blunt reality is that a majority of Muslims do not consider Hindustan to be their own and co-existence with the Kafir Hindus strikes their conscience badly. This is sadly the root of the whole communal cauldron. Barring some broad-minded and sensible Muslims, many want to Islamize India just as Turkey, Iran or Afghanistan. Just day before yesterday Barrister Amin said in a public meeting in Delhi that in the next 10 years it was the bounden and religious duty of every Muslim to convert a minimum of at least 3 Hindus, so that when India gets swaraj, the dream of the establishment of a Muslim country can be realized. It is this attitude that strikes at the foundation of national unity and becomes the core of the Hindu-Muslim conflicts. The fact that most Muslims are not vocal against such tendencies is also part of the problem. And to compound that, our own leaders including Gandhiji spout such nonsense that 'What is the need or use of numerical strength?' Even at this time of a heinous murder, Gandhiji has not mustered sufficient courage to unequivocally condemn these tendencies. Had it been some hot-blooded Arya Samaji who dared to answer a Barrister Amin, by now all hell would have broken loose and like an angry school headmaster Gandhiji would have unleashed the sword of his pen on all of us. This attitude of his is what hurts us Hindus. He would be well-advised to begin his charity at home and sit with his favourite Ali Brothers of the Khilafat fame, remind them of those peace-loving verses of the Koran and bind them by it completely, rather than make the inflammatory speeches that they have been doing. Yet, Gandhiji's silence even on proven atrocities like in Kohat, and his lack of courage to tackle this problem from the roots, is bound to create serious problems for the country in years to come.[30]

It was with this baggage of intellectual differences of opinion and also their historical rivalry, that Savarkar received a message from Gandhi, expressing a desire to meet him. He was coming to Ratnagiri on 1 March 1927. In his letter, Gandhi wrote:

> We cannot have long talk today, but you know my regard for you as a lover of truth and as one who would lay down his life for the sake of truth. Besides, our goal is ultimately one and I would like you to correspond

with me as regards all points of difference between us. And more. I know that you cannot go out of Ratnagiri and I would not mind finding out two or three days to come and stay with you if necessary to discuss these things to our satisfaction.[31]

Savarkar replied: 'I thank you, but you are free and I am bound, and I don't want to put you in the same case as I. But I will correspond with you.'[32] The stage was set for these long-time opponents to come face-to-face, nearly eighteen years after they had met last in London. Much water had flowed down the Narmada since then. The Congressmen requested Savarkar to share stage with Gandhi at a public meeting of the Ratnagiri Municipality. But Savarkar refused to do that. He was moreover convalescing from high fever at that time and invited Gandhi to his home instead. At the public speech, Gandhi referred to Ratnagiri as a place of pilgrimage as it was the birthplace of Lokamanya Tilak and now the residence of Vinayak Damodar Savarkar.[33] Knowing well the political sentiment around shuddhi and sangathan in Ratnagiri at that time, Gandhi brought it up towards the end of his speech himself:

> I am asked to take part in the shuddhi movement. How can I, when I wish that its Muslim and Christian counterparts should also cease? It is unthinkable that a man will become good or attain salvation only if he embraces a particular religion—Hinduism, Christianity or Islam. Purity of character and salvation depend on the purity of heart. I therefore say to the Hindus, 'Do whatever you like, but don't ask a man like me, who has come to his conclusions after the maturest (sic) thinking, to take up what he cannot.' Man's capacity is after all limited. I can do what is within my power, not what is beyond it. I cannot do a hundred or even half a dozen things at a time. I would think myself blessed even if I can do one thing well at a time. If you agree with me that the charkha is the best sangathan that is possible, give me as much help as you can render.[34]

After this public meeting, Gandhi went to meet Savarkar at his house, along with his wife Kasturba. Savarkar's wife Yamunabai welcomed the honoured guests with the traditional arati. The two giant ideologues met fondly and discussed several political issues and burning considerations—from the eradication of untouchability to swadeshi to political freedom for India. Finally, the matter veered around to shuddhi. Savarkar proactively brought this up and asked Gandhi what his views were about this contentious issue. Gandhi replied that the belief that a man loses his religion was an absurdity for him. Savarkar agreed with this proposition but said that given the traditions of the caste system that have laid out the norms of loss of caste or religion and which have come down the ages, it was necessary as part of reform to adopt rites and rituals that restored the reclaimed individual to his or her original society. As long as these notions of a person falling from one's religion existed, shuddhi was a necessary tool and the only remedy. What harm could accrue of this, he asked, when it gave mental satisfaction to both the reconverted and the society. Gandhi replied saying that he had no qualms about such ceremonies that could go on and those who were forcibly or through allurements converted, ought to be brought back. His problem was with reconverting individuals whose ancestors had changed faiths decades ago. He however added: 'Nor do I uphold the conversions of persons from other religions. Because I believe that it is better to die while observing one's own religion than to embrace another religion. None should be persuaded to change his or her faith. It should be left to the will of the person.'[35]

Savarkar fundamentally agreed with this proposition. He had never been an advocate of forcible shuddhi. He reiterated this to Gandhi that a person needed to weigh carefully what his good was and, where his happiness lay and, with that freedom of thought, make a choice. He also subtly countered Gandhi when he remarked that Hinduism was too vast an ocean of thought and its message was both spiritual and practical. While on one hand it did advocate, as Gandhi did, that one needed to die under the domain of one's own religion, on the other it also spoke of transforming the world into Aryan thought and faith. Gandhi put a quick end to this by agreeing that both their goals were the same. They both strove for the glory of Hinduism and Hindustan.

Gandhi then expressed a desire to meet Savarkar's wife Yamunabai. When she came, he turned to his wife Kasturba and said: 'Let us bow to this saintly woman who showed immense courage in facing all tribulations when her husband was sentenced to 50 years imprisonment.'[36]

While taking leave, Gandhi told Savarkar that quite noticeably they disagreed on several issues but he hoped that the latter would have no objection to his making experiments to deal with the issues on hand. Savarkar sternly replied: 'Mahatmaji, you will be making these experiments at the cost of the nation.'[37] R.K. Gavande, president of the Malvan Taluka

Congress Committee, who was present, realized the awkwardness of the moment. He quickly intervened to hail the two leaders by saying, 'Gandhi plus Savarkar equals Swaraj.'[38] At this, Gandhi laughed heartily and took leave—cognizant all the while that there was no meeting ground between him and his ideological opponent. This was the last personal meeting that these two great men had, though they continued to differ with each other vociferously in their approach to shape the future of the nation in the mould of their dreams and ideologies.

Irrespective of the inherent dangers involved in movements such as shuddhi, Savarkar continued his association with it. He appealed to his followers that an apt revenge for Swamiji's assassination was not counter-violence, but continuing his work of shuddhi for which he laid down his life, with added vigour. He implored Hindu society to accept those who had been reclaimed. He also opined that entering the Patit Pavan Mandir was enough to be 'purified'. 'My brothers and sisters,' he said, 'if you do just that, it would suffice. This does not need money, bombs, machine guns, armies or workers. No more efforts are needed. Just say that those who are converted are welcome in the Hindu society. That is all.'[39] In an article, he narrated the anecdote of a letter he had received from a recently converted Hindu. The man informed Savarkar that even though he had gone back to his original faith from Christianity, the missionaries continued to send him and his family sweets during the occasion of Hindu festivals such as Makar Sankranti and presents for his children. They also kept enquiring about the family's well-being. The man confessed that he knew their game, but was exasperated that while the foreign missionaries were being so kind to him and his family, the society he had been reclaimed into never accepted him completely. When he or his children were spotted on the road, Hindus openly ridiculed or abused them. They were not invited to social gatherings or people's homes, nor were even mere greetings sent on festive occasions. He wrote to Savarkar that his only satisfaction of being back home was philosophical and it translated to almost nothing on ground when it came to the society.

Addressing this very real social malaise, Savarkar asked the Hindus:

Don't you feel anguished at such feelings expressed by converts? It is entirely in your hands to remove the frustration and the neglect they feel. Does it cost you anything to be merely nice to them? All that you have to say is that they are welcome to the Hindu fold. You do not face imprisonment for that. Remember, millions are waiting for just such a warm welcome. Just say openly, 'I will welcome any convert to Hindu Dharma. I shall shake hands with him, hug him, offer him sweets.' This is what we need to do to commemorate Swami Shraddhanand's memory.[40]

Shuddhi for the sake of it without emotional integration back into the parent community was meaningless for Savarkar, as chances of the neo-converts getting back on being frustrated by the incessant non-acceptance was high. This was not a movement merely to bolster the numerical strength of communities, but a true emotional cohesion of Hindu society. This approach is reflected in both the shuddhi and untouchability eradication movements.

He undertook shuddhi movements whenever and wherever the opportunity arose, beginning May 1925. For instance, on 25 May 1926, he got one Dhakras family in Ratnagiri converted back to Hinduism. The family of eight had become Christians about fifteen years before. In May 1927, however, the Hindus of Kharepatan ex-communicated the Dhakras. Savarkar organized a public meeting and said, 'You may not be able to carry out valorous deeds like Shivaji, but at least follow his example in the field of Shuddhi. Remember how Shivaji converted Netaji Palkar, who was forced to become a Muslim by Aurangzeb, back to Hindu Dharma?' This convinced nearly fifty Brahmins of the town and they agreed to share tea with the Dhakras and readmit them into the Hindu fold.[41] Soon several relatives of the Dhakras family, who had converted out of frustration, slowly began contemplating a return. They influenced other friends who had embraced Christianity and thus the movement had a ripple effect.[42] In a daring move, Savarkar arranged for the sacred thread ceremony of two sons of Dhakras. Local Brahmins were invited for the event and they dined with members of other castes. This further boosted the confidence of the Dhakras that they were indeed being accepted by their parent community.[43]

Many 'fallen women'[44] were prevented from being swallowed by the conversion factories by arranging help for them.[45]

In October 1926, he converted one Prof. Pinto of Lucknow University into the Hindu fold. Prof. Pinto, who had an MA degree from Cambridge, was attracted to Hinduism after having studied comparative religion.[46]

In January 1928, the maharaja of Indore, Tukoji Holkar, wanted to marry an American girl, Miss Miller. There was opposition from orthodox Hindus about this and there were murmurs about how the maharaja might convert to Islam just to marry the girl he was madly in love with. Savarkar and the Hindu Mahasabha members strongly supported the maharaja's desire to wed the woman he loved and offered to perform her shuddhi ceremonies. With the help of the Shankaracharya, Dr Kurtkoti, Savarkar managed to organize a priest to officiate the marriage. So pleased was the maharaja that he gave a generous grant of Rs 2,00,000 to the Shankaracharya for undertaking shuddhi work in particular.[47]

~

In 1922, while in prison, Savarkar composed an epic poem titled *Gomantak*. This was in addition to two other epic poems he wrote as a prisoner— *Kamla* and *Virahochchhvas*. *Gomantak* was not just a literary piece but also his foresight on events that were to unfold in Goa. The shuddhi movements done there in the wake of Portuguese colonialism and stranglehold were something Savarkar imagined while in captivity. But these eventually turned out to be prophetic. The first half of the poem runs into about 911 verses. The second half, in two parts, is in a non-verse, free-flowing metre. He also wrote several articles and an eponymous novel, all dealing with the issue of the Portuguese conquest of Goa and the persecution and conversion of Hindus there.

Savarkar's article 'The Birth anniversary of Baji Rao I' was published in the *Lokamanya* newspaper on 7 June 1925. Here too he exhorted all Maharashtrians to turn their attention towards Goa—go to Vasai and liberate Hindus who had been forcibly converted. He wrote:

In Vasai, Thane, Mahim and other localities, there are thousands of our people who are Christians in name only. They are eager to come back into our fold. It is our fault that we do not welcome them back. Had the Portuguese succeeded in their design, no Hindu would have been left in the territory they controlled. Baji Rao's brave soldiers put a stop to that monstrous design. It is now our ordained duty to complete his work and bring those forcibly converted Hindus back into our fold. All the Hindu Sabhas should concentrate on this work this year, without any excuses. Arya Samaj managed to convert 60,000 Malkana Rajputs back to Hinduism. Are we saying that we cannot achieve what the Arya Samaj did? Let us not assume that this is an impossible task without giving a try with the same fervour that Baji Rao's brother Chimaji Appa put in to defeat the Portuguese in 1739. A lion lying with its mouth wide open will not have its prey enter into its mouth automatically—it needs to go out and hunt for it. Let us do the same and exert ourselves for this task.[48]

Savarkar's plea, his poem and writings had an immense impact on Vinayak Maharaj Masurkar, the head of a Vaishnava ashram in Satara district's Masur. He began a massive campaign to reconvert the Gawda tribals who had become Catholics. With his disciples, he toured villages inhabited by the Gawdas, singing devotional songs and performing Hindu rituals. This created considerable interest among the tribes who expressed their fervent desire to convert back to Hinduism. Despite vehement opposition from the Roman Catholic Church and the Portuguese government in Goa, an en masse shuddhi was conducted on 23 February 1928. They were given new Hindu names. Around 4,851 Catholic Gawdas from Tiswadi, 2,174 from Ponda, 250 from Bicholim and 329 from Sattari became Hindus in this ceremony. The total number of converts to Hinduism was nearly 7,815.[49] Of course Hindu society refused to accept them back in their fold and these neo-converts formed the community of 'Nav Hindu Gawdas'.

On 1 March 1928, his editorial in *Shraddhanand* was titled, 'Don't forget Gomantak'. He lamented that India did not mean just British India and hence the mainland had forgotten the travails of the smaller colonies within the country that were under Portugal, Netherlands and France. There were no representatives from Goa, Pondicherry or Nepal in the Congress and their voices too were seldom heard. He lamented the lack of integration of these places in the larger imagination of an independent India. From Nepal to Sri Lanka, an integrated, well-knit and united India was Savarkar's vision. He embarked on an ambitious shuddhi mission from Vasai to Goa. In October 1928, several members of Goa Hindu Sabha met Savarkar in Ratnagiri and, under his guidance, shuddhi of about thirty-two Gawdas was undertaken.[50]

On 9 March 1930, Savarkar gave a speech to the Christians of Malvan on 'How Hindus were converted'. He postulated that conversions happened in Goa as much due to Portuguese excesses as they did because of Hindu orthodoxy and a refusal to accept back those Hindus who had been converted by force. He also attended a reception organized for him in the Christian locality where he spoke about how their ancestors were converted with force or deceit. This inspired several shuddhi ceremonies in the region.

Savarkar walked the talk when it came to his core beliefs. And he asked his followers too to do the same—act as much or more than you talk. In his article 'March to Vasai' in June 1925, he wrote:

> Time has come for various movements to progress from seminars and resolutions to doing something practical. People make resolutions to the effect that we need to raise volunteer force for the protection and preservation of our dignity or that we need to start orphanages. But what is the point in merely passing resolutions? Afterwards the question arises, 'Where is the money for putting into practice these resolutions?' But then, why do these delegates waste money in travelling and organizing seminars? Stop that waste and use the money thus saved to raise the volunteer force and open orphanages.[51]

Similarly, at the commemoration of Chhatrapati Shivaji's 300th birth anniversary in May 1927, he admonished the scholastic arguments that were abuzz about whether Shivaji was born in 1627 or 1630. How does it matter even if we celebrated his tri-centenary twice, he asked. What was more important according to Savarkar was to do tangible work that would make the great king proud of his followers.[52]

~

In the early part of 1925, Savarkar was greatly delighted to meet his long-lost friend and comrade in revolution, V.V.S. Aiyar. Their last meeting in London's Brixton jail had been an emotional one. The two friends did not know if life would give them a chance to meet and embrace each other again. Aiyar called on an ailing Savarkar at Ratnagiri. It was a joyous reunion where they reminisced so many stories gone past, the vicissitudes of life that they had to face and the challenges of the present. But sadly, just two months later, on 3 June 1925, V.V.S. Aiyar drowned in the Papanasam waterfalls, trying to save his daughter Subhadra. Savarkar was overwhelmed by grief and wrote a touching tribute to his friend in the *Mahratta*. Among other things he said:

> I met Shriyut Aiyar a couple of months ago . . . We forgot for a while the bitterness and the keen pangs of the afflicted and tortured past and lightly gossiped as boys fresh from schools, meeting again after a

really long holiday. He took my leave. I watched him disappear and said to myself: 'Now I can call him again any time I like.' Alas, that was not to be![53]

However, a cause of some cheer for the Savarkar family was the birth of a son to Yamunabai and Savarkar in March 1928 in Bombay. He was named Vishwas. Another daughter that they had, named Shalini, was a sickly child and died early.

~

Meanwhile, with 1929 looming, the five-year restrictions that were placed on Savarkar during his conditional release were coming to an end. He was desirous of being freer in his movements and political activities and to express his creativity and thoughts. He sent a petition on 16 July 1928 to the Governor of Bombay seeking the removal of strictures before he vacated office the following December. However, he received a reply on 28 August 1928 from the district magistrate of Ratnagiri that the government was not prepared to consider the removal of any restrictions 'before the five years specified in the second of the two conditions from which he was released from jail have expired'. This referred to his abstention from political activities for five years.[54]

At around the same time, the Bengal Provincial Hindu Sabha held its fifth session at Dacca on 27 and 28 August 1929 with N.C. Kelkar presiding over it. A resolution was passed there, which was forwarded by the secretary, Padmaraj Jain, to the Home Department of the Government of India:

> This Conference calls upon the Government to remove all restrictions placed upon the liberty of Mr. Vinayak Damodar Savarkar, Bar-at-Law, who has already undergone imprisonment and internment for 20 years, and thereby restore to the Hindu community one of its most honoured members, and feels that it is sheer vindictiveness to maintain the restrictions any further.[55]

Despite all the pressures and petitions, the government passed its order on 31 December 1928. H.F. Knight, secretary to the Government of Bombay, wrote to the district magistrate of Ratnagiri:

I am directed to state that the Governor-in-Council, after consideration, has decided that it is not at present desirable to cancel the first condition of release, requiring Savarkar to reside in Ratnagiri, but that, though no period was attached to this condition, Government will again consider the desirability of its cancellation after a period of two years from now. With regard to the second condition of release requiring V.D. Savarkar's abstention from political activities for a period of five years, such restriction being renewable at the discretion of the Government, at the expiry of the said term, I am to state that Government now renews this restriction for a period of two years from the 4th January 1929, such restriction again being renewable at the discretion of Government on the expiry of the period. I am to ask you to communicate the above orders of Government to V.D. Savarkar before the 4th January 1929.[56]

It was clear that the British were keen on ensuring that Savarkar did not join mainstream politics or extend his influence beyond the confines of Ratnagiri.

All through his conditional captivity, Savarkar had absolutely no means of employment or earning a livelihood. Given that his degrees had been withdrawn and that he had been explicitly directed not to take up employment or practice at the courts, there was no source of income for him other than the books, plays and freelance journalism that he undertook with several newspapers and magazines. These writings too were under constant surveillance of the government and hence there was no guaranteed stream of income. It was not as if the government was unaware of the problems that Savarkar and many such political internees who were under strict house arrest conditions faced. The government had therefore fixed a financial support structure for several political internees—Rs 1.5 per day as food allowance and Rs 34 per person per year to purchase clothes. This totalled up to about Rs 100 a year as a pension or allowance. The political internees in Bengal received an additional Rs 20 to Rs 30 a year as sustenance amount.[57]

When Savarkar made a request for a similar allowance to be paid to him as well, as were the norms of the government towards political prisoners, immediately after his release in 1924, it was summarily rejected by the government. After the government decided to extend the period of his restriction from the initial five-year span to two more years, in 1929, they sought a report from the district magistrates of Ratnagiri and Nasik and also the Police Commissioner of Bombay to estimate the monthly expenses of Savarkar and his family. The district magistrate of Ratnagiri recommended a monthly allowance of Rs. 150, given his growing family. The Home Secretary in Bombay decided to halve this amount to Rs 75 per month. Eventually when the recommendation reached the desk of the Governor of Bombay, the final orders stipulated a further reduction to Rs 60 per month, payable to Savarkar till the restrictions remained on him. Accordingly a monthly sustenance allowance of Rs 60 was paid to him starting 1 August 1929. Though the orders of 1929 stipulated an extension of restrictions on him for two years only, each time the matter came up for consideration of the government, they were reluctant to withdraw the restrictions and kept extending them for a period of two years. Thus, similarly worded extension orders on his restrictions came up in 1931, 1933 and 1935 till he was finally set free in 1937. Consequently the allowance was paid to him from 1929 till his eventual release on 10 May 1937.[58]

~

Ever alert about the various developments in different parts of the world, Savarkar warned of a possible global conflict that could erupt into a world war, way back in 1928. In a series of four articles for the *Shraddhanand,* he prophesied this and also advised India to take the maximum advantage of this confusion to win herself freedom. These are obviously not written as a direct prescription of what India needed to do vis-à-vis the British (though a couple of articles do count as what might be considered 'seditious'), but stated as generic war strategies that fit aptly with the Indian scenario.

In the first of the series that is titled 'Best Opportunity to Strengthen India' that appeared in the *Shraddhanand* on 16 February 1928, Savarkar stated that the best opportunity for any country to win its freedom was when its rulers were engaged in war with another powerful enemy. He stated that had the Indian leaders understood this earlier, India would have been long free. An enslaved nation, he advised, must always remain alert, watch political developments across the world and in its borders, befriend border countries and make common cause and alliances with them if the ruler gets embroiled in a major conflict. In such a scenario, weakening the ruler from within and destabilizing their regime was the only way out to win freedom, just as America, Germany or Italy had done. The enslaved nation must also spread true (or even false) stories about inhuman practices of the rulers as that catch global attention. He lamented that the Indian leadership had never thought on these lines so far. Savarkar wrote:

India was given the place in the League of Nations after the First World War. But the opportunity of snatching freedom was lost. The incompetence and ignorance of the Indian Leaders were responsible for it. The World War may provide such an opportunity once in 50-75 years, which was lost by India. The Indians continued to suffer for years thereafter, without even having the courage of uttering the word 'Freedom.' An important opportunity was thus lost in the last German war . . . Now is the most opportune time to weigh our strengths and weaknesses and prepare ourselves to take India to unreachable heights, unequalled by any nation.[59]

In the second of the series, on 23 February 1928, Savarkar traced the genesis of the armed revolutionary struggle in India and its various warriors. In the wake of an impending large-scale conflict, he advocated a strong militarization for India, for her to be able to be of consequence in global realpolitik.

In his third article dated 1 March 1928, Savarkar held out his strategy for the future. He prophesied that while the First World War was a German war, the second one would have a strong locus in Asia with Russia also possibly getting involved in a major way. Given that a major scene of war would be Asia, India's strategic importance would increase all the more. Whether she realizes and uses this position to her advantage would depend entirely on India and her leadership. He stated that if the underground revolutionary movement made common cause with border states like Nepal or with the enemies of the British, driving the colonial power out of India would be an easier task. Getting to more details, he writes:

In 1917, Germans were ill equipped to fight the war either on land or on the seas or in the air. The British Rule in India, therefore, could continue unabated. The Gurkhas were the backbone of the British army. However, if Russia instigates and supports Nepal to usurp the North Eastern part of India, the British may be put into a very difficult and irreversible position. The Gurkhas in the British army would refuse to fight for them since Gurkhas owe their life-long allegiance to their King. If they are asked to fight their King, they will march to Calcutta without any difficulty. The underground Indian revolutionaries could join them to uproot the British regime in India. One can imagine the damage to the British Empire if such a plan is really executed jointly by Nepal and Russia. But truth be told, the British are cunning, discreet and shrewd. For generations, they have conquered, manipulated, ruled, enslaved and manifested their instinctive supremacy. Since 1857, they used Nepal against India. Neither Nepal nor India was capable of assessing their own strengths and their importance in the British Empire. None of the Indian leaders too ever realized the importance of Nepal, and they still do not. Nepal's strategic location and Hindu ideology will prove to be of great advantage. India must realize it and assist Nepal and build a lasting and unbreakable relationship with Nepal.[60]

In the final article of the series, published on 8 March 1928, Savarkar held that in the event of an Anglo-Russian war, many countries like Afghanistan, Turkey, Iran, etc., would ally with Russia. This would work to India's advantage by weakening the British Empire. He concluded his piece with the following prescription for a 'path to victory':

It is evident that the whole of Asia will rise against Britain. All the bordering nations of India will attack Britain to eliminate the British threat to their existence. Japan may or may not join them. Their policies are uncertain and unknown. Britain does not have any friend in Asia and no nation will stand by it. All the Asian nations, at some time or the other, were enslaved and ill-treated by Britain making them detest the Empire . . . India, therefore, must prepare itself to be stronger than before, more united than before, more organized and consolidated than before. India must plan and decide its own course of action and execute it shrewdly but with firm commitment. It is not very long for India to declare herself as Maha-Bharat (or the Great India).[61]

~

Meanwhile, in 1925, one of Savarkar's important works, *Hindu Pad Padashahi: A Critical Review of the Hindu Empire of Maharashtra*, was published. In his foreword to the book dated 20 December 1925, historian R.C. Majumdar praised his efforts and said:

The author has soared high above the matter-of-fact history and drawn [in] bold relief the spirit lying behind it. He has justly observed that the Hindu revival, in order to be complete, required not only freedom from political bondage, but also liberation from the superstitions that had gathered round it in course of centuries. He had shown that the Marattas, while successfully achieving the first, made an earnest effort to secure the latter. They initiated the revolutionary movement of *Suddhi* (sic) in order to re-admit the apostates into the Hindu fold, but could not achieve a large measure of success in this direction. 'The lesson is,' as the author remarks, 'that although fetters of political slavery can at times be shaken off and smashed, yet the fetters of cultural superstition are often found far more difficult to knock off.' The author has further shown that the result of the combat between the English and the Marattas was a foregone conclusion—for the Marattas, along with other Indians, lacked in those 'public virtues' which the English nation possesses to an eminent degree. Here are two important lessons, which modern India should not ignore.[62]

Savarkar's work, as he himself put it in his author's prologue of 15 February 1925, was a continuum of the work done by eminent historian Vishwanath Kashinath Rajwade and Justice Mahadev Govind Ranade. The latter's *Rise of the Maratha Power* was in English and it gave the non-Marathi speaking readers a wonderful insight into the history of the Maratha Empire. Savarkar felt that the 'Indian public, not to speak of that of any other nation, has still very dim, curious, and even perverted notions regarding both the heroic principles that animated the Maratha movement, as well as the far-reaching effects it had on the course of the larger history of the Indian people'.[63] He had begun this work in London itself, after the work on the history of the Sikhs that sadly never saw light of day. Following the chaotic events and his subsequent incarceration, it took almost fifteen years thereafter for the *Hindu Pad Padashahi* to be published. Like his work on Mazzini and the 1857 uprising, this too was the result of intense research and was undertaken with the objective of using history as an effective tool to create awareness, pride and mobilization. The aim and glory of the Hindu Empire of the Marathas was sought to be contextualized in the India of the 1920s that had seen so many communal upheavals. According to Savarkar, this history transcended provincial limits and was of a pan-Hindu importance across India and the world. Being aware that the historical conflicts between the Marathas and the Mughals could create discomfort among his Muslim readers, he addressed this specifically.

He also holds out a very timeless advice of how history needs to be narrated, without contemporary prejudices and biases and what its eventual aim ought to be:

To our Muhammadan readers, however, a word of explanation is needed. The duty of a historian is primarily to depict as far as possible the feelings, motives, emotions and actions of the actors themselves whose deed he aims to relate. This he cannot do faithfully and well, unless he, for the time being, rids himself not only of all prejudices and prepossessions, but even of the fears of the consequences the story of the past might be calculated to have on the interests of the present. That latter end he should try to serve by any other means than the falsification or exaggeration or underestimation of the intentions and actions of the past. A writer on the life of (Prophet) Muhammad, for example, would be wanting in his duty; if he tries to smoothen down the fierce attacks on 'Idolatry' and the dreadful threats held before the 'Unbelievers' by that heroic Arab, only to ingratiate himself with the sentiments of those of his fellow-countrymen or readers who do not belong to the Moslem persuasion. He should try to do that by being himself more tolerant, or even by drawing a moral more in consonance with reason and freedom of thought and worship, if he can honestly do so, after he has faithfully recounted the story of that life with all its uncompromising episodes.

If he cannot do that, he had better give up the thought of writing the life of Muhammad altogether. Just as this responsibility lies on the shoulder of an honest biographer of Muhammad, there is a corresponding obligation on the part of those of his readers who do not fully, or at all, contribute to the teaching of Muhammad, which they owe to the writer. They too ought to know that an author, who in the discharge of his duties as a historian of yesterday, of Muhammad or Babar or Aurangzeb, depicts their aspirations and deeds in all their moods, fierce or otherwise, faithfully, and even gloriously or appreciatingly (sic), need not necessarily be wanting in the discharge of his duties as a citizen of today, may even be most kindly disposed to his fellow-countrymen or fellowmen of other religious persuasions or racial lineage. In dealing with that period of Hindu History when the Hindus were engaged in a struggle of life and death with the Muhammadan power, I have never played false to my duty of depicting the great actions and their causes in relation to their environments and expressing the sentiments of the actors almost in their own words, trying thus to discharge the duty of an author as faithfully as I could. Especially our Muhammadan countrymen, against the deeds of whose ancestors the history under review was a giant and mighty protest, which I hold justifiable, will try to read it without attributing, solely on that ground, any ill feeling to us towards our Muhammadan countrymen of this generation or towards the community itself as such. It would be as suicidal and as ridiculous to borrow the hostilities and combats of the past only to fight them out into the present, as it would be for a Hindu and a Muhammadan to lock each other suddenly in a death-grip while embracing, only because Shivaji and Afzulkhan had done so hundreds of years ago.

We ought to read history, not with a view to find out the best excuse to perpetuate the old strife and stress, bickering and bloodsheds whether in the name of our blessed motherland, 'of our Lord God,' that divided man from man and race from race, but precisely for the contrary reason of finding out the root causes that contributed to, and the best means to the removal of that stress and strife, of those bickerings and bloodsheds, so that man may be drawn towards man because he is man, the child of that our common father God—and nursed at the breast of this our common mother—Earth—and wield humanity in a World-Commonwealth.

But, on the other hand, the brilliance of this ultimate hope ought not to dazzle our eyes into blindness towards the solid and imminent fact that men and groups, and races in the process to consolidation into larger social units have, under the stern law of nature, to get forged into that larger existence on the anvil of war through struggle and sacrifice. Therefore, before you make out a case for unity, you must make out a case for survival as a national or a social human unit. It was this fierce test that the Hindus were called upon to pass in their deadly struggle with the Muhammadan power. There could not be a honourable unity between a slave and his master. Had the Hindus failed to rise and prove their strength to seek retribution for the wrongs done to them as a nation and a race, even if the Muhammadans stretched out a hand of peace, it would have been an act of condescension and not of friendship, and the Hindus could not have honourably grasped it with that fervour and sincerity and confidence which a sense of equality alone breeds. But the colossal struggle which the Hindus waged with those who were then their foemen in the name of their *Dev* and *Desh* really paved the way to an honourable unity between the two combating giants.[64]

The prose is in Savarkar's usual lyrical style and literary flourish—often given to dramatization and exaggeratedly flowery language. Yet it covers the entire span of Maratha history from the birth of Shivaji, the martyrdom of his son Sambhaji, the chivalry of Peshwa Baji Rao I, Madhav Rao I, Kanhoji Angre, Sawai Madhav Rao, the diplomacy of Nana Phadnavis and the chivalry of Mahadji Shinde (Savarkar considered Phadnavis and Shinde as the two pillars of the Maratha Empire), to the establishment of Hindavi Swaraj and a pan-India Hindu Empire. The rich quality of the research, official papers of the Peshwa daftar and archival documents lend the book a lot of historical credence. Added to this, the narrative style makes it a highly accessible research.

Savarkar repeatedly invokes the concept of 'Maharashtra Dharma'. This term appears in various Marathi texts. It draws its origins in a couplet ascribed to Saint Ramdas, the spiritual guru of Shivaji: '*Maratha tituka melavava, Maharashtra dharma vadhavava*' (Bring together the Marathas, spread the Maharashtra dharma). Nationalist historians of the Marathas have interpreted this term as the expression of Maratha nationalism. Hindu right-wing historians, including Savarkar, have construed this as not just Hindu nationalism, but one centred on the protection of cows and sacred spaces from Muslim attacks. It could however be argued to refer to the 'Maratha way' of living and doing things.

It must be mentioned here that there have been several prominent, and often contesting constructs of Maratha history, especially centring on the heroic figure of Shivaji. Various social groups and political ideologies appropriated and branded him (and continue to do so) to suit their politics. Social reformer Jyotiba Phule (1827–90), the prominent leader of the non-Brahmin movement in Maharashtra, visualized Shivaji in his ballad of 1869 as a 'guardian of the peasantry'.[65] Portraying him as a self-made hero, raised by his equally heroic mother Jijabai, he was sceptic about the role of his Brahmin mentor and political guide Dadoji Kondadev. In his own magnum opus, *Sarvajanik Satya Dharma Pustak* (1891), Phule was critical of the Brahmin saint Ramdas (1608–82) who is generally seen as Shivaji's guru. He accused Ramdas of misleading Shivaji and inciting him against Muslims.[66]

Phule's disciple Krishnarao Arjun Keluskar (1860–1934) published the first biography of Shivaji from the perspective of the depressed classes. Yet again, in his narrative, there was a hotly contested debate with Justice Mahadev Govind Ranade (1842–1901) when it came to the role of

Saint Ramdas. A Kshatriya status was accorded to the monarch in this narrative, as opposed to the stands of Hindutva historians such as V.K. Rajwade (1863–1926), who denied a Kshatriya status to the Chandraseniya Kayastha Prabhus (CKP) and the Maratha castes. Prominent among Keluskar's aides was Keshav Sitaram Thackeray (known by his pen-name Prabodhankar Thackeray), a writer and social reformer of the CKP caste, and father of Shiv Sena founder Bal Thackeray.

As mentioned earlier, Justice Ranade's work on the Maratha Empire was an important milestone in the historiography of the region. It was an intellectual rebuttal of sorts of British historian James Grant Duff (1789–1858) who had portrayed Shivaji as an unscrupulous adventurer.[67] The liberal Ranade also opposed Phule's stand that sought to strip Shivaji's story of any spiritual foundation, rooted especially in the bhakti movement and Saint Ramdas. 'Shivaji's chief adviser,' opined Ranade, 'was Ramdas, who gave the colour to the national flag and introduced a new form of salutation, which displayed at once the religious character of the movement and the independence of the spirit which prompted it.'[68] In fellow-nationalist Justice K.T. Telang's (1850–93) imagination, Shivaji's crusade emerged as a movement for 'the preservation of the Hindu religion against foreign aggression'.[69] It was this idea that was built upon by Tilak, even as he strove to institutionalize the legacy through the Shivaji Jayanti festivities.

The communists too made Shivaji a hero of their ideological stand. Prominent Maharashtrian communist leader Shripad Amrit Dange (1899–1991) stressed on the path-breaking changes that Shivaji had brought about in terms of ownership of land from feudal lords to the cultivating peasants.[70] In his article of April 1958 in the weekly *Yugantar*, titled '*Shivarayache Athavave Swarup*', Dange argued that Shivaji's administrative reforms and abolition of hierarchical bureaucracy reinforced the image of a monarch of the masses and downtrodden. Quite interestingly, despite being a communist, Dange had acknowledged Savarkar as one of the greatest mentors and influencers in his life for his stellar role against the British through revolution.[71]

Hindutva historians such as Rajwade extended Justice Telang's thesis to conceptualize Shivaji as a bulwark against Muslim tyranny and founder of a grand Hindu kingdom that posed a challenge to the alien Mughal rule. Interestingly, the bhakti element of Ramdas was downplayed and a dose of chivalry and the cause of Hindu empowerment were added as prominent motifs.

Savarkar belonged to this school of Maratha historiography too and cemented Rajwade's arguments. 'This word 'Hindavi Swaraj',' argued Savarkar, 'coming from the pen of Shivaji himself, reveals, as nothing else could have done, the very soul of the great movement that stirred the life and activities of Maharashtra (for a hundred years and more). Even in its inception the Maratha rising was neither a parochial nor a personal movement altogether. It was essentially a Hindu movement in the defence of Hindu Dharma for the overthrow of the alien Muhammadan domination, for the establishment of an independent, powerful Hindu Empire.'[72] While Shivaji had founded a Hindu-centric principality, it grew into the vast empire that it did under his successors, Savarkar postulated. The Peshwas were thus seen as the legitimate torch-bearers of this hallowed objective and their being Brahmins was thus not an impediment in this glorification. An integral part of the Hindutva construct was also visualizing him as a 'go-brahmana samrakshak' or the protector of cows and Brahmins. All of these were in consonance with the burning issues of the twentieth century—cow protection, Hindu sangathan and shuddhi. They needed a historical justification and Shivaji was the rallying point, a beacon of hope and an icon to emulate.

Thus, in Shivaji we see the fascinating malleability of historiography and narrative constructions to progress agendas of contemporary politics. One man, one king, meant myriad things to so many different people depending on which side of the political ideology spectrum they stood. It is in this context that we must evaluate *Hindu Pad Padashahi* and Savarkar's contribution in creating this dominant Hindutva-centric narrative of the seventeenth-century monarch and his successors.

4

Making the Deaf Hear

February 1928

Sir John Simon was arriving in British India as the head of a seven-member delegation of British parliamentarians. It was called the Indian Statutory Commission and was popularly referred to by the name of its chairman as the 'Simon Commission'. The Government of India Act of 1919 contained a provision that at the end of ten years, the constitutional reforms would be evaluated by a commission, which would examine the effects of these reforms and chalk out a future road map. Several Indian leaders had been pressing for an evaluation before the statutory ten years since the passing of the Act, by December 1929. The government somehow kept procrastinating. But the British prime minister, Stanley Baldwin, sprang a surprise on everybody by announcing this commission to visit India for the study. The reasons were obvious to most people. The term of the House of Commons in Britain was to expire in 1929. The ruling Conservative Party apprehended an imminent defeat in the hustings at the hands of the Labour Party. It was commonly believed that Labour governments had been more sympathetic to the Indian cause and a future government might concede a lot more than what was beneficial to British interests.

But this was not the main reason for the opposition that the Simon Commission faced all over India with cries of 'Simon, Go Back!' The non-inclusion of a single Indian member in this seven-member commission that was to deliberate and draft the future constitution of India was unacceptable to Indian leaders cutting across political ideologies. The All-India Muslim League (AIML) too supported the boycott of the Commission. The Congress reiterated the demand that it had been making since 1920 of a Round Table Conference of all Indian stakeholders or a convention of

Parliament to deliberate on the constitutional draft. The Congress also listed possible measures to deal with this situation—mass demonstrations across India the day the Commission set foot here, refusal of legislatures to elect committees that would cooperate with the Commission and a social boycott of the members of the Commission.

The Congress organization made the mass agitations a huge success. When the Commission was to land in Bombay on 3 February 1928, strikes, black flag protests and 'Go Back, Simon' placard marches dotted the entire country. Over 50,000 people gathered at Bombay's Chaupatty beach and leaders of all political parties condemned the decision in one voice. Nationalist leaders walked out of committees that were to be formed by various provincial legislatures. The Indian leaders decided to make their own attempts of drafting their constitution. In a committee meeting of all political parties under the chairmanship of Motilal Nehru (popularly called the Nehru Committee), held in Lucknow during 28–31 August 1928, several recommendations were made. It sought a responsible form of government where the executive was responsible to a popularly elected legislature. The sovereign Parliament was suggested to be bicameral with a Senate and a House of Representatives—200 members of the former elected by provincial councils based on proportional representation and 500 members of the latter elected by popular adult franchise. The powers of the Parliament were to be similar to those of the Dominions within the larger Empire. On the representation of communities, it recommended mixed legislatures for the House of Representatives and the provincial legislatures. No reservation of seats was mandated in the House of Representatives, except for Muslims in provinces where they were in a minority and non-Muslims in the North-West Frontier Province (NWFP). Punjab and Bengal were not to have any reservations, while other provinces would have reserved seats for minorities on the basis of population, with right to contest additional seats.

But the consensus in Lucknow evaporated in merely four months when the Nehru Committee met in Calcutta on 22 December 1928. The Muslim leadership came up with new, unprecedented demands and it was here that Muhammad Ali Jinnah emerged as a strong voice of the community's interests. Jinnah pushed for one-third representation for Muslims in the Central legislature. He pressed for Muslim representation on the population basis in the Punjab and Bengal legislatures for ten years. Residuary powers were recommended to vest in the provinces and not the Centre. Acrimonious debates and dissent led to a defeat of his amendments. Frustrated, he walked out and later confabulated with other Muslim groups led by Aga Khan and Muhammad Safi in Delhi on 1 January 1929. Sections of Sikhs, depressed classes, Christians and other groups too opposed the Nehru Committee recommendations. But all groups seemed to agree on one common principle though that there was a need for total freedom and a responsible government.

Building on this sentiment, Gandhi suggested that the Dominion status be accepted, provided the British Parliament accepted the Nehru Committee recommendations within a year, failing which the Congress would embark on non-violent non-cooperation movements again. Dominion status meant the formation of autonomous communities within the British Empire that would be equal in status but owe an allegiance to the Crown; in other words independent but not fully sovereign. Gandhi moved this resolution in the Congress annual session in Calcutta in December 1928. Several young members of the Congress itself, like Jawaharlal Nehru and Subhas Chandra Bose, opposed this move by Gandhi. They moved an amendment in the Congress resolution that India would be content with nothing short of total independence. Bose opposed the additional one-year handle given to the British and sought an instant negotiation, given the prevailing sentiment. But his amendment was defeated as Gandhi's supporters made it out to be a prestige issue and declared that he would retire if his formula was not accepted. Votes in favour of Gandhi's plan numbered 1350, while Subhas managed to garner a decent 973. 'The Mahatma,' lamented Bose, 'did not see light and his temporizing resolution . . . only served to kill precious time . . . The decision that should have been made soon after the appointment of the Simon Commission—and certainly not later than the Calcutta Congress—was not made till the Lahore Congress in December 1929. But by then the situation was to deteriorate.'[1]

United Provinces, 1924

While this compromise resolution of Gandhi in Calcutta halted the feverish pace of political frenzy that was building up in the aftermath of the Simon Commission, rumblings of a different nature were brewing. The lull that the revolutionary movement had seen in the immediate aftermath of the First World War and the many failed attempts of the revolutionaries in collusion with Germany suddenly saw a gradual revival.

Sachindranath Sanyal who had been let out from the Cellular Jail got together with a group of revolutionaries from north India and Bengal and formed a united platform, the Hindustan Republican Army (HRA). In 1924, Sanyal drafted the HRA's constitution and declared the establishment of a 'Federated Republic of the United States of India by an organized and armed revolution' as its aim.[2] Based at Benares, the HRA was headed by Sanyal and Jogesh Chandra Chatterjee. It was hardly able to move much beyond the stage of fund-raising, mostly through dacoities. The most daring attempt was at Kakori in the United Provinces on 9 August 1925 where the revolutionaries attacked a train transporting a cache of government funds. The perpetrators were arrested and after a two-year trial, four members of the group—Ashfaqullah Khan, Ramprasad Bismil, Roshan Singh and Rajendra Lahiri—were executed. Others were transported for life or awarded jail terms.

Just as the incident of the Chapekar execution had inspired young Savarkar into revolution, the Kakori case became an inspiration for a new generation of revolutionaries who were perhaps just waiting in the wings— Chandrashekhar Azad, Bhagat Singh, Sukhdev and Rajguru among others. Bhagat Singh had been in touch with the HRA in Kanpur from 1923–24. He took it upon himself to organize revolutionary movements all over India under a single umbrella. Calling for a meeting of revolutionary groups from the United Provinces, Bihar, Punjab and Rajasthan at Delhi's Ferozeshah Kotla during 8–9 September 1928, he decided to rechristen the HRA as Hindustan Socialist Republican Association (HSRA).[3] The Yugantar and Anushilan Samiti of Bengal, however, did not join forces, as they preferred to work independently. This new group was largely influenced by communism and trade union ideologies and the inclusion of socialism in the name of the organization too was revealing. The HSRA slowly began spreading its tentacles across Kanpur, Agra, Delhi and Lahore and had satellite branches in Calcutta, Benares, Jhansi and other places. The Central Committee had Bhagat Singh as the general secretary, Bhagwati Charan Vohra as propaganda minister, Chandrashekhar Azad as the all-India coordinator, while Virabhadra Tiwari, Sukhdev and Kailashpati were in charge of the United Provinces, Punjab and Delhi respectively.[4]

The immediate trigger to the revolution was a protest against the Simon Commission being held in Lahore on 30 October 1928. James A. Scott, the senior superintendent of police in Lahore, ordered a massive lathi charge on 7 November against all the non-violent protesters. The great leader of Punjab, Lala Lajpat Rai, was grievously wounded after being hit on his head. Ten days later he succumbed to his injuries. Along with Bal Gangadhar Tilak and Bipin Chandra Pal (of the Lal-Bal-Pal trio), Lala Lajpat Rai was among the tallest and most respected leaders of the country. His death, that too in this manner, sent shock waves all over India. The whole of India plunged into mourning.

Savarkar wrote a stirring piece on this unfortunate episode on 20 December 1928. He mocked the committee that the government set up to probe the attack on Lalaji. Quoting from the Bible lines that seemed apt in this case, he wrote: 'They then spat at him in his face and did buffet him. They smote him in the face with the palms of their hands and jeeringly asked: prophesy unto us, Oh Christ, who of us smote thee!' It just remained to replace the word 'Christ' with 'Lalaji', said Savarkar, adding that this committee was a hogwash to ask a dying man: 'Prophesy unto us, Oh Lala ji! Who of us smote thee.'[5] In a condolence meeting organized in Ratnagiri, Savarkar spoke glowingly of Lalaji's contribution and appealed to the people that the best way to pay tribute to Lala Lajpat Rai was to work the way he did.

To make matters worse, when the matter was raised in the British Parliament, the government denied any role in Lalaji's death.[6] The Young Turks of the HSRA were however not content with mere editorials and protests. The wife of the late Congress leader C.R. Das, Basanti Debi, issued an open challenge: 'I, a woman of India, ask the youth of India: What are you going to do about it?'[7] The HSRA took on the cudgels of avenging this murder. Bhagat Singh, his Maharashtrian revolutionary associate Shivaram Hari Rajguru, and Chandrashekhar Azad plotted to kill Scott. But in a case of mistaken identity, Singh and Rajguru ended up gunning down John P. Saunders, an assistant superintendent of police in Lahore on 17 December 1928, before making an escape. Saunders was a part of the lathi charge brigade and hence the group was satisfied that they had fulfilled their vow. Azad shot an Indian constable Channan Singh who gave him chase.[8] Disguising himself, Bhagat Singh boarded a train to Calcutta and went underground.

By February 1929, the HSRA regrouped in Agra and set up a bomb factory there. They planned two attacks—one on the Simon Commission in Delhi (which never materialized)[9] and another on the Legislative Assembly. On 8 April 1929, Bhagat Singh and Batukeshwar Dutt went into the Assembly and from an elevated position in the visitor's gallery threw two low-intensity bombs, fired two pistol shots, scattered HSRA propaganda leaflets and shouted slogans of Inquilab Zindabad (Long Live the Revolution!). Their main intention was not to kill anyone but to 'make a loud noise' so that the 'deaf may hear'. The duo allowed themselves to be arrested. Several members of the HSRA were rounded up and the plot, including Saunders's murder, slowly began to unravel in a long-drawn trial that came to be known as the Lahore Conspiracy Case.

Prisoners under Bhagat Singh's leadership began an intensive hunger strike in jail, protesting against the ill-treatment meted to them. This received wide press coverage, and demonstrations began to be held all over the country on more humane treatment to the prisoners. Jawaharlal Nehru met the strikers; Muhammad Ali Jinnah defended them in the Assembly. Strangely it was Gandhi who kept a studied silence, especially on a matter related to hunger strikes, of which he was an expert. The government was shaken to its foundations. One of the strikers, Jatindranath Das from Bengal, died in the hunger strike on 13 September 1929. Even here, Gandhi refused to acknowledge the martyrdom of Jatin Das in his speeches or writings in *Young India*.[10] A month after Jatin Das's martyrdom, Bhagat Singh led a marathon 116 days of hunger strike. He ended it on 5 October 1929. His courage made him a national hero, beyond Punjab.

But Jatin Das's sacrifice did not go in vain. The government was forced to revise their regulations about political prisoners. They were divided into three classes (A, B, C or Divisions I, II and III) in respect of their treatment in confinement—a demand that Savarkar had long advocated during his incarceration in the Cellular Jail through his several petitions. Despite the government's changed attitude vis-à-vis political prisoners, not much however changed on the ground, barring for a few high-profile ones.[11] Explaining this categorization, Subhas Chandra Bose wrote:

C class prisoners would be treated exactly like ordinary criminals; B class prisoners would be treated slightly better than C class in the matter of food, letters, interviews and other facilities—while A class prisoners would be treated somewhat better than B class. The distinction at the time of classification would be made according to the social status of the prisoner. When these rules were applied in practice, it was found that at least 95 per cent of the political prisoners were classed as C; about 3 or 4 per cent were classed as B and less than 1 per cent as A. The effect of the new rules therefore was to give somewhat better treatment to a microscopic minority in order to break the solidarity of the political prisoners. The principle of 'divide and rule' was thus extended to the domain of prison administration. The only welcome feature in the new rule was that it abolished in theory the classification of certain prisoners as 'European', who used to get better food, clothing and accommodation than Indians of the highest rank.[12]

Savarkar took on Gandhi for his silence on Jatin Das's martyrdom. In an article dated 12 October 1929 in the *Shraddhanand*, he lamented that the incident had sent shock waves across the country and moved even the insensitive British government to act.[13] Savarkar quoted the Hindi daily from Calcutta, *Swatantrya*, that mentioned that even distant Ireland had expressed its sorrow on the tragic death of a young man. Despite this, Gandhi's mouthpiece *Young India* maintained a curious silence on the matter, though the smallest of incidents in the Sabarmati Ashram warranted huge editorials and columns. Savarkar wondered if Gandhi's omission meant that he considered Jatin too as a violent upstart, though the latter's definition of violence and non-violence was contrary to the Hindu tenets and had therefore earned him disapproval from large sections of people. Savarkar exclaimed sarcastically that after all Jatin had done no major feat than merely laying down his life for his country that a Mahatma of Gandhi's stature would waste his time and effort to condole his martyrdom. Moreover, he was not Abdul Rashid either who had fired at Swami Shraddhanand and immediately won both the sympathy and the title of 'my dear brother' from Gandhi. Exposing the hypocrisy in Gandhi's stand, he wondered how it could be a tenet of non-violence for the Mahatma to wholeheartedly support all those Indian soldiers who were dispatched with his blessings during the First World War to fight Germany and shed German blood—supporting a nation that had colonized our country, and attacking those who had never raised their finger against us. While the Moplahs could be commended as 'brave people', revolutionaries like Jatin Das, Bhagat Singh or Batukeshwar Dutt and their acts were 'dastardly' and acts of cowardice for the Mahatma, Savarkar noted.

Even as Savarkar termed Jatin's bravery as 'laudable, respectable, praiseworthy', he considered it as an act that was 'not to be emulated'. He argued that dying will not bring the goal of freedom any closer, but staying alive will allow freedom fighters to work towards it. He gave an example of when Aurangzeb imprisoned Shivaji, the latter did not die fasting in protest. He bided his time and escaped to build an even greater kingdom than before. This, according to Savarkar, was the strategic need of the hour.

Evidently, Savarkar was not the only one to question Gandhi's silence on such an important matter. Rumblings of discontent were heard from within the Congress too. Subhas Chandra Bose mentions:

> In this connection the attitude of the Mahatma was inexplicable. Evidently the martyrdom of Jatin Das, which had stirred the heart of the country did not make any impression on him. The pages of *Young India* ordinarily filled with observations on all political events and also topics like health, diet etc., had nothing to say about the incident. A follower of the Mahatma, who was also a close friend of the deceased, wrote to him inquiring as to why he had said nothing about the event. The Mahatma replied to the effect that he had purposely refrained from commenting, because if he had done so, he would have been forced to write something unfavourable.[14]

Faced with a deluge of queries, Gandhi finally broke his silence in an article in *Young India*, dated 17 October 1929, a full one month after Jatin's martyrdom. Titled 'My Silence', it said:

> I had hoped that by this time my correspondents had realized that, if I was silent on any question that agitated the country, the silence was maintained in its interest or on similar valid grounds, and that therefore they would not deluge me with inquiries and protests regarding my deliberate silence over the self-immolation of Jatindranath Das and the question of hunger-strikers generally. At Gorakhpur in one of the addresses received by me the question was directly put to me, and I was in courtesy bound to answer it. My answer was that the silence was observed entirely in the national interest. I had felt that an expression of my opinion was likely to do more harm than good to the cause for which brave Jatindra fasted unto death. There are occasions when silence is wisdom. This I hold to be such an occasion. I may inform the reader that there are very many important questions affecting the nation on which, though I hold strong and decided views, I maintain absolute silence, for I believe that it often becomes the duty of every public man to be silent even at the risk of incurring unpopularity and

even a much worse penalty, as it undoubtedly becomes his duty to speak out his mind when the occasion requires it, though it may be at the cost of his life. So far as the philosophy of hunger strikes is concerned, I have given the fullest expression to my general views in these pages more often than once. It is therefore unnecessary for me to expound them any further. I regret that I can give my numerous correspondents no further satisfaction. I may however give them this assurance that my silence has no connection whatsoever with Jatin's crime or innocence. For I hold that even a criminal is entitled to decent treatment and decent food. I also hold that an under-trial prisoner must be presumed at least by the public to be innocent, and for that matter what I have heard about Jatindranath Das is all in praise of him, and I have been assured that he was no more capable of doing or contemplating violence than I should be myself.[15]

A few weeks later, when the questions did not cease, a piqued Gandhi remarked:

I have already written about Jatin Das. He has been praised all over the country and abroad. It is the special dharma of *Navajivan*[16] to sing praises of those poor but heroic men and women whom no one knows nor would care to know. It is my firm belief that we are going to achieve true *swaraj* or *Ramarajya* with the help of such unknown people. Those who believe that without self-purification such *swaraj* is impossible should preserve such articles.[17]

This incensed Savarkar further. In his rebuttal in the *Shraddhanand* dated 16 November 1929, he wondered why Gandhi could not gather the moral courage to address a young man who was being praised from Kashmir to Rameshwaram, as 'Martyr Jatin' or 'Brave Jatin' or even 'Brother Jatin' as Abdul Rashid had been elevated.[18] He scoffed at Gandhi's condescension of not considering him a criminal, saying Jatin Das really did not need his certificate of non-criminality. He noted a deep insecurity in Gandhi that any fulsome praise to the revolutionaries might reduce his own stature and respect, as also that of his philosophy of non-violence among the masses. Hence, he was perennially parsimonious in his admiration and even called them cowards and perpetrators of dastardly acts. When the youth of India were celebrating the brave acts of revolutionaries, including the recent bomb heroes of Dakshineshwar—Anant Hari and Pramod Ranjan—was Gandhi's *Young India* out of tune with the voice of the young? Was it 'Old India' run by a sixty-year-old editor? Savarkar asked. The newspaper needs to be retitled as a 'Back Number' of the voice of *Young India*, or even 'Old Dying India', he suggested. He pointed the readers' attention to Gandhi's opposition to the collection of public funds for finding legal help to defend the revolutionaries of the Meerut Conspiracy case. But in a volte-face, sensing the public mood, Gandhi visited the revolutionaries in jail. When asked about his earlier reservations, he remarked that this was merely to ensure a lawyer would come to fight the case driven by his pure conscience and not by the lure of money. Savarkar remarked in exasperation that a man, who openly sought funds for the khadi initiative, was being delusional in assuming a lawyer would fight such an important case for free. Why did Gandhi not wait for Indians to voluntarily join the British forces during the First World War and why did he go marching from village to village recruiting soldiers, he questioned. The ideological differences between Gandhi and Savarkar were thus increasing with every major political incident in the country.

~

Meanwhile, by June 1929, the Labour Party came to power in Britain and it summoned Viceroy Lord Irwin to London for consultations. While Lord Irwin was there, Gandhi gave a call to the Congress members in different legislatures to resign their seats and boycott the legislative councils. Leaders like J.M. Sengupta and Subhas Bose stoutly opposed the move. Much to the surprise of the younger brigade in the Congress, Motilal Nehru, who mostly held contrarian views on this matter with Gandhi, also acquiesced. This shocked many like Bose who commented:

> One has to remark with great regret that Pandit Motilal Nehru who was the only man who could influence the Mahatma either way at that time, did a positive disservice to his country by actively supporting the Mahatma in his policy of reviving the boycott of the Legislatures. The harmful effect of this boycott became more and more evident in the years to come. To say the least, it was tactically a great blunder to boycott the Legislatures when the new Constitution was under consideration, especially when it had been demonstrated the year before that because of

the presence of Congressmen in the Assembly, that body had been able
to repudiate the Simon Commission.[19]

Sensing opposition from the Young Turks, especially Jawaharlal Nehru,
who were all for total independence and not Dominion status, Gandhi
decided to win him over by offering him to preside over the All-India
Congress Committee. Till then, young Jawaharlal, who had returned from
Europe in 1927, called himself a socialist and often expressed disagreements
with Gandhi's views. But his crossover eventually alienated Jawaharlal from
his comrades in the 'Left Wing' within the Congress, including Bose who
lamented: 'The Mahatma took a clever step in supporting the candidature
of Pandit Jawaharlal Nehru and his election as President opened a new
chapter in his public career. Since then, Pandit J.L. Nehru has been a
consistent and unfailing supporter of the Mahatma.'[20]

In October 1929, Lord Irwin returned to India and issued a statement
on 31 October that Britain favoured the attainment of Dominion status
for India and that a Round Table Conference was to be called in London
of all the parties to discuss the Dominion constitution, after the Simon
Commission submitted its report. To secure an assurance on the Dominion
status from the viceroy on this promise, Gandhi and Motilal Nehru
met him on 23 December, but had to return disappointed, as there was
nothing forthcoming. There was much consternation over the viceregal
announcement back in Britain of assuring Dominion status to India with
opposition from Churchill, Lord Birkenhead, Lord Reading and others.
Irwin was hence playing his cards cautiously.

Gandhi and his ardent supporters were left in a bind. They had bought
time for a year with the assurance that if Dominion status was not granted
by then, they would launch an agitation for total independence. With the
viceroy's non-committal attitude, the Lahore Congress of 1929 under
Jawaharlal Nehru advocated for total independence and Gandhi decided
to launch the Civil Disobedience movement. There was however no clear
plan of action for the attainment of either of these goals. Jawaharlal Nehru
had strongly advocated the proposal for complete independence in the
Madras session of the Congress way back in December 1927, but it had
not found favour with Gandhi and the proposal was defeated.

As before, Gandhi's might prevailed completely in the Congress again
and he managed to have his way in deciding members of the All-India
Congress Committee. Naysayers like Srinivasa Iyengar and Subhas Bose

were deliberately dropped and a compliant group of fifteen members was announced to ratify every future political move of Gandhi. The Lahore Congress marked another complete takeover of the Congress by Gandhi in what was seen as a deft political move and a marginalization of the Left Wing and Young Turks who were opposed to him.

On 26 January 1930, the flag of independence was unfurled and a clarion call for Poorna Swaraj or complete independence was given by the Congress. But barely had the ink on the Congress resolution dried than Gandhi made a shocking offer to the viceroy with a set of eleven demands, which if the government agreed to, they would 'hear no talk of Civil Disobedience; and the Congress will heartily participate in any Conference where there is a perfect freedom of expression and demand'.[21] This could have been the practical politician in Gandhi trying to keep the door open with the government for negotiations if the resolution of total independence proved to be a stumbling block. But since he took none into confidence, the vacillation shocked most of his supporters who had enthusiastically unfurled the flag of complete independence.

A month later, in February 1930, the Congress Working Committee (CWC) met and again passed a resolution favouring civil disobedience to attain Poorna Swaraj. After much prevarication, even as the enthusiasm of the country and large groups of mobilized young men and women had peaked, Gandhi decided to launch the movement by violating salt laws by undertaking a march at Dandi, a village on the sea coast of Gujarat. Here too, contradicting the points of the Lahore resolution, Gandhi wrote to the viceroy on 2 March 1930 reiterating his eleven demands and announcing the launch of the movement. In his letter, while rightly enumerating his reasons for calling British rule in India a curse, Gandhi contradicted the collective resolution of the Congress as agreed upon in Lahore:

But the Resolution of Independence should cause no alarm, if the word Dominion Status mentioned in your announcement had been used in its accepted sense. For, has it not been admitted by responsible British statesmen that Dominion Status is virtual Independence? What, however, I fear is that there never has been any intention of granting such Dominion Status to India in the immediate future.[22]

. . . I have no desire to cause you unnecessary embarrassment, or any at all, so far as I can help. If you think that there is any substance in my letter, and if you will care to discuss matters with me, and if to that end you would like me to postpone publication of this letter, I shall gladly refrain on receipt of a telegram to that effect soon after this reaches you. You will, however, do me the favour not to deflect me from my course unless you can see your way to conform to the substance of this letter. This letter is not in any way intended as a threat but is a simple and sacred duty peremptory on a civil resister.[23]

Even Gandhi's protégé Jawaharlal Nehru was perplexed by this somersault and wondered: 'What was the point of making a list of our political and social reforms when we were talking in terms of independence? Did Gandhiji mean the same thing when he used this term as we did, or did we speak a different language?'[24] The viceroy was not amused and he refused to meet Gandhi and regretted that the latter was contravening the law.

But the magical effect of Gandhi's call on the nation was something even the government did not foresee. Men, women and children came out in humungous numbers to participate in the movement. Even by official figures, more than 60,000 civil resisters were imprisoned.[25] Special prisons had to be improvised at short notice but they were filled up in no time. As the seriousness of the campaign dawned on the government, it embarked on a ruthless and brutal repression policy. Untold atrocities were committed on the resisters by the police and the military and every province had its tales of woe. Unarmed satyagrahis were mercilessly hacked, private parts of men hit with lathis, horses ridden over agitators, pins thrust into people's bodies, houses and property burnt, and lives of countless people were lost. The Press Ordinance was passed in April 1930 to muzzle the press and prevent any form of communication especially among the agitators. Gandhi himself was arrested by the government in May 1930.

Ratnagiri

On his part, Savarkar continued to remain critical of the many flip-flops of Gandhi and the Congress. In his article dated 19 March 1929,[26] he compared Gandhi's ultimatums to the empty threats of a weakling in school who gets routinely thrashed by the stronger boys of the class. And each time they beat him up, the weakling threatens them with mere words: 'If you touch me again, you will see what I will do to you!' Even before the weakling could complete his threat, the second thrash would have landed on his cheek! He ridiculed the long rope that Gandhi gave to the British and trusted them till the night of 31 December 1929 to grant India her Dominion status. 'If Gandhi threatened the British, "Give us Dominion Status, else I will spin the charkha more" or "Give us poorna swaraj, else I will wear Khadi more" will this move the British Government?' questioned Savarkar. It will on the other hand heartily entertain the British, he contended. What kind of 'strong, contextual and natural' civil disobedience was this that takes place alongside dinner meetings and socializations with the viceroy, Savarkar wondered.

He was scathing of Gandhi's ambivalence towards the concept of 'Total Independence' right from the Madras session of 1927. On 28 June 1928, he wrote:

> Of the two people who were angered by the Freedom resolution—The British and Gandhi—it was natural that the British got angered, most people understood that. But Mahatma Gandhi—a born Indian, a patriot, who set out to get freedom in one year, as soon as India decided to throw off the bounds of the British rule, why should he get so angry, this puzzled many. His followers also could not solve this puzzle.[27]

He was also biting in his attack on Gandhi for what he considered as the latter's abject surrender to the British during the Zulu conflict, the Boer War and the First World War. A significant part of his very long article has been reproduced here to give an insight into the nature of the intellectual animosity and differences of opinion that Savarkar had with Gandhi's tactics:

> The tussle between the Zulu people and British had started. The Zulus had not done anything to the Indians, nor was Gandhi understanding what they had done to the British. Rather the whole world knew that it was the British who had snatched the Zulus' wild freedom, and threatened them with their English nails! But the British attacked the Zulus . . . He [Gandhi] went along with the British as volunteers for the attack. He was watching the British being crueler than animals in killing the Zulus. It was clear that the British were taking away the freedom of the Zulus. But the kind Gandhi did not resign from his job as a volunteer from the British army! The way his heart would pine for the British kingdom that even the brutal killings of the Zulus could not deter his love. This is one experiment of Truth.

Let us not speak about the Boer War. To attack the freedom of that strong country, these sons of India, themselves losing their freedom at the hands of the British, honestly and inherent slave qualities pushed their way into the British Army! Not one or two but they took along another fifty-sixty people with them! The whole world was pained by the loss of the Boers in the war of independence, and shunned the British victory. But the British awarded all those whose hands were covered with the blood of the Zulus, and then Gandhiji also received one and a medal too—he wore that honest and flattering belt of Slavery with great pride around his neck. This was the second experiment.

Even then this self-enslaved person who lost his own freedom, went about the whole world trampling other persons' freedom for the third person who had in the first place enslaved him and taken his freedom. These were the experiments of truth that went on in the Beautiful Africa. Only the actual India remained to be vaccinated by this truth serum.

Then very kindly in order to display these experiments of truth in India at the time of the last World War, this person who sold his own honour and loyalty to the British Empire—i.e. India's Slavery—began his exhibition of dishonest stupidity in India. At the time of the World War, Lokmanya Tilak's National Party was trying to acquire as many Indian rights as possible from the British taking advantage of the World War and on the other hand the Abhinav Bharat Revolutionary organisation was trying to take over the royal spectre, that held all the rights, and shouting 'kingdom by strength' blowing away the planned plots was entering the war zone; at that time Gandhiji writes in his autobiography or 'Experiments of Truth' that, 'At that time I was faced with the question, what do I have to do with this war of Germany . . . According to a lot of Indians, these English are our molester lords, we are slaves because of this relation between us, we should take advantage of their crisis and make way towards our freedom, but how could this decision go down my throat! Because I did not find my condition to be like that of a slave. My belief was that, it is the fault of the way the British rule and of most British Officers. These faults can be removed with love. The rule was faulty, but it was not as unbearable then as it seems today. But today, as much as I have lost confidence and faith on the rule, those who felt that way then began trying to get as many rights to freedom as possible at that time. How would they support the British? But I found the idea of let alone snatching our rights, but even demanding them at the time of their crisis very uncivilized and short-sighted. And I decided that giving England unconditional support as our first and foremost duty.' To fulfill this 'far-sighted and righteous duty' Gandhiji first gathered around 80 men and started applying for their permits to volunteer in the army. But finally within the crowd of thousands of men, the clever British politicians found that these handfuls of innocent Indians were like a poppy seeds in the sea; and they would be more useful in India to destroy the plans of Lokmanya Tilak's National Party. Hence they immediately diverted these 'far-sighted and righteous volunteers to India. These righteous, decent truth dramas are extremely famous.

This non-violence became a 'Volunteer recruiting officer' that sent the poor farmers' army from India to be sent to the British Army's butchery to kill the Germans in the armed war! The old code of ethics sometimes writes, 'violence for the religion is not violence. The violence done to protect the decent people is non-violence'. The old definition is wrong, the Mahatma who claims unexceptional non-violence is the only non-violence now defines non-violence as follows: Violence undertaken for the British Empire is not violence! The violence involved in recruiting men to kill the Germans, Zulus, Boers, whoever were fighting against the British Empire is acceptable to the righteous unexceptional non-violence!

During the last World War, Gandhiji tried to create as many obstacles as possible in the plans of the National Party and was a little successful. The British only expected that he would be able to hinder Lokmanya Tilak's work. Because they knew that the revolutionaries did not find Mahatma Gandhi's non-violent righteous and far-sight, worth a penny . . .

Seeing this tradition the Madras Resolution that is called by Gandhiji as childish and short-sighted today, tomorrow he himself will come forward and call his comments as childish and the fact that he made them a Himalayan Mistake. But that is after some years! What the world sees today, he sees after a few years! Far-sighted! A vision that shows the past closer when gone far ahead![28]

In another article dated 30 March 1929, Savarkar quoted several British newspapers including *Pioneer* and *Manchester Guardian*.[29] They had all started addressing Gandhi as 'Mahatma ji' and he wondered how the same press that abused him as 'swollen headed' and welcomed his arrest had suddenly discovered the virtues of the man in loincloth. He quoted the *Pioneer* that said:

> There can be little doubt but that the wide spread conservative elements in the land will once more rally round the Government and among them the foremost would be Mahatma ji! The revolutionary movement in the country would be isolated and left in the air and there would be still a chance to preserving India for the British Commonwealth of Nations. If no such step is taken, the future would be black indeed.

The manner in which the English press had been advocating that the British government put no restrictions and penalties on Gandhi as he was their most effective bulwark against the armed revolutionary movement to free India should give people an indication as to where the Congress movement was headed, argued Savarkar. When the press of your enemy country chants the mantra of 'Rally around Gandhites' as the British newspapers had, it does create a sense of alarm. Was this why Gandhi had not a word of sympathy for the many brave hearts who had taken up arms against the British, he asked. The title of the article 'The British Collaborators' made Savarkar's intention and assessment of the entire movement clear.

~

Even as the political ferment in India carried on, the Simon Commission submitted its report on 7 June 1930. It recommended a federal constitution for India, full autonomy in the provinces with overriding powers vested in the Governor, an enlargement of the provincial legislative councils, an enlarged Lower House of the Central legislature elected by the provincial councils but not responsible to the Central government, and a separation of Burma from India. These recommendations were unsatisfactory to most stakeholders. The Congress issued a statement on 15 August 1930 that it stood for India's right to secede from the Empire and form a responsible, national government that controlled the country's finance and defence. The British Government paid no heed to the Congress's protests or demands and instead went ahead and convened a First Round Table Conference on 12 November 1930. This was attended by eighty-nine members—sixteen from British parties, sixteen from Indian princely states and fifty-seven from British India. The Congress was unrepresented. The

marathon meetings went on till 19 January 1931 under the chairmanship
of British prime minister James Ramsay Macdonald. The broad consensus
that emerged among the Indian delegates was that British India and native
states form a federal union ruled by a parliamentary system of government.
The British delegates stoutly opposed the immediate grant of Dominion
status or even the introduction of a parliamentary system in the country.
Several subcommittees were formed to discuss the modalities of creating a
federal structure.

But there were thorny issues too related to election of members
belonging to minority communities. The matter was further complicated
with the demand by Ambedkar that for electoral purposes the depressed
classes be treated as a separate community. Attempts to work out joint
electorates between communities that also helped foster social harmony
were totally foiled by Sir Fazl-i-Hussain, a member of the viceroy's
Executive Council. Several Muslim delegates supported this move and
made it clear that meeting their demands was a precondition to accepting
Dominion status. Muhammad Ali, the celebrated associate of Gandhi in
the Khilafat movement, articulated this mindset in a candid manner: 'Make
no mistake about the quarrels between Hindu and Mussalman, they are
founded only on the fear of domination . . . I belong to two circles of equal
size but which are not concentric. One is India and the other is the Muslim
world . . . we are not nationalists but supernationalists.'[30] By the end of
the conference the entire Muslim delegation that included Jinnah spelt
out that 'no advance is possible or practicable, whether in the Provinces or
the Central Government, without adequate safeguards for the Muslims of
India, and that no constitution will be acceptable to the Muslims of India
without such safeguards'.[31]

By the end of the conference, the broad steps that were laid out included
the creation of an All-India Federation of Indian states and British India,
in a bicameral legislature. Defence and external affairs were to rest with
the viceroy (Governor General). The provincial legislatures were to be fully
responsible. The greatest degree of self-government was assured with the
rejig of provincial subjects, while the federal government was to concern
itself with those matters of all-India concern. Minority issues were left for
more threadbare discussion and consensus. As Subhas Bose summed it up:

> The net result of the first session of the Round Table Conference was the
> offer to India of two bitter pills—Safeguards and Federation. To make

these pills eatable, they were sugar coated with 'Responsibility' . . . to make matters worse, the anti-Nationalist Moslems who were present at the Round Table Conference declared that they would agree to responsible Government with Federation and Safeguards, only if the communal question was decided to their satisfaction.[32]

That the entire conference concluded without the representation and views of a body as pan-Indian as the Congress discredited the very outcome of the deliberations. The government slowly decided to open doors of negotiation with the Congress and Gandhi. The no-tax campaigns and the Civil Disobedience movement had shaken the economic base of the Empire. Also, as Miss Ellen Wilkinson, a former member of the British Parliament, stated in her opinions after visiting India in 1932 as a member of the India League Deputation: 'Gandhi was the best policeman the Britisher had in India.'[33] Lord Irwin was shrewd enough to realize that there was no point in embittering the equation and not taking the concerns of Gandhi and the Congress on board. Gandhi and other members of the Congress Working Committee (CWC) were unconditionally released and he was soon called for talks with the viceroy to reach a settlement.

On 4 March 1931, Gandhi and Irwin sat across the table in Delhi and signed what came to be known as the 'Gandhi–Irwin Pact'. Gandhi had put the terms of the pact in front of the CWC and stated that he would not proceed till they were unanimously agreed upon. Jawaharlal Nehru had reservations but decided to give in to the terms as an 'obedient soldier'.[34] It was later when the Pact was published and created a public uproar that Jawaharlal Nehru voiced his disagreements. Gandhi offered to call off the Civil Disobedience movement and participate in a future Round Table Conference to draft a Constitution of India on the basis of federation, responsibility, adjustments and safeguards necessary for India's interests. He also decided to forego demands for any investigations into police atrocities across the country. The viceroy also conceded release of all political prisoners incarcerated in connection with the non-violent movement and restore any property of theirs that was confiscated or sold. Emergency ordinances were to be withdrawn and manufacture of salt, free of duty, permitted for those living close to the seashore. In effect not only had the Congress given up on the demand for total independence that it so heroically championed from the Lahore Congress, it also eschewed its demand for Dominion status that was so dear to Gandhi. Why then did it reject participation in the Round Table Conference in the first place or even launch the Civil Disobedience movement, one may be forced to ponder. What purpose did the untold sufferings of thousands of Indians who enthusiastically took part in the movement to great personal and physical harm serve? After the conference, the CWC had pooh-poohed the resolutions as vague and general to justify any change in its policy vis-à-vis the British government. Yet, in barely two months, it had come around to agreeing to the very terminologies agreed upon at the conference by parties that it had ridiculed as non-representational of Indian opinion. The pact of course elevated the status of the Congress as being worthy of a solo confabulation and agreement with the viceroy of India, and that too with a man whom they, till not too long ago, detested as a half-naked fakir (as Churchill called him disparagingly). The silver lining was the awakened political consciousness among common Indians who were now willing to endure any amount of suffering to ensure freedom. This moral regeneration of the Indian spirit is certainly something that one must attribute to Gandhi's charismatic leadership and his ability to touch the hearts and minds of countless Indians who were ready to act on his call.

But as Nehru recounted in exasperation in his afterthought about the anticlimax of the Civil Disobedience movement:

Was it for this that our people had behaved so gallantly for a year? Were all our brave words and deeds to end in this? The independence resolution of the Congress, the pledge of January 26, so often repeated? So I lay and pondered on that March night, and in my heart there was a great emptiness as of something precious gone, almost beyond recall.[35]

The next day, a closed-door meeting with Gandhi was planned to assuage his agitated mind. It perhaps helped, as Nehru himself reminisced:

The merits of the agreement apart, I told him [Gandhi] that his way of springing surprises upon us frightened me, there was something unknown about him which, in spite of the closest association for fourteen years, I could not understand at all and which filled me with apprehension. He admitted the presence of this unknown in him, and said that he himself could not answer for it or foretell what it might lead to. For a day or two I wobbled not knowing what to do. There was no question of opposing or preventing the agreement then . . . So,

I decided, not without great mental conflict and physical distress, to accept the agreement and work for it wholeheartedly. There appeared to me to be no middle way.[36]

The Gandhi–Irwin Pact dominated the Congress's annual session at Karachi, held on 29 March 1931 and presided over by Sardar Vallabhbhai Patel. Interestingly, despite the terms of the Pact, the resolution passed stated that 'the Congress desires to make it clear that the Congress goal of Purna Swaraj remains intact'. How this squared with what had been agreed between Gandhi and the viceroy was an open conundrum. Subhas Bose, who stoutly opposed the terms of the Pact, had an opportunity to confabulate with the Mahatma in Bombay and also travel with him by rail to Delhi. Bose made him assure that the terms of the Pact would be put up for discussion at the Karachi Congress, that these would not contravene the spirit of total independence and that he would strive for total amnesty for all political prisoners.

But a larger shadow loomed on the Congress session. This was the government's decision to execute Bhagat Singh and his comrades in the Lahore Conspiracy case. Pressure was brought upon Gandhi to save the lives of the young men and he did try his best. Subhas Bose had urged Gandhi to make the amnesty of Bhagat Singh, Sukhdev and Rajguru a breaking point for the agreement with the viceroy, as similar instances had occurred with the Sinn Fein of Ireland and the British government. As Bose rued: 'But the Mahatma who did not want to identify himself with the revolutionary prisoners, would not go so far and it naturally made a great difference when the Viceroy realized that the Mahatma would not break on that question.'[37] The viceroy merely communicated to Gandhi that he had received a petition signed by several eminent people seeking commutation of the death sentence and that the government would consider postponement of the execution.

But just six days before the Congress session, the country woke up to the horrific news that the young revolutionaries had been hanged on 23 March 1931. Reports abounded of how their bodies too had been disposed of unceremoniously. When Gandhi alighted at Karachi, he was greeted with loud protests, black flowers and black garlands as people felt that he had let Bhagat Singh and his comrades down.

~

Savarkar's house in Ratnagiri that always had the saffron flag atop it as a notable identifier had a black flag hoisted to grieve for the young brave hearts. Savarkar also composed a poem in honour of Bhagat Singh immediately after the news of his execution trickled out. The poem was sung in different parts of Maharashtra where tribute meetings for the martyr were held. Children in Ratnagiri also took out a procession singing this poem.

> Ha, Bhagat Singh, hi ha!
> You galloped on the gallows, oh hai for us!
> Rajguru, you ha!
> Veer Kumar, martyr in National warfare
> Hi ha! Jai Jai Ha!
> This ah of today will win tomorrow
> Royal crown will come home
> Wore you crown of death before that.
> We will take arms in our hands
> The ones with you were killing the enemy!
> Who is a sinner?

Who does not worship the unmatched sanctity of your intentions,

> Go, martyr!
> We take oath with testimony.
> The fight with arms is explosive,
> We are remaining behind you
> Will fight and win freedom!!
> Hi Bhagat Singh, Hi Ha![38]

Four months later, Savarkar wrote another article in *Shraddhanand*, reminding people of Bhagat Singh and his associates and their brave martyrdom.[39] This was in line with the several articles that Savarkar routinely wrote in the *Shraddhanand* in support of revolutionaries. For instance, on 15 February 1930, he wrote a piece in support of the martyr of the Kakori case Ashfaqullah Khan titled 'Janatecha Pyara Ashfaq' (The darling of the masses Ashfaq).[40]

Meanwhile shortly after the Congress session, the new CWC met on 1 and 2 April 1931 and decided that Gandhi would be the sole representative of the Congress in the upcoming Second Round Table Conference—this, despite the government being willing to accommodate about twenty members of the Congress. Gandhi made his participation in the conference contingent on total amity between Hindus and Muslims, given that around the time of the Karachi session, violent communal riots had scarred Kanpur. Subhas Bose laments that this only added fuel to the fire of reactionary leaders of the Muslim community whose might had somewhat been stifled after the viceroy's solo pact with Gandhi:

> In private and in public, he [Gandhi] began to say that his going to the Round Table Conference depended on his ability to solve the Hindu-Moslem question beforehand. Along with this statement, he also began to say that if the Moslems made a united demand on the question of representation, electorate etc. in the new Constitution, he would accept the demand. The effect of these statements was a most tragic one. After the Delhi Pact, the reactionary Moslems had been somewhat overawed by the strength and power of the Congress and they were in a mood to come to terms with that body on a reasonable basis. The first statement of the Mahatma immediately changed that mood and made them feel that they held the key position, since if they refused to come to an understanding with him, they could prevent his attending the Round Table Conference. The second statement of the Mahatma made the reactionary Moslems feel that if only they would remain firm and secure the support of the Nationalist Moslems, the Mahatma could be forced to accept all their extreme demands. After the above statements had been made, the Mahatma had a Conference with some reactionary Moslem leaders in Delhi in April. I was in Delhi at the time and I went to see him the same evening, after the conference. He seemed to be in a depressed mood, because they had presented him with the fourteen demands made by Mr. Jinnah [known in India as Jinnah's fourteen points], and he felt that an agreement would not be possible on that basis. Thereupon I remarked that the Congress should only care for an agreement between Nationalist Hindus and Nationalist Moslems and that the agreed solution should be placed before the Round Table Conference as the Nationalist demand and that the Congress need not bother what other anti-Nationalist elements thought or said . . . Soon after this, the Mahatma issued a public statement saying that he could not accept the demands

made by communalist Moslem leaders, since the Nationalist Moslems were opposed to them.[41]

The CWC's statement of 20 July 1931 stressed that joint electorates shall form the basis of representation in the future Constitution of India. For the Hindus in Sindh, the Muslims in Assam and the Sikhs in the Punjab and NWFP, and also for the Hindus and Muslims in any province where they were less than 25 per cent of the population, seats would be reserved in the federal and provincial legislatures on the basis of population, with an additional right to contest more seats.[42] But the British government, and the new viceroy, Lord Willingdon, were quite determined to scuttle the outcome of any conciliatory discussions at the Second Round Table. The new viceroy turned down all the demands made by Gandhi about the complete violation of the terms of the Gandhi–Irwin Pact. Gandhi threatened to call off his attendance at the Round Table, but was later convinced to meet the viceroy for a compromise. Despite the government not giving in to any major demands, Gandhi eventually agreed to sail to England for the conference in September 1931. Over the next several months, the Round Table meetings ended in precious little despite a spirited representation put up by Gandhi. He found himself cornered by other delegates who had been carefully selected by the government. The British had also cleverly pitted the communal problem as an important component of the meeting and the divide was out in the open despite Gandhi's attempts at a rapprochement. The conference ended in December 1931 making little or no progress on the constitutional modalities for India. Subhas Bose sums up the tragedy of the failed conference:

> His [Gandhi's] goodness, his frankness, his fairness, his humble ways, his profound consideration for his opponents—not only did not impress John Bull, but was construed as weakness. His habit of putting all his cards on the table was all right for India and the Indians, but damaged his prestige among British politicians. His proneness to confess his ignorance on intricate questions on finance or law would have been all right in the company of truth-seeking philosophers, but lowered him in the estimation of the British public who were accustomed to see their leaders more wise than they really were . . . If . . . the Mahatma had spoken in the language of Dictator Stalin or . . . Mussolini or Fuehrer Hitler—John Bull would have understood and bowed his head in respect.

As it was, the Conservative politicians began to think: 'Is this frail man in loin-cloth so formidable that the powerful British Government should yield to him? India was being ruled by a man who was fit to be a bishop and so we had so much trouble. If only we had a strong man at Delhi and at the India Office—everything would be all right. The secret of political bargaining is to look more strong than you really are. Indian politicians, if they want to match themselves successfully against their British opponents, will have to learn many things which they do not know and unlearn many things which they have learnt.[43]

By the time Gandhi returned to India to a hero's welcome in late December, the animosity between the Congress and the government, and the latter's violation of the Gandhi–Irwin Pact, had reached its climax, forcing him to resume civil disobedience—something that the British government put down with brute power and unleashing an unprecedented reign of terror.

Ratnagiri, 1930

Meanwhile, back in Ratnagiri, Savarkar had a young visitor calling on him. Vasudev Balwant Gogate was a student at the Fergusson College in Poona. As a student at the Miraj High School, Gogate had been deeply influenced by Savarkar's revolutionary activities in London. As a teenager, he had read Ranade's biography of Savarkar and was mesmerized by the Savarkar brothers. In 1922, when Babarao came to Sangli to recuperate from illness, young Gogate managed to meet him through the mediation of his friend Bidesh Tukaram Kulkarni. Their meetings increased and Babarao made a deep impact on the young man's mind. Their meetings continued even as Gogate took admission in Poona at the Fergusson College. Babarao inspired him to create a group of young revolutionaries in the college and also encouraged them to read revolutionary literature and get trained in arms. The students were so beholden to Babarao that they even managed to raise funds for him, which he used for the expenses incurred in trials of revolutionaries.

By the time Gogate came to Fergusson College in 1929, the political situation in India was surcharged with the brave exploits of Bhagat Singh and his associates. Their execution incensed thousands of youth, including Gogate. The Youth League of Fergusson College that included members such as Yusuf Meharally, S.M. Joshi, K.M. Phadke, A.R. Bhatt and others got photographs of Bhagat Singh, Sukhdev, Rajguru and Savarkar printed and distributed among the students. Gogate himself got more than 1000 photographs of his hero, Savarkar, printed and distributed. He then ventured to Ratnagiri to meet Savarkar, stayed at his house for a few days and had long discussions with him. Savarkar asked the young man to determine his goal: 'If you want to be an editor, you can do that. But my view is that whatever political consciousness is created by writing in a newspaper is of much less effect than the political awakening which is created by sacrifice, like that of Bhagat Singh and Rajguru. So unless you first determine your goal, you should not step in politics. But once you do that, then certainly you will have to join politics.'[44] Gogate then went on to quiz him on whether revolution, which was also termed as 'terrorism' by the government, was the right approach. To this, Savarkar replied: 'The method of terrorism is right, because so long as India is in bondage, the only way to fight the British will be by revolutionary activities. The other activities will lead to mass agitation. But the revolutionary activities will create an effective point. The slogan of "Bande Mataram" given by the martyrs on the platform of execution, that is the platform on which the martyrs were hanged, has created greater political awakening than ten sessions of the Indian National Congress.' Savarkar reminisced about his former colleague in London who had been similarly martyred for the cause of the country's freedom, Madan Lal Dhingra, and his statement: 'So long as British are ruling India, there is a War between the British and the Indians. An open War was rendered impossible. I attack by surprise. And the only lesson that India wants to learn is how to die and that can best be taught by dying ourselves. Therefore, the revolutionary philosophy states that if revolutionaries came together and made an active effort, they will be able to drive the British out.'

The discussion then veered around to the question of whether individual acts of shooting down a British officer here and there was prudent. To this, Savarkar opined: 'Shooting a Governor here and there certainly would not bring freedom but there are times when the atrocities reach such a point that unless you register your protest by such an effective action, the atrocities do not stop.' He jokingly added, 'Every British man who is good enough to rule India is bad enough to be killed!' But he believed that if revolutionary activities were carried on a large scale, if armies are raised, especially when the British were in difficult times, the goal of freedom would be nearer. On the question of the state of mind of a man possessed by revolutionary zeal,

Savarkar took the example of Anant Laxman Kanhere and said: 'When a martyr intends to take an action, then nobody can stop him. The mental posture of Anant Kanhere at that time was such that even had I asked him not to take this action, he would not have listened to me. The mind of a martyr comes to such a pitch. His conviction becomes so certain that nothing on earth can prevent him from doing this.'

This meeting deeply inspired Gogate. His thoughts went to the immediate political ferment in Maharashtra, in Sholapur. The freedom fighters there had gathered in a large mob that the police tried to disperse. They went off the city limits, cut palm trees and blocked the police's path. The police opened fire and many were killed. The mob was so agitated that they used their might against the police force, overpowered them and even burnt down the police station. The collector of Sholapur consulted Home Member Ernest Hotson who recommended Martial Law to be imposed in Sholapur from 12 May 1930. Several freedom fighters, editors of newspapers and nationalists were rounded up, unfairly tried and meted out punishment ranging up to several years of rigorous imprisonment. Gogate slipped away to the Hyderabad state where his brother worked as a medical practitioner. Being a princely state, there was no Arms Act there and he procured two revolvers—a nickel-plated and a blue-steel. He assiduously practised shooting in the jungles of the Deccan and managed to achieve proficiency in hitting a target from a distance of 10–15 yards.

By July 1931, Hotson was appointed as the acting governor of Bombay Presidency and was scheduled to inaugurate the legislative assembly on 20 July 1931. Gogate managed to get an entry pass to the assembly. But as his luck could have it, Hotson skipped that event. The following day, Babarao paid a visit to Gogate who stayed at the Vaidikashram area of Poona, but the latter did not disclose the plans he had about assaulting Hotson.

Quite serendipitously, on 22 July 1931, Hotson was paying a visit to Fergusson College. Gogate quickly kept both the revolvers in his pocket and also photographs of Hotson, since he knew how revolutionaries in the past had mistakenly attacked wrong targets. As he recounts:

> I had also kept in my pocket the photograph of Sir Ernest Hotson. I had read the stories of revolutionaries and I found that some revolutionaries made a mistake between the Europeans. They could not identify them correctly because, for us Indians, all Europeans are practically alike.

I thought to myself that I should not commit such a mistake, and therefore, I had kept a photograph of Sir Ernest Hotson in my pocket.[45]

Gogate sat in the Wadia Library waiting for his prey. Hotson and his entourage came right to the library and were being shown the photographs there. Closing the book that he was pretending to read, Gogate got up from his seat, took out his nickel-plated revolver and shot point-blank at Hotson, hitting him near his heart. But Hotson managed to survive since he wore a bullet-proof armour. He instead managed to attack the young assailant who fired again. They tumbled over each other. Gogate was arrested. Several students turned amuck and tried to assault Hotson and smashed the glass panes of his car. He was somehow escorted out in haste by the college authorities. Gogate was tried and sentenced to eight years of rigorous imprisonment and sent to the Yerawada Central Prison.

While he was in prison, Mahatma Gandhi too was jailed at Yerawada. Through a common prisoner friend Parchure Shastri, the case of Gogate was narrated to Gandhi who wrote back to him: 'It was a happy, happy tragedy. Happy because the assailant was punished and not the assailed.' Gogate also got to know that his case was hotly discussed even in the Congress Working Committee. Subhas Bose had pleaded his case that though not his actions, but the patriotic intent behind them deserved acknowledgement. This was flatly refused by Gandhi. When Bose questioned him about why he had acknowledged similar actions of Bhagat Singh, Sukhdev and Rajguru but was unwilling to do so in the case of Gogate, Gandhi replied that he had committed a grave mistake by doing so then and did not wish to repeat it. Gogate served his sentence till 1937 and was released thereafter.

Savarkar and his works inspired revolutionaries across India. Bhagat Singh had the fourth edition of Savarkar's book on 1857 secretly published in India.[46] There are references of how Bhagat Singh was deeply influenced by a small English biography of Savarkar that he read in the Dwarkadas Library of Lahore.[47] Copies of the book were found in the course of the raids on all the members of the Hindustan Socialist Republican Association (HSRA) who were accused in the Lahore Conspiracy case (1928–31), including Bhagat Singh. This fact is bolstered by a first-person account given by Durga Das Khanna in an interview in 1976.[48] Khanna was the former chairman of the Punjab Legislative Council in independent India, but was a revolutionary in his youth days. He recalls his first meetings with Bhagat Singh and Sukhdev. During their recruitment drive for the organization, they had met Khanna, spoken to him on politics and a wide range of issues to gauge his political orientation, and also suggested several books to read. These included Nikolai Bukharin and Evgenii Preobrazhensky's *The ABC of Communism* (1920), Daniel Breen's *My Fight for Irish Freedom* (1924) and Chitragupta's *Life of Barrister Savarkar*. It hence becomes clear that Bhagat Singh and his associates expected new recruits to the HSRA to not only read about the Russian Revolution and the Irish Republican Army, but also the life story of Vinayak Damodar Savarkar.

In fact, six quotes from Savarkar's book *Hindu Pad Padashahi* were noted down by Bhagat Singh in his own handwriting in his *Jail Diary*. The quotes are as follows:

1) Sacrifice was adorable only when it was directly or remotely but reasonably felt to be indispensable for success. But the sacrifice that does not ultimately lead to success is suicidal and therefore had no place in the tactics of Maratha warfare (*Hindu Pad Padashahi*, p. 256).

2) Fighting the Marathas is like fighting with the wind, is to strike on the water (*Hindu Pad Padashahi*, p. 254).

3) That remains the despair of our age, which has to write history without making it, to sing of valorous deeds without the daring abilities and opportunities without actualizing them in life (*Hindu Pad Padashahi*, pp. 244–45).

4) Political slavery can be easily overthrown at any time. But it is difficult to break the shackles of cultural domination (*Hindu Pad Padashahi*, pp. 242–43).

5) No freedom! whose smile we shall never resign. Go tell our invaders, the Danes, 'That's sweeter to blood for an age at thy shrine. Than to sleep but a minute in chains!' (*Hindu Pad Padashahi*, p. 219, Savarkar quoting Thomas Moore.

6) 'Rather get killed than converted.' This was the prevalent call among Hindus at that time. But Ramdas stood up and exclaimed, 'No, not thus. Get killed rather than converted is good enough but better than that. Do not get either killed nor get violently converted. Rather, Kill the violent forces themselves and get killed while killing to conquer in the cause of righteousness' (*Hindu Pad Padashahi*, pp. 141–62)[49]

In an article titled 'Vishwa Prem' published twice in the *Matwala* of 15 and 22 November 1926, Bhagat Singh had this to say about Savarkar and what he perceived as the latter's tender heart despite being a revolutionary: 'World-lover is the hero whom we do not hesitate a little to call a fierce insurgent, staunch anarchist—the same heroic Savarkar. Coming in the wave of world-love, he used to stop walking on the grass thinking that the soft grass would be mowed under the feet.'[50] In March 1926, Bhagat Singh also wrote about Savarkar and his equation with his protégé in London, the martyr Madan Lal Dhingra:

The impact of the Swadeshi movement reached England as well and Mr. Savarkar opened a house called 'Indian House'. Madan Lal also became its member. . . . One day, Mr. Savarkar and Madan Lal Dhingra were talking for a long time. In a test of daring to give up his life, Savarkar pierced a big needle in his hand by asking Madan Lal to lay his hands on the ground, but Punjabi Veer did not even say ah. Tears filled the eyes of both. The two hugged each other. Oh, how beautiful that time was. How invaluable and indelible that teardrop was! How beautiful that match was! So glorious! What should we know about that emotion, what cowardly people who are afraid of even the thought of death, know how high, how holy and how revered are those who die for the sake of the nation! From the next day, Dhingra did not go to the Indian House of Savarkar and attended the Indian students' meeting organized by Sir Curzon. Wylie. Seeing this, the boys of the Indian House got very agitated and started calling him even a traitor, but their anger was reduced by Savarkar saying that after all he had tried to even break his head to run our house. And due to his hard work, our movement is going on, so we should thank him! On July 1, 1909, there was a meeting at the Jahangir Hall of the Imperial Institute. Sir Curzon Wylie also went there. He was talking to two other people, that was when Dhingra suddenly pulled out a pistol. He was put to sleep forever. Then after some struggle Dhingra was caught. What to say after that, there was a worldwide cry! Everyone started abusing Dhingra wholeheartedly. His father sent a telegram from Punjab and said that I refuse to accept such rebel, rebellious and murderous man as my son. The Indians held large meetings. There were big speeches. Big proposals moved. All in blasphemy! But even at that time Savarkar was the hero who favored him openly. At first, he offered an excuse for not letting the motion pass against him that he is still on trial and we cannot call him guilty. Finally, when the vote was taken on this proposal, the Speaker of the House, Mr. Bipin Chandra Pal, was saying that if it is deemed to be unanimously passed by everyone, then Savarkar Sahib stood up and started the lecture. Just then, an Englishman punched him in the mouth and said, 'Look, how straight the English fist goes!' A Hindustani young man put a stick on the head of the Englishman, and said, 'See, how straight the Indian club goes!' There was a noise. The meeting was left in between. The proposal remained unpassed. Well![51]

Quite evidently there was mutual admiration between these two revolutionaries—Bhagat Singh and Savarkar. An article published in Savarkar's *Shraddhanand* titled 'The Real Meaning of Terror' was published by Bhagat Singh and colleagues in *Kirti* in May 1928.[52] An article written by Savarkar expressing solidarity and support for Bhagat Singh and his companions was titled 'Armed but tyrannical'. A similar article on the name of the bomb's philosophy was published by Bhagat Singh's HSRA and Bhagwati Charan Vohra on 26 January 1930.[53] The article was given final shape by Bhagat Singh in jail and was distributed across the country.

Several young revolutionaries kept their contacts with the Savarkar brothers, more so with Babarao who was not put under stringent surveillance by the British as Savarkar was. Babarao's health had been ravaged due to the incarceration at Cellular Jail. His knees had given in completely and he could barely walk. He had contracted tuberculosis in the Andamans and spasms of cough continued to dog him all his life. This was compounded later with tuberculosis of the intestines and bones too, along with constant fever, anaemia, heart problems and diarrhoea. He travelled to several places to recuperate and seek treatment—Bombay, Yeola, Nagpur, Akola, Calcutta, Kashi, Jamkhindi and Sangli—but this did not help much. During all these travels, he still managed to somehow clandestinely meet revolutionaries or help them in some way, including in raising funds.

While in Kashi, Babarao came in contact with a young revolutionary from Varhad (Berar) in Maharashtra—Shriram Balwant Savargaonkar, who was ostensibly in the holy town to study Sanskrit but was networking in the underground revolutionary movement. The latter put Babarao in contact with another daring revolutionary from Poona's Khed district, Shivaram Hari Rajguru who was to later become the associate of Bhagat Singh. Babarao was deeply impressed by the daring nature of Rajguru and decided to organize the physical training for him at Amravati. Thereafter Rajguru also stayed for a while at the RSS headquarters in Nagpur and advanced his training. Rajguru then joined the HSRA and Bhagat Singh in his activities.[54] Given the total lack of documentation due to obvious reasons around secrecy, a lot of the activities of the revolutionaries are not clearly deducible. The dots need to be connected to deconstruct the larger picture of their clandestine network and in this attempt, the role of all the three Savarkar brothers becomes clear.

Babarao had also visited Gandhi at his ashram in Wardha on 15 February 1931, a day before Gandhi was to meet Lord Irwin. He pleaded with Gandhi to take up the cause of Bhagat Singh, Sukhdev and Rajguru and their clemency with the viceroy. Given Gandhi's non-committal response, Babarao was miffed and walked away unsatisfied from the meeting.

During another daring attempt made by the revolutionaries in Bombay, Babarao's house in Khar was their rendezvous. Durga Devi Vohra (known as Durga 'Bhabhi' or sister-in-law), the wife of Bhagwati Charan Vohra, had stayed with the Savarkars. In fact, Narayanrao's wife Shanta recounts how she had taught Durga the art of disguise by dressing up in a traditional Maharastrian nine-yard sari.[55] Durga had left her eight-year-old son Hari at Babarao's house. She had played a crucial role in abetting Bhagat Singh's escape from Lahore after Saunders's murder in December 1928, by posing as his wife.

Writing about the association with the Savarkars during this episode one of the protagonists Prithvi Singh 'Azad' who was also an associate of Savarkar in the Cellular Jail says:

I reached Bombay at nine o'clock and made for the clinic where Vinayak Damodar Savarkar's brother, Narayan Damodar Savakar, was practising as a well-known dentist. His compounder accompanied me to his house for which he had left earlier. He was very much astonished to see me at his house at about eleven o'clock when he was about to retire. He looked questioningly at me. I put him in mind of a piece of news in the morning papers of the escape of a prisoner from police custody last night in a railway train. It was I, Prithvi Singh. His astonishment changed into concern for me. He assured me that I was safe in his hands, and he went out of the room. His compounder came in with a meal for me. While I ate my supper, I fell a-thinking: 'Why did my host go out? Why has he not come back? Am I really safe in his hands?' These questions were born of suspicion and fear in my heart . . . I was lost in mental turmoil when

Savarkar returned in an hour, and with a young lad of about eighteen, full of verve. Savarkar asked me to accompany him with a perfect sense of security. A room was vacant on the upper story of the police station in Princess Street. The young man took me there. It is rather a long story to write whom I met and where and what transpired between me and others. Later I was taken to Poona and lodged in a house, the name of the master I could learn incidentally in the course of a conversation . . .

In disguise, after Poona, I went to Belgaum and thence to Goa but at no place did I like to stay for long. I returned to Bombay. Dr. Savarkar arranged for my stay at Bhavnagar in Saurashtra at the house of his friend Ganesh Raghunath, known as Tatya Saheb Vaishampayan, a telegraphist (sic), in whose company I found a very kindred soul of an old revolutionary.[56]

Durga 'Bhabhi' and Prithvi Singh 'Azad', along with other revolutionaries such as Swami Rao and Sukhdev Raj then drove on the midnight of 8 October 1930, heavily armed, towards the residence of Sir Malcom Hailey, who had been the Governor of Punjab from 1924 to 1928 and then the Governor of the United Provinces. He was on a visit to Bombay and the revolutionaries had planned to assassinate him. Finding the house heavily armed by the Punjab Police personnel, they changed their plans and decided to attack the Lamington Road Police Station and kill Police Commissioner Sir Patrick Kelly. On failing to locate him, Durga Bhabhi shot at Europeans who were coming out of the police station and in this Sergeant Taylor and his wife were injured. This incident was etched in the annals of anti-imperialism in India as 'the first instance in which a woman figured prominently in a terrorist outrage'.[57]

The car later drove away and was found abandoned in Andheri. The driver was later caught and he confessed to the crime. However, the case (known as the 'Lamington Road Shooting Conspiracy Case' or 'Lamington Road Outrage') collapsed and resulted in an acquittal of all the accused and other co-conspirators such as Shankar Narayan Moghe, Shivram Vitthal Deodhar, Purushottam Hari Barve and Ganesh Raghunath Vaishampayan (all close associates of the Savarkar brothers from the Abhinav Bharat days). Given the police round-ups of all suspects, Babarao managed to quickly shift Durga Bhabhi's son Hari to a safer place.

On 25 February 1931, Babarao was in Kashi where he sauntered through its narrow lanes to a small, decrepit house hidden from the thoroughfares. It belonged to a priest of the holy town. After a while, a massively built man arrived at the house. The priest and his family knew that there was something extraordinary about this imposing man and left him with Babarao. The two of them confabulated for nearly two-and-a-half hours so silently that their voices were barely heard outside. At the end of their meeting, Babarao called the priest and told him that the visitor was a great man and that the latter's house had been blessed by his visit, that he was in difficulty and needed some help. Without thinking twice, the priest went inside and brought in a hundred-rupee note and handed it over to the man, along with his son's dhoti that was out for drying. The visitor thanked him profusely and made haste. It later turned out that he was none other than the great revolutionary Chandrashekhar Azad.[58] Azad had been in regular touch with Babarao through the latter's young aide Savargaonkar. The young man even managed to smuggle in revolvers from Hyderabad State for Azad. He had been elated by the youngster's bravery and hugged him tight exclaiming: 'He is a true Maratha follower of Shivaji Maharaj!' Savargaonkar was inducted into Azad's secret revolutionary group and given a pseudonym of 'Engineer.'[59]

Two days after meeting Babarao in Kashi, Azad met two of his revolutionary comrades at Alfred Park in Allahabad. He was betrayed by an informer who had leaked information of his whereabouts to the British police that surrounded the park. Azad fought valiantly and even shot three policemen. Sensing his own release as being impossible, Azad shot himself with the last bullet in his revolver and kept his pledge of never being caught alive by the British. The news of his death reached Babarao through Nana Damle, the son of Bhaurao Damle at whose house he was staying. In an article in the *Kesari* dated 7 March 1931, Bhaurao Damle recollected: 'Nana brought Chandrashekhar's news and on hearing it, Babarao clutched his head and sat down speechless for some time! . . . We could not make head or tail of his action.'[60]

On 25 March 1933, a bomb was thrown in the Empire Cinema of Bombay injuring one person. A few days later, on 6 April 1933, a bottle containing chemicals and pellets was thrown in the same place, but the missile did not explore. The investigations revealed the handiwork of Janardhan Balkrishna Bapat who had also been a part of the Lamington Road shooting case. The searches yielded bomb manufacture pamphlets and somehow the needle of suspicion pointed to Babarao, given his antecedents in similar cases in Nasik. The police raided Babarao's house in Khar and arrested him. He was put on trial but acquitted for lack of firm evidence. However, the police were not willing to let go of Babarao so easily. Even as he walked out of the trial on acquittal, he was arrested under the provisions of a special ordinance and kept imprisoned for two months. The first three weeks were spent in Bombay's Byculla Jail and the remaining five weeks at the Nasik Jail. He was finally released on 17 June 1933. He was prohibited from leaving Nasik municipal limits and taking part in any kind of political activity, directly or indirectly, or participating in public meetings. The restrictions that were initially supposed to be for a month were extended to four long years, till May 1937.

Towards the end of 1931, Savarkar's former colleague during his London days, Pandurang Mahadev Bapat or 'Senapati' Bapat, came to visit him in Ratnagiri. After his participation in the Mulshi Satyagraha, he was arrested for several years and released in 1931. He was made president of the Maharashtra Pradesh Congress Committee, but he openly spoke in favour of the revolutionaries and differed with the Congress ideology on several occasions. Though he had come to preside over the Ratnagiri District Political Conference, he refused to attend to any of those engagements till he paid his respects to his former comrade. It was an emotional reunion for the two associates. Bapat's fiery speeches thereafter and his advocacy of Gogate landed him in trouble and he was sentenced to seven years' rigorous imprisonment.

Meanwhile on 27 April 1934, there was an attack on Mr Sweetland, a warrant officer attached to the Auxiliary Force India (AFI). Sweetland was cleaning his motorcycle in the AFI quarters when Waman Baburao Chawan of Ratnagiri hurled a dagger at him that struck him in the cheek. Chawan then shot at him from his revolver repeatedly but missed the target each time. He was eventually caught and stated that his intention was to avenge the execution of Bhagat Singh. He had been staying with Gajanan Vishnu Damle, a revolutionary of Benares. Chawan was sentenced to seven years' rigorous imprisonment.

The government's suspicion over any acts of revolution in Bombay Presidency pointed towards Savarkar or Babarao. Following the 'Sweetland Shooting Case', on 7 May 1934, Savarkar was arrested, his house was searched and documents were confiscated. He was later released on 21 May. In a letter written by him on 4 November 1934 to the deputy commissioner of police, Special Branch, Bombay, he states:

Sir, in the month of May 1934, my house was searched in my absence by the Bombay Sub-Inspectors Messrs. Kamat and Divekar and a number of documents and other articles were taken possession of in connection with the investigation then being conducted by the Police arising out of the Sweetland Shooting case in Bombay. Now that the case in point has already been tried and finished, will you kindly return those articles to me intact? And in case some of them are to be withheld, will you please let me know the reasons for refusing their delivery together with a list of articles to be returned to me as well as those; if any, to be withheld by the Police?[61]

In September 1931, the Ratnagiri Hindu Sabha had invited Thakur Chandan Singh, president of the All-India Gurkha League, and Hemchandra Shamsher Jung, a representative of the royal family of Nepal. The League had been founded by Thakur Chandan Singh in Dehradun on 15 February 1924 as a national forum for all Gurkhas and to integrate them into the national mainstream. Branches of the League soon mushroomed across India, from the North-Western Frontier Province to Kashmir, Assam, Manipur, Sikkim, Calcutta, Burma, Bombay, Bhutan, Patna and even Fiji. Thakur Chandan Singh (1887–1968) was a gifted writer, an accomplished journalist, an eloquent orator and a committed freedom fighter. He was opposed to both the colonial British rule and also the ruthless dynasty of the Ranas of Nepal. He was the editor of *Tarun Gurkha*. His campaign, through the League, was to address the indifference of both the British and the Rana Government of Nepal, towards the plight of the Gurkhas.

Nepal had always been an important and strategic ally for politicians in Maharashtra. Way back in 1902, Tilak had sent his associates Vasukaka Joshi, Krishnaji Prabhakar Khadilkar, Hanmantrao Murkibhavikar of Kolhapur and others to Nepal to open an arms factory there. The maharaja of Baroda, Sayaji Rao Gaekwad, and Kashinath Pant Chhatre of the famous Chhatre Circus had sponsored the whole project. But the plans were revealed to the British and they had to be wound up. Vasukaka Joshi had then tried to establish contacts with the Japanese through the help of the king of Nepal to train Indians in warfare and to smuggle arms—a dream that was fulfilled decades later by the Indian National Army of Rash Behari Bose and Subhas Chandra Bose.[62]

Prior to this plan of starting an arms factory in Nepal, Tilak had been introduced to the king of Nepal through the intercession of Mataji

Tapaswini, a distant niece of the heroic Rani Lakshmi Bai of Jhansi. Contact had been established with the prime minister of Nepal, Chandra Samsher Bahadur, and his cousin Kumar Narasimha Rana. Ranganath Govind Tikhe, whose brother Vinayak had been convicted in the Nasik Conspiracy case, stayed on in Kathmandu to further the association.

Nepal being a sovereign Hindu kingdom was always high in the Hindutva imagination as the defender of the Hindu faith, drawing perhaps from the concept of the pan-Islamic ummah or brotherhood that had been given a further fillip after the Khilafat movement. The constant invocation was to the glorious past of Nepal's bravery, especially in the Sino-Gurkha War (1788–92), where the Nepali Gurkhas under Bahadur Shah plundered the combined armies of the Tibetan Tamangs and the mighty Chinese Qing dynasty. Rekindling this warrior spirit was thought of as the ultimate panacea to help liberate neighbouring Hindu India from colonial rule through an armed rebellion. That Nepal had been recognized by the British as an independent, sovereign nation through the Treaty of 1923 (signed on 21 December 1923 in Kathmandu) bolstered its status in the eyes of the Hindutva exponents of India. A Hindu king from Nepal, presiding over a future independent India and forming a strategic caucus with the Buddhist nations of South-East Asia, was imaginatively envisioned as an effective bulwark against the Khilafat of the Middle East and the pan-Islamic conglomerates. Savarkar advocated a resolution to be passed by the All-India Hindu Mahasabha in 1924–25 to congratulate Nepal on its attainment of sovereignty in view of this larger vision.[63]

The Ratnagiri Hindu Sabha sent rakhis to the king of Nepal and several other prominent leaders there on the occasion of the Hindu festival of Raksha Bandhan. The king accepted the gift and also sent a letter of appreciation and gratitude. Activists and leaders from Nepal were regular attendees to several Hindu Mahasabha annual conferences across Maharashtra. For the Delhi session of the Hindu Mahasabha in 1926, the king of Nepal was invited to preside and a letter of invitation from Babarao was also published in a Delhi newspaper named *Arjun*. All the state chapters of the All-India Hindu Mahasabha withdrew their nominees for the president of the session to pave the way for a unanimous selection of the Nepal monarch. But due to several reasons, the king could not accept the invitation, but sent his address that was read out at the session. Among other things, he said: 'In the progress of Hindus is my progress, in the deterioration of their condition, is mine too.'[64]

There are copious correspondences between the Ratnagiri Hindu Mahasabha and members of the Nepal royal family as well as political activists of the All-India Gurkha League in Nepal, between 1924 and 1937. Savarkar had actually compiled an entire book on the Hindu Sangathan movement and Nepal between 1924 and 1930. It was a collection of about thirty-three essays, most of which were written by him. The book, with a preface by Babarao, was published in 1937. These essays were also translated and published in Nepali newspapers and magazines like *Tarun Gurkha* and *Himalayan Times*. In his preface, Babarao mentions:

> In the quiver of Hindu Sangathan, the invincible Ram-Baan (Lord Rama's arrow) is Nepal. But that arrow is now slightly rusted and its owner too has forgotten the utility and strength of his own possession. If not the ability to unfurl the Hindu flag over the sub-continent, Nepal could play an important role in arousing the consciousness of one crore Hindus and organizing them into a potent political force and a cultural entity. The British understand the strategic importance of Nepal and hence an author like Perceval Landon has compiled an exhaustive two volume series on Nepal, its geo-political, historical and religious context in the twentieth century, while we in India, have neglected Nepal completely.[65]

Some of the essays in this book also quote Thakur Chandan Singh who exemplified the need for Hindu Sangathan movement in the geopolitical context that India found herself in, bound by three nations of three different religious orientations: Afghanistan, Nepal and Siam. Despite Nepal sharing a close border with a large part of northern and eastern India, there was a sad lack of communication or of awareness, rued Singh. While Christian nations and Islamic states were powerful across the world and Buddhist countries like China, Siam and Japan too were on the rise, there was no united Hindu caucus, according to him. He felt it was the duty of the kingdom of Nepal to take a lead in establishing such a Hindu country too that could hold its stead in the comity of nations.[66] Inspired by Swami Shraddhanand and the Shuddhi movement, Thakur Chandan Singh spearheaded a similar reconversion programme in Nepal too.[67]

In an article dated 11 January 1928, Savarkar writes:

> If in the future, there were a major conflict between Britain and Russia, which it seems like what might erupt soon into a global conflict, then

Nepal and Afghanistan would emerge as two strategic centres of any war. As India is bound by these two nations, the key to power in India would be fought on the battlefields of Nepal and Afghanistan. The British realize this and hence in a span of a few days, the Amir of Afghanistan and the King of Nepal Maharaja Chandra Shamsher Jung Bahadur have been invited to meet the Viceroy and the entire military establishment in Bombay and Calcutta respectively . . . the visit of the King of Nepal must be utilized by us Hindus and the Gurkhas to widen the cause of Hindu Sangathan . . . it is a matter of pride for all of us Hindus that in such a short span of their existence the Gurkha League has already been termed as a 'seditious body' and come under the scanner of the C.I.D. for suspicious activities. This shows the awakening that has happened among the Gurkhas in particular and the Nepalis in general. This feeling must not go in vain . . . there are about 10 Lakh Nepalis living in British India. If the Sikhs can send their representatives to British meetings such as the Round Table Conferences, the Nepalis too should be in a similar position to, as they have been disadvantaged of their rights both in Nepal and in India.[68]

The visit of Thakur Chandan Singh and Hemchandra Shamsher Jung to Ratnagiri in 1931 was thus the result of several years of friendship that had been cultivated between Maharashtra and Nepal. At the Hindu Mahasabha conference at Akola on 22 September 1931, the two special guests from Nepal were felicitated. They also gave lectures at various places including Nagpur and Amravati on 'Nepal and its role in the Hindu Sangathan movement'. At the Conference, the flag of an independent Hindu nation—the saffron *Bhagwa Dhwaj* that Savarkar had designed with the sacred symbols of the Kundalini and the Kirpan (dagger of the Sikhs) was unfurled. A song composed by Savarkar that referred to the masses of organized Hindus leading to an armed war for their independence from colonial rule, and also promised that they would aid other nations too in their struggle for freedom after being unshackled, was openly sung.[69]

On the occasions of birthdays of the monarch Tribhuvaneshwar Bikram Dev and others, proclamations and greetings were sent from the members of the Ratnagiri Hindu Sabha wishing a long life for the emperor of 'the lone, independent Hindu Kingdom'.[70] There are letters from the general secretary of the Gurkha League, Subedar Sher Bahadur Khatri, from their headquarters in Dehradun to the president of the

Ratnagiri Hindu Sabha, Mahadeo Ganapat Rao Shinde, acknowledging with gratitude donations received from the latter.[71] Thakur Chandan Singh also alerted the Ratnagiri Hindu Sabha about certain cautions that need to be kept in mind, as in his letter dated 20 March 1930 to Shinde:

> It is very encouraging indeed to see you all trying to do so much to awaken Nepal to its sense of duty. But let me tell you frankly that when you would be in a position to study the actual state of our country and its rulers and its people, you will then realize that we cannot expect all that we need and want from present rulers of Nepal who form a class by themselves as imperialistic in their outlook as the rulers of Germany. What we want our co-religionists in India to do is not so much to court the goodwill of the rulers, for that would be a sheer waste of time and attention, but to encourage and assist as far as possible the movement of the young gurkhas who are working for an immediate evolution, not a bloody revolution, mind you, in our country, so that Nepal may not only obtain its honoured position among the sovereign and free nations of the world, but that it may also give a new life to the decaying forces of the great Hindu civilization . . . great ideal of creating a federation of powerful, peace-loving Hindu nations from the Himalayas to Ceylon, and from Sindh to far off Java. The menace of Islam is still hanging over our land as the sword of Damocles. Christianity and its activities in India threaten to wipe away whatever is left of us now.[72]

About his impending visit to Ratnagiri and the position of the Gurkhas, Chandan Singh wrote to Shinde:

> We occupy almost the same position as do the Sikhs in the body politic of India and if the Moslems insist upon separate communal representation, we want the Hindu Mahasabha to treat us as a special minority claiming special representation for the 3 million British Indian Gurkhas who are domiciled in India permanently. If the Moslems give up the idea of separate representation, we shall abide by the ruling passed in the Hindu Mahasabha on this subject, this year . . .[73]
>
> I do understand the importance of my visit to Ratnagiri where I hope to have the high honour and privilege of seeing and meeting brother Vinayak Savarkar also, whose name and fame is now a bye-word (sic) in the whole of enlightened India. I am reading his books, the Hindu Pad

Padshahi at present and I cannot but admire the soul-stirring patriotism and feeling of undaunted courage and catching spirit with which every word and letter of the entire work is deeply permeated. Kindly send me a complete list of the works of Vinayak Savarkar . . . as I am anxious to read them all before I have the pleasure of being received by him. The Gurkha League has also been thinking of sending a Deputation of its working to the various provinces of India to help the Hindu Sangathan movement and at the same time to enlist public sympathy and support of the Hindus to the Gurkha League's cause.[74]

Chandan Singh was a great admirer of Savarkar and his works and had got many of his writings translated and published in the *Tarun Gurkha* and *Himalayan Times*. The two met in Ratnagiri at the Patit Pavan Mandir. Presiding over the gathering, Savarkar exhorted the Gurkhas and other Hindus to work towards the pan-Hindu consolidation movement and to root out social evils. Chandan Singh pledged the support of the Gurkhas as defenders of the Hindu faith and of their defence against any external and internal threats to a united Hindustan. Several newspapers like the *Pioneer* of Allahabad carried reports of this meeting, expressing grave concern over such gatherings. This was enough to raise the suspicions of the British government that always kept a hawk's eye on Savarkar's movements and utterances. The Home Department of Bombay asked him for an explanation and the district magistrate summoned him to his office to explain the gist of his speech. The government was not satisfied with his defence and he was let off with a strong warning that any such moves would mean a continuance of his transportation for life for another thirty-seven years.

It was another matter that the bonhomie with Chandan Singh was short lived. He was disillusioned when the Ratnagiri Hindu Sabha seemed disinclined to reimburse the travel expenses for his entire delegation to Ratnagiri.[75] The continued courting of the king of Nepal by the Hindu Mahasabha might have been another point of discord between them.

The attitude and strategy of the Ratnagiri Hindu Sabha vis-à-vis Nepal and its monarch is exemplified in these letters by R.V. Chiplunkar of the Mahasabha:

The Ratnagiri Hindu Sabha on the occasion of the celebration of its 10th anniversary this month begs to tender its tribute of faithful devotion to His Majesty the King of Nepal as the only independent Hindu monarch and all our Hindu countrymen and co-religionists there. The Sabha takes this opportunity to congratulate Your Excellency on initiating the policy, as has been long advocated and pressed by the Sabha, of establishing international relations with advanced nations in the world by sending out an Embassy to England and holding friendly interviews with the Heads of Government of France and Italy as well. The Sabha begs to urge that His Majesty be pleased to open Embassies in Japan, China and Siam in particular and in America and Russia also, as soon as it is found practicable to do so. In fact the flag of an independent Hindu kingdom must be kept flying in every great capital in the world.

The second fact that the Sabha begs to bring to the notice of the Government of Nepal today refers to the crying need of opening a sort of a 'Nepal Publicity Board.' Now that the awakening of the Pan-Hindu consciousness is making us Hindus in Nepal and outside realize the oneness of our life as an integral, undivided and indivisible nation, Hindus outside Nepal are getting as much interested in the news from Kathmandu as from Calcutta, Poona or Madras. It is therefore imperative to see that a Publicity Board in Nepal issues to all publicists regular and reliable news about public activities in Nepal in all directions of life.[76]

The theme of appealing to Nepal and its monarch to assume a larger-than-life role by realizing the power of co-religionists stayed on in the Hindu Mahasabha. In meetings, Savarkar often addressed the king of Nepal as the 'only Hindu Chhatrapati of Nepal and the Pan-Hindu movement'. The following resolution of the Ratnagiri Hindu Sabha of 16 March 1937 elaborates this:

This meeting of the Hindu citizens of Ratnagiri held to commemorate the Silver Jubilee of the Maharajadhiraj of Nepal tendered its loyal homage to His Majesty as the only independent Hindu monarch and the cultural head of Hindudom as a whole and hopes that His Majesty's government will proclaim and assert their position as an independent Hindu power amongst the independent nations of the world by establishing Nepali legations flying the Hindu flag in every capital in Europe, Asia, and America, and raise the military and aerial strength of the Kingdom to an up to date efficiency so as to be able to realize the mighty goal which the Pan-Hindu movement has set its heart on.[77]

~

During his internment in Ratnagiri, in addition to the extensive social reforms and quasi-political activities, Savarkar produced a copious amount of literature in the form of books, articles, plays and essays. The written material during this time runs to a staggering 2225 pages.[78] His books included *Hindu Pad Padashahi*, *My Transportation for Life*, *Language Purification*, *Script Reformation*, *The Revolt of the Moplahs*, *Kalepani*, *Essays on Abolition of Caste* and so on. He wrote regularly for *Kesari*, *Kirloskar* Magazine, *Stri*, *Manohar*, *Nirbhid*, *Shraddhanand* and other periodicals. The sheer magnitude of his contribution to Marathi literature would take anyone a lifetime to accomplish.

When the annual Marathi literary conclave, the Marathi Sahitya Sammelan, was to be held in Nagpur in 1924, several friends and well-wishers of Savarkar such as Dr Keshav Baliram Hedgewar, Vishwanathrao Kelkar, Dr B.S. Moonje, Dadasaheb and Babasaheb Khaparde and others suggested his name to preside over the meet. The Sammelan, started by Justice Ranade in Poona, had grown in stature and held annual meets in several towns across Maharashtra. Litterateurs, politicians, princes and bureaucrats considered it a great honour to be associated with and invited to the Sammelan. The position of the president of the Sammelan was a prestigious and much coveted one. The daily *Swatantrya* that was founded by Dr Hedgewar and Kelkar was at the forefront of canvassing Savarkar's name for the president.

But there was stiff opposition against him by the literary community. The reasons were twofold. He was considered to be too young to preside. This argument was ironically put by G.T. Madkholkar, the founder editor of the Marathi daily *Tarun Bharat*, which was an active proponent of Hindutva and the RSS.[79] But more importantly, given his strained relations with the government that saw him with deep suspicion, it was felt that elevating him to this position would keep away many delegates, especially from the government side. One of Savarkar's supporters, Vasudevrao Phadnavis, wrote: 'This is a festival of Goddess Saraswati, who is adored and worshipped by Brahma, Vishnu and Mahesh. Her devotees cannot be so naïve and submissive. I have to state this that those who fear participating in the festival for this reason, are not true devotees of the Goddess.' An election was held and there were four other candidates—Riyasatkar G.S. Sardesai, Krishnaji Prabhakar Khadilkar (a Tilak acolyte and former editor of *Kesari*), Dr S.V. Ketkar and Vasudevrao Apte. Savarkar won the election with thirty-four votes, while Sardesai came a close second with thirty-two. Khadilkar, Ketkar and Apte bagged fourteen, one and one vote respectively. After Savarkar's win, the head of the Reception Committee of the Sammelan and a staunch moderate Congressman, Sir Gangadharrao Chitnavis, resigned in a huff.[80] Irregularities were alleged in the polling process, which later turned out to be false. Given the bad blood, the Sammelan was deferred and was later held in Bombay in 1926. Savarkar of course kept away from it after all the unsavoury episodes that occurred.

One of Savarkar's important contributions to Marathi language during this time was the movement of *Bhasha Shuddhi* or language purification that he commenced. Though he had begun working on this since his incarceration in the Cellular Jail, his first article on the subject came up in the *Kesari* on 21 April 1925. It was the occasion of the birth centenary of Swami Dayanand Saraswati, the founder of the Arya Samaj. In another article on the same day, in the *Mahratta*, Savarkar urged the Hindu youth of Punjab to draw inspiration from Swamiji's life and avoid the usage of the Arabic script, but rather use Devanagari or Gurmukhi. It was shameful that in the year of Swamiji's centenary, Hindu poets and writers were writing their poems in an alien script, he argued.[81]

The key elements of this 'language purification' project were as follows:[82]

1. Resurrect the usage of old, Sanskritised words in all languages including the Dravidian languages.
2. Create a national corpus of such indigenous words from various languages and eschew the usage of words from foreign languages such as English, Arabic, Persian and Urdu. Create words for scientific terminologies in Sanskrit and Indian languages if they do not exist.
3. If those words from foreign languages that have crept into our linguistic usage because those objects did not hitherto exist in India (e.g. Coat, Suit, Jacket, Tennis etc.) then they can be co-opted into the national linguistic pool.
4. If the style and usage of any foreign language seems easy and interesting, there should be no objection to its adoption.

A significant part of his work on language purification consists of debunking claims of an indigenous or original language of the Muslim community. He documents the tussle between Arabic and Persian in the regions where Islam originated and how they kept fighting with one another for linguistic supremacy.[83] Urdu for him was a language that grew from the intermixing of Muslim invaders into India and their Hindu slaves who spoke Hindi or Punjabi.[84] Urdu was merely a distorted version of Hindi, according to him—this despite his proficiency in the language to compose patriotic ghazals in it during his incarceration in the Cellular Jail. He noted with alarm the increasing usage of Arabic and Persian words in north Indian languages and feared that in times to come these languages would completely dry out their indigenous vocabulary. The shuddhi that was propagated in religious reconversion to Hinduism was extended to linguistic purification too, to reclaim those original words and create a sense of cultural identity and ownership.

What Savarkar was advocating was not new in the Maharashtrian cultural imagination. Language and its purity had always played an important cultural marker in Maharashtra's history. Savarkar himself noted that it was Chhatrapati Shivaji's reign that saved Marathi from the disaster that her north Indian sister languages faced. Shivaji appointed Raghunath Pandit as his lexicographer to create a *Rajya Vyavahar Kosh* or a glossary of Marathi terms for use in administration. The result was a sweet resurgence of original Marathi words or Sanskritized words that one found in the letters of Peshwa Nana Saheb or even in the poetry of Moropant—undiluted by the influence and intrusion of foreign (Islamic) words. However, the loss of political power of the Maratha Empire also meant the decay of cultural and linguistic identities. Words such as *Pradhan, Amatya, Sachiv, Mantri, Sumant, Nyayadhish, Senapati* and so on were coined by Raghunath Pandit to describe various positions in the Maratha kingdom, that were hitherto referred by Urdu or Persian equivalents.

The second wave of linguistic colonization of Marathi came with the onslaught of English. This too was stemmed by the efforts of scholars such as Vishnu Shastri Chiplunkar through his seminal work *Nibandhamala*. He rued how the language that is spoken in large parts of northern and north-western India was actually Hindi, but it was written in Persian script and hence seemed alien to many. This trend also brought into the language a torrent of foreign words and corrupted the original language. Savarkar saw in this a cultural hegemony and imposition of soft power by the Muslims and sought a reversal of the trend. One of the elements of a strong nation, according to him, was the pride one has in one's language.

Hence for political purposes he advocated an official language of free India that was Hindi in its original and pristine Sanskritized form, devoid of Arabic, Persian, Urdu and English influences that had crept into it.

Savarkar compiled an exhaustive dictionary of new words of daily usage that could be used as alternatives to the ones in vogue.[85] These were categorized under various heads, related to education, business and trade, war, publishing, postal services, public gatherings, legal, geographic, film and entertainment, and so on. For instance, Cinema House would be *Chitra Griha* or *Chitrapat Griha*; terms such as *Veshbhusha* (Costume), *Chhayachitra* (Photograph), *Digdarshak* (Director), *Daak* (Post), *Panji* (Register), *Doordarshan* (Television) and so on—many of which are in actual usage today.

Closely linked with the language purification project was the script rectification that Savarkar embarked upon from 1927. He consulted several scholars such as Deodhar who had done work in the field of reforming the Devanagari script in which languages such as Hindi, Sanskrit and Marathi are written. The goal was to make this script publishable on a large scale, so that the goal of elevating Hindi to the status of a national language could be realized. The alphabets needed to be more compositor-friendly on typewriters, linotypes and monotypes.[86]

~

The years 1932 to 1935 saw intense political ferment in India. Even as the Congress restarted the Civil Disobedience movement, the British government, more prepared with its modus operandi and not caught unawares as in the previous time, crushed the movement with brute force, repressive laws in the form of ordinances and sheer barbarity. All the important national leaders including Gandhi were put behind bars. As Pandit Madan Mohan Malaviya stated:

> It is estimated that nearly 1,20,000 persons, including several thousand women and quite a number of children have been arrested and imprisoned during the last fifteen months. It is an open secret that when the Government started repression, the official expectation was that they would crush the Congress in six weeks' time. Fifteen months have not enabled the Government to achieve the object. Twice fifteen months will not enable it to do so.[87]

In the midst of the peak of the movement, Gandhi decided to pledge his cause against the Communal Award that British prime minister Ramsay Macdonald announced on 17 August 1932. As per the Award, Muslim, European and Sikh voters were to elect candidates by voting in separate communal electorates. The situation would be reviewed in ten years with the assent of all the communities. Depressed classes however were given voting rights in general constituencies and also special constituencies where only depressed classes were in numerical strength and were qualified to vote. A person voting in these special constituencies was also entitled to vote in a general constituency. Gandhi announced a fast unto death from 20 September 1932 against this Award, from Poona where he was jailed. The news caused alarm across the country. The Congress prevailed upon Ambedkar, the most prominent leader of the depressed classes, to meet with the fasting Gandhi and arrive at a compromise to ensure the latter's survival. On 25 September, five days after the fast began, Ambedkar and Gandhi ironed out an agreement commonly known as the Poona Pact. Ambedkar had actually managed to secure a better deal in the bargain. As Subhas Bose accounts:

> As long as the Mahatma was on fast, rational thinking was completely suspended and the one thought of his countrymen was how to save his life. Once he was out of danger, people began to examine the Poona Agreement in the cold light of reason. Then it was realized that while the Communal Award had provided 71 seats in the Provincial Legislatures for the Depressed Classes, the Poona Agreement had provided 148. These additional seats would be given (to) them at the expense of the rest of the Hindu community. In provinces like Bengal, where Hindus had already been unjustly treated in the Award, the Poona Agreement was regarded as a further injustice by the rest of the Hindu community—particularly in view of the fact that the depressed classes problem hardly existed there. Moreover, it was realized that the Poona Agreement had not done away with separate electorate altogether. People began to ask seriously if after all it was worthwhile for Mahatma Gandhi to have staked his life for such an issue, especially when the Communal Award was from start to finish an objectionable document.[88]

Gandhi's trusted lieutenant Jawaharlal Nehru was himself deeply frustrated by these repeated flip-flops each time the movement aimed to peak to its crescendo. He writes:

I felt annoyed with him [Gandhi] for choosing a side issue for his final sacrifice. What would be the result on our freedom movement? Would not the larger issues fade into the background, for the time being at least? And, if he attained his immediate object and got a joint electorate for the depressed classes, would not that result in a reaction and a feeling that something has been achieved and nothing more need be done for a while? And was not his action a recognition, and in part an acceptance, of the communal award and the general scheme of things as sponsored by the Government? Was this consistent with non-cooperation and civil disobedience? After so much sacrifice and brave endeavor, was our movement to tail off into something insignificant? I felt angry with him at his religious and sentimental approach to a political question, and his frequent references to God in connection with it. He even seemed to suggest that God had indicated the very date of the fast. What a terrible example to set![89]

Despite the speed breaker, the movement lingered on with some enthusiasm in the following months. But not for too long. Even as the Civil Disobedience movement was slowly picking up again and the public resistance to government brutalities kept gaining momentum, Gandhi yet again recommended a suspension of the movement altogether. On 8 May 1933, he announced a twenty-one-day fast, this time for the cause of eradication of untouchability and for the welfare of the Harijan brethren. The reasons given seemed hardly convincing:

1. The whole purpose of the fast will be frustrated if I allow my brain to be occupied by any extraneous matter, that is any matter outside the Harijan work.
2. The secrecy that has attended the movement is fatal to its success.
3. Fear has seized the common mass. The Ordinances have cowed them down, and I am inclined to think that the secret methods are largely responsible for the demoralization. The movement of Civil Disobedience does not depend so much on the quantity as on the quality of men and women taking part in it.
4. During these three weeks (of fast) all civil resisters will be in a state of terrible suspense.[90]

Gandhi's appeal to Viceroy Lord Willingdon to release all civil resisters and withdraw the repressive ordinances in return of his call for suspension of movement was rebuffed by the new viceroy who was a diehard politician. The days of Lord Irwin who was ever-willing to negotiate and mollycoddle the Congress, especially Gandhi, were seemingly over. It was realpolitik at play now and Willingdon refused to budge. He even refused to grant Gandhi an interview, as sought by him and the Congress. Despite this humiliation, the Congress withdrew the movement for six weeks initially and another six weeks thereafter. Instead, individual civil disobedience, rather than a mass one, was considered as the alternative. Given the lack of clarity on what this actually meant or sought to achieve, the movement slowly died its natural death by early 1934. A dispassionate assessment of the many twists on turns to the Non-Cooperation and Civil Disobedience movements, right from 1921 to 1933, leaves one confused as to why in a fight to the finish and when the goal was in sight, brakes were repeatedly put to abort the momentum.

K.F. Nariman, the committed and zealous Bombay Congress leader, was scathing in his attack of the tapering away of such an effective mass movement and of the allegations of secrecy that Gandhi had made. 'By what rule of modern warfare or sport are we bound to disclose our plans and schemes beforehand to the enemy? But I forget, it is a religious fight and not political, so neither the rules of sport nor the canons of modern warfare apply!'[91] On the irrationality of 'Individual Civil Disobedience', Nariman scoffed saying: 'Does it need an Indian National Congress to tell an individual to break laws on his own responsibility and take the consequences? . . . the eternal liberty to act as he likes and take the consequences is given to man since the days of Adam!'[92] Nariman asked in anguish: 'How can we induce Gandhiji to rid himself of this incorrigible habit . . . this perpetual blundering, blending of religion and politics?'[93] As if offering a solution to the problem, Nariman contended that they needed to find for Gandhi, in place of the late Pandit Motilal Nehru, a taskmaster of realpolitik, 'a plain-speaking outspoken giant and not lip-sealed mummies who always shake their heads like spring dolls, perpendicularly or horizontally, according as the Mahatma pulls the strings straight or sideways'.[94]

~

The British government, meanwhile, was undeterred by all the political drama that was unfolding among the Indian players. They stuck to their resolve of drafting the Indian Constitution. After the third and last Round Table Conference in London on 17 November 1932, they got down to the act in right earnest. After several bureaucratic procedures, a bill was introduced in the British Parliament on 19 December 1934. Despite opposition from the Conservatives led by Winston Churchill, it was passed as the Government of India Act of 1935 on 2 August 1935. As per the Act, Burma was separated from India; two new provinces of Orissa and Sindh were created. In view of the federal form of government envisaged at the Centre, the provinces were endowed for the first time with a legal personality. Diarchy was abolished and provincial subjects were passed on to popular control. Bicameral legislatures were established in Madras, Bombay, Bengal, the United Provinces, Bihar and Assam, while unicameral legislatures were established in other provinces.

The federal chamber was to have two houses where the Indian princes could nominate two-fifths and one-third of the members. Only seventy-five out of the 260 seats in the Upper House were open to general election from an electorate that comprised 0.05 per cent of the population of British India. Eighty-six out of 375 seats were open for general election in the Lower House, accounting for about one-ninth of the Indian population. The powers of the legislatures were highly limited. Defence and foreign policy were the preserve of the viceroy. With financial policy, control of bureaucracy and the police too considered to be out of the competence of the legislature, there was precious little left at the federal level. The viceroy was vested with sweeping discretionary powers to veto decisions, appoint and sack ministers, dissolve legislatures and suspend the Constitution itself.

In the eleven provinces of British India, there were appointees from the Indian princes, and given a wider franchise, they were slightly more representative. But here too sensitive subjects such as secret police were under the governor who held emergency powers. General seats were left open, numbered 657 out of the total of 1585 seats in the eleven provinces. The rest were reserved on communal basis.

There was no change in the allocation principle of seats among different communities and special interest groups. The Communal Award, as modified by the Poona Pact, regulated the distribution of seats among communities. Muslims were to get one-third representation in the federal legislature as far as British India was concerned. The country was not thought to be ready yet for complete transfer of responsibility at the

Centre, and hence a diarchic executive was provided for, as was hitherto prevalent in the provinces.

The new Constitution was rejected by Indians, and particularly the Congress, as this was seen as no genuine attempt at self-government, but rather an indirect ploy at 'maintaining British rule . . . through the help of Indian Princes and sectarian, reactionary and pro-British organizations'.[95]

Ratnagiri, 1934

Back in Ratnagiri, the date of the extension of Savarkar's conditional incarceration (that had already been extended twice by a period of two years each, once in 1931 and the next in 1933) was fast approaching expiry in January 1935. Savarkar sent in a petition seeking his release. In reply, the government rejected the suggestion and decided to extend his restrictions for another two years. The intelligence reports about the active and tacit support to revolutionary movements and the political stances that he had taken obviously went against his favour. This was the government's official response through the district magistrate of Ratnagiri:

Memorandum
Camp Chiplun, 19 December 1934

In continuation of this office letter dated 17 January 1933, communicating to him Government decision to continue the two conditions for his release for a period of two years from 4 January 1933. Mr. Vinayak Damodar Savarkar is informed that the period of the two years specified in the letter referred to is due to expire on the 3rd January next and that Governor-in-Council has again given careful consideration to the question of the removal of the restrictions. But, in view of the fact that Mr. Savarkar's conduct during the last two years has not been wholly satisfactory, he has come to the conclusion that it would not be in the interests of public tranquility to withdraw them. He has accordingly decided that both the conditions should continue for a further period of two years from the 4th January 1935 and that before the expiry of that period the question again be reviewed.[96]

District Magistrate (Ratnagiri).

But Savarkar was relentless. In view of the silver jubilee of the accession of Emperor George V and Queen Mary, the British government had planned number of celebrations across Britain and her colonies from 6 to 12 May 1935. Many political prisoners were released as a gesture of goodwill on this occasion. Savarkar petitioned the government in March 1935 to seek his release as well. However, this was rejected.

Dated: 11 April 1935

With reference to his petition dated the 19th March 1935, addressed to His Excellency the Governor-in-Council praying to show mercy on the occasion of the forthcoming celebrations of Their Majesties' Silver Jubilee and to release him from all restrictions, Mr. Vinayak Damodar Savarkar of Ratnagiri is informed, under instructions from the Government, that his prayer cannot be granted.[97]

District Magistrate (Ratnagiri).

The extended two-year period too was soon coming to an end and by December 1936, Savarkar sent another petition to the governor seeking his release from the conditions that had been put on him since 1924, initially for just a period of five years, but perpetually extended thereafter for twelve years.

To

His Excellency the Governor General in Council India 2-12-1936
The Humble Petition of Vinayak Damodar Savarkar of Ratnagiri
Most humbly showeth:

1.   That the petitioner, after being sentenced to transportation for life in 1911 March, put in 14 years of imprisonment in the Andamans and was then interned in Ratnagiri District in 1924. Since then, he had up till now passed some 12 years under restrictions. During this long period of internment he had kept his activities so scrupulously within the letter of the terms of restrictions as to not to give any cause to the authorities concerned to cancel the facilities granted. The last terms of extension of the internment for a further period of 2 years more in

1934, is now nearing termination and therefore the petitioner begs to request that the Government be pleased to restore the petitioner to full liberty—which a citizen is entitled to enjoy in India.

2. The petitioner has been frequently informing the Government of his intention to serve the nation through all constitutional and legitimate means and try his best to work out the latest political reforms to their logical conclusion.

Hoping that this petition may find favour in the eyes of the Government and the petitioner is released from the internment and restrictions, which are to end on 3rd instant December 1936, unless they are extended to a further new term.

He begs to remain His Excellency's most obedient servant
Vinayak Damodar Savarkar[98]

In reply to his petition, the government sent an almost identical reply that they had been for the past several years—that in the larger interest of public tranquility they were not in a position to release Savarkar as yet and his conditional captivity was to continue for another two years, till 1939.

13 December 1936

The Governor in Council has again given careful consideration to the question of removal of the restrictions and has come to the conclusion that it would not be in the interests of public tranquility to withdraw them. Both the conditions of your release should accordingly continue for a further period of 2 years from the 4 January 1937 and before the expiry of that period, the question should again be reviewed.

G.K. Joshi Esquire
District Magistrate, Ratnagiri.[99]

However, with the elections of 1937 and the coming to power of a government in Bombay that was more Indian in character than before, Savarkar's fortunes too seemed to change for the better. Barrister Jamnadas Mehta, who represented the Tilak ideology and the Democratic Swarajya

Party, was going to play an important role in the formation of the ministry in Bombay. Having been an ardent champion of Savarkar's release, Mehta made this an important precondition for his support. Hence, merely five months after communicating their decision of not securing his release, the government seemed to have a change of mind. In May 1937, the district magistrate of Ratnagiri, G.K. Joshi, met Savarkar and conveyed the government's decision to withdraw the restrictions that had been placed on him since 1924.

10 May 1937

Sir,

I am directed by His Excellency the Governor of Bombay to inform you that in exercise of his powers conferred by Section 401 of the Code of Criminal Procedure, 1898 and in modification of Government Home Department, Resolution No. 724 dated 4 January 1924, His Excellency the Governor of Bombay is hereby pleased to direct that the conditions subject to which the unexpired portion of the sentences of transportation for life passed upon you was remitted, are withdrawn.

G.K. Joshi Esquire
District Magistrate, Ratnagiri.[100]

Savarkar was highly sceptical about the new order and sought written confirmations from the district magistrate about the terms of the withdrawal of restrictions and if he was truly a free man.

10 May 1937

Sir,

After receiving the Government communication from you regarding the removal of conditions restricting my liberty and reading the language therein through the light of your oral assurance to the effect that 'I was a free man,' I feel it would contribute to a definite and clearer understanding if the District Magistrate could give the same assurance in writing, which he gave orally while interpreting the government communication and be pleased to let me know clearly in writing that in consequence of the withdrawal of the conditions, 'I am unconditionally released.'

Vinayak Damodar Savarkar[101]

The district magistrate responded quite contemptuously.

11 May 1937

Sir

With reference to your letter dated 10th May 1937, I have the honour to state that I have nothing to add to or retract from the language of my letter No. S.D. 1251 dated 10th May 1937 addressed to you. I am further to state that I gave you no oral assurance yesterday nor have I the power or authority to give you any oral assurance. I think that I have made this quite clear to you when I handed over to you the decision of the Government in this matter. As regards your request for a written assurance to the effect that you are unconditionally set free, I am first to enquire what meaning you attach to the words 'unconditionally set free'.[101]

G.K. Joshi Esquire
District Magistrate, Ratnagiri

Thus after thirteen and a half years since his release from prison, and coincidentally on the anniversary of the 1857 War of Independence, on 10 May 1937, Savarkar was to be a free man. A new world beckoned him where the restrictions of confinement to Ratnagiri district alone and eschewing all political activities were finally withdrawn. He was now free to chart a new course in his life and that of the political history of his nation.

5

The Hindu Mahasabha Years

Ratnagiri, 1937

With the thirteen-year-long exile at Ratnagiri coming to an end in May 1937, Savarkar bid a tearful farewell to the town that had housed him for so long and which had been the laboratory of all his social reforms.

On 18 June 1937, in a public speech, Savarkar paid his tributes to Ratangiri and its people. The eminent citizens of Ratnagiri—Moropant Joshi (editor of *Balwant*), V.G. Shetye (litterateur and legal expert), A.S. Bhide Guruji, Devrukhkar and Rao Bahadur Parulekar—made speeches on the occasion. A citation and a purse of Rs 501 were also conferred on Savarkar as a sign of the goodwill and affection of the citizens of Ratnagiri. Savarkar was acutely aware of how the dominant political players of the time, including the Congress, were wooing him to join their ranks given that the strictures on his political participation no longer existed. Hence, in his acceptance speech, he clarified:

> I have always had to say and do things that are unpopular. Today, the kind of opposition I face when I say that untouchability must be abolished there was similar opposition when I was young and talked about freedom. But I always did what I thought was the right thing. Whatever I do next, I will do it by keeping the good of the nation in mind. Whichever party I join, I will never abandon the party [cause] of the Hindus. I am not just a friend of the Hindus, but also a son. Hence, I will not join the Congress till it is dominated by its current perverse Muslim appeasement politics.[1]

Packing his bags for good from Ratnagiri, Savarkar made an extensive tour of western Maharashtra. His first stop was Kolhapur—the seat of power of the descendants of Chhatrapati Shivaji Maharaj. An enthusiastic crowd of more than 150 to 200 people, which included the eminent film personality of the time, Baburao Pendharkar, welcomed him here. He was taken in a grand procession through the streets of Kolhapur where nearly 20,000 people walked along the cavalcade of motor cars on both sides of the street for several miles. Savarkar then gave a stirring speech to the masses assembled there on the need for Hindu sangathan. Quite in consonance with his political and social views, Savarkar's family and he were thereafter taken to the local theatre for a screening of the popular classic of the times, *Achhut Kanya* (The Untouchable Girl), starring Ashok Kumar and Devika Rani.

During his visit to Pendharkar's Hans Pictures Studios, Savarkar was saddened to see the English signboards. He requested Baburao Pendharkar to replace them with easy Marathi words, and suggested replacements to words like director (*digdarshak*), theatre (*kalagruha*), photography (*chhayachitran*), movie (*chitrapat*), sound recording (*dhwani lekhan*) and so on. Interestingly, these words have remained in vogue in Marathi (and to an extent Hindi) cinema too, though few know about the man who coined these terms! The Hans Pictures Studios were keen to record his voice message on this occasion. Complying with this request, Savarkar said:

> After 27-28 years of imprisonment and captivity, today I am a free man and have this opportunity to give a message to my countrymen and women. I have lots to share but I will refrain from pontificating on lofty ideals and poetical flourish that speeches are these days. I have only this to say—our country no longer needs speakers, but doers. Each time I have embarked on any programme, be it revolution or social reforms, many have been apprehensive about how their family or society would react if they participated in this. I want brave hearts who do not care about what others say and have only and only our country's complete independence as their objective and are ready to walk the talk for this and not merely give grand speeches. This is my only message not just to the people of this town but across India.[2]

In his public speeches he commended the often neglected or maligned role of the princely states in the cause of good governance and social reforms. He commended the role of Chhatrapati Shahuji Maharaj in eradicating untouchability; the contribution of the Gaekwad of Baroda for popularizing Hindi and that of some other states for their industrial progress. These

Hindu princely states were, according to Savarkar, the latent sources of future power once the British relinquish their control.[3] Mass inter-caste dining programmes or shuddhi campaigns normally followed most of his public speeches.

Proceeding to Miraj, Savarkar stoked a major controversy in his speech there at Khare Mandir, in a meeting presided over by a Congressman, Balkrishnapant Vitthal Shikhre. Attacking the Congress's pusillanimous attitude, he quoted the instance of a debate in the Central Assembly where Hindu Mahasabha leader Bhai Parmanand had brought up the issue of the kidnap and molestation of four Hindu girls in the NWFP by Muslim men. Press reports abounded that a prominent legislator Dr Abdul Jaffar Khan, elder brother of the famed 'Frontier Gandhi' or Khan Abdul Ghaffar Khan, blatantly dismissed this incident as being inconsequential and that these girls should have been handed over to their abductors. At this preposterous statement, Congressmen had giggled away uncontrollably, according to Savarkar. He likened this shameful act of the Congress to the scene in the Kaurava court and the behaviour of Duhshasan and other Kauravas when Draupadi was being disrobed. This was an act most suited for national-level eunuchs, he thundered.[4] This was enough to set the cat among the pigeons. All hell broke loose thereafter. Congressman N.V. Gadgil resigned in protest as the head of a reception committee panel in Poona to welcome Savarkar. Wherever Savarkar went, along with flower petal showers, black flag protests by Congressmen welcomed him too. The Congress boycotted all reception meetings of Savarkar and also got information regarding him blacklisted in the press that was sympathetic to it. The seeds of Savarkar's constant acrimony and hostility with the Congress were sown in Miraj.

Even when contacted by newspapers for clarifications, Savarkar maintained that while he has the greatest regard for the Congress that had leaders like Tilak, Malaviya, Gandhi, Nariman and others, he would not mince words when it came to the party's silence on atrocities on Hindus. His words castigating the Congress could be considered dropped if indeed the news that Dr Khan made these disparaging comments—of the incident being just an issue of a few boys and girls and that the girls should be returned to their abductors—was false. Bombay's daily *Prabhat* of 26 June 1937 explained that this explosion in the Savarkar–Congress relationship was bound to happen and the Miraj incident was a mere trigger:

The Hindu Sangathan work that Barrister Savarkar had undertaken in Ratnagiri was something that several Congressmen had routinely frowned upon. Still, they hoped that after the restrictions on him were taken away, given his stature and popularity, co-opting him into the Congress, putting a white cap on his cap and making him scream '*Gandhi ji ki Jai*' would only benefit the party. But his farewell speech at Ratnagiri itself dampened the hopes of many people and Miraj sealed the deal.[5]

From Miraj, Savarkar proceeded to the holy temple town of Pandharpur and paid his respects to all the saints of Maharashtra. Here, along with the welcome he received, he also faced protests from the orthodox who despised his social reforms and untouchability eradication programme in Ratnagiri. Black flags were raised and parched popcorn was thrown at the procession that took him around.[6] Undeterred by the protests that marred all his travels, Savarkar proceeded to Sangli and thereafter to Poona on 25 June 1937. In this historical city, he was yet again greeted by a massive victory procession. In one of his interactions, when asked why he was so insistent on Hindu dharma, Savarkar replied, 'If the world will move towards the end of all religions, I too will stop advocating Hinduism, but till that day dawns, I will continue to advocate my religion.' Renowned Marathi writer, poet, playwright and educationist Prahlad Keshav Atre ('Acharya' Atre, as Savarkar reportedly addressed him) stoutly supported him. To the protesting Congressmen he had words of advice that for a man like Savarkar who did not get petrified by Kala Pala, what were their Kala Nishan (black flag) going to achieve.

The hounding of Savarkar by both Congress supporters and the orthodox elements continued in Poona too. Atre had organized an inter-caste dinner in Poona in Savarkar's honour. But since some youth Congress workers tried to attack the meet and even mortally harm Savarkar, the meet was abruptly cancelled. Savarkar was scheduled to leave for Bombay by train. When Atre came to know that a Congress group was waiting to create a scene at the railway station, he drove him to the next station on the route, Talegaon, and made sure his guest was carefully sent off.

The metropolis of Bombay awaited Savarkar after Poona. At the city's Dadar station, the three brothers—Vinayak, Babarao and Narayan—met as free men for the first time since Savarkar's departure to London. The newspapers were agog with information about the public reception

that awaited Savarkar in Bombay. As the *Kaiser-i-Hind* reported on
27 June 1937:

> As previously announced, Mr. Vinayakrao Savarkar will arrive here
> this morning. Mr. Savarkar will be taken in procession from Azad
> Maidan to Krishna Cinema. The procession will start at 9 A.M. today
> and terminate at the Krishna Theatre at 10 A.M. At the Krishna
> Theatre at 10 A.M. Mr. Savarkar will be accorded a Public Reception
> and Address by the Bombay Savarkar Reception Committee.
> Mr. Laxmidas Tairsee will preside at the function and prominent
> leaders, including Messrs. K.F. Nariman, S.K. Patil, President and
> General Secretary of the Bombay Provincial Congress Committee,
> Mr. Jamnadas Dwarkadas, Mr. M.N. Roy, Mr. Silam will attend and
> address the gathering.[7]

Several eminent citizens under the leadership of Barrister Jamnadas
Mehta, who was instrumental in ensuring Savarkar's release after his own
election to the Bombay Provincial Legislative Assembly, decided to give a
rousing public reception. A committee was formed for this and, unlike in
the rest of Maharashtra, was supported by the Bombay Pradesh Congress
Committee. This committee requested several political leaders to give
their messages on this occasion. Some of these messages were published in
the *Lokmanya* dated 27 June 1937. Congress president Jawaharlal Nehru
sent his greetings saying: 'Welcome and respect to Vinayakrao Savarkar.'[8]
Subhas Chandra Bose in his statement said: 'I heartily welcome Barrister
Savarkar who is returning to Bombay now as a free man. I hope that he
will join the Congress and support the freedom movement. He has a bright
future ahead of him.'[9] C. Rajagopalachari said:

> The vigour and organizing abilities of Mr. Savarkar is something I can
> never forget. It also brings waves of memories of his phenomenal plan
> of escaping by jumping into the sea near Marseille under the nose of
> the guards when he was being escorted from England to India, and
> France then handing him over to British by violating the International
> Law is fascinating even today. According to me he is someone who has
> always been a fighter who will keep the torch of independence burning.
> He must be called an embodiment of heroism, courage, adventure, and
> nationalism.[10]

Rajagopalachari also revealed that he had written a biography of Savarkar about twenty years ago. 'What can I now add,' he wondered, 'to a biography of his that I had penned nearly twenty years ago, because since then his intellectual prowess must have only deepened by his prolonged introspection during his extended internment.'[11] This gave further credence to the often-held view that the first English biography of Savarkar titled *Life of Barrister Savarkar* written under a pseudonym 'Chitragupta' and published from Madras in 1926 was either written by Rajagopalachari or supported by him. Savarkar's close associate in his revolutionary days, V.V.S. Aiyar too was in the Madras Presidency during that time, before his untimely death in 1925. So one is unsure if Aiyar contributed to this biography as its author or as a first-hand eye-witness. Given that the work dealt with underground revolutionary activities at a time when all such literature would be proscribed by the government as seditious, the mysterious author chose to write it under a pseudonym. The details of Savarkar's early years, childhood and youth are sparse and sketchy, while his London days come alive with more details, further indicating that it could be someone who was with him during those stormy years. A publicity note announcing the release of a new book published by Madras based B.G. Paul Publications, appeared in the *Bombay Chronicle*, July 1927. This note further bolsters the claim of the book being written by a close accomplice, possibly Aiyar. Priced at Rs. 1-8-0, the book, the advertisement said, 'The story of the life of this famous patriot, written by a close friend' and 'is packed with thrilling incidents of how as a leader of a revolutionist party he had led the movement in India and England; how he was arrested and his dramatic escape at Marseilles by jumping out through the port-hole of the ship. A book of enchanting interest and full of interesting lessons to our New India.'[12]

On the occasion of the Bombay felicitation, Manvendranath Roy, the revolutionary, and the founder of the Communist Party of India, said in his message:

Savarkar is a leading freedom fighter of the 20th century, who had dedicated his life to the freedom the country. He didn't care that he could have been hanged or jailed in Andaman. I disagree with Savarkar's political ideology but I have the utmost respect for him as he is one of the few patriots who risked his life and whose sacrifice, bravery and his philosophy demands respect. I welcome his return to full freedom.[13]

M.S. Aney, Central Legislative Assembly member, said:

> Due to the release of Savarkar, the influential people in India have
> reached a state that demands aligning of Savarkar's idea of cultural
> independence and the three political ideas existing in India. The three
> right political ideas are Gandhi's idea based on absolute love and ahimsa,
> nationalist principles of Nehru with a colour of socialistic nationalism
> and the revolutionary socialism of the Roy school. Thus the thought that
> integrates the above-mentioned ideologies can be the ideology that will
> play a definite role in achieving national independence of India.[14]

These were certainly different times in the history of Indian politics where
political opponents were not personal enemies and one could differ with
another's political ideology and yet have charitable assessments of their
contributions.

A massive public reception was organized in Bombay to welcome
Savarkar. After a grand procession from Azad Maidan to Girgaon,
Savarkar was felicitated at Krishna Cinema. He was given a citation in
a silver trophy and garlanded on behalf of forty-one different national
organizations. Several renowned personalities such as Congressmen K.F.
Nariman and S.K. Patil, and M.N. Roy of the CPI spoke on the occasion.
Patil made an earnest appeal that Savarkar take over the reins of the party
that looked at him with the hope of much-needed guidance and support
at this juncture.[15]

In his thanksgiving speech, Savarkar expressed his gratitude and said:

> This is a unique ceremony as people of different ideologies have gathered
> together to welcome me. I will try my best to fulfill your expectation of
> working towards the national good. I have had a lot of ups and downs in
> my life and I am used to facing difficulties. If communists are asking for
> a religion-less society, I would support them, but I cannot accept injustice
> heaped on only one religion in the name of equality. I would urge the
> Congress to not deny the rights of a particular community while giving
> special privileges to another. I do not expect the Congress to turn into
> Hindu Mahasabha, but it should not turn into an outfit that treats Hindus
> unfairly in order to safeguard the interests of other communities.[16]

The *Bombay Chronicle*, while welcoming his release, summed up the
exhilaration with which he was being received across cities and towns:

Savarkar is almost a legendary figure to the modern generation. His career reads almost like a romance, and though the struggle for freedom has received a new orientation during the last quarter of a century under the leadership of Mahatma Gandhi, there will not be a true nationalist in India who will not feel happy today . . . not sure that he will not be the object of attention of the all-pervading C.I.D.[17]

Bombay was to become Savarkar's permanent home henceforth, like it was for his brothers. He stayed for a year or so at Bhaskar Bhavan in Dadar, where all the brothers lived independently within the same premises. He continued his political tours across Maharashtra for the remainder of 1937 too, to ascertain the pulse of the people and his well-wishers, before he could take a final call on his own political future.

He made repeated visits to Poona to ideate with several groups of people there on charting the next course, both for himself and for the country, as he saw it. Meeting a delegation of untouchables in Poona, he urged them not to fall for the bait of conversion as that was not going to solve their social, cultural or economic woes. Instead, if they joined hands with him in the manner of social reforms that he had spearheaded in Ratnagiri, he was confident of rooting out untouchability in about a decade thence. As always, inter-caste dinners were a common feature after all these meetings to send out a strong, symbolic message of the irrelevance of caste.

On 24 July, Savarkar left for Nasik and then to Bhagur, his birthplace, on 26 July, where the entire population of the village gathered to give him a rousing reception. Back in Poona on 31 July, he was joined by his former colleague Senapati Bapat who had met him six years ago in Ratnagiri. During this visit, Savarkar addressed a group of young students at the Hindmata Mandir who strongly disagreed with his views. They wanted the old 'Revolutionary Savarkar' and not the one who harped on Hindu Sangathan. In his reply, Savarkar said:

You say you disagree with my views and that you want the Savarkar of 1908 back. But how many of you know that even the Savarkar of 1908 was not accepted by many. It has taken you so many decades to accept those views now. If even five young brave hearts from among you can get the courage of a Madan Lal Dhingra or Anant Laxman Kanhere, then I could consider our country as being fortunate. Can any of you raise your hands to commit this kind of daredevilry? What then to talk about revolution? Though you oppose me, in reality, have you understood my views fully? I hold that view that India should get total and complete freedom. Do you disagree?[18]

When some irate students tried to disrupt his speech, Savarkar calmly told them:

I have heard you now patiently, and it is your turn to hear me. I hold the view that we should try every means available to get full freedom, including getting military training and joining the British army. Do you disagree with this? I also hold that in the future constitution of a free India, whenever that comes about, every human being should be equal in the eyes of the law, irrespective of the caste or religion he belongs to. I am not demanding 5 votes for 4 Hindus in the Assemblies. Today, in our Assemblies, for 4 Muslims, there are 6 votes cast. Is this not unfair and should I not raise my voice against such blatantly communal injustice or appeasement? Religion in politics is a recipe for disaster and I will fight to remove that and ensure equality for all—not just have the Hindu community bear the albatross of these discriminatory terms and conditions, but create a common benchmark.[19]

He urged the students to start training in arms. He implored them to start with rifle classes so that they could at least handle air guns. 'There is scope,' he said, 'for drama, poetry and literature in life. But when the mother is on her death-bed; it is a sin to go out for a change of climate, or to enjoy life, and the stars![20]

~

On 1 August 1937, Savarkar attended a programme to commemorate Tilak's death anniversary. Quite opportunely, Savarkar announced his decision to join the Democratic Swarajya Party. The political malleability of the times gave ample space for numerous such political outfits to thrive within the Congress rubric. The first Democratic Swarajya Party was established as an informal platform within the Congress by Tilak. After his death in 1920, his supporters in the Congress, such as N.C. Kelkar, M.R. Jayakar, Bhaskar Bhopatkar and others, continued their association with this group. Nationally, the Swarajya Party members included leaders such as C.R. Das, C. Rajagopalachari and Motilal Nehru who used this platform as a pressure group against some of the views and decisions of Mahatma Gandhi after the collapse of the Non-Cooperation movement. The unit in the Bombay Presidency was revived on 29 October 1933 with the aim of attaining Poorna Swaraj or complete independence. The old Tilak faction within the Congress was frustrated with Gandhi's flip-flops and also the boycott of councils following civil disobedience. The chief protagonists were interestingly a melange of leaders who belonged to the Congress and the Hindu Mahasabha, many having joint memberships as well. N.C. Kelkar, B.S. Moonje, Madhav Shrihari Aney and Jamnadas Mehta were instrumental in breathing life back to this umbrella party.

Struggling to survive, the Democratic Swarajya Party decided to relaunch itself with much fanfare through a 'Tilak Week' that was organized in various parts of the Bombay Presidency between 24 July and 1 August 1937. As government intelligence reports mention, these 'meetings were poorly attended'.[21] At an exhibition of swadeshi products in Poona, party veteran Lakshman Balwant Bhopatkar inaugurated a volunteer corps. But 'only 15 persons enlisted in the corps'. A modest gathering of 150 people had assembled on 1 August 1937 that included Jamnadas Mehta, L.B. Bhopatkar, N.C. Kelkar and Dr B.S. Moonje where Savarkar made his declaration. It was decided that active steps needed to be taken to revive the party. A sum of Rs 10,000 was intended to be collected for this purpose before the end of October 1937. Of this, an amount of Rs 4500 was subscribed on the spot. The plan of action for the next few months included enlisting 10,000 members, establishing a branch in every taluka and to hold a conference in Sholapur in November. A Hindu Yuvak Sangh or youth league was also started with 'the object of carrying out the programme of the party and of organizing Hindu youths against any attack on their religion'.[22] The Sangh was to 'follow V.D. Savarkar's teaching that caste differences among Hindus should be abolished'.[23] Speaking about Savarkar's elevation in this party, the intelligence report states:

V.D. Sawarkar [sic] was accepted as a leader of the party, but in this connexion [sic] several speakers expressed the view that Sawarkar should confine himself to political activities and avoid propaganda in respect of his controversial social views. It is understood that Sawarkar will receive a monthly salary of Rs. 200/-. He will not, it seems, hold any official position, but will take an active part in organizing and developing the party.[24]

In this meeting, Savarkar exhorted the members not to be complacent or satisfied by the limited governing mechanisms that had been facilitated by the British through the Government of India Act of 1935. Just having governments in a few provinces gave the Congress a false sense of satisfaction of having achieved the goal, he opined. One would be a true ruler only when the country got total, absolute and complete political independence, through any means, from the colonial power. When that happened, the names and heroism of the numerous brave revolutionaries such as Barrister Sardar Singh Rana, Virendranath Chattopadhyay and others who were or are still struggling all their lives for this objective would be popularized and taken with gratitude. He expressed happiness that the patriotic song '*Vande Mataram*' by Bankim Chandra Chatterjee was being sung in the legislative assemblies. He recounted how this song and the very term was the life blood of the brave revolutionaries; how the first flag of Indian independence that Madame Bhikaji Cama unfurled in 1907 at the International Socialist Congress in Germany had these hallowed words that gave goose pimples to every patriotic Indian. Yet, he cautioned that there might well be a day when this same Congress that is so steeped in Muslim appeasement and its leader Gandhi might decide to scrap this song in case some members of the Muslim community oppose the Hindu iconography in the verses. The party needed to guard against such tendencies too, he cautioned.[25] His statement was to be quite prophetic as that was precisely what the Congress did by eventually junking the song and adopting '*Jana Gana Mana*' of Rabindranath Tagore as the national anthem of free India. A regeneration of the Hindu community and eradication of caste barriers was also stressed upon. He asserted that his conception of Hindutva was broad-based, inclusive and non-theological and thereby different from Hinduism. Speaking about this, Savarkar postulated:

> Let Hinduism concern itself with the salvation of life after death, the concept of God and the Universe. Let individuals be free to form opinions about the trio. The whole universe from one end to the other is the real book of religion. But so far as the materialistic and secular aspect is concerned, the Hindus are a nation bound by a common culture, a common history, a common language and a common country.[26]

A week later, Savarkar visited Sholapur to meet eminent citizens of the town. The Congress protests continued against him. Ramakrishna Jaju, a local Congress leader, sent out threats that the minute Savarkar stepped into Sholapur he would be given a grand procession on a donkey. To this, 'Acharya' Atre, gave his characteristic repartee that if that was indeed the intention, there could be no one better than Jaju to carry Savarkar on his shoulders.[27] But things went beyond such sarcasm and turned more serious and violent in Sholapur. As the motorcade carrying him went through a procession, several attempts were made by Congress workers to attack and physically harm him. Shoes, stones, ash and sewer water were hurled at the car, damaging it to an extent, though Savarkar managed to remain both unharmed and undeterred. One of the hosts, Vishnupant Patil was injured and fell unconscious, and another 8–9 people were rushed to the local hospital for treatment. Even when Savarkar reached his host's house, a mob surrounded the building and kept banging the doors violently till the police came in and dispersed the crowd. About seventeen Congressmen were arrested for rioting, creating nuisance and causing grievous harm to life.[28]

Similar unruly scenes marred his visit to Barshi. A ruffian who had been jailed in the Andamans for crimes and murder was employed to mortally hurt Savarkar. But when he came to know who his victim was supposed to be, he had an immediate change of mind and instead became a bodyguard for Savarkar in Barshi. Later, during an interaction with the press, when asked if not joining the Congress cost him his popularity and also denied him grand receptions, Savarkar said:

> For the sake of grand welcomes, I cannot sacrifice the welfare of the country and of Hindus. If I had complied with the British, don't you think I would have earned grander receptions, positions and perks? Yet, since my youth, it is only national interests that have guided my every action. I have no regrets or fear when I am attacked like this by Congressmen in every town that I visit. They are such a peace-loving, non-violent bunch after all![29]

The hectic travels, public lectures and the tension caused by the violent disruptions affected Savarkar's health. On his return to Bombay on 11 August, he came down with a high fever. He was diagnosed with typhoid and was confined to bed for more than a month.

On 26 October 1937, the Democratic Swarajya Party decided to celebrate 'Vande Mataram Day' in Poona. L.B. Bhopatkar presided over a gathering of nearly 1200 people. Senapati Bapat was present on this occasion. A convalescing Savarkar addressed the crowds after he unfurled the first flag of Indian independence of green, saffron and red silk with 'Vande Mataram' inscribed in the middle. This flag had been sent by Sardar Singh Rana from Paris to Tilak's grandson G.V. Ketkar. In his speech Savarkar recounted the London days when Hemchandra Das of the Anushilan Samiti had visited them at India House and had designed this flag, which was the one that Madame Bhikaji Cama had courageously unfurled in Germany, thirty years ago, in 1907, to proclaim Indian independence. He also demanded that efforts needed to be made to repeal the Arms Act. He refused to furnish details of what he and other revolutionaries, including Madame Cama, had done whilst in Europe. Thereafter, nearly thirty institutions of the city came forward and garlanded this flag.[30]

A few weeks later, on 18 November 1937, addressing a meeting of the Swarajya Party in Dadar, Bombay, Savarkar criticized the Congress for its egoism and contended that the majority in the Congress belonged to the toiling masses. These were the real people who truly deserved credit for whatever political progress vis-à-vis the British administration that the country was witnessing. He implored the gathering not to suffer under the illusion that the Congress had achieved Swaraj, because the real power still rested in the hands of the viceroy and the governors. He also urged the Hindus to work hard to remove the scourge of untouchability. Referring to the cult of non-violence, he said that although it was a good one, it was of no avail when opposed by violence. For liberating India from British rule, only an armed conflict could effect any tangible result. The Hindus must eschew this non-violent path that emasculates them and instead fit themselves for the defence of India against any foreign invasions, he suggested. Whether one liked it or not, an army was absolutely necessary for protecting the country. Nations gained respect with guns, and peace could not exist without guns, he said. He called for a rallying of international help and pro-Indian sentiment where the goal of independence had to be much more important than ideology. First the country needs to be strong to be independent. He argued that it was not important whether Japan, which conquered China, was right or wrong. The world took care of its own countries and India must not count on help from any other country. He believed that people had the right to possess arms for self-defence and hence young Indians must agitate with the slogan 'Down with the Arms Act' to facilitate this.[31]

The contents of Savarkar's speech made their way to the most unlikely recipient, far away in Japan. Deshpande, a resident of Japan who had earlier visited Savarkar secretly in Ratnagiri, was in the audience that evening. He narrated the transcript of the speech to the daring Indian revolutionary Rash Behari Bose when he got back to Japan. On 23 December 1912, Rash Behari Bose burst into prominence for his alleged role in the bomb attack on Viceroy Lord Hardinge, just as the latter was entering the new Indian capital of Delhi on the back of an elephant. While his accomplices were arrested, tried and executed, Rash Behari Bose went underground. During the First World War, he confabulated with Indian revolutionaries across the world—America, Canada, Germany—to instigate an uprising in the British Indian Army and even in Singapore, similar to that in 1857. Lahore was selected as the spot for this outbreak on 21 February 1915. But surveillance and strict British intelligence foiled all these plots and Rash Bihari Bose came under intense scrutiny. Disguising himself as a relative of the Nobel laureate and poet Rabindranath Tagore, Rash Bihari Bose set sail for Japan from the port of Calcutta on 12 May 1915, never to return to the country he loved so much. Japan's success in the Russo-Japanese war of 1905 had enhanced its stature as a nation for restoration of global balance to the East and to pan-Asiatic supremacy. Though Japan was a British ally between 1902 and 1923, it had kept its doors open to revolutionaries who wanted to end the rule of the Empire in different Asian countries. In Tokyo, Rash Bihari Bose met Sun Yat Sen, the head of the revolutionary army of China who was also in exile there and plotting an armed revolution in his home country. Sun introduced Rash Bihari Bose to Mitsuru Toyama who led the pan-Asianist group Gen'yosha. Bose even married a Japanese to further integrate himself into Japanese society. Right from 1931, he had organized an Independence League in Japan to attain independence of India by all possible means. A journal titled *New Asia* was also brought out in Japanese and English. He wrote fiery articles urging the Japanese government to ally with the United States, China and the Soviet Union to eliminate the colonial hegemony of the British Empire in Asia. As relations between Britain and Japan deteriorated, Rash Bihari Bose's propaganda became louder and bolder.[32] He was soon to establish what became well known as the Indian National Army (INA).

On 29 December 1937, Savarkar unexpectedly received a letter from Japan, written to him by Rash Behari Bose. The contents of the letter were as follows:

The speech that you gave at Dadar on the current political climate of the country, published in Kesari, was read to me by a Marathi speaking colleague of mine as I do not speak Marathi. On reading your speech, I am of the firm view that India needs a leader like you today. Your knowledge and understanding on geo-politics is profound and I hope India produces more leaders like you. As for the Congress, they are doing the same things that they were doing 20 years ago. I do not think India can ever achieve independence through the Congress methods. I fear that the Congress leadership is playing into the hands of the British knowingly or otherwise seem to have strengthened the position of the British Government in India. I was delighted by your criticism and rebuttal of the Congress ideas and politics. This gives me hope and fills me with excitement. I hope that you will create a group of true patriots and continue this great national work with full responsibility.[33]

Yours truly,
Rash Behari Bose

The foundations were thus being laid for a continental alliance of two individuals who held similar views when it came to the methods to attain freedom in India—through an armed uprising instigated within the Indian Army.

Savarkar continued his whirlwind travels through November and December 1937, visiting Arvilla, Deoli, Wardha, Chanda, Baroda, Bhatna, Mulgaon, Rajuri, Navargaon, Tilodi, Raipur, Bilaspur and other towns and villages across Bombay Presidency, Baroda state and Central Provinces. He also travelled to Nagpur and paid a visit to the Rashtriya Swayamsevak Sangh (RSS) shakha headquarters there on 12 December 1937. The erstwhile associate of Babarao and founder of the RSS, Dr Hedgewar, garlanded him and said, '[it] was a lucky day for the Sangh that a brave freedom fighter, patriot and leader like Savarkar visited it'.[34]

It was around this time that Savarkar made the decision to end his brief flirtation with the Democratic Swarajya Party that did not seem to be going anywhere. He was invited to become the president of the All-India Hindu Mahasabha and preside over its annual conference in Karnavati (Ahmedabad) in December 1937. His ascendancy to this position gave the Mahasabha a new vigour and heralded a completely unprecedented era in its history. It had all along remained a loose confederation and a kind of an amorphous group within the Congress and stitching together Hindu movements largely in the United Provinces and Punjab. As Richard Gordon states:

> In its first phase before 1922, the Hindu Mahasabha was not an all-India organization in any real sense, either in the extent of its organization or in the scope of its activities. It was, at most, an inter-provincial organization linking Hindu movements in the U.P. and the Punjab. As its conferences were held in conjunction with the annual Congress, it attracted casual platform support from other provinces.[35]

Savarkar's decision to transform this platform into a political party of national stature that could pit itself against both the Congress and the Muslim League gave it a new breath of life. There is a lack of clear evidence on what prompted his ascension. The common view is that a faction within the Mahasabha was itching to catapult it to a national party status from the decrepit platform, run by two northern Indian factions, that it had remained. Maharashtra now became the organizational hub of the Mahasabha, even though its head office continued to operate in Delhi. Through Savarkar's efforts not only did the Mahasabha enunciate a clear national vision and strategy but also enhanced its footprint across India with party branches in many parts of the Bombay Presidency and Central Provinces. His efforts were strongly supported by veterans and activists such as Dr B.S. Moonje, L.B. Bhopatkar, Bhai Parmanand, Chandragupta Vedalankar, Ganpat Rai, Indra Prakash and others. Savarkar's presidency years coincided with the most sensitive period of both Indian as well as international history and geopolitics in the twentieth century—India on the threshold of her freedom and the world at the brink of a catastrophic world war.

Thus, at the nineteenth annual session of the Hindu Mahasabha at Karnavati on 30 December 1937, Savarkar was elected as its national president. In his presidential address he outlined the broad principles on which he wished to steer the party under his leadership.[36] 'Hindudom' as he called it was to be 'simply identified with best interests of Hindustan as a whole'. The Hindudom's ultimate mission was to be one where the Motherland was set completely free and consolidated into an Indian state in which 'all our countrymen to whatever religion or sect or race they belong are treated with perfect equality and none allowed to dominate others or is deprived of his just and equal rights of free citizenship as long as everyone discharges the common obligations and duties which one owes to the Indian Nation as a whole'. Interestingly, he began the speech with tributes and greetings to the king of Nepal, Yuddhsamsher Ranaji, its prime minister and people, and also co-religionists and countrymen across various countries from America, Africa, Mauritius and Bali to those in colonies within India termed as 'French India' and 'Portuguese India'.

> The Hindusthan of tomorrow must be one and indivisible, not only a united but a unitarian nation, from Kashmir to Rameshwar, from Sindh to Assam. I hope that not only the Mahasabha but even the Congress and such other national bodies in Hindusthan will not fight shy of claiming Gomantak, Pondicherry, and such other parts of Hindusthan as parts as inalienable and integral of our Nation as is Maharashtra or Bengal or Punjab.[37]

Labouring on his own hypothesis in the codification of Hindutva and whom he defines as a 'Hindu' by those yardsticks through a cultural and nationalistic prism and not a theological one, he also defined the ambit of the Mahasabha. 'The Mahasabha,' he said, 'takes its stand on no dogma, no book or school of philosophy whether pantheist, monotheist or atheist . . . The Mahasabha is not in the main a Hindu-Dharma-Sabha but it is pre-eminently a Hindu-Rashtra-Sabha and is a Pan-Hindu organization shaping the destiny of the Hindu Nation in all its social, political and cultural aspects. Those who commit the serious mistake of taking the Hindu Mahasabha for only a religious body would do well to keep this distinction in mind.'[38]

Conscious of the tag of the Mahasabha being a parochial and communal organization, Savarkar explained:

> No movement is condemnable simply because it is sectional. So long as it tries to defend the just and fundamental rights of a particular nation or people or community against the unjust and overbearing aggression of other human aggregates and does not infringe on an equal just right and liberties of others, it cannot be condemned or looked down simply because the nation or community is a smaller aggregate in itself. But when a nation or community treads upon the rights of sister nations or communities and aggressively stands in the way of forming larger associations and aggregates of mankind, its nationalism or communalism

becomes condemnable from a human point of view. This is the acid test of distinguishing a justifiable nationalism or communalism from an unjust and harmful one. The Hindu Sangathan movement, call it national, communal or parochial as you like, stands as much justified by this real test as our Indian Patriotism can be.[39]

The overall objective for the Hindu Mahasabha was 'absolute political independence of Hindusthan'. This independence was not mere geographical freedom of the piece of land called India, but one where for Hindutva there was religious, racial and cultural identity and independence. He chided the 'Mohammedans who are nowhere to be found while the national struggle goes on and are everywhere to be found in the forefront at the time of reaping the fruits of that struggle',[40] and who are 'often found to cherish an extra-territorial allegiance, moved more by events in Palestine than what concerns India as a nation, worries himself more about the well-being of the Arabs than the well-being of his Hindu neighbours and countrymen in India'.[41] The broad generalization, particularly of the second characteristic of the Indian Muslim, was certainly worrisome and would do little to help the Mahasabha build any bridges or even tactical compromise with the Muslim community or its leadership. This excessive codification and a formulaic definition of 'Hindu' and 'Hindutva', however rational and logical it might have been, contributed in alienating several sections from accepting the Mahasabha's viewpoint.

What position was Savarkar then envisaging for non-Hindus (Muslims, Christians, Parsis and Jews according to him) in this grand construct of a Hindu Rashtra, the Hindu Nation? Were they to be relegated to the state of tenants or second-class citizens within a majoritarian regime? Here he posits a more egalitarian and modern view of a secular nation state where he vouches for equal rights for everyone.

Let the Indian State be purely Indian. Let it not recognize any invidious distinctions whatsoever as regards the franchise, public services, offices, taxation on the grounds of religion and race. Let no cognizance be taken whatsoever of man's being Hindu or Mohammedan, Christian or Jew. Let all citizens of that Indian State be treated according to their individual worth irrespective of their religious or racial percentage in the general population. Let that language and script be the national language and script of that Indian state which are understood by the overwhelming majority of the people as happens in every other state in the world, i.e., in England or the United States of America and let no religious bias be allowed to tamper with that language and script with an enforced and perverse hybridism whatsoever. Let 'one man one vote' be the general rule irrespective of caste or creed, race or religion. If such an Indian State is kept in view the Hindu Sangathanists will, in the interest of the Hindu Sangathan itself, be the first to offer their wholehearted loyalty to it. I for one and thousands of the Mahasabhaites like me have set this ideal of an Indian State as our political goal ever since the beginning of our political career and shall continue to work for its consummation to the end of our life. Can any attitude towards an Indian State be more national than that? Justice demands that I must plainly proclaim that the mission and policy of the Hindu Mahasabha with regard to an Indian state have been more national than the present-day policy of Indian National Congress itself.[42]

Referring to the belligerent speeches and resolutions of Jinnah and the Muslim League in their Lucknow session in October that year, Savarkar claimed that it laid bare their 'anti-national attitude' and 'Pan-Islamic ambitions'. The clamour for Urdu being made the national language, the use of the Arabic script over Devanagari or opposition to 'Vande Mataram' or such other songs was indicative of a deeper malaise, according to Savarkar, something that the 'unity-hankers' would never manage to understand. These clashes pointed to a more fundamental 'strife of different cultures and races and nations and these trifles are but the passing and outward symptoms of the malady deep-seated in the Moslem mind.'[43] The notion of being the erstwhile rulers of the country and hence subjugating their former subjects was central to such tendencies, he claimed. He severely castigated the emergent demand in the League circles of a Muslim state of Pakistan that cut through the 'body politic of our Motherland.' These audacious demands sprung from the constant hankering on the side of the Hindus that freedom cannot be won without Muslim support or without Hindu–Muslim unity. The results of such appeasement were there for all to see, according to Savarkar.

When an overwhelming majority in a country goes on its knees before a minority so antagonistic as the Mohammedans, imploring them to lend a helping hand and assures it that otherwise the major community is doomed to death, it would be a wonder if that minor community does not sell their assistance at the higher bidder possible, does not hasten the doom of the major community and aim to establish their own political suzerainty in the land. The only threat that the Mohammedans always hold before the Hindus is to the effect that they would not join the Hindus in the struggle for Indian freedom unless their anti-national and fanatical demands are granted on the spot. Let the Hindus silence the threat once for all telling point blank: 'Friends! We wanted and do want only that kind of unity which will go to create an Indian state in which all citizens irrespective of caste and creed, race and religion are treated all alike on the principle of one man one vote. We, though we form the overwhelming majority in the land, do not want any special privileges for our Hindudom; nay more, we are even willing to guarantee special protection for the language, culture and religion of the Mohammedans as a minority if they also promise not to infringe on the equal liberty of other communities in India to follow their own ways within their own respective houses and not to try to dominate and humiliate the Hindus. But knowing full well the anti-Indian designs of the pan-Islamic movement, with a link of Moslem nations from Arabia to Afghanisthan bound by their recent offensive and defensive alliances and the ferocious tendencies of the frontier tribes to oppress the Hindus out of religious and racial hatred, we Hindus are not going to trust you any longer with any more blank cheques . . . We are not out to fight with England only to find a change of masters but we Hindus aim to be masters in our own house. A Swarajya that could only be had at the humiliation and cost of Hindutva itself is for us Hindus as good as suicide. If India is not freed from foreign domination the Indian Moslems cannot but be slaves themselves. If they feel it to be true, if and when they feel they cannot do without the assistance and the good will of the Hindus let them come then to ask for unity and that also not to oblige the Hindus but to oblige themselves. A Hindu–Moslem unity which is effected thus is worth having. The Hindus have realized to their cost that in this case seeking unity is losing it. Henceforth the Hindu formula for Hindu-Moslem unity is only this: 'If you come, with you; if you don't, without you; and if you oppose, in spite of you'—the Hindus will continue to fight for their National Freedom as best as they can![44]

He exonerated the other minorities—Christians, Parsis and Jews—of any such anti-national tendencies and opined that they could contribute to 'national consolidation' as 'honest and patriotic citizens'. But he sounded another warning bell to the country about the Muslim separatism and supremacy:

> I warn the Hindus that the Mohammedans are likely to prove dangerous to our Hindu nation and the existence of a common Indian State even if and when England goes out. Let us not be stone blind to the fact that they as a community still continue to cherish fanatical designs to establish a Moslem rule in India. Let us work for harmony, let us hope for the best, but let us be on our guard! As it is, there are two antagonistic nations living side by side in India. Several infantile politicians commit the serious mistake in supposing that India is already welded into a harmonious nation, or that it could be welded thus for the mere wish to do so. These our well-meaning but unthinking friends take their dreams for realities. That is why they are impatient of communal tangles and attribute them to communal organizations. But the solid fact is that the so-called communal questions are but a legacy handed down to us by centuries of a cultural, religious and national antagonism between the Hindus and the Moslems.[45]

Savarkar postulated that just wishing the malady away does not make it go, but by recognizing that there is a fundamental problem of clash of civilizations, we can at least attempt a solution, a cure in the larger national interest and for peace. However, brushing this under the carpet and constructing a false narrative that these problems do not exist at all is little short of suicidal. In this speech he proclaimed that India could not be considered a 'Unitarian and homogeneous nation' but there were two nations in the main 'Hindus and Moslems'.[46] As 'unpleasant' as it was to hear, it was a bitter truth, he contended. But the solution to that was not a vivisection of the country on religious lines, but the model adopted world over when faced with diverse ethnicities. And that was the welding together of a united nation state where 'none is allowed any special weightage of representation and none is paid an extra-price to buy his loyalty to the State'.[47] He exhorted the Hindus of the country to not be apologetic about being called a 'Hindu' or of their past and heritage just to make any community feel happy and safe. Even as he guaranteed complete protection to the religion, culture and languages of the minorities, he would not 'tolerate any aggression on their part on the equal liberty of the Hindus to guard their religion, culture and language as well. If the non-Hindu minorities are to be protected, then surely the Hindu majority also must be protected against any aggressive minority in India.'[48]

The text and tenor of the inaugural speech as president of the Hindu Mahasabha was to lay the ground for the politics that he and his party were to follow over the next five years under his stewardship.

Over the next few months, in 1938, Savarkar embarked on a marathon tour across various parts of India, meeting and understanding the political viewpoints of different protagonists and the masses, and to propagate the Hindu Mahasabha views that he had articulated at Karnavati. On 6 February 1938, the capital city of Delhi braced itself for a grand reception for Savarkar. After a massive procession and rally, several eminent Hindu Mahasabha leaders such as Dr B.S. Moonje, Lala Narayan Dutta, Bhai Parmanand, Ramsingh, Dr M.R. Jayakar, M.S. Aney and others accompanied him. After several public meetings and speeches, Savarkar made his way to Bhopal and Nagar.

Meanwhile, the new Congress president Subhas Chandra Bose came calling to Bombay in end-February that year. He addressed several meetings in Vile Parle, Ghatkopar and Kurla. He also met with leaders of the Democratic Swarajya Party—Jamnadas Mehta and L.B. Bhopatkar— over dinner at the former's bungalow in Malabar Hill. They told Bose that barring a few issues, there were hardly any differences between the two parties and hence they were keen on merging their party with the Congress. Bose assured them of placing the matter in front of Gandhi and the Congress Working Committee for its consideration.[49] He also expressed a desire that Savarkar change his mind and join the Congress to strengthen his and the party's hands. In his response, Savarkar sent him a letter explaining his position:

> The Constitution of the Congress and the Congress norms dictate that no member of the party can be part of any 'communal organization'. When they say this, they speak only about the Hindu Mahasabha but there are people in the Congress who have declared themselves openly as supporters or members of the Muslim League and even gone on to occupy leadership position in the party, despite this. People in positions of power have been notified not to take part or be associated with the Hindu

Mahasabha and/or any movement organized by it. Joining the Congress in such circumstances would mean that I am a Hindu Mahasabhaite only in name, not in action, which to me would be a betrayal of Hindu interests. Swarajya according to me is the full independence of myself, my *tatva* [essence], which is Hindutva. Even when it is obvious that Indian interests are inevitably Hindu interests, the Congress actively forbids it, it concedes to every demand of the Muslim, sometimes even when they are against national interests or human morality. I feel it is impossible for me to work in such an organization until the mindset is changed. Hindu Mahasabha does not forbid any of its members from being part of the Congress. I hope that the Congress is also as open minded. If they are willing to guide Hindus with their wisdom, they should also be ready to protect their rights [Hindutva], advocate their just demands and oppose any anti-national, separatist movements and policies. When that happens, I promise to lend my voice and support fully to the Congress. My opinion on the suggestion of a united front against the Empire as a member of the Hindu Mahasabha is that I would not even blink and jump into any such movement assuming national character, irrespective of which party leads the movement. I can even work with the Socialists and the Bolsheviks to a certain extent. One can contribute towards the national cause without being a member of the Congress and hence we have decided not to yoke ourselves to the membership of the Congress and its ideals, but instead work towards the national cause with even more vigour and inspiration. The Congress needs to come clear on its position regarding Hindu Sangathan and Shuddhi movements.[50]

A few months later, in April, he embarked on an extensive tour of the United Provinces. Supporters in Lucknow, Agra, Faizabad, Kanpur and Barabanki rose in large numbers to welcome him. At Lucknow, he visited his comrade from the Cellular Jail times, fellow convict and revolutionary Sachindranath Sanyal. The latter threw a party in honour of the distinguished visitor. Sanyal seems to have been the active conduit between Savarkar and Rash Bihari Bose in Japan and encouraging the two to work more collaboratively. Sanyal and Savarkar had been in constant touch since their Cellular Jail days. In fact, in April 1928, when Sanyal's mother Kshirodvasini, who participated in the Kakori conspiracy passed away, Savarkar wrote an editorial in her memory, titled, *'Veer Maa Kshirodvasini'*, applauding her courage and patriotism.[51] For the historian of the 1857 uprising (that he had called as the 'First War of Indian Independence' in his seminal work), it was an emotional moment for Savarkar at Kanpur on 3 April 1938 when he visited the Massacre Ghat and the Shiva Temple from where Tatya Tope blew his bugle calling for war. In his stirring speech there, he said:

> This very Cawnpore has witnessed the defeat of the British forces at the hands of Tatya Tope. Since my childhood I have been cherishing an irresistible yearning for visiting this city as the venue of the scenes of revolution and visiting Kashi as the ultimate holy city of Hindustan. Since my arrival here, I have been haunted by the spirits of Nana Sahib, Tatya Tope, the war cries raised by their battalions and the thunder of their cannons.[52]

On his return to Bombay, he was informed of his election as the president of the twenty-second Marathi Sahitya Sammelan, the same organization that had earlier rejected his nomination for the position due to internal politicking. The idea of the literary conclave as a potent platform to voice not only concerns related to the language and its contemporary challenges, but also the politico-social conditions of the times was mooted by the reformer, Congressman and legal luminary Justice Mahadev Govind Ranade in the 1880s, along with another allied institution called the Granthottejak Mandal. Only two *sammelan*s were held in his lifetime and the idea got a fillip under Tilak from 1905. Several rulers of princely states, such as the maharaja of Indore and Gaikwad of Baroda were active patrons and even presided over past conferences. The conclaves were most often marred by internecine quarrels, personal jealousies and provincial feuds of Bombay versus Poona and so on. It was not rare for politicians with a literary flair to be invited to chair such conferences. Mahatma Gandhi and K.M. Munshi were often invited to preside over Gujarati conferences of similar nature. With Savarkar, his political affiliations, his opposition to the Congress and his extreme views on subjects such as the Marathi language purification caused some consternation among the members. The tensions and issues surrounding Savarkar's election by an overwhelming majority to preside over the Sammelan are lucidly detailed by one of the forces behind the Sammelan, advocate Datto Appaji Tulzapurkar, in his letter to Justice M.R. Jayakar who was elected the chairman of the Reception Committee:

> Barrister Savarkar is now the elected President of the Sammelan. His varied literary activities are well known. He is a powerful writer and a most effective speaker. Politically he has allied himself for the present with the

Democratic Swarajya Party of Poona and that is why he is not in the good
books of the Congress leaders. In a way I am also a Congressman! But the
politics have nothing to do with social and literary functions. Why should
we not all Maharashtrians unite on a common platform? Savarkar holds
some extreme and puritanic [sic] views on the language question. Since his
release he has given a great impetus to that question by his forceful writings
and speeches. He has converted orthodox Pandits like Prof Madhavrao
Patwardhan (Madhav Julian) who was President of the Jalgaon Sammelan
to his view. But there is a large section of Marathi writers who are opposed
to his extreme views. I am one of them. This question is bound to figure
prominently in the coming Sammelan. It is the topic of the day. During
the last few months, Savarkar had to preside over two Provincial Literary
conferences—one at Nagpur and the other at Baroda. His speeches there
were no doubt excellent but there too he found two great opponents to
his views. At Nagpur my son-in-law Prof. Behere was the Chairman
of the Reception Committee and the Prime Minister- Dr. Khare who
inaugurated the proceedings. Both in their own ways criticized Savarkar's
views. At Baroda there was a climax—Rajaratna Vasudeorao Joshi who was
the Chairman of the Reception Committee in his welcoming speech itself
very humorously, but mercilessly, attacked the new cult of the 'Marathi
Bhasha Shuddhi' sponsored by Savarkar and others. Possibly we may also
have some very interesting discussions on this and other questions.[53]

The conference held on the grounds of the Robert Money School in
Bombay drew a huge attendance of over 3000 delegates. In his hour-long
presidential address, Savarkar touched upon all the themes that plagued
Marathi literature. He emphasized that the countrymen need to abandon
their lethargy and instead spur to action. Philosophical and intellectual
debates were important, he said, but so much time was wasted in merely
talking that 'we have become feeble in practice, we have lost our kingdoms
time after time. We have succumbed to foreign aggressors'.[54] He elaborated
on his favourite themes of script reforms and language purification, despite
several well-wishers advising him to steer clear of these contentious issues.
He mooted a Maharashtra Committee for the reform of the Devanagari
script that would have branches in every town and village. They should keep
a record of people who use the new script and also propagate the message
through schools, newspapers and various institutions. These reforms in
the script would make the Devanagari more effective and cheaper to print.

He criticized the suggestion of the Congress president Subhas Chandra Bose that the Roman script be made the national script of India as 'slavish mentality'.[55] He also suggested a similar Maharashtra Bhashashuddhi Mandal for language purification. The existing set of Marathi words that he had coined as a replacement for Urdu words in vogue needed to be expanded and organized. English words too that had crept into Marathi parlance needed to be resurrected. The Mandal could be tasked with the work of publishing extensive dictionaries of words and also go around people's houses to make them vow that they would not use the older words. The Arya Samaj had done similar work for the Hindi language and it was time that Marathi too stood up to be counted. He spoke of an ambitious All-India Bhasha Shuddhi Conference where Indian languages could come together to reclaim their vocabularies. Simultaneously, keeping in view the need of the times, scientific terminologies in Indian languages for subjects such as physics, chemistry, biology, astronomy and mathematics needed to be taken up on war footing. He suggested that across India if scholars sat together and put their minds to it, in about three to four years this could be achieved through an action-oriented plan. He floated the idea of a national university that looked at translations of literary works between Indian languages and also English. A Maharashtra University was also envisaged that would work towards issues of social importance such as compulsory primary education for all, imparting of moral values and so on. 'The University,' he postulated, 'we need is a modern, up-to-date one on the lines of those in America and Europe. But it must be for practical subjects. This is not the time for Philosophy, Logic, Social Sciences, but for subjects such as Chemistry, Radiology, Ballistics and Military Engineering.' His constant theme was on taking action and not merely talking about it in conference after conference. 'Let us stop' he said, 'passing five hundred resolutions, making five hundred futile discussions, five hundred wishful thinking each year. Let us be practical and concentrate on limited objectives and direct all our energy on them.'[56]

But the main punch of his speech that caught the attention of everyone and created a huge stir in the Marathi literary circles was reserved for the end:

The absence of poetry and poets, novels and novelists would not be felt during the coming decade. Austria and China suffered not because they lacked good literature, but because they lacked military power. Did you not hear, O! Learned men and scholars, the last pathetic shriek of the President of Austria? He said, 'We yield under German bayonets' and not under German sonnets! If literature is part of the national life, its primary aim ought to be the security of national life. I absolutely admire the advocates of the principle of 'Art for Art's sake.' But when a theatre is ablaze it is the duty of the true worshipper of Art to rush out to extinguish the gathering flames. What worth is literature then if a whole nation is writhing with pain under the oppressor's heel? . . . Did you forget the fate of Nalanda and Takshashila, the seats of learning, and other great libraries that were turned into smouldering ruins? . . . it was the triumphant sword of Shivaji that made Maharashtra safe for poets and philosophers. I say therefore with all the emphasis at my command that the crying need of our times is not men of letters, but soldiers. It does not matter even if the whole decade is barren in respect of literature. Let there not be a song sung, or a sonnet composed. But let the streets resound with the thud of the feet of thousands of soldiers marching with modern rifles on their shoulders . . . so my message to you, literary men, is that you should abandon your pens in favour of guns; for literature can never flourish in a slave country. It has been well said that the pursuit of sciences is possible only in a free nation protected by the power of arms.[57]

One can only imagine what the howlers of reactions would have been when the president of a literary conference advises a delegation of litterateurs to 'break your pens and hold guns instead' since literature is subservient to national interests! The issue was a constant feature in newspapers and debates for several months. But Savarkar had made his point loud and clear.

~

Around this time, Savarkar built a house of his own at Bombay's Dadar area, near the famous Shivaji Park through money loaned by his younger brother Dr Narayanrao Savarkar. It was named 'Savarkar Sadan' and the brothers began living there from June 1938—Savarkar on the first floor, Babarao and Narayanrao on the ground floor. Later, Jamnadas Mehta got him a car that he used for a year and then sold it off during the time of the Second World War.

Savarkar continued with his whirlwind tours across India. On 3 May 1938, he embarked upon a journey to Punjab, which was ruled by Sir Sikandar

Hayat Khan, an old friend and colleague from the Abhinav Bharat days. Hayat Khan promised to aid his old comrade in any way he can including supplying his own personal elephant for a public procession! Hayat Khan could not meet Savarkar officially, both due to his now elevated political status and the fierce sentiments against Savarkar that the Congress held. But according to an article in the English daily from Delhi, *Organiser*, he met his old friend disguised as a postman.[58] In this trip, Savarkar visited Lahore, Amritsar, Hoshiarpur and Ajmer. Everywhere he spoke, he talked about the need for Hindu unity, for the Hindu youth to take military training and join the British forces so that they could defect and oppose from within. Garlanding a statue of Lala Lajpat Rai and visiting the historic Shahid Ganj of the Sikhs, he addressed several press conferences. He took pains to clarify that he and Jinnah of the Muslim League were not birds of the same feather because while he stood for equality and no concessions, Jinnah favoured more and more concessions. He opined that there should either be joint electorates without any reservation of seats for any community in any legislative body, or there must be joint electorates with seats reserved for minorities on the basis of population weightages that applied equally to all minorities. The *Tribune* reported his Lahore visit:

> As a matter of fact Mr. Savarkar's anchor as a sincere and true nationalist holds as ever. The several speeches made by him during the last three days, show unmistakably both the general soundness of his political views and the fervor and intensity of his love of country and freedom. His conception of a modern nation and an ideal state is that of a nation and state in which no difference is made between one person and another on the score of community, religion or caste. Holding this view, and this is undoubtedly the only correct view, it is only right that he should want the Congress, which is India's supreme national organization, not to recognize religion, class and community and stand for the equal rights of all citizens.[59]

In a public speech at Amritsar, Savarkar said:

> The more you hanker after the Hindu-Muslim unity, the further it runs away from you. Plainly speaking, there does not exist any minority problem worth the name. The Parsis, the Jews and the Christians inhabiting this land never claimed special rights and they have declared more than once that they do not want separate electorates.[60]

Towards the end of the month, he visited Gwalior and in August 1938, he visited Sindh, where he was given a massive reception in Karachi that took five hours to wind its way. The Sindh Hindu Conference was held in Sukkar with Savarkar presiding it where he exhorted the Hindus to unite against the Congress's appeasement follies. Even the *Sind Observer*, a newspaper of Congress persuasion, declared: 'He came, he saw, he conquered.'[61]

Around this time news began trickling in of Savarkar's former comrade during the revolutionary times, Virendranath Chattopadhyay, being arrested in the Soviet Union by the Stalin administration. His name appeared in the list of 184 prisoners who were to be executed. Savarkar wrote letters to all the Congress ministries in various provinces urging them to put pressure on the viceroy to aid Chattopadhyay in these tough times:

> You have attained these Ministries today only because of the sweat, toil and sacrifice of the armed revolutionaries who have been fighting relentlessly for the cause of India's freedom for several decades now, across continents. It is now your responsibility to raise your voice to save them when they are in dire conditions.[62]

His colleague M.S. Aney also raised questions in the legislature about the condition of Indian revolutionaries abroad, particularly Chattopadhyay. But none of this led to anything tangible. Unfortunately, Chattopadhyay was eventually executed by the Soviet Union.

The following year, Lala Hardayal died in Philadelphia on 5 April. The news of his death was largely ignored by Indian newspapers. Savarkar wrote a scathing editorial in *Vividhvrutt* about the media's apathy towards Lalaji's death.

> We heard about Lalaji's death in a two-line telegram sent by Reuters. Indian newspapers carry detailed bulletins if Jawahar has influenza, if Gandhi's Blood Pressure fluctuates, newspapers report about his pulse rate and where Dr. Gilder has kept the thermometer like sacrosanct stories from the *Mahabharat* or *Illiad*. But the news of Lala Hardayal's death is disposed off in two lines—because Lalaji did not fast, Lalaji did not live on grapes and oranges, Lalaji did not lean on the shoulders of young girls and Lalaji did not ingratiate himself to the British, so why would the newspapers be concerned about him?[63]

Earlier, Shyamji Krishna Varma had died in 1930; Madame Bhikaji Cama who was in exile in Europe till 1935 had suffered a stroke and died in 1936. With Chattopadhyay's execution, an entire era of the early Indian revolutionaries who had staked their lives for their nation by their struggle abroad came to an end.

Bhagnagar (Hyderabad), 1938

Since the beginning of the year, news of communal trouble brewing in the Nizam's state of Hyderabad (or Bhagnagar) kept making its way to newspapers of the time. On 3 March 1938, the *Marathwada*, a Marathi weekly from Poona, flagged this simmering issue first:

> The Hindu Standing Committee in its memorandum has made a clear assertion that 'the recent whirlwind propaganda of proselytization, carried out by a powerful Muslim organization with its headquarters in the capital of Hyderabad, in a sympathetic atmosphere of Muslim officials and Government servants all over the State specially in the Revenue, Judicial and Police Departments, has created a strong sense of suspicion and insecurity of life and property in the mind of Hindus.' No reply at all to the said assertion is given in the memorial submitted by the Muslims as an answer to the Hindu Standing Committee's said memorandum. It was necessary that the Hyderabad Government should have given an answer to the said charge; but it is not as yet anywhere published that the Government has issued a reply to it. The Hyderabad Government has now a well-managed Information Bureau through which many dubious or wrong assertions are even corrected now and then. It is a matter for surprise that why then there should not have been issued a Government Press Note in respect of such a serious charge made by the Hyderabad Hindu Standing Committee. The misunderstandings, if any, entertained by the public are likely to become more firm-rooted by not issuing such an authentic statement [by the government]. Nay, if the Government remains silent without giving a reply to the assertion made about it, it is very much probable that the meaning of this attitude will be even taken as its [government's] 'half-consent'. As we do not consider that this charge made by the Hindu Standing Committee is admitted by the Government, it is necessary that it [government] should issue a statement in this regard . . . we, on our part, cannot even imagine that the Hindu

society in Hyderabad trespasses upon the rights of the followers of other religions. This helpless Hindu society, instead of retaliating injustice, is found to be copying the lesson of suffering silently. The only exception to this thing is that at some places owing to the propaganda carried on by Aryasamajists this wicked tendency to suffer injustice appears to have been disappearing and that the tendency to offer resistance to it is being gradually strengthened. It is also seen that these incidents are happening in a greater proportion in those very parts of the State i.e. the districts of Bidar and Osmanabad.[64]

Hyderabad posed a peculiar communal challenge. Ruled by Nizam Sir Osman Ali Khan, the seventh descendant of the Asifjahi dynasty, it was a Hindu-majority state, with Hindus comprising nearly 85 per cent of its population. Quite under the influence of pan-Islamic idealism, it is said that the Nizam even 'entertained an idea of becoming the Khalipha of the whole Muslim world'.[65] His executive council made of seven members had just one Hindu. The administration was deeply personalized with the Nizam's writ running over all matters of state and he being viewed as the fountainhead of all state authority. The legislative council was hardly representative; the subjects of the state did not even enjoy the privilege of managing their own municipal affairs. No criticism of state authority, the ruler or the mechanisms to elicit public opinion was encouraged, and the ruler had absolutely no accountability towards anyone. The British maintained a position of coy neutrality and as long as the Nizam was ready to follow the advice of the British Resident, they were on amicable terms with him. In that sense the state was almost akin to a British protectorate. As long as the Nizam did not interfere in the policies and prestige of the British government all over India, they gave him all the freedom to manage his administration in the way that he wished. All posts and positions of eminence in the bureaucracy and landed gentry was handed over by the Nizam only to his co-religionists.

When Osman Ali became the ruler, the prime minister was a Hindu, Sir Kishan Prashad. But in 1912 he was forced to resign and Nawab Salarjung III was appointed as the new prime minister. The Hindus were also disenfranchised from the civil services. In 1885, whilst there were 4949 Hindus and 2882 Muslims in the civil list, by 1920 the numbers flipped to 2393 Hindus against 5174 Muslims.[66] Positions were kept vacant till qualified Muslim candidates applied, most recruits coming in as immigrants to the state from the Aligarh Muslim University. In all departments of administration, law and order, education, military and judiciary the extraordinarily high proportion of Muslims, even if they were not Hyderabad natives, was alarming. Cultural subjugation was an important component of this hegemonic, communal administration. Even though Urdu was the mother tongue of merely 10 per cent of the population and more than 86 per cent of the state not even understanding the language, Urdu was made the official language of the state and the courts, even as the vernacular Telugu remained unfavoured. Though the budgetary outlay on education increased under Osman Ali with the founding the Osmania University in 1918, the literary levels among Hindus plummeted. Only 2.6 per cent of the majority community of the Hindus was literate, as against 8.9 per cent of the Muslims and the government made little efforts to correct such imbalances.[67] Active efforts for conversions and religious subjugation was undertaken and encouraged through state departments like the Ecclesiastical Department. Bans on religious discourses and meetings of the Hindus was carried out with impunity. Hindu religious festivals were to be strictly observed only in the confines of one's home and never in public. Music or processions were not allowed. Permissions were seldom granted to build new temples or repairs of existing ones. A note of the Ecclesiastical Department stated this in no uncertain terms:

> The public are hereby informed that everywhere, whether in Hyderabad City or outside it, or in the Nizam Dominions, where the population of the followers of Islam is considerable, the existing old temples and Maths should not be extended or improved, and should remain in the condition as in the past.[68]

Ruffians were often encouraged by the state to harass the Hindu community or molest its women, with no one being held accountable.[69] Large-scale riots in Hyderabad in January 1938 that were allegedly fanned by state actors seemed the last nail in the coffin.

Slowly, the Hindu population began to wake up to the tyranny and hegemony under which they were being placed. Still in the absence of any press or platforms of protests or even mild criticism, their hands were severely tied. Organizations such as the Arya Samaj and the Hyderabad Hindu Subjects League slowly began to work against the enormous tide.

The latter comprised more of Maharashtrians and held their conference in
Partud in 1937. They passed resolutions urging the new prime minister,
Sir Akbar Hyderi, to redress the grievances of the Hindu community.
None of these met with any success.

These groups naturally then turned towards the Hindu Mahasabha with
entreaties to support their just agitation for civil rights. The Mahasabha
decided to send a delegation to meet the Nizam's government and relate
the grievances of the Hindus of the state. But the government refused to
even grant an audience to any such delegation. Bhai Parmanand managed
to meet Akbar Hyderi in a personal capacity but the latter disparaged and
rejected all the charges against the Nizam's government as being motivated.

Several refugees of the January 1938 riots met Savarkar and urged
him and the Hindu Mahasabha to represent their cause and help them.
He assured them that he would do all that was in his power to redress
their grievances. The Maharashtra Provincial Hindu Sabha sent an
inquiry committee consisting of S.R. Date, V.S. Modak and G.R. Kale to
investigate the riots and also the grievances of the Hindus. They toured the
length and breadth of the Hyderabad state and met a vast cross section of
people—pleaders, teachers, bankers, merchants, traders, zamindars, priests
and others. The report was a comprehensive one that laid bare the pitiable
misery that the Hindus of the state suffered under the despotic Nizam. It
stirred the conscience of several leaders across India. Senapati Bapat was
one of them. He announced an ultimatum to the Nizam's government to
cease its tyranny and grant civil liberties, failing which he would launch a
massive Civil Disobedience movement. He knew that it was futile to even
wait for the Nizam government's response and without wasting much time
indicated the launch of the Civil Disobedience movement on 23 September
1938. Supporting this decision, Savarkar wrote:

> Every patriot cannot but acclaim the lead that Senapati Bapat has given
> in starting the Civil Disobedience Movement with regard to the fanatical
> and oppressive orders of the Nizam. Soldiers of civil liberty all over
> India and especially in Maharashtra, it is for you now to follow up his
> heroic lead irrespective of party considerations and continue the Civil
> Disobedience Movement without letting it lag even for a moment. I
> request the Nizam Government once more to see the wisdom of giving
> up religious persecution and the intolerable communal oppression to
> which the Hindus in the State have been subjected to for years in the

past, and to restore the fundamental rights of citizenship to all alike irrespective of caste or creed. I hope even against hope that this request is granted forthwith and the Nizam receives Senapati as a friend instead of as a foe.[70]

Issuing a statement to the press about his intentions and also the need for the movement, Bapat reached Hyderabad on 24 September. But he was immediately taken into custody by the Nizam's government and moved to the Lingapalli Jail and thereafter sent back to Poona. Bapat issued another statement that he and his supporters would regroup and launch the movement again on 1 November. But the movement from within the state too was gaining momentum and was led by a young leader Yashwantrao Joshi, without expectations of immediate responses from the government. Joshi had met Savarkar in Poona and was assured of full support. When the group was denied the rights to take out a procession in memory of their leader Wamanrao Naik, they decide to break the law, despite vehement opposition from the state Congress that asked Joshi to adhere to the rules laid down. To avoid conflicts with the state Congress that he was loosely associated with, Joshi formed a separate association named Nagarik Hindu Swatantrya Sangha (Hindu Civil Liberties Union). They chose 21 October 1938 as the date for breaking the prohibition against the meeting and procession and decided to commemorate the memory of Wamanrao Naik from the Rama Mandir in Gauliguda in Hyderabad. After delivering a fiery speech where he laid threadbare the facts of the manner in which the government obfuscated details to deny Hindus their basic civil rights, he led a group of over 3000 people in a procession. The police officers asked them to disperse but when they refused, the police resorted to forceful eviction, which the protestors bore with equanimity. Mass arrest was effected, including that of prominent leaders of the Union—Yashwantrao Joshi, Dattatreya Rao Jukkulkar, Sadashiv Dusange, Narahari and Satyanarayan. They were produced before a magistrate on 26 October and tried and sentenced with fines under various sections of the law.

But the movement had caught up with a definite momentum. Several batches of young Hindu men came forward fearlessly in an unprecedented manner, offered civil resistance and broke the law by taking out processions or reading banned newspapers. Severe police atrocities were unleashed and each day brought in the news of arrests of agitators. The Hyderabad State Congress decided not to be left behind in this moment of public upsurge and jumped into the movement. Meetings were organized at Sholapur, Pandharpur and Dhulia where its members encouraged the formation of Hyderabad Hindu Satyagraha Mandals, Congress Satyagraha Camps and Hyderabad Satyagraha Shibirs.[71] Both the Congress and the Hindu Mahasabha eyed the nineteen seats in the federal legislature, which was certain to be filled only by Muslims if the Nizam had his way.[72] The state Congress thought that their party's influence in British India could help them find a solution to this problem at the earliest. However, the state unit was in for a shock when they received a 'cold and curt reply'.[73] The high command 'admonished the State Congressmen for their audacity in starting the movement at all, and displeasing His Exalted Highness; and then they advised them to sue immediately for peace and forgiveness'.[74] With no other option left, Kashinathrao Vaidya of the state Congress issued a telling statement announcing withdrawal of the party from the movement:

> The Working Committee of the Hyderabad State Congress, after a great deliberation, has decided upon a temporary suspension of satyagraha which was recently launched and which has already resulted in imprisonment of more than four hundred satyagrahis. Sentences range from one month to 3 ½ years . . . the decisive cause for suspension was advice given by Mahatma Gandhi, Pandit Nehru and other Congress leaders that in order to make our position absolutely clear, it was essential that we should suspend civil disobedience. They say that suspension would give the Government of His Exalted Highness the Nizam, an opportunity to review the situation. We could not disregard the advice of the leaders whose sympathy and support was [sic] a valuable asset in the conduct of the struggle for Swaraj within the State . . . we wish to draw the attention of our people that there are two arms to non-violent Swaraj movement, the remedial and the constructive. Civil Disobedience is remedial and therefore in its nature temporary. The other is constructive and permanent . . . the constructive activities include hand-spinning, hand-weaving, and like productive pursuits of activities of promoting heart unity between the Hindus and the Muslims and different communities composing the subjects of H.E.H.[75]

Yet again, even as a civil movement was reaching its peak, the Congress in its characteristic fashion put the brakes on halting it. It was quite foolhardy to assume that the Nizam's government was planning to have a rethink about its repressive policy if the movement was suspended.

Unmindful of the Congress's flip-flop, the Arya Samaj and Hindu Civil Liberties Union carried on with their movement. Savarkar requested the lawyer and president of the Maharashtra Hindu Sabha, L.B. Bhopatkar, to fight the case on behalf of Yashwantrao Joshi and get him released. New waves of the movement under several other leaders like Balayya Sriramulu Naidu, Babu Shyama Desai, Hanmanthrao Mukhed, Keshavrao Deshpande and others kept emerging. Savarkar wrote several letters and articles, and spoke extensively on the need to keep the civil rights movement in Hyderabad going for the cause of the suffering Hindus there. On 15 October 1938, speaking at a regional session of the Nasik and Khandesh District Hindu Mahasabha held in Nandgaon, he articulated that there were three main foes that the Mahasabha had to fight—the British, a united and aggressive Islamist tendency and the Congress and its Muslim appeasement policy.[76] He remonstrated with the arguments put forth by several Muslim leaders, particularly of the Congress, that the movement would breach the harmony between people of the two communities. Resolutions were passed by all the regional Hindu Sabhas of their unalloyed support to the Hyderabad agitation. 'Their conception of a communal harmony,' Savarkar said, 'seems to be borrowed from the argument of a wolf in a sheep's skin who remonstrated with his victim for disturbing the peace and public tranquility of the neighbourhood by raising an untimely hue and cry.'[77] He went on to attack the insinuation of the movement being a communal one:

> We ask what else can it be? Whenever a community is singed out to be tyrannized over by another community, all efforts to defend and liberate the victims must have reference to that singled out community alone, and the struggle cannot but be communal in that aspect. Take the case of removal of untouchability. The untouchables have to undergo, as a community, certain disabilities. The efforts to remove these disabilities must have reference to that community in the main. But does that make the question of removal of untouchability communal in a reprehensible sense of unholiness (sic) or antinational? The same is the case with the movement of the civil resistance started by the Hindu Sangathanists in Hyderabad State. It is a lie to say that civil liberty is denied in the Nizam State to all communities alike. To the Hindus, all civil liberties

of speech, association, worship are denied. It is the Hindus alone who are banned from having any share in the public services or any voice in the administration of the State. The Muslims enjoy all civil liberties with a vengeance, monopolize public services and offices, and control all administration in spite of the fact that not only they but the Hindus contribute almost all the revenues and taxes that replenish the State Treasury. It is the Hindus alone who are threatened with extermination, as a race, religion, and culture. The Hindu Mahasabha, therefore refused to fight under lying colours of a common Hindu-Moslem movement and means to enter the list in defence of their Hindu brethren in the State under an unalloyed Hindu flag. Whether this attitude of the Hindu Mahasabha is called by the tyrants of the pseudo-nationalist Congressites as anti-national or communal or parochial or otherwise, we care a fig for the name.[78]

Charged by his call, several volunteers of the Hindu Mahasabha and other Hindu organizations in Poona, under the banner of the Hindutva Nishtha Nishastra Pratikar Mandal (literally, Hindutva Faith Unarmed Resistance Group) with G.V. Ketkar as its president, made their way to Hyderabad right from November 1938. The team was led by a young and springy man who was the secretary of the Mandal, Nathuram Vinayak Godse. Godse had extensively toured several towns and villages to muster support and gather funds. Most of the teams and their members, including Godse, were arrested and sentenced for months and years upon their entry into Hyderabad.

The fervour of the surcharged times inspired the Hindu students of the Osmania University to put up a massive defence against the attempts to prevent them from singing the national song, 'Vande Mataram' on the campus on the grounds that it was 'offensive to the Muslim sentiment'.[79] The orders of the government and the pro-vice-chancellor were defied by the students who decided to continue to sing the song that they held so dear, even at the cost of being expelled from hostels for committing this 'crime'. More than 800 students joined the 'Vande Mataram struggle'. They were summarily rusticated from the university and had to leave for Nagpur where the vice chancellor of Nagpur University admitted them warmly and assured them of no discontinuance of their study. The reactions to the Nizam government's ban on 'Vande Mataram' spread like wildfire across the state and everyone—from jails to homes, schools and colleges—took to

its singing to defy the despot. Interestingly, the state Congress sided with
the Nizam's decision and admitted that the song 'should not be sung in
the public if opposed by anybody'.[80] Seeing the mass movement that it was
snowballing into, the Nizam caved in and rescinded the ban on the song.

Issuing a statement to the press on 25 November 1938, Savarkar
condemned the despotism of the Nizam. He equally took to task the
Congress for its appeasement that prevented it from coming out openly
in support of civil rights. He taunted them about how they had 'shed
so many tears in sympathy with the harassed Arabs in Palestine, the
Abyssinians, the Czechs, and almost every body in the world, but . . . they
could hardly spare a single tear . . . over the bloodshed and persecution of
thousands of Hindus in Hyderabad or Bhopal State, even in the name of
the so-called "National" civil liberty!'[81] While it had raised concerns over
alleged persecution of subjects in Hindu princely states such as Mysore,
Travancore, Kashmir, Rajkot, etc., it had kept a studied silence when it
came to Muslim princely states such as Hyderabad or Bhopal. He warned
that the movement would be made into a national one after the annual
session of the Hindu Mahasabha if the Nizam's government did not
see reason soon. Even Aurangzeb could not face the united attack from
Maratha forces, he warned. As always, these threats and appeals fell on
deaf ears when it came to the Hyderabad administration.

Hindu Pratikar Mandal branches came up across several places—
Dadar, Nasik, Barshi, Pandharpur, Sholapur, Chalisgaon, Dhulia, Akola,
Nagpur and so on. Massive information propaganda through the national
press to let citizens across the country know the pitiable state of the Hindus
in Hyderabad was also launched. The agitation simmered on relentlessly.

Savarkar attended the All-India Aryan Congress called by the Arya
Samaj at Sholapur from 25 to 28 December 1938 under the presidentship
of M.S. Aney, member of the Central Legislative Assembly. The agenda
was specifically to launch a mass civil resistance movement in Hyderabad.

~

Meanwhile, amidst the Bhagnagar struggle, the annual session of the
Hindu Mahasabha came up from 28 to 30 December. It had no parallel
in the annals of the Mahasabha with more than 50,000 delegates who had
gone there specifically with the agenda of civil rights of the Hindus in
the Nizam state.[82] Presiding over the twentieth session held in Nagpur

in December 1938, Savarkar obviously had the Hyderabad agitation on the back of his mind and made fervent calls to resurrect Hindudom from the 'sepulchre' into which the Hindu Rashtra found itself buried. He criticized the British for denying the due rights of the Hindus who formed the majority of the country by not following the principle of legislative representation in proportion of the population strength. They had also broken up the Hindu society into so many watertight compartments. Discriminatory laws such as the Land Alienation Act in Punjab and divisive laws in Bengal that reserved 60 per cent of government jobs for Muslims were seen as the pernicious agenda of the British. The denial of civil rights to Hindu citizens in Muslim-ruled states such as Hyderabad and Bhopal where riots against Hindus of the kind witnessed in Malabar or Kohat went unnoticed was a further act of belittling Hindu concerns, he said. Equally reprehensible for him was 'the Pseudo-Nationalism of the Congressites'[83] who condoned such acts or rationalized it as being driven, not by any anti-Hindu sentiment, but economic reasons. He criticized the Congress for offering blank cheques to the Muslims, but giving ultimatums to the Hindus with the diktat: 'Get looted, but don't report; get stabbed, but don't shriek; get repressed as Hindus but don't organize to resist it as Hindus; or else you will be damned as traitors to the cause of our Indian nationalism.'[84] In such a scenario if a body like the Hindu Mahasabha raised the legitimate concerns and issues facing the majority community of this country who had been short-changed by everyone else—the British and the Congress—why should it be dubbed as communal, he sought to know. He harked back on his favourite theme of history to deduce that for 5000 years the ancestors of Hindus were always shaping the formation of the people into a religious, racial, cultural and political unit. This nation was not a 'mushroom growth' and barring China, few others could claim such unbroken civilizational continuity. Of course, like any other nation would, this Hindu nation too had its sects and sections, its differences and dissimilarities, yet welded together by that spirit of nationhood.

He blamed the British squarely for undermining the solidarity and strength of the Hindu nation through several means, including using the Muslims as handy pawns. Through English education they had themselves admitted to opening the doors to conversion to Christianity for several young Hindus by creating a disdain for his own native culture and religion. This new generation of English-educated Hindus was slowly distanced from their moorings and blindly admired anything that was

Western. They even borrowed the concept of nationhood from the West
as a territorial unit where one inhabits. They argued that all people in
India—Hindus, Muslims, Christians, Parsis and others had inhabited
this territorial unit called India for centuries and hence they must be a
nation by themselves. The corollary was also true—if we were all to be
called Indians, we cease to be Hindus, Muslims, Christians and Parsis.
Hence, they were the first ones to disown their Hindu-ness, though none
of the other communities, especially the Muslims, followed similar suit, he
postulated. This disappearance of Hindu consciousness greatly favoured
the British who had been wary of a Hindu resurgence right from 1857
to the armed conflicts of men such as Vasudev Balwant Phadke. They
ensured that the Muslim community did not catch the 'contagion of this
new Indian nationalist cult' because if that happened and the Hindus and
Muslims united as a nation, their interests as the colonial rulers would be
immensely impacted. The nightmares of 1857 where this briefly occurred
haunted them. Hence through appeasements and encouraging fanatic and
hateful tendencies among the Muslims, they kept this unity at bay.

The more insistent the Congress became in calling upon all Indians to
merge their racial and religious individuality into an Indian nation defined
by territorial unity, the more distrustful and enraged the Muslims felt,
according to Savarkar.[85] He also made no bones of praising the benefits
that Hindus reaped through their association with the Congress. He felt
that, quite inconsequentially, it had contributed to the consolidation of
Hindudom by rubbing away provincial, linguistic and sectional angularities,
given them a common national platform and animated them with the
consciousness of a common national being with the goal of a united central
state. But he hastened to add that just as the benefits that Hindus had
received through English education or contact with the West was despite
the evil British rule, so also this outcome was in spite of the Congress's
attempts to suppress and undermine Hindu consciousness itself altogether.
These 'territorial patriots,' he explained, 'wanted us to cease to be Hindus
at least as a national and political unit. Some of them actually gloried in
disowning themselves as Hindus at all! They were merely Indians, thinking
that they had set a very patriotic example in that which they fancied would
persuade the Moslems too to renounce their communal being and also
merge themselves in that territorial Indian Nation beyond recognition.'[86]
But such an expectation was fanciful according to him. Having largely sat
on the fence and staying away from freedom struggle, the Muslims, in his

opinion, jumped to gather their pound of flesh only after all the struggle and efforts by others had forced the British to climb down and begin granting concessions. Things had come to such a pass now that a separate non-Hindu state for the Muslims was being discussed, and this only went to show the thoughtless beliefs of the Hindu patriots of welding everyone on to a common nationhood through the bond of territorial unity that had eminently proved itself to be futile. The root cause of this failure was the Congress's failure to understand that in the formation of a nation state, religious, racial, cultural and historical affinities count more than mere territorial unity or a common habitat. He quoted examples from England, Austria-Hungary, Ireland, Spain, Germany to buttress his argument of this being a natural human trait and not a political one. The Congress blindfolded itself to the communal tendencies of the Muslim community in the false hope that they would eventually come around through the former's goodwill and generosity. But that was not to be.

Diagnosing this alleged antipathy of the Muslims, he elaborated:

The Moslems in general and Indian Moslems in particular have not as yet grown out of the historical stage, of intense religiosity and the theological concept of state. Their theology and theocratical [sic] politics divide the human world into two groups only—The Moslem land and the enemy land. All lands which are either entirely inhabited by the Moslems or are ruled over by the Moslems are Moslem lands. All lands, which are mostly inhabited by non-Moslem power are enemy lands and no faithful Moslem is allowed to bear any loyalty to them and is called upon to do everything in his power by policy or force or fraud to convert the non-Moslem there to Moslem faith, to bring about its political conquest by a Moslem power. It is no good quoting sentences here or there from Moslem theological books to prove the contrary. Read the whole book to know its trend. And again it is not with books that we are concerned here but with the followers of the book and how they translate them in practice. You will then see that the whole Moslem history and their daily actions are framed on the design I have outlined above. Consequently, a territorial patriotism is a word unknown to the Moslem—nay is tabooed, unless in connection with a Moslem territory. Afghans can be patriots for Afghanisthan is a Moslem territory today. But an Indian Moslem if he is a real Moslem—and they are intensely religious as a people—cannot faithfully bear loyalty to India as a country, as a nation, as a State, because it is today 'an Enemy Land' and doubly lost; for non-Moslems are in a majority here and to boot it is not ruled by any Moslem power, Moslem sovereign. Add to this that of all non-Moslems the Hindus are looked upon as the most damned by Moslem theologians. For Christians and Jews are after all 'Kitabis', having the holy books partially in common. But the Hindus are totally 'Kafirs' as a consequence their land 'Hindustan' is pre-eminently an 'enemy' and as long as it is not ruled by Moslems or all Hindus do not embrace Islam . . . What wonder then that the Muslim League should openly declare its intention to join hands with non-Indian alien Moslem countries rather than with Indian Hindus in forming a Moslem Federation? They could not be accused from their point of view of being traitors to Hindusthan. Their conscience was clear. They never looked upon our today's 'Hindusthan' as their country, nation. It is to them already an alien land, and enemy land—'a Dar-ul-Harb' and not a 'Dar-ul-Islam!!'[87]

He called upon Hindus to consider themselves as a nation because religious, racial, cultural and historical affinities bind them into a nation, in addition to the gift of territorial unity. Just as the Germans were the nation in Germany and the Jews a community, Savarkar averred that the Hindus were the nation in India and the Muslims a community within it. Elaborating on the accusation made on the Hindu Mahasabha of being a communal organization and a mirror image of the Muslim League, he said:

The fact is that Nationalism and Communalism are in themselves either equally justifiable and humane or not. Nationalism when it is aggressive is as immoral in human relation as is Communalism when it tries to suppress the equitable rights of other communities and tries to usurp all to itself. But when Communalism is only defensive, it is as justifiable and humane as an equitable Nationalism itself. The Hindu nationalists do not aim to usurp what belongs to others. Therefore, even if they be called Hindu communalists they are justifiably so and are about the only real Indian Nationalist. For, a real and justifiable Indian Nationalism must be equitable to all communities that compose the Indian Nation. But for the same reason the Moslems alone are communalists in an unjustifiable, anti-national and treacherous sense of the term. For it is they who want to usurp to themselves all that belongs to others. The Indian National Congress only condemns itself as an anti-national body when it calls in

the same breath the Hindu Mahasabha and the Muslim League as bodies
equally communal in the reprehensible or treacherous sense of that term.
Consequently if to defend the just and equitable rights of Hindus in their
own land is communalism then we are communalists par excellence and
glory in being the most devoted Hindu communalists which to us means
being the truest and the most equitable Indian Nationalists![88]

This assertion of equal rights for Hindus, he prescribed, must be led from
the most local issues to the more important ones of the Indian federation
and its foreign policy. The foreign policy needed to be guided purely by
the interests of the nation: oppose anyone who opposes the interest of
this Hindu nation; ally with anyone who is friendly to it; be neutral to
those who do neither. He called for eschewing merely academic political
ideologies or 'empty slogans of democracy or Nazism or Fascism' as the
guiding light for such an international policy. If a nation that had similar
ideology but was opposed to your interest, it made no sense to ally with it.
Hence national interest was the only paramount. Taking a dig at the earlier
Congress policies, he said: 'No more Khilafats or Palestine-afats can dupe
us into suicidal sympathies and complications. Our relations with England
also will be guided by the same Hindu policy, having the absolute political
independence of the Hindu Nation in view.'[89]

He reiterated the declaration of the Karnavati session of how this
Hindu Nation did not wish to trample the legitimate rights of any
community. It did not seek any 'preferential treatment and special
prerogatives' for the majority on sheer virtue of their enhanced numbers.
In the same breath it also abhorred 'preferential treatment, weightages
and special favours over and above what the major community obtains' to
any minority groups.[90] A true sense of democracy was what was needed
of 'One Man, One Vote' and no enhanced weightage to a citizen's vote
based on his/her religion. He exhorted the Muslim community to see
reason and the benefit of such an equitable and amicable resolution and
join hands in future nation building. If it did not, he had his favourite
formula handy: 'If you come, with you; if you don't, without you; but if
you oppose, in spite of you, we Hindus will fight out the good battle of
achieving the independence of India and herald the rebirth of a free and
mighty Hindu nation in the near future!'[91] About the minority policy in
particular he said: 'The Hindus will assure them all that we hate none,
neither the Moslem nor the Christians nor the Indian Europeans, but

henceforth we shall take care to see that none of them dares to hate or belittle the Hindus also.'[92] He exonerated the Christian community from any extraterritorial political designs and as one that is amenable to political assimilation. The only guard that he wanted the Hindu nation to keep was against attempts to proselytize by the church and political designs in the Travancore state.

His prescription to the Hindu sangathan movement to achieve these objectives was to capture political power in municipalities, boards and legislatures to successfully implement this agenda. He hastened to add that though the Congress being made what it is by the Hindus had forgotten its commitment towards them, his intention was not to spite the Congress institution itself or its leaders but to fight the mindset, hypocrisy and appeasement. In his characteristic sarcasm, he took a dig at the Congress remembering Hindus and their votes only during elections:

> Next election when they come to your Hindu doors to beg for votes tell them in all honesty and humility 'Sirs Congressmen you are Indian Nationalists; but I am a Hindu and this is a Hindu Electorate? Then how can you accept a vote so tainted by communalism? Please go to a truly "Indian Nationalist electorate", to beg for votes wherever you may find it; and if you find it nowhere in the world today please wait till a pure and simple and truly "Indian electorate", comes into being!' Do you think you will find a dozen Congress candidates honest enough to do so? None, none![93]

He pointed out the dichotomy in the Congress approach where they eschew their Hindu identity but during elections not only appeal to the same sentiment, but also stoke caste pride and identity. Candidates too are set up in an attempt to woo particular caste combinations and arithmetic, making them 'the worst communalists' during election time. But after winning the polls, they don the robes of Indian nationalism and hit back at the very Hindus who have voted them to power and feel ashamed of calling themselves Hindu. Unless a politically relevant constituency was created, the Congress would not sit up to take notice. Hence, he called for a boycott of Congress or its ticket and to vote only for an avowed Hindu nationalist. He called for a grand union of all groups and parties that spoke for the larger Hindu cause and also of an alliance with the Sikhs in Punjab and with Ambedkar in Maharashtra. Allying with every shade of political opinion with the simple prerequisite of protection of legitimate Hindu rights was his simple formula for the Mahasabha.

The Congress's garnering of the Hindu votes and its taking on the mantle of being their voice rattled many in the Hindu Mahasabha who viewed themselves as the prime representatives of Hindu interests. Conscious of this, Savarkar added:

> Let no Hindu Sangathanist pay a single farthing or lend a single member or register a single vote for the Congress ticket. We know by experience that even a staunch Hindu has to act against Hindu interests as soon as he is tainted by a Congress ticket under the Congress discipline and for the selfish fear that he would lose his job . . . It is worst on the part of a Congressite who got himself elected on Hindu votes, it is downright treachery![94]

A resolution was passed specifically on carrying on a massive fight in Hyderabad and this was vehemently supported by all the attendees. Several youngsters enlisted their names as volunteers in the open session and thousands of rupees came pouring in as voluntary donations. Amidst loud cheers the following resolution was adopted:

a) In view of the fact that the Hindus in the Hyderabad State are not enjoying religious liberty and other civic, cultural and political rights and that the Government of H.E.H. the Nizam has taken no steps to concede the legitimate demands of the Hindus and has thereby compelled the Hindus, in and outside Hyderabad, to resort to civil resistance, this Sabha records its full support to the civil resistance movement started against the Nizam's government and calls upon all Hindus to continue it vigorously and actively until all the rights are conceded to the Hindus in accordance with their numerical strength in the State.

b) The Mahasabha censures the attitude of the Congress authorities in weakening the movements by advising the State Congress to suspend the movement and out of fear of Muslim opposition and thus once again betraying the fundamental rights of the Hindus.

c) That a Committee should be appointed by the Working Committee to consider the ways and means of this active civil resistance movement.[95]

Immediately after the Nagpur session, the Hindu Mahasabha Working Committee got to action. A pan-India committee was constituted to strategize the ways and means to conduct the civil resistance in Hyderabad. It consisted of Gokulchand Narang (Lahore), Bhai Parmanand (Lahore), Indra Prakash (Delhi), Chandakiran Sarda (Ajmer), Anandpriya (Baroda), Patwari (Ahmedabad), L.B. Bhopatkar (Poona), G.V. Ketkar (Poona), G.M. Nalvade (Poona), Padmaraj Jain (Calcutta), Talapade (Bombay), L.R. Tairsee (Bombay), B.S. Moonje (Nagpur), Mamarao Joglekar (Akola) and Masurkar Maharaj (Satara). The Hindu Pratikar Mandal merged itself into the Mahasabha. The resolutions passed at the Nagpur session and the Sholapur conference were sent from the office of Savarkar in his capacity as the president of the All-India Hindu Mahasabha to the prime minister of Hyderabad Sir Akbar Hyderi on 11 January 1939:

I take the liberty to assure you and through you, H.E.H. the Nizam, that the Hindu Mahasabha has no ulterior motives against the Nizam or the Nizam State or against the Muslims as a community in this movement. The Mahasabha does not aim and has no grudge against any equitable treatment being dealt with the Muslims in the State, nay, its very standpoint is that all subjects including the Muslims be equitably treated and should enjoy freedom of association, freedom of speech, freedom of worship, and should be represented in the Legislatures and the Public Services according to the strength of their population or if that suits the Nizam Government, even on merit alone without any distinction of caste or creed. Nothing could be more just or national and non-communal than this attitude taken up by the Mahasabha.

Fervently, I therefore appeal to you to cast all administration of the Nizam State in consonance with the above just and equitable principle and policy, and remove all inequitable laws, rules and regulations under which the Hindus are being systematically, and in cases even fanatically oppressed and restore to them all civic, religious and political rights which such a non-communal and just policy, as indicated above, involves.

The Hindu Mahasabha genuinely wishes to arrive at a peaceful settlement of this question. Therefore, I request you to grant all the religious and civic demands detailed out in the enclosed copy of the resolution passed at the Aryasamajists' Conference at Sholapur, usher in immediately political reforms, introduce a Legislature and grant a free representation to the Hindus in it, and the Public Services as well in proportion to their population. But if even this appeal fails to persuade H.E.H. the Nizam to concede all these demands immediately, then the Hindu Mahasabha having exhausted all constitutional means, will have no other course left but to continue the civil resistance movement which has already been launched in the Nizam State on a mass scale, and not to call it off, whatever the cost, till the demands as enumerated in the resolution of the Hindu Mahasabha and the Aryasamajists are fully conceded.[96]

In a nonchalant reply, dated 15 March 1939, Akbar Hyderi kept mum on the grievances that the Hindus faced and blamed the Hindu Mahasabha for supporting the civil resistance movement in the state. He however gave a casual assurance of introducing in a few months' time, some reforms that would address any legitimate grievances of any community, not necessarily Hindu alone.

In his counter-reply on 15 March 1939, Savarkar urged the Nizam state to promulgate these reforms as quickly as possible so that the Hindu Mahasabha could evaluate whether they met the legitimate demands of the Hindus of the state. Only if these reforms substantially guaranteed the fundamental civic rights of the Hindus, gave them constitutional representation on some equitable basis and assured them of equality of treatment sans humiliation or persecution would the Mahasabha and Arya Samaj back out, he laid out. He also emphasized that often it was not the laws alone, but their implementation and right intent, which also needs to be put in place. He hence urged Akbar Hyderi to put pressure on the officials to administer these equitable laws to all citizens without communal considerations.

Even as these diplomatic communications were going on between Savarkar and Akbar Hyderi, the civil resistance movement on the ground kept gathering momentum. The twenty-first day of every month was observed as civil resistance day not only in Hyderabad but also all over Maharashtra. The Congress on its part kept trying to discourage and wean away volunteers by spreading ill will and rumours and also dissuaded the Arya Samaj from participation. These intentions were revealed in an article written by a Congressman named Damodardas in the *Sanjeevani* newspaper dated 16 March 1939.

If the Arya Samaj movement stops, the Hindu Mahasabha will have no other alternative than an enforced inanition . . . considering their (Arya Samaj) talks with us, most of us hoped that they would give urgent consideration to this matter . . . in that case, we hoped that there will be scope for the Congress to restart its national movement.[97]

But he chastised the Samaj for going ahead with its support to a blatantly 'communal organization' like the Mahasabha, participating in a movement that was confined to a particular 'social class in the greater Maharashtra' and was detrimental to the people of Hyderabad and also the entire nation. Despite all attempts by the Congress to dissuade the Arya Samaj from associating with the Mahasabha, the latter was steadfast. In April 1939, they called for a meeting with Savarkar in Sholapur where he told them point-blank that he was aware of the pressures being put on them by the Congress. He also declared that even if the Samaj withdrew from the movement, he and the Mahasabha were planning to go ahead with it, full throttle. But the Arya Samaj dismissed all such fears and rooted their support to the Mahasabha efforts.

Batches of volunteers kept trooping inside Hyderabad from the end of January 1939. They were not only arrested, but also brutally assaulted by the police. Reports kept pouring in on violent attacks on peaceful civil resisters raising alarm across the country. Savarkar remonstrated to Akbar Hyderi again about these barbaric attacks.

I am convinced by unimpeachable testimony that the Nizam police in complicity with Muslim mobs have been assaulting, as a set policy, the Mahasabha and Arya Samaj Hindu volunteers who offer peaceful civil resistance to the anti-Hindu bans in the Nizam State . . . Setting aside even the rigid laws of the Nizam State, when armed Muslim mobs and the police are allowed to take law in their own hands . . . as was in the case at Tuljapur, Vaijapur, Gavliguda and other places and where these criminal Muslim mobs and police are not brought to book by any higher State authorities, I feel it my duty to warn the Nizam Government of the serious consequences that such outrages are bound to bring in their trail. I hope your Honour will take a serious note of this matter, punish the outrageous miscreants and put a stop to this barbarity.[98]

The remonstrance too fell on deaf ears. Considering these attacks were happening more in smaller villages, the Mahasabha decided to send their larger teams to bigger cities and smaller groups of four to five members to villages. Nearly forty batches of volunteers kept pouring in till April 1939 and the number of volunteers soared to over 2000.[99] The Congress kept spreading rumours that the two organizations were losing their morale and the movement had been called off—thereby creating utter confusion among the volunteers on ground. It necessitated Savarkar to issue a statement on 8 April 1939 removing these misapprehensions and to state 'unreservedly and definitely that so far as the Hindu Mahasabha is concerned, it is not going to suspend, much less call off, the movement unless and until the reforms which the Government has been promising . . . are actually announced and the Hindu Mahasabha is in a position to judge, if they concede in some substantial measure, if not in full, the demands put forward . . . at Nagpur.'[100]

With all these negotiations leading nowhere, the Mahasabha decided to go for the big push. L.B. Bhopatkar declared that he would lead a batch of 200 volunteers to Hyderabad forthwith. The call of such a senior functionary created massive goodwill and more than 300 people signed up to accompany him—so much so that many had to be restrained to be sent in future batches. Groups of volunteers joined in from Bengal and the United Provinces under Ram Bharose Shivahare. Members of the Shiromani Gurudwara Prabandhak Committee of the Sikhs from Punjab too joined in, as did Arya Samaj members from as far as Kashmir. The Nizam's government sent a terse warning that they could not assure the peaceful protestors of any security and that they were not to be held responsible for any untoward incidents. Savarkar wrote in exasperation to the government on 24 April 1939:

To Mr. Bhopatkar's letter last week informing Nizam Government of his intention to offer civil and non-violent resistance, the Nizam Government's latest reply has virtually admitted that they could not guarantee security from mob violence in Nizam State. Against this astounding reply, which amounts to veiled violent threat, Hindu Mahasabha records its strongest protest. Civil resisters may be dealt with under whatever laws that prevail under the Nizam Government. But no Government can resign its legal authority to mob violence. The responsibility of communal tension lies primarily and entirely on anti-Hindu policy of Nizam Government. Mr. Bhopatkar goes to protest and oppose it with peaceful resistance. So responsibility of any mob violence and consequent criminal assault on his party will lie on the Nizam Government alone, which is duty-bound to order the police and military to see that legal functions of

Nizam Government are not usurped by violent mobs. Please take serious note of this as the results of abdicating Government's legal power to mob fury cannot but exasperate discontent and disorder in the State instead of terrorizing civil resistance movement. Removal of just grievances of the Hindus can alone restore peace and content.[101]

The letter and also the propaganda on the issue across the country had its impact. The mobs were contained by the Hyderabad police. Bhopatkar was allowed to make a speech and immediately thereafter he and his entire group of resisters were arrested. This only gave further impetus to the movement. Through the months of April and May 1939, batches of volunteers came under the leadership of eminent personalities—Anantrao Gadre, a well-known leader of the anti-untouchability movement, D.K. Sathe, Keshavrao Kelkar and others. Nearly 4000 volunteers offered civil resistance on behalf of the Mahasabha. The jails in Hyderabad were insufficient to house the prisoners and many had to be shifted to Gulbarga and Aurangabad. Jail administration, sanitation and water supply collapsed as the numbers swelled. Trying them in courts also proved to be a big ordeal for the administration. Young boys in the age group of 12–14 were also part of the movement and they were mercilessly treated and sentenced to 1–2 years of rigorous imprisonment under the most torturous and inhuman jail conditions. In the prisons, the police, aided by the mobs, dealt with the volunteers in the most barbaric fashion and many were beaten up black and blue. As jail kitchens ran out of supplies most of them were left to starve for days on end. More than 150 undertrial volunteers were fettered in manacles and crossbars, and flogged.[102] In fact the jails exhausted their stock of fetters and new orders had to be placed. The tales from the jails of hell in the Nizam state filled the people of Maharashtra and India with utter horror. Savarkar issued a statement expressing horror at the turn of events and also an appeal to other Hindus:

If the Nizam Government knew that its resources or wretched administration was really so incompetent to supply room, food and water to its prisoners inspite of a fortnight's notice of their coming to defy the anti-Hindu laws in the State, why did the Nizam Government arrest them at all? Even barbarous States feel it a moral duty to feed even their criminals they imprison and sentence. Even under armed warfare each belligerent is held responsible by public code of war to give human

treatment to the respective armed prisoners of war. But here hundreds
of Hindu civil resisters unarmed and immune from the slightest tinge
of crime enter the Nizam State having informed of their intention to do
so, weeks ago only to assert rights of fundamental civil liberties. They
are formally arrested by the Nizam Government, pent up in the prison,
which gets so overcrowded as to render the black hole myth a reality and
then for two days denied food and water . . . outrageously lathi-charged
en masse and then again individually assaulted in their cells with lamps
out, in darkness, so mercilessly that their lives are held in suspense . . .
the only effective response therefore that ought to be returned to this
challenge of the Nizam Government cannot but be the still more
vigorous intensification of the Hindu movement to assert our birth rights
in that State . . . Let Sanatanists, Aryasamajists, HinduSabhaits, Sikhs,
Jains and others who constitute Hindudom as a whole, rise up and march
on to the front, not only in hundreds as was done up till now, but in
thousands . . . Arise then, in your millions, and join ranks to press on this
Dharma Yuddha.[103]

Simultaneously the echoes of the horrors of Hyderabad were heard in state
and central legislatures, and also in the House of Commons.[104] Pamphlets
about the issue were distributed in London by one Mr Tamhankar. No
newspapers were willing to publish anything against the Nizam, as it was
alleged that many of them were on the secret payrolls of the richest Indian
monarch. Tamhankar distributed leaflets to British members of Parliament
and stirred their conscience to raise the issue in the House. It was then
that news of the Hyderabad happenings began to trickle into London
newspapers including the *Guardian*. The Welsh member of Parliament in
the House of Commons, David Rhys Grenfell, who represented Gower
constituency for the Labour Party, took up the matter in Parliament on 10
July. He was not satisfied with the British government's reply, especially
since he had received a telegram from India about more than 10,000
detainees in Hyderabad and their pitiable plight. Despite representations
even to the viceroy there had been no action, the telegram from a member
of the International Aryan League had claimed. Grenfell had read up
extensively on this issue and deduced that 12,000,000 Hindus in the
Nizam state were being systematically persecuted on religious grounds.[105]
In his statement to the *Manchester Guardian*, Grenfell wrote on 18 July
1939: 'It is apparent that the Hindus in the Hyderabad State are denied

the most elementary civil liberties, such as freedom of speech, press, assembly, or religion. A Hindu must not celebrate his marriage if the appointed day happens to coincide with a Muslim festival.'[106] He urged for some prompt and immediate action from the British government and its counterpart in India. All of this pressure from various quarters further galvanized the movement. The Government of India too began exerting its pressure on the Nizam. Finally, the Nizam capitulated and, on 19 July 1939, brought in the much-delayed reforms, a kind of a 'Magna Carta' of civil liberties for the Hindus, including 50 per cent reservation in certain administrative jobs.

Celebrating the victory of a long-drawn bloody struggle, Savarkar released a statement guardedly welcoming the reforms:

I welcome the announcement of Reforms by the Nizam Government as a wise move betokening on their part the change of heart for the better. In spite of the ugly fact that the Reforms are tainted from the beginning to the end by an underlying assumption that the Muslims though in a 10% minority in the State are to be politically recognized on an equal basis with the Hindus who form 90% majority, not on account of any special merit but only because they are Muslims, which assumption belies the Nizam's professions of treating all his subjects with equal justice, irrespective of race or religion; and in spite of the fact that the seemingly disinterested claim in theory advanced by the Government that they have framed electorates on economical and functional basis in order to eliminate all communal bias, stands exposed in the face by the astounding self-contradiction, which consists in the very next breath in reserving 50% seats in the Legislature for Muslims as Muslims, I shall feel no hesitation in stating that even these Reforms, halting as they are, do constitute a substantial advance over the old rotten order of things and open out a constitutional channel, which if the Nizam Government would only help the Hindus in all sincerity to work out, may lead to future expansion and fuller freedom. Thanks to the brave sufferings and sacrifices undergone by those thousands of our civil resisters, the Hindus have succeeded at last in effecting a constitutional breach in the citadel of fanatical autocracy, wide enough for a triumphant march of forces of progress into its very heart. And therefore, I reciprocate the hope expressed by H.E.H. the Nizam in 'a spirit of accommodation and response' for which he pleads, and assure him that the Hindus will never be found wanting in responsive cooperation with the Government to bring about restoration of peace and amity provided that the peace and amity are not to be bought at the cost of their birth-rights as Hindus or subjugation to any racial humiliations in future.[107]

On 8 August 1939, the Nizam's government brought out another communiqué clarifying the concessions it had laid out in terms of religious gatherings, associations, processions and places of public worship. A substantial amount of freedom was granted to the Hindus through this order. All prisoners were released by the Nizam the same month. The Working Committee of the Hindu Mahasabha under Savarkar accordingly passed a resolution withdrawing the civil resistance movement and paying tributes to all the martyrs and brave hearts who participated in it. Thus ended the Hyderabad struggle under the leadership of Savarkar, the first successful mass movement that the Hindu Mahasabha had undertaken.

~

Buoyed by the success, Savarkar continued his travels across the country garnering support for his party and its ideology. Earlier that year, in February 1939, he made a visit to Bengal to preside over the regional Hindu Mahasabha conference. He was welcomed warmly by several leaders such as Syama Prasad Mookerjee, Ramananda Chatterji, Ashutosh Lahiri, Nirmalchand Tarji, Padmaraj Jain and others. The *Amrit Bazar Patrika* noted the enthusiasm with which he was received in Bengal:

> Thousands of Hindus from the remotest villages came and there was a record attendance of delegates from all parts of Bengal to honour Bar. Savarkar and take part in the conference. The President-elect Bar. Savarkar did what he said. He dined with so-called untouchables and high-caste Hindus. He was given an honour, which Hindu kings and princes accorded to Brahmarshis like Vasista. If that honour means anything it should mean a revolution in Hindu society not in the distant future but here and now.[108]

Savarkar addressed several public meetings and receptions in Calcutta and Khulna. In his speeches, he stressed on the unity of Hindu society regardless of caste or gender and the need to vote for leaders who have the interests of Hindus in mind. He also addressed large student gatherings in the city, including one at the Albert Hall. Reporting this, the *Amrit Bazar Patrika* said:

> Half an hour before the scheduled time for the meeting, the spacious hall was packed to suffocation. Every inch of the floor of the gallery was occupied. People perched themselves dangerously on the windows and some of the more venturesome and resourceful ones climbed up to the ventilators, smashed the glass panes and made their way through them. The arrival of Sjt. Savarkar was greeted with deafening prolonged cheers. Standing under the orange-coloured Hindu Flag which floated overhead, Sjt. V.D. Savarkar addressed the assemblage in pin-drop silence for nearly an hour.[109]

At the end of the speech the youngsters cheered him loudly with slogans of 'You are taking Bengal with you!' This visit of Savarkar galvanized the Mahasabha's presence in Bengal to a great extent and also laid the foundations in a way for his protégé Syama Prasad Mookerjee's political career in the state.

In March 1939, he travelled to Bihar to mobilize the party there and to organize the general session of the Bihar Hindu Mahasabha at Monghir. He delivered a stirring speech at the session where he presided. The *Indian Nation* of Patna reported the event:

> It was a stirring speech. He made an impassioned appeal to Hindus to unite, to resist inroads and revive their lost glory . . . his speech was heard with rapt attention and created an atmosphere of great enthusiasm among Hindus. He spoke with feeling and the audience was also greatly impressed with the arguments he gave in support of his conclusions.[110]

On 1 August 1939, Savarkar spoke at a public meeting organized at Tilak Smarak Mandir in Poona. In his speech, he talked about the three different schools of thought prevalent in the Congress, led by three different leaders—Gandhi, Subhas Bose and Manabendranath Roy—and how it is different from the school of thought of the Hindu Mahasabha. He said:

> In today's Congress, there are three schools of thought . . . Gandhian school of thought has truth and non-violence as its key ideas. But

Gandhian non-violence is inimical to Hindutva. Hindu philosophy says
violence for violence sake is bad, but violence is permissible to destroy evil
and protect the good, and such violence is good conduct. But Gandhian
thought makes no such distinction. They believe in non-violence under
all conditions. Second school of thought is led by Subhas Bose and the
Forward Bloc. His policies and means used are similar to our thought
process and we could work together on certain issues, but even they are
obsessed with this mirage of Hindu-Muslim unity. The third school of
thought is of Manvendranath (sic) Roy and that is not acceptable to us at
all. They believe in the policy of active Muslim appeasement. The Hindu
Mahasabha has the interests of Hindus in mind always.[111]

In end-September 1939, Savarkar visited Karnataka and addressed rallies
in Dharwar, Hubli, Hosur, Gurla Hosur, Bailahongal and other places.
He then campaigned for the Hindu Mahasabha candidate, Maharaja
Krishna, in the Meerut by-elections in October 1939, during which time
his cavalcade was attacked by alleged Muslim goons.

Evidently the Hindu Mahasabha was quite keen to ensure that given
his popularity, Savarkar travelled a lot more across the country. The over-
dependence on his personality and popularity was becoming a handicap
for the party that had just recently got its political influence. In a letter
addressed to the secretary of the Hindu Mahasabha, Ganpat Rai, dated
11 July 1939, Savarkar outlines the problems that he and the organization
personally faced due to such over-dependence on him:

> You know from newspapers that I am almost constantly going on tours
> far and wide in different provinces and almost all districts in Maharashtra
> besides attending to the Hindu Maha Sabha work. The Nizam Civil
> Resistance Movement has cost the Hindu Maha Sabha some 75,000
> Rupees in cash. All this fund had to be raised and thousands of volunteers
> whose number now has reached to 4000 approximately has taxed all my
> time and energy and now that the movement is thickening all the more
> new fronts of Hindu Maha Sabha activity are opening in Madras and in
> London, the pressure of the work is bound to grow heavier and intenser
> (sic). Interviews with the leaders from the Nizam State and the spasmodic
> and endless talks to be conducted require me from time to time to hurry
> back to Bombay. I have to preside over a conference at Poona at the end
> of this month where all the Maharashtra, Berar and C.P. leaders are to

assemble. Then in all probability I have to go to Bengal to preside over the Hindu Rally to usher in United Hindu Bengal Party and in the first week of September I have to preside over the U.P. Hindu Conference. At the end of September, the Madras Hindu Conference is almost sure to take place and in and between all this a heap of correspondence lying in arrears is to be disposed of with one single typist at my disposal. How do you expect me under these circumstances to tour Punjab and Delhi? From every quarter letters pour in 'if you want our province or city to contribute any funds or volunteers you must personally visit this place'. That is, you will admit, an impossible condition. I cannot be at two places simultaneously at one and the same hour. I feel grateful for the public trust and kindness, which makes them depend on a single individual. But I want to impress all our friends and workers in all Provinces that no one man and least of all, my humble-self can meet the emergency unless and until the Hindus as a people rise equal to the occasion and learn to depend upon themselves and do their bit each on his own initiative and comes forward to go to the front in this Dharma Yuddha without waiting for someone else to tell him to do so.[112]

He therefore advised Rai to find prominent leaders in Delhi and Punjab or even volunteer himself, to lead from the front and carry on the propaganda as well as the fund-raising for the party. As president he was willing to send a big *jatha* (rally) of people from Maharashtra to accompany these leaders on their tours. Anticipating a victory in Hyderabad, he also advised Rai to cultivate a large contingent of local leaders from all provinces whose presence in the eventuality of victory would add grandeur and a pan-India appeal to the Mahasabha.

But since the time of the Nagpur session and the Hyderabad struggle, the Mahasabha had hardly caught any attention of the British government. It was after Nagpur that for the first time British intelligence took cognizance. In an extract, it noted that the session, attended by more than 30,000 members, was a 'sensational success' by all its past standards.[113] It spoke about the spectacular reception that delegates received at the railway station, an aeroplane scattering flowers from the sky and a grand display by volunteers with swords and lathis. It went on to add:

The President Mr. Savarkar, who was the recipient of a very enthusiastic welcome, spoke mainly against the Congress and the Muslims, and urged

organization among the Hindus for the protection of their rights. Among
the more important resolutions passed at the conference were those
according support to federation, supporting the satyagraha in Hyderabad
state and condemning the Congress for advising its suspension,
demanding extension of military training to Hindus, and establishment
of arms at factories, urging the opening of all provinces for recruitment
to the Army so as to obviate the possibility of any treachery on the part
of the Punjab Muslims, appointing a Hindu National Parliamentary
Board to fight the next elections, asking Hindus to deal only with Hindu
shops, protesting against the declaration by the Congress of the Hindu
Mahasabha as a communal organization and threatening to start civil
disobedience in Bhopal State.[114]

There was cautious optimism tinged with scepticism as well about whether
the Mahasabha was at all a serious political contender in the Indian scene.
Sir Francis Wylie, governor of the Central Provinces, in his report to the
viceroy, mentioned that he found it difficult 'to take the Hindu Mahasabha
very seriously. They are so blatantly communal that their programme cannot
these days commend itself very much to the better class of Indians, while in
the political field the Congress of course overshadows them completely.'[115]

~

Even as these new tidings were under way in the Indian political scenario,
the September of 1939 saw the world getting entangled into a new global
strife. The Battle of Westerplatte saw the invasion of German army, navy
and air force into Poland, gradually drawing the entire world in its wake of
war and destruction. Britain and other European nations were inevitably
drawn into this conflict that came to be known as the Second World War.

On 10 September 1939, the Working Committee of the Hindu
Mahasabha met in Bombay under Savarkar's leadership and passed
resolutions related to the impending global outbreak. Several top leaders of
the Mahasabha from different provinces including Babasaheb Khaparde,
Syama Prasad Mookerjee, Varadarajulu Naidu of Madras, Yashvantrao
Joshi, Barrister Jamnadas Mehta, Dr B.S. Moonje and others participated.
The main points of the resolution were that the Indian Army is not
British Army but the army of Indians, and that the government should
make all efforts to inculcate this feeling. This was the only way that they

could enlist the support of the troops in any global conflict. It called upon the British government to expand the Indian Territorial Forces and the Universities Training Corps and 'to establish such military organizations in the provinces where they do not exist at present'.[116] It urged the British to Indianize the army by abolishing the distinction between 'warrior and non-warrior' castes; that Indians should be inducted in all branches of the Indian defence forces and they should enjoy equal rights and privileges as the British soldiers. The meeting also called upon Hindus to organize 'Hindu National Militia' (*Hindu Sainikikaran Mandals*) in their respective provinces for Hindu youth between the ages of eighteen and forty to seek admission there. The government, the resolution added, should encourage production of arms and ammunition in India.

Commenting on his own much-repeated stance of an 'India-First' foreign policy, Savarkar commented that there was no point picking up ideological battles with Hitler or his associates. Hitler, he said, knows how to be independent and what he needs to do. Nazism and Fascism might be appropriate for Germany and Italy, and India need not meddle in their internal affairs. What India needed to do was to first create its independent government. India did not have power like Japan, Germany and Italy, and its people wanted independence. He averred that the British claim of independence being a threat to democracy was a lie. He called for British soldiers to leave India so that Indians could create their own nation. The Mahasabha, he declared, supported Indian independence and regarded all those who opposed it as enemies. For those who were neutral to Indian interests, India too must be neutral. Our policy to British must be decided this way, he concluded.[117]

The stance of the Mahasabha won appreciation from several quarters including from across the border, in distant Japan. Rash Behari Bose who had been keeping a close watch on Savarkar and his ideology wrote a letter to him on 22 September expressing his complete support to the idea of militarization. The revolutionary dream of building on the 1857 model of creating disaffection in the minds of the natives who served in the British Indian Army against their colonial masters, creating thereby a nationwide uprising in the army and heralding the end of the Empire, was potent as ever. Rash Behari Bose also expressed his deep apprehensions about whether this will indeed materialize, given that 'the British Empire's biggest supporter in India, Mahatma Gandhi, was strongly opposed to such a move'.[118]

Rash Behari Bose had volunteered to start a Japanese arm of the Hindu Mahasabha in the summer of 1938. On 14 November 1938, Savarkar had sent in his consent to this idea with the caveat that the organization there must be subordinate to the Indian office.[119] Bose had in fact written a lengthy article on Savarkar in a Japanese magazine named *Dai Ajia Shugi* (Greater Asianism) in its March and April 1939 issues. Giving a detailed biographical sketch of Savarkar who was described as 'a rising leader of New India,' the article extolled him for his, 'heroism, valour, adventure, and epitome of patriotism . . . to praise him is to praise the spirit of sacrifice'. He [Savarkar] was the one 'who always kept the fire of India's freedom burning; he is a patriot who risked his life for the freedom of India in the early 20th century and is a founder exponent of the doctrine of cultural independence in the current times'. After writing in detail about Savarkar's views on Hindutva and his policy of militarization of Hindus, Rash Behari Bose sums up the article by saying, 'If you agree with Savarkar, you will have political power, and he has a strong position in the Indian independence movement.'[120]

The militarization concept that Savarkar envisaged was well in line with that of his predecessor Moonje, which would be worth taking a closer look at. Since the early 1930s, Moonje was advocating the founding of a military school and college for Hindu youth, which among other objectives would serve as a feeder institution for recruitment to the armed forces. A sturdy man with a stern look and a flowing beard, Moonje was a man in a hurry. He also gave the unconventional call to Hindus to take to non-vegetarian diet like the Kshatriyas of yore to improve their strength for self-defence.[121]

There was merit in the apprehensions of men like Moonje and Savarkar on the communal composition of the Indian Army. Ambedkar, who studied this aspect, mentions that by the year 1930, Muslims composed about 36 per cent of the Indian infantry and about 30 per cent of the Indian cavalry.[122] Intriguingly, the government suppressed all information about this composition after 1930. Around 1940, Ambedkar said:

It is impossible to know what the proportion of the Muslims in the Indian Army at present is. There is no Government publication from which such information can be gathered. In the past, there was no dearth of publications giving this information. It is very surprising that they should have disappeared, or if they do appear, that they should cease to contain this information. Not only is there no Government publication containing information on this point, but Government has refused to give any information on the point when asked by the Central Legislative Assembly.[123]

Ambedkar states that the estimates that some people had was that the pre-war proportion of Muslims in the army was 60–70 per cent, while others pegged that number around 50 per cent.[124] He goes on to state that even if one assumed it was the latter figure, 'it is high enough to cause alarm to the Hindus'.[125] Elaborating further, Ambedkar writes clinically and bluntly:

The Indian Army today is predominantly Muslim in its composition . . . the Musalmans who predominate are the Musalmans from the Punjab and the N.W.F.P. Such a composition of the Indian Army means that the Musalmans of the Punjab and the N.W.F.P. are made the sole defenders of India from foreign invasion. So patent has this fact become that the Musalmans of the Punjab and the N.W.F.P. are quite conscious of this proud position, which has been assigned to them by the British, for reasons best known to them. For, one often hears them say that they are the 'gate-keepers' of India. The Hindus must consider the problem of the defence of India in the light of this crucial fact. How far can the Hindus depend upon these 'gate-keepers' to hold the gate and protect the liberty and freedom of India? The answer to this question must depend upon who comes to force the gate open. It is obvious that there are only two foreign countries, which are likely to force this gate from the North-West side of India, Russia or Afghanistan, the borders of both of which touch the border of India. Which of them will invade India and when, no one can say definitely. If the invasion came from Russia, it may be hoped that these gate-keepers of India will be staunch and loyal enough to hold the gate and stop the invader. But suppose the Afghans singly or in combination with other Muslim states march on India, will these gate-keepers stop the invaders or will they open the gates and let them in? This is a question, which no Hindu can afford to ignore. This is a question on which every Hindu must feel assured, because it is the most crucial question . . . Will they (the Muslim soldiers) respond to the call of the land of their birth or will they be swayed by the call of their religion, is the question, which must be faced if ultimate security is to be obtained. It is not safe to seek to escape from these annoying and discomforting questions by believing that we need not worry about a foreign invasion so long as India is under the protection of the British. Such a complacent attitude is unforgivable to say the least.[126]

Ambedkar's fears were shared even by British educationalist and member of the Council of India, who had served as the director of the University of London Institute in Paris, Theodore Morrison, whom he quotes as having said way back in 1899:

> The views held by the Mahomedans (certainly the most aggressive and truculent of the peoples of India) are alone sufficient to prevent the establishment of an independent Indian Government. Were the Afghan to descend from the North upon an autonomous India, the Mahomedans, instead of uniting with the Sikhs and the Hindus to repel him, would be drawn by all the ties of kinship and religion to join his flag.[127]

Ambedkar postulated that during the Khilafat agitation in 1919, the moves to invite the amir of Afghanistan to invade India were actively supported by the leaders of the movement and this strengthened the theory that Morrison had put forth.[128] He also wonders whether the Indian government would be free to use an army that had a communal composition of this kind and whether it could rest assured on its loyalty. He considered this too high a risk to leave this matter to the speculation of whether some such eventuality might occur as it dealt with important national security.

Ambedkar however quotes the Secretary of State's report of 1943 where finally the government did release the details of the religious composition of the army: 50 per cent Hindus and Gurkhas, 34 per cent Muslims, 10 per cent Sikhs and 6 per cent Christians and others.[129] Apart from the relaxation in recruitment that the British introduced during the Second World War to swell the numbers of the soldiers fighting from India in the war, the major contribution to the spurt in the proportion of the Hindus in the army was thanks to the constant militarization drive that was pushed with a vengeance by Moonje, Savarkar and other leaders of the Hindu Mahasabha as a tenet of inherent faith. From the point of view of security and sovereignty of India, which Ambedkar had flagged, such a tilt in composition was undoubtedly a need of the hour. The Congress with its romanticized preoccupation with non-violence had not given suitable attention to this important element, despite warnings from leaders such as Ambedkar, Savarkar or Moonje.

Moonje was involved in deliberations that led to the foundation of the Indian Military Academy (IMA) in Dehradun. This was a follow-up of the deliberations of the First Round Table Conference that sought progressive Indianization of the armed forces. The Indian Military College Committee was set up under the commander-in-chief of India, General Sir Philip Chetwode. Moonje who was part of the Round Table Conference became a natural part of this eighteen-member committee. In 1931 the committee drew up a detailed scheme to train at least sixty commissioned Indian officers every year and the IMA came up in 1932.

On his way back from England that he visited for the Round Table Conference, Moonje made study tours of military schools in England, France and Germany. Notably, he visited Italy between 15 and 24 March 1931, making a detailed assessment of the Military College, the Central Military School of Physical Education, the Fascist Academy of Physical Education, and Mussolini's Balilla and Avanguardisti there. In his diary, Moonje notes: 'India and particularly Hindu India need some such institution for the military regeneration of the Hindus: so that the artificial distinction so much emphasized by the British of martial and non-martial classes amongst the Hindus may disappear.'[130] He even mentions that something close to this exists in the form of his favourite disciple Dr Hedgewar's organization, the Rashtriya Swayamsevak Sangh but it needs a lot more developing on similar lines. Moonje also met the Italian dictator Benito Mussolini in Palazzo Venezia, the fascist government's headquarters on 19 March 1931 and was hugely impressed by the resurgence of Italy under his leadership. The fascination for a strong dictator-like leader—'Shivaji of old or Mussolini or Hitler of the present day in Italy and Germany'—comes up repeatedly in his public meetings and speeches after his return to India.[131] Even the British had taken note of this fascination and in an intelligence report said, 'It is perhaps no exaggeration to assert that the Sangh hopes to be in future India what the "Fascisti" are to Italy and the "Nazis" to Germany.'[132]

Moonje founded his own Central Hindu Military Education Society in Nasik in 1935 and later started the Bhonsala Military School in 1937. The aim of the society was 'to bring about military regeneration of the Hindus and to fit Hindu youths for undertaking the entire responsibility for the defence of their motherland . . . to train them in the science and art of personal and national defence.'[133] The Military School received funds from Indians, as well as the British overlords. Industrialist Ghanshyam Das Birla considered Hindu self-defence as an important tenet and offered constant help to the school.[134] Moonje had in fact even met Viceroy Lord Willingdon on 16 March 1936 and explained the aims of the school. The viceroy donated Rs 250 to the school along with a letter of appreciation that the school 'would prove to be a most useful organization in training its pupils to do good service for the British Empire in future years'.[135] The school became an important destination for many Hindu youths who were desirous of gaining entry to the IMA.

The visage of a strong leader of a centralized nation, in the form of Hitler or Mussolini, undoubtedly attracted the Hindu nationalists in the run up to the Second World War, though this was to change once the horrors of the war and ethnic cleansing began to get clearer. A declaration from the Hindu Mahasabha on 25 March 1939 makes this fascination for the renegade countries taking on the might of the colonial Empire clearer:

> Germany's solemn idea of the revival of the Aryan culture, the glorification of the Swastika, her patronage of Vedic learning and the ardent championship of the tradition of Indi-Germanic civilization are welcomed by the religious and sensible Hindus of India with a jubilant hope. Only a few socialists headed by Pandit J. Nehru have created a bubble of resentment against the present Government of Germany, but their activities are far from having any significance in India. The vain imprecations of Mahatma Gandhi against Germany's indispensable vigour in matters of internal policy obtain but little regard in so far as they are uttered by a man who has always betrayed and confused the country with an affected mysticism. I think that Germany's crusade against the enemies of Aryan culture will bring all the Aryan nations of the world to their senses and awaken the Indian Hindus for the restoration of their lost glory.[136]

Savarkar seems to have kept close secret contacts with the Axis powers—Rome, Berlin, Tokyo—through several emissaries and their local agents and/or consulates in Bombay. These did not bring about too many noticeable results possibly because the war regulations had already struck in and tighter security and surveillance had been imposed by the government. The British were keeping a close watch on these foreign connections with the Hindu Mahasabha leaders. An intelligence report talks about the regular correspondences between Savarkar and Rash Behari Bose:

In the meantime, the maintenance of the connexions (sic) between Japan and the Hindu Mahasabha is shown in a letter recently written by Rash Behari Bose in Tokyo to Indra Prakash, Secretary of the Hindu Mahasabha, New Delhi, at the instigation of Savarkar asking for Hindu Sabha literature to be sent to Japan from India.[137]

Another report details:

In June 1938, two parcels of literature were received by a well-known revolutionary in India from a member of the Japanese Legation, Kabul. This information came to light in the course of secret censorship. The Japanese Foreign Office arranged for the production in Calcutta of a Quarterly Review entitled 'New Asia'. Indian extremists such as Prof. Benoy Sirkar and V.D. Savarkar were asked to contribute articles. The intention of the Japanese Vice-Consul was to expound political, rather than cultural, views, and to conceal the propagandist nature of the journal.[138]

From the Hindu Mahasabha, Jugal Kishore Birla was a conduit man to connect with the Axis powers,[139] while the two Germans who undertook the liaison with the Indian side were G.L. Leszczynski and P. Pazze. The former was a representative of a German news agency and the latter the manager of a company located in Bombay. They had got Savarkar's articles and speeches printed in the German press including the *Volkischer Beobachter*. Leszczynski also dispatched a copy of Hitler's autobiography *Mein Kampf* to Savarkar.[140] The British had kept a watch on these 'suspicious players' as well:

G.L. Leszczynski- Mark Haren, Strand Road, Apollo Bunder, Bombay; Head of Commerce Branch of the N.S.D.A.P. Bombay; In-Charge of the German India Institute, which publishes monthly reports on the commercial situation in India; Has a good knowledge of commercial, economic and political matters in India. In touch with Savarkar, President of Hindu Mahasabha, whose note on President Roosevelt he cabled to German News Agency and a copy to Hitler.[141]

Another interesting character that the Savarkar brothers, especially Babarao got acquainted to was Savitri Devi.[142] Originally a Frenchwoman of Greek-English birth, born as Maximiani Julia Portas in Lyons, France, she grew up to become a deep admirer of the German National Socialism and the Nazi-Aryan race theory. She soon began to venerate Adolf Hitler as a veritable supernatural incarnation. When all of 27, in 1932, she landed in India and it was love at first sight with the country, its culture and the dominant Hindu religion, in which she saw the perfect synthesis of her evolving views—a living civilization that personified the Aryan legends that she grew up fantasizing. She travelled across the country— from Rameswaram, Tiruchirapalli, Amritsar to enrolling as a student at Rabindranath Tagore's Shantiniketan, before settling down in Calcutta by the end of 1936 and converting to Hinduism, rechristening herself as Savitri Devi. Here she got closely associated with the Hindu Mission and its president Swami Satyananda, and through them got introduced to the idea of Hindutva and Savarkar. She began writing extensively on Hindu philosophy and nationalism and a lot of these ideas echoed those of Savarkar's earlier works. Her book *A Warning to the Hindus*, written in 1939, cautioned the community against its own social evils and the external threats from other religions, especially Islam. Babarao wrote the preface to this book and heaped praises on her:

> She has one advantage over the usual workers from within the Hindu fold. She was Greek by nationality. It is, owing partly to her appreciation of Hindu art, thought and 'dharma,' and partly to deeper reasons that she was drawn to our society and that she adopted what we call Hindutva, for the rest of her life. But naturally, being a European, she could, though from within, study the condition of the Hindus in a detached manner. And this book contains the mature and thoughtful conclusions drawn by her, conclusions which, in no case, can be taken as the outcome of that partial attitude, which one of the born-Hindus may be said to possess.[143]

Regular correspondences between her and Babarao from 1939 till 1942 have come to light, and some communication with Savarkar as well.[144] Most of these are replete with profuse veneration for Savarkar, his philosophy and political stances on matters related to Hindu nationalistic identity and a strong, militarized nation that could stand on its own to defend itself. In a letter dated 21 November 1941, she writes to Babarao about a plan they discussed about starting a nationalistic publication that could be used for widespread public propaganda for the cause and that how she would be willing to help 'with ready zeal' to tour the country and spread the message.[145] She adds there: 'Non-Hindus must not take this movement for a "Hindu propaganda" before they can realize that they themselves have all rights to be called Hindus culturally.'[146]

Providentially, in Calcutta, she met a man who shared, and perhaps exceeded her admiration for Aryan racism and Hitler, a publisher with strong pro-German sympathies, Asit Krishna Mukherji. He was the editor and proprietor of *The New Mercury*, a fortnightly National Socialist magazine published from Calcutta with the support of the German consulate. She married him in 1940 in a Hindu wedding ceremony. The couple became an active conduit of the Axis Powers, operating as underground spies to undertake clandestine work—possibly even working as double agents, as nothing else can explain how they managed to do all of this with such impunity and still remain untouched in Calcutta by the British Government. Mukherji and Devi developed close links with Subhas Chandra Bose and claimed to have played an important role in encouraging him to meet Savarkar and also connecting him to the German and Japanese authorities, with whose help Bose eventually met Hitler and also eventually led the Indian National Army (INA).[147] It is these dots that one can manage to connect to map out an otherwise hazy account of underground and revolutionary activities and the networks between its various protagonists.

The militarization strategy of the Hindu Mahasabha and Savarkar during the Second World War had multiple objectives. As mentioned earlier it was to create that ultimate push towards freedom by infiltrating the British Indian Army and creating disaffection there. Simultaneously, there seems to have been preparation for a post-British scenario as well where the Hindus would be in direct clash with the Muslims who had already begun murmurs of a separate land of their faith. In such a scenario, where the Muslim strength in the army exceeded that of the Hindus, particularly in sensitive provinces such as the NWFP and the Punjab, without arming oneself militarily, it would mean a surrender to a powerful and theocratic opponent. As Walter Andersen points out, this was 'motivated by a belief that Hindus had to prepare for the eventual struggle for power between Muslims and Hindus when the British finally vacated India'.[148] Another element of the Mahasabha strategy was to overtly earn the goodwill of a beleaguered government, even as it hobnobbed with its adversaries abroad covertly. The Mahasabha was always annoyed that the British considered only the Congress and the Muslim League as the voices of representation in India and that they were seldom on the high table of negotiations with the government that those parties managed. They wanted to establish themselves, as against the Congress, as being the sole representative of Hindu popular opinion in the country that the government must sit up and take notice of. Hence, within India, the olive branch was extended through support to militarization as well as responsive cooperation in administrative functions and to increase Hindu representation in government councils. Here too the idea was that when the British left India, the Hindus would be in superior positions both in the government as well as in the army. Moonje in fact openly made claims about this:

> The importance of the move lies in the fact that when after the War, the Government will again take in hand the question of Federation, it is the question of recruitment that will count at the time. The balance between the two rival communities, the Hindus and Musalmans, competing for power and domination, will be struck mainly on the numbers for recruitment supplied by each community.[149]

Moonje also called upon the Government to trust the Mahasabha as the most suited to provide the lead in the difficult wartime in securing the defence of India.[150] The Congress's decision to oppose any cooperation in the war efforts and the Muslim League's ambiguity had created a political impasse that was ripe for the Mahasabha to exploit. Moonje articulated this when he dismissed the Congress as being 'steeped in Mahatma's philosophy of non-violence and non-cooperation' and hence an ineligible partner in the war efforts. The Muslim League on the other hand with its 'extra-terrestrial patriotism would be sitting on the fence facing both ways, ever ready to jump on the winning side'.[151] In such a circumstance it was only the Mahasabha that was openly willing to cooperate in extending the Viceroy's Executive Council and the War Advisory Council as they offered 'opportunities for the general militarization of the Hindus and the organization of Defence of India on sound and scientific lines'.[152]

The British government on its part latched up the offer as it seemed like a counterweight to the Congress and its agitation politics, with the hope of giving it a better bargaining power with the Congress too at a

later date and keeping the League at tenterhooks. Of course, many in the
colonial set-up were wary of openly flirting with the Hindu Mahasabha, at
a time when the government was giving concessions to the Muslims and
the League. Jinnah himself revealed this fear among the Muslims about
this new alliance in a conversation with Reginald Coupland of the Oxford
University Press: '. . . the Muslims were mortally afraid that the British
would fall into trap because . . . the attitude of "another brother" [Savarkar]
who represented himself before the British public as more reasonable than
the "Congress brother", was more subtle and more dangerous'.[153]

Savarkar sought and obtained an interview with Viceroy Lord
Linlithgow in Delhi on 6 October 1939. Linlithgow was to later record
that while he found his guest 'a not very attractive type of little man', but
he was 'definitely interesting' and that they had a 'very friendly talk'. In a
secret correspondence the very next day, Linlithgow detailed the contours
of his meeting with Savarkar and seemed rather wary of him:

> The situation he [Savarkar] said was that His Majesty's Government
> must now turn to the Hindus and work with their support. After all,
> though we and the Hindus had a good deal of difficulty in the past, and
> was equally true of the relations between Great Britain and the French
> and, as recent events have shown, of relations between Russia and
> Germany, our interests are now the same and we must work together.
> Even though now most moderate of men, he had himself been in the
> past an adherent of a revolutionary party . . . but now that our interests
> are so closely bound together that essential thing was for Hinduism and
> Great Britain to be friends and old antagonism was no longer necessary.
> The Hindu Mahasabha, he went on to say, favoured an unambiguous
> undertaking of Dominion Status at the end of the War. It was true,
> at the same time that they challenged the Congress claim to represent
> anything but themselves. The Congress has accepted office under false
> pretence and on an understanding that they were doing so in order to
> wreck the constitution. But we Hindus were waiting for them. There was
> a great deal of Congress policy, which it was impossible for the Hindu
> Mahasabha to oppose because it was essentially a Hindu policy, but for
> all that the Mahasabha was determined to have them out. If he could, he
> could produce much better men to the places so vacated. He went on to
> urge a repeal of the Arms Act and a national militia, of the compulsory
> military training for the educated youth of the Hindu community and the

readjustment of the plan of recruitment for the ordinary Indian Army in
favour of classes at present without a real chance of securing admission in
the army. It was of utmost importance, he said, that we should chastise
the frontier tribes. He could only think that we have some arrangement
with the Afghans, which prevented us from taking a strong line with
them. But the chastisement must be with Hindu troops, the only troops
on which we could rely.[154]

The viceroy's meeting with Savarkar was part of a series of marathon
sessions with fifty-two leaders from all over India by mid-October.[155] The
reason for these meetings being the extreme reactions that his declaration of
4 September—just days after the formal outbreak of the war—had caused
across the country. On that day, Linlithgow had declared unilaterally that
India would be a combatant and an ally in a war that had largely been, till
then, a European conflict. His constitutional position was that India being
a subject country was automatically at war when the overlord nation was
involved in one. He also suspended the Federation plan of the government,
as envisaged by the 1935 Act.

The Congress was a bitterly divided house on these pronouncements.
In a meeting with the viceroy on 5 September 1939, Gandhi broke down
imagining about the possible destruction in the war of the grand buildings
of the Houses of Parliament and Westminster Abbey in London, whose
visits kindled fond memories for him.[156] India's deliverance, he said,
was not on his mind at the time but how the world could be saved from
the destruction of war. Nehru favoured an unconditional support to the
British in the interests of democracy against fascism while Rajagopalachari
advocated responsive cooperation in return of the promise to grant
Dominion status after the war.

In May 1939, in a classic Machiavellian party coup, Gandhi had
managed to oust Subhas Bose from the post of Congress president. Bose
now had formed a new rebel group called the Forward Bloc and it favoured
using the opportunity to launch a massive mass movement against the
government. Eventually, the Congress Working Committee, after four
days of deliberations, resolved on 15 September 1939 that India would
not associate with a war that was said to be for democratic freedom when
that same freedom was denied to her. The war collaboration aims and the
declaration of independence was a prerequisite for the Congress support,
it said.[157]

Linlithgow's reiteration in October 1939 of the old British promise of the grant of Dominion status and the only post-war concession being getting all stakeholders on to the table for a discussion on the contours of constitutional governance riled the Congress. This was going back to the Simon Commission and the Round Table Conference days that preceded the 1935 Act. Between end-October and the middle of November 1939 all the Congress ministries resigned in protest. This was a huge strategic blunder on their part as it lost its bargaining power with the government. As long as its ministries were in office, Linlithgow could not afford to ignore a party that governed eight out of the eleven British Indian provinces. But with the ministries bowing out, the viceroy's attitude too changed for there did not seem to be a tearing hurry to placate the Congress for now. Parliamentary governance being suspended in the Congress-ruled provinces, the administration came directly under the governor, making war efforts actually much easier. On its part, the Congress was willing to cooperate in the formation of a national government provided the British gave a commitment towards independence after the war, something that the latter was reluctant to amidst all the turmoil that existed.

The Muslim League, late in 1939, did not come out openly in support of the war efforts but did not oppose it as well. Some of its ministries in provinces like Sindh, Bengal and Punjab in fact offered unconditional support even before Jinnah made his decision known. But in its own ambiguous resolution of 18 September 1939, the League promised support on the condition that no constitutional advance in India could be made without taking the Muslim League on board.

Linlithgow found it expedient to befriend the League and encourage it to become a rival of the Congress on the all-India scene. As Jinnah was to recount:

> After the war began . . . I was treated on the same basis as Mr. Gandhi. I was wonderstruck why all of a sudden I was promoted and given a place side by side with Mr. Gandhi . . .[158] There was going to be a deal between Mr. Gandhi and Lord Linlithgow. Providence helped us. The war which nobody welcomes proved to be a blessing in disguise.[159]

It was this very vacuum created by the exit of the Congress that both the League and the Mahasabha tried to fill in by getting on to the good books of the viceroy. Linlithgow on his part chose the League, even while keeping the Mahasabha at close quarters to hedge his bets. The viceroy acknowledged this support from Jinnah:

> He (Jinnah) had given me very valuable help by standing against the Congress claims and I was duly grateful. It was clear that if he, Mr. Jinnah, had supported the Congress demand and confronted me with a joint demand, the strain upon me and His Majesty's Government would have been very great indeed. I thought therefore, I could claim to have a vested interest in his position.[160]

For public consumption, the viceroy created a smokescreen by inviting Gandhi, Rajendra Prasad and Jinnah for a meeting to work towards a national government and an expansion of the Governor General's Council at the Centre. The Congress refused to accept the proposals saying these still did not satisfy its original demand from the government. Jinnah put such a premium for his support with conditions that he knew well the Congress would never accept. Even as the Congress–League talks stood precariously, the viceroy got to claim that they had broken down on the communal issue and that he had personally begged them all to unite to a compromise solution, while in reality the British were determined to prevent the two from joining hands.

Meanwhile, even as negotiations were on between Jinnah and Nehru, the former came up with a humiliating celebration called 'Deliverance Day' on 22 December 1939. It was supposed to mark the deliverance from the 'tyranny, oppression and injustice during the last two and a half years'[161] of Congress rule in different provinces. Several non-Congress leaders—including B.R. Ambedkar and the Independent Labour Party leader E.V. Ramaswamy Naicker (Periyar), as also Parsis and Anglo-Indians—joined the League's nationwide celebrations marking the collapse of Congress governments. Needless to say, the Nehru–Jinnah talks ended right there and the League went straight into the lap of the viceroy. He asked them to put forward their concrete proposals to counteract the Congress demand for independence and a constituent assembly to frame a constitution or amend the 1935 Act. Notably, the League had no plans of its own till then despite its opposition to the 1935 Act. But the results of the 1937 elections clearly showed them that despite separate electorates and reservation of seats, the League was in no position to play a decisive role in the proposed federation and sticking on to such a system would be disadvantageous to them. They were pushed to think resolutely about what they had always wanted to, but never really mustered the political will, partitioning India.

The celebration of Deliverance Day found its echoes in the Hindu Mahasabha's annual session in end-December 1939 at Calcutta. Savarkar in his presidential address said:

> The Deliverance Day of today is but the inevitable logical consequence of the Khilafat Day so gaily observed by the Congress yesterday. It is you who have initiated the Moslems into the belief that the more they demand the more you yield, the more they frown, the more you placate, the more they pocket the more you offer, the more thankless they grow the more afflicted you are with craving for their thanks. Did you not offer them blank cheques? Why then get startled, now that they begin to fill them up with whatever ransom they are pleased to demand! Dr. Moonje, Bhai Parmanand and other leaders of the Hindu Mahasabha protested against the Khilafat Policy, against your blank cheques, against your meaningless 'neither accept nor reject vagaries', but you then denounced them all as wicked communalists, looked down even upon Shivaji and Pratap as misguided patriots, because they conquered by the sword and you gave yourself out as new messiahs who have come to conquer by the love alone, as world guides in direct communications with the inner voice. And now how pitiable it is to find you so sorely afflicted for want of guidance for yourselves to find out a way to appease and win over by love alone a single individual, the President of the League, that you should stand imploring at the gates of all the British Governors and the Viceroys to lend you a helping hand.[162]

Savarkar advised the Congress to counter the League's Deliverance Day with its own Rectification Day, where it should change its policy of appeasement. That the Congress would no longer recognize people as Hindus, Muslims, Christians, etc., but only as Indians and thereby support no special communal, religious or racial interests; that it would stand by 'one man one vote' principle with no special reservations, and public services would go by merit alone.

He also dwelt briefly on the economic principles of the Hindu Mahasabha which, as he mentioned, needed detailed exposition when their election manifesto came up soon. Countering Nehru's famous socialist idea of even communal issues squaring down to economic questions of hunger and 'Dal Bhat' (rice and lentils, meaning basic human needs), Savarkar considered it reductionist and one-sided to maintain that man had no urges other than hunger. Man was a complex being and a range of urges drove him to action and not just economic ones. These ranged from intellectual, social, cultural, to the sensual, sentimental, personal, some natural and some acquired urges. Everything was not just about the economics of food and shelter. If economic progress were the only panacea for all ills, the countries of the West that had invested in economic progress would not be facing any strife. He underpinned economic questions to religious and racial complications. A nationalistic economy and a 'national coordination of class interests' was his economic prescription. Being the machine age, he welcomed the rapid and widespread mechanization and spread of industrialization, deriding the fanciful means of hand-spun charkha that Gandhi espoused. The peasants and working class formed the fulcrum of the national wealth and hence their well-being and a reinvigoration of the villages where they lived to make them hubs of economic growth needed to be the goal. But even these classes must keep in mind that being an integral and important part of the nation, they must conscientiously share their responsibilities and obligations towards national wealth creation and national industry.

The interests of both capital and labour, in Savarkar's world view, were however subservient to national interests and requirement. Just as in times of profits, labourers share a large portion of it, in times of distress, losses also need to be borne in a way that the overall national industry may not be undermined by the selfish needs of either the capitalists or the labour. He advocated nationalization of key industries and manufactures if the government felt that it could do better than private enterprise.

A similar approach was sought for agriculture too where the interests of the landlord and the peasant needed to be coordinated in such a way that it positively impacted the national agriculture and its production. The government could plan to take over land if it felt it could introduce state cultivation and train peasants in modern mechanized farming to improve their productivity. Strikes and lockouts aimed at crippling national economic activity needed to be arbitrated quickly in special courts or quelled. Private property needed to be held in general as inviolate and in no case there should be any expropriation of the same by the state without adequate recompense to the holder. A protectionist approach was also suggested where the national government needed to make all attempts to protect the fledgling national industries against foreign competition. The national economic strength must grow and the nation must be economically self-sufficient—these were his two cornerstones. Equally important was the protection of economic interests of Hindus when threatened by others, especially in states like Hyderabad, Bhopal, Assam, Punjab, etc., where there was aggressive competition backed by state patronage. Class differences among Hindus needed to be sorted out to unify against such aggression.

Outlining the programme for the next two years, he said the war was the most important focus for the Mahasabha. He exhorted the British to make a definite and immediate declaration of grant of Dominion status to India at the end of the war as the only way to elicit Hindu sympathy and support and to 'ensure the willingness even of an independent India in the future to continue a partnership in the Commonwealth on equal terms'.[163] He criticized the strategy of the government of waiting for bridges to be built within the two major communities as a prerequisite for granting Dominion status.

No amount of political sophistry can disarm Indian discontent and make her tolerate the humiliation of continuing as a British dependency. Do you expect any longer to dupe her into the belief that it is only the want of an understanding between the Indian majority and minority, the Hindus and Moslems with regard to such details as the percentage in representation, etc. that justifies England in delaying the grant of Dominion Status forthwith? The British Statesmen have recently stated that their conscience forbids to thrust an understanding on the minority, the Moslems, in India, against their will and would not move an inch till the Hindus and Moslems have produced a willing compromise and a common demand for a progressive constitution. It was really a news [sic] to learn that English Statesmen have grown so god-fearing and Democratical [sic] almost overnight as not to be willing to thrust on any people anything against their own will! But may it be asked that when you thrust your unmitigated political autocracy on India, was there any plebiscite taken to a certain Indian opinion? Or did you take a plebiscite or receive a united request from the minority and the majority when only a couple of months ago you scrapped up the provincial autonomy at a stroke and invested Governors with powers to conduct

the Government at their own discretion and in their own judgment? And
if you could thrust undiluted autocracy, a vassalage on India and hold
her as a dependency, can you not thrust a Dominion Status on her in
spite of the will of a minority and especially so when the majority has
unanimously demanded it? The sooner the British people cease to have a
resort to these transparent political subterfuges and to utilize the Moslem
minority to camouflage their own unwillingness to grant Hindusthan her
birthright, her Swarajya, while she is still treading on an evolutionary
path of political progress the better for England, the better for India. If
the evolutionary path is thus altogether closed to the Hindus in particular
by empowering the Moslems with a definite veto on all equitable progress
a deadlock may ensue, but only for a while. Because nature hates vacuum:
and if evolutionary progress is denied, the gathering forces of Time Spirit
cannot but take the other and more dangerous turn.[164]

He called upon the Hindu Mahasabha volunteers carry out a whirlwind
campaign across the country towards three main points: Removal of
untouchability and thereby consolidating crores of Hindus; compelling
schools, universities and colleges to make military training compulsory,
enabling enrolment in armed forces; and finally preparing the Hindu
electorate to vote only for the Hindu sangathanists who would safeguard
their interests and not the Congress that had a history of betraying them.
Returning a favourable representative would help the Hindus in the most
likely event of a constituent assembly being formed soon to draft a new
constitution, he prophesied. Reassuring the minorities he added:

As we have no grudge against the Moslem minority in so far as their
legitimate rights are concerned and as the Hindu Sangathanists are ever
willing to live in an honourable friendship and amity with their Moslem
countrymen in Hindusthan, the Moslem minority too will have every
protection in the exercise of its legitimate rights.[165]

Savarkar wished to 'relieve our non-Hindu countrymen of even a
ghost of suspicion... that the legitimate rights of minorities with regard
to their religion, culture and language will be expressly guaranteed : on
one condition only that the equal rights of the majority also must not
in any case be encroached upon or abrogated. Every minority may have
separate schools to train up their children in their own tongue, their own
religious or cultural institutions and can receive Government help also

for these, but always in proportion to the taxes they pay into the common Exchequer. The same principle must of course hold good in case of the majority too.'[166]

The *Amrit Bazar Patrika* that covered the session and Savarkar's address opined:

Whether one agrees with all his views or not, Mr. Savarkar compels attention by the boldness and clarity of his utterances. He knows no doubt or hesitation. His logic is merciless, his humour caustic, and his irony effective. He is a man with a mission. The faith that burns in him throws a halo all around and he seems as he delivers his message and advances like a conquering hero, sweeping away from his path like cobwebs all time-worn theories and personalities . . . In Indian politics we have at least a man who is not afraid to call a spade a spade . . . one consideration is that the Congress has lost its hold over Bengal. We shall not go into the story today but it is an admitted fact that it is the non-communal outlook of the Congress, which has failed to satisfy the Hindus of this Province.[167]

The curtains thus came down on what was an eventful and turbulent year in Indian and world history, ushering in the fourth decade of the twentieth century—one that would see unmitigated disasters and suffering for the subcontinent.

6

Tumultuous Times

23 March 1940, Lahore

There was a sense of inexplicable excitement coupled with nervousness in the rank and file of the Muslim League as it met for its annual session in Lahore in 1940. The session was to see a landmark resolution being adapted by the League. It was moved by Abul Kashem Fazl-ul-Haq whose Krishak Praja Party (KPP) was in coalition with the League in the government in Bengal. Chaudhry Khaliquzzaman of the League was asked by Jinnah to second it. The sum and substance of the resolution drew from an earlier plan by one Rehmat Ali and the Urdu poet Sir Mohammad Iqbal way back in 1930–33. The scheme had advocated a division of British India into Pakistan and Hindustan on the basis of religion. In the original scheme, Pakistan included Punjab, NWFP, Kashmir, Sindh and Baluchistan. The proposal for these five independent Muslim states had even been circulated to the members of the Round Table Conference but never officially put forth. The Lahore Resolution enlarged this to include Muslim-majority areas in the east as well, in Bengal and Assam. Rejecting the Federation Plan of 1935, the resolution, among other things, noted:

> Resolved that it is the considered view of this Session of the All-India Muslim League that no constitutional plan would be workable in this country or acceptable to the Muslims unless it is designated on the following basic principle, viz. that geographically contiguous units are demarcated into regions, which should be so constituted with such territorial readjustments as may be necessary, that the areas in which the Muslims are numerically in a majority as in the North-Western and Eastern zones of India should be grouped to constitute 'Independent

States' in which the Constituent Units shall be autonomous and sovereign.[1]

The next morning newspaper headlines were agog claiming that a 'Pakistan Resolution' had been passed, though this word itself had never been used by anyone in the speeches or in the body of the resolution. The resolution however rendered all issues that had been hotly contested hitherto—separate electorates, composite cabinets and reservation of seats—totally irrelevant. This was the culmination of a long bitterness and distrust that the League shared with the Congress in particular and more so after the 1937 elections.

The League had hoped that the Communal Award of the British government would seal its fortunes for the better. The Award had allowed the Muslims to retain weightage and separate electorates, in addition to giving them the statutory majority of seats in those provinces where they constituted a majority of the population. But the 1937 results demonstrated that neither the Congress nor the League could claim to be truly representative of the Muslims. The League managed to get 108 seats out of the 485 Muslim seats. The Congress contested fifty-eight Muslim seats and won twenty-six.[2] The Congress refused to have any truck with the League and refused to form a coalition government with it in the United Provinces. Ridiculous conditions were put to form such a coalition including that in UP the League must cease to function as a separate group; dissolve its Parliamentary Board; abide by the CWC guidelines and 'the members of the Muslim League in the U.P. shall become part of the Congress Party and will fully share with other members of the Party their privileges and obligations as members of the Congress Party'.[3] Such preposterous demands were obviously rejected not only by the League, but also several pro-Congress Muslim groups such as the Ahrars and members of the Jamiat-ul-Ulema. The strategy they felt was to deny the Muslim League the position of being the sole representative of Muslim voice in India. This thinking in the Congress was led by its president, Jawaharlal Nehru, who along with his socialist friends in the party tried to underplay the whole communal issue of Hindu–Muslim differences. Under Nehru's handpicked leaders who were avowed socialists and communists in their orientation—Kunwar Mohammad Ashraf, Z.A. Ahmed and Sajjad Zaheer—a new Muslim narrative was sought to be crafted. The communal issue between Hindus and Muslims was portrayed as one of economic class

conflict and competing interests over the same, shrinking economic pie[4]—
something that Savarkar had ridiculed at the Calcutta session of the Hindu
Mahasabha in December 1939.

The Congress began its ambitious programme called 'Muslim Mass
Contact Programme' (MMCP) to enlist thousands of Muslims into its
rank and file and to make its ideology appealing to them. They sought to
reach out mainly to the peasants and labourers among the Muslims and
declared that the so-called 'Muslim culture' only referred to the aristocratic
and landed gentry, most of whom were either associated with or were
patrons of the Muslim League. By creating this cleft within the Muslim
society on economic grounds, it sought to attract to its folds several fence-
sitters of the community who were obviously not with the League as the
election results had proved. Stressing on common emotional bonds between
Hindus and Muslims, it tried to create a narrative where none existed.
Promotion and propagation of Hindustani as the composite language of
the two communities were launched aggressively. In its new education
policy called the Wardha Scheme that was adopted in the Haripura session
in 1938, these features were elaborated, causing quite a stir within the
League. They saw this as an attempt by the Congress to indoctrinate young
minds into the Congress (read Hindu) culture, stress on ahimsa or non-
violence and propagate the new creature called Hindustani at the cost of
Urdu. To propagate the new education policy, the Vidya Mandir scheme
of new schools was to be launched in 1939. Protests about this broke out
in several provinces from the Muslim side. The Congress's acceptance of
'Vande Mataram' as a national song and its singing in schools was fiercely
opposed as being anti-Muslim given the rich iconography of the nation
as the Mother Goddess. This went contrary to the fundamental Muslim
belief of adherence to a single God, it was argued.

Denouncing the Congress's MMCP, Jinnah thundered in 1937: 'The
Congress under the guise of establishing mass contact with Muslims is
calculated to divide and weaken and break the Mussalmans and is an effort
to detach them from their accredited leaders. It is a dangerous move and it
cannot mislead anyone.'[5] While running a mass contact programme with
any demographic was the natural and fair right of a political party that was
keen on expansion of its footprint, these steps gave the League a convenient
excuse to arouse Muslim fears and apprehensions. With minuscule power
in a few provinces if the Congress could, by subterfuge, impose a Hindu raj
on them, what fate could befall the community if the country became free

under the majority, it was argued. The federal part of the 1935 Act, it was declared, would hurt the Muslims more as the government in the Centre would be dominated by Hindus (Congress).

Sadly for the Congress, the MMCP was a disastrous failure right from the start, as it did not encourage the Muslim masses to join the party. It pushed the League more and more to take on the mantle of being the messiah of the community. With a life and death challenge for its organizational future, the League decided to reinvent itself in terms of its structure, policies and programmes and the results were to be seen quite early. In the UP by-elections where the League had hitherto little impact, out of five seats (Jhansi, Bijnore, Moradabad, Seherampur and Bulandshahar), the Congress won just one at Bijnore and the rest went to the League. By January 1938, the League demonstrated an impressive 3,00,000 Muslims in its membership rolls, as against 1,00,000 of the Congress.[6]

Congressmen themselves began to write to Nehru in alarm to rescind this scheme that specifically targeted one community. Pushed to the corner through such attempts of its target vote base, the beleaguered League actually rose from the ashes of 1937 with a lot more influence and power. If it was not pushed to the wall, it might have meandered along in coalition governments. But with an acute existential crisis, the urgency to prove itself as the sole voice of the Muslims propelled it into action. It was this antipathy of the League towards the Congress that showed itself in the celebration of Deliverance Day too in December 1939. The war and Viceroy Linlithgow's soft corner for Jinnah and the League were further encouraging stimuli at a time when Shia–Sunni conflicts over theological issues that manifested in the form of the *Madhe Sabaha* agitations in UP were almost threatening to blow the League away.

~

The tendency of separatism among the Muslims has often been ascribed to the British policy of 'divide and rule'. But there was an inherent problem deep-rooted among a vast section of the Muslims, especially its clergy and leadership that bred this separatism.[7] Right from Sir Syed Ahmed Khan's advocacy of Muslims being a separate nation in themselves and the clamour for partitioning Bengal to the Lucknow Pact, the Communal Award and finally the Pakistan Resolution of 1940, the trajectory seems predictable. Many political commentators pointed out this tendency to overemphasize on the divide and rule policy. That the Congress had to stress on the need for Hindu–Muslim unity as a goal in itself showed that this unity was lacking and needed to be achieved (after all they had no Hindu–Christian or Hindu–Parsi unity goals). Savarkar was one such commentator who called this spade a spade. In the 1939 Hindu Mahasabha address in Calcutta, he spoke about this:

> It is also instructive and therefore, necessary to point out here that this theory of 'the third party' also constituted a Congress superstition which was responsible for so many of its errors. They always used to fancy that the Moslems, if left to themselves, would never have indulged in any anti-national, ulterior, anti-Hindu designs. The Moslems-including Messrs. Jinnah, [Fazal-ul] Huq [sic], and [Sikandar] Hayat Khan, were very simple-minded folk incapable of any political subterfuges and as devotes of Islam, peace and goodwill, had no aggressive political aims of their own against the Hindus. Nay, even the Frontier tribes, the 'brave brothers Moplas', the Moslem populations in Bengal or Sindh who indulge in such horrible outrages against Hindus have no taste for it all, nursed within themselves; but were almost compelled to rise and revolt against the Hindus by 'the third party' the Britishers [sic]. When the British did not step in we Hindus and Moslems lived together in perfect amity and brotherly concord and Hindu-Moslem riots was [sic] a thing simply unheard of. Thousands of Congressite Hindus are observed to have been duped in to this silliest of political superstitions. As if Mahamad Kasim, Gazanis, Ghoris, Allauddins, Aurangzebs were all instigated by the British, by this third party, to invade and lay waste Hindu India with a mad fanatical fury. As if the history of the last ten centuries of perpetual war between the Hindus and Moslems was an interpolation and a myth. As if the Alis or Mr. Jinnah or Sir Sikandar were mere school children to be spoiled with the offer of sugar pills by the British vagabonds in the class and persuaded to throw stones at the house of their neighbours. They say, 'before the British came, Hindu-Moslem riots were a thing unheard of'. Yes, but because instead of riots, Hindus-Moslems wars was the order of the day.[8]

Inarguably, the most clinical and ruthless analysis of the theological, political and sociocultural dimensions of this malaise was done by Babasaheb Ambedkar. In his seminal work *Pakistan or the Partition of India,* he devotes chapters to analyze this threadbare. On the divide and rule policy, he states:

> The Hindus say that the British policy of divide and rule is the real cause of this failure and of this ideological revolution . . . but [the] time has come to discard the facile explanation so dear to the Hindus. For it fails to take into account two very important circumstances. In the first place, it overlooks the fact that the policy of divide and rule, allowing that the British do resort to it, cannot succeed unless there are elements which make division possible, and further if the policy succeeds for such a long time, it means that the elements which divide are more or less permanent and irreconcilable and are not transitory or superficial. Secondly, it forgets that Mr. Jinnah, who represents this ideological transformation, can never be suspected of being a tool in the hands of the British even by the worst of his enemies. He may be too self-opinionated, an egotist without the mask, and has perhaps a degree of arrogance, which is not compensated by any extraordinary intellect or equipment . . . At the same time, it is doubtful if there is a politician in India to whom the adjective incorruptible can be more fittingly applied . . . The real explanation of this failure of Hindu-Muslim unity lies in the failure to realize that what stands between the Hindus and Muslims is not a mere matter of difference, and that this antagonism is not to be attributed to material causes. It is formed by causes, which take their origin in historical, religious, cultural and social antipathy, of which political antipathy is only a reflection. These form one deep river of discontent which, being regularly fed by these sources, keeps on mounting to a head and overflowing its ordinary channels.[9]

Delving dispassionately into the theological roots of the issue, Ambedkar states:

> Hinduism is said to divide people and in contrast Islam is said to bind people together. This is only a half truth. For Islam divides as inexorably as it binds. Islam is a close corporation and the distinction that it makes between Muslims and non-Muslims is a very real, very positive and very alienating distinction. The brotherhood of Islam is not the universal brotherhood of man. It is brotherhood of Muslims for Muslims only. There is a fraternity, but its benefit is confined to those within that

corporation. For those who are outside the corporation, there is nothing but contempt and enmity. The second defect of Islam is that it is a system of *social* self-government and is incompatible with *local* self-government, because the allegiance of a Muslim does not rest on his domicile in the country which is his but on the faith to which he belongs. To the Muslim *ibi bene ibi patria* is unthinkable. Wherever there is the rule of Islam, there is his own country. In other words, Islam can never allow a true Muslim to adopt India as his motherland and regard a Hindu as his kith and kin. That is probably the reason why Maulana Mahomed Ali, a great Indian but a true Muslim, preferred to be buried in Jerusalem rather than in India.[10]

According to the Muslim Canon Law, the world is divided into two camps, Dar-ul-Islam (abode of Islam) and Dar-ul-Harb (abode of war). A country is Dar-ul-Islam when it is ruled by Muslims. A country is Dar-ul-Harb when Muslims only reside in it but are not rulers of it. That being the Canon Law of the Muslims, India cannot be the common motherland of the Hindus and the Musalmans. It can be the land of the Musalmans—but it cannot be the land of the 'Hindus and the Musalmans living as equals.' Further, it can be the land of the Musalmans only when it is governed by the Muslims. The moment the land becomes subject to the authority of a non-Muslim power, it ceases to be the land of the Muslims. Instead of being Dar-ul-Islam, it becomes Dar-ul-harb.[11]

One cannot dismiss away the analyses of leaders such as Savarkar or Ambedkar through the modern idioms and narratives such as 'Islamophobia', but must see these as views of thinkers who actually took the bull by the horns. However, Ambedkar was not entirely supportive of Savarkar's stands when it came to his attitude towards the two-nation theory. He says:

Strange as it may appear, Mr. Savarkar and Mr. Jinnah, instead of being opposed to each other on the one nation versus two nations issue, are in complete agreement about it. Both agree, not only agree but insist, that there are two nations in India—one the Muslim nation and the other the Hindu nation. They differ only as regards the terms and conditions on which the two nations should live. Mr. Jinnah says India should be cut up into two, Pakistan and Hindustan . . . Mr. Savarkar on the other hand insists that although there are two nations in India, India shall not be divided into two parts . . . that the two nations shall dwell in one country and shall live under the mantle of one single constitution; that the constitution shall be such that the Hindu nation will be enabled to occupy a predominant position that is due to it and the Muslim nation made to live in the position of subordinate cooperation with the Hindu nation . . . the rule of the game, which Mr. Savarkar prescribes is one man one vote, be the man Hindu or Muslim. In this scheme a Muslim is to have no advantage which a Hindu does not have. Minority is to be no justification for privilege and majority is to be no ground for penalty. The State shall guarantee the Muslims any defined measure of political power in the form of Muslim religion and Muslim culture. But the State will not guarantee secured seats in the Legislature or in the Administration and, if such guarantee is insisted by the Muslims, such guaranteed quota is not to exceed their proportion to the general population . . . this alternative of Mr. Savarkar to Pakistan has about it a frankness, boldness and definiteness which distinguishes it from the irregularity, vagueness and indefiniteness which characterizes the Congress declarations about minority rights. Mr. Savarkar's scheme has at least the merit of telling the Muslims, thus far and no further. The Muslims know where they are with regard to the Hindu Maha Sabha [sic]. On the other hand, with the Congress, the Muslamans find themselves nowhere because the Congress has been treating the Muslims and the minority question as a game in diplomacy, if not in duplicity.[12]

Ambedkar, however, picks bones with Savarkar's formula where he concedes these rights and privileges to the Muslims whom he calls a separate nation within the larger Indian rubric by terming it as 'illogical, if not queer'.[13] In fact, he terms these concessions that Savarkar accords to the Muslims of following their culture and religion, and having their flags, etc., as creating a 'dangerous situation for the security and safety of India'.[14] Ambedkar mentions that history has shown only two ways in which a major nation has dealt with a minor nation that exists within it. The first way is for the former to destroy the nationality of the latter and assimilate and absorb it within itself. This would be done 'by denying to the minor nation any right to language, religion or culture and by seeking to enforce upon it the language, religion and culture of the major nation'.[15] The other alternative is to let the minor nation separate itself into an autonomous and sovereign entity. Evidently, Savarkar was doing neither of the above. As Ambedkar postulates:

> He [Savarkar] does not propose to suppress the Muslim nation. On the contrary, he is nursing and feeding it by allowing it to retain its religion, language and culture, elements which go to sustain the soul of a nation. At the same time he does not consent to divide the country . . . he wants the Hindus and Muslims to live as two separate nations in one country, each maintaining its own religion, language and culture . . . Why Mr. Savarkar, after sowing this seed of enmity between the Hindu nation and the Muslim nation, should want that they should live under one constitution and occupy one country, is difficult to explain . . . Suffice it to say that the scheme for Swaraj formulated by Mr. Savarkar will give the Hindus an empire over the Muslims and thereby satisfy their vanity and their pride in being an imperial race. But it can never ensure a stable and peaceful future for the Hindus, for the simple reason that Muslims will never yield willing obedience to so dreadful an alternative.[16]

Thus, India was headed towards a complex situation and there were competing thought processes and philosophies on how to deal with it. If one were to fault Savarkar for his attitude during this time, it would rest on the fact that he never attempted to open bridges or conversation with the Muslims or the League or even meet/cultivate a personal rapport with Jinnah whose animosity for Nehru was legendary. His formula was, as Ambedkar analyzed, one where he formulated a scheme and threw it at the 'face of the Muslims with the covering letter "take it or leave it"'.[17] A tactful co-option of Jinnah and weaning him away from the British or the Congress might have held a different course for Indian history, though rife with the perils that Ambedkar prophesied for the future security and sovereignty of the country.

Viceroy Lord Linlithgow meanwhile realized that his earlier offers had struck no chord with any political formation of India. In a speech at Bombay's Orient Club on 10 January 1940, he said that Britain's object was Dominion status of the Westminster model. Three days later he assured the Congress in particular that there was merely a difference in name when it came to Dominion status and independence. According to the Statute of Westminster of 1931, Dominions were promised freedom to manage their internal and foreign affairs, have their own diplomatic contingents and separate representation in the League of Nations. Laws passed by the British Parliament would not automatically be adopted in the Dominions till the latter consented to them. Both Gandhi and Savarkar seemed enthused by these announcements. Savarkar called them as clear and definite; Gandhi met the viceroy on 5 February 1940. These talks were inconclusive largely because of the antagonistic views of the British government back in London. Prime Minister Neville Chamberlain, Chancellor of the Exchequer Sir John Simon and First Lord of the Admiralty Sir Winston Churchill all thought that the viceroy was pusillanimous and gave too much to Gandhi and the Congress. The stalemate was to continue for a few more months.

On his part, Savarkar carried on with his whirlwind countrywide tours. Despite his failing health, he travelled to West Khandesh in mid-March 1940 making speeches for several Adivasi communities in Takarkhed, Shahade, Prakashe and Talode. He later embarked on a tour to Salem and Madras in south India. On 20 March 1940, Savarkar travelled to Salem to attend the Tamil Nadu Hindu Conference. In his speech, he said:

I am asked that since there is no injustice against Hindus in South India, why do we need a body like the Hindu Mahasabha here. And this question is not asked by Muslims or Christians, it is asked only by Hindus, mainly by Hindus supporting the Congress. Can these people answer me why does the brain feel the pain if a thorn is stuck in the foot? As a Hindu you should feel the pain of Hindus anywhere. The CM of Sindh, Allah Baksh himself admitted that in the recent anti-Hindu riots in Sindh, 10 Hindus were burnt alive, millions were made refugees, 150 Hindus were killed. If you neglect it by calling it a problem of 'North India', in another 100 years, Madras will face the same thing. In the past too, Hindus of the South didn't do anything when the Muslim invaders were attacking Punjab and Sindh and Islam reached this region as well. If we keep doing the same thing again, Hindus will be a minority everywhere. And it is a myth that there is no problem of Islamic persecution in India. The Moplah rebellion happened in the Malabar; right now the Nizam's forces are discriminating against the Hindus in Hyderabad State. In Mysore State, Muslims form 6 % of the population but their numbers in the army are over 60%. Congress leaders like Sikandar Hayat Khan, Fazlul Haq and others attend Muslim League sessions. Even the so-called nationalist Muslim leaders of the Congress like Maulana Azad say openly that they will not compromise on the interests of Muslims in India. Have you heard any Hindu leader talk about Hindu interests so openly? If a Hindu starts speaking like this, the Congress will start calling him communal. Isn't this unfair?[18]

In mid-April 1940, he embarked on a tour to Travancore. At the Hindu Conference held at Changanacheri on 5 May 1940 he spoke about the Hindu Mahasabha's philosophy with regard to untouchability, princely states and militarization. From there he made his way to Madurai where he was accorded a grand reception at the famed Meenakshi temple.

The viceroy sought to meet Savarkar on 5 July 1940 to discuss the proposals related to the formation of a national government of all parties. Savarkar called the meeting as frank, considerate and impartial. He made it known to the viceroy that while he favoured a national government, he would want fresh elections to decide the composition as much had changed in the political landscape of the country since 1937 and forming a government by drawing from hitherto elected members of the legislatures was not truly representative of the current will of the masses. The viceroy gave no assurances but promised to consider all options.

It was largely believed that the Congress would take to mass civil disobedience after its resignation from the ministries. But none of this happened as the British tried to keep them engaged. Apart from the viceroy's confabulations, writer Edward Thompson and Sir Stafford Cripps were sent in October and December 1939 respectively to speak to and win over Congress leaders. It was however Subhas Bose and his Forward Bloc that kept up the fire for a Civil Disobedience movement. In the National Week that was declared by him from 6 to 13 April 1940, the Bloc commenced its Civil Disobedience movement across the country to give a final push towards freedom. Interestingly, the same Congress that had given out belligerent statements against the British government bitterly criticized Subhas's move. On 20 May 1940, Nehru stated: 'Launching a civil disobedience campaign at a time when Britain is engaged in a life and death struggle would be an act derogatory to India's honour.'[19] Gandhi too concurred: 'We do not seek our independence out of Britain's ruin. That is not the way of non-violence.'[20]

Bose toured the country to seek support for his views and in the course of it met Jinnah first. Interestingly, Jinnah asked him to meet Savarkar to elicit the latter's views. Accordingly, on 22 June 1940, Bose and Savarkar had a meeting that lasted for nearly three hours. In his memoirs, Bose was least charitable to both Savarkar and Jinnah:

> Mr. Jinnah was then thinking only of how to realize his plan of Pakistan (division of India) with the help of the British. The idea of putting up a joint fight with the Congress, for Indian Independence, did not appeal to him at all though the writer [Bose] suggested that in the event of such a united struggle taking place, Mr. Jinnah would be the first Prime Minister of Free India. Mr. Savarkar seemed to be oblivious of the international situation and was only thinking how Hindus could secure military training by entering Britain's army in India. From these interviews, the writer was forced to the conclusion that nothing could be expected from either the Muslim League or the Hindu Mahasabha.[21]

Savarkar's secretary Balarao, however, recounts that in this meeting the former strongly advised Bose to not run behind the mirage of Hindu–Muslim unity but seek the help of the enemies of Britain in the war, such as Japan, Italy and Germany. He advised Bose to flee India and move to either Germany or Japan, get the captured Indian soldiers released and raise an army that would attack British India via the Bay of Bengal. His view was that this was the only way that the British could be forced out of the country and not through mass protests or demonstrations.[22] This was the same model that the Indian revolutionaries had attempted during the First World War and failed. Corroborating this is a letter from Balarao, dated 2 June 1954:

> It may be mentioned here that it was at a private and personal meeting between Netaji Subhas Babu and Savarkarji at Savarkar Sadan Bombay that a definite suggestion was made to Subhas Babu by Savarkarji that he should try to leave India and undertake the risk of going over to Germany to organize the Indian forces there fallen in German hands as captives and then with the German help should proceed to Japan to join hands with Sri Rash Behari Bose. To impress this point Savarkarji showed to Subhas Babu a letter from Sri Bose [Rash Behari] to Savarkarji written just on the eve of Japanese declaration of war.[23]

As later events were to prove, in about six months thence, Subhas Bose took precisely this route by disappearing from India in January 1941 from

his house on Elgin Road in Calcutta and eventually joined Rash Behari
Bose. On his mysterious disappearance, Savarkar issued a statement: 'May
the gratitude, sympathy and good wishes of a nation be a source of never-
failing solace and inspiration to him wherever he happens to be. Wherever
he happens to be, I have no doubt he will continue to contribute his all,
even health and life to the cause of Indian freedom.'[24]

~

A major part of 1940 turned out to be very difficult for Savarkar personally
as his health took a complete beating with all the whirlwind travel across
the country. Following his long incarceration in Cellular Jail, his health
was already fragile. The pressures of public life compounded this further.
He came down with high fever and excruciating sciatica in his legs. He was
homebound for nearly four months. Letter correspondences between the
viceroy and the Hindu Mahasabha leaders including Moonje and Savarkar
however continued even during this period. After a Working Committee
meeting of the Hindu Mahasabha on 21 and 22 September in Bombay,
Savarkar issued a statement revising the terms of cooperation from the
Mahasabha. He urged the viceroy to reject any scheme to partition the
country and also the League's demand for 50 per cent reservation of seats
on an expanded Executive Council. There was talk that the government
was in favour of giving the League two seats on the Executive Council and
six on a proposed War Advisory Council. The Mahasabha demanded three
times that number for itself on the population proportion formula, i.e.,
six on the Executive Council and fifteen on the War Advisory Council.
The Mahasabha was willing to give two seats from its six seats on the
Council—one to the Sikhs and another to the depressed classes. Moonje
wrote to the viceroy about this formula, trying to put out a case for the
Mahasabha being a better choice of an ally in the war in his letter of 26
September 1940:

> I may repeat here my conviction that between the two communities, the
> Hindu Mahasabha, which represents the Hindus, will be in a position
> to give immensely large help both in men, material and intellect than
> the Muslim League can hope to do, in organizing the defence of India
> on modern scientific lines. Besides, the inherent loyalty of the Moslems
> based on the conceptions of their religion, for Muslim countries outside

India, which may at any time in the course of the war, join hands with the enemies of the British Empire, is always a standing potential danger. In contrast with this fundamental fact, the loyalty of the Hindus to their own sacred land, Hindusthan, surrounded as it is on the Western and north-Western frontier by its traditional enemies of the last more than one thousand years, is the one stable factor in its choice of its allies for its permanent safety and prosperity. It will naturally lead the Hindus to look up to Britain, in spite of its quarrels with it for constitutional powers. Thus Hindusthan and Britain are allied together in unshakeable bond of union for long, long years to come. Thus this fundamental contrast between the two loyalties, the Hindus and the Muslim, is the chief pivot of the situation, which should never be allowed to fade away from Your Excellency's mind.[25]

The viceroy turned down most of the demands, including those of the League, and proposed a seat each for the Hindu Mahasabha, the Sikhs, the depressed classes and a Muslim party. What is commonly known as the 'August Offer' was declared on 8 August 1940: 'It goes without saying that His Majesty's Government could not contemplate the transfer of their present responsibilities for the peace and welfare of India to any system of government whose authority is directly denied by large and powerful elements in India's national life.'[26] This put a huge premium on the veto that the League wished to have on constitutional reforms without settling the communal issue. Unless the minorities were on board, the British would not be willing to consider any transfer of power. The 'August Offer' also stipulated the formation of a representative constituent body to frame India's new constitution in accordance with Dominion precedent and opening the way to the attainment by India 'of that free and equal partnership in the British Commonwealth which remains the proclaimed and accepted goal of the Imperial Crown and of the British Parliament'.[27]

Barring the Mahasabha and Ambedkar's Independent Labour Party, all others, especially the Congress and the League, rejected the offer. Rather than an outright rejection, Savarkar reiterated this support in principle to the 'August Offer' in his letter to the viceroy on 2 October 1940, but decided to negotiate on the qualified encouragement to Muslim separatism that was implicit in the offer.[28]

The Hindu Mahasabha suggested to the viceroy to create his council with the help of disgruntled members within each of the main parties.

Moonje in his letter to Linlithgow dated 3 October suggested that 'if the
Congress does not come in, there is the Congress Nationalist Party which
is doing good work in the Legislative Assembly' and could be incorporated
as it represented 'a great deal of whatever realism and patriotism' there was
within the Congress. As for the Muslim League, he suggested that there
were lots of differences between the Shias and the Sunnis, and that these
divisions must be made use of to weaken the League, rather than view the
Muslims as a monolithic community. He drew the viceroy's attention to
the differences between Sikandar Hyat Khan and Jinnah, and the former's
complaint about the arrogant, dictatorial style of the latter. These factions,
along with the Shia Association and the Independent Moslem Conference
Association, could be co-opted by the viceroy instead of the League. He
also argued in favour of both the Hindu Mahasabha and the princes of
India who should not be taken as rubberstamps. Moonje wrote:

> As for the Hindu Mahasabha, it would be wrong to take a narrow
> view of its status and importance as compared particularly, with the
> Muslim League, its competitor, for authority and power, from the
> mere fact that it has not fared well in the last general elections as
> compared with the Congress. The Hindu Mahasabha truly represents
> the communal and religious sentiments of the Hindus generally, not
> excluding the Hindu Princes also, who are no insignificant supporters
> of the war efforts. Circumstances oblige the Princes to be dumb and
> perhaps even deaf publicly, but that is all the more reason to attach
> overwhelming importance to what they say when they break their
> silence in complete confidence within closed doors. Thus, from the
> vital point of view the status and importance of the Hindu Mahasabha
> in relation to the work in hand, is immeasurably greater than that of
> the Congress. We cannot, therefore, afford to alienate and antagonize
> the Hindu Princes.[29]

The Congress meanwhile was in a bind. Even as it was negotiating with
the viceroy, the Forward Bloc under Subhas Bose had been carrying out a
successful Civil Disobedience campaign in the country. It feared a loss of its
relevance in both the corridors of power as well as in the mass movement.
Gandhi was being pressed to start a mass movement of his own, given all
talks with the viceroy had led to nothing. But instead of a mass movement,
he came up with a peculiar campaign from 17 October 1940 called

representative satyagraha. Individuals were to be selected to go on to streets across the country, shout anti-war slogans, attract the ire of the police and get arrested. Nearly 600 people were packed off to jails, including Congress president Maulana Abul Kalam Azad and C. Rajagopalachari—some being sentenced even for twelve months. The futility of such a campaign was recognized by many, including Congress workers who urged Gandhi to launch a more robust and impactful movement, but this was not to be. As Bose recounted:

> During the year 1941, the Civil Disobedience Movement continued—but without much enthusiasm on the part of Gandhi and his followers. The Mahatma had calculated that by following a mild policy, he would ultimately open the door towards a compromise—but in this, he was disappointed. His goodness was mistaken for weakness and the British Government went on exploiting India for war purposes to the best of its ability. The Government also exploited to the fullest extent such agents as the erstwhile Communist leader, M.N. Roy, who were prepared to sell themselves to Britain.[30]

Despite serious ideological differences with Gandhi and Nehru, Savarkar was deeply critical of the British government when Nehru was arrested and subsequently sentenced to four years' imprisonment. Describing the move as a vindictive one that was 'a painful shock to every Indian patriot' he held that he had nothing but 'deep appreciation of the patriotic and even the humanitarian motives which had actuated Pandit Jawaharlalji throughout his public career'. Savarkar added:

> In spite of differences as to principles and policy, which compel both of us to work under different colors, I shall be failing in my duty as a Hindu Sabhaite if I do not express my deep appreciation of the patriotic and even the humanitarian motives which had actuated Pandit Jawaharlalji throughout his public career and my sympathy for the sufferings, which he has consequently had to face.[31]

He, however, was quick to remind the Congress that it never had the large heart to utter a single word of sympathy or protest when patriots like Senapati Bapat or Subhas Bose and others who differed from the Gandhian philosophy were similarly held under the draconian Defence of India Act ever since the war broke out. He urged the government to introspect 'why a man like Pandit Jawaharlalji who, as soon as the war broke out, was impulsively carried off his feet as to declare that India should offer unconditional cooperation to the British who were out to fight the cause of world democracy . . . should feel so embittered'.[32] Repression on the part of the government could thus do nothing to help achieve responsive cooperation. Instead, a timeline for the grant of Dominion status could help build bridges between the Indian political opinion and the British government.

A clear articulation of the Hindu Mahasabha's attitude towards the war efforts came in Savarkar's presidential speech at the annual session in Madurai in end-December 1940. He was still convalescing and was brought to the dais on a chair. He rubbished the British claims, and those initially of Congress leaders like Nehru, that the war was a crusade for strengthening democracies and that England, Germany, Japan, China, USSR or any country could not make such claims. The Mahasabha had outlined this in its September 1939 Working Committee resolution long back that the war was not 'actuated by any moral, democratic or altruistic considerations' and all the belligerents were only interested in 'self-interest and self-aggrandizement'.[33] He attacked the viceroy's speeches to this effect and quoted the instance of Hitler who when asked to vacate Poland by Chamberlain said that he would do so when Britain decided to vacate India. 'Thieves alone can trace the footsteps of thieves best,' he mocked. Hence the Congress demands to make the British spell their 'war objectives' was just idle talk since their objectives were clear to anyone who wished to see. So, it would be a suicidal folly for India, he warned, to be taken in by all these lofty slogans or political philosophies ('isms' that each of the war participants follow), and one should only see what their attitude towards India, her goals of freedom and a democratic constitution is and base one's support or opposition on that alone to serve India's own interests to the maximum.

> We should neither hate nor love Nazists [sic] or Bolshevists [sic] or Democrats simply on the ground of any theoretical or bookish reasons. There is no reason to suppose that Hitler must be a human monster because he passes off as a Nazi or Churchill is a demi-God because he calls himself a Democrat. Nazism proved undeniably the saviour of Germany under the set of circumstances Germany was placed in; Bolshevism might

have suited Russia very well and we know what the English Democracy has cost us.[34]

Savarkar also dismissed the fears aroused by the British and others that if India did not support Britain, Hitler and Germany would invade and take over India as being 'unreal, ridiculous and crafty'.[35] He said, '. . . if ever the English really come to feel so helpless that without our help they were sure to lose India, they would offer us themselves not only the Dominion Status but some of their colonies and possessions as they are doing today in the case of America.'[36] He, however, cautioned against any false sense of complacency and bombast and prescribed eternal vigilance on the fluid and perpetually changing global situation in order to calibrate a self-interest-based response.

In passing, Savarkar mentioned an armed revolt on a national scale as a sure-shot way of dependent nations emerging free when their oppressor was caught in a global mess. He however maintained that this was not possible in India at the moment given the state of disunity where the country was disorganized and disarmed. The astute politician in him also stated that talking openly about an armed revolt as an objective from the platform of a political party was not prudent. But at the same time, the other extreme of total and complete non-violence, even in these charged circumstances, as advocated by Gandhi, was 'monomaniacal senselessness'.[37] Relative ahimsa, he claimed, was a virtue, but the absolute ahimsa of the Gandhian variety was a veritable crime that even had a moral perversity to it. Quoting the scriptures of religions like Buddhism and Jainism that stress on non-violence, he claimed that even they allowed taking up of arms in defence of a just and righteous cause. Does saintliness demand just spinning the wheel to free India of foreign yoke or abdicate her right as an independent nation in future to have an army, warships or armed soldiers, he tauntingly questioned. Training his guns further on the Mahatma, he said:

When things have come to such a pass that such quixotic souls are sent as accredited spokesmen by the credulous crowd to the round table conference and even in foreign lands such senseless proposals are seriously advanced by them in the name of the Indian Nation itself in so many words to the great merriment of the foreign statesmen and the general public in Europe and America, the time has surely come to take this doctrinal plague quite seriously and to counteract it as quickly as possible. We must tell them in no apologetic language but in firm accents that your doctrine of absolute non-violence is not only absolutely impracticable but absolutely immoral. It is not an outcome of any saintliness but of insanity. It requires no ingenuity on your part to tell us that if but all men observe absolute non-violence, there will be no war in the world and no necessity of any armed forces. Just as it requires no extraordinary insight to maintain that if but men learn to live forever mankind will be free from death. We denounce your doctrine of absolute non-violence not because we are less saintly but because we are more sensible than you are. Relative non-violence is our creed and therefore, we worship the defensive sword as the first saviour of man. It was in this faith that Hindus worship the arms as the Symbols of the Shakti, the Kali, and Guru Govind Singh sang his hymn to the Sword.[38]

Savarkar reiterated his demand for a military awakening among the Hindus and a concerted campaign to enhance militarization amidst them. Within a year of beginning the policy of militarization the results were there for all to see with more Hindu youths enlisting in the armed forces, he maintained. Hitherto, while almost 75 per cent of the army was comprised of Muslims, among the new recruits the ratio was skewed in favour of the Hindus: 60,000 Hindus vis-à-vis 30,000 Muslims.[39] A similar rise in the numbers was seen in the air force and navy too and this was thanks to the efforts of the Mahasabha. In the navy, communities of Maharashtra like the Agris, the Bhandaris, the Kolis and others, who had been at the forefront of the naval strength of the Maratha army that had at one time challenged British forces, were now being reinvigorated to rediscover this martial spirit among them and applied in large numbers to the navy, he averred. He accused the Congress of following its non-violence policy to the extent that it had killed the martial instinct of the Hindus and brought about an alarming decline in their numbers in the armed forces.

The British policy of raising the army or industrialization was not being done by some altruistic motives to help Indians, but to eventually help the Empire. Savarkar said:

We are also participating in these war efforts, or at any rate are not out to oppose them, with no intention of helping the British but of helping ourselves. I have put the situation almost bluntly in the above manner to disarm the political folly into which the Indian public is accustomed to indulge in thinking that because Indian interests are opposed to the British interests in general, any step in which we join hands with the British Government must necessarily be an act of surrender, anti-national, of playing into the British hands and that co-operation with the British Government in any case and under all circumstances is unpatriotic and condemnable.[40]

Scoffing at the attempts by Congress to dub the Mahasabha offer of support to the war as being collaborative with the British, Savarkar said:

It is all the more amusing to find that this spirit of silly bravado is more rampant amongst those very Congressites [sic] who did not hesitate to serve the British Government by conducting their Provincial Ministries swearing loyalty and allegiance to the British Domination in the oath of allegiance which they had to take; who wept over the fancied destruction of Westminster Abbey, only the other day and had served the British Government as their recruiting officers during the last war and are even now promising full co-operation to the British, if but they get some of their fadist [sic] demands satisfied and assure the British that they would do nothing even as it is to embarrass the British.[41]

He exuded confidence in the political wisdom of the Hindu sangathanists to not be duped by British statecraft as the Congress had always been and that any political alliance with anyone is cemented on the principle of achieving common interests and is never one-sided.

About the prospects that militarization held for India and Hindus in particular, Savarkar said that in view of the war, the government had an urgent need for technicians to produce military equipment, rifles and tanks on a large scale and had made arrangements to train 15,000 Indian candidates as technicians immediately. Some of them were also going to be sent to England to be trained in up-to-date technology, staying and working along with British experts and being treated on par in terms of pay scales and stature, at a cost footed by the government. The government similarly had plans to expand the Indian Army to half a million Indians, trained in all arms, to assist in future war efforts. With the increase in the required count in the armed forces from some two lakh to almost ten lakh Indian soldiers, there was an increased demand for creating commissioned officers. To manufacture war equipment on a large scale quickly, the government reluctantly permitted industrialist Seth Walchand Hirachand to open India's first shipyard at Visakhapatnam and had plans for aircraft manufacture to be set up in Bangalore. Other allied industries such as chemicals, paper, etc. too would be seeing a spurt. Savarkar questioned if this scaling up of Indian participation in the military or industry would have been possible only through the efforts of political parties like the Mahasabha or Congress. It was the government's role that helped in this scale-up. To be prudent was to participate in these efforts for our own good in the long run rather than being foolhardy in boycotting a golden opportunity that presented itself before the nation, he claimed. He also cautioned that the British were doing all this not merely because the war was being fought far away in Europe, but because they knew that trouble was brewing closer home with Japan's inevitable entry into the skirmish and the threats that posed for them in India. While they were caught in war in Europe with the Nazi and Fascist forces, an Indian invasion by Japan would make it impossible for Britain to send their forces from there to assist the Indian Army. Hence, local armies and technology were being developed in such tearing haste.

> Now again I ask you, shall we lose this golden opportunity to acquire this military strength which our interests also demand and British interests compel Britain to help us in that task simply because some fadists [sic] call it an act of violence or some fools condemn it as cooperation with Imperialism? Or shall we take the wisest step of allying ourselves with Britain on this point alone and to the extent to which it serves Hindu interests and flood the new army to be raised with Hindu Sangathanists and re-animate our race with martial spirit and regain the military strength and status we had lost?[42]

He called upon the Hindus to help in the militarization and industrialization of India and if they lost the opportunity, it would be up for grabs for the Muslims and would prove perilous. The counter move to this is the Congress satyagraha of shouting slogans in the streets, that too by individuals, and then get arrested for it. He dismissed it as a stunt at best that might bring some dividends in the next elections.

Courting arrests or launching a civil resistance movement as a counter to these stunts, just to win elections, was what the Hindu Mahasabha was being called upon to do. But this was counterproductive to the long-term Hindu or national interests and hence 'it is our clear duty to lose the elections rather than try to win them by pandering to the follies of the electorate to the detriment of the Hindu cause',[43] he claimed. The Nizam movement had proved that the Mahasabha volunteers were braver than the Congress when it came to undergoing sufferings and jail terms under abhorrent conditions. There was no need to stretch on the same when it was of no use to the country or its ultimate goal of achieving freedom. The government had agreed to the Mahasabha demands substantially in terms of grant of Dominion status after the war and not breaking the integrity of India. The only issue of conflict was the government's demand for a consensus among the majority and minority to draw out a new constitution and Savarkar exuded confidence in being able to convince them out of this 'specious' argument too in right time. In any negotiation, achievements were counted incrementally and not in absolute measure.

On the political front, Savarkar congratulated the Mahasabha for increasing its footprint across the country. From a membership in mere thousands, it had now swelled to several lakh and branches had sprung up in such areas where the party was not even heard of before. Organizations that had similar objectives as the Mahasabha had now either merged or affiliated themselves closely with it. He made mention of the Travancore State Hindusabha and the Shuddhisabha; the Kolhapur State Hindusabha and the Shuddhisabha, the Bhopal State Hindusabha, the Nizam State Hindu Mandal, the Gwalior State Hindusabha, the Cutch-Kathiawar State Hindusabha among others.[44] The Bengal Hindu Mahasabha had come out with flying colours in the Calcutta Corporation elections and challenged the once-held monopoly of the Congress, while in Sindh it had wrested majority from it as well. Importantly, he asserted that the British had finally woken to the fact that it was not just the Congress and the League, but that 'The Hindu Mahasabha, the League and the Congress = the sum total of Indian representation'.[45]

Summarizing the immediate action points for the party, Savarkar concluded:

(a) To secure entry for as many Hindu recruits as possible into the army, navy and the air forces.

(b) To utilize all facilities that are being thrown open to get our people trained into military and mechanical manufacture of up-to-date war materials.

(c) To try to make military training compulsory in colleges and high schools.

(d) To intensify the organization of the Ram Sena.

(e) To join the civic guard movement with a view to enable to defend our own people against foreign invasion or internal anarchy, provided always that the civic guards are not used against any patriotic political movements in India or in any activities detrimental to the legitimate interests of the Hindus.

(f) To start new industries on large scales to capture the market where foreign articles to defeat the entry of new foreign competitors.

(g) To boycott foreign articles to defeat the entry of new foreign competitors.

(h) To set on foot an all-India movement to secure the correct registration, in the coming Census, of the popular strength of the Hindus including Tribal Hindus such as Santhals, Gonds, Bhils, etc., and to secure their enlistment as Hindus instead of as Animists or Hill Tribes and by taking every other step necessary to secure the object in view.[46]

The Mahasabha adopted a resolution in Madurai that clearly enunciated its stand on the political developments in the country. It stated that 'while reiterating its faith in the goal of complete independence of India . . . was prepared [to] accept the Dominion Status of Westminster Statute as an immediate next step . . . that this be conferred on India within one year after the termination of the war'.[47] It demanded the framing of a constitution that ensures the integrity and indivisibility of India as a state and a nation, along with 'providing legitimate safeguards for the protection of the rights and interests of the minorities on the lines laid down by the League of Nations'.[48] Simultaneously, it called for a guarantee against any adverse impact on the rights and interests of the majority in India. The resolution criticized the British government for delaying the constitutional scheme until it was agreed by the Muslim minority as it felt such a condescending attitude was vesting them with the veto power—something that was clearly 'preposterous, undemocratic in theory and is bound to be most detrimental to the legitimate Hindu interests in practice.[49] 'Even as it praised the attempts of the government to increase Indian strength in the army, it found these efforts as being 'inadequate and insufficient for the protection of India from external aggression and for the maintenance of internal order'.[50] The Mahasabha resolved that the defence policy must be actuated first by the considerations of the welfare of India and not be subordinated to the interests of the British. Along with making military training compulsory in schools, colleges and universities, it also sought a repeal of the Arms Act to enable acquisition of arms by Indians. The resolution also sought an encouragement and establishment of 'factories in India with Indian capital and under Indian control where all implements of War, e.g. aero-engines, aero-planes, motor engines, tanks, modern armaments and equipment will be manufactured and also to provide for and assist in ship building in India without further delay'.[51] It urged the British government to be firm and unequivocal in its criticism and dismissal of any Pakistan scheme and also pledge to protect the lives and rights of the Hindu minority in Muslim-majority provinces such as the North-West Frontier Province, Punjab, Sindh and Bengal. It adopted a policy of responsive non-cooperation with the government and gave it a three-month window until 31 March 1941, failing which the Mahasabha threatened direct action to get its demands fulfilled. A committee was constituted to strategize such a direct action and it included Savarkar, Syama Prasad Mookerjee, B.S. Moonje, B.G. Khaparde, V.G. Deshpande, L.B. Bhopatkar and Bhai Parmanand.

The British had kept a keen watch on the Mahasabha session and its proceedings, perhaps for the first time. Viceroy Linlithgow sent a report to the Secretary of State, Lord Leopold Amery, on 31 December 1940:

Open Session of All India Hindu Mahasabha at Madura on 29 December passed resolution of which following is summary . . . Mahasabha appreciates recognition by Viceroy and Secretary of State that political situation cannot be satisfactorily solved without cooperation of Mahasabha. While reiterating faith in goal of complete independence, Mahasabha is prepared to accept Dominion Status as immediate step. But declarations made from time to time by Viceroy and Secretary of State are vague, inadequate and unsatisfactory, and Mahasabha contemplated in-statute of Westminster will be within one year of termination of war, and that constitution will be so framed as to ensure integrity and individuality of India, and while providing legitimate safeguards for minorities, will not in any manner adversely affect rights and interests of majority. Mahasabha condemns British Government for not making clear announcement of opposition to Pakistan scheme and urges immediate declaration that Pakistan will not be tolerated. After referring to Sind, Bengal and Punjab, and demanding compulsory military training for Indian youths and promotion of war industries, resolution announces that if government fail before 31st March next to make satisfactory response to demands contained in resolution, Mahasabha will start movement to Direct Action, and names eight persons as Committee to devise ways and means of starting and conducting it immediately after time limit expires.[52]

Following up on the resolutions of the Madurai session by way of negotiations, Savarkar elaborated the demands of the Hindu Mahasabha in a detailed letter to the viceroy on 20 February 1941. The first demand was that the government must 'try its best to grant Dominion Status to India in such a way as to ensure her free and equal co-partnership in the Indo-British Commonwealth, within a year after the cessation of the war'.[53] This was to be akin to similar rights being exercised by Canada, Australia and other self-governing colonies. To achieve this end, he demanded that the government bring to the discussion table, as soon as the war ends or even earlier, all leading political parties and voices of India, especially the triumvirate of the All-India Hindu Mahasabha, the Congress and the Muslim League to frame the contours of the Constitution. He prescribed that such a constitution must guarantee, 'every legitimate protective to the religion, language, script and such other fundamental special interests . . . to all citizens and communities alike, whether they be in majority or minority . . . no party or community would be allowed to follow such obstructive tactics as to affect the legitimate and equal rights of any other community or party or threaten to hold up all further constitutional progress'. This was a clear barb aimed at the nuisance tactics that the League had been adopting since long. Savarkar also stressed that constitution needs to be 'founded on the basic principle of the indivisibility of India as a Nation and a state with a Central Government strong enough to maintain this integrity against any attacks from outside or inside'.[54]

In the same letter, Savarkar outlined the outrages perpetrated against the Hindus in Sindh, the NWFP and Bengal. He chided the governors of these provinces for turning a blind eye to the sufferings and religious persecution that the Hindus were facing. He prevailed upon the viceroy to issue a solemn and public assurance to the Hindus that their lives, property and faith would be safeguarded and the murderous, fanatic tribes that were persecuting them would be duly brought to book. If the ministries failed to live up to this duty, the provincial autonomy should be suspended and the governors should assume the administrative powers in their hands. He also called upon the viceroy to finalize the expansion plans of the Executive Council and War Advisory Council, to Indianize these completely and not point out to the 'excuse that a party here or there is still refusing to participate in it'.[55] Such representation as a reflection of the population mix would be ideal, according to Savarkar. The Hindu Mahasabha, the Liberal League, the All-India Christian Federation and several other political parties were in favour of such an expansion and hence further procrastination on this matter could prove detrimental.

Elaborating on all of Savarkar's demands, the viceroy replied on 7 March 1941. Regarding the Dominion status, he claimed that his speeches as well as those of the Secretary of State, Amery, and the debates in the British Parliament had made it 'crystal clear that the proclaimed and accepted goal of the Imperial Crown and of the British Parliament is the attainment of India of free and equal partnership in the British Commonwealth'.[56] To devise the framework of the new Constitution, the government was willing to set up a representative body, immediately after the war, which would comprise all the 'principle [sic] elements in India's national life'. The objective of the British government remained leading India to the 'proclaimed goal of Dominion Status and that as early as may be immediately after the War'. He did not give a specific commitment of the timeline that Savarkar had sought of a year after the cessation of the war but merely added that the sincerity of His Majesty's government on this matter should not be in doubt for any party whatsoever. On the demand for the indivisible nature of India that Savarkar had stressed upon, the viceroy concurred that the principle was evident in the speech of the Secretary of State, Amery, titled 'India First' and added: 'By India, I mean India as a whole; India as nature and history have shaped India with its infinite diversities and underlying unity.' He assured Savarkar that the governors of Sindh, NWFP and Bengal would be advised to prevail upon the ministries in their provinces to ensure protection of the Hindu minorities and see to it that there is no 'victimization and that where any community commits act of aggression against another, the full powers of Government will be used to maintain public order and the rights of all sections of the community'.[57] The viceroy expressed his inability to go ahead with the expansion of the councils as 'no sufficient support has come forward from the Indian public parties' to enable such a step.

Referring to an earlier letter dated 11 January 1941 where Savarkar had forwarded the proposals related to militarization and industrialization, as postulated in the Madurai conference, the viceroy explained certain limitations that the government faced when it came to military training in schools. These pertained to the shortage of rifles and instructors, which could not be diverted from the requirements of the regular army, caught as it was in the midst of a real war. The syllabus for such training was however under the active consideration of the government, he claimed.

~

Meanwhile, Savarkar's health continued to remain a matter of concern for him in the early months of 1941. By the middle of March, however, he managed to gather himself to participate in an important initiative that was being heralded by Sir Tej Bahadur Sapru. Sapru was a leading intellectual, jurist and legislator who had worked extensively on the drafting of the Constitution from 1927 onwards. Though a member of the Congress initially, he left it to join the Liberal Party of India. Sapru was an active part of the Round Table Conferences and his services were always invoked to build bridges during times of distress, including between Gandhi and Ambedkar during the Poona Pact. Under his leadership a conference was convened to create consensus among the Indian political players regarding the constitutional deadlock that was being faced since the outbreak of the war. On 13 and 14 March 1941, the conference was held at the Taj Mahal Hotel in Bombay and the attendees included Savarkar, Syama Prasad Mookerjee, B.S. Moonje, M.R. Jayakar, Sir Jagdish Prasad, Sir Nripendranath Sirkar, Sir Chimanlal Setalvad, Loknayak M.S. Aney, Pandit Kunzru and other prominent public intellectuals and political leaders. The agenda was to set a road map towards the formation of a provisional national government in India. Jinnah was highly critical of the conference and dubbed it as one being engineered by the agents of the Congress and the Hindu Mahasabha. Sapru was however undeterred by any such misplaced criticism. He met the viceroy too and apprised him of the conference proceedings. He felt 'more than gratified that men like Savarkar and Moonje, who were present at the conference, played the game and accepted the resolution. They were men of strong party convictions and yet, for the sake of settlement, they subordinated their party feelings to the common goal we had in view.'[58] He also recommended to the viceroy to call for a meeting that had Gandhi, Jinnah and Savarkar in it so that all issues could be discussed threadbare and a consensus reached.

Around this time the occasion arose for the national census. Savarkar was deeply critical of the Congress attitude of boycotting such an important exercise—one that would influence political, constitutional and legislative decisions for the coming decade from the view of population proportions of different communities in India. On the eve of the census, he appealed to all Hindus, including the tribal communities such as Bhils, Santhals and others to get themselves correctly enumerated. He appealed to the Arya Samajists, Lingayats, Jains and Sikhs to maintain their distinct identity but come under the larger rubric of 'Hindu' as Arya (Hindu), Lingayat (Hindu), Jain (Hindu) and Sikh (Hindu).

District and provincial Hindu Sabhas were asked to participate fully and cooperate with the census authorities and also supervise against any potential mischief or tinkering. A perusal of the census documents of the times right from 1881 to 1931 is elaborative of some of the fears of the Hindu political leadership.

	HINDU				
	1881	1891	1901	1921	1931
INDIA	74%	72%	70%	69%	65%
BRITISH PROVINCES	72%	70%	69%	66%	64%
STATES & AGENCIES	83%	80%	78%	77%	67%
	MUSLIM				
	1881	1891	1901	1921	1931
INDIA	20%	20%	21%	22%	27%
BRITISH PROVINCES	22%	22%	23%	24%	28%
STATES & AGENCIES	10%	12%	14%	13%	26%

	1881		1891		1901		1921		1931	
	HINDU	MUSLIM	HINDU	MUSLIM	HINDU	MUSLIM	HINDU	MUSLIM	HINDU	MUSLIM
INDIA	74%	20%	72%	20%	70%	21%	69%	22%	65%	27%
BRITISH PROVINCES	72%	22%	70%	22%	69%	23%	66%	24%	64%	28%
STATES & AGENCIES	83%	10%	80%	12%	78%	14%	77%	13%	67%	26%

Hindu-Muslim Population percentages from 1881 to 1931, Source: Census Data of Government of India. https://censusindia.gov.in/DigitalLibrary/browseyearwise.aspx

Since the time of the first pan-Indian census in 1881 to the last census conducted till then in 1931, the Hindu population numbers were on a steady decline nationally, as also in the British provinces as well as the princely states and agencies.[59] The corresponding figures for the Muslim community during the same time showed an upward trend. These trends were more marked in provinces such as NWFP, Punjab, Assam, Ajmere-Merwara [sic], Rajputana, United Provinces, Central Provinces and Berar, and the central Indian states. Even in areas such as Mysore state that was deemed the 'most Hindu' in 1881 with a population of 95 per cent in 1881 had fallen to 77 per cent in 1931, as against the corresponding Muslim population pegging itself at 16 per cent in 1931 vis-à-vis 5 per cent in 1881.[60] The reasons for these population shifts could be varied—changing demographics due to religious conversions or incorrect enumeration by the respondents. Bengal was a case in point of the latter reason.

For the longest period of time, from 1881 to 1921, Bengal had shown a predominance of the Muslim community in its population mix. The 1931 census, however, revealed that several population groups that identified themselves as Hindu had hitherto gone uncounted. As Syama Prasad Mookerjee noted in his diary about the errors in the Bengal census figures:

> We wanted to check the growing tendency among the Scheduled Castes people to regard themselves outside the Hindu fold—their antagonism to Caste Hindus was being slowly nurtured on political consideration— Caste Hindus were the enemies of the Scheduled Caste's progress etc. We wanted that Hindu solidarity must grow; we wanted that caste prejudices should disappear. We therefore declared that we should not indicate our castes but call ourselves Hindus in our census returns. This was bitterly opposed by a section of Scheduled Castes people. Still our propaganda had great educative value. We not only got all Hindus to take an active interest in the census but united them as far as possible.[61]

Bengal's prime minister, Fazl-ul-Haq, saw the Mahasabha's move as a 'sinister design to reduce the Muslims of Bengal to a minority'.[62]

Given the political situation in India with the grant of the Communal Award where population proportions of different communities determined state policy, government formations and representation in the legislatures, an accurate determination of the population strength of each community was extremely vital. Hence, Savarkar's call and insistence on a proper enumeration of the Hindu populace to safeguard its interests during this crucial phase of transition of power from the British gained more significance. With the Muslim League's clamour for sovereign, autonomous units in provinces that had Muslim majority, the issue became all the more important to ascertain what the true numbers actually were. To boycott the census as a 'communal issue' as the Congress did, was immature, given they had signed up for the Communal Award that guaranteed these provisions to Indian communities on the basis of their population strength.

~

The April of 1941 saw a war of words between Jinnah and Savarkar. The twenty-eighth Annual Session of the All-India Muslim League was held in Madras on 11 April 1941. Flanked by several Dravidian leaders including E.V. Ramaswamy Naicker (Periyar), Jinnah openly advocated another separate state—Dravidastan or a coalition of southern states. Periyar and Ambedkar had stood by Jinnah during his campaign of Deliverance Day against the Congress on its resignation from ministries. Periyar had hoped that Jinnah would reciprocate by being a force multiplier to his demands for a separate nation for the Dravidians. In his speech, Jinnah said:

> In this subcontinent, you have two different societies, the Muslim society and the Hindu society and particularly in this land, there is another nation, that is Dravidastan. This land is really Dravidastan, and imagine its three percent of electioneering, three percent of them should secure a majority. Is this democracy or is this a farce? Therefore, I have the fullest sympathy and give my fullest support to the non-Brahmins, and I say [to] them: 'The only way for you to come into your own is to live your own life, according to your culture, according to your language- thank God that Hindi did not go very far here and your own history is to go ahead with your ideal. I have every sympathy for you and I shall do all I can to support you to establish Dravidastan. The seven percent of Muslims will stretch their hand of friendship to you and live with you on lines of equality, justice and fair-play.[63]

Under immense pressure from the Muslim clergy, Jinnah however conveniently backtracked from any support to Periyar's political moves, stating that he was only concerned about the interests of the Muslims of India and if Periyar felt strongly about this demand, he must mobilize people to assert those claims.

In his presidential address at Madras, Jinnah compared the situation in India to that in Yugoslavia and said that following the German capture of Zagreb, the Yugoslav province of Croatia had been proclaimed as an 'Independent State' according to a German news agency, and a Croat general had called upon all officials, army officers and non-commissioned officers to take an oath of allegiance to the 'New State'. Just like Yugoslavia took this unilateral decision through the actions of the three groups of Croats, Slovenes and the Serbs, in India Hindustan of the Hindus, Pakistan of the Muslims and Dravidastan of the Dravidians were the three stakeholders. 'Are you going to wait and allow somebody else to come here and do the job for you or are you going to do it yourselves?'[64] he asked rhetorically. He threatened the eruption of many Pakistans out of undivided India if the government did not accede to their demands. Jinnah also derided the Hindu Mahasabha as an absolutely incorrigible and hopeless body.

Joining issue with him, Savarkar stated that he considered Jinnah's diatribe against the Mahasabha as a tribute to the unalloyed patriotism of the organization and warned the Congress to open its eyes and read the writing on the wall—a balkanization of India into several splinters that was being propounded openly. If the state of the Croats was indeed an ideal for him, Savarkar asked Jinnah to read about the history of these three communities. He asserted that any pan-Islamist attack on India would be stoutly resisted by a Hindu–Buddhist alliance from Jammu to Japan. Invoking the thousand years of invasions, he said all those attempts to Islamize India had failed due to the valour and the resistance that had been offered by the Hindus of the country. 'The same fate,' he asserted, 'shall these, your petty parasites of your Pakistan states meet after a miserable existence for a time, even if they ever come into existence . . . history avers to the ever-abiding truth in India: Pakistans may come and Pakistans may go, but Hindustan goes on forever.'[65] Postulating his stand regarding a united India, Savarkar said:

> There is consequently only one way for the Indian Moslems to secure
> their safety, peace and prosperity as a community in India; and that is to
> get themselves incorporated wholeheartedly and loyally into an Indian
> nation, which can only be done on the following basic principles: 1)

Independence of India and indivisibility of India as a Nation and State, 2) Representation strictly in proportion to the population strength, 3) Public services to go by merit alone, and 4) the fundamental rights of freedom of worship, language, script etc. guaranteed to all citizens alike.[66]

Savarkar's correspondences with the viceroy continued throughout this time and give an important insight into his and the Mahasabha's views on critical issues that the country faced. The viceroy's earlier letter was put before the Working Committee of the Hindu Mahasabha, held on 11 March. Savarkar wrote to the viceroy on 27 March on the points raised by the Committee. He lauded the government for its continued pledge towards the attainment of a free and equal partnership in the British Commonwealth and disregarded the conflicting aims of objectives of principal parties and interest groups. As far the Mahasabha's stand was concerned, he welcomed the move and asserted that its 'objective remains to lead India to the proclaimed goal of the decision status and that as early as may be'.[67] But he pushed for a fixed and definite timeline for this rather than keeping it vague as 'Immediately after the War' or 'And that as early as may be'. A definite timeline of a year or so would help build confidence in the minds of all Indian parties, he averred. He expressed his happiness on the steps taken towards militarization and industrialization of India, the removal of the humiliating ban on the 'Non-Listed' caste and classes in the army and the freeing of recruitments. He however felt these were tardy and betrayed a lack of confidence in Indians on the part of the government and needed to be speeded up. Even as he thanked the government for its unequivocal and definite assurances on protecting the lives of minorities in the Muslim-majority provinces of Sindh, NWFP, Punjab and Bengal, Savarkar called for 'immediate chastisement and utter subjugation and annexation of the lawless tribal tracts'.[68] Claiming that when leaders in Bengal of the stature of the prime minister (Fazl-ul-Haq) were openly stating an intent to tyrannize Hindus, Savarkar said that the onus was on the government to dismiss such people from positions of power and safeguard the life and properties of minorities. He expressed concern on the government's lack of a definitive response on the indivisibility of India and a criticism of the Pakistan scheme and called upon them to make a clear declaration against any vivisection of the country. He requested the government to disregard the obstacles that the Congress was putting in the way of expanding the Executive Council and the War Advisory

Council and not use their tantrums as an excuse to postpone progressive reforms. Referring to the conference in Bombay under the leadership of Sir Tej Bahadur Sapru, Savarkar stated that several participants of eminence including men like M.S. Aney, Pandit Hriday Nath Kunzru, B.R. Ambedkar and other leaders of the Mahasabha who represented hundreds and thousands of voters and their interests were keen on such an expansion. Hence their demands for such an Indianization of the two councils were more important than the vacillating stand of the Congress. The Hindu Mahasabha, he concluded, would be happy to 'concentrate all its energy during the war period on its militarization and industrialization programme and extend a whole-hearted cooperation with the war efforts of the government, with a view to express the common objective of defending India from any alien invasion or internal anarchy and the common immediate goal of rearing up an Indo-British Commonwealth'.[69]

On 13 April 1941, the Hindu Mahasabha's Working Committee meeting was held at Nagpur under the presidentship of Savarkar. One of the important considerations that were deliberated here was the question of Direct Action that the Mahasabha's Madurai resolution had warned in the wake of the government not acceding to the Dominion status demand by 31 March 1941. In the light of the regular correspondences between Savarkar and the viceroy and the latter's firm assurance on the grant of such a status, the Working Committee decided to defer the decision to the All-India Committee of the Mahasabha that was slated to meet later in the year in Calcutta. There were rumblings of discontent in the Mahasabha during this meeting. As British intelligence managed to gather, 'the younger section of the Hindusabhaites is not satisfied with the present leadership. Dr. [Varadarajulu] Naidu of Madras is being criticized for "hobnobbing" with Mahatma Gandhi. Dr. Munje [sic] is being accused of "sabotage" and even Mr. Savarkar is not spared caustic criticism'.[70] The possible reasons for this could be the vacillating stands taken by the Mahasabha and Savarkar on the issue of both Direct Action as well as the conference chaired by Tej Bahadur Sapru. Savarkar had been writing to the viceroy claiming that this conference was an important counter against the Congress, while at the same time, a view was expressed in the Working Committee that the Hindu Mahasabha 'is not officially connected with Bombay Conference and that Mahasabha will be free to take its own decision on any settlement that may arise out of those negotiations'.[71] It led the viceroy to conclude in his letter to the Secretary of State that the 'Bombay Conference has insufficient substance behind it and Congress has been leading Sapru up the garden path'.[72]

Further, General Secretary Varadarajulu Naidu, who was a staunch Gandhian and a former Congressman who had joined the Mahasabha in 1939 due to disillusionment with the Congress, was viewed with suspicion. Even as Savarkar was writing to the viceroy in his capacity as the president of the Mahasabha, Naidu was issuing statements that the 'Mahasabha will not cooperate in any scheme for expansion of Central Government unless communal proportion of Indian populations reflected in the Council'.[73] On his part, Savarkar remained tight-lipped on these contradictions, thereby creating rumblings of confusion and dissent.

Even as the Working Committee was meeting in Nagpur, communal riots intensified in Dacca and several thousand Hindus were rendered homeless. These riots had sparked off in mid-March and only grown in scale over the following weeks. Savarkar sent a strongly worded letter directly to the Secretary of State alleging that the ministry in Bengal was incapable of affording any protection to the minorities there and that the governor must be instructed to dismiss the ministry and assume direct control. The Secretary of State sought the advice of the viceroy on how he needed to respond to this and also wished to know if he could quote this to show 'how instinctively Indians still demand our intervention to solve difficulties and how little direct government is really resented'.[74] He however added that he would not make any reference to an individual or political party if the viceroy thought it might embarrass him in relation to Savarkar. The viceroy advised him to 'avoid any direct association either with Savarkar or the delicate Dacca situation',[75] especially since he had been in regular communication with him.

The British government was keeping a close watch on the Hindu Mahasabha and its activities. Following up on the Nagpur meeting, a draft resolution that Rao Bahadur S.K. Bole of the Mahasabha had circulated among its members was intercepted by the government intelligence. This draft sought the opinion of members of the Mahasabha and their acceptance through signatures on the planned Direct Action. Given the multiple voices within the Mahasabha after the Madurai resolution, this was seen as an attempt to generate consensus ahead of the crucial All-India Committee meeting in Calcutta during 14–15 June 1941. The draft appreciated the stand taken by the British government of granting equal co-partnership to India with Britain after the war, assured protection to

minorities in Muslim-majority provinces and turned down explicit demands
of the League on vivisection of the country on religious lines. However, in
the wake of continued attacks on the Hindus in Sindh, NWFP, Punjab
and Bengal, particularly the Dacca riots—in all of which the government's
actions did not match its words of assurance—and the hesitation of the
government to set a timeline for granting Dominion status for India or
expanding the viceroy's council, the Hindu Mahasabha was contemplating
Direct Action. It however clarified that such a civil resistance was 'no
programme of seeking jail on a mass scale on the futile Congress line' and
that any such move must entail the more effective step of an 'economical
British boycott on an All-India scale'.[76] The steps contemplated for such
an economic boycott were as follows:

> Let every Hindu take up a pledge to boycott all British articles, British
> business concerns, British banks, British films, British Insurance
> Companies etc. in so far as it is not detrimental to our own interests. This
> boycott is not only to operate during the war period but will continue to
> gather momentum and intensification after the war, in particular when
> the British imports will be pouring in India with a vengeance. This
> meeting warns the Government that along with this economical British
> boycott, more stringent steps would be taken in due course to render this
> civil resistance movement as effective as possible in case the Government
> does not satisfy the Hindu Mahasabha demands in full and does not
> raise India to the status of an equal and actual co-partnership with Great
> Britain and the self-governing dominions within a year, at the latest, after
> the cessation of the war and thus transform the British Commonwealth
> into a variable Indo-British Commonwealth, which may serve as an
> immediate step ahead on the path of our ultimate political goal.[77]

The draft had initial signatures of Rao Bahadur Bole, Narayanrao Savarkar,
D.G. Abhyankar, Ganesh Damodar Savarkar and B.N. Bhagwat.
Considering the emphasis that the Mahasabha and Savarkar had all along
been placing on industrialization and the Hindu participation in it, the
economic boycott was a sure step to coerce the British government to
accede to its demands.

On the eve of his fifty-ninth birthday on 28 May, Savarkar coined his
new catchphrase, 'Hinduize all politics and militarize Hindudom.' In his
statement, he said:

The Hindus should henceforth test all national and international politics
and policies through the Hindu point of view alone. Whatever policy
or political event contributes to safeguard and promote Hindu interests
must be backed up by the Hindus and whatever is likely to prove
detrimental to Hindu interests must be condemned and opposed by the
Hindus. In as much as the Hindus do not ask anything more than what
is legitimately due to them on principles of equity and equality, Hindu
interests must of necessity be consistent with the demands and contents
of genuine nationalism, and even humanism. Let the Hindus therefore
as an immediate step to give effect to this Hinduised political progress,
elect only those Hindus to represent them in the Legislatures and all
other political bodies as Hindu representatives who pledge themselves
openly and uncompromisingly to safeguard, to defend, and to promote
uncompromisingly the interests of Hindudom as a whole. Thus firstly
Hinduise all politics. And secondly, as the first and immediate step to
militarize Hindudom, let every Hindu youth who is capable to stand the
test, try his best to enter the army, the navy and the air force or get the
training and secure employment in the ammunition factories and in all
other branches connected with war crafts. Unforeseen facilities are being
thrown open to you. Unexpected opportunities have presented themselves
before you. You help no one else more than you help yourselves if you
utilize these facilities and opportunities to militarize Hindudom! This
done, everything else shall follow: if you miss this, nothing else shall avail!
This sums up the whole programme and the supreme duty of the hour.
Hinduize all politics and militarize Hindudom!!—and the resurrection of
our Hindu Nation is bound to follow it as certainly as the Dawn follows
the darkest hour of night.[78]

The much-awaited All-India Committee meeting of the Mahasabha took
place in Calcutta during 14–15 June 1941 with Savarkar presiding. About
200 out of the 400 members were present. Four initial resolutions were
adopted. These were related to expressing sympathy with cyclone victims
in Bengal, Assam, Malabar, etc., condemning the Bengal government's
interference with census operations, one-man one-vote principle for
communal amity, etc.[79] The main resolution was moved by Moonje. It
referred to the correspondences between Savarkar and the viceroy and
appreciated the government stand on several demands made by the
Mahasabha, including the actions taken to curb the violent Khaksars in

Punjab and NWFP from attacking the Hindus. However, the call for postponement of the Direct Action that disconcerted several members was a damp squib. Savarkar explained the rationale for this by positing that at a time when war was knocking at the doors on both frontiers, it would be in the best interests of Hindus to postpone any foolish jail-seeking programme, taking a lesson from the Congress fiasco. This was stoutly opposed by many and on 15 June, amendments permitting the Mahasabha to launch a campaign of economic boycott and giving provincial committees full discretion to launch such a direct action whenever they deemed it necessary in order to safeguard Hindu interests were moved by V.G. Deshpande and Syama Prasad Mookerjee. However, these amendments were lost by an overwhelming majority.

Mindful of the immense and sharp criticism that the postponement of the Direct Action drew from all quarters, Savarkar issued a lengthy statement on 24 June 1941 explaining the stand. Ironically, Savarkar who always criticized the numerous flip-flops of Gandhi and the Congress was now elaborating his own retraction. He termed the criticism as being purposive and malicious. Elaborating on the meaning of the term 'Direct Action' itself, Savarkar maintained that it could mean anything and everything from 'an active and armed revolt down to the passive non-cooperation inaction'.[80] If it meant the former, there was obviously no way this could be discussed so openly and in such detail. Given the popularity of the Congress movements, it might have been the general perception that such a Direct Action meant undergoing self-tortures by voluntary jail-seeking programme, something that the Mahasabha found 'queer and immoral'. 'By Direct Action,' explained Savarkar, 'the Hindu Mahasabha means resistance to aggression offered in such a wise way as to inflict a deterrent punishment to the wrong doer, to make the aggressor suffer more in the long run than their own forces.'[81] Terming this as a tactical retreat for the time being, he laboured to postulate that he and the Mahasabha—

. . . never contributed to the general superstition, which fancies that going forward must always be an act of bravery or falling backward of cowardice. If your forces, while marching on, find themselves suddenly on the point of a dangerous precipice, it cannot be an act of bravery, but of criminal fool-hardiness to persist still in going forward and hurl them into an abysmal depth of destruction. The first principle in politics as well as in warfare lay it down that consistency is to be judged in relation to the ultimate goal and not in relation to the movements and maneuvers. These are truisms. But the public sense and view have been blurred to such an extent by the fantastic exhibitions of the so-called Gandhist 'Technique' during a couple of decades in the past that even such political truisms require to be re-taught as original truths.[82]

Savarkar explained in detail why carrying on Direct Action only to secure a timeline for grant of constitutional provisions for post-War India, while other demands were being met by the government, was not a good strategy:

The demand that equal co-partnership in the Indo-British Commonwealth should be granted within a year after the cessation of the War, the Government made a promise in response to this demand that such a co-partnership would be granted but they refused to bind themselves by any time limit [sic]. Would the Hindu Mahasabha have been well-advised to take up this issue immediately in hand here now and to launch an all-India campaign sending thousands on thousands of Hindu Sangathanists to brave imprisonment, to pay lacs [sic] upon lacs of Rupees as fine to the Government, and all this merely to demand a promise that equal co-partnership will be granted within one year after the cessation of the war? Even supposing that after such an enormous cost to us, we succeeded in squeezing out, say after a year, a promise to this effect from the Government, could it be more than a promise? Do we not know what mere promises mean in politics and how they are not worth a moment's purchase between all-powerful nations? Then again, what certainty there is as to how long the war is likely to last? Even the best of the German and the English statesmen differ in their forecast and put down the duration of the war from some 3 years right up to some 30 years term? Are we to continue to send thousands on thousands to jail and to continue to face untold and unforeseen sacrifices year in and year out till it suits Europe to end this war after some 3 to 30 years? And to undergo all this enormous loss for the fun of securing a promise . . . as a policy it would have been stupid and as a strategy suicidal!!! And what greater pressure can any of the puny efforts on the part of Indians, Congressites and others bring to bear on international political situation than what the mighty Mars is already executing on the battlefields in Europe? Is it not better to wait till Fate casts her fine decisive die and we can see again where and how we ourselves and others do exactly stand?

Consequently, the All India Committee of the Hindu Mahasabha took the only sensible and far-sighted course, which could be taken under the circumstances in the best interests of Hindudom and decided that in view of the dangerous and rapid approach of war towards both the Eastern and Western frontier of our land from outside and the anti-Hindu Moslem riots threatening peace and order throughout India inside the country, Direct Action in connection with the Constitutional demands which . . . must be carried on an all-India scale should be postponed at any rate till the end of the war when we are all in a position to know exactly where we stand and where England stands along with other nations on the map of the world when it emerges out of this crucible of a world battlefield. Then only a tangible question of constitutional framing can really arise and we shall be in a position to test the sincerity of the promises made by the Government regarding the equal co-partnership. That will be the right and most effective time for us to exercise whatever pressure we are able to bring to bear upon the Government by resorting, if necessary, to a campaign of civil resistance or even otherwise.[83]

Savarkar postulated that the Calcutta resolution did not prevent the Hindu Mahasabha or its provincial units from carrying on any Direct Action to safeguard Hindu interests. Drawing attention to the movements in the Nizam state and continuing efforts by the Mahasabha and its members to protect Hindu lives, rights and property in Sindh, Bengal, Bihar and the recent Dacca riots, he claimed that it was the Mahasabha that had been at the forefront. Several of its members had been stabbed, killed and imprisoned and despite that the Mahasabha had worked hard to rescue Hindus, provide for their relief, offer free legal help to victims and given voice for every Hindu grievance. Even on the preposterous Pakistan claims, he claimed that the 'Congress has not passed even a single official resolution to condemn Pakistan in unequivocal terms. It was the Hindu Mahasabha alone, which stirred up the whole Hindudom and put forth a determined opposition to each and every question detrimental to Hindu interests'.[84] Was this less than any Direct Action, he wondered.

However, few in the Mahasabha were convinced by Savarkar's logic. Syama Prasad Mookerjee was exasperated. 'The withdrawal of the Madura resolution,' he said, 'was a severe blow on the prestige of the Mahasabha, and made people feel that we could only talk big but ran away from the field of action. This had a very disheartening effect on my mind.'[85] And Mookerjee was not wrong in this assessment. The bravado of Madurai was in the wake of all the events that Savarkar had postulated in this lengthy explanation. The war, its uncertainty, its duration and the non-committal position of the British government were what it was in December 1940 in Madurai, as it stood in Calcutta in June 1941. A retreat at this important juncture also meant ceding the space for mass movement to the Congress and to lose the bargaining power of the Hindu Mahasabha with the government. Ironically, it was akin to what several Congressmen, especially the Young Turks, held as a grouse against Gandhi for grandiose announcements and mobilizations of mass movements and then retreating in the interests of back-channel talks with the viceroy. A nationwide civil resistance could have helped the Hindu Mahasabha to be taken more seriously on future negotiation tables, even with the British, since electorally it did not count for much importance. It would have also posited the Mahasabha as a crusader for national issues such as setting into motion a constitutional process and the future of India that were not restricted to the agitation themes of only Hindu interests as hitherto. The stage was thus getting set for a schism within the Hindu Mahasabha and for anti-Savarkar voices to gather steam into separate factions.

The first breakthrough in the political deadlock in the country came on 22 July 1941 when Viceroy Linlithgow finally announced the composition of his new Council. While British officials held important portfolios of home, finance and communications, for the first time a majority of eight out of the thirteen members were Indians. This was however just a matter of numerical satisfaction since the Indian members were neither responsible to the Legislature nor to any political party. The Defence Council (also called War Advisory Council) that was established was also merely an advisory body that had twenty-two British Indians mostly drawn from the provincial legislatures and nine members from the states. It failed to make much impression on Indian political opinion. There was hardly anything tangible to convince Indians of the bona fides of the British offers and promises to grant Dominion status and further fuelled the suspicions about the usual British doublespeak and insincerity.

The non-inclusion of Sikhs or the depressed classes in the Council was conspicuous and was resented by several leaders including Ambedkar. Savarkar stepped up his support for Ambedkar and wired the viceroy stating that 'the British Government could find no more capable a gentleman to fill that post than Dr. Ambedkar himself'.[86]

In the wake of these limited political reforms, leaders met under the leadership of Tej Bahadur Sapru for the second time in Poona on 26 July 1941. Savarkar insisted and managed to get the conference to pass a United India resolution that unequivocally opposed any move to vivisect the country.

~

On 14 August 1941, the United States of America and Britain jointly issued the 'Atlantic Charter' as a statement of their war policy. Among other things, Article 3 of this charter declared that 'they respect the right of all peoples to choose the form of Government under which they will live; and they wish to see sovereign rights and self government restored to those who have been forcibly deprived of them'.[87] The statement was obviously welcomed with cheer by Indians across the political spectrum. However, the joy was short-lived as British prime minister Winston Churchill punctured the balloon in his speech in the House of Commons on 9 September 1941. He declared that the Atlantic Charter had no application to India and referred only to European nations under Nazi rule. It did not relate to 'the development of constitutional government in India, Burma or other parts of the Empire'.[88] The 'progressive evolution of self-governing institutions in the regions and peoples who owe allegiance to the British Crown'[89] was to be distinguished from the emancipation of Europe from Nazism, he asserted. Even the advice of the US ambassador to Britain, Guy Winant, to whom he sent an advanced copy of his speech, could not influence Churchill. Winant believed that the denial of the Charter clauses to India 'would simply intensify charges of Imperialism and leave Great Britain in the position of a "do-nothing policy"'.[90] But Churchill was adamant and refused to modify the passage. If the expansion of the viceroy's Executive Council merely fuelled Indian suspicions, Churchill's speech was the proverbial last nail in the confidence of Indians about British promises. There was never a wider gulf between India and Britain than what had now emerged. All along Britain seemed to be making empty promises to bribe India to do her utmost to help the war efforts with a promise that they had no intentions to honour either during or after the war.

Savarkar cabled US president Franklin D. Roosevelt on 20 August seeking a clarification on the American stand:

As President Hindu Mahasabha, the all-India Hindu body, exhort you to declare explicitly if Anglo-American announcement war aims covers India's case. Whether America guarantees full political freedom of India within one year after the end of this war STOP if America fails to do that India cannot but construe this declaration as another stunt like war aims of the last Anglo-German war meant only to camouflage imperialistic aggressions of those who have Empires against those who have them not and are out to win them.[91]

This was the second cable that Savarkar had sent to Roosevelt. Earlier in the year on 23 April 1941, he had sent him a message in the wake of the latter's appeal to Hitler to ward off the impending colossal damage to the human civilization. Savarkar had said then:

If your note to Hitler is actuated by disinterested human anxiety for safeguarding freedom and democracy from military aggression, pray ask Britain too to withdraw the armed domination over Hindustan and let her have a free and self-determined constitution. A great nation like Hindustan can surely claim at least as much international justice as small nations do.[92]

Savarkar's correspondences with the American president drew varying political reactions. Subhas Bose's elder brother Sarat Chandra Bose who was the leader of Opposition in the Bengal Legislative Assembly sarcastically remarked that in the days of yore, Indian leaders would look to the Liberals and Radicals of England to make them a 'gift of independence', but Savarkar's overtures had led him 'almost breathless by surprise' given his dependence on Roosevelt's 'generosity', predicting that his 'disillusionment will be complete soon'. He saw no way that Savarkar could either 'cajole or intimidate' Roosevelt with his telegram.[93] Savarkar was quite surprised by such an innuendo and replied that 'there is a difference between demanding an explanation of a diplomatic statement with a view to exposing its underlying casuistry and political hypocrisy and expecting any help'.[94] He reminded Bose of how not too long ago the Congress had sent Sarojini Naidu to America to drum up support for India there. He also added that unlike the Congress, the Forward Bloc and the communists, the Mahasabha did not view the Soviet Union as a symbol of 'anti-imperialistic innocence' and held a very realistic view of their motives that had been vindicated by their war actions.

~

Meanwhile, things were moving rapidly on the war front and took an alarming turn so far as India was concerned, with the entry of Japan into the conflict and siding with the Axis powers. The rapidity with which the once impregnable Singapore fell to the Japanese, as also Malaya bringing them right to the Indian gates at Burma made the spectre of a Japanese invasion of British India a foregone conclusion. The war was no longer confined to Europe alone but having percolated to Asia made the strategic importance of India more pronounced than ever before. Also, the Japanese victories considerably lowered British prestige and shattered the myth of their invincibility.

Savarkar reiterated his call to action to the Indian people and his demands to the British in the wake of the fall of Singapore:

Of all events in the war till now, the fall of Singapore affects most vitally the question of Indian defense. Nothing now can prove so effective a measure to counteract this defeatist shock and rouse the Indian people with war-like spirit to fight to a finish but an unambiguous proclamation on the part of the British Government that India is granted forthwith co-partnership and status in every respect equal with other self-governing constituents including Great Britain herself, in an Indo-British Commonwealth. Every functional step to nationalize the Government in India to materialize this proclamation must also be immediately and actually taken. I urge the British Government not to underrate the blunt truth that if Japan is allowed to forestall the British Government in this case and to proclaim, as soon as and if her invading forces reach the borders of India that their immediate objective is to free and guarantee the independence of India, such a proclamation on their part cannot but capture the popular imagination of the Indian people by storm and usher in incalculable political complications. The sooner the British forestall the invaders in making India feel that fighting in alliance with Britain is fighting for Indian political freedom the better for all of us concerned.[95]

While the younger lot within the Hindu Mahasabha including those like Syama Prasad Mookerjee strongly favoured an all-out mass movement akin to that of the Congress, the 'old-guard' continued to impress upon the viceroy that at such a critical juncture if the British government wishes to protect its important colony from external invasion, it had little option but to befriend the Hindus, win their trust and concede their demands. Moonje in his letter to the viceroy on 12 September 1941 elaborated on this point that for the Hindus there was no country beyond the frontiers of India that they can call as their home and hence if not for Britain's interests, but for their own interests, they will ensure the territorial sovereignty and security of the nation. But in contrast, given the extraterritorial allegiances that the Muslims had with the larger Muslim brotherhood, they might well encourage 'Moslem nations outside India'[96]to a possible invasion on India from the western front even as the eastern front remains tense with Japan. Contrasting the attitude of the two communities, Moonje said:

> The Moslems generally cannot look at the Indian problems from any point of view other than that of their narrow communal interests, which unfortunately, they believe, are more wedded with the destinies of the Muslim nations beyond the frontiers of India than with that of the Hindus though they are part and parcel of their own blood and bones. As for these Moslem nations for which England had always entertained a delicately soft corner in its heart, and to England they have every reason to be grateful for their very existence as independent nations, none of them appears to have any friendly feeling for England in its hour of trial. Some of them are openly hostile and playing the game of England's enemy such as Iraq and Iran and others such as Turkey, Afghanistan and Egypt are neutral, only waiting for an opportunity to jump on the winning side. It is either by the actual exercise of force or by a determined show of force that England can keep them under control . . . the attitude of the Hindus is quite the opposite. They will quarrel with England for their constitutional rights almost to the bitter end but will immediately go over to the side of Britain when any crisis involving the question of life and death arises because they are aware of the fact that there is no other ally than Britain for them.[97]

There was also a sign of despair and frustration in his letter where he mentioned that right from the time of Lord Minto every effort was made to placate and appease Muslim interests by giving them separate electorates, then weightages in representation and services and finally the Communal

Award. But nothing seemed to satisfy them and 'they are getting more and more arrogant and are now demanding Pakistan . . . besides sowing the seed of a terrible civil war'.[98] Despite all the positive assurances from it, Moonje felt dejected by the fact that the British 'looks upon it [Hindu Mahasabha] as of no value, if not with contempt'.[99] He urged the viceroy to revise the British policy towards Muslim appeasement and also of their inclusion in the army to about 25 per cent and fill the rest with Hindus who would fight with greater loyalty for the sovereignty of their only motherland.

The Mahasabha in its Working Committee meeting held in Delhi on 12 October also endorsed this view as also Savarkar's move to cable Roosevelt. It also took a jibe at the Congress and other parties who had 'fancied at the outbreak of war that Britain was defending democracy and freedom throughout the world and vindicated unerring and often repeated view of Mahasabha that every belligerent including even Russia and America was out for self-interest and self-aggrandizement alone. India too must consequently adopt that policy alone, which safeguards and promotes own national interests'.[100] As Savarkar stated:

There is no question of cooperating or non-cooperating with the British Government in their war efforts. The only question that you have before you is to find out how best you can turn this inevitable cooperation with the British as profitable to your own country as it is possible under our present circumstances to do. Because let it not be forgotten that those who fancy that they can claim of not having cooperated with the Government and helped the war efforts either on account of the demoralizing and hypocritical fad of absolute non-violence and non-resistance, even in the face of an armed aggression as a matter of policy simply because they do not join the fighting but indulging in self-deception and self-complacency. They pay taxes, serve in the railway, postal, legal and even police department and are openly out to pool up as much profit as they can in supplying directly to the military departments, clothing, blankets, food and all other articles. Thus they too provide the Government with the very sinews of war. For all practical purposes they too cannot but cooperate with the British Government with this only difference that their policy of boycotting the army deprives the nation of the only outstanding benefit it could have received in return for this inevitable co-operation. But if we Hindusabhaites utilize this opportunity to the largest measure possible by extending military co-operation with the British

Government in a responsive spirit and measure we shall do a double
service to Hindudom. The first being that we shall be able to defend
our own country, hearths and homes, if we are actually attacked by alien
forces from outside or by an internal anti-Hindu anarchy, secondly in
addition to this immediate benefit we shall be able to press on the Hindu
Militarization movement to such an extent as to secure permanently a
dominant position for the Hindus in the Indian army, navy and air-force
wherein today the Moslems are almost monopolizing and the Hindu
element is woefully subordinated as a result of the criminal negligence
towards and even a downright condemnation of military life which the
Congress under the Gandhist lead had been guilty of.[101]

Savarkar expressed satisfaction at how the suppressed martial feeling among
the Hindus was being rectified as evidenced in the increasing enrolment
in thousands of the heroic Gurkhas, Sikhs, Jats, Rajputs and Marathas
in the armed forces. The humiliating distinction of listed and non-listed
classes and castes too was lifted making the entry into the army open
for all. Simultaneously several others were being trained in ammunition
manufacture, ordnance factories, shipyards and other war crafts. However,
this was just the beginning and more needed to be done.

Savarkar outlined a detail plan of action to achieve this. The Hindu
Mahasabha would set up a Central Hindu Militarization Board at its
head office in Delhi with Ganpat Rai as its convenor. A Central Southern
Hindu Militarization Board was formed under the chairmanship of
L.B. Bhopatkar in Poona. A subcommittee with powers to co-opt any
other Hindu members of the Defence Council was to be created with
the following members and their regional jurisdictions: Sir Jwala Prasad
Shrivastav (United Provinces), Barrister Jamnadas Mehta (Bombay and
Maharashtra); Mr V.V. Kalikar (Berar and Nagpur), Lala Ram Saran Das
(Punjab) and Rao Bahadur Rajah (Madras). The subcommittee was to be
in contact with the civil defence member of the Executive Council of the
viceroy and move him to sanction military appointments. The different
Hindu Sabhas and local Hindu Militarization Boards would collect
complaints, grievances and queries from across the country and forward it
to the members who would then sort and examine them. Those deemed
important would be forwarded to the respective government departments
for redress. The office of the subcommittee and its members was to have at
all times tabulated information regarding the number of Hindus vis-à-vis

the Muslims in the army, navy, air force, and ammunition, ordnance and other military-related manufacturing factories. He also recommended as a 'matter of urgent importance that must be taken on hand immediately'[102] an overseas visit to the theatres of war wherever Hindu soldiers were fighting, of the member(s) of the subcommittee, as also some prominent Hindu princes. This would give them a ground report of the issues that were being faced. All the answered queries and information about admission rules, training requirements, the regulations in the different schools in Mahu, Bangalore, Dehradun, etc., were to be compiled, translated into all Indian languages and printed as booklets that were available for free in all leading bookshops, stands, the Hindu Sabha offices and at festivals and fairs.

Savarkar thereafter toured Assam in November 1941 and addressed several meetings at Gauhati, Jorhat, Dibrugarh, Shillong and other places. Along with the usual political statements of the Hindu Mahasabha, he also criticized the mode of census enumeration in Assam, urging the Central government to reject the numbers compiled by the government of Assam and conduct the process in a fair and transparent manner. He also expressed public support to the Hindus of Nellore in the Madras province who had been fighting for their just political and civil rights. His meetings drew crowds ranging from 600 to 5000 in several places. His attention was drawn to Pandit Nehru's statement regarding the Muslim influx in Assam that migrations are inevitable since nature hates vacuum. Savarkar retorted that Pandit Nehru was neither a philosopher nor a scientist and did not know that nature also abhors poisonous gases! Two ministers in the government of Assam, Rohini Chaudhuri and Hirendra Chakravarty, met with Savarkar on 26 November and expressed their desire to join the Hindu Mahasabha on the assurance that they would be nominated as candidates in the next general election.[103] Savarkar told them that he was happy to nominate them if they succeeded in replacing the present ministry in Assam by one with a Hindu majority and thereby nullify all the anti-Hindu measures that it had hitherto adopted.

~

Trouble had been meanwhile brewing for long in the Bengal government. Abul Kashem Fazl-ul-Haq had been in power for over three years by then but his position was becoming increasingly untenable in the coalition government that his Krishak Praja Party had formed with the Muslim

League. He was being arm-twisted by League veterans such as Huseyn Shaheed Suhrawardy. On one hand, Haq was mounting anti-Hindu propaganda and actions but on the other he was deeply suspicious of his coalition partner the League's machinations. A no-confidence motion against his ministry in August 1941 was only narrowly defeated. As it rejected the League offer to form a coalition in UP, the Congress and its leaders like Sarat Chandra Bose rebuffed Haq's overtures in 1937 to form a ministry together. Had the Congress joined hands with Haq to form a ministry in 1937, the Krishak Praja Party would not have fallen prey to the League and its agenda of Islamizing Bengal. A similar situation had pushed Sikandar Hayat Khan of the Unionist Party in the NWFP into the lap of the League to form a ministry. Like Haq in Bengal, Hayat Khan too was opposed to many things that Jinnah and the League propounded but the Congress did not exploit these differences between the allies.

The strategy of Savarkar and Mookerjee was that it made realpolitik sense to split the Muslim political leadership and ally with non-League Muslim parties to create a wedge among them rather than let them consolidate. However, at times, he also contradicted this stand of isolating the League and even let the legislators join League ministries as well when opportunities arose, citing protection of Hindu rights and giving a voice to the Hindu minority in the corridors of power. Right from the time Congress members started resigning from legislatures starting October 1939, Hindu Mahasabha legislators began to join the ministries in several Muslim-majority provinces like Sindh, Bengal and NWFP. Savarkar had said: 'In the Hindu-minority provinces whenever a Muslim Ministry seemed inevitable—whether it was sponsored by the Muslim League or otherwise—and Hindu interests could be served better by joining it, the Hindusabhaites should try as a matter of right to capture as many seats as possible in the Ministry and do the best they can to safeguard the interests of the Hindu minority . . . boycotting a ministry was more often than not highly detrimental to Hindu interests.'[104] He even sent a telegram to the Akali leader Tara Singh urging Hindus and Sikhs to join the League Ministry in Punjab and 'transform it into a coalition ministry'.[105] It was natural for his political opponents to dub these vacillating stands as hankering for power and being an opportunist. The Congress severely criticized this move of the Mahasabha of being 'out for the crumbs'. Congress leader Pattabhi Sitaramayya admonished Savarkar's strategy of joining League ministries as a 'return gift to the nation, which had presented to him a purse of about three lakhs of rupees'[106] while other Congress leaders called the Mahasabha legislators 'job-hunters'.

Savarkar had responded to these charges of political opportunism against the Mahasabha by the Congress:

> Another argument, which forms the stock-in-trade of the libelous criticism and propaganda of the Congressites with regard to the policy of the Hindu Mahasabha of occupying centres of political power, howsoever limited it be, springs back upon themselves and unlike the boomerang hits only themselves hard. The Hindu Mahasabha through its elected or supported representatives has now come to occupy responsible positions in political councils, committees, ministries, legislatures, municipalities and such other centres of political power and it is this fact which has pre-eminently contributed to the outstanding political importance which the Mahasabha has throughout India as never before. It is human that some of the unemployed Congressites should get irritated to find that so many of the 'Jobs' should have fallen into other hands and should make them accuse the Hindu Sangathanists as mere 'Job-hunters'. We pity them for their irritation. But we cannot excuse them for making a virtue of necessity and go about posing as so many suffering saints who never cared a fig for these very worldly and servile 'Jobs'. For, was it not only the other day that the Congress from one end of India to the other went on such 'job-hunting'? They agreed to act as Ministers—not as Kings! But servilely enough as ministers to the Governors, who in their turn were servants of the British Crown. They, who now accuse the Hindusabhaites as helping imperialism took oaths of allegiance to the British Imperial Crown, accepted salaries, invited whole troops of their followers and hangers-on to get the loaves and fishes of the Offices, posts and positions distributed only among themselves. They could do only those things, which the Governors permitted at their pleasure in the last resort. They laboured under the constitution, which they had pretended to despise. Whenever they failed to satisfy this or that section of public they either pointed out to the limitations under which they held office or they sallied out firing and delivering lathi charges on those of their countrymen who disobeyed them or picketed them. If anybody fasted at their doors in protest of their actions they told him bluntly, 'You may lie there comfortably till you die, I must attend my office and do my duty as I choose.' Did not Rajagopalachari himself, the foremost of those

ministers, who 'followed the Mahatma', tell the world in blunt accents in general justification of the actions of the Congress Government that the first duty of the Government was to govern! Do you condemn the Congress for this 'job-hunting' and rough-riding? Or do you justify all this as patriotic? Do the Congressites explain it all away on the ground that larger public interest demanded that even under limitations the Constitution should be worked out to squeeze whatever public good you can get out of it? If you say 'yes' to the latter, then in justifying yourselves you justify the Hindu Mahasabha too in its policy of capturing centres of political power, limited though it be to begin with and standing on that point of vantage, try to leap over and occupy more effective centres of power.[107]

To keep the League away and defang it and thereby save the Hindus of Bengal, Savarkar and Mookerjee felt that it was prudent to join forces with Haq at a time when he was facing a political existential crisis. Accordingly, with the consent of Savarkar the new 'Progressive Coalition' ministry was sworn in on 12 December with the Krishak Praja Party and the Mahasabha coming together. Mookerjee was the sole representative from his party, appointed the finance minister of Bengal.

Politics being the art of the possible, every political party seemed to justify its actions on the basis of some hallowed principle. It was ironic that in 1940, the Subhas Chandra Bose faction within the Bengal Congress had first attempted to align with the Hindu Mahasabha for the Calcutta Corporation elections in March 1940. The municipal polls had come in the wake of the Haq government's blatantly communal action of passing the New Calcutta Municipal Amendment Act of 1939 that sought to end Congress monopoly over the civic body and also reserved separate electorates for the Muslims. Bose had then tried to woo Syama Prasad Mookerjee and form a united Hindu front to fight the elections. However, Bose faced strong opposition from the Congress for this alleged compromise and subversion of Congress principles through a dalliance with the Mahasabha. When the talks failed between the two, the official Congress even ridiculed the whole exercise of a joint front as 'a nine days wonder'.[108] When the results came in, of the eighty-five seats in the Corporation, the Hindus won forty-seven and the Muslims twenty-three. Of the forty-seven, the Bose faction won twenty-one while the Mahasabha won sixteen seats. The League performed well and won eighteen of the twenty-three Muslim seats. Bose then shifted his focus and strangely allied with the same League that he was critical of. The 'Bose-League Pact' of 1940 was bitterly criticized by all shades of political opinion, within and outside Bengal. The Mahasabha leaders, who till the other day were keen on allying with Bose, went all out to castigate his move as one that had sold out 'the interests of the Hindus'.[109] The official Congress mouthpiece, *Forward*, too criticized Bose for not fulfilling his promise of a 'raging and tearing campaign against the Calcutta Municipal Amendment Act, and instead going on to form a pact with the authors of the iniquitous legislation' and even termed it as 'a surrender of nationalism to sordid consideration' and to serve his own 'narrow careerism'.[110]

Thus, in these early years of Indian electoral politics, alliances were formed and broken by all players on sheer arithmetic considerations, couched of course with ideological justifications and the invocation of sanctimonious and lofty principles—both real and imagined.

~

Around this very time, the war took a catastrophic turn. On 7 December 1941, the battleship USS *Arizona* was sunk in the naval base of Pearl Harbour in Honolulu, Territory of Hawaii, by the Imperial Japanese Navy Air Service. The US had hitherto been a neutral country in the war, but this incident dragged America too into this global conflagration. The very next day the Allied powers declared war on Japan. The increasing threat that the Empire's most prized colony, India, faced in the Asian bastion reshaped the strategies of the British government, as also the Indian political players, as the events of the future were to demonstrate.

The Bhagalpur Affair

As the year drew to a close a new clash was brewing between the government and the Mahasabha. The twenty-third session of the All-India Hindu Mahasabha was to be held in the last week of December 1941 in Bhagalpur in Bihar with Kumar Ganga Nand Singh as the working president and Rai Bahadur Sukhraj Roy as the general secretary. The deliberations had been marred by several factional fights in the Bihar Provincial Hindu Sabha and it was left to the astute negotiation skills of Ashutosh Lahiri, the all-India secretary of the Mahasabha to iron out the differences. But by

end-September the commissioner of the Bhagalpur Division summoned
the Sabha members and communicated to them his decision to ban the
session in Bhagalpur, Monghyr, Patna, Gaya, Shahabad, Muzaffarpur
and Darbhanga apprehending communal flare-ups in view of the Bakr-
Eid festival that fell around the same time. Savarkar wrote to the Bihar
governor on 25 September 1941 seeking a reversal of this decision. He
averred that it was a denial of the legitimate rights of freedom of speech
and association for the Hindus and that could not be infringed upon by the
state only because it felt that the Muslim community would get inflamed
by the conduct of such a session. He drew the governor's attention to the
Muslim League session that was held that year in Madras, where a delicate
communal situation prevailed, and the administration had 'prohibited the
Hindus from holding any conference or assembling in numbers or making
any demonstrations etc. in that restricted area'[111] by imposing Section 144
of the CrPC. Even if this unjust act was taken up as a precedent, the onus
was on the Bihar administration to ensure that similar concessions were
provided to the Hindu community and any trouble-makers are kept at bay
through efficient maintenance of law and order, rather than penalizing
the Hindus each time. He assured the governor that being a responsible
national party, the Mahasabha would ensure that nothing would be done
or said to 'offend other communities'[112] or fan communal passions. He
chastised the government saying 'it is this policy, which puts a premium on
goondaism and criminal aggression on one hand and alienates the sympathy
and confidence of the law-abiding on the other'[113] that was abhorrent.

In the replies from the Bihar government, W.G. Lacey, the secretary
to the governor, quoted Rule 56 of the Defence of India Act as also
the history of communal strife in those districts of Bihar during the
festivals of both communities as a reason to seek postponement of the
session to a date after 10 January 1942. Tensions had prevailed in these
districts right from 1924 where religious processions around Kali Puja
or Muharram and issues of cow-slaughter on Bakr-Eid had vitiated the
atmosphere. Rath Yatra processions of the Hindus had been obstructed
by the government repeatedly since it would offend Muslim sentiments.
On these occasions, Hindus had resorted to satyagraha to demand their
legitimate religious rights.

The Working Committee of the Reception Committee decided on 9
October that unwanted restrictions on the exercise of legitimate civil rights
of the Hindus would be rejected and they demanded the conduct of the

Bhagalpur session from 24 to 27 December, given the possible dates of Bakr-Eid were after 29 December depending on the sighting of the moon. Savarkar conveyed the same to the governor with the further concession that they could try to wind up the session by 26 December so that the administration gets enough time of three to four days for redeployment of forces by the time the Bakr-Eid festival begins on 30 December or thereafter. However, this proposal was flatly rejected by the government, which also issued a warning to him that any 'challenge to authorities will be met by all the resources at the command of Government'.[114]

As several letters went back and forth, Savarkar chastised the Bihar government for succumbing to the perceived pressure and apprehension of violence by a fanatic section of a community. He wrote on 8 November:

> It is the fundamental and unchallengeably [sic] established principle on which alone law and good government can ever securely rest that a man or an association can not be convicted for or prevented from doing a lawful act even if it seems likely that it may cause a ruffian or a fanatic to commit an unlawful act. The duty of the government in such a case is to hold in check and chastise the lawless one and not to flourish the bludgeon in the face of the law-abiding to stop them from exercising their legitimate rights . . . it is extremely humiliating to the government itself to acknowledge its inability to check and chastise the suspected Moslem section at a single town like Bhagalpur . . . the Government correspondence makes it clear that the Government of Bihar has forces sufficient enough to force their ban on the thousands of Hindus and hundreds of most responsible Hindu leaders who are likely to gather at Bhagalpur for the Session and yet the Government maintains that it would be very difficult to check and chastise the fanatical section of the Moslem population at a single town like Bhagalpur. This paradoxical line of argument and action shows clearly that the underlying idea why the Government thinks it cheaper and more convenient to prohibit the Hindus from their law-abiding activities rather than restrain the Moslems for their lawlessness must be the usual presumption that the Hindus as [a] rule are more amenable as gentlemen to law and order . . . and yet this perverse policy of maintaining peace and order not by suppressing the lawless Moslem fanaticism but by placating it at the cost of the civic, religious and political rights of the Hindus continues to be the order of the day throughout India.[115]

He maintained that since the Bihar government had invoked a national Act such as the Defence of India Act to maintain the law and order of a single town, it no longer remained a local issue. The Mahasabha had therefore decided to defy the ban and also seek the viceroy's intervention on the matter, as it was no longer a provincial issue. It was decided to observe 14 December as All-India Bhagalpur Day throughout India to protest against the unjust imposition of the ban with meetings, rallies and resolutions urging the viceroy to intervene and lift the restrictions.

Even as the Hindu Mahasabha continued to carry on with the arrangements for the session, an offer was made by the maharaja of Darbhanga at the behest of the viceroy that he was willing to bear the entire expenses of the session on the dates proposed by the Mahasabha provided they shifted the venue from Bhagalpur to Darbhanga. Though Darbhanga too was among the list of banned districts due to its alleged sensitive communal situation, this strangely did not seem to be a deterrent. In a haste, the Bihar Hindu Sabha's Kumar Ganga Nand Singh and Pandit Bharat Misra agreed to this offer without the consent of the national president. Statements were issued to the press. Savarkar squarely put down the proposal and refused to cower to either the threats of the Bihar government or the fanatics in Bhagalpur.

Meanwhile, thousands gathered for protests at the venue for the session, Lajpat Park in Bhagalpur, criticizing the government ban on the 'Bhagalpur Day' of 14 December. A complete hartal was observed and no shops remained open. An outpouring of the sentiments of several common Hindus too was on full display against what was seen as a deliberate encroachment of their legitimate political rights. Quite effortlessly and possibly unintentionally, the Bhagalpur fiasco took on the shape of a Hindu civil resistance movement. The police sprang into action. Members of the Hindu Sabha were arrested and the pandals at the Lajpat Park destroyed and the venue taken under government custody.

A fierce factional war was also brewing within the Bihar Hindu Sabha with personal animosities and egoes having been let loose in this entire drama. V.G. Deshpande and Nathuram Godse were dispatched by Savarkar to go to Bhagalpur and personally oversee the situation and report back. They tried to soothe all ruffled feathers within the party and returned to Bombay. Massive arrangements needed to be made for the stay of the delegates and the civil resisters in various hotels, private residences and dharmashalas and the kitchens to serve food to all attendees during the session, all in stealth to avoid government vigilance. The Bihar government had deployed a thousand-strong police force to curb the session and the DIG, Northern Range, was placed in charge of the police arrangements. Prohibitory orders were issued and searches were carried out in the houses and offices of the office-bearers of the Bihar Hindu Sabha. The press where pamphlets and propaganda material for the session were being printed was raided. All public meetings, processions and assembly of people were banned in the seven districts till 4 January 1942. N.P. Tripathi, secretary of the Bihar Provincial Hindu Sabha, said:

> This act of high-handedness and action in pursuance of anti-Hindu policy of the Government is bound to have repercussion over the disorganized and disunited Hindus . . . the Government have done their worst to the Hindus. It is now for the Hindus in general and Hindusabha workers in particular to show to the world their intrinsic worth and face bravely the situation in which they are thrown . . . in the name of God and in the name of humanity let me proclaim that the results that will come out will bring life in the Hindu community and I prophesize today that the Government will have to repent for their act.[116]

But the delegates started making preparations to leave for Bhagalpur and issued statements to the government to not interfere with their peaceful and legitimate programme. Raja Maheshwar Dayal Seth of Kotra, a prominent member of the Mahasabha, said in an interview to the press in Lucknow before leaving for Bhagalpur:

> The attitude of the British Government towards the only political organization cooperating with it at present is clear from what is happening at Bhagalpur. I refuse to believe that the Government of Bihar alone is responsible for it. The policy is the same whether it is Lucknow, Bhagalpur or Nellore. Those who are opposed must be appeased and humoured and to please their friends must be humiliated and kicked because they are friends and are expected to remain such inspite of all kinds of insulting treatment. This is the policy of the British Government, which we, the landlords, learnt to our cost three years ago.[117]

He appealed to the Hindus to offer civil resistance in a united front and defend Hindu honour.

Delegates and civil resisters started trickling into Bhagalpur by 23 December and were mainly accommodated in the Debi Prasad Dharmashala. But several eminent members of the Mahasabha, including N.P. Tripathi, Ashutosh Lahiri, V.G. Deshpande, as well as delegates and resisters were arrested the moment their trains got into Bhagalpur station. But unmindful of the repression, nearly 1200 delegates and civil resisters reached Bhagalpur by 23 December. Significantly, prominent Muslim leaders of Bhagalpur were themselves deeply critical of the government's high-handed attitude. Qasim Hussain, the vice chairman of the Bhagalpur Municipality, issued a lengthy statement terming the act of the government as unwise and uncalled for.

> The attitude taken by the Government of Bihar so far as the holding of Hindu Mahasabha at Bhagalpur is concerned, is one of grave concern and anxiety for every Indian. The leader of the Hindu Mahasabha, Mr. Savarkar, has all along been exhorting the Indians to help in the war effort and to get themselves enrolled in the Army and the Navy and the Air Force in order to help the powers who are fighting on the side of democracy. And at a time when the war is at the very gate of India, in my humble opinion the Provincial Government would have done better to find out a peaceful solution instead of taking recourse to drastic steps. This has acted as a spark, which set ablaze the whole of India. It has become an all-India question.[118]

The unambiguous statements by several other Muslim leaders in Bihar and outside that they never sought this ban nor did they appreciate their festival to be trotted out as an excuse for it was a terrible embarrassment for the government.

Support began pouring in for the Mahasabha from several quarters. The Liberal Party leaders V.S. Srinivas Shastri, P.S. Sivaswami Iyer and T.R. Venkataramana Shastri issued strong statements of camaraderie. 'The clear right of one community ought not,' they said, 'to be placed at the mercy of another community.'[119] They called upon the viceroy and the Bihar Governor to rectify the situation before it turned more explosive. Raja Narendranath, president of the Punjab Provincial Hindu Sabha, and Sir Gokal Chand Narang sent a joint telegram to the viceroy:

> Bihar Government's order banning Mahasabha session has created wave of deep resentment throughout India. It is considered and rightly

considered great insult to Hindu community that Hindus forming over 90% population in Bihar should not be allowed to hold Mahasabha session. In Madras, Muslim League session was allowed and Hindus were asked to keep indoors although forming 95% of the population. This apparently savours [sic] of invidious distinction and partiality. We do not believe that there was any danger of breach of peace, but even if there was any danger, control should have been exercised over those from whom any attempts to cause disturbance were expected. If Bihar Government can collect 1000 policemen to disperse Hindu Sabha delegates, much smaller number would have been sufficient to maintain peace and order. Bihar Government's order, unless reversed, is sure to create serious repercussions. Earnestly request Your Excellency to advise Bihar Governor to remove ban.[120]

Amidst all this, Savarkar left for Bhagalpur by train on 22 December with over 400 volunteers and delegates from Bombay and Poona. Huge crowds gathered at the Bombay station to see him off with shouts of '*Hindu Dharma ki Jai*' and '*Veer Savarkar ki Jai*' (Victory to the Hindu faith and to Veer Savarkar) reverberating. At every station en-route, crowds gathered to have a glimpse of the man. On the morning of 24 December, when the train reached Gaya at 2 a.m., the Bihar Police arrested Savarkar under Section 26 of the Defence of India Rules. He was detained at the Gaya Central Jail. Through the rest of the day, over sixty-five people were taken into custody, including several eminent Hindu Mahasabha leaders such as B.S. Moonje, B.G. Khaparde (an ex-minister of the Central Provinces), N.C. Chatterji, Varadarajulu Naidu, Rai Bahadur Harishchandra, Hakim Ganga Prasad Gupta, S.K. Chakravarti and several others. As the Congress-friendly newspaper *Searchlight* reported about the arrests:

> 10 from Madras, 8 from Naokhali [sic], 8 from Allahabad and Moradabad, 12 from Comilla, 1 from Chapra and several local men . . . 5 ladies were also arrested while marching in procession. As the arrested leaders were taken away, men, women and children lined the streets cheering them to the echo and rending the sky with shouts of '*Savarkar ki Jai.*' As police reinforcement pour in, delegates are also trooping from all parts of the country. Over 400 have arrived from Bombay and C.P. Arrests on a mass scale have started and are proceeding.[121]

Savarkar's arrest in Gaya sparked off nationwide protests in Madras, Madurai, Ajmer, Calcutta, Wardha, Lucknow and other places. On 27 December, in the open session of the National Liberation Federation Srinivas Shastri moved a resolution on the Bhagalpur ban holding the move as one that denied the fundamental rights of citizens without any justification. Undeterred by the outcry from all quarters, the government arrests continued. Bhai Parmanand, Sir Gokul Chand Narang and Captain Keshab Chandra were all arrested upon landing in Bihar along with their large contingent of delegates and volunteers from Punjab. The working president of the Mahasabha and the new finance minister of Bengal, Syama Prasad Mookerjee, who had always been a votary of such mass Civil Disobedience movements, was apprehended at Colgong, a wayside station near Bhagalpur. Savarkar had advised him not to involve himself in the Bhagalpur affair and concentrate instead on the new ministry that he had become part of. However, after Savarkar's arrest, Mookerjee decided to enter the fray himself. When he refused to alight, the bogey in which he was travelling was detached from the main engine and he was packed off to the Dak Bungalow. The same Rule 26 was applied on him and he was directed to leave the province of Bihar with immediate effect.

In quite a tongue-in-cheek remark on his political opponent following his approach of civil resistance, Gandhi expressed his indirect support as well: 'It fills me with delight to find Vir Savarkar, Dr. Moonje and others being arrested in their attempt to assert the very primary and very fundamental right of holding an orderly meeting subject to all reasonable restrictions about the preservation of public peace.'[122]

Bhagalpur was meanwhile turned into an effective fortress with all its approaches by rail, road and rivers being strictly guarded by the police. But as the press reported, 'the Mahasabha leaders had a better organization to deal with the "thoroughness" of the Bihar Government, keeping every move of theirs as a guarded secret'.[123]

On the directions of Savarkar from the jail two groups were created— one that went to the Lajpat Park, the designated venue for the Session and another to the Debi Prasad Dharmashala where delegates were put up. The former was declared as the formal annual session of the Mahasabha with the vice-president of the Bihar Provincial Hindu Sabha, Krishna Ballav Prasad Narayan Singh, presiding over the meeting. Savarkar's written speech as the all-India president was read out and copies distributed among members. Shortly after they finished reading Savarkar's speech, the police detained them. Sessions began to be held in batches with new presiding officers. Lala Narayan Dutt, the treasurer of the All-India Hindu Mahasabha, presided over the next session with nearly 2000 volunteers trooping in to attend. And this process continued throughout the day. As newspapers reported:

> The whole town of Bhagalpur was the meeting place of the session of the Mahasabha. Never was a banned meeting held in a better style and thoroughness. Never had an order of a ban been more thoroughly trampled, torn to pieces and scattered to the winds. Nearly 1000 delegates and leaders were arrested by the night of the second day of the session. So plentifully did people offer themselves for arrest that the Government was forced to abandon the method of arrest on the third day. The intensity of lathi charges also was less.[124]

Some volunteers were taken in police vans and forced to get down several miles away from Bhagalpur. On the third day, many *Prabhat Pheris* or morning processions were taken out defying all ban orders. Arrests were going on all the while at Ranchi, Arrah, Monghyr, Champaran and Samastipur. The last day's session was presided over by G.V. Ketkar, secretary of the All-India Hindu Mahasabha, who termed this session as 'momentous and memorable' and one that was unprecedented in the annals of not only the Mahasabha but any other political party of India.

> The spirit of resurgent Hindudom has during the last five years under the leadership of Swatantryaveer V.D. Savarkar grown from strength to strength and the whimsical pranks of any provincial satrap cannot in the least affect its progress . . . remember that the mission of Hindudom is not merely that of removing the ills of the foreign Raj but to repair mistakes and set aside difficulties, which have clogged its legitimate and logical progress during several centuries past and requires an alertness and vigilance from every individual Hindu man, woman and child.[125]

Even as sessions were being held at Lajpat Park and the Dharmashala, parallel sessions and meetings were being held even inside the various jails where the leaders had been detained. Rai Bahadur Mehar Chand Khanna, ex-minister of NWFP, explained the deplorable condition of the Hindus in his province, while Gokul Chand Narang and N.C. Chatterjee spoke about Punjab and Bengal respectively. As Rai Bahadur Khanna exclaimed: 'We had a grand time in jail! The government gave us an opportunity to be together for over 10 days and has allowed us to forge the links of the All-India Hindu Mahasabha stronger.'[126] On 25 December, the jail session was presided by Moonje who advised N.C. Chatterjee to read out Savarkar's presidential address. Early in the mornings, Arya Samaj prayers and Vedic chants, followed by a havan or fire ritual created a serene atmosphere. RSS members unfurled their flag to express solidarity and Sanatan Dharma meetings too were held. And so this jail life that resembled more of a camp was spent in enlivened talks, national songs and devotional prayers, an opportunity that a conventional session would have never created.

The *Amrit Bazar Patrika* reported on 27 December:

> Bhagalpur has now fought to the last and won. The instructions of Vinayak Damodar Savarkar to the effect that the session must be held at all costs and against all oppositions have been thoroughly carried out. The Government, despite all advice and suggestions from far and near, remained adamantine and stuck to their false vanity. But these four days at Bhagalpur have made it clear that to the will of the mass, bureaucracy has to bow down. The most moderate and loyal section of the Hindus who happened to witness the four day session which was held amidst frequent lathi and baton charges, said that now Mahasabha had been infused with a new life . . . though Hindu leaders, delegates and volunteers who defied the ban are in prison, yet great satisfaction is in evidence among the Hindus who realize that the great task has been accomplished and they have done their duty.[127]

Syama Prasad Mookerjee issued a statement to the press on 27 December:

> I shall have to issue later larger statement making many disclosures, which will be of no credit at all to any civilized government. Today I offer my heartfelt gratitude for the bold and resolute stand the Hindus of India took on this momentous occasion. The Bhagalpur session of the Hindu Mahasabha has been held in spite of the ban imposed by the local Government and held in a manner, which will electrify the entire Hindu population in India. There is no power in Bihar or anywhere in India, which can arrest the progress of the gigantic Hindu Mahasabha

movement, which is based on sound national principles, which are now shaping one part of the country to another. The greater the resistance, the greater the movement will be. All that we need is calmness, courage, unity and determination so that the goal of national freedom may be reached much earlier than what our enemies and detractors dream of. As regards our future course of action no decision would be taken by any of us individually. As soon as the leaders are set at liberty a meeting of the Working Committee of the All-India Hindu Mahasabha should be called and should be attended by all the leaders now under detention. The meeting of the Working Committee of the Bihar Hindu Sabha should also be held simultaneously and decision should be finally arrived at. The meeting of the Working Committee should be held somewhere in Bihar, as decided by Veer Savarkar.[128]

For Savarkar, it was a moral and political triumph that enhanced his status within and outside the Hindu Mahasabha. It cleared some of the misapprehensions within the party about his diffidence towards mass civil resistance in the wake of rescinding the call to Direct Action. The years ahead however had more political challenges and landmines awaiting everyone, circumstances that would alter not only individual destinies but also those of the entire subcontinent.

7

'Leaning on a Broken Reed'

The Cripps Mission

Within a month and a half of the attack on Pearl Harbour, on 15 February 1942, General Arthur Percival, commander-in-chief of the British forces in Singapore, surrendered to General Yamashita of the Japanese invading army. Rangoon was to fall soon on 8 March. And it seemed like a matter of time before British India would be attacked by the Axis powers, especially Japan. Bombs were lobbed at Kakinanda, Visakhapatnam and Calcutta causing considerable alarm to the British. When Japanese ships were sighted a few miles off the coast of Madras, the Governor of Madras, Arthur Oswald James Hope, collected his British staff and fled to Ootacamund. Lord Wavell, the then commander-in-chief, was sufficiently angered to send a strong admonishment in a wireless message 'upbraiding him for this unworthy and unbecoming abandonment of post'.[1] Gandhi too had written to Patel that an 'attack on Orissa seemed likely since the Government had massed troops there'.[2] India was top priority for the Allied forces. In the same month, the president of the Republic of China, Chiang Kai-shek, paid a visit to India to deliberate on the war strategy with the viceroy. He was shocked by the political situation in the country and termed the danger as being extreme and that 'if the British Government does not fundamentally change their policy towards India, it would be like presenting India to the enemy and inviting them to quickly occupy India'.[3] The increasing attempts to break the constitutional and political deadlock in India were thus accentuated. Churchill too was given this clear and unambiguous message, especially by America, when he was in Washington in December 1941.

But Churchill was obstinate. On 7 January 1942, from Washington, he warned his colleagues not to talk about constitutional issues when the enemy was knocking at the doorstep. With an obvious reference to the Muslim community and their large numbers in the Indian Army, he said: 'The Indian troops are fighting splendidly, but it must be remembered that their allegiance is to the King Emperor, and that the rule of the Congress and the Priesthood machine would never be tolerated by a fighting race.'[4] The viceroy too concurred and in a correspondence of 21 January affirmed a need to make no further moves especially because India 'was hopelessly, and I suspect irremediably split by racial and religious divisions which . . . become more acute as any real transfer of power by us draws nearer'.[5] The Secretary of State, in a paper submitted to the War Cabinet on 28 January summarized the Indian political situation:

> The political deadlock in India today is concerned, ostensibly, with the transfer of power from British to Indian hands. In reality it is mainly concerned with the far more difficult issue of what Indian hands, what Indian Government or Governments, are capable of taking over without bringing about general anarchy or even civil war.[6]

While there was a broad political consensus in Britain over grant of Dominion status to India in Westminster terms, it was believed that to effect that grant, a modicum of agreement needed to prevail politically in India and that was totally missing, making these succession plans difficult. This view was held on in Britain despite the mounting calamities in the war. On 4 March 1942, Churchill cabled Roosevelt:

> We are earnestly considering whether a declaration of Dominion Status after the War, carrying with it, if desired the right to secede should be made at this critical juncture. We must not on any account break with the Muslims who represent a hundred million people and are the main army elements on which we rely on for the immediate fighting.[7]

He added that India had other diverse groups such as forty million untouchables and eighty million inhabitants of princely states, all of whom were not too friendly with the Congress. 'Naturally,' he added, 'we do not want to throw India into chaos on the eve of invasion.'[8]

But the American advice, as also a small section of British statesmen wanted Britain to take the lead in ironing out these differences through some act of foresight and statesmanship. Roosevelt replied to Churchill's cable on 10 March 1942 suggesting the setting up of what could be termed a temporary government in India, headed by a small representative group that could be recognized as a temporary dominion government. 'Some such method,' Roosevelt hypothesized, 'might give a new favourable slant in India itself, and it might cause the people there to forget hard feelings, to become more loyal to the British Empire, and to stress the danger of Japanese domination, together with the advantage of peaceful evolution as against chaotic revolution.'[9]

The British public opinion and the Labour Party lobby within the Cabinet was inclined towards greater freedom for India. In a memorandum to the War Cabinet, on 2 February, Clement Attlee, the Lord Privy Seal, suggested that Britain send to India someone of standing who could be entrusted with the express task of bringing Indian political leaders together. 'There is,' he said, 'precedent for such action. Lord Durham saved Canada to the British Empire. We need a man to do in India what Durham did in Canada.'[10]

And that man who was chosen by Britain to lead the mission to India was Sir Stafford Cripps. Cripps was no stranger to India and had visited the country in late 1939–early 1940 and held extensive, informal meetings with Indian political leaders. He had been particularly friendly with Nehru and wanted to use that old bonhomie to create history both for himself and for the subcontinent. Cripps was handed a Draft Declaration by the War Cabinet to discuss with Indian leaders across the political spectrum the issue of dominion settlement for India, albeit after the war. 'The object,' it said, 'is the creation of a new Indian Union, which shall constitute a Dominion, associated with the United Kingdom and the other Dominions by a common allegiance to the Crown, but equal to them in every respect, in no way subordinate in any aspect of its domestic or external affairs.'[11] The new Union was free to decide its relationship with other members of the Commonwealth and even choose to secede, if it so wishes. It stipulated the formation of a body to create the Constitution after the creation of the new Union. Indian states would be invited to appoint representatives on the basis of population proportions. Further, in an attempt to assuage the Muslim League, it held that those Indian states that were unwilling to adhere to the new Constitution would retain their existing relations with the paramount power until a revision of treaty agreements was effected. The new Union was to also sign a negotiated treaty with the British Government on all matters relating to complete transfer of responsibility from British to Indian hands, especially the protection of racial and religious minorities. Until the new Constitution was framed, the British government was to retain control of the defence of India as part of their world war efforts. Cripps landed in New Delhi with this document on 23 March 1942 with a plan to spend two to three weeks in India in negotiations. He began a series of meetings with leaders of the Congress, the Muslim League, the Hindu Mahasabha, the depressed classes, Sikhs and the Chamber of Indian Princes.

In preparation of the forthcoming political activity, the All-India Committee of the Hindu Mahasabha met in Lucknow on 1 March. Four resolutions were passed by the Committee that outlined the exact stand of the Mahasabha on the fluid political situation in the country—a summary of which is as follows:

1. Britain has failed to convince people of Hindustan of sincerity of her intentions. Tragic reverses in Far East can be prevented in Hindustan by England granting fullest political freedom to India and securing wholehearted support and cooperation of Hindus. Only effective measure to rouse Indian people is bold and unambiguous proclamation, which must be made immediately by the British Government that India is granted full independence and co-partnership equal with Great Britain in Indo-British Commonwealth. Committee demands abolition of India Office and India Council, complete nationalization of Government of India on democratic lines, concentration of political sovereignty in India and transfer of entire administration of India to Indian hands, including defence, finance, foreign affairs and relations with Indian States.

2. In view of deplorable unpreparedness of India, Committee calls upon Hindu Sabhas, particularly in threatened areas to organize civic defence parties and raise and equip national militia for preventing ravages caused by possible air attacks, anti-Hindu hooliganism and internal commotion. Mahasabha defence organizations should act in cooperation with authorities and with defence organizations. Government should repeal Arms Act and provide members of defence organizations with arms.

3. Hindu Mahasabha calls upon the government to
   a. Relax administration of Arms Act so that every Indian can, without difficulty, secure a rifle and learn its use to shoot down

invaders and thus support the government defence by guerilla warfare.

b.   Encourage and provide funds for organization of national militia.

c.   Establish immediately factories for manufacture of aeroplanes, motors and warships.

d.   Provide rifles to schools and colleges.

4.   Mahasabha apprehends that Congress may accept some anti-democratic and anti-national agreement to placate Muslims. If any such agreement is arrived behind the back of the Hindu Mahasabha, it will be stoutly resisted by every possible means.[12]

To the open threats and war cries that were becoming frequent in the Muslim press about 'Pakistan is our deliverance, defence, destiny . . . Pakistan is our only demand . . . and by God, we will have it!'[13], Savarkar issued a statement from Lucknow on 1 March accepting these challenges:

Why hold your threat in abeyance, why not come out with it today? Hindus have an ancient culture and have withstood numerous revolts. They are four times the Muslims numerically and have the same arms and penal codes to defend themselves, which Muslims have . . . The Mahasabha, like the Congress, demanded full independence, but unlike it, was ready to cooperate with the Government in making preparations for defence.[14]

Savarkar was cautiously optimistic about the forthcoming meeting with Cripps. He said:

Hindu Mahasabha cannot attach much importance to endless discussions and conferences even if conducted by member of British War Cabinet like Cripps unless and until we have definite proclamation bringing into operation immediately status of co-partnership equal with Great Britain in Indo-British Commonwealth and representation of Hindu majority and Muslim minority, which is perfectly democratic and in proportion to population. I welcome Cripps, but regret that scheme itself should have been still a 'cat in the bag'.[15]

The Mahasabha delegation comprising Savarkar, Moonje, Syama Prasad Mookerjee, Jwala Prasad Srivastava and Ganpat Rai met Stafford Cripps at his Queen Victoria Road residence in New Delhi on 28 March. Savarkar and the delegation conveyed to Cripps in the most unambiguous terms that while they accepted the first part of his draft proposals, the clauses that put secession on a platter and virtually signed the death knell for a unified free India were totally unacceptable to them. Cripps opined that self-determination was a right that was normally granted to all countries and even in Canada or South Africa such discretion was given to the constituent units while forging a new state. To this Savarkar retorted that the example of Canada was a wrong equivalence since the units there were already distinct and they were being called upon during the Durham Mission to decide on whether they wished to forge themselves into an organic state, federal or otherwise. But in the case of India, the states were already welded into one central unit. 'The question before us today,' he said, 'is not to form out of separate and independent States or constituents a new nation or a federation or a confederation. India is already a Unitarian State.'[16] Cripps quipped back that India according to him was never a unitarian state. In his sharp response, Savarkar maintained:

> To the Hindus, it is an article of faith that India, their Motherland and Holyland, is a cultural and national unit undivided and indivisible. Let alone the cultural unity, which you may not grasp during this short period of the interview, but you will agree that politically and administratively the British Government admits and calls the Government of India, the Indian Government; the Army and Navy are called the Indian Army and Indian Navy, and Bombay and Bengal are called provinces. All these factors prove that India is an undivided, centralized nation and a State. And as for the principle of self-determination, it is a right to be given to a nation as a whole and not to a part thereof.[17]

Throughout the interview, Cripps was left with not much of an opportunity to talk as he himself recounted later that Savarkar 'spent most of his time lecturing me upon the principles of majority determination and of fallacies in the document'.[18] The meeting ended in an unequivocal rejection of Cripps's proposal by the Mahasabha on account of the secession proviso that it contained. One of the possible reasons for the disenchantment of the Mahasabha with Cripps could possibly be what a secret note exchanged between Sir Tej Bahadur Sapru and Sachchidananda Sinha of Patna, dated 2 April 1942, revealed:

'As for the Hindu Sabha and other parties, I think Cripps handled it badly and alienated them by saying that he had come to secure the consent only of the Congress and the Muslim League.'[19]

Emerging from the meeting Savarkar addressed the press and in a major giveaway of what the provisions might have contained announced: 'We shall fight out Pakistan to the last.'[20] The fact that the Pakistan scheme that had not been publicly stated by the Mission had come up for discussion and had led to a breakdown of talks between Cripps and the Mahasabha. It portended ominously of what was to follow with other political parties in India. As the *New York Times* stated that this breakdown was 'the first public intimation of anything other than smooth sailing in Sir Stafford's fulfillment of his mission'.[21] The road to reconciliation seemed to have broken completely as the Hindu Mahasabha leaders refused to have any more parleys with Cripps.

Savarkar's unequivocal stand won him a lot of appreciation, including from the Congress mouthpiece the *National Herald*:

> Profoundly as we disagree with Savarkar's politics, we freely admit that he is one of the few men of our age who have made history and contributed to a reawakening of our people . . . he showed the old fire in him, when he took up the thoughtless challenge thrown to the Hindu Mahasabha by the Government of Bihar, and obtained a resounding victory at Bhagalpur. With Sir Stafford Cripps he crossed swords, which the former will never forget.[22]

Cripps held marathon meetings for over a week with Nehru and Maulana Azad from the Congress side. Roosevelt's personal representative Colonel Louis Johnson too was involved in the deliberations, as was Lord Wavell, the commander-in-chief. The Congress took up the question of defence first as it was anxious to retain its control over the important portfolio. After a lot of back and forth, a formula was worked out that war operations would remain with the commander-in-chief and the new Indian defence member in the viceroy's council would keep under his charge the defence department along with other subjects dealt with by the defence coordination department.[23] An imminent breakthrough seemed possible going by the public statements of Congress leaders, especially Nehru and Rajagopalachari. British newspapers such as *The Scotsman* confidently put out headlines in its 10 April edition that said: 'Mr. Nehru may be India's first defence minister: Negotiations for National Government continue; hammering out new formula.'[24]

But the fact was that several of these concessions, as also the Congress's demands for an agreed share in the national government that in effect sought fundamental changes in the Constitution and a break to the viceroy's veto powers, were carried on by Cripps without taking Viceroy Linlithgow into confidence. Even as the Congress was busy making public pronouncements that 'we [Congress] are prepared to assume responsibility if national government is formed with full powers',[25] as Azad did on 9 April, they angered Linlithgow. Angry telegrams were exchanged between the viceroy and London about Cripps exceeding his brief.

At the same time, there were apprehensions of an internal sabotage to the Mission in the Congress given Gandhi's stiff opposition to it. Gandhi had told Cripps early on in the discussions: 'Why did you come if this is what you had to offer? If this is your entire proposal in India, I would advise you the next plane home!'[26] Gandhi famously trashed the Mission and its proposals as 'a post-dated cheque on a bank, which is obviously going broke',[27] emphasizing his early prophecy of Britain losing the war. It was the younger lot within the Congress who seemed eager to share power in the new proposed national government that made them oblivious to the stark threats to national unity that Cripps's proposals had embedded within it. Thus, despite all the public display of confidence about a breakthrough soon, Nehru seemed a diffident man after 9 April. Gandhi's writ seemed to have run internally in the party and Professor Reginald Coupland, a constitutional expert and Cripps's confidant in Delhi saw Gandhi's undeniable hand in thwarting the proposals.[28]

Interestingly, the Muslim League whose pet scheme of Pakistan was bolstered by the Mission also rejected it as it felt that there was no clear enunciation of Pakistan and its contours. That Pakistan was only an implication as far as the proposals were concerned, the League declared it an impossibility to work in a constituent assembly that had representative members based on population strength, thereby having to kowtow to the majority community. The depressed classes found inadequate safeguards of their interests in the scheme.

The British official view conveniently put the blame on Gandhi's pacifist and non-violent approach and his refusal to cooperate with war efforts as stipulated in the plan. But that was far from the complete truth. American and British correspondences on this matter till the very end show the obstinacy with which Churchill held on to his determination not to grant any concessions to India and to thwart Cripps's attempts. On 11 April, Churchill cabled Roosevelt claiming that the British had tried their best but the Indian political opinion was too divided and obdurate for any considerations. In his long reply, Roosevelt told him on 11 April:

> I most earnestly hope that you may find it possible to postpone Cripps' departure from India until one more final effort has been made to prevent a breakdown in the negotiations. I am sorry to say that I cannot agree with the point of view set forth in your message to me that public opinion in the United States believes that the negotiations have failed on broad general issues. The general impression here is quite the contrary. The feeling is almost universally held that the deadlock has been caused by the unwillingness of the British Government to concede to the Indians the right of self-government, notwithstanding the willingness of the Indians to entrust technical, military and naval defense control to the competent British authorities. American public opinion cannot understand why if the British Government is willing to permit the component parts of India to secede from the British Empire after the war, it is not willing to permit them to enjoy what is tantamount to self-government during the war.[29]

But this was not to be. Cripps left India by mid-April totally defeated in his grandiose mission and with his dreams of becoming the Lord Durham for India completely shattered.

Even as the Cripps Mission was undertaking its negotiations with the Congress, a faction of the party was busy conducting backroom discussions with other political parties including the Hindu Mahasabha. British intelligence reports that while the Working Committee meeting of the Mahasabha was to be held in Delhi on 3 April, in the wake of the Cripps interviews, it was changed to 1 April and was attended by Savarkar, Mookerjee, Moonje, Bhai Parmanand and others. One of the reasons that it attributes for this urgent meeting was 'to accommodate some members of the Congress Working Committee like Sardar Patel, who wanted the Hindu Mahasabha to give some indication of its attitude, so that the Congress Working Committee itself should not yield to the proposals or waver in favour of acceptance.'[30] According to the report, the Patel group within the Congress strongly believed that 'if the Hindu Mahasabha alone rejects the proposals, the Congress will lose much of its influence with the Hindu masses to the Hindu Mahasabha. The Patel Group has been privately meeting Hindu Mahasabha and Sikh leaders to exchange views.'[31]

~

The Mahasabha Working Committee that met on 1 April resolved that the primary fact that needed to be emphasized and recognized was that India 'is an indivisible, inviolable and integral unity, which must be maintained and strengthened at all costs'. It harked back to both the cultural unity of the nation and its people, as also the political and administrative integration of the country that several dynasties of the past and the British Empire too had brought about. The Mahasabha explained that the fact that India is a unitary state did not mean that it does not have different races, religions or languages. These differences had to be 'fully recognized and protected on principle by a comprehensive scheme of cultural autonomy, which is seen in operation in its best form in the Turkish Constitution. The scheme has also been elaborated by the League of Nations.' It also illustrated the example of the Soviet Union where as many as twenty-seven different communities, people and religions were brought together to form a centralized unitary state, dissociating statehood from race and religion. In the USSR, none of the constituent units were permitted the freedom to secede from the Union. The resolution referenced the American Civil War too where the question of secession of the individual states was vital for the Union. Abraham Lincoln had then said: 'I hold that the Union of these States is perpetual. No State, upon its own mere action, can lawfully go out of the Union.'[32] The resolution concluded with the Hindu Mahasabha's firm declaration of not being 'a party to proposals aiming at the dismemberment of India as an established Unitary State, which has been up to now functioning as a living organism. The Hindu Mahasabha has been throughout supporting the Government in its war effort and is of the opinion that it may be much more increased by making the people feel that it is as much a war for their own freedom as it is that of any of the Allied Nations.'[33]

On 6 April, Savarkar dashed off a telegram to Cripps, one that was carried in all the major newspapers in London as well. In a terse manner Cripps was told that '. . . if you depend on any Congress-League pact alone, to which the Hindu Mahasabha is not made a willing party, then you will be *leaning on a broken reed* [emphasis mine] . . . Such a pact can only alienate the largest part of the Hindus, who would have welcomed the scheme if the vivisection of India clause had been omitted.'[34]

The Mahasabha leaders Savarkar, Moonje and Mookerjee met the maharaja of Bikaner and confabulated on the prospect of what position the Indian princes, particularly the Hindu provinces would take in the event of a transfer of power. A few other Hindu princes whom the Mahasabha leaders met assured them that they need not fear any alignment with Jinnah. 'Some of the Hindu Mahasabha leaders had unfounded fears on this account,' mentioned a British intelligence report, 'not having had previous contact with the princes'.[35]

On reaching Bombay on 9 April, Savarkar issued a brief press statement further emphasizing the Hindu Mahasabha's position:

> Hindu Mahasabha's rejection of Cripps' scheme in no way means that Mahasabha has given up policy of militarization of Hindus. Principle of responsive cooperation, which guides Mahasabha policy implies any means calculated to defend and advance legitimate interests of Hindudom. Scheme of British war cabinet was highly detrimental to Hindu interests and had therefore to be rejected. But Hindu interests demand our joining Government military forces. We must intensify militarization movement and join in as large numbers as possible Army, Navy, Air Force, A.R.P., Civic Guards, Ordnance Factories etc. throughout India. Thus only will Hindus be in position to defend homes from ravages of war and to suppress any internal anti-Hindu anarchy. Martial mentality and capacity thus developed will prove invaluable asset to national strength even after war.[36]

Savarkar even cabled to the editor of the *New York Times* on the Hindu Mahasabha's stand given the active interest among the American leadership and public opinion in securing for India her long-awaited freedom. He also warned Cripps that no tacit or secret understanding that he might have secured or would secure in future with the Congress and the League would be ever binding on the Mahasabha. He wrote:

> The Hindu Mahasabha partially accepted the Cripps proposal and welcomed the promised grant of equal co-partnership with Britain; but the scheme made it all conditional on granting freedom to provinces to secede and break up India into a number of independent States with no

Central Indian Government . . . Americans in particular who went to war even with their kith and kin on the question of secession and saved the integrity of their union, cannot fail to appreciate and uphold the Hindu opposition to the vivisection of India. Hindus are prepared to guarantee legitimate safeguards to the minorities, but can never tolerate their efforts to create a State within a State as the League of Nations put it.[37]

Despite the stiff opposition to the Cripps Mission by the Mahasabha, Savarkar was also interviewed by the Governor of Bombay, Lawrence Roger Lumley, on his return. He reiterated the same views of the Hindu Mahasabha's willingness to join the national government provided the secession clause of Cripps was annulled. An interesting secret note that Lumley had compiled as brief points for the viceroy throws light on how the British government actually viewed Savarkar:

A temporary ally, but a dangerous friend; Anti-Muslim but equally Anti-British; Is anti-Gandhi because opposed to Gandhi's non-violence for internal politics; Believes in individual killing and guerilla warfare. If Congress does not come into expanded Executive Council and if Hindu Mahasabha and Muslim League come in—dogfight will ensue. Jinnah will fight on question of Indianization of Army, which would at present mean stronger Muslim element from the Punjab. Savarkar will want a Hindu Army. Other questions too, there will be continuous dissentions.[38]

Following the Cripps Mission, Savarkar and the Mahasabha came well in the attention of international press that had hitherto been swayed or preoccupied only with the views of Gandhi and Jinnah for the Indian perspective. For the first time, editors of various international newspapers sought Savarkar's time to elicit the Hindu Mahasabha's standpoint on the Indian problem. American journalist of the weekly *Nation* of New York, Louis Fischer, interviewed Savarkar and pressed him on about the latter's opposition to the Pakistan scheme. Savarkar asked him nonchalantly whether a demand for a separate Negro state within or separate from the USA could be thought of or entertained. Fischer exclaimed that that was an anti-national demand to make. 'Exactly Mr. Fischer! Granting Pakistan will be anti-national and undemocratic in India as would be the granting of Negrostan in the U.S.A.,' quipped Savarkar.[39] In a threatening tone, Fischer then told Savarkar not to forget the debacle of Panipat and that it could be repeated if the Muslims felt offended and short-changed. Savarkar immediately reminded him of the recent debacles that the Allied forces had suffered in the war in Dunkirk and Crete, leaving Fischer speechless.

Lawrence Brander of the British Broadcasting Corporation, London, too interviewed Savarkar who reiterated the demands that the Hindu Mahasabha had been making of the British Parliament. A Hindu Mahasabha communiqué states that on 18 June 1942, an 'outstanding Negro leader of the Ethiopian movement from America'[40] met Savarkar at his residence (name of the leader not stated). He is supposed to have shared with Savarkar the difficulties that his community was facing in America; that they were not allowed to join the White forces or even command the separate battalions that were raised of the Blacks.

On 19 May 1942, John Paton Davies, the second secretary of the American embassy attached to the staff of the general commanding the American army forces in China, Burma and India, interviewed Savarkar for over an hour. During the interview Davies stated that the American press and the public were realizing the growing strength of the Hindu Mahasabha as a major representative organization of the Hindus and wanted to know more about its ideology and political attitude.[41]

~

An interview he gave a year later to American war correspondent Tom Treanor went on to become popular when the latter recounted it in his memoirs. Treanor recounts how 'Savarkar was not specially dressed for the occasion. He looked his worst. His sunken cheeks were unshaven, his perfectly round metal-rimmed eye glasses were specked, and he was dressed in a soiled length of cloth, which looked like a nightgown and was insecurely fastened in front with silver studs, some of which were missing.'[42] Savarkar evidently did not seem to care, even as Treanor himself rationalized that he was more interested in ideas, though 'American people consider political ideas dull'.[43] 'His voice would become like a phonograph,' wrote Treanor, 'and he would go on and on, braiding and unbraiding a tired handkerchief while he carried on about the Hindu Mahasabha.'[44]

Savarkar was quite taken aback when Treanor questioned him about his revolutionary past and whether he had thrown bombs that killed high officials in England and India. Savarkar denied doing any of these himself but attributed the acts to his revolutionary friends. When asked about

Viceroy Lord Hardinge being hit by a bomb in the Delhi Conspiracy Case of 1912 and if it hurt him, Savarkar quipped with neither a sense of contentment nor regret, 'It knocked him off an elephant . . . he was six months in hospital with his spine.'[45] When quizzed more of his 'terrorist' antecedents, he shot back, 'Would you wish that I confess to you everything?'[46]

Making his opposition to the Pakistan demand clear, Savarkar termed it as non-negotiable. The following conversation occurred between the two:

Treanor: How do you plan to treat the Mohammedans?

Savarkar: As a minority, in the position of your Negroes.

T: And if the Mohammedans succeed in seceding and set up their own country?

S: As in your country (waggling a menacing finger), there will be civil war.[47]

On the issue of Gandhi and his non-violence, Savarkar was respectful of the Mahatma but mentioned, 'If a fast is so effective, why doesn't Churchill fast against Hitler? What would Hitler say?'[48] Not waiting for Treanor to gather much of his thoughts, he answered it himself, 'He'd say something rude.' Savarkar was clear in his head that it was permanent national interests that guided any country's foreign policy. 'The world is run by self-interest, not the Bible. What is your self-interest in India?' Again answering it for Treanor, he hypothesized that India was a strategic fighting base for America now and in the future since it would be a while before the world settled down to normality and having Indian goodwill was a smart thing to do for the USA. 'So why not oblige India? You will need her some day!'[49] he quipped.

In his assessment of Savarkar, Treanor wrote:

Savarkar is quite a sight to Western eyes . . . I suppose he is a little fanatic for our taste. But he has a certain power of personality and is definitely a figure of some importance on the Indian political scene, particularly now that many of the leading Hindus are in jail along with the Mahatma . . .

> Despite all this confinement [*referring to the Andamans and Ratnagiri for twenty-eight years*] he was enough in tune with the spirit of the times to get into a political whirl and come on the top of a strong minority party. He's a real story, is old man Savarkar.[50]

Despite his steadily failing health, in July 1942 Savarkar undertook an extensive trip of Jammu and Kashmir, a province that he hailed as 'Hindudom's Northern Watchman'.[51] In the Hindu-majority Jammu, more than 40,000 people welcomed him in mammoth public procession and rally. In Muslim-majority Kashmir and Srinagar too there was enthusiasm on Savarkar's visit. The pro-Partition political party, the Jammu and Kashmir Conference, and its delegates presented a memorandum to him asking him to specify if his oft-repeated principle of majority rule applied in Kashmir too, where the population was Muslim largely and was ruled by a Hindu king. In his statement later, Savarkar told then that the Hindu Mahasabha's national principle was that '. . . all citizens who owe undivided loyalty and allegiance to the Indian nation and to the Indian state shall be treated with perfect equality and shall share duties and obligations equally in common, irrespective of caste, creed or religion, and the representation also shall either be on the basis of one man one vote or in proportion to the population in case of separate electorates and public services shall go by merit alone.[52]

The prerequisite for claiming rights was unalloyed allegiance and loyalty to the nation. But when these parties openly call for seceding from India and also overtly talk in support of Pakistan, how could they expect the Indian state to grant them any privileges or even look upon them as citizens at all, Savarkar wondered. No country could tolerate the concept of a 'state within a state' as that would be dangerous for its integrity. Also, he questioned that if such a 'national formula' needs to exist in Kashmir, would the Muslims of Kashmir make common cause and openly back the rights of the Hindu majority in princely states such as Bhopal and Hyderabad that were ruled by a Muslim monarch.

> The Hindus cannot think of the Hindus in Kashmir as cut off and apart from Hindudom as a whole, just as the Kashmir Moslems feel themselves inseparably connected with Islam outside Kashmir and even outside India and do not fail at times to call upon these outside Moslems to help them, at times even in their treacherous designs

to capture the Hindu State and annex it to their airy ambitions of a Pakistani Federation.[53]

He drew the attention of the Muslims of Kashmir to the plight of Hindus in Muslim-ruled provinces and concluded that their lives and properties were, in comparison, much safer and secured in Kashmir.

> In Kashmir, the security of life and property the Moslems enjoy is a thing unknown in the Nizam state as far as the Hindus are concerned, who are attacked, killed, looted at this place or that by the riotous Moslem mobs almost from month to month. The Moslems have in Kashmir fifty per cent representation already in the legislature while in the Moslem states there are no legislatures at all in working order.[54]

Constantly on Savarkar's radar of ire was Sir Mirza Ismail who had served as the dewan or prime minister of the Hindu princely state of Mysore and was then appointed as dewan of Jaipur in 1942. Citing his antecedents in Mysore where Savarkar claimed that Ismail had packed the police, military and other administrative services with Muslim officers beyond their population ratio, Savarkar said, 'To give more to the Moslems than what is due to them on the basis either of merit or population is to rob the Hindus of their legitimate rights and all this happening in a Hindu state which ought to be predominantly manned and officered by the Hindus themselves.'[55] He urged the maharaja of Jaipur to reconsider this appointment.

> Where shall we then find one who will patronize the Hindu cause if, even the Hindu princes and at that a Rajput prince like the Maharaja of Jaipur does not defend even the legitimate interests of the Hindus and should fail to find a single Hindu able and trustworthy enough amongst the 30 crores of Hindus to act as the Minister of Jaipur![56]

The Thorn of Pakistan

Given the imminent push to the cause of Pakistan as evidenced in Cripps's proposals, the Hindu Mahasabha decided to launch an offensive against the idea. On 10 May 1942, which was also the momentous anniversary of the 1857 War of Independence, it observed an 'Anti-Pakistan Day' across the country. From Jammu, Peshawar, Poona, Amritsar, Lahore to Delhi, Lucknow, Patna, Calcutta, Bombay, Nagpur down to Madras, almost all capital cities and hundreds of towns and villages responded to the Mahasabha's call. In Bombay, cycle processions were held across the city with slogans of '*Hindustan Zindabad, Pakistan Murdabad!*' (Long Live Hindustan; Death to Pakistan!). Buttonhole flags with a map of India on it, signifying Indian solidarity and unity were sold in large numbers by Mahasabha and Arya Samaj volunteers all day. In the evening, a procession began from the Mahasabha office and culminated in a meeting at the Chowpatty Beach with over 25,000 people attending. The picture on the dais was a big map of India, above a naked sword with the inscription: 'My India will ever remain one and undivided.'

After a speech by Jamnadas Mehta who presided over the event, Savarkar delivered a stirring address, interjected several times by a charged audience who chanted shouts against Pakistan. In the course of the speech, he said:

> I am glad that thousands of Hindus have assembled here today. From one end of Hindusthan to the other, every Hindu will take a solemn oath today that he will fight and preserve India un-divided, whatever may befall him. Today India is divided into several parts such as French Hindusthan, Portuguese Hindusthan, British Hindusthan etc. and consequently this war for Akhand Hindusthan will be going on from generation to generation, till the object has been achieved.[57]

Recounting his own laborious study of British documents to write about the 1857 War of Independence, Savarkar mocked Rajagopalachari who claimed that he was deeply inspired by his book. The latter had said that during 1857, Hindus and Muslims had fought together under one banner and had questioned Savarkar how without such a Hindu–Muslim unity could the fight against imperialism happen again. Savarkar asked him:

> My counter question to him is whether the battle for freedom should be stopped, because the Muslims are not prepared to join? There must have been some strong reason for this unity. The Hindus were strong and had a very big army and that was the real reason for this unity. The Muslims did not dare to go against Nanasaheb Peshwa, Laxmibai of Jhansi, Tatya Tope and others. If Rajaji says he derived inspiration from this book, he should read it once more. Rajaji has not understood the main reason for the Hindu-Muslim unity of that time even after reading my book.[58]

He reminded Rajagopalachari that the real example of the unity of the two communities was to be seen in Bengal where after the Haq–Mookerjee alliance in government, Haq who had hitherto been anti-Hindu in its utterances and actions was today permitting anti-Pakistan rallies and processions in Bengal without any government permission. Haq had also admitted that the Pakistan scheme would not be successful in Bengal and it did not have his concurrence. This, according to Savarkar, was the real Hindu–Muslim unity and its ultimate objective, rather than merely 'pamper the Muslims by respecting their whims' and making them 'swollen-headed'.[59] The meeting ended with the resolution moved by Jamnadas Mehta, unequivocally condemning the Pakistan scheme, being adopted unanimously amidst chants of the motherland.

Savarkar's antipathy and references to Rajagopalachari were driven by the latter's moves that had even embittered several Congressmen towards him. Ever since the outbreak of the war, Rajagopalachari was keen to broker a truce between the Congress and the government. With the Cripps Mission failing, he was convinced that no progress was possible in the political deadlock until and unless the gulf between the League and the Congress was bridged. To attempt this, he embarked on a rather preposterous move, and on 23 April got the Madras legislature pass a resolution that Congressmen should acknowledge the Muslim League's claim for separation if it persisted during the time of framing the Constitution. It called for immediate start of negotiations with the League for the 'purpose of arriving at an agreement and securing the installation of a national government to meet the present emergency'.[60] The resolution urged that 'to sacrifice the chances of the formation of a national government for the doubtful advantage of maintaining a controversy over the unity of India is the most unwise policy'[61] and hence the lesser evil needed to be chosen. The resolution was recommended for deliberation when the All-India Congress Committee was scheduled to meet in Allahabad later that year. The League was overjoyed at this unexpected support from a veteran within the Congress and an entire provincial legislature supporting its claim even without its explicit demand for the same. This however created a huge stir in political circles, including within the Congress, and hence the supporters of the united-India campaign like Savarkar made no bones about castigating Rajagopalachari at all forums. This, despite Rajagopalachari having been an admirer of Savarkar, whose biography too he had penned.

The anxiety was further exacerbated by the vacillating stands often taken by Gandhi and the Congress on the whole issue of Pakistan since the time it was vaguely mooted in the Lahore Resolution in 1940. In the *Harijan* of 4 May 1940, he had said: 'I would any day prefer Muslim rule to British rule . . . the partition proposal had altered the face of the Hindu-Muslim problem . . . Pakistan cannot be worse than foreign domination.'[62] His earlier statements were vague at best where he had said: 'As a man of non-violence, I cannot forcibly resist the proposed partition if the Muslims of India really insist upon it . . . but I can never be a willing party to the vivisection.'[63] On another occasion, he had declared in a rather emotional manner: 'Vivisect me before you vivisect India.'[64] But in the wake of no negotiations with the League or the government on the matter or even a public admonishment of the Pakistan scheme, the Congress and Gandhi were giving mixed signals on their acquiescence.

But close on the heels of the failure of the Cripps Mission, the Congress's stand on Pakistan began to become more pronounced. Its Working Committee proclaimed in its resolution in Delhi in April 1942 that 'the Congress could not think in terms of compelling the people of any territorial unit to join the Indian Union against their declared and established will'.[65] As Congress leader Pattabhi Sitaramayya himself admitted about this particular CWC Resolution: 'It is evident that the passage concedes the division of India into more than one State and gives the go-by to the unity and integrity of India.'[66] But even as the CWC was passing this resolution, Gandhi was declaring in the *Harijan* of 24 May 1942: 'I consider the vivisection of India to be a sin.'[67] In the same edition, Gandhi wrote that the 'Indian Army will be disbanded with the withdrawal of the British Power'.[68] There was little clarification on how then would the new Indian state deal with external aggression or the scenario of internal anarchy and civil war.

Reacting sharply to the resolution of the CWC, Savarkar issued a statement on 21 April 1942:

> For the last three years or so I have been publicly warning the Hindus that there was every likelihood that the Congress would servilely surrender to the Moslems on the issue of Pakistan even as it did on the issue of Communal Award and would even have the crazy audacity of parading this treacherous act itself as an acid test of Indian patriotism. The Congressite Hindus continued to challenge and a large section of the non-

Congress Hindus also used to doubt the accuracy of these assertions on my part. They wanted evidence to prove my assertions. Now here comes the evidence with a vengeance. Here is an authoritative declaration by the Congress framed in a resolution, which they have passed, signed, sealed and delivered to the envoy of the British War Cabinet that they admitted the right on the part of the Muslim Provinces, nay, for the matter of that any provinces whatever, to cut themselves off from Hindustan and create independent States of Pakistans or any other *Stans* they choose . . . the Congress, which calls itself 'Indian National Congress' has in these few lines stabbed at a stroke, the unity and integrity of the Indian Nation itself in the back.[69]

Despite the CWC resolution, when the AICC met in Allahabad on 29 April, the resolution of Rajagopalachari and the Madras legislature was defeated by an overwhelming majority of 120 votes against fifteen. Congress leader Babu Jagat Narayan moved a counter resolution on 'Akhand Hindustan' or Undivided India in the same AICC declaring that, '. . . any proposal to disintegrate India by giving liberty to any component State or territorial unit to secede from the Indian Union or Federation will be highly detrimental to the best interests of the people of different States and provinces and the country as a whole and the Congress therefore cannot agree to any such proposal'.[70] The resolution went through despite the Muslim members of the AICC voting against it. However, leaders like Nehru and Azad were at pains to stress in their letters to Sayyid Abdul Latif of Hyderabad on 6 August 1942 that the Delhi resolution of the CWC conceding the right of self-determination to the provinces superseded any Akhand Hindustan resolution that the AICC might have passed.[71]

Hence where exactly the Congress and its top leadership stood on the issue of Pakistan was an enigma. By their actions though, they seemed to have conceded the idea even before having a tough bargain with Jinnah or to coerce him to drop the idea off the agenda or to split Muslim political opinion on the proposed Partition.

'Quit-India' and Thereafter

The collapse of the Cripps Mission gravely accentuated the rumblings within the Congress. The views of one P. Subbaroyan, a Congressman and supporter of Rajagopalachari, on the power mechanics within the Congress that led to the failure of the Cripps Mission, are in the words of a British Secret Report, 'little more than academic importance':

> From the very beginning C. Rajagopalachari informed the Congress Working Committee at Delhi, that it [was] no use prolonging negotiations with Cripps. The proposals should be accepted and worked out. The Gandhi Group never allowed him to see Cripps. According to Dr. Subbaroyan, the whole affair was sabotaged by the Gandhi Group. They made a fool of Jawaharlal who never knows his own mind, and is not prepared to oppose the wishes of the majority of the Working Committee for fear of losing popularity. Dr. Subbaroyan thinks that Jawaharlal's love of popularity plays the most important part in his political life. The Gandhi Group had no intention of accepting the Cripps' proposals.[72]

Gandhi, who had been virtually sidelined within the party for a brief while, resurrected his hold over the party. He was ruminating the launch of a new Civil Disobedience movement that forced British withdrawal from India. This went in tangent to the views of several Congress leaders including Nehru and Azad who were sympathetic to the Allied forces and wished to align with the British war efforts against their alleged fight against fascism and for the cause of democracy globally. Gandhi on the other hand believed that Japan's quarrel was not with India and if the British left, Japan may not even attack India and even if it did, it would be dealt with through non-violent civil resistance. In his writing on 24 May 1942, Gandhi postulated:

> Leave India in God's hands . . . in modern parlance, to anarchy and that anarchy may lead to internecine warfare for a time or to unrestrained dacoities. From these a true India will rise in place of the false one we see.[73] . . . I have not asked the British to hand over India to God or in modern parlance to anarchy. Then all the parties will fight one another like dogs, or will, when real responsibility faces them, come to a reasonable agreement. I shall expect non-violence to arise out of that chaos.[74]

This was a prescription that obviously had no takers among sane and sober statesmen within the Congress, leave alone the British. The British saw these utterances of Gandhi as being suggestive of his being on the verge of taking decisions 'when overtaken by signs of loss of faith in his leadership, to stage civil disobedience campaign or personal fast'.[75]

These contesting viewpoints clashed several times in the meetings of the All India Congress Committee (AICC) and the Congress Working Committee (CWC) in Allahabad (29 April to 2 May 1942) and in the CWC meeting in Wardha (6 July 1942). In Wardha, Gandhi floated his idea of a 'Quit India' movement that shocked most Congressmen, including Nehru, Azad and Rajaji. Giving an account of the tumult within the party, the Congress resident of the time, Maulana Azad says:

I could not believe that with the enemy on the Indian frontier, the British would tolerate a movement of resistance. Gandhiji seemed to have a strange belief that they would. He held that the British would allow him to develop his movement in his own way. When I pressed him to tell us what exactly would be the programme of resistance, he had no clear idea . . . Gandhiji held that the British would regard his move for an organized mass movement as a warning and not take any precipitate action. He would therefore have time to work out the details of the movement and develop its tempo according to his plans. I was convinced that this would not be the case . . . Apart from Jawaharlal, who often agreed with me, the other members were generally content to follow Gandhiji's lead. Sardar Patel, Dr. Rajendra Prasad and Acharya Kripalani had no clear idea about the war. They rarely tried to judge things on their own, and in any case, they were accustomed to subordinate their judgment to Gandhiji. As such, discussion with them was almost useless. After all our discussions, the only thing they could say was that we must have faith in Gandhiji. They held that if we trusted him he would find some way out. Gandhiji's idea seemed to be that since the war was on the India frontier, the British would come to terms with the Congress as soon as the movement was launched. Even if this did not take place, he believed that the British would hesitate to take any drastic steps with the Japanese knocking at India's doors. He thought this would give the Congress the time and the opportunity to organize an effective movement. My own reading was completely different . . . never before had our difference been so complete. Things reached a climax when he sent me a letter to the effect that my stand was so different from his that we could not work together. If Congress wanted Gandhiji to lead the movement, I must resign from the Presidentship and also withdraw from the Working Committee. Jawaharlal must do the same.[76]

The British obviously keenly watched the developments in the Congress with utter disdain. In their assessment, the possible impact of the movement 'may make British task more difficult, but will neither expel them nor reconcile minorities, while it would assist Japanese plans to invade India'. British reports summarize what they term as Congress's frustration in poetic flourish by comparing it to a Persian proverb: 'I will not eat it myself, nor will I give it to someone else to eat, but I will let it rot, so that I can throw it to the dogs.'[77]

But even by Gandhi's own past standards, the proposed Quit India movement seemed to lack all planning and preparedness or any clear sense of strategy. This is what baffled the saner elements within the Congress who tried in vain to convince him against such a precipitant move during a juncture as critical and sensitive as the one India was facing then. However, Gandhi in his characteristic manner managed to bulldoze his personal whim on the Congress party. The Congress Working Committee on 14 July 1942 passed the long 'Quit India resolution' urging the British to withdraw from the country and allow responsible men and women to then come together and form a provisional government and a constituent assembly. The Congress, it said, 'had no desire whatsoever to embarrass Great Britain or the Allied Powers in their prosecution of the war, or in any way encourage aggression in India or increased pressure on China by the Japanese or any other power associated with the Axis group. Nor does the Congress intend to jeopardize the defensive capacity of the Allied Powers. The Congress is therefore agreeable to the stationing of the armed forces of the Allies in India, should they so desire, in order to ward off and resist Japanese or other aggression, and to protect and help China . . .'[78] If the British failed to accept this 'very reasonable and just proposal' the Congress would be compelled to utilize all the 'non-violent strength it might have gathered since 1920, when it adopted non-violence as part of its policy for the vindication of political rights and liberty'.

There was discontent within the Congress on the idea of asking the British to quit India but leave their army behind. Rajagopalachari, himself a votary of amicable settlement with the government, wrote to Gandhi:

Your proposal that while the civil power may be withdrawn, the British and allied forces may continue in India in anticipation of a treaty with a

Courtesy: Swatantryaveer Savarkar Rashtriya Smarak (SSRS), Mumbai.

Courtesy: Team of www.savarkar.org (Dr Shreerang Godbole, Late Himani Savarkar, Shreedhar Damle, Chandrashekhar Sane and Akshay Jog)

A portrait of Savarkar in Ratnagiri, dated 1928.

Picture depicting the killing of the demon of untouchability, Ratnagiri, February 1933.

Courtesy: Team www.savarkar.org

Sacred thread ceremony of ex-untouchables at Malvan, 1929, under the leadership of Savarkar.

The Harijan Bhajan Mandal raised by Savarkar in Ratnagiri.

Undated photograph of Savarkar in Ratnagiri.

The first Sahabhojan or inter-caste dining in Ratnagiri, 1930.

Members of the Ratnagiri Hindu Sabha with Savarkar, 1936. Standing: Narayanshet Khatu, M.V. Patkar, Palukaka Joshi, Shrikrishna Sheth Gandhi, D.D. Sawant. On seats: Acharekar, Achyutsheth Malushte, Dr Shinde, Chiplunkar, Savarkar, G.V. Patwardhan and Athavale. Seated on ground: Gajanan Damle, Dattoo Sheth Jali & Tatyarao Damle.

First procession in Pune after unconditional release from Ratnagiri; also seen are uniformed RSS volunteers; sitting next to Savarkar is Maharashtra provincial RSS Sanghachalak K.B. Limaye; sitting next to the driver in front is J.S. Karandikar; 25 June 1937.

Felicitation of Savarkar in Bombay by students at the Shrikrishna Theatre, Girgaon, after his release from Ratnagiri, 1937.

Grand reception at Ajmer during the Rajasthan tour, May 1938.

Speech by Savarkar; Keshavrao Jedhe in the background.

Savarkar with J.S. Karandikar (L) and Senapati Bapat (R).

Savarkar with
Dharamveer
L.B. Bhopatkar.

Photograph in Nasik
during a Shuddhi
ceremony; seated on
ground at left most is
Babarao Savarkar; on
chair, third from left,
L.B. Bhopatkar, to
Savarkar's left Masurkar
Maharaj, and Dr B.S.
Moonje to his right.

Presidential Speech
at All India Hindu
Mahasabha session,
Karnavati, 1937.

Savarkar with Bhai Parmananda in the Presidential procession at All India Hindu Mahasabha session, Karnavati, 29 December 1937.

Tour of Ahmednagar, Maharashtra, 14 February 1938.

Grand welcome reception in Calcutta, 1939.

With anti-Nizam Hindu activists at Umarkhed in Vidarbha, close to the Nizam territory; 7 June 1939.

Savarkar addressing the mammoth meeting in Town Hall, Calcutta, on 17 February 1939.

At Salem on occasion of Tamil Nadu Hindu Parishad, March 1940; standing with stick in the hand is Madras RSS Sanghachalak and Hindu Sabha leader Varadarajulu Naidu.

Meeting Subhas Chandra Bose at his Bombay residence in Dadar, 22 June 1940.

Savarkar with Sir Stafford Cripps, New Delhi, 23 March 1942.

The Hindu Mahasabha delegation comprising of Savarkar, Dr Moonje (bearded), Dr Syama Prasad Mookerji, Sir Jwala Prasad Srivastava, and Lala Ganpat Rai coming out after meeting Sir Stafford Cripps. They ran into the incoming Congress delegation comprising of then Congress President Maulana Azad.

With Seth Gulabchand Hirachand at Balachandranagar.

At the Shimoga Hindu Mahasabha Conference, 1944.

With the 'Nightingale of India', Bharat Ratna Lata Mageshkar.

With the accused in the Gandhi Murder Trial at Red Fort, New
Delhi, 1948.

After release from the Belgaum Jail, 1950.

Public unfurling in Pune of the first national flag hoisted by Madam Cama in Stuttgart.

Speech at Tilak Smarak Mandir, Pune. N.C. Kelkar also seen.

Felicitation at Miraj, 30 July 1941, N.C. Kelkar seated to Savarkar's left.

At the public event to dissolve the Abhinav Bharat in Pune, 1952. Senapati Bapat also seen.

Inspecting a printing press; on the left is personal secretary Balarao Savarkar, on the right is Jayantrao Tilak, Lokmanya's grandson.

Sindhi Hindu Sabha volunteers felicitate Savarkar on his 50th birthday on 28 May 1952.

Public Reception in New Delhi to commemorate the centenary of 1857 First War of Independence.

Felicitation in New Delhi by N.V. Gadgil.

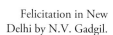
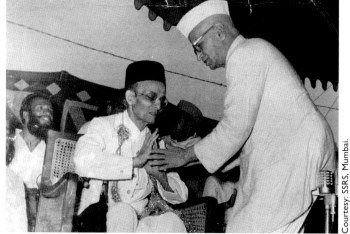

Outside the Patit Pavan Mandir, Ratnagiri.

Tilak Death Anniversary, Pune.

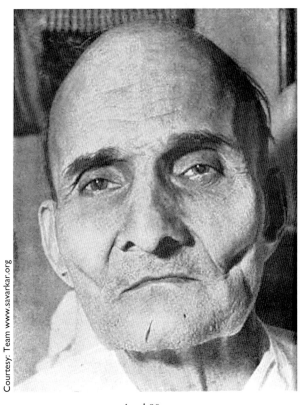

Aged 80 years.

problematic provisional Indian government will only lead to the exercise of all Government functions by military forces. This will happen if only for their own safety and effective functioning. They are further likely to be urged towards this step by local chieftains and suffering people. This would be the reinstallation of the British Government in the worst form.[79]

When Gandhi's staunch adherent Miss Slade, popularly known as Mira Ben, was sent to meet the viceroy to appraise him of the Congress resolution, the latter refused to even entertain her on the premise that this smacked of an open rebellion and that the government was not willing to tolerate any rebellion during the war, be it violent or non-violent, or even speak to representatives of parties that propagated such thoughts.[80] Azad's prophecy seemed to be coming true and Gandhi realized that the British were not so flexible this time. A mass struggle was however launched on 7 August 1942 after the AICC met in Bombay. The British were told in no uncertain terms to 'Quit India' and the clarion call of a fight to the finish was given to Indians to 'Do or Die', within of course the limits of non-violent struggle. The people were told to carry on the movement on their own initiative and wisdom if the top leaders were clapped in jail.

No government, especially one that was faced with imminent external aggression, was to take such an openly rebellious move quietly. Keeping a close track on the AICC developments, within a week of the resolution being passed, all Congress leaders were hauled up and jailed. The AICC and all the Provincial Congress Committees except in NWFP were declared unlawful organizations. Congress headquarters in Allahabad was seized, all its funds confiscated and its publications including Gandhi's *Harijan* were suspended. Brute force was used to suppress all agitations and mass movements that emerged in large numbers across the country. The sufferings, police brutalities, rapes and property damages were numerous and untold. As Nehru recounted:

Official estimates of the number of people killed and wounded by police or military firing in the 1942 disturbances are: 1028 killed and 3200 wounded. These figures are certainly gross underestimates for it has been officially stated that such firing took place on at least 538 occasions, and besides this people were frequently shot at by the police or the military from moving lorries. It is very difficult to arrive at even an approximately correct figure. Popular estimates place the number of deaths at 25,000, but perhaps this is an exaggeration. Perhaps 10,000 may be nearer the mark.[81]

Expressing his sympathies on the arrest of the entire Congress leadership, Savarkar released a press statement:

> The inevitable has happened. The foremost and patriotic leaders of the Congress Party including Mahatma Gandhi, Pandit Jawaharlal Nehru and hundreds of other leaders of the Congress Party are arrested and imprisoned. The personal sympathies of the Hindu Sangathanists go with them in their sufferings for a patriotic cause. I warn the Government once again that the only effective way to begin with, to appease the Indian discontent, can not but be an unequivocal declaration by the British Parliament to the effect that India is granted a political status of a completely free and equal partner in the Indo-British Commonwealth with rights and duties equal with those of Great Britain herself and that this should be immediately implemented by investing India with actual political powers as envisaged in the above declaration.[82]

But there was no clear policy formulated by Gandhi before he was arrested on 9 August. As Azad, supported by Nehru, said:

> Neither in public nor in private at the meetings of the Congress Working Committee did he [Gandhi] hint at the nature of action he had in mind, except in one particular. He had suggested privately that in the event of failure of all negotiations, he would appeal for some kind of non co-operation and a one-day protest hartal, or cessation of all work symbolic of a nation's protest. Even this was a vague suggestion which he did not particularize for he did not want to make any further plans till he had made his attempt at settlement. So neither he nor the Congress Working Committee issued any kind of directions, public or private, except that people should be prepared for all developments and should in any event adhere to the policy of peaceful and non-violent action.[83]

Provincial Congress Committees adopted varied stands depending on what they understood of 'Do or Die'. Going against the tenets of non-violence, many advocated violent rioting too. Andhra Congress, for example, outlined a detailed plan to cut telephone lines, telegraph wires, railway lines and demolition of bridges.[84] These measures impeded the government's war efforts when communication during times of emergency was crucial. How these acts were any less abominable or violent than the Chauri Chaura police station burning that had led Gandhi to call off the Non-cooperation movement in the 1920s, one might wonder. The instinctive revolutionary and violent tendencies of people that had been bottled up for long spilt over in every conceivable fashion, more so in the absence of a clear leadership or guidelines. Bombs and pistols were recovered from numerous places. The extreme government repression that followed had only the common masses bearing the brunt. Even Nehru regretted that 'the people forgot the lessons of non-violence, which had been dinned into their ears for more than twenty years'.[85]

The government hypothesized that the turn the movement had taken, had left most Congressmen in a quandary. 'They cannot,' they felt, 'openly claim as Congress-inspired an obviously violent movement; but they cannot very well oppose it since its success or failure will, in popular estimation, be a victory or a defeat for the Congress.'[86]

The movement was crushed by force by the government within two or three months and failed to achieve any solid or tangible results, not to speak of course of the immense sacrifices and sufferings that Indians endured in its wake. While the non-violent nature of the struggle that Gandhi had envisaged might not have made much impact on the government, the widespread people's agitation and upsurge, the violent outbreaks and the rumblings of rebellion in the Indian Army too that came to the fore during this period certainly made the government realize the extent and nature of popular discontent.

Gandhi possibly understood the miscalculation on his part and undertook a twenty-one-day fast for self-purification. Azad observed about this: 'He accepted the responsibility for what had happened and as was usual with him, he was planning to undergo the fast as an expiation for the situation. I could not see any sense in his fast or any other hypothesis.'[87]

The political reactions to the Quit India movement were varied. Jinnah and the Muslim League denounced it at the very outset. He said:

The latest decision of the Congress Working Committee on July 14, 1942, resolving to launch a mass movement if the British do not withdraw from India is the culminating point of the policy and programme of

Mr. Gandhi and his Hindu congress of blackmailing the British and coercing them to concede a system of government and transfer power to that government, which would establish a Hindu Raj immediately under the aegis of the British bayonet, thereby throwing the Muslims and other minorities and interests at the mercy of the Congress Raj.[88]

Less than a week before launching the Quit India movement, Gandhi had written to Jinnah and even declared on 2 August, much to the alarm of the country, that, 'he had no objection to Britain handing over power to the Muslim League or any other party, provided it was real independence'.[89] But he perhaps caught even Jinnah by surprise by launching the movement without even waiting to solicit a response from Jinnah to this generous offer. Most Muslim leaders of all political shades hence kept away or maintained a cautious distance from the movement. As Khaliquzzaman recounted about the dilemma that Jinnah and other leaders in the League faced:

> . . . if we allowed the campaign to succeed, so enabling Congress to coerce the British Government to yield to its demand to concede independence without any settlement of the Pakistan issue, the Muslim cause would go under forever; but on the other hand if we opposed the movement, there was a great risk of communal riots and widespread violence. After great cogitation, we came to the conclusion that complete neutrality in the fight should be observed by the Muslims and no attempt should be made from their side to disturb the peace of the country.[90]

They were bewildered by Gandhi's actions given his own earlier statements that any civil resistance launched at this point without a resolution of the communal issue would be tantamount to a civil resistance against the Muslims of India. Yet, despite no such resolution in sight and the Rajagopalachari resolutions that had raised the League's hopes being trashed by the AICC, the launch of the same movement that was described by its protagonist as being detrimental to Muslim interests made them extremely wary and suspicious.

Liberal Party leaders such as Sir Tej Bahadur Sapru and Srinivasa Sastri appealed to the Congress to abandon the Civil Disobedience movement at this juncture since it would be 'prejudicial to the best interests of the country in respect of defence and other matters'.[91] Ambedkar, who had been inducted as a member of the viceroy's council on 2 July 1942, was deeply critical of the Quit India movement. In a telegram to the Secretary of State dated 23 July 1942, the viceroy stated Ambedkar's position:

Ambedkar made a strong speech last night declaring civil disobedience at this time as 'treachery to India' and 'playing the enemy's game' and urging all Indians as a patriotic duty 'to resist with all the power and resources at their command any attempt on the part of Congress to launch civil disobedience.[92]

The case of the Communists of India was a curious one. The secret correspondences exchanged between P.C. Joshi, the general secretary of the Communist Party of India (CPI) and Sir Reginald Maxwell, the home member of the Government of India, make it clear that they 'acted as stooges and spies of the British Government, and helped them against their own countrymen fighting for freedom'.[93] S.S. Batlivala, a former member of the Central Committee of the CPI revealed in an interview on 22 February 1946 that, 'the various political drives undertaken by the Party in the name of anti-Fascist campaigns were a part of the arrangement, which helped the Government of India to tide over certain crises'. He also declared that P.C. Joshi and a few designated senior politburo members had been 'in touch with the Army Intelligence and supplied the C.I.D. chiefs with such information as they would require against nationalist workers who were connected with the 1942 struggle or against persons who had come to India on behalf of the Azad Hind Government of Netaji Subhas Chandra Bose'.[94] Joshi's letters revealed how 'unconditional help' was being offered to the government to fight the underground workers and Bose's Indian National Army soldiers, and how the CPI received financial aid from the government and had a secret pact with the League to undermine the Congress activity in several ways.[95]

Even while it officially disassociated itself from the Quit India movement, the Hindu Mahasabha in its Working Committee meeting from 29 to 31 August passed a resolution that declared:

If the British Government still persists in its policy of callous indifference to India's national aspirations and does not respond to this demand for the recognition of India's freedom and the formation of a National

Government, the Hindu Mahasabha will have no other alternative but
to revise its present programme and to devise ways and means whereby
Britain and her Allies will realize that India as a self-respecting nation
can no longer be suppressed.[96]

Savarkar maintained that while he agreed with the 'Quit India' slogan if it
implied independence in the truest sense, but he found its interpretation by
Gandhi as being 'wholly inadequate and unsatisfactory'.[97]

   While the Quit India movement might not have achieved any tangible
political goals, the upsurge of popular discontent that it brought to the fore
had become bipartisan, making it a people's mass movement. To oppose it
on the grounds of opposing Gandhi or the Congress at a time when it had
captured the imagination and emotions of the people at large was politically
imprudent. This move hence threw wide open the fledgling schisms within
the Hindu Mahasabha and brought to the fore the beginning of Savarkar's
dwindling hold over the organization after helming it for five years. Being a
bitter opponent of Gandhi and his ways, Savarkar dismissed the movement
as a ridiculous jail-seeking programme that was not about 'Quit India'
but 'Split India'.[98] Savarkar viewed the timing of the movement as being
extremely problematic as the Japanese had already bombed the Indian ports
of Visakhapatnam and Kakinada in Andhra on the eastern cost. Yet he
offered to support the Congress's movement provided Gandhi withdrew
his statement of unconditional support to Jinnah's secession claims and
also press for the British Army to stay on in India even after their political
leadership quit.

   But it perhaps shocked him too to see the anti-Congress edifice within
the Mahasabha crumbling after August 1942. The calls to boycott the
Congress programme were ignored and several provincial leaders as well
as activists of the Mahasabha participated eagerly in the upsurge following
the arrest of Gandhi and other leaders. Opposing Savarkar's views, a
political alliance of sorts was brewing between the Mahasabha members in
the Central Provinces and the local Congress. Local Hindu Sabha leaders
of the Central Provinces were getting restless too with the unending
negotiations between the viceroy and Savarkar and were demanding the
launch of a mass movement if the government did not accede to their
demands.[99]

   A prominent Mahasabha member and general secretary of the
Maharashtra unit, S.R. Date, said: 'At that time . . . I was supporting the

movement for Non-Cooperation and Quit India on one hand, we were supporting the recruitment on the other. That we were carrying on a dual role by supporting the freedom movement on one side and by supporting the [recruitment] movement.'[100] (Reference here is to the military recruitment drive that Savarkar had stressed on.)

Savarkar's trusted lieutenant Syama Prasad Mookerjee toured Punjab immediately after the Working Committee meeting in Delhi, and on 9 September 1942 announced that the Mahasabha might be forced to launch its own mass Civil Disobedience movement, not on the Congress lines but its own form of 'direct action' whose contours were undecided yet. Mookerjee had written a letter to the viceroy on 12 August, just three days after the Quit India movement was launched:

It is therefore essential that India's free status should be recognized immediately and the people of the country called upon to defend their own country in co-operation with the Allied Powers, and not merely look upon Britain to fight the impending aggression. The demand of the Congress, as embodied in its last resolution, virtually constitutes the national demand of India as a whole . . . you [have] a similar duty to ensure that there can be no just cause for discontent and disaffection resulting in chaos and disorder. Repression is not the remedy at this critical hour.[101]

The viceroy's blunt reply rebuffing him had in fact made his continuance in the Bengal government untenable and his resignation was just a matter of time. Mookerjee was soon to exit the Haq ministry in Bengal on 20 November 1942, less than a year since the grandly touted alliance between the Mahasabha and the Krishak Praja Party.

Bengal was sounding the discordant note. Heated arguments were witnessed at the Bengal Provincial Hindu Sabha meeting of 17 September. One of the leaders Narin Das favoured the Mahasabha launching a campaign independent of the Congress, but Ashutosh Lahiri and others felt that they could not make much headway unless they cooperated with the Congress.[102] Ratindra Nath Chakravarty, an important functionary in the Bengal Hindu Sabha, wrote to Mookerjee that their movement against the British in the event of non-consideration of demands must include economic measures such as 'withdrawal of money from government and European banks, refusal to accept paper currency, resistance to the imposition of collective fines even if such action involved clashes with the authorities' and so on.[103]

N.C. Chatterjee, one of Savarkar's close colleagues in the Mahasabha, vented his frustration in a letter to Moonje:

> The entire Hindu population is with Gandhiji and his movement and if anybody wants to oppose it, he will be absolutely finished and hounded out of public life. The unfortunate statement of Veer Savarkar [opposing Quit India] made our position rather difficult in Bengal. It is rather amusing to find that Mr. Jinnah wants the Mussalmans not to join the Congress movement and Mr. Savarkar wants the Hindus not to join the same. Even when the Congress movement has made a great stir and it shows that it has got thousands of adherents.[104]

Colonial authorities too noted with alarm the participation of some Mahasabhaites in the Quit India movement. They began to keep a closer watch on the party and its activities given such an ambivalent stand.

However, there was a strong pushback by the 'Savarkarite' faction within the Mahasabha. Back in Savarkar's home city of Bombay, members of the All-India Hindu Mahasabha Committee, M.B. Udgaonkar, D.G. Abhyankar and Nathuram Vinayak Godse, wrote a letter to Moonje stressing on the following points, which according to them was to save the Hindu Mahasabha from 'being engulfed in a bottomless pit', presumably an attack on all the proponents of mass movements and direct action within the party. These had the blessings of prominent Mahasabha leaders such as L.B. Bhopatkar, G.V. Ketkar, Captain Keshav Chandra, Varadarajulu Naidu, B.G. Khaparde and others:

a) No resolution passed by the Mahasabha should in any way compel Hindus to start civil disobedience or 'direct action' involving an endless strife at this most inopportune time and on such a fundamentally radical issue as 'independence'.

b) The policy of Hindu 'militarization' and 'industrialization' must be continued. All positions of importance in municipalities, local boards, Councils and services must be captured and everything should be done to strengthen the Hindu position in relation to Muslims. No resolution against this policy should be passed.[105]

Towards end-September, the Savarkar faction managed to have its way. The Bombay Provincial Hindu Mahasabha put forth the following view for the consideration of the All-India Working Committee:

This meeting of the Working Committee of the Bombay Provincial Hindu Mahasabha lends its full support to the demands made in the resolution passed by the Working Committee of the All India Hindu Mahasabha at Delhi on August 31 and is of the opinion that direct action at this juncture would be harmful to Hindu interests and expresses its full confidence in the leadership of Veer Savarkar, the President of the Hindu Mahasabha.[106]

The need for the explicit expression of confidence in the president was in itself an indication of the vast differences of opinion that had come to plague the organization, ever since the call to Direct Action was postponed by Savarkar.

The repeated equivalence that was being drawn between him and his bitter opponent Jinnah, even from within his own party, must have been deeply disconcerting for Savarkar. He constantly attempted to fight off this equivalence that he was not comfortable with. A newspaper quoted him on 15 August 1943 as having said: 'I have no quarrel with Mr. Jinnah's two-nation theory. We, Hindus, are a nation by ourselves and it is a historical fact that Hindus and Muslims are two nations.' Within four days, on 19 August 1943, Savarkar issued a clarification saying his views had been distorted and presented. Further in an interview with the daily *Kaal* dated 19 August 1943, Savarkar clarified that either deliberately or due to lack of space, the distorted and misleading idea that he supported the 'Two-Nation Theory' had been published. He clarified that in his view, Muslims all over the world had always considered themselves as a religious state under the rule of the Khalifa and it is in this sense that he believed that the Muslims consider themselves a separate nation. But in reality, from the point of view of political democracy, Hindus have always been the nation as they have lived here since time immemorial, while Muslims had been an aggressive minority, he surmised. The threat of Partition was created due to this approach of the Muslims, or a section of them at least, and he was opposed to this very idea. He had hence ordered the party workers of the Hindu Mahasabha to actively oppose Partition.[107]

Savarkar must have been doubly anguished when, on 31 August 1942, in a broadcast from Germany over the Azad Hind Radio, Subhas Bose issued a joint appeal to Savarkar and Jinnah, putting them again on the same pedestal. Bose said:

> The British Empire is in any case doomed; and the only question is as to what will happen to us when its final dissolution takes place. Shall we obtain our freedom as a right from other Powers or shall we win it by our own effort? I would request Mr. Jinnah, Mr. Savarkar and all those leaders who still think of a compromise with the British to realize once for all that in the world of tomorrow there will be no British Empire. All those individuals, groups or parties who now participate in the fight for freedom will have an honoured place in the India of tomorrow. The supporters of British imperialism will naturally become nonentities in a free India. In this connection, I will appeal earnestly to all parties and groups to consider this and to think in terms of nationalism and anti-imperialism, and to come forward and join the epic struggle that is going on now.[108]

Even Rash Behari Bose who continued to have unadulterated veneration for Savarkar had written to him from Tokyo in March 1942 itself, much before the launch of the Quit India movement and the Cripps Mission. This however seems to have been a premature reaction to Savarkar's militarization drive as being supportive of the British, as these views of the INA leaders were to change subsequently, as later documents show, once the benefits of the militarization to the swelling of their ranks became more evident. Rash Behari wrote:

> Please do not let your vision be blurred at this critical moment. That England is in extreme difficulties must be known to you. That England's difficulty also offers the golden chance for India's independence must also be known to you . . . I have, therefore, decided to mobilize all my Indian brothers in East Asia in a supreme effort to strike at the fetters that have hitherto reduced our Motherland to a state of national slavery. But, I know that I shall not succeed in my attempt unless yourself and other leaders at home support me at the right time . . . At this stage, Britain may offer all kinds of temptations to Indians—she might even offer independence. But please do not accept even independence if it

would involve India in a war with which she has got nothing to do. For, fighting on the side of England in a war in which Britain is sure to lose, would mean for India all that accrues from a military defeat . . . why not side with Japan and destroy the British power, which alone is responsible for the present miserable state of India?[109]

Despite the internal bickering within his party and remonstrance from those who hitherto supported his views, Savarkar stuck to his stand vis-à-vis the British on the future status of India. On 5 July 1942, he issued a statement to the press in India where he appreciated the expansion of the Viceroy's Executive Council to include members such as Sir C.P. Ramaswami, Sir Jwala Prasad Shrivastava (president of the Agra and Oudh Provincial Hindu Sabhas and a member of the Working Committee of the All-India Hindu Mahasabha), B.R. Ambedkar and others. He reiterated the demand that 'the British must offer voluntarily so complete a political freedom and power to India as to render it impossible for any enemy to offer anything more alluring to lead India astray'.[110]

Savarkar also sent out a statement to the British Press where he stressed that India's cooperation could only be secured if the British Parliament made an immediate declaration to the effect that—

1) India is raised to the position of a free nation in the Indo-British Commonwealth having equal status with that of Britain herself,
2) during the war period this declaration should be immediately implemented by Indianization of the Central Executive Council whose decisions would be binding on the Viceroy with the only exception of matters military and strategical [sic] in connection with suppression of any internal anarchy and defending India against external invasion, 3) military forces should be fully Indianized as early as possible, 4) Provincial Governors should also have Executive Councils similar to the Central, and 5) after the end of the war, a conference should be immediately convened to frame a national constitution for India, so as to give full effect to the declaration referred to above.[111]

Referring to this statement, the London correspondent of the *Bombay Chronicle* mentioned in his dispatch of 26 August 1942 that it was 'prominently featured by the leading newspapers like *The Times, Manchester*

Guardian, Daily Herald, News Chronicle and *Yorkshire Post*.[112] The correspondent further added:

> The appeal has been the topic of discussion among a section of the political leaders here and it is felt that an early initiative on the part of the British Government on the lines suggested by Mr. Savarkar is well worth making and with goodwill and cooperation on both sides, a satisfactory way out of the present Indian deadlock may yet be evolved . . . Mr. Savarkar's statement also came up for informal discussion among the Indian residents in London who gathered last night in a public meeting of the Indian League in the Central Hall.[113]

The All-India Working Committee of the Hindu Mahasabha met and further pressed these demands for an immediate grant of independence to India by the British. It urged the government to initiate negotiations with all the principal political players in India to resolve the deadlock, which is impeding war efforts also widening the cleavage between India and Britain. It called for the formation of a national government of composite character and with representatives of all parties, to whom all power must be transferred by the British. Similar governments were to be formed in the provinces too. Coming hard on the murmurs about the Muslim League being the sole invitee to a proposed national government given the ban on the Congress and the imprisonment of its entire top leadership, the Working Committee squarely rejected any such moves and condemned 'the anti-national attitude adopted by the Muslim League' and profoundly regretted 'that it is still pursuing a policy which will intensify the strife and bitterness between the communities, calculated to help the continuance of foreign domination in India'.[114] In a firm message to the British, the resolution said:

> The time has come when the Hindu Mahasabha must warn the British Government that although bayonets may suppress the violent outburst of popular discontent for the time being, they can never appease or remove the fundamental cause of India's discontent. The only way to secure the willing co-operation of India in the titanic struggle against the present menace is to recognize India as a free country and to respond to India's demand for a National Government . . . If the British Government still persists in its policy of callous indifference to India's national aspirations

and does not respond to this demand for the recognition of India's freedom and for the formation of a National Government, the Hindu Mahasabha will have no other alternative but to revise its present programme and to devise ways and means whereby Britain and her Allies will realize that India, as a self-respecting nation, can no longer be suppressed.[115]

Despite the proactive overtures of the Mahasabha, the British and the viceroy did not seem to give its views and vetoes much importance. This was evident in the attitude of Cripps, as is in a lengthy thesis on the political situation in India by Viceroy Linlithgow to his predecessor, Viscount Halifax, who was serving as the Secretary of State for Foreign Affairs. Even as he chided all the Indian political parties for not coming up with any concrete alternatives to Cripps's proposals that they had summarily rejected in a grandiose manner, Linlithgow claimed that 'Hindu opinion is substantially behind Congress, and Muslim opinion behind Jinnah'. He held that 'the claims of the communities are irreconcilable and a solution can be imposed on either only if we are prepared to back one or the other in a subsequent civil war'. He was not too keen on forming a national government with just the Mahasabha and the League given the shaky nature of such a coalition with all the inherent antipathy and mutual suspicions that would be likely to 'weaken rather than strengthen war effort'. 'The trouble,' he said, 'is not our reluctance to transfer power, but the difficulty of finding people ready to accept the transfer, and capable of discharging the obligations power involves.' Making clear the limited role he saw of the Mahasabha itself, he said, 'I am the last to underestimate the political importance of the principal Indian parties: Congress, Muslim and *to some extent* [emphasis added] the Mahasabha.'[116] Even as Savarkar seemed to be hopeful about the ongoing correspondence and negotiations with the British over the last two years, many times at the cost of his own goodwill amongst his supporters and party members, the British did not seem to give his party much credence beyond what they thought it deserved.

In the midst of the political ferment in India, Churchill gave a pompous speech at the House of Commons on 10 September that seemed to assure the members of Parliament that there was nothing serious about the Indian situation. His speech was unilaterally condemned by all Indian politicians as being provocative, insensitive and extremely reactionary. London newspapers carried Savarkar's brief quote about the speech: 'Thrice blessed be they if they retired pleased with a sense of self-complacency and security.'[117] He reminded Churchill that just a week before the fall of Singapore, the British were similarly assured and complacent of it being an impregnable fortress that guarded the Far East of the Empire and would withstand all storms that blew. 'The future of India does not lie in the lap of Mr. Churchill but it lies in the lap of War Gods!' he declared.[118]

Efforts were meanwhile on to coalesce non-League Muslim parties that were more nationalist and favouring a united India in their approach. Parties such as Krishak Praja Party, Unionist Party, Sind Ittehad Party, All-India Momin Conference, Jamiat Ulema-e-Hind and others formed a larger banner known as the Azad Muslim Conference or Board with Sir Allah Bux Muhammad Umar Soomroo, the former premier of Sind as the president. Allah Bux was a strong votary of a united India and he termed the Partition plan as being un-Islamic. The League and the Congress had joined hands to defeat his government in Sind in a no-confidence motion in 1940, following which he was co-opted into the National Defence Council of the viceroy. Parties such as Krishak Praja Party and Unionist Party were already in positions of power in provinces like Bengal and NWFP, with the Mahasabha. Curiously, this 'coalition' had several pro-Congress groups and socialist leaders such as K.M. Ashraf. In fact, on 19 April 1940, the Azad Muslim Conference celebrated 'Hindustan Day' to counter the League's separatist 'Pakistan Day' call.

With the entire Congress leadership behind bars after the Quit India suppression, the political field was left open to the Mahasabha and the League. The Mahasabha tried to stitch together a pan-India alliance of all votaries of united India, including the parties of the Azad Muslim Conference. Informal talks were held in early October 1942 between Mahasabha leaders and the conference stalwarts such as Allah Bux, Fazl-ul-Haq, Zahiruddin Ahmed, Shaukatullah Shah Ansari, Prof. Humayun Kabir, K.M. Ashraf and others to find a solution to the domestic communal problem.

The Working Committee of the Mahasabha met again in Delhi from 3 to 5 October and expressed satisfaction about the negotiations that were on with different political parties by the special committee that was constituted under Mookerjee. In view of these, the Committee resolved that these negotiations be continued 'in the larger interests of the nation' and called upon 'Hindu Sangathanists throughout India to keep themselves in readiness to respond to any call that may be given by the Hindu Mahasabha in accordance with the aforesaid resolution'.[119]

Savarkar even cabled Churchill on 9 October about the outcome of these confabulations with other political entities in India:

Hindu Mahasabha succeeded in producing national demand on fundamental points, namely, immediate recognition by the British Parliament of India as an independent nation; national coalition government during wartime, leaving Commander-in-Chief free in military operational matters as Allied War Council dictates; and all Constitutional and controversial details to be decided by a post-war All-Party Conference. The Sikh leaders, Presidents of Christian Federation, Momin and Azad Moslem Conferences, three Premiers of Provincial Governments of Sind, Bengal and Orissa, of whom two Moslems, one Hindu, and prominent Liberal leaders, several other bodies and personalities signed and supported it. Congress Resolution too being more or less on same lines, this demand is as representative of Hindus, Moslems, Christians and others, as any demand could be and consequently entitled to be recognized as all-India national demand. In view of repeated assurances, the British Government should transfer power, now that a joint national demand is framed by Indians, and enable India to put forward whole-hearted and unstinted war effort in defending herself against invasion.[120]

On the basis of the Working Committee resolution of the Hindu Mahasabha, Syama Prasad Mookerjee was assigned the task of trying to iron out differences with all political parties. Moonje, N.C. Chatterjee, Raja Maheshwar Dayal Seth, Rai Bahadur Meher Chand Khanna and Prof. V.G. Deshpande of the Mahasabha were part of the negotiations committee. Savarkar appealed to 'all patriotic parties and all prominent leaders in India to join hands with Dr. Shyama [sic] Prasad Mookerji, the Working President of the All-India Hindu Mahasabha and members of the sub-committee who are exerting themselves to bring about an agreement as regards the demand we should place before the Government, on behalf of India'.[121]

However, strangely he asserted his position by specifically sending Mookerjee and Moonje a telegram on 3 September 1942: 'I, as President issue this instruction that President Moslem League must not be interviewed or negotiated with on behalf of the Hindu Mahasabha unless he invites STOP Letter follows.'[122]

But Mookerjee disregarded this diktat and decided to meet Jinnah in Delhi in his personal capacity. The meeting was supposedly facilitated through the intervention of Mahasabha general secretary, Raja Maheshwar Dayal Seth of Kotra, who was an ardent supporter of Mookerjee. Seth had been having secret discussions with Jinnah on resolving the deadlock. This act by Mookerjee was another breach in the already tenuous relationship that existed between him and his party president. In his dairy Mookerjee records that Jinnah and he spoke their minds out very frankly to each other. The Mahasabha pledged to concede the fullest measure of autonomy to provinces and the maximum protection to minorities for the pursuit of their religion, language and customs. But Jinnah was adamant on his demand for Pakistan and there seemed little meeting ground. The meetings turned out to be quite fruitless as the ideological differences were too wide to be bridged. Mookerjee's confabulations with Sir Sikandar Hayat Khan too were not very fruitful as the latter expressed serious misgivings about the fate of an independent India unsecured against Axis oppression by the essential prerequisite of internal unity.[123]

Jinnah effectively sealed an epitaph on the efforts of the Azad Muslim Conference as also of the Mahasabha to negotiate with him through his unequivocal message on the occasion of Eid.

> We, the Muslims of India, are determined to attain our national freedom and independence by establishing our own independent and sovereign states in the North Western and Eastern parts of this sub-continent where we are no less than 70 millions of souls and which are our homelands where we are in a majority. I appeal therefore to every Muslim to stand solidly by our goal of Pakistan for it is a matter of life and death to us and the future destiny of Muslim India. Either we achieve Pakistan or we perish.[124]

The death of Sir Sikandar Hayat Khan by the end of the year and the untenable position of Fazl-ul-Haq in Bengal (which was caused by the differences leading to the eventual resignation of Syama Prasad Mookerjee from the coalition) helped consolidate and cement Jinnah and the League's role as the sole credible voice of the Muslims of India.

~

Interestingly, a meeting between Savarkar and Jinnah never materialized. An attempt was made first in 1940 when Jinnah was to meet Ambedkar, and it was decided that Savarkar too would be invited to the meet. But that did not fructify. In 1943, however, another opportunity arose for these staunch opponents to meet. This time it was Jinnah making the overtures. Journalist M.S. Mantreshwar Sharma notes in his memoirs that even the steely man of iron, Jinnah, once lost his nerve.[125] He contemplated meeting Savarkar to figure out a League–Mahasabha pact, given that his meets with Gandhi had led him nowhere. He quietly broached the topic with Hemandas Wadhwani, minister for public health in the Sind government and a Mahasabha member. Wadhwani dashed to Bombay and returned with a favourable response from his party president. Jinnah was at that time in Karachi and at a tea party. Sharma accosted him and nonchalantly asked him if he had plans of meeting Savarkar in Bombay. Sharma recounts that Jinnah was shocked and blurted out: 'What is this nonsense you are speaking about?'[126] Jinnah was worried that Wadhwani would leak information of their conversations to the press. Sharma calmed him down and told him that this information came to him through his sources in Bombay and not through Wadhwani and that he intended to carry it in the next day's newspaper. Jinnah supposedly requested Sharma: 'Please do not publish the news. But you are at liberty to suggest that it would be good for the country if "I and Savarkar" [not 'Savarkar and I'] could meet and review the situation in the interests of the country's peace.'[127] Sharma kept a lookout at the news to see if the meeting had indeed taken place, but there were no updates.

Sharma was given to understand that a lot of back and forth had happened on who was to call on whom. Jinnah had proposed that being the senior among the two, it should be Savarkar who should be calling on him at his Malabar Hill bungalow in Bombay. Savarkar had been insisting that Jinnah rather called on him at his Shivaji Park residence in Dadar. Savarkar was finally convinced to give up his insistence and call on Jinnah—sometime after dusk. But as luck could have it, even as Jinnah was readying to receive Savarkar, a ruffian turned up at his house the same morning with the intent of killing him with a big knife. Jinnah parried the attack and the murder was averted. But this incident demoralized both leaders and no more attempts seem to have been made to meet. Both instead turned their residences into veritable fortresses to prevent similar attacks. As Sharma notes: 'After that incident, it was far easier to gain access to the Viceroy's House in Delhi than get anywhere near Jinnah or Savarkar. A visitor was invariably subjected to all kinds of harassments and scrutiny before he was admitted to the presence of either of the two slaves of the devil of communalism.'[128]

On his part, Savarkar sent Jinnah his enquiries on 27 July 1943 where he wrote:

> I am extremely pained to learn of the murderous attempt made on the life of Mr. Jinnah and felicitate him on his narrow escape. It is very natural that he should have been touched by the quick, by the fact that a Moslem should have tried to take the life of one who has been the foremost advocate of the Moslem cause. Such internecine, unprovoked and murderous assaults, even if their motive be political or fanatical, constitute a stain on the public and civic life and must be strongly condemned.[129]

Jinnah acknowledged and thanked Savarkar for his sympathetic statement in his letter dated 1 August 1943. That is where the interaction between the two leaders began and ended.

~

Meanwhile, Savarkar was keen on sending Hindu Mahasabha deputations to foreign countries such as America, England, Russia and China to put forth its views to the leadership and the people there. He constituted a delegation of Mahasabha leaders under Moonje, S. R. (Mamarao) Date, M.N. Ghatate and Babarao Khaparde who represented Maharashtra, Bombay, Central Provinces and Berar Hindu Sabhas, to travel to the USA to acquaint the leaders there with the Mahasabha's views and ideology. He was trying to convince reluctant Mahasabha leaders such as Gokul Chand Narang and Syama Prasad Mookerjee to undertake similar deputations to England or China.[130] In his individual letters to these leaders he urged them to undertake these deputations to convince those countries that 'the Hindus need to extend actual military cooperation in a responsive spirit by joining Army, Navy, Air Forces etc. in our own interest for the defence of India herself and that the policy of militarization will continue [despite] whatever constitutional complications [may] arise'.[131] While he was quite sure that the government might not approve the issuance of the passports, he saw such a refusal by the government too as serving the cause of 'attracting American attention to the Hindu Mahasabha, its demand and its status as the foremost representative body of the Hindus'.[132]

In the official request to the viceroy on the issuance of passports for the delegation, he stated that the general feeling in America was that the Congress represented the interests of the Hindus, but since the Congress itself repudiated any such 'charge' brought against it, it was necessary for the Mahasabha as the sole representative of legitimate Hindu interests to put forth its viewpoints. 'Any constitutional change, which is ratified by the Congress and the League alone cannot be looked upon as a compromise and agreement between the Hindus and the Muslims without the sanction or ratification by the Hindu Mahasabha,'[133] he said. He wanted this delegation to also explain to the American public that quite in the same way as they would not approve of the Negro minority of the country demanding the secession or creation of a 'Negrosthan', the demand to vivisect India and create Pakistan was also illegitimate. The Mahasabha had been following a policy of responsive cooperation and of supporting the war efforts through its calls for militarization and this policy was in consonance with Cripps's proposals, barring the secession clause for provinces.

The government was however wary of such a move. It informed Moonje that since the general objective of the delegation seemed to be the solicitation of the American public support to the views of the Mahasabha on controversial Indian questions on which the American government had neither any solution nor locus standi, they found it unnecessary to grant such a permission.[134] A move by the Azad Muslim Conference to send such a delegation abroad too was rejected by the government.

~

On his part, towards end-October 1942, Rajagopalachari came up with a preposterous solution to the political deadlock. He suggested to the viceroy that the latter form a provisional government and nominate five Congress leaders to it. Jinnah could be asked to choose 'as many League Ministers as he wishes to make sure that the Pakistan issue is not prejudiced'. The Congress and League ministers would then choose three other ministers from the remaining major political elements. He also recommended setting up a United Nations Mission in London 'to consider what would be the best thing to do with the present Indian Government for the war period'.[135]

He volunteered to go to England and explain these proposals in details, if need be. These were met with unanimous condemnation and rejection by all parties. Jinnah called them 'pretty pretty' proposals that were akin to 'kite-flying', while Savarkar and the Mahasabha rejected them wholly. Bhai Parmanand, vice-president of the Mahasabha, was caustic in his criticism and told Rajagopalachari that if he was indeed planning to go to England 'to secure the transfer of power to the League, he should abandon the idea at once and save himself from the sin of proving a traitor to his country as well as to his community'.[136] Ambedkar felt sorry for Rajagopalachari whom he likened to an 'orphan in the storm keenly fighting for the kith and kin whom he deserted in search of greener pastures' and felt that 'nobody can accept his proposals'.[137] The British too saw through the game in Rajagopalachari's proposal that seemed to be directed wholly at Jinnah and not at any other players such as the Mahasabha, the princes or the other minority and special interest groups'

> If Mr. Jinnah refuses he is proclaimed to the world as the wrecker, the man who will not compromise; if he accepts, he comes into a game in which the trumps are in the hands of the Congress; for by virtue of its strength in the Legislature, Congress can either get its own way or force a fresh constitutional crisis for which the responsibility can be placed on the Viceroy or the Muslims or both. Nor for nothing has Mr. Rajagopalachari the reputation of being the most astute politician in India.[138]

It was to counter Rajagopalachari's moves in England that Savarkar was keen that Gokul Chand Narang too led a Mahasabha delegation to that country. In his letter to him dated 7 November 1942, Savarkar wrote: 'You will realize that in case Rajaji is allowed to proceed with his absurd, but nevertheless most harmful proposals, we cannot afford to leave him to roam in political circles in England unchallenged on the spot there, especially on the question of Pakistan.'[139]

~

Towards end-November, Syama Prasad Mookerjee's position in the Bengal government became highly untenable given the increased interference of the governor in the working of the ministry. He finally resigned in a huff. In a strongly worded letter, Mookerjee said:

The British Prime Minister and the Secretary of State have from time
to time taken pride in declaring that even today, millions of Indians
are living under a system of administration where the functions of the
Government are in the hands of Ministries responsible to the Legislature.
Let me tell him without any exception whatsoever that the Constitution
that functions under the so-called system of Provincial Autonomy is a
colossal mockery.[140]

~

Amidst the colossal political turmoil, the stormy year ended with the
twenty-fourth Annual Session of the Mahasabha in Kanpur. Delivering
his sixth consecutive presidential address, Savarkar stressed on his reasons
for opposing the Quit India movement whose timing, goals and the means
to achieve them were all suspect or non-existent. He found the Congress
strategy of asking the British to quit, but leave their army back in India,
along with the Americans too making the country their base, all of this
coming at a cost of vivisection of the country too, as being a total loss game.
He said he would have willingly supported the Congress movement if it
had been aimed at genuine independence and also not fanned secession and
a breakup of the country. He quoted Gandhi's letter to Jinnah around the
same time that he was launching the Quit India movement and wondered
how any sane nationalistic Hindu could approve of this:

In all sincerity, let me explain it again that if the Moslem League cooperated with the Congress for immediate independence, subject of
course to the provision that Independent India will permit the operations
of the allied armies in order to check Axis aggression and thus to help
China and Russia, the Congress will have no objection to the British
Government transferring all the powers today . . . to the Moslem League
on behalf of the whole of India . . . The Congress will not only not
obstruct any Government which the Moslem League may form on behalf
of the people, but will even join the Government. This is meant in all
seriousness and sincerity.[141]

He expressed his deepest sympathies for all the sufferings that the movement
had brought about on the masses, and also the jail terms that Congressmen
were undergoing. 'But patriotism itself demands,' he cautioned,

. . . that it is a national duty of all of us Hindus to see to it that sympathy with patriotic sufferings must not be allowed to get the better of our judgment and drive us headlong and blindfolded on a path, which we conscientiously believe to be detrimental to the best interest of our Hindu Nation. To make a common cause on a wrong issue or a line of action, which is bound to lead to national disaster, simply to present a 'United Front' is not the essence of patriotism, but amounts to a betrayal of national duty. It will be well of those who criticize the Hindu Mahasabha either through indiscretion or impudence for not following the Congress rightly or wrongly for the sake of Unity and because the Congress was actuated by patriotic motives, would do well to remember that patriots also are no exception to the general rule that it is human to err.[142]

With a clear target on his detractors within the party, Savarkar asserted:

Some of these critics seem to be irritated at the thought that the leaders of the Hindu Mahasabha did not jump over the walls of the jail the very day Gandhiji and others were arrested for raising such a momentous cry as 'Quit India but keep your army here.' So far as the 'Quit India' is concerned, it is enough to point out that some of the outstanding Mahasabha leaders and followers today had been amongst those handful of revolutionists, who publicly raised the standard of Indian Independence for the first time in current history and rose in an armed revolt when Gandhiji and some of the present leaders of the Congress were singing Hallelujahs to the British Empire, extolling its blessings and thinking it their duty as loyal citizens and subjects of that Empire to take its side against Zulus and the Boer who were fighting for their freedom. When further on as a consequence of their revolutionary activities, these Hindusabhaites of today had some of them to stand under the shadow of the gallows and others were undergoing the sentences of transportation for life, rotting in Andamanese dungeons for decades on decades if we reason as you do now, were not the present outstanding Congress leaders including Gandhiji 'guilty' for not making a common cause with the revolutionists merely for the sake of 'United front' and for not seeking the gallows or getting themselves locked in the cellular jails in the Andamans? Coming nearer, what have you to say regarding the Congress when it not only kept itself at a respectable distance from imprisonment but actually joined hands with the Nizam and took up a pledge 'not to embarrass His Exalted Highness' while thousands of Hindu Sangathanists were carrying on a deadly struggle with the Nizam for the most legitimate rights of the Hindus and were facing lathi charges, imprisonment and tortures at the hands of the Nizam's Government? Far from sharing these sufferings with the Hindu Sangathanists, were not the leaders and followers of the Congress strutting about as Ministers of provinces under the British Crown, some drawing fat pays, others rolling in the lap of luxury? And what about Bhagalpur? When for the defence of fundamental civil liberties of freedom of speech and freedom of association not less than one hundred thousand Hindu Sangathanists carried on an active struggle with the Government of Bihar throughout the six districts which came under the ban, against all the forces which the Bihar Government could draw upon, firings, bayonetting, cavalry charges, not to speak of whippings, imprisonments, etc., did not the Congressites stand totally unconcerned and aloof without uttering a word of sympathy with the struggle for civic liberty which the Hindu Sanghatanists were carrying on against the foreign Government or of condemnation of that Government?[143]

He emphasized that it was only the Mahasabha that had taken on the mantle of conducting genuine and open negotiations with all shades of Indian political opinion in a genuine attempt to maintain the unity of the country and also resolve the deadlock. Hence the oft-repeated charge against the party of being driven by narrow communal agendas that did not feature the larger national picture no longer held true. He strongly defended the idea of sending delegations abroad and pooh-poohed those who condemned the move as being akin to washing India's dirty linen of communal tangle in open public. The coverage that the Cripps Mission and its failure on account of the communal problem and the fact that so many American and Chinese army officials were in India and had their eyes and ears open to the ground situation had already made this problem known internationally.

The provincial redistribution within the Indian Federation that the Mahasabha was negotiating was markedly different from the provincial self-determination translating to seceding from India entailed. It was the latter that the Congress and some of its leaders like Rajagopalachari, whom Savarkar dismissed as 'exerting himself (for the cause of Pakistan) with more sincerity and perverse fanaticism than any mad-Mullah known to history' were doing.[144] Giving provinces the free will to secede or stay on was hugely dangerous for the future of the Indian Union, he averred. At a later date, a province that had merged with the Union could easily be swayed by forces of disintegration or by Pakistan to demand secession and break away. He warned about the perils of handing over the frontier states to the Muslims, who after getting free from the control of the Central government, could 'within measurable time join hands with the tribals and form a contiguous Pathani State from Hindukush to the very banks of Zelum'.[145]

Rejecting the very need to concede to Muslim demands for Pakistan, Savarkar wondered whether this should be done at all, especially with the hallowed view of gaining their goodwill. And if creating this amity was indeed the motivation, what guarantee was there that after getting their pound of flesh, the new state of Pakistan would maintain friendship and peace with its parent country and not covet more and more territory from it? Today, being weak, they were threatening a civil war to get their demands through. But, he warned,

> . . . once they get an independent footing as a State, sufficient time and liberty to organize themselves and entrenched on the powerful frontier-ranges, grown stronger precisely in the proportion your position grows weaker by the withdrawal of your frontier. Unity, when it lays our nation exposed to more dangerous position is worse than open hostility.[146]

He also dismissed the economic mandarins who predicted doom and gloom on the proposed Pakistan on the basis of the laws of economics that poverty and unsustainability would eventually make them repent their secession demand and come back to the table begging for a merger.

> So long as we continue to be so cowardly as to yield to any preposterous demand on the part of the Moslems to keep up the show of unity and so terribly afraid of Moslems' discontent as to allow even the integrity of our Motherland to get broken up into pieces, is it not more likely that this very financial and economical starvation of these would-be Moslem states may goad them on to encroach once more on our Hindu provinces and instigated by the religious fanaticism, which is so inflammable in the frontier tribes even now and urged on by the ideal of a Pathanistan under the lead of the organized forces of the Ameer, may threaten to

invade you if you do not handover to them the remaining parts of the Punjab right up to Delhi to make them financially and economically self-supporting?[147]

Poverty and bankruptcy could well heighten the fanaticism further and lead to systematic attacks on India's national security and sovereignty, Savarkar theorized.

Summarizing the Indian political problem at the moment, Savarkar said the belief had been that England was not going to bestow us Swaraj or self-rule that we sought until and unless there was a united demand and univocal Constitution drafted by both Hindus and Muslims together. Since the Muslims had made it clear that they would not join hands with the Hindus in this effort until their demand to vivisect the nation was conceded, the popular Hindu sentiment had been to quietly agree to satisfy the Muslims and accede to those demands to obtain Swaraj. Terming this chain of logic as fallacious, Savarkar said the fundamental definition of that Swaraj needed to be one where not only all citizens were united and equal in the eyes of the law, but also one that did not allow any community or group to break up the integrity of the nation. He also dismissed the supposition that once such a united charter was presented to them Britain would fold up and leave, as long as India remained helpless, disarmed and unable to protect herself. Increasing one's bargaining power with the British by arming oneself had a much surer chance of success than abjectly surrendering to Muslim demands of vivisection only to secure the doubtful grant of freedom from British.

No minority in India shall be allowed to demand to break up the very integrity of Hindusthan from Indus to the Seas as a condition of their participation in the Central Government or Provincial ones. No province whatsoever, by the fact that it is a province shall be allowed to claim to secede from the Central State of Hindusthan at its own sweet will. Hindusthan as a nation can have a right of self-determination but a Province or a District or a Taluka can have no right to run counter by the strength of their own majority to the law and the will of the Central Government of Hindusthan.[148]

And the only political organization that could look the League in the eye and say thus-far-and-no-further was the Hindu Mahasabha, he concluded.

Savarkar noted with satisfaction that while at the start of the war
the percentage of Muslims in the armed forces was an alarmingly high
62 per cent, through the concerted efforts of militarization by the Hindu
Mahasabha, that number had come down to 32 per cent with more and
more Hindus joining the army. That drive must hence continue in the
Mahasabha initiatives without wavering, he opined. He also stressed on
his favourite issue of social reform and said even as freedom was seeming
at close sight now, the war against untouchability must be taken up with
more vigour and a pledge made to eradicate it completely from the country
in about five years thence. Given the unpredictability of the war and its
outcome all that India could do was to wait and watch as to which way
the dice of destiny would roll and how best a situation can be created that
serves India's and Hindu interests the most.

Savarkar's presidential address, however, disappointed many,
including the Hindu press that criticized his views. The *Hindustan
Standard* noted, 'Now that the Congress is compulsorily removed from
the political field, it was expected that Mr. Savarkar would voice the
Congress demand for independence from his own platform with all his
characteristic vigour. Unfortunately, this is where he has failed us.'[149] The
Ananda Bazar Patrika said:

> With much of what Mr. Savarkar said Indian nationalists are in entire
> agreement, but we are afraid he was not quite fair to the Congress leaders
> when he accused them of having indirectly accepted the Muslim League
> demand . . . Mr. Savarkar has not accepted the ideal of mixed nationalism,
> which has been adopted by the Congress. We do not think that people
> will see eye to eye with Mr. Savarkar in this view.[150]

The Muslim press was obviously antagonistic. 'No amount of fire spitting,'
said the *Star of India*, 'by Hindu communalists of the type of Mr. Savarkar
can relegate the one hundred million who constitute the great Muslim
nation of India to the category of a community.'[151] The *Azad* reported:

> By uttering empty shibboleths, Mr. Savarkar has, on the one hand
> made his claim to establish an undivided India ridiculous and, on the
> other, lowered his own prestige and that of his organization. The Indian
> problem will not be solved in this way—it will only complicate the already
> complicated situation.[152]

The *Morning News* held:

> To question self-determination whether on the basis of area or faith
> and to ask his hearers to accept Sovietization [sic] is, to say the least,
> ridiculous. The President had better look to Lenin's solution of the
> Muslim problem in Central Asia . . . if he feels that his Mahasabha will
> be the Presidium of the Comintern and the Indian world will bow to it,
> he is sadly mistaken.[153]

Commenting on the resolutions passed in the session, the *Statesman* was
slightly more generous:

> The Hindu Mahasabha has done one good thing at an otherwise rather
> unsatisfactory session. It has appointed a committee to draft a charter
> of rights and responsibilities of Indian citizens in general and of the
> minorities and such sections as the workers and peasants in particular.
> If the Muslim League did the same and the contents of the lists were
> found to coincide at any rate in their main items, further progress could
> be hoped for.[154]

The Kanpur session was held amidst troublesome developments of
Savarkar rendering his resignation from the post of the president of the
Mahasabha. This was actually the third time that he had offered to resign
citing his rapidly failing health. In August 1940 itself, months before the
Madurai session, he had decided to step down due to his ill health but was
convinced by all to continue. Even as he contemplated doing the same the
following year in 1941, the Bhagalpur episode ensured that there was no
change at the helm. Savarkar again offered to step down on 31 July 1942:

> The year is drawing to a close and the presidential election would be
> shortly held. I think that this is the most suitable time to tender my
> resignation of the Presidentship of the Hindu Mahasabha. Firstly,
> because the continuous strain for the last five years of the presidential
> duties have naturally told on my health and secondly, because I feel it a
> duty that I should myself come forward to help my colleagues in shifting
> the burden and responsibility of the presidential office to some stronger
> and broader shoulders and entrust the leadership of the Hindu Mahasabha
> to some worthier hands. I rejoice while tendering this resignation to see

that I have been able to do so while. I am in possession of the fullest confidence and affectionate regard of the Hindu Sangathanist public throughout India. I thank the Hindu Sangathanist public most cordially for their overwhelming kindness and the forbearance they showed for whatever shortcomings they might have noticed in me. It is also a matter of intense delight, pride and hope to find that during these five years of my presidential tenure the Hindu Mahasabha should have, through the combined efforts of one and all, continued its march onward with strides of a giant and should have been able to bring about a veritable mental revolution in the Hindu World. The Hindu has recovered once more his national soul and self-consciousness and has risen to assert it under the pan-Hindu colours. This has been noticed even by those who ever evinced but a scant sympathy for the Hindu cause. Witness for example, what Prof. Coupland, a member of the Cripps Commission, admits in his latest work 'The Cripps Mission' published by the Oxford University Press. The Hindu Mahasabha, says he, has come to be a militant organization of the Hindus and has been growing fast in membership and influence. Mr. Cripps himself has written that so influential an organization as the Hindu Mahasabba cannot be left out of account when constitutional questions arise. But the most eloquent compliment that could be desired was paid to the Hindu Mahasabha by Mr. Jinnah himself, when he said at Madras in his presidential speech, 'The Hindu Mahasabha is an absolutely incorrigible and hopeless body and I would have nothing to do with it.' I have no doubt whatsoever that if the Mahasabha persists in marching on keeping in full view the Hindu ideology it has adopted as its guiding star, it is bound to occupy the position of the most dominating and even the dictating factor in the Indian politics before long. The motto of this ideology as well as my parting message is no other than this.[155]

But the rank and file of the party, despite the internal bickering, prevailed upon him not to precipitate matters at a time as fluid as this. From Syama Prasad Mookerjee and Jwala Prasad Shrivastava to Meherchand Khanna, Raja Maheshwar Dayal Seth, Rai Bahadur Harishchandra of Delhi, stalwarts of the Mahasabha implored him not to relinquish the charge of the party at such a fluid and crucial situation of crisis. Savarkar was also aware of the possible machinations that the Congress was doing to capture the Mahasabha and make it comply with its idea of conceding the Pakistan demand.[156] After the meeting that Mookerjee had with Jinnah despite a clear directive from Savarkar not to engage with the League, there was a growing suspicion that the Congress, and in particular Rajagopalachari, was getting close to Mookerjee, were infiltrating the Mahasabha by propping him up against Savarkar and also wished to see him as the president. Gandhi had in fact told Mookerjee when he had met him on a visit to riot-hit Bengal in February 1940, 'Patel is a Congressman with a Hindu mind, you be a Hindu Sabhaite with a Congress mind.'[157] The Mookerjee faction in the Mahasabha had the backing of influential landed magnates like Meherchand Khanna of Punjab and Raja Maheshwar Dayal Seth of Kotra. Seth was seen as pro-Congress by many Mahasabha leaders. Mookerjee soon began to have the backing of most factions of the party, especially members from Punjab and the United Provinces who were not too happy with Savarkar's leadership. Raja Maheshwar Dayal and Mookerjee were in regular touch with each other after the latter resigned from the Bengal ministry. These correspondences also show that Mookerjee was to play an important role in the Standing Committee called by Sir Tej Bahadur Sapru in Allahabad to resolve the political stalemate.[158]

When Mookerjee held talks with Gandhi on 5 August 1942 at Sewagram, just before the launch of the Quit India movement to 'discuss the political situation',[159] Savarkar had made it clear that the involvement of any Mahasabha leader in mass agitations that were not ratified by the party's Working Committee was only in an 'individual capacity' and not as a representative of the organization.[160] Mookerjee and his supporters tried to toe a more balanced line rather than the outright denouncement of the Congress and Gandhi that Savarkar attempted. Both factions had a rationale for their belief. Given the overlap that the Mahasabha in its early history had with the Congress along with common membership too, Savarkar was keen to craft for the party an ideology and programme that was distinct from the Congress and not one similar to it. But given the mass base and popularity that the Congress drew, Mookerjee and his supporters were eager to not appear blatantly and viscerally opposed to the Congress, especially when the Quit India movement garnered huge public support. On some political spheres while this faction highlighted the differences with the Congress and its programmes, on several others they demonstrated their sympathies and concurrences.

Bowing to popular pressure within the party, Savarkar decided to stay on but offered to contest the election to the president's post before the

Kanpur session. He won the poll unopposed. It was his way of stamping his authority over all the factions that had mushroomed within the party. But he knew that it was just a matter of time before he departed from the position.

The Saffron Brotherhood

Another internal strife was brewing within the Hindu Sangathan world and this was between the Hindu Mahasabha and the RSS. As mentioned earlier, the Savarkar brothers, especially Babarao, had an important role to play in the formation of the RSS in 1925 with Dr Hedgewar as the head of the fledgling organization. British intelligence reports note that it was Dr B.S. Moonje of the Mahasabha who reorganized the RSS corps in 1927 in the four Marathi-speaking districts of the Central Provinces (CP) to 'defend Hindus during communal outbreaks'. It also mentioned that the RSS was 'accorded official recognition by the All-India Hindu Mahasabha' in 1932. In fact, by the end of that year, the CP government had debarred government servants from joining or taking part in the activities of the Sangh.[161]

It is said that it was Savarkar's influence on the nascent Sangh that festivals such as Hindu Samrajya Divas that commemorated the coronation of Chhatrapati Shivaji Maharaj were incorporated into the Sangh's annual calendar of celebrations.[162] On 13 November 1939, Narayanrao Savarkar addressed a gathering of 300 Sangh volunteers at Nagpur and told them that they were 'the allies of the Hindu Mahasabha and the Arya Samaj in the fight against the enemies of Hinduism, viz. the British Government, the Muslims and the Congress'.[163]

Right from its inception, the Sangh was clear in its view of steering away from active politics and did not want to become a mere arm or a youth brigade of the Mahasabha. Since Moonje was his mentor, Hedgewar and the Sangh volunteers actively assisted him when he contested elections to the Central Legislative Assembly in 1934. Moonje was an important guest of honour at the Sangh's tenth anniversary celebrations in 1935.[164] Hedgewar even officiated as the secretary of the Hindu Mahasabha from 1926 to 1931.

As one of the founding members of the RSS, Babarao was deeply venerated by the Sangh, especially Hedgewar. Babarao too donned the mantle of an elderly adviser for the Sangh. In his book

Hindu Rashtra Poorvi, Aata, Aani Pudhe (Hindu Nation Past, Present and Future), Babarao had both praise and some advice for the Sangh:

> The birth of the Sangh and the fact that it has taken upon itself the task of securing freedom for the country is an event that signifies the future glory of the Hindu Nation. The Sangh has brought many people together and has organized millions and millions of orderly swayamsevaks in military-like discipline. This contribution of the Sangh is truly remarkable. Future historians will have to record this contribution in letters of gold. The contribution of the Sangh in keeping Hindutva alive is likewise incomparable. It cannot be matched. But henceforth, an organization such as the Sangh cannot remain satisfied with mere numbers of disciplined individuals. The Sangh should gradually find occasions to test its strength. It should create experts in every aspect of the polity so that freedom may be won and maintained. The Sangh followers have taken a pledge to protect '*jati-dharma-samskriti*'. To make this pledge meaningful and to serve society and gain its support, the Sangh should protect people from riots and foreign aggression. Only if this happens will the Sangh progress and expand. Else, the Sangh will shrink and the hopes of the Hindu society will be dashed![165]

Savarkar and Hedgewar too were on cordial terms with the latter accompanying him on his Vidarbha tour in December 1937, following which Savarkar even addressed the Sangh members at Nagpur on 11 December 1937. Commending the work of the Sangh and Hedgewar, Savarkar is said to have suggested (as quoted in a British intelligence report) that the 'Hindus should keep guard over the "thief in their midst" i.e. the Muslims and then expel the "foreign dacoits"'.[166] Even when Hedgewar passed away on 21 June 1940, Savarkar had expressed his deepest anguish and condolences. He instructed Hindu Sabhas across the country to observe 30 June as a day of mourning.[167] Narayanrao Savarkar played a pivotal role in the expansion of the Sangh in Bombay city.

Differences between the two organizations crept in around 1938–39 when Moonje was told in no uncertain terms by Hedgewar and others in the RSS not to misuse the Sangh platform to deliver vitriolic anti-Congress speeches.[168] Moonje was incensed enough to vow to never speak at any RSS event and in due course even launched his own volunteer corps, the Ram Sena, in 1939. The attitude of Mahasabha veterans in treating the RSS as one of its affiliate appendages that could be taken for granted riled the latter. The Sangh volunteers were as it is going all out to help Mahasabha leaders in electoral politics, be it the case of Moonje mentioned earlier or during the 1936 general elections to provincial assemblies where it campaigned actively for the Mahasabha's L.V. Paranjape against the Congress's Khare.[169]

However, the Mahasabha considered this almost as a natural right since it believed that it was their efforts that helped the RSS expand from a tiny pocket of Maharashtra to other parts of the state and the country. Bhai Parmanand's invitation to Hedgewar to attend the Karachi session of the Hindu Yuvak Parishad in 1932 gave the latter an opportunity to establish contacts with Hindu leaders of Punjab and Sind, creating inroads for his organization there. Babarao acted as a bridge between the Mahasabha and Sangh activists in Delhi and Benares, helping the RSS expand in these areas. By the 1940s, it had branches across India—NWFP, Punjab, United Provinces, Madras, Bihar, Bombay, Sind, Bengal, CP and Berar, Gwalior, Indore, Hyderabad, Mysore, the Deccan States and elsewhere.[170] By 1941, there were 700 branches across the country and about 1,50,000 members, though the precise numbers were uncertain given the extreme secrecy that was maintained in matters of organization and membership.[171]

Given the symbiotic relationship between the Mahasabha and the Sangh, even the colonial government reports mention the close links and the assumption of the RSS being almost the youth wing of the Mahasabha. The fuzzy roles and associations between the Mahasabha, the RSS and the Democratic Swarajya Party, and the porous borders of membership between them, were known to all. The British feared that the 'Sangh might be drawn into pro-Japanese activity through its connections with the All India Hindu Mahasabha, if the latter itself initiates or develops such activities'.[172] It termed it as an anti-British body that was also the 'Hindu answer to the Khaksars'—the violent Muslim tribes of the NWFP and Punjab.

During 30 April–1 May 1938 over 3000 men and women attended the first session of the Maharashtra Hindu Youths' Conference in Poona that was presided over by Hedgewar and attended by Savarkar, Moonje, L.B. Bhopatkar and Senapati Bapat.[173] Speaking on the occasion, Savarkar had outlined the activities of the Mahasabha as the political arm of the Sangathan movement. The conference had concluded with resolutions that recognized the Mahasabha as the sole voice of the Hindu aspirations in the political arena, as also militarization, the favourite topic of Savarkar.

But Savarkar and the Mahasabha leadership were peeved when the RSS refused to associate in an official capacity in the Hyderabad agitation that had brought the Mahasabha and other Hindu organizations such as the Arya Samaj close to each other for a joint Hindu battle.[174] Hedgewar's permission to Sangh volunteers to take part in an individual capacity, under one Bhaiyyaji Dani who also got arrested in the Hyderabad agitation, was not sufficient enough.[175]

After Hedgewar's death, the leadership of the RSS came under the ascetic-minded Madhav Sadashiv Golwalkar, who was commonly known as Guruji. Trained as a biologist and a professor of zoology, he was Hedgewar's handpicked successor. The normal belief is that Golwalkar's ascent to the position of the supreme head or the Sarsanghchalak of the RSS cemented the final breach in the organization's relations with the Mahasabha.[176] As Walter Andersen notes, 'Savarkar, the blunt revolutionary-turned-politician, and the ascetic Golwalkar were not particularly close to one another. Very few letters either from or to Golwalkar are in the Savarkar Files, unlike the fairly large number between Hedgewar and various Mahasabha leaders.'[177] Golwalkar's insistence on an apolitical stance for the Sangh that focused more on the organization's social expansion possibly clashed with Savarkar's requirement for a strong Hindu cadre in the political and electoral arena in the troubled war years. Many staunch Savarkarites of the Hindu Mahasabha, including Nathuram Godse who had joined the RSS in 1930, deserted it in later years, being disillusioned with the body's apolitical nature.[178] In a private discussion in Sangli State on 14 July 1942, Golwalkar is said to have stressed to the local leaders of the Sangh that the 'Sangh was an independent organization, free from party politics and was not the creation of the Hindu Mahasabha'.[179]

Even during the Quit India movement, speakers at Sangh events would be urged, 'to keep aloof from the Congress movement'.[180] The British, who kept a close watch on the Sangh's activities, noted that 'these instructions were generally observed: a notable exception was the notorious Chimur case in which Sangh volunteers joined Congress volunteers in stirring up mobs which brutally murdered certain Magistrates and Police Officers'.[181]

Yet, it was not as if the two organizations and its top leadership were entirely divorced. It was under Guruji's leadership that Savarkar inspected about 500 members of the Sangh and the Rashtriya Sevika Samiti at Amravati on 1 August 1943 and urged them to strive for Hindu unity.[182] Savarkar was invited to preside over the Sangh's most important annual graduation ceremony of its cadets, the Officers' Training Camp (OTC) or the *Truteeya Varsh Sangh Shiksha Varg* in Poona on 26 and 27 April 1943. Over 2000 volunteers had gathered from all over Maharashtra and over 6000 spectators for the drill and lathi exercises that were held.[183] Savarkar was given a 'general salute of the volunteers and was entertained to a demonstration of *lathi* drill and physical exercises'.[184]

Despite its avowed apolitical stance, the British who had managed to gather intelligence on the activities of this curious organization and infiltrated some of its members, noted something interesting. Through the statements of one Ram Rakha Mal, an important member of the RSS in Punjab, it deduced the following policy of the Sangh vis-à-vis participation in politics and public life:

> No interest is to be taken in politics unless the All-India organization claims 3% strength of the entire population of India. Till then there should be no aspiration for office acceptance. In short, the Sangh should remain unassuming till the necessary strength is obtained. The Sangh should not come into conflict with the Government till their strength is not up to the mark. No part should be taken in communal riots.[185]

In 1940, it was revealed by the British intelligence through an insider's account that at the end of the annual forty days' training selected members of the Sangh were, as a rule, tried for a period of three years in different capacities. Only the most reliable of them were then 'unobtrusively introduced into various departments of Government, such as the army, navy, postal, telegraph, railway and administrative services in order that there may be no difficulty in capturing control over the administrative departments in India when the time comes'. Even as the British dismissed these as exaggerated claims that could not be accepted literally, it conceded that 'the Sangh has been for some years working out a long term policy of steady preparation for the attainment of its ultimate objective of Hindu supremacy'.[186]

The alarm on the Sangh infiltration into government and possibly the army too started getting accentuated with time. A secret report of the government dated 30 November 1943 detailed these concerns:

> Members of the Sangh are believed to exist in Government services and (according to an unconfirmed report, intentionally omitted for the

survey pending verification) in the armed forces as well. In the Central Provinces, the Sangh claims among its members, a number of employees serving in certain security installations. Such information as we have been able to collect of its secret activities suggests that this organization is both intensely communal and anti-British in outlook and that its tone is becoming increasingly militant.[187]

The government had noted with some degree of confusion the relationship between the Mahasabha and the Sangh. On the one hand, the Sangh's collections in Badaun for the Bengal famine relief were sent to the Provincial Hindu Mahasabha and members of the Bihar Hindu Sabha were particularly interested in furthering the Sangh's growth in their province. However, during this time, clashes too were reported between the Sangh and Mahasabha volunteers since August 1942.[188] The Mahasabha depended heavily on the contributions of a few wealthy businessmen and landlords. Over the issue of Bhai Parmanand using the Mahasabha head office, The Mahasabha Bhawan in Delhi, for one of his service ventures, the Mahasabha's chief patron, Jugal Kishore Birla, had threatened to stop all funding. The controversy dragged on for a few years even as the Mahasabha tried its best to placate its financier. The bad blood that ensued even pushed Parmanand to resign in a disgusted huff. The RSS bore the brunt of the collateral damage of these developments as it was prevented from using the parade grounds of the Mahasabha office. However, in due course, in the elections held after the war, a majority of the RSS members campaigned or even voted for the Mahasabha candidates. But Golwalkar denied permission to the Sangh volunteers from attending guerilla warfare classes in Moonje's Bhonsala Military School at Nasik.[189] These clashes and differences of opinion amazed even the colonial government that exclaimed about the RSS that its 'relations with the Hindu Sabha are somewhat puzzling; one would have expected more or less open co-operation between the two, unless there was some underlying cleavage in aims'.[190]

The Mahasabha 'had no viable youth, labour, or farm organizations and was poorly financed'. Barring J.K. Birla or Raja Maheshwar Dayal Seth and Meherchand Khanna, who in turn was fanning the Mahasabha's factional feuds, the financial crunch that the organization was facing was real. These shortcomings of the Mahasabha were also well-known to the government that however ascribed curious reasons for the organization's weakness and the strains in the relationship with the RSS. 'I have no doubts,' says an official noting on one of the British intelligence reports of 1943, 'about the objectives of the Sangh . . .'

> . . . The Shivaji tradition is the key to the problem. That is also the explanation of why the Sangh is strongest in Maharashtra and of why there is no closer bond between it and the Mahasabha. The latter has no real roots. It is the offspring of the desire for supremacy of persons who are not willing to fight for such supremacy. J.K. Birla and Maheshwar Dayal Seth wd. [sic] be the shining lights of the Sabha; the Sangh wd. [sic] be led by a different type.[191]

In such a scenario, it was but natural for Savarkar and his faction to expect the wholehearted support of the RSS and its cadre, given the shared ideological moorings. As Savarkar himself admitted in 1943: 'We have a programme, but we want more men and means.'[192] These were real, ground-level problems that the Mahasabha was facing in the wake of its transition from an amorphous appendage of the Congress to a fighting-fit political entity that hoped to be at the high table of negotiations with the British. The Sangh's refusal and inability to shoulder the burden were what possibly made Savarkar blurt out that much-quoted abuse for the non-utility of a Swayamsewak, as he perceived it: 'The epitaph on a Sangha Swayamsewak will be: He was born; he joined the R.S.S.; he died.'[193]

Attempts made by the Mahasabha to create their own parallel youth cadet corps and not rely on the RSS did not however make much headway. Moonje's Ram Sena had a grand vision but lacked the organizational strength and the discipline that the RSS had instilled amongst its volunteers.[194] It was confined to Nagpur and a few pockets of Central Provinces and Berar and had very limited reach or appeal.

In a speech delivered on 15 May 1942, Savarkar stressed on the need to create another youth movement to protect Hindu interests. As a secret intelligence report of 23 May 1942 states: 'The R.S.S. Sangh [sic] was designed to safeguard the interest of the Hindus and to create an inspired youth, but it was chiefly a "scholastic" body and could not take up active work.' The Savarkar adherents such as V.B. Gogate, Nathuram Godse and N.D. Apte formed the Hindu Rashtra Dal. As an intelligence report states:

The Hindu Rashtra Dal is an independent body of volunteers founded by V.D. Savarkar to carry on the secret. But the Dal remained a small, insulated group, akin to the revolutionary secret societies that Savarkar had started early in his life such as the Mitra Mela and Abhinav Bharat. By 1944, its membership was just 160, 120 of whom came from Poona and the rest from Ahmednagar. In its second annual training camp, quite like the OTC of the Sangh, in May 1943, about 70 cadets from all over Maharashtra, Bombay city, princely states of Miraj, Sangli and Indore were present. The curriculum consisted of Indian games, physical exercises, shooting practices with air guns and so on. By 1947, the Dal's strength had increased to 1200.[195]

These moves by the Mahasabha to create their own youth corps further embittered their relations with the RSS.

But the chief handicap with these corps was their intense dedication to individuals—Ram Sena to Moonje and Hindu Rashtra Dal to Savarkar. This was also the fundamental difference between the Sangh and the Mahasabha. In fact, the Savarkarite model of Hindutva idolized heroes. From Rama and Krishna to Shivaji and Sambhaji as heroic, war role models, it was an intensely person-centric ideology of hero-worship and exaggerated adulation. It presented to the Hindus the perfect ideological foil or counter narrative to the dictatorial Gandhi-centric Congress that had gained strength in the country and caught the imagination of the people. Quite on the contrary, the RSS model of Hindutva desisted from idolizing individuals as heroes and also avoided scenarios where the masses started rallying around an individual than a cause or institution. The RSS strongly seemed to believe that to tie the fortunes of an organization to the rise and fall of an individual hero would be suicidal for the organization in the long run. Rather, adherence to a cause, a philosophy and ideology would make it immune to the comings and goings of heroes and leaders. Instead of having one towering behemoth, it perhaps preferred a million midgets, all of them thinking alike in the right direction and marching in small baby steps in absolute coherence and consonance with one another. This also gave the RSS the flexibility to own and disown leaders, ideologies and political philosophies from across the spectrum at will, and customize it to its own liking and advantage. Hence, while it was easy for a Swayamsewak to find something creditable and worthy of emulation in a Gandhi or the Congress, this would be anathema for the Savarkarite Hindu Mahasabha member whose loyalties were strictly bound to the personal likes and dislikes of his idol. This adaptability trait was what kept the RSS alive, especially in turbulent times of its history, while the Hindu Mahasabha gradually petered down and ceased to exist in due course.

In its early decades, the RSS drew vastly from the traditional, *sanatani* and orthodox elements of Hindu society, especially the upper castes. Savarkar's revolutionary thoughts of social reforms, caste eradication, inter-caste marriages and dining and views on cow worship—all of which caused considerable consternation even within the Hindu Mahasabha's traditionalist elements that always urged him to tone down—might have been deeply disconcerting for the Sangh too.

An assessment of the Mahasabha–RSS relations was made in a detailed intelligence report of the British, after which they also began to solicit nationwide reports from all the provinces on the extent of the Sangh organization and actions there:

The Hindu Mahasabha is evidently anxious to take the R.S.S. under its wing but it is still not clear if M.S. Golwalkar will agree to subordinate his personal ambitions to those of the Mahasabha leaders by merging his organization into the larger body. Although he will probably have no objection to lending the services of his volunteers to the Hindu Mahasabha if and when required for any special purpose. Although Golwalkar seems shrewd enough to recognize the disadvantage of coming into open conflict with Government, he and his followers have time and again defied the Government ban on the wearing of uniforms and performance of drill of military nature. It is clear from the summary of the Sangh's more recent activities that Golwalkar's outward compliance with orders is no more than a smoke screen behind which to carry on secretly or in a modified form the very activities that he has renounced. On the basis of available information, however it would be difficult to argue that the R.S.S. constitutes an immediate menace to law and order and therefore it is doubtful if a case can be made out for banning the organization under the Criminal Law Amendment Act. At the same time, it is clear that Golwalkar is rapidly building up a strong body of volunteers, sworn to secrecy and complicit obedience to orders and prepared to serve 'wherever required' and presumably in any capacity (subversive or otherwise) that the leader may choose to assign. The whole set up suggest the Khaksar model, the difference being that while Inayatullah[196] is an unbalanced and blustering megalomaniac, Golwalkar is a wary, astute and therefore by far the more capable leader. Although on the face of it the danger arising from Golwalkar's activities may at present seem comparatively remote, it would be . . . unnecessary to leave his activities unchecked and to allow him to establish himself as the undisputed leader of a disciplined corps capable of being used in a manner subversive to the public peace.[197]

Golwalkar was also deeply critical of Savarkar's militarization drive. This caused an upheaval within his organization too. On 29 April 1943 Golwalkar issued a circular to RSS branches announcing the indefinite suspension of military training. He said:

You are aware that since August 1940, in view of the [Government] orders which came into existence then we have discontinued that part of our training, which for want of a more suitable and expressive word used to be denominated as 'military.' Indeed the training we used to impart under that head was quite preliminary and such as served us to inculcate the spirit of brotherhood and a high sense of civic discipline. But even this we discontinued to keep our work clearly within bounds of law, as every law-abiding institution should . . . hoping that circumstances would ease early, we had in a sense only suspended that part of our training. Now, however, we decide to stop it altogether and abolish the department wholly without waiting for the times to change. If they do change we will certainly adjust ourselves then, but now we do not wait. The department being abolished, all posts concerning it naturally cease to exist.[198]

The *sanghchalak* (local district head) of Satara, Bhaurao Modak, and the *prant sangh chalak* (provincial head), K.B. Limaye, allegedly resigned from their posts in protest against Golwalkar's public criticism of the Mahasabha and of military training.[199] Veteran Hindu Sabha members like Vishnu Shripad Dandekar and Madhavrao Bhide tried their best, in vain, to convince Golwalkar to tone down his diatribe.

But all these efforts drew a blank and widened what was seemingly emerging as a permanent wedge between the two saffron brothers.[200]

8

Hurtling towards Disasters

The political deadlock in India was showing no signs of resolution. The situation was getting murkier with the decision of Gandhi to go on a fast towards end-January 1943. The government offered to release Gandhi even while he was undertaking the fast. But he refused this concession offered to him. There was a lot of political uproar with prominent Indian leaders pressing the government to release Gandhi and other Congress leaders, given that they had spent more than six months in imprisonment after the Quit India movement. The non-party leaders under Sir Tej Bahadur Sapru met during 9–10 March in Bombay to discuss the situation that arose due to Gandhi's fast at the Aga Khan Palace in Poona where he had been housed, and also create some rapprochement between political players. There were forceful arguments on the need for the Indians in the viceroy's Executive Council to resign in protest to force the government's lenience towards Gandhi. Savarkar issued the following statement regarding the proposed fast:

> The time has come that all those who are deeply concerned regarding the serious condition of Gandhiji's health and desire to leave no stone unturned to spare his precious life should realize immediately that whether we like it or not, the only way now, which is likely to prove more effective than any other in saving Gandhiji's life is to issue a national appeal to Mahatma Gandhi himself to break his fast before the time of his capacity to bear the strain is stretched out to the breaking point. Even now it is dangerous to depend on chance. We have tried our best to persuade the Government to release Gandhiji and to spare his life. It is of no use now hoping against hope that the fast or its moral or human appeals would bring about any change of heart of the Government. They have made it quite clear that they have washed their hands clean of all

responsibility for any further consequences, however fatal they may be. But now the sands of time are running so fast that we cannot waste a moment in only resenting and protesting. No appeals, resignations or resolutions addressed to the Governments can secure Gandhiji's release. We must now turn our faces from the aliens and unsympathetic doors of the Viceregal Lodge to the bedside of Gandhiji himself and request him to break his fast in the very national interest to serve which he must have undertaken it. There is no moral question that may stand in the way of breaking this fast before it proves fatal. Apart from the fact that moral questions when they are made to serve political ends must after all be mainly judged by their political utility, Gandhiji himself when he took up the fast did so subject to two conditions. The first was that he was not going to risk his life but wished to survive the ordeal. Consequently, this was only a capacity fast. He mentioned no doubt, a set number of days, but that was a haphazard calculation subject to two main limits referred to above. Secondly, apart from this aspect, there is a higher objective, which must override all other verbal hair-splitting. That objective is that the nation, which Gandhiji wants to serve by his fast even at the risk of his life does itself feel that his precious life at this juncture is of immeasurably greater value than his loss to it. There are certainly more chances of his yielding to this national will than yielding of the Government to our irritations or cajolings [sic]. Because we know Gandhiji has more than once allowed higher national objectives to override any moral quibbling involved in vows and broken by him as in the case of Rajkot and several other penances.[1]

Local committees of the Hindu Mahasabha passed resolutions seeking his unconditional release. Savarkar had issued strict directives that members such as Sir J.P. Shrivastava should not resign from the council in protest against the government.[2]

Savarkar had been a part of these Leaders' Conference meetings for quite some time now and was convinced of their futility. So even while he attended the meetings, he was seated there nonchalantly reading 'a newspaper all the time, and when he was asked for his views at the end, remarked that he had always said that the British had no intention of parting with power and the conference could achieve nothing'.[3] He viewed the conference as bending backwards to give a way out to Gandhi to avoid loss of face, even as he advocated for his release by the government.

He skipped the second day of the conference. The resolution of the conference, dated 10 March 1943 was as follows:

> We are of the opinion that the deplorable events of the last few months require a reconsideration of their policy both by the Government and the Congress. The recent talks which some of us have had with Gandhiji lead us to believe that a move for reconciliation at the present juncture will bear fruit. It is our conviction that if Gandhiji is set at liberty he will do his best to give guidance and assistance in the solution of the internal deadlock and that there need be no fear that there would be any danger to the successful prosecution of the war. The Viceroy may be approached on our behalf to permit a few representatives to meet Gandhiji to authoritatively ascertain his reaction to the recent events and to explore with him avenues for reconciliation . . . the following leaders were present at today's meeting held at Mr. Jayakar's residence: Sir Tej Bahadur Sapru, Mr. M.R. Jayakar, Mr. C. Rajagopalachari, Mr. G.D. Birla, Sir Purushotamdas Thakurdas, Mr. Bhulabhai J. Desai, Mr. K.M. Munshi, Sir Ardeshir Dalal, Mr. J.R.D. Tata, Mr. S.A. Brelvi, Mr. Walchand Hirachand, Sir Chunilal Bhaichand Mehta, Sir Homi Mody, Mr. Devdas Gandhi, Master Tara Singh, Mr. S. Ramanathan, Mr. G.L. Mehta, Mr. Allah Bux, Sir Jagdish Prasad and Mr. Kasturbhai Lalbhai and Dr. Mackenzie. Mr. V.D. Savarkar who was unable to be present at the meeting has signified his assent to the statement issued. Besides, the following leaders who could not be present in Bombay are also stated to be in agreement with the statement . . . Mr. K. Srinivasan, Mr. C.R. Srinivasan, Mr. N.R. Sarker, Dr. Syamaprosad Mookerjee, Mr. Amritlal V. Thakkar, Raja Maheshwardayal Seth, Mr. P. Subbarayan, Pandit Hirdaynath Kunzru, Sir Abdul Halim Ghuznavi, Mr. N.M. Joshi, Sardar Sant Singh, and Mr. M.S. Aney.[4]

When he found his name too as a signatory in the resolution that the conference came up with, Savarkar issued a quick rejoinder distancing himself:

> I read in this morning's papers a report that I had signified my assent to the statement issued following the Conference of Leaders last evening. The report is incorrect. I could not be a party to it as I did not attend the Conference on the second day and I attended on the first day in my

individual capacity and not as the President of the Hindu Mahasabha and due to the pressure of some friends.[5]

In public speeches Savarkar also castigated the Leaders' Conference as being 'promoters of that Conference to fall at the feet of Jinnah and accept Pakistan as a means of relieving the deadlock'.[6] This naturally annoyed the conference leaders. M.R. Jayakar and Sir Tej Bahadur Sapru exchanged several angry letters about the 'distasteful comments' of Savarkar and an attempt by him to spread 'total falsehood'.[7] The rupture seemed final and Savarkar was slowly beginning to antagonize and alienate not only members within his party, but in the larger political fraternity too.

With Savarkar's formal disassociation, the government too knew that the conference was 'nothing more than a number of leaders without any followers'.[8] The government remained firm in its resolve not to release him and Gandhi survived the fast, even as he continued to remain in house arrest at the Aga Khan Palace.

~

Savarkar's strategy of stitching together alliances with non-League Muslim parties in the earlier years and cohabit even with the Muslim League from 1943 onwards drew a lot of ire. The political ferment in different provinces arising out of the death of Sikandar Hayat Khan, the assassination of Allah Bux allegedly by League goons, and the collapse of Fazl-ul-Haq's ministry in Bengal, brought the League back in pole position to form the ministry in those very provinces (Bengal, Punjab, NWFP and Sind) that they wished to carve out to create Pakistan.

On 3 March 1943, the president of the Sind Muslim League G.M. Syed passed a resolution in the Sind Legislative Assembly recommending to the viceroy that Muslims in India were a separate nation and the creation of Pakistan for them was a non-negotiable item. The resolution, the first of its kind passed in a provincial legislature stated that the Muslims were entitled 'to have independent national states of their own, carved out in the zones where they are in a majority in the sub-continent of India'.[9] It also mentioned that 'no constitution shall be acceptable to them that will place the Muslims under a Central Government dominated by another nation' and any such attempt would result in 'disastrous and unhappy consequences'.[10] The resolution was carried by a majority of twenty-four votes against three. Of the three, two were Hindu ministers of the Mahasabha and one a Hindu parliamentary secretary. Although the Mahasabha ministers protested against the resolution and voted against it, the resolution was adopted and they too continued to remain in the government.

Questions were therefore obviously being asked of Savarkar and his policy of 'practical politics' to safeguard Hindu interests. However, Savarkar held on to his view. On 10 June 1943, he issued a lengthy statement justifying the Hindu presence in several Muslim-majority ministries, even if it meant allying with the Muslim League. He said that wherever an opportunity arises in a Muslim majority ministry, the Hindu members should capture positions of power and influence to better voice the concerns and legitimate rights of their community. Their presence would act as an effective bulwark against any possible anti-Hindu activities that the ministry might undertake, he believed.

> But they (Hindu Ministers) should oppose publicly every attempt on the part of the Moslem Ministry to support Pakistan or the treacherous principle of Provincial self-determination to secede. The Provincial Hindu Sabhas should be left free on all other details to agitate against any anti-Hindu step on the part of the Ministry in its collective capacity and if the Hindu Ministers are known to have recorded their protest against such steps, they should not be asked to resign their seats on the Ministry. The leading principle which must be emphasized is that boycotting the Ministry altogether is bound to be more often than not highly detrimental to Hindu interest.[11]

He prescribed a coalition model with the Muslims even in Hindu-majority states if and when such opportunities arise there, but with the fundamental idea of non-support of Pakistan and secession. 'Within the scope of these leading principles the formation of ministries and adjustment to the special circumstances prevailing in each province should be left to the discretion of the respective provincial Hindu Sabha.'[12]

When the Akalis were faced with the confusion of whether or not to ally with the League in forming a government in the NWFP, Savarkar prevailed upon them too to form the coalition with the League. Akali leader S. Ajit Singh accordingly joined the ministry. His letter to Ajit Singh that was intercepted by the British intelligence is quite instructive of what Savarkar thought about forming these alliances even with the bitter opponent, the League:

It must be remembered, in a minority province the Hindu-Sikh ministers must be in a minority unless indeed we re-conquer the province and establish our own rule. If we must continue in minority in the ministry, we cannot every day stop every bill getting passed, which the Muslim majority votes for, nor can we protect the Hindu-Sikh interest as fully and completely in every case in the majority Muslim population. Under such circumstances the minority has either to surrender absolutely to the majority and not enter the councils or the ministries, or utilize whatever seats in the Legislatures, Ministries, Army and in fact all points of vantage to render our resisting power more and more effective. I believe that the latter course is the only policy, which will strengthen the minority. The first course of leaving even those positions of authority and vantage can only leave the whole field absolutely unchecked to majority and amount to voluntary surrender and complete subjection. Look, how the Muslims act. Even in the provinces where they are 10 or 4% minority, they insist on entering the councils, having more seats, forming their independent blocks in the Councils and acting always as a thorn in the sides of the Hindus to [the] best of their power. They never completely and always boycott the councils or ministries simply because they are in a minority of even one or two and they can depend on the majority of other Muslims in other provinces to back them up.

The Hindu-Sikh can also follow this policy, which in fact every one follows to make the best of a bad job. But the Congress mentality, pseudo-nationalistic and almost always therefore anti-Hindu-Sikh and suicidal had blinded even the instinctive urge of self-preservation in our Hindu-Sikh public. To boycott the councils or ministries permanently on account of every detail is a slogan as foolish and absurd as 'To win Swaraj by the Charkha' or India requires no military forces at all because we would not invade anybody, nobody else will invade us, or 'to write a letter to Mr. Churchill when Germans were supposed to invade England after Dunkirk fiasco to lay down arms if he wanted to conquer Hitler,' and all this Gandhistic Puran.

Yes, in one case only a Hindu-Sikh minister may resign, under these present circumstances and that is when the Governor openly announces his determination to scrap up the whole Muslim ministry altogether

under Section 93 if the majority of Muslim ministers cannot secure
Hindu-Sikh representatives to partake in the Ministry.[13]

The Hindu press attacked the Akalis of deserting their principles and
betraying Sikh interests in return for illusory benefits under a Muslim
regime.[14] But considering how the presence of the Hindus in the ministry
in Sind could not prevent the Pakistan resolution from being passed,
there were obvious questions raised of Savarkar, if this was not merely
an opportunistic and power-hungry arrangement of 'job-hunters' as the
Congress derided them.

But unfazed by these criticisms, Savarkar warned the Hindus of
NWFP in a statement on 3 September 1943 and asked them to vote
decisively for the Hindu Mahasabha henceforth if they needed a strong
political voice to protect their rights:

> Moslems have learnt to vote solidly for the Moslem League [sic] not
> because it has any very well-disciplined organization or extensive
> membership or work to recommend it but only because the Moslems
> have been taught and trained from their very cradle that their first duty
> is to enable Islam to dominate even politically over the non-Islamic
> world. To them the Moslem cause is the only patriotic, the only national
> nay, the only human cause. That is why the Moslem electorate, almost
> instinctively, backs up the candidates of any Moslem organization
> whether it be the Khilafat movement or the League as soon as that
> body pledges itself to defend and promote even aggressively this innate
> ambition of the Moslems. The League has most uncompromisingly
> raised the standard of Pakistan and Moslem electorate backed it up by
> · voting for it solidly and invested it with the unquestionable right of being
> the representative body of the vocal and powerful Moslem sections.
> But the Hindu electorate on the contrary has been subjected to the
> perverse and degenerating influence of the pseudo-nationalistic tenets
> of the Congress. Anybody or any organization that tries to advocate
> the Hindu cause is immediately dubbed as unpatriotic, something sinful
> and any one or any organization that plays ducks and drakes with even
> the legitimate Hindu rights or with Hindu honour is invested with
> humanitarian magnanimity and saintliness. Owing to this mentality the
> Hindu electorate continued to entrust their representation in the hands
> of that very body which stands openly pledged not to defend Hindu

rights as Hindu rights, and publicly maintained that 'Nationalism' requires it to betray the Hindu rights. The result is that the Hindus are now hemmed in on all sides by anti-Hindu forces and Pakistan and the cursed principle of Provincial self-determination to secede which is worse than Pakistan—have now become life-issues. But if the Hindus even now learn the stem lesson which the determination of Moslem electorate to vote only for the most aggressive Moslem candidate implies and rally round the only organization which has been strenuously, faithfully and effectively advocating the Hindu cause then even now the Hindus would regain much that they have lost and find themselves in a dominant position in the political field. The Congress cannot and will not recognize itself as a Hindu body and cannot therefore advocate the special rights and interests of the Hindus. Nay, on the other hand the Congress is always bound to indulge in letting down the Hindu case if only to prove more emphatically its pseudo-nationalistic pretensions . . . If today the Hindu cause is not defended or promoted as strongly and rapidly as it ought to have been it is only due to the suicidal mistake of the Hindu electorate in voting for this very Congress. Let the Hindu electorate try at least once to cast their votes for the Hindu Sangathanist candidates and it will immediately see that the Hindu Mahasabha and the Hindu Front in general grows a dozen times more in strength than the League or the Moslem Front as a whole.[15]

Yet the Mahasabha in its Working Committee meetings of 9–10 May 1943 and 7–8 August 1943 opined that it was not 'prepared to cooperate with the Muslim League and form a coalition ministry until the Muslim League agrees that the Pakistan issue should be shelved during the period of war'.[16] It further added that if the Muslim Ministry did bring in a Pakistan resolution (like Sind did), the Hindu ministers would oppose it tooth and nail on the floor of the House. It concluded with some degree of ambiguity that should such a Pakistan scheme be carried on despite the Hindu protests, 'the Hindu Sabha ministers will resign, if the Provincial Hindu Sabhas concerned, were so to decide'. It was left to each provincial Sabha to also work out the coalition model with the League or any party, based on the ground situation there, rather than through the diktats of the party high command.

~

Meanwhile, across the country his well-wishers and fans greeted Savarkar on his 61st birthday. Grand celebrations and felicitations were held all over India. In the evening, on 28 May 1943 in Poona he was presented with a purse amount of Rs 1,22,912. Further, he was gifted a sum of Rs 41,500 in Bombay and Rs 30,000 from elsewhere.[17] After receiving these purses, Savarkar stopped receiving the monetary help that was coming to him from the very generous philanthropist Raja Narayanlal Bansilal and the Hindu Rashtriya Nidhi. The Kesari Trust too used to send some monthly allowance for sustenance. Despite now being well-to-do, monetarily, it was possibly the extreme poverty consciousness of his early life and imprisonment he suffered from that made Savarkar careful of keeping his wealth intact and not sharing it even with those who served him faithfully. A very telling and blunt mention of this is made as a flaw in his character by an otherwise glowing biographer Dhananjay Keer:

> But having now ample money at his disposal, Savarkar did not think it proper to raise the monthly pittance he paid to his private secretary Gajananrao Damle, his bodyguard Appa Kasar and his secretary Bhide Guruji. Though poorly paid they all served him loyally. The private secretary and the bodyguard suffered silently. But Bhide had his children to support. He was not being paid even a junior clerk's salary. So he requested his master to consider the question. But the master, who was always afraid that his family would come to want, blankly refused to do so, although on a previous occasion he had raised the pittance by Rs. 25. Bhide thereafter resigned his post from October 1, 1944 to start an independent political life and an English weekly. Savarkar knew not the use of a good secretary or a good office. He gave interviews to eminent journalists and held discussions with statesmen in his bedroom, which almost all visitors described as shabby.[18]

The Nagpur University conferred on Savarkar a Doctorate of Letters in appreciation of his literary prowess and contributions. In the public felicitation in Poona, Savarkar explained how 'he had been consistent in his political ideology though he had to alter his tactics according to the times'.[19] Interestingly, he held that 'he had an abiding faith in armed revolution, which he would not hesitate to raise if circumstances required'.[20] He also exhorted all Maharashtrians to take advantage of military training 'to enable them to defend India against any foreign invasion'.[21] In a thanksgiving message to the nation in June 1943, he sounded prophetic about what the future might have in store for him in terms of imprisonment and captivity yet again:

> A note of caution also must be struck. It is true that these celebrations have added one more romantic touch to my personal story. The irons that hound [sic] me hand and foot in the prison cells have more or less literally blossomed up in flowers and the steel-plated steamer 'Morea' which was meant to carry me to the gallows has suddenly been transformed into a silver and gold model to enclose a public address to be presented to me, expressive of the national rejoicings on my passing unscathed through the ordeal of Death. Still, even while I was moving on, loaded with garlands, through the pressing and cheering crowds on my 61st birthday I continued to feel in a mood of aloofness that it was but a romantic accident on the path of life and I must he prepared to face a counter transfer-scene at any moment when all this blossom and silver and gold might once again get transformed and hardened into iron and steel and fiery ordeals. Let therefore those who want to join the fight for a New Truth know before-hand that they must not do so with a certainty that every one of them would find his path strewn with blossoms and silver, at some step of life, as happens to be the case with one in a million. Every pioneer, every soldier of God, should take up his cross and march on determined to fall fighting if need be fameless and nameless. For, to the pioneers of Truth, immediate success or honour is an accident, unrecognized sacrifice.[22]

Linlithgow meanwhile retired from his viceroyalty in October 1943 after holding the position through such tumultuous times for seven-and-a-half years—longer than any other viceroy. He was succeeded by Lord Wavell, who was serving as the commander-in-chief of India during the Cripps Mission times and the Quit India movement. His term was to bring about new developments to the story of India's ultimate liberation. Many leaders sought an appointment with him to understand his mind and also share their thoughts with him. Savarkar too did and met him in end-November. Wavell however did not seem to have too good an opinion about him. As he reported in his letter to Secretary of State, Amery: 'Savarkar, the Mahasabha leader, also asked to see me, and I granted him an interview.

I thought him an unpleasant, intolerant little man, full of communal bitterness and with no constructive ideas.'[23]

In November 1943, the Marathi theatre was celebrating its centenary year and Savarkar was invited to preside over the celebrations that were held in Sangli. The rich contribution of Marathi theatre to the social and cultural life of Maharashtra and the many thespians it produced was an odyssey in itself. Savarkar presided over several of these literary and theatre sessions, in line with his first love that was literature.

~

The years 1943 and 1944 saw one of the most horrendous famines in Bengal. India's foodgrains were exported to Ceylon and to other war fronts, European stockpiles in Greece and elsewhere so that food supplies could be kept ready in cases of prolonged hostilities, as also post-war scenario. Britain conveniently turned down offers of American and Canadian food aid and even as millions were starving in India, their food was snatched away from them. Lord Leopold Amery mentioned in the House of Commons of the death of close to three million people due to starvation in the famine.[24] By the time the famine ended another million had been added to the death toll in Bengal.[25]

Savarkar courted controversy during this time through some of his remarks and observations regarding the famine. He alleged that there was a massive Muslim conspiracy to convert several hundreds of starving Hindu women and children to Islam with the lure of food:

> The Moslem proselytizers would not give a morsel of food to the dying Hindu mothers or their children, would rather stand watching them breathing their last and would save them, from that dire agony only if those unfortunate Hindu women and children renounced their cherished Hindu faith and accepted the Moslem religion before they fell victim to death. These nefarious activities are glorified as religious conversions and cherished tacitly or otherwise as justified means of gaining further political strength by the Moslem community as a whole. Hundreds of famished Hindu children are bought as you buy vegetables or picked up by the roadside and sent to conversion centres by those proselytizing Moslem agencies. The public every now and then shudders to read incidents reported from these starving parts to the effect that vultures or

foxes or wolves keep watching the dying human beings and drag children even before they breathe their last to feast themselves on human flesh. Are these wild hearts anyway more beastly than those human beings who as religious apostles keep watching helpless Hindu women and children suffering from the terrible agonies of hunger but would not rescue them unless and until they were spiritually dead and these servants of God could drag them into their Islamic fold.[26]

He called upon Hindus to contribute in large numbers to the Bengal relief programme through the aegis of the Hindu Mahasabha or organizations like the Ramakrishna Mission so that such conversion attempts could be checked.

There was an obvious outcry against this statement. M.A.H. Ispahani, MLA of Bengal and member of the Working Committee of the League stated to the press:

I am amazed at how a public figure of Mr. Savarkar's prominence can make a statement so unrelated to facts. Being closely associated with the biggest Muslim relief organization in the Province, namely the Muslim Chamber of Commerce Relief Committee and knowing how all other Muslim relief organizations and individuals in the Province have rendered yeoman service to suffering humanity without distinction I can categorically state that the allegations of Mr. Savarkar are utterly false. They also constitute an aspersion on Islam, because Islam abhors forcible conversions. There is also a cruel irony about Mr. Savarkar's statement. He is probably aware more than anybody else that if Muslims even tried to play the sort of game he has attributed to them, they could not, as they do not have the wherewithal to do it. With their limited resources they would be happy if they could help their Muslim brethren and save them from the possible fate, which Mr. Savarkar pretends to fear for Hindus. I consider Mr. Savarkar's action in rushing to the Press without satisfying himself . . . highly deplorable. It is also mischievous, as it will have the inevitable effect of fanning the fire of bitterness between Hindus and Muslims.[27]

The new prime minister of Bengal who succeeded Fazl-ul-Haq, the League's Sir Khawaja Nazimuddin, issued an emphatic denial to all the allegations. He added in his statement to the *Dawn* on 27 December 1943 that neither Syama Prasad Mookerjee nor any other Hindu Sabha leader had mentioned such a thing to him, directly or indirectly. He said it was extraordinary that 'a responsible leader of a section of the Hindus should give currency to such a baseless charge'.[28]

However, Moonje, who was on a visit to Bengal to overlook the relief operations, insisted that Savarkar's statement was true. He maintained that this state of affairs was going to have an adverse effect on the Hindu community as their numbers were bound to suffer in the next census. About Mookerjee he said the latter was 'aware of this movement of the Muslims but he was not prepared to do anything at the time. His whole efforts being mainly directed to save the lives of Bengalees irrespective of caste and creed',[29] but would take up the matter in due course.

The government took serious note of Savarkar's statement and even mulled prosecuting him under various sections of the law. Eventually the legal advisers of the government told them to drop the idea of prosecution, which could lead to unnecessary precipitation of the matter.

~

Meanwhile, in July 1943, Savarkar tendered his resignation from the position of the president of the Mahasabha yet again, on health grounds. The Working Committee once again appealed to him to stay on till further arrangements were made. Just around the time of the Mahasabha's annual session in Amritsar, Savarkar came down with a bad bout of acute bronchitis and was advised strictly by his doctors not to undertake any journey. The Amritsar session was a significant silver jubilee one of the Mahasabha. For all practical purposes, with his health failing rapidly, the working president, Syama Prasad Mookerjee, was the de facto president of the Mahasabha. He was asked to officiate on Savarkar's behalf in Amritsar.

Around the same time, at the Aga Khan Palace, Gandhi's wife Kasturba's condition had been worsening. A patient of chronic bronchitis, she suffered two heart attacks in January 1944. She soon contracted pneumonia. A huge argument broke out between Gandhi and his son Devdas about the course of treatment, with the latter insisting on administering penicillin that he had arranged from Calcutta for his mother and Gandhi putting his foot down firmly. Eventually, Kasturba died on 22 February 1944. In his telegram conveying his condolence, Savarkar wrote to Gandhi: 'With a heavy heart I mourn the death of Kasturba. A faithful wife and an affectionate mother, she died a noble death in the service of God and man. Your grief is shared by the whole nation.'[30]

However, the bonhomie seemed short-lived. When Congressmen started a Kasturba Gandhi Memorial Fund inviting donations from Indians and proposing that the money so collected was to be handed over to Gandhi to utilize it in any way he deemed fit for the emancipation of women or social causes, Savarkar opposed this bitterly in a harsh statement that was released on 14 May 1944, even as lakhs of rupees started pouring into the fund. His premise was that 'Hindu Sangathanists should not contribute a single pie to the Congressite Kasturba Fund'. Expanding on his reasons for the same, Savarkar said that while her death was universally mourned and more so as she was 'sharing political imprisonment with her revered husband', there ought to be a 'sense of proportion'. What does the country then do for the thousands of women and girls whose husbands were martyred or sent to the gallows or transported for life to dungeons, he asked. Those young girls had suffered in anonymity and borne these catastrophes bravely. Kasturba's sufferings were 'insignificant relatively' to this, he claimed. 'Has the Congress,' he asked, 'ever cared to keep even the list of the addresses of these women sufferers?'[31] He held that if a fund is to be started at all to honour patriotic Indian women sufferers, it ought to be for all whom we can yet remember. He prescribed the formation of a committee of all parties equally represented to locate such brave women and help their cause.

> But as it is, their martyred husbands, sons, or brothers have actually been condemned vociferously by the Congress and by Gandhiji in particular, as murderers, anarchists, as a curse, as a blot on the 'Indian' culture and the Ahimsa Charkha politics. And these brave women sufferers were consequently not thought worthy of even grateful recognition. Has the Congress said a single word in commemoration of the heroic Madam Cama who championed the cause of Indian independence publicly, when the Congress could not dare even to claim Home Rule and Gandhiji was dancing to the tune of the British Imperial Anthem and prided himself on his hearty loyalty to the chains that bound Mother India![32]

Savarkar reminisced that in the past too the Congressmen who had spent all their lives 'vilifying and exterminating the Tilakite principles and parties', had created a Tilak-Swaraj Fund on his death. The proceeds of that fund

happily found its way to finance the Khilafat movement that had proved
itself to be so pernicious for the country, according to him. Similarly, the
Kasturba Fund was a euphemism and a trick by Congressmen to dupe the
nation. He was apprehensive that considering it was left to Gandhi's sole
discretion to use the money from this fund, it would be—

> . . . spent directly and indirectly in propagating and popularizing the
> 'regional' vivisection of India, perhaps especially among the women just
> as a large part of it will flow under-channel into the Moslem pockets
> as well . . . Under Gandhiji's leadership the ahimsa, charkha, Hindu-
> Moslem unity and vote for the Congress can not but be the chief planks
> on which he wants women also to work organizedly [sic]. We can have
> positive proof of them in the ashrams conducted up to this time on those
> lines.

The particular tough period that the country was going through
with famine raging in provinces, the need of the hour, according to
Savarkar, was to gather funds from all sources to provide succour and
relief to the teeming, starving millions. In a rejoinder statement on 1
June 1944, he added:

> Congressites alone who believe in the utility of the fund may contribute
> to it by lacs (sic) and even crores and spend it as they like and the Hindu
> Sangathanists who have grown wiser after being made dupes to such
> Congressite pseudo-nationalistic labels, should not contribute a pie to
> this Congressite Kasturba fund by mistaking it for a 'national fund'. Let
> every Hindu Sangathanist see to it that every pie he can spare for charity
> is contributed to strengthen the Hindu Cause, to help the Shuddhi
> Sabhas, Hindu Rescue Homes and such other institutions spread all
> over Hindusthan under auspices of Hindu Sabhas, Arya Samajas or
> other Hindu Sangathanist institutions which are doing excellent work
> for the relief, rescue, nursing and education of exclusively Hindu women
> and children. Such Hindu Sangathanist institutions which on that very
> account are extremely hard-pressed for funds must have first claim on
> Hindu charity.[33]

Savarkar was bitterly criticized by several Congress leaders and their
sympathizers for his alleged lack of grace and a spirit of generosity. This

further widened the breach between him and the Congress in general and Gandhi in particular.

Around this time, on 8 February 1944, the American vice consul Thurston met Savarkar to solicit his views on the political situation in the country. The following day, Consul Howard Denovan sent a secret dispatch to the Secretary of State, Cordell Hull, in Washington detailing the discussions that were held. Among a host of other things, Savarkar had made it clear that he and his party were stoutly opposed to Partition and that they did not see eye-to-eye with the Congress. Savarkar described Gandhi's policies as 'dreamy nonsense', his non-violence theories as 'stupid' and Rajagopalachari as a 'Congress Pakistanite'. He apprehended that once released, the important Congress leaders might 'all sign up for Pakistan'[34] and that his party needed to be vigilant about this. The report also mentions that Savarkar evinced a great deal of interest in American policy towards India, as also the immense publicity that the Mahasabha was receiving in American press. He is supposed to have told them that among the four great powers—Britain, Japan, USSR and United States—independent India would prefer to have the closest and strongest bond with America that was a natural ally, particularly so in the commercial field. Free India would like to import machinery and manufactured goods from the USA without any political obligation. If he had his way, Savarkar wanted to send 10,000 young Indians to the USA for technical training. He also warned America against any imperialist ploy against India or plans to annex a portion of the country to build a naval base against Japan. Instead, America must focus on winning the friendship of India, he added.

~

Meanwhile, trouble was brewing in the Jaipur state where, as Savarkar had apprehended earlier, the alleged acts of the new dewan, Sir Mirza Ismail, in demolishing temples for town planning but leaving mosques untouched, or the stifling of Hindi and Nagari script to give preference to Urdu caused popular unrest. A local Hindu Sangathanist leader, Pandit Ramachandra Sharma, undertook a fifty-four-day fast in Delhi to protest against Ismail's directives. In his staunch support of Sharma, Savarkar issued a statement on 6 June 1944. He said that in states such as Hyderabad, Bhopal, Junagarh, Sind, NWFP, Punjab, Kashmir, Ramgarh and so on, by virtue of the rule of their monarch or their majority status, Muslims had managed to coerce

Hindus directly or indirectly to eschew the Nagari script or the Indian languages and adopt Urdu for all purposes. But in Jaipur,

> . . . where 93% are Hindus and even the Ruler happens to be a Hindu, a Moslem Minister dares to render it compulsory for all Government and its script. It is good of him he did not make it compulsory even for the Maharajah and his descendants to know how to read and write Urdu to be eligible to inherit the 'Gadi'. Under these circumstances all those Hindus who recognize the Nagari-Hindi their national or mother tongue must declare a war on Urdu on a Pan-Hindu scale throughout India. We can surely checkmate this danger which has not only a linguistic but also a political aspect, detrimental to the Hindu Cause.[35]

Savarkar urged the Hindi Sahitya Parishads, Nagari Pracharani Sabhas, the Hindi Mandals, the Hindi Granthalayas and Hindi linguistic institutions to spread out throughout the United and Central Provinces and Mahakosal to fight and lead a Nagari–Hindi agitation. He also urged for a massive public campaign through newspapers, articles, cartoons and also delegations to the maharaja of Jaipur to put pressure for the withdrawal of the order requiring all government servants to learn Urdu with its script. An anti-Urdu week was also called for from 15 to 22 June 1944 and about 1000 volunteers of the Hindu Mahasabha kept on standby in case the government of Jaipur repeats the actions as were committed by the Nizam to crush any agitations or deputations to the state.[36]

'The Constitution of the Hindusthan Free State'

The Hindu Mahasabha meanwhile was indulging in an interesting and significant exercise. A committee comprising D.V. Gokhale, L.B. Bhopatkar, K.V. Kelkar and M.R. Dhamdhere was set up to deliberate on the contours of a possible constitution for free India. It met for the first time on 31 May 1944 and had thirty-five sittings in all. The crux of the deliberations made its way into a detailed, hundred-page published document titled 'The Constitution of the Hindusthan Free State'. The committee consulted the constitutions of almost all the countries of the world and also the official and unofficial documents related to India in this matter. Issues such as the minorities, Indian states and India's future relations with Britain were all considered with an open mind. It stated:

Hindusthan must be free and independent at the earliest possible moment, as it would at no distant date, be called upon to play an important part in the maintenance of the peace and order of the world . . . a free and unfettered Hindusthan was as it were the *sine qua non* of the world peace and world order. It was an independent Hindusthan, and not one bound to the chariot wheels of British Imperialism that would surely be one of the few powers in the world strong enough to hold the scales even between warring interests, and thereby to avoid world wars and the consequent holocaust of all human values . . . frame a constitution on the basis of Hindusthan being a free state and not a servient [sic]member or even a partner of any other State or Commonwealth.[37]

The following were the points on which the committee raised the superstructure of the proposed Constitution, submitted on 15 July 1944:

1. The name of the free country to be Hindusthan and not India.
2. The relationship that should exist between Hindusthan and Britain—one of alliance rather than partnership, which would be beneficial to both parties concerned.
3. Hindusthan to remain one indivisible entity—the terms of the constitution were applicable to the entire nation including the proposed and demanded Pakistan.
4. The form of government to be democratic, republic and federal with the residuary powers at the Centre.
5. Legislature to be bicameral both at the Centre and in the provinces.
6. Formation of the two chambers at the Centre and in the provinces.
7. The executive to be responsible to the legislature, and both to be responsible to the people.
8. Referendum, initiative and recall. Mechanism to instill popular sovereignty by initiating people's proposals for laws or constitutional amendments (initiative), people's scrutiny of Acts before the Legislature passes them as laws (referendum) and people's rights to remove an unsatisfactory representative before the end of term (recall).
9. Fundamental rights of the citizens.
10. Provision for admission into and training in the army, navy and air forces without distinction of martial and non-martial races.

The Constitution proposed by the Mahasabha recommended adult franchise for all irrespective of sex and on a 'one man, one vote' basis. Voting age was to be twenty-one and there was no question of weightage or reservation of seats. All matters of governance were to be divided into two legislative lists between the Centre and the provinces. The Federal Legislative List was to contain only 'such subjects as are common to all the provinces and as are of national importance'.[38] Provincial Legislative List comprised those of provincial interest and importance, though the reserve of the powers was to vest with an empowered Centre. Legislative, executive and judicial powers were demarcated.

The comprehensive document had five parts to it. An entire section was dedicated to defining a citizen and his/her fundamental rights. Another was on the federal legislature, the process of voting, disqualification, salaries, privileges of members, prorogation and dissolution of legislature sessions, voting and quorum, annual budgets and its details, rights of the Speaker, money bills and ordinary bills, auditing and so on. It detailed the powers and boundaries of various instruments of state—the president and his rights and powers, the salaries and emoluments to the president, the process of removal of the president, the Council of Ministers and their equation with the president, bills and ordinances, the establishment of a Supreme Court, its functions and the judicial process and the role and structure of the army. A similar structure for the provinces was detailed and its relationship with the Centre defined.

The preamble of the proposed Constitution said:

Whereas all sovereignty rests in the people, and

Whereas the people of Hindusthan including the people in territories at present ruled by Indian Princes and Chiefs are the sole source of all State power in Hindusthan Free State, and

Whereas the people of Hindusthan constitute free, independent and indivisible State, and

Whereas it is the inalienable right of the people of Hindusthan to have freedom and to enjoy the fruits of toil and to have the necessities of life, so that they may have full opportunities for self-expression and growth, and

Whereas the people of Hindusthan are inspired by the determination to establish their realm in freedom and justice, to be of service to the cause of peace at home and goodwill abroad and to further progress in all aspects[39]

In the definition of a citizen, no mention or distinction of religion, caste, creed and gender was made.

> Every person, without distinction of sex, domiciled within the limits of the jurisdiction of the Hindusthan Free State at the date of the coming into operation of this Constitution, who was born in Hindusthan or either of whose parents was born in Hindusthan or who has been ordinarily resident within the limits of the jurisdiction of the Hindusthan Free State for not less than seven years is a citizen of the Hindusthan Free State, and shall within such limits enjoy the rights and privileges and be subject to the obligations of such citizenship.[40]

The list of sixteen fundamental rights envisaged for such a citizen is also illustrative of a modern, egalitarian, secular state:

i) All men and women shall have equal rights as citizens.

ii) All citizens are equal before the law and possess equal civic rights. There shall be no law, civil or penal, substantive or procedural, of a discriminative nature.

iii) All citizens have an equal right of access to, and use of, public roads, public wells and all other places of public resort.

iv) All citizens have the right to free elementary education, and of admission into any educational institution maintained or aided by the State without any distinction of caste, colour or creed.

v) Every citizen shall have the right to keep and bear arms in accordance with the regulations made in that behalf.

vi) The state shall make suitable laws for the maintenance of health and fitness for work of all citizens, securing of a living wage for every worker, the protection of motherhood, welfare of children, and the economic consequences of old age, infirmity and unemployment, and the state shall also make laws to ensure fair rent and fixity and permanence of tenure to agricultural tenants.

vii) All persons are by nature equally free and independent and have certain inherent rights; viz., the enjoyment of life and liberty with the means of acquiring and possessing property and pursuing and

obtaining happiness and safety without any exploitation of man
by man.

viii) The liberty of the person is inviolable and no one shall be
deprived of his liberty of person except in accordance with law.
The privilege of the writ of Habeas Corpus shall not be denied
to any person, unless, in case of rebellion or invasion, the public
safety requires such denial and then only in such manner as shall
be prescribed by law.

ix) No person's dwelling or property shall be entered, sequestered or
confiscated save in accordance with law.

x) The right of free expression of opinion, as well as the right to
assemble peaceably and without arms, and to form associations or
unions, is hereby guaranteed for purposes not opposed to public
order or morality.

xi) Freedom of conscience and the free profession and practice of
religion and the protection of culture and language are, subject
to public order and morality, guaranteed to every citizen, and
no law shall be made either directly or indirectly to endow any
religion, or prohibit or restrict the free exercise thereof, or give
any preference or impose any disability on account of religious
belief or religious status.

xii) No person attending any school receiving state aid or other public
money shall be compelled to attend the religious instruction that
may be given in the school.

xiii) No person shall, by reason of his colour, caste or creed, be
prejudiced in any way in regard to public employment, office of
power or honour and the exercise of any profession, trade or calling.

xiv) No public money or property shall ever be appropriated, applied,
donated or used directly or indirectly, for the use, benefit or support
of any sect, denomination, sectarian institution or association
or system of religion, or for charitable, industrial, educational or
benevolent purposes not under the control of the state.

xv) There shall be no state religion for the Hindusthan Free State or
for any of its provinces.

xvi) Every citizen shall have the right to petition to the Supreme Court
in respect of any infringement of his fundamental rights, and the
decision of the said court shall be final and binding on him, the
State and the Provinces concerned.[41]

It mentioned that the proposed Constitution guaranteed to the citizens of free Hindusthan freedom from what President Roosevelt had termed as 'Four Freedoms': freedom from fear, freedom from want, freedom of expression and freedom of worship.[42] While going over all the terms of this exhaustive document and its various clauses and provisions might be well beyond the scope of this work, it would suffice to say that the broad vision, terms and structure of this Constitution seems to have found its resonance in the eventual Constitution of India. In fact, in the Constituent Assembly debates, the document of the Mahasabha was also referenced. Congress leader Narhar Vishnu Gadgil mentioned in the Constituent Assembly debates after Independence:

I have singled out two parties in the country—the Socialists and the Hindu Mahasabha. Both the parties have put down in writing their ideas about the Constitution for this great country. One is published under the title 'Drafting Constitution of Indian Republic' and it is red in colour, which is rather the monopoly of the communists with something different by way of an emblem. The other party—the Hindu Mahasabha—has also published a book called the 'Constitution of the Hindustan [sic] Free State'. I went carefully through both these documents and I find that there is agreement on the main features of the Constitution that ought to prevail in this country . . . The Socialists as well as the Hindu Mahasabha, are agreed that the Federal State, or the Centre must be strong.[43]

~

Gandhi, meanwhile, was released from jail in May 1944. Expressing his satisfaction at the release, Savarkar issued a press statement on 7 May 1944:

The whole nation feels a sense of relief at the news that the Government has released Gandhiji in view of his advanced age and declining health owing to his recent serious illness. It was a human act. I wish Gandhiji a speedy recovery. I hope that the Government will now release Pandit Nehru and all those gentlemen who have been incarcerated without being tried for political activities, or put publicly on trial so that the country may know what are the definite charges that the Government has against them.[44]

In a series of press interviews thereafter, Gandhi pledged not to renew his campaign of civil disobedience during the war and promised instead to help the Allied war efforts.[45] In another interview to the *News Chronicle*, London, he reiterated:

> It was his [Gandhi's] purpose to help and not hinder the Allied war effort. He had no intention of offering civil disobedience. History could never be repeated; he could not take the country back to 1942. The world had moved on during the last two years and the whole situation had to be reviewed de novo. Today he would be satisfied with a National Government in full control of civil administration and would advise the Congress to participate in such a Government, if formed.[46]

On 27 July he wrote to Lord Wavell that he would advise the Working Committee of the Congress to publicly renounce civil disobedience and cooperate in the war efforts provided a declaration of immediate Indian independence was made and a national government formed with the proviso that during the pendency of the war, military operations should continue as it was but no financial burdens on India.[47] The Secretary of State to India rebuffed the suggestions the very next day in the House of Commons, stating that Gandhi's proposals 'obviously did not form even the starting point for a profitable discussion'.[48] So, in effect, all the parties had gone back to where they began in 1939 and after all the enormous sufferings and strife that the people of the country had endured during the Quit India movement. The British wanted a united demand from all Indian political players; the Congress wanted an upper hand in any future government; the Muslim League was adamant on Pakistan as a prerequisite and the Mahasabha rejected the vivisection plan.

Pushed to the wall, Gandhi eventually decided to engage with Jinnah in negotiations, egged on by his associate Rajagopalachari, who had all along suggested several prescriptions, some preposterous, to solve the communal problem and the Pakistan demand. It became known that Rajagopalachari had been in constant touch and negotiations with Jinnah even after his aborted attempt of acceptance of the Pakistan scheme in 1942. The terms of this formula were that the Muslim League should endorse the demand for independence and cooperate with the Congress in the formation of a provisional interim government for the transitional period. After the war, a commission was to be appointed to demarcate the contiguous districts of the north-western and eastern frontiers where

Muslims were in a majority and a plebiscite was to be conducted there to decide on the issue of secession from India. In the event of separation of provinces if so desired in the plebiscite, a mutual agreement was to be entered into for defence, commerce, communications and essential purposes. A transfer of population was on voluntary basis. The terms were binding only in case of transfer of power to India by the British.

Even when these correspondences and terms began to become public knowledge and political leaders expressed their concerns, Savarkar said there was nothing astonishing in the fact that

> . . . Rajaji with the explicit and often repeated consent of Gandhiji himself expressed readiness to accept the principle of provincial self-determination to secede from the central Indian Government, and had actually made an offer of the northwestern and eastern parts of Hindusthan to Jinnah if he agreed to cooperate with the Congress in conducting the national Government which was still in the land of dreams.[49]

He reiterated that all along the Congress had been fooling people with slogans such as Quit India, whereas he had foreseen their true intentions much earlier. The Congress, he averred, rejected the Cripps Mission too, not on the issue of provincial self-determination and a potential dismemberment of the Indian Union, but on the reluctance of the government to hand over the defence and military control. 'Even after he was imprisoned did not Gandhiji,' asked Savarkar, 'write to the Viceroy expressing gratitude to see that "he was not fallen from His Excellency's grace", to the effect that Mr. Jinnah should be entrusted with cent percent Governmental power and should be left free to govern as he chose at his own sweet will?'[50] In view of all that had happened at the CWC and AICC resolutions, why would it come as any surprise to anyone that immediately after his release, Gandhi should get down to fructifying this deal, he wondered. In his characteristic style, Savarkar lambasted the whole scenario thus:

> The Hindu Mahasabha had foretold that just as the Swaraj-Khilafat movement ended in strengthening the Khilafat forces and gave birth to the Pan-Islamic movement so also this Swaraj-Pakistan movement can only result in strengthening the Pakistani forces. Had I been hypocritical enough to claim to possess any super-human 'Inner Voice,' I could have very well claimed this warning now as an oracular prophecy!! So true it has come out to the letter. So completely justified had been the

policy, which refrained the Hindu Mahasabha from being duped into the movement of 'Quit India, But Keep Your Army Here,' which has now ended in such miserable fiasco. From 'Quit India' the Congress has inevitably landed on 'Split India'. Those who want to know the reasons which made me foresee this miserable end of the Congressite 'Quit India' movement should do well to read my Presidential address delivered at Cawnpore, December 1942 . . . It is really unjust to look upon Rajaji alone as the villain of this tragedy. His fault is that he allowed himself to play as a willing tool in the hands of Gandhiji, who long before Rajaji's 'Sporting offer' of seceding a few provinces to the Moslems, had once abetted even the conspiracy to instigate the Amir of Afghanistan to invade India under the pressure of the Ali Brothers, as has been evidenced by no less a trustworthy and saintly authority than the late Swami Shraddhanand-ji himself. The fact is that a Moslem Raj in India has always been looked upon by Gandhiji and a large number of the Congressite monomaniacs as a cent-per-cent 'Swa-Raj'. Let Rajaji remember that he is a 'Raja' in name only and that the Indian provinces are not his or Gandhiji's private property, to make a gift of them to any one they like. There stands the Hindu Mahasabha and the whole Hindu Sangathanist world in India to challenge all those self-seekers or the spineless simpletons or the treacherous pseudo-nationalists who dare to cut off an inch of this our Holy-Land and Fatherland.[51]

Savarkar also cabled the Secretary of State for India, Leo Amery, about his party's reservations on 26 July 1944, something that was not even acknowledged by Amery:[52]

Hindu Mahasabha the only all India representative body of Hindus condemns emphatically Gandhiji's proposal to vivisect India allowing Moslems to form separate independent states. Gandhiji or the Congress cannot represent Hindus. Thousands of resolutions and meetings of Hindusabhaites continue to condemn the demand of provincial self-determination to secede from the central government. Hindusabhaites can never tolerate breaking up of union of India their fatherland and holyland.[53]

Voices began to rise from the Sikh community too. Giani Sher Singh, a prominent Akali leader, thundered that if Gandhi and Jinnah got down to cutting the country up into two parts over a table, the Sikhs too would demand an independent sovereign Sikh state that would include '4,000,000 Sikhs out of the total population of 4,165,000 Sikhs in British India'.[54] Ambedkar raised the pitch for the Scheduled Castes who made up nearly '60,000,000 of the population—more than the population of England'.[55] Ambedkar feared that in the event of the formation of a Dominion, the British government would have no right to interfere in the drafting of a new constitution. At that time, the depressed classes would be at the mercy of the Congress, whom he could not trust and hence it was a situation of 'now or never'.[56] Said Ambedkar:

> Mr. Gandhi's whole life, his political life and political strategy were directed at bypassing the demands of the Minorities. The Civil Disobedience Movement, the breaking of the salt law and all these 'tamashas' that Mr. Gandhi had been performing had no other purpose; Mr. Gandhi has now come to realize that it was not possible to bypass the political demands of all minorities and that he must make a treaty with Muslims and with Sikhs. But he had no desire to recognize the demands of the Scheduled Castes community.[57]

The confirmation of the Gandhi–Jinnah talks thus evidently exacerbated adverse political reactions from all players. All protagonists knew that the time of reckoning had finally come after all the dalliance for so many years now and that if they did not hold on to their demands firmly now, it would just be too late. The tension was palpable on all fronts as to which way the scales would turn at the end of the meetings between two mercurial and unpredictable national leaders.

One of the harshest opposition to any potential surrender by the Congress and Gandhi to the Pakistan idea was provided by the Mahasabha and Savarkar. On 1 September, a week before the proposed talks were to begin, Savarkar announced an 'Akhand Hindustan and Anti-Pakistan Week' throughout India. Five thousand meetings were held and 50,000 signatures collected of those protesting the Rajagopalachari formula.[58] British intelligence reports quote Savarkar's instructions to Mahasabha members and volunteers to 'create disturbance in pro-Pakistan meetings organized by the Congress and other parties with a view to their ending in a fiasco'. He even advised them to be ready to court arrest or face criminal procedures if need be. Savarkar is supposed to have sent 'verbal instructions to Sabha leaders in Poona to enroll volunteers for offering "Satyagraha" at Wardha in order to prevent Mr. Gandhi from going to Bombay to meet Mr. Jinnah'.[59]

Narayanrao Savarkar addressed a public meeting in Miraj on 30 August and held that the very idea of Pakistan originated when Gandhi began the Khilafat agitation in 1919. Stressing the 'evils' of the Communal Award, the system of separate electorates and the disproportionate weightage granted to Muslims in public life, he criticized the 'Neither Reject, Nor Accept policy of the Congress' with regard to these divisive schemes. He added that the idea that without Hindu–Muslim unity the attainment of independence was impossible was a fallacy and urged the youth of the country to fight for the nation's indivisibility at all costs. 'However great might be the Mahatma,' he added, 'the ideal of undivided India was greater still.'[60]

Moonje, then the vice-president of the Mahasabha, said in a press conference in Lucknow on 14 September, 'Hindu Mahasabha will certainly oppose such a demand, which granted Pakistan to the Muslims, but it will work for the attainment of independence for India as strenuously as ever.'[61] He stated that if the British acceded to the demands of the Muslims, it was but natural then for similar demands from Sikhs, Christians and other communities. Yielding to this would lead to the complete balkanization of India and there could be no room for formation of what might be called a Central national government.

Still, many meetings organized by the Mahasabha hardly elicited much public response. For instance, the meetings of 15 and 16 August at Sholapur and Ahmedabad to denounce the Rajaji formula drew only 500 and 150 people respectively. As a British report notes about the Bombay Province:

Speaking of the Province as a whole, the recent activities of the Hindu Mahasabha appear to have failed to arouse much more than a very superficial impression on the public mind. This is possibly due in part to the still enormous influene of Mr. Gandhi and in part of the fact that Pakistan does not raise in this Province issues of such complexity as in the Punjab and Bengal.[62]

On 7 September several leaders signed a joint statement opposing any attempts to vivisect the country on communal lines. They included V.D. Savarkar, S.P. Mookerjee, Sir Jwala Prasad Srivastava, Sir Chimanlal Setalvad, Sir Nripendra Nath Sirkar, Sir P.S. Sivaswamy Iyer, V.S. Srinivasa Sastri, N.B. Khare, Sir Homi Mehta, Faiz B. Tyabji, N.C. Kelkar, Sir Sultan Chinoy, N.C. Chatterjee, L.B. Bhopatkar, Pandit Rajnath Kunzru,

Sir C. Ramalinga Reddy, B.S. Kamat, Dewan Bahadur K.G. Brahma, Raja Maheshwar Dayal Seth and several others. The text of the statement was as follows:

> While yielding to none in the desire to secure the freedom of India from foreign domination at the earliest possible moment, we are clearly of the opinion that the proposal to divide India into two or more sovereign states with no central organization to control subjects of vital interest to the whole country, and having their own separate armed forces, is not only against the best interests of the country, but is fraught with dire consequences in the future and will imperil the very independence of the country, to secure which the proposed partition of the country is professed to be undertaken. Such partition will, instead of solving the problem of minorities, accentuate it and will not be in the interest of Muslims themselves. We are of the opinion that coalition governments, both at the Centre and in the provinces, should be established and effective safeguards for the special interests of substantial minorities should be provided. We therefore earnestly urge upon the leaders engaged in present negotiations on the footing of partition of the country to review the whole situation calmly and dispassionately and to arrive at a compromise solution which, while giving complete protection to all interests concerned, will maintain the unity of India, which alone can make her voice effective and respected among the nations of the world and keep her free from the danger of foreign domination in the future.[63]

Meanwhile, in a tone completely in contrast to the highhanded rebuff that the Congress under Nehru had earlier offered Jinnah in the aftermath of the 1937 polls, Gandhi wrote to the League president on 17 July calling for talks with his usual style: 'I have always been a servant and a friend to you. Do not disappoint me.'[64] Even as he rejected Rajagopalachari's proposals as being a 'shadow and a husk, a maimed, mutilated and moth-eaten Pakistan',[65] Jinnah agreed to sit across the table with Gandhi with fresh proposals. He very well knew that he had the upper hand in the negotiations and that all players were getting restive about attainment of freedom, which the British were unwilling to give till he came on board. Hence, he put an obvious premium on his support and upped his bargaining power.

This olive branch from Gandhi could not have come at a more opportune time for Jinnah who was battling political crisis in Punjab that was vital for his Pakistan scheme. After Sikandar Hayat Khan's death in December 1942, Khizr Hayat Khan of the Unionist Party became the premier of Punjab. Jinnah's strong-arm tactics to subsume the Unionists within the League caused huge consternation, leading to severe instability in the government there. League ministries in other crucial provinces for Jinnah such as Sind, Bengal and NWFP were all at various stages of collapse and instability. Jinnah's dictatorial attitude in dealing with coalition allies had lowered his prestige and he was facing a crisis at a time as crucial as this when he was manoeuvring the redrawing of borders with these very provinces. But Gandhi's invitation to him was a providential boost to him politically when his capital was lowering and was thus not appreciated by several Congressmen themselves.[66]

The marathon talks between the two leaders began on 9 September and went on till 27 September. Gandhi travelled every day to Jinnah's bungalow at Mount Pleasant Road in Bombay and the two were closeted in meetings for hours and hours, even as the anxious press gathered outside to collect sound bites. Despite all these meetings, no agreement emerged and the talks were suspended indefinitely.

~

The stage was now set for more political confrontations. Savarkar decided to form a broad anti-Pakistan political front that included his party, all the Sikh parties, the Liberal Party, the Arya Samajists, the Democratic Swarajya Party and others to float an 'Akhand Hindusthan Leaders' Conference'. He began to write to several leaders of other parties seeking their support to be a part of this pressure group. He also used this opportunity to firmly put in his resignation to the post of the president of the Hindu Mahasabha, stating that his efforts needed to be focused now on the Anti-Pakistan Conference. He requested his name to not be included even in 'the first panel of five names' and that 'under no circumstances' could he accept the responsibilities of the president of the Mahasabha from the following year.[67]

Syama Prasad Mookerjee was slated to take over from him as the new president. Mookerjee came to Poona on 1 August to discuss the details of the forthcoming annual Mahasabha session in Bilaspur. Savarkar sent out a telegram to L.B. Bhopatkar, the chairman of the reception committee welcoming Mookerjee's ascent:

I join you in welcoming Dr. Mookerji. Hindudom is indebted to him so much for his monumental services and his recent condemnation of Provincial self-determination to secede from the Central Government and his determination to oppose Indian vivisection that I for one wish that the crown of thorns of the Presidentship of the Hindu Mahasabha, the highest honour that Hindudom can offer be bestowed on him next year.[68]

By the end of the year, though, when the Mahasabha annual session was held at Bilaspur, Savarkar inaugurated it and let Mookerjee preside over it. But rather curiously, he chose to stay away from the proceedings and, in what seemed like a calculated move, decided to address a parallel rally just outside the Mahasabha session pandal protesting the banning of the *Satyarth Prakash* of Swami Dayananda Saraswati by the Sind government. This, even as Mookerjee was delivering his presidential address. Mookerjee was 'naturally perturbed by his leader's strange action',[69] though Savarkar perhaps felt it apt to hit back at his hitherto detractors within the party.

~

On 7 and 8 October 1944, the 'Akhand Hindusthan Leaders' Conference' was held at New Delhi at the Hindu Mahasabha premises under the presidentship of Sir Nripendra Nath Sirkar, former law member of the Government of India. The conveners were Savarkar, N.C. Kelkar, Syama Prasad Mookerjee, George S. Arundale of Madras, S.M. Parande (president of Varnashram Swaraj Sangh), Sir Gokul Chand Narang, Moonje, P.N. Bannerji (MLA and leader of the Nationalist Party), B.G. Khaparde (MLA and ex-minister of Berar) and others. It was evidently lopsided in its composition, including as it did, more Hindu Mahasabha leaders. Stating the reasons and objectives of such a grouping, Savarkar elaborated:

This Conference had from its very inception almost nothing to do to the beginning or ending of the Gandhi-Jinnah Talks. It is an independent effort to consolidate those who stand by the Integrity of India into a common front. Many of those Congressites and others who had secret sympathy with Gandhiji's unholy mission either through conviction or want of foresight tried their best to frustrate the efforts of holding such an Akhand Hindusthan Leaders Conference till the Gandhi-Jinnah Talks were over simply because Gandhiji said 'Let no one speak against the Gandhi-Rajaji Proposal till we are trying to arrive at a compromise with brother Jinnah'. But the organizers of the Akhand Hindusthan Leaders' Conference did not yield to these efforts simply because the very starting point of those Gandhi-Jinnah Talk was the acceptance in this or that form of the treacherous concession to Pakistan. It was impossible as the Rt. Hon. Sreenivasa Shastriji said, for a genuine Indian nationalist to remain tongue-tied while the integrity of our Motherland and Holy land was being openly sold at auction. Even now that the Gandhi-Jinnah talks are over for the time being none should overlook the point that Gandhiji had made it quite clear that they are only adjourned sine die.

I earnestly request those Congressites and other leaders who wanted to wait till the Gandhi-Jinnah talks were over but were in their heart of hearts against the Pakistani proposal to take courage in both hands to conquer their own inferiority complex and come forward to condemn all further efforts to vivisect India and attend the Akhand Hindusthan Leaders' Conference to consolidate the Anti-Pakistan Front. They would doubtlessly be welcomed in the Conference by each and every one who has consented to attend it. But even if some of those do not find themselves able to do so, the Akhand Hindusthan Leaders' Conference will meet in Delhi irrevocably on the 7th and 8th of October next. The prominent Leaders of our Sikh brotherhood, the Mahantas of different Mathas and Ashrams, His Holiness the Shankaracharya of Puri, the Sanatanis, the Arya Samajists and hundreds of Hindu Sangathanist Leaders and other personalities occupying prominent positions social and political have already consented to attend the Conference. I hope that specially in view of the adjournment of the Gandhi-Jinnah talks and the consequent commitment which Gandhiji and almost all the Congressite Press and the Congressite following have now made to accept this or that proposal to vivisect India, it is all the more urgent to consolidate the anti-vivisection party. As a first step towards it the genuine national leaders all over India will not fail to join the Akhand Hindusthan Leaders' Conference at Delhi.[70]

Not much came out of these conferences, however, beyond self-congratulatory messages, since they were largely attended by personalities who had limited or no mass appeal or social backing. Also, Savarkar kept using some of the anti-Pakistan platforms to campaign hard for the

Mahasabha in the forthcoming elections, urging the electorate to vote for them if they wanted to avert the disasters of Partition. From the platform of one such conference on 10 December, Savarkar exhorted Hindus to 'consolidate themselves and whenever the question of election comes they should give their votes to those Hindus who will give the pledge of guarding the interests of the Hindus'.[71] The few political parties that had coalesced with the conference too would obviously drift away eventually from such an overtly partisan programme.

~

The year 1945 brought with it some personal turmoil for Savarkar. His elder brother, and his source of inspiration and support all his life, Babarao's health had been steadily declining. By May–June 1943, he moved from Bombay to Sangli to recuperate and stayed at the residence of the Gundwades. The younger brother Narayanrao and his family moved in to nurse him. Even in his ill health he managed to write a book titled *Hinduness of Christ* and also met several visitors including the RSS chief, Golwalkar. By July 1944, his health reached breaking point with his anaemia worsening, leading to excruciating cramps in the calves. He would in fact tie up his calves in ropes to alleviate the pain. Finally, he was shifted to Bombay to undergo blood transfusion. He insisted on moving back to Sangli where his health worsened. He however wrote a moving article for the weekly titled *Vikram* towards end-November 1944 detailing the journey of his struggles for the liberation of the country. It turned out to be his final statement to his country and its people. He ended the note with a dash of poignancy:

> I must have had many deficiencies; I may have committed many mistakes in my personal and public life and I may have hurt many individuals and opposed them. All these individuals should forgive me for the unavoidable deficiencies in my life. I am offering this overview of my service to the *Rashtra Devata* along the course of the observance of my duty, at her feet. I tasted success in very few of the different fields of national progress, failure came my way in most of the things I attempted. These failures are proofs of my attempts. Through this statement, I am offering the garlands of both my broken and incomplete failures and my unbroken and complete successes at the feet of the *Rashtra Devata*. I shall

continue to do the same in future given the strength. Those I invoked while taking the pledge are capable of extracting its observance from me. The leisurely time I have ahead of me may be short, or may even become permanent. So at this moment, may my salutation reach the feet of the *Rashtra Devata*.[72]

On 8 February 1945, Savarkar visited his ailing brother at Sangli. As the *Vikram* dated 10 February reports: 'Babarao was lost in a happy semi-conscious state while Tatyarao (Savarkar) was recalling their mutual life-history and touching Babarao's feeble body again and again. After some moments had thus passed, Tatyarao got up on Babarao's instructions.'[73]

Babarao's condition steadily deteriorated. On 16 March, after prolonged suffering, this great patriot breathed his last and with that ended an important era in the history of India's armed revolutionary struggle. A moving letter that Savarkar wrote to his brother in his last days was made public on 21 March 1945:

> Baba, we three brothers had a common life-mission. We have repaid our ancestors in our generation. When the history of Bharat is written, this chapter will have to be necessarily written in letters of gold. Our detractors have already called it the 'Savarkar Epoch'. I had written regarding duty in yesterday's letter. But I had not spoken about the fruit because of the sentiment of '*Maa Phaleshu Kadaachana*' [expect not the fruit as per the Bhagwadgita]. But if one were to speak relatively, we along with our associates have twice changed the course of our national life from the adverse to the favourable. The first revolutionary slogan '*Swatantryalakshmi ki Jai*' [Hail the Goddess of Liberty] was ours and the second slogan of '*Hindusthan Hinduon ka, nahi kisike baap ka*' [Hindusthan belongs to the Hindus, not to anybody's father] that complemented it was also ours! We have twice brought about a revolution in the nation's thought and actions. People may remember those warriors who fought and gave their lives in this battle for a few days. As for others, their names will remain unknown. But both deserve credit in equal measure. If at all a statue is to be erected, it should be of selfless *karma yogis* like you! The first thing is that the death that is holding your hand is not an enemy but a friend. Our life is fulfilled. We never gave up the childhood pledge of freedom. Hellish torture, sorrow!—and likewise joy as well. On one side was the Andamans; on the other side was the flag of victory that

was unfurled on the peaks of the Himalayas, in Kashmir, Haridwar and Assam to the thunderous cries of millions of our own people! But the revolutionary flag of freedom of the Hindus did not once fall in the face of joy and sorrow. We fought a lifelong battle to the extent possible for any individual. We stood at the hangman's noose while under-thirty but continued fighting. What contentment in doing this! . . . The sacrificial fire of freedom that we first lit has engulfed the whole nation. When the body of a brave warrior such as yourself who has been fighting for sixty years falls, it will not be a mere mortal body but a great and effulgent offering! It is a matter of such great contentment that with the conclusion of your personal life an effulgent offering of a body that has attained fulfillment is being made! Let us welcome death that has come visiting as a friend . . . A warrior steeped only in his duty without regard to fame, one who has spent a lifetime in the service of the people has the right to contentedly pass into *Yoganidraa* [Yogic sleep] by controlling the mind in a spirit of '*Aapule maran paahile mayaa dolaa*' [I saw my own death].

Hitherto, death had knocked in our twenties, thirties and forties but that was more in the nature of a challenge. The spirit at that time was 'Come if you will, who is scared?' What is termed as happiness and fulfillment in today's world is also scattered around you. You met your near and dear ones once again. The work that was interrupted in the confines of the prison is now at peace after drinking from the water of all the sacred rivers throughout this land of Bharata, from the Sindhu-Ganga-Yamuna to the Southern Ocean. Our children are laughing and playing in our homes and outside. Now it is not death that has come but the time has come to set off for the Great journey. Hence, hold the hand of death as one would that of a dear friend! Not in a spirit of challenge but in happiness! In that void where nothing from the past or future remains, where all thirst is quenched, where only silence prevails after all worldly events, greed, anger, relations are quelled, where the Self also vanishes, into such a void, O Karma Veer, merge yourself with a sense of complete fulfillment.[74]

Gandhi sent his condolences too to 'Bhai Savarkar' in his telegram of 22 March, which he curiously dispatched to the wrong address, Savarkar's earlier home in Ratnagiri. 'I write this,' said Gandhi, 'after reading the news of the death of your dear brother. I had done a little bit for his release and ever since I had been taking an interest in him. Where is the need to condole with you? We are ourselves in the jaws of death. I hope his family are all right.'[75]

~

The political situation in the country was meanwhile heading towards a decisive turn. The viceroy, who had been closely watching the developments since the breakdown of the Gandhi–Jinnah talks, decided to take the initiative himself to create a post-war settlement. Wavell decided to leave for London to finalize the contours of this arrangement. Sir Tej Bahadur Sapru and his group submitted a draft constitution to Wavell before he departed for talks in London. This was rejected by both Jinnah and Ambedkar on the grounds that it rejected the creation of Pakistan and for not taking care of the depressed classes in the proposed Constituent Assembly, respectively.

Meanwhile, Bhulabhai Desai of the Congress and Liaquat Ali Khan of the League presented a pact to Wavell, which they claimed had the blessings of both Gandhi and Jinnah. This called for a creation of an interim government under Desai and Khan with 50 per cent representation to both parties and all positions, except that of the Governor General and commander-in-chief to be held by Indians.

Savarkar was quick to criticize the pact and remind the Congress of the epithets of 'job seekers' and 'traitors' that it had hurled against the Mahasabha when it tried to form coalition ministries with the League. He asked of the Congress:

> If you justify your action by the principle that capturing political power and thus preventing it from falling into worse hands is a better policy than a futile boycott of it, well then, those patriots who entered the Executive Council stand justified by your own principle. This was the very reason, which made me call upon the Hindu Sangathanists to support the Hindu ministers who joined the Executive Council in those dark days when the Congress had anathematized all cooperation with the Government except perhaps in securing military contracts which enabled them to pocket millions![76]

He criticized the pact that gave a community in India which had about 22 per cent population strength a right of 50 per cent in the governance and administration of the country, calling it a betrayal of Hindu interests. 'The League of Nations,' he claimed, 'which represented the wisdom of almost all prominent nations of the world has laid down that no minority should be allowed any concession so as to enable it to claim equality with the "National majority" which in fact forms the Nation.[77]

Savarkar even wrote to Amery on 29 March 1945:

Any pact between the Congress and the League giving the Moselm minority of twenty two percent seats in the legislatures or administration equal with the Hindu majority of seventy five per cent is outrageously undemocratic. The Congress on its own confession does not and cannot represent the Hindus as Hindus. The Congress regime itself had trampled on Hindu rights and sentiments. The Congress-League Coalition therefore cannot but be a hundred times more detrimental to the Hindus. Consequently, no pact or constitution framed without consulting the Hindu Mahasabha, which alone represents the Hindus can bind them. The Hindus in no case would concede to Moslem minority any representation more than what its population strength justifies. Freedom, indivisibility of Hindusthan and representation according to population proportion are the fundamentals on which the Hindu Mahasabha takes its stand.[78]

But clutching on to the Desai–Liaquat Pact, Wavell rushed to London to discuss the plan with the War Cabinet on 23 March 1945. But even as those negotiations were on in London, Jinnah openly feigned ignorance of giving assent to any such pact. When Congressmen like Nehru and Patel too expressed their serious misgivings about the pact, Gandhi washed his hands off it. Desai and Rajagopalachari became the scapegoats and it marked their exit from active politics. But the plan was seized by Wavell to pronounce his personal achievement of a major breakthrough in the Indian deadlock. In a broadcast to the nation on 14 June, upon his return from London, Wavell put forth his plan for the resolution of the Indian deadlock. Gandhi was critical of the use of the expression 'Caste Hindus' in the broadcast, whom the viceroy averred that the Congress represents. Gandhi wondered:

Let alone the Congress, which seeks to represent the whole of India which is yearning after political independence, does Veer Savarkar or

Dr. Shyamaprasad [sic] or Dr. Moonje of the Hindu Mahasabha represent Caste Hindus? Do they not represent all Hindus without distinction of caste? Do they not include the so-called Untouchables? Do they themselves claim to be caste Hindus? I hope not![79]

Jinnah held that the 50 per cent Muslim composition of the new Council should be comprised completely of League leaders and no other Muslim parties. Wavell called for a political conference of twenty-one leaders of all parties to be held in Simla on 25 June 1945 to discuss the composition of the Viceroy's Executive Council to be constituted anew.

Interestingly, unlike Linlithgow who had been in regular communication with the Mahasabha and with Savarkar, Wavell snubbed them by not even including them in the all-parties conference at Simla. This was also indicative of the changed stance that the government was taking towards the Mahasabha, especially after the ascent of Mookerjee to its helm. He was seen as being too close to the Congress and its ways of functioning, making the viceroy suspicious of the party's motives and stance. 'The Mahasabha,' wrote Wavell, 'is a curious body; many of its rank and file seem to be Congress men, and on big political issues will follow Gandhi rather than Syama Prasad Mookerjee or Savarkar.'[80] In a telegram to London, the viceroy shared his thoughts on the near convergence of views of the Mahasabha and the Congress, as evidenced in Mookerjee's presidential address of December 1944. 'The annual session of the Hindu Mahasabha,' he wrote, 'was remarkably insignificant. The Presidential address of Dr. Shyam Prasad Mukerjee [sic] might as well have been delivered from the Congress platform. His solution of the political deadlock was that His Majesty's Government should renew the Cripps offer without the partition clause.'[81]

This exclusion marked the beginning of the end of the British government's active engagement with the Mahasabha. The Savarkarite faction in the party felt vindicated that it was Mookerjee's mass agitation aspirations and his softness towards the Congress that had led to the increasing irrelevance of the party at the high negotiations table. The Mahasabha met during 23–24 June and passed several resolutions denouncing Wavell's exclusion of their party. The younger members of the Mahasabha once again urged for Direct Action, but that was not ratified by the Working Committee. A protest week against the 'Wavell Plan' was however organized across India from 1 to 7 July 1945.

As Savarkar's otherwise complimentary biographer Dhananjay Keer also notes about the inability of the Mahasabha to seize the opportunity to launch a mass direct action:

Had the Hindu Mahasabha done this [launch a mass direct action], it would have risen in the eyes of the public. It must be admitted that Savarkar failed in his promise to resort to direct action at the opportune time. He said right things at the right time, but at this critical time he failed to do the right thing. It was here that the rudder of the ship of the Hindu Mahasabha broke down and the ship was swept down along with the new captain (Mookerjee) into the trough of the popular estimation in the election held soon thereafter. But the fact that the Hindu Mahasabha was the only political organization that stood stubbornly against the anti-national Wavell Plan will be recorded in history. Times needed a stronger action and efforts than they put in. Their protests were not powerful enough to bring down the prestige of the leaders of the Congress . . . mere condemnation could not crush out the Congress misdeeds at the Simla Conference. It was thus that what the Hindu Mahasabha had won at Bhagnagar and Bhagalpur, it lost at Simla. The Mahasabha really missed the bus.[82]

Cognizant of the change in the government's attitude, even Mookerjee slowly began to toe a Savarkar line in his public criticism of the Congress and putting on a more strident Hindu nationalist image. The Mahasabha slowly also began taking a harsh stand towards the government, which further embittered the relationship. But all of this was too little, too late.

Savarkar cried foul about this rebuff from the government and claimed that the Mahasabha was not called only because it was the only party that had stood its ground in a principled and unwavering opposition to the Pakistan scheme. In the *Free Hindusthan* weekly that he had started, he said,

The Congress would clearly cease to be the Indian National Congress if it would accept this Government offer and thus recognize itself as a representative body of a section of Hindus by letting the League, the Depressed Classes, etc. to be represented as different communities. The Congress will sign its own death warrant as the Indian National Congress by its own hands. But the Hindu Mahasabha takes its stand most definitely on the principle of representation to all alike on either as one man-one vote or communally in proportion to the population strength. This is the only national and democratic formula. It neither robs most atrociously, as the Congress does, the majority of its dues nor does it deny the Moslem minority any of its dues. That is why the Government cannot call the representative of such a body to the conclave where the Hindu, interests are to be butchered.[83]

The conference though was doomed from the start as all parties squabbled on the terms that Wavell tried to offer. The failure of the conference however strengthened the League's position as the ultimate veto power in any move towards constitutional drafting or independence.

~

May 1945 saw the war in Europe coming to an end with a complete and unconditional surrender of Germany to the Allied powers. Japan was however still menacing in the South-East Asian and Indian frontiers. 'Victory Day' was celebrated at the British behest in several parts of India. Savarkar however refused to participate in any celebrations and rejoicings till India was made free.[84] Soon, Japan too surrendered in August 1945, following the dropping of two atom bombs on the country, ending the catastrophic war. Churchill quit after the Labour Party secured an absolute majority in the House of Commons and Lord Clement Attlee became the new prime minister of Britain. After a quick visit to London, in September 1945, Wavell announced fresh elections in India. This was going to test the mettle of all political parties and the public estimate of them during this crucial time and make it thereby to the new Constituent Assembly. Savarkar issued several statements to the Hindu electorate to think several times before casting their vote during such a critical poll that would decide the future fate of the country and its indivisibility.

But right in the midst of all these global changes at lightning speed and the election blitzkrieg, Savarkar once again fell grievously ill. After having had all his teeth removed in 1945, he had already stopped tours and public speeches and confined himself largely to bed and to his writings. 'My nerve system has been literally shattered for the last two years,' wrote Savarkar to his Mahasabha colleague N.C. Chatterjee in late 1945, 'it has now collapsed.'[85] The intense nervous exhaustion also made him slip in and out of delirium, occasional memory lapses and nightmares of crowds banging at his door or attempting to break open the walls of his home with iron pickaxes.[86] Savarkar moved to Walchandnagar in Poona for rest and treatment in January 1946 and was tended there by his admirer Gulabchand Hirachand, brother of the industrialist Walchand Hirachand. On 20 January 1946, Savarkar suffered a severe heart attack and a second one in quick succession. For a large part of the first half of 1946, Savarkar was confined to the bed and suffered problems of vomiting, even as the woes of his devastated intestines continued. For a while he was again hospitalized to the Sassoon Hospital in Poona and after eight long months managed to return to Bombay in August 1946, battered and shattered.

With the absence of strong leadership and the series of miscalculated decisions that had been taken by the party, the Mahasabha suffered a massive rout in the elections and failed to make any mark anywhere. Mookerjee's confidence was completely shattered by the results. The Mahasabha, as also M.N. Roy's Radical Democratic Party and Ambedkar's Scheduled Castes Federation were literally wiped off the political map of India. The League secured all the thirty-two seats in the Central Assembly and even defeated the Congress's Muslim candidates. In the provincial legislatures the League won a massive 427 out of 507 seats.[87] It was a timely needed shot in the arm for Jinnah at such a crucial juncture of the subcontinent's history. Dhananjay Keer notes with disappointment that during these crucial elections, even the larger saffron family such as the Arya Samaj or the RSS did not stand by the Mahasabha. He writes:

Let it be said to the credit of the small per cent of those defenders of the Hindu Nation from these two organizations that they did help the Hindu candidates far-sightedly enough, but let it also be recorded that the majority from these two great institutions of Hindu hope and faith kept culpable neutrality over such a life and death struggle in which the Hindu Nation was involved, while the majority of them were reported to have voted for the Congress.[88]

The ending of the war and the changed political situation in Britain brought in a wave of transformation as far as the Indian problem was concerned. As British journalist and historian Leonard Mosley states:

From the moment, in 1945, when the war was over and the post-war world began to reshape itself, no one of clear mind had any doubt that

the Indian people would achieve the independence from British rule . . .
Even the Government of Winston Churchill had grumblingly and
reluctantly conceded—not, it is true, without some goading from the
United States—the need to accord to India the same hopes of freedom
as those with British and Indian soldiers fought to achieve in Europe and
Asia. With the advent in Britain in 1945 of a Socialist Government under
Clement Attlee, the question of India's freedom was never in doubt . . . it
was a policy with which the bulk of the electorate at the time agreed; and
from a purely practical point of view, even the diehards at home and the
imperialist British in India could do little to stop it . . . the British troops,
which might hold the country against rebellion and insurrection, were
clamouring after years of fighting, to go home. And above all, British
power and prestige, in spite of victory, had been diminished by war. The
campaigns in Asia had shown up Britain's weaknesses. After Singapore,
Burma and the sinking of her finest ships by the Japanese, Britain would
never be able to demonstrate in Asia the background of strength and
influence . . . which had for so long enabled her to rule a million people
with one man-on-the-spot.[89]

What Mosley mentions in passing about Indian troops and glosses over
the details is the impact of the Indian National Army (INA) or Azad
Hind Fauj spearheaded by Subhas Chandra Bose and the manner in which
it rattled the vitals of the Empire. Bose had reached Berlin from India
where he was received well by Joachim von Ribbentrop, minister of foreign
affairs of Nazi Germany and the right-hand man of Hitler. Germany soon
encouraged Bose to create legions of the army in India that could turn
against its own imperial masters. Indian prisoners of war in North Africa
were recruited after a lot of persuasion by Bose and two units were ready by
1942. Bose was also allowed to make regular radio broadcasts from Berlin.
Free India Centres began to come up in Rome and Paris with over 3000
men. The Japanese success in the war made him change the strategy and
decide to turn to the Far East as a better option for possible invasion of
British India.

Rash Behari Bose was at the same time holding a Tokyo Conference
during 28–30 March 1942 where it was resolved to form an Indian National
Army under the direct command of Indian officers who would conduct
the campaign to liberate India. An Indian Independence League (IIL)
was established and its conference held in Bangkok in June 1942.

Over 100 delegates participated from Burma, Malaya, Thailand, Indo-China, Philippines, Japan, China, Java, Sumatra, Hong Kong and the Andamans. The conference raised the tricolour flag of free India and also invited Subhas Bose to East Asia. Indian soldiers who had been captured by the Japanese in the war but had now sworn allegiance to liberate their motherland and eschew the British, were also recruited into this group. More than 25,000 volunteers swore to join the INA that was formally set up on 1 September 1942. But several handicaps prevented Rash Behari Bose from being able to take the full plunge and it was only after Subhas came to the East that the INA got a bolster. Subhas was made the leader of the Indian independence movement and hailed as Netaji by his followers, with the war cry of 'Jai Hind' resonating the frontiers. A Provisional Government of India was also established from Singapore and India was declared free. This government was to take control over India once the Japanese invaded. Japan, Italy, Germany, China, Philippines, Burma, Thailand and Manchuria accorded recognition to the Provisional Government of Azad Hind. Japanese premier Hideki Tojo announced on 6 November 1943 that the Andaman and Nicobar Islands that were occupied by the Japanese would be handed over to the provisional government, which renamed them Shahid and Swaraj islands. Regiments of the INA joined hands with Japan in their campaign against British India. By mid-1944, the troops reached Kohima, preparing for the fall of Imphal, cross the Brahmaputra and invade the heart of Bengal. But change in the war strategy with the Japanese Air Force diverted to fight the Americans in the Pacific area depleted the strength of the forces on the Indian frontiers, waiting to strike. With a strong counter-attack from British Indian forces, the INA withdrew. The Japanese did not give wholehearted support to the troops and the valiant men became easy targets of the British counteroffensive. Several men of the brigade, nearly 4000, were killed and several others captured in the Imphal campaign.

Bose believed that with the capture of Imphal he would be able to induce more Indian soldiers in the British Army to join the INA and bolster its capacity. But the sudden monsoon and the changing fortunes of the war on the global scale tilted the scales against the INA. The British evacuated the Arakan Yoma and Rangoon, which were under the control of the INA, by May 1945. The INA soldiers were taken prisoners and this in effect dealt a death blow on the Indian independence movement in South-East Asia. Netaji Bose left Burma for Japan with the hope of renewing the fight for a later date, one that never came. His disappearance following an air crash remains shrouded in mystery till date with no definitive conclusions on his fate thereafter. Despite its apparent failure, the INA episode jolted the British. They could no longer rely on Indian soldiers for maintaining their hold on India. A repeat of 1857 seemed imminent. It had already seen the public upsurge in the wake of the call for 'Quit India' by Gandhi, where the army, the revolutionaries and the public at large relinquished all calls of non-violence and took to violence and anarchy to root out colonial occupation. The subsequent trials of the captured INA officers held in Delhi, known as the Red Fort Trials, made the brave attempts of these Indian soldiers known to the public at large and aroused great sympathy and passion.

Savarkar cabled British prime minister Clement Attlee on 1 December 1945 seeking a general amnesty for all the captured soldiers as a gesture of goodwill:

> In view of general convention of international treatment dealt out to war prisoners and in view of the very deep discontent aroused in the public mind, which could not be easily appeased I implore apart from any question of right that every Indian under arrest of those war prisoners whether they belong to the Subhash Sainiks or outside of it should be released without any humiliating conditions as an act of grace by declaring a general amnesty. STOP. I may remind here that there is an important precedent to justify this step on the part of the British Government. STOP. At the cessation of war of 1857 when it was found that a whole nation could not be wisely sentenced or appeased the British Government declared as an act of clemency a general amnesty to all those fighters who surrendered their arms on a given day and returned to peaceful and loyal life. STOP. Thousands who were likely to be hanged under martial law were released forthwith. STOP. Several foremost British officials and historians justify this general amnesty on grounds of justice, equity and farsighted policy. STOP. Following this precedent a general amnesty now will doubtless satisfy equity, touch the heart of the people and make hundreds of homes happy and grateful.[90]

Nearly 25,000 Indian soldiers as prisoners of war who were part of the INA offensive were rounded up after the collapse of the Japanese Army in Burma. Charges of sedition and war against the emperor were slapped on them in varying degrees and a fast-track trial ordered by the British government. There were two broad categories among the soldiers—the core INA regiment made up of about 20,000 men of the Indian Army and another 23,000 civilians and the 950 regiments of Hitler's Indian Foreign Legion (HIF's) of some 3000 people. The former composed the forces that were under the leadership of Subhas Bose and formed part of the Japanese Army, while the latter were part of the German Army. The government initially categorized the soldiers into Whites (those whose loyalty was beyond question and were to be treated as POWs), Greys (who were loyal but got swayed by propaganda) and Blacks (traitors who merit trial for criminal offence and whose release would be dangerous).[91]

But as Wavell recounted:

> As soon as it became known to the public that trials were about to commence, all the main political parties, especially the Congress made the INA a prominent political issue. The Indian Press is full of articles extolling the INA as heroes. This, together with the fact that popular ministries will be set up in the Provinces by April, make it highly desirable, if not essential to dispose of the INA problem during the next six months.[92]

Official correspondences thereafter show the alarm with which Government functionaries viewed both the public sympathy for the INA trials and the political capital that parties like the Congress were trying to derive out of this with elections just round the corner. The repeated diktat from London was that the trials need to be disposed off soon and the soldiers needs to be treated with utmost leniency. Any seemingly repressive measures or stringent, large-scale punishments had the potential of an explosive mass flare up and a rebellion across India that would be tough to control. As it is, popular demonstrations had erupted across the country against the persecution of these patriots—from Calcutta to Lahore and Bombay, Lucknow to Madras and Madurai protests erupted everywhere.

But more than public protests, it was what the British feared as their worst nightmare that seemed to be fructifying. By 18 February 1946, massive mutinies broke out in the Royal Indian Navy (RIN) in Bombay. Twenty thousand sailors of the RIN serving on seventy-eight ships mutinied. Across Bombay people held processions with portraits of Netaji and 'Jai Hind' slogans and brought down the Union Jack. This was followed by rebellions in the Royal Indian Air Force and the British Indian Army units in Jabalpur. There were 2.5 million Indian soldiers in the British Indian Army, controlled by about 40,000 British overlords. If more of the former turned mutineers, it would have resulted in a tremendous catastrophe for the Empire. The fire of public anger soon spilt over in Bombay, Karachi, Madras and Calcutta. The British were anxious to redeem the situation and evict themselves out of this wreckage. Quite coincidentally, within a few weeks, a Cabinet Mission was sent to India in March 1946 to discuss the details of a transfer of power.

The relationship between the INA and Savarkar has remained shrouded in mystery in the wake of insufficient or contradictory source materials in this matter. Rash Behari Bose in a radio address had said this about Savarkar: 'In saluting you I have the joy of doing my duty towards one of my elderly comrades in-arms. In saluting you, I am saluting the symbol of sacrifice itself.'[93]

Savarkar's biographer Dhananjay Keer states rather emphatically that on 25 June 1944, Subhas Bose made a mention of Savarkar in his radio broadcast from Singapore. A reference to this address by Netaji was reported in the *Free Hindusthan* newspaper of 27 January 1946. Further, Savarkar himself referred to this address in his article on Netaji titled *'Netaji Subhas Babunchi ni Maajhi Shevati Bhet Aani Nantar.*[94]' This is what Bose is supposed to have said, according to Keer:

> When due to misguided political whims and lack of vision almost all the leaders of the Congress party are decrying all the soldiers in the Indian Army as mercenaries, it is heartening to know that Veer Savarkar is fearlessly exhorting the youth of India to enlist in the Armed Forces. These enlisted youth themselves provide us with the trained men from which we draw the soldiers of our Indian National Army.[95]

Nowhere does this address or its text appear in the 'Testament of Subhas Bose,' which was published in 1946 as a 'complete and authentic record of Netaji's Broadcast speeches, Press statements etc'.[96]

However, even if one might dismiss Keer's citation or find its sources as being suspect, some recent findings that have come to light portray a picture that is similar to possibly what Keer was trying to build a case for. Kapil Kumar, former professor at Indira Gandhi National Open University (IGNOU) stumbled upon some letters of the INA Trials and Military

Intelligence Reports. A letter in his collection, dated 31 May 1946, is from a soldier to the INA Relief Committee and is addressed to Sardar Patel:

Sir,

I am very glad to inform that the C-in-C in India has now permitted to read any newspapers prohibited since a long time . . . Sir, there are Indian soldiers who still raise their rifles against their own brothers, for example Srinagar. Simultaneously, there are men who have I.N.A. at heart and worshipping 'Netaji' as their God, and waiting for the order, who joined the Army by the advice of Barrister Savarkar in 1942. Still the same light is in the lamp . . . Awaiting such arrangements that a committee would visit all major units in India.

S/d
K.N. Rao Sirai
An Ambitious Soldier
For the present my Unit is located in Bengal area.[97]

Through his compilation of the letters of the time, Professor Kumar asserts that several of the soldiers of the INA were from Maharashtra and were seemingly inspired to join the Indian National Army through the call given by Savarkar for militarization.[98]

N.B. Khare, eminent Congressman who later joined the Hindu Mahasabha after independence, writes in his memoirs about the INA:

In this enterprise Subhash Bose took his inspiration from Sawarkar's [sic] book on Indian War of Independence of 1857. In one of his speeches Subhash Bose has freely admitted this. He also distributed copies of this book freely amongst all the army personnel. He named one of his regiments as Rani of Jhansi regiment and he borrowed the slogan *Chalo Delhi* from the Indian soldiers in Meerut who marched on Delhi from there on the 10th May of 1857.[99]

Khare further writes:

According to his policy of militarization, Veer Sawarkar [sic] was carrying on propaganda in favour of recruitment. The Congressmen called him

an unpaid recruiting agent. I was also a member of the Provincial War
Committee and I was also ridiculed by the Congress, but it was surprising
that the All India Spinners' Association, an ancillary organization of the
Congress, supplied thousands of blankets to the Indian sepoys. When
this activity of the All India Spinners' Association was criticized as help
to war efforts, Mahatma Gandhi replied that it was not helping the
War efforts, but it was only carrying on trade and business. This reply
of the Mahatma was clever but unconvincing. The Congress policy of
opposition to war efforts was also lukewarm and the British had recruited
over 20 lacs of Indian sepoys during wartime, the great majority of whom
consisted of Hindoos.[100]

~

Meanwhile, even as Gandhi refused to acknowledge the two-nation theory,
Jinnah was making a passionate case for it:

> The differences in India were far greater than those between European
> countries and were of a vital and fundamental character. Even Ireland
> provided no parallel. The Muslims had a different conception of life from
> the Hindus. They admired different qualities in their heroes; they had a
> different culture based on Arabic and Persian instead of Sanskrit origins.
> Their social customs were entirely different. Hindu society and philosophy
> were the most exclusive in the world. Muslims and Hindus had been
> living side by side in India for a thousand years, but if one went into any
> Indian city one would see separate Hindu and Muslim quarters. It was
> not possible to make a nation unless there were essential uniting factors.
> How would His Majesty's Government put 100 millions of Muslims
> together with 250 millions whose whole way of life was so different? No
> government could survive unless there was a dominant element, which
> could provide a 'steel frame.' This frame had hitherto been provided by
> the British, who had always retained the key posts in the Civil Service,
> the Police and the Army . . . there were in India two totally different and
> deeply rooted civilizations side by side and the only solution was to have
> two 'steel frames,' one in Hindustan and one in Pakistan.[101]

The League passed a resolution in April demanding the sovereign state
of Pakistan comprising the six provinces of Bengal and Assam in the east,

Punjab, the NWFP, Sind and Baluchistan in the West with two separate constitution-making bodies. These terms were non-negotiable for the League and any attempt to impose a constitution or an interim government was to be rejected and resisted with all the force at their command. Lengthy communications took place between the Cabinet Mission and the Congress and League representatives. Squabbles continued even for the formation of the interim government. The viceroy finally issued his own list of a fourteen-member Executive Council on 16 June 1946 that included six from the Congress, five of the Muslim League, one Sikh, one Indian Christian and one Parsi. Nehru and Jinnah were to be part of the interim government. Wavell went out of his way to placate every whim of Jinnah. A plan known as the 'State Paper of May 16' was worked out that repudiated Jinnah's claims for division, contemplated a Central Union/Federation with powers restricted to external affairs, defence and communications and full autonomy to provinces. A constituent assembly was to be elected by the provincial legislatures to frame the constitution of the Indian state and an interim government to be sworn in with representatives from all communities and groups.

But at this critical juncture, Nehru's conduct ruined any last hopes of peaceful settlement. As historian R.C. Majumdar notes:

> Unfortunately at this critical moment, when a peaceful settlement of India's future was almost within sight, it was upset by some indiscreet utterances of Pandit Jawaharlal Nehru. In 1937, his outright rejection of Jinnah's offer of Congress-League Coalition Ministry ruined the last chance of a Hindu-Muslim agreement. His observations in 1946 destroyed the last chance—though a remote one—of a united India.[102]

At a press conference too on 10 July, Nehru qualified his views as the new Congress president in a manner that naturally scared Jinnah away. Nehru admitted that the Congress was bound by the procedure set down for election of members to the Constituent Assembly. But what the Congress would do once it got into the Assembly was entirely its wish and it was not bound by any directives of the agreed 'State Paper' of May 16.

As Leonard Mosley states:

> Did Nehru realize what he was saying? He was telling the world that once in power, the Congress would use its strength at the Centre to alter

the Cabinet Mission Plan as it thought fit. But the Muslim League (as had Congress) had accepted the plan as a cut and dried scheme to meet objections from both sides. It was a compromise plan, which obviously could not afterwards be altered in favour of one side or another. In the circumstances, Nehru's remarks were a direct act of sabotage. Whether he meant them to be so, in the mistaken belief that Jinnah and the Muslim League were not really a force to be reckoned with or whether they were the ham-handed remarks of a politician who did not know when to keep his mouth shut will never be known.[103]

There was unequivocal condemnation of Nehru's intemperate remarks even from within the Congress. But Jinnah had simply had enough. The League decided to resort to 'Direct Action' for the attainment of Pakistan in end-July. In many League-ruled provinces this was interpreted as an all-out war to snatch Pakistan. Particularly in the unfortunate province of Bengal under its premier Huseyn Shaheed Suhrawardy an organized mass loot, arson and indiscriminate genocide of the Hindus was conducted, even as the governor and the Central government sat watching helplessly. In retaliation, in the absence of any government support to maintain law and order, the Hindus too resorted to violence leading to the ugly spectre of a civil war. Mosley notes that 'between dawn on the morning of 16 August 1946 and dusk three days later, the people of Calcutta hacked, battered, burned, stabbed or shot 6000 of each other to death, and raped and maimed another 20,000'.[104]

Even as Calcutta and the rest of the Bengal burned, Nehru was busy negotiating terms with the viceroy on the formation of the interim government, now solely comprised of the Congress, as the League had refused to be a part of it. Nehru, Sardar Patel, Rajendra Prasad, Asaf Ali, Rajagopalachari, Sarat Chandra Bose, John Mathai, Sardar Baldev Singh, Sir Shafaat Ahmed Khan, Jagjivan Ram, Syed Ali Zaheer and Covesji Hormusji Bhabha were named as part of this government on 24 August. It took a lot of convincing on the part of Wavell to get the Congress and League to dine at the same table and finally on 14 October, the League sent its nominees Liaquat Ali Khan, I.I. Chundrigar, Abdur Rab Nishtar, Ghazanfar Ali Khan and Jogendra Nath Mandal to be a part of the interim government. The government though remained ineffectual as both blocs were deeply suspicious of each other and completely non-cooperative.

Large-scale communal violence and riots erupted in the Noakhali and Tipperah districts of East Bengal, many of these engineered by the League. Two of the League's representatives in the interim government made openly belligerent speeches that the events in East Bengal were part of the all-India battle for creation of Pakistan.[105] This was followed by Hindu reprisals in Chapra, Ahmednagar and Ahmedabad. The Bihar violence was especially ghastly and subsided with Gandhi's threat to go on a fast unto death and by very heavy governmental force at Congress's behest, unlike the League ministry of Bengal that let the Bengal carnage go on. Citing all these incidents and several other excuses, Jinnah conveniently rescinded on his promise to be a part of the new Constituent Assembly that was to meet in December 1946. The viceroy's negotiations with Jinnah made him particularly irate, concluding that the British were keen on subjugating the Muslims to a Hindu rule gradually by asking him to be a part of the Constituent Assembly where the Congress had an upper hand and that he would have to negotiate for their rights. If the British were leaving India, they better leave at once or do so by awarding a constitution, he opined. The British 'should give the Muslims their bit of country however small it might be, and they would live there, if necessary on one meal a day!',[106] he added. When the viceroy disregarded these objections and sent invitations to members, including those of the League, to the Constituent Assembly meetings, the League members even threatened to resign from the Interim Government, though they had put no such precondition to joining the government in the first place. The stalemate did not end even after Nehru, Jinnah, Baldev Singh and Liaquat Khan conducted parleys in London, with the viceroy joining them there.

To push all parties towards conciliation, Prime Minister Attlee decided to hold out a deadline for the transfer of power to India. With the looming threat of the interim government breaking apart, and large-scale communal riots and civil war, with the army on the tenterhooks fearing an uprising, he announced in the House of Commons on 20 February 1947: 'The present state of uncertainty is fraught with danger and cannot be indefinitely prolonged. His Majesty's Government wish [sic] to make it clear that it is their definite intention to take necessary steps to effect the transference of power to responsible Indian hands by a date not later than June, 1948'.[107] To decide the delicate task of 'whom the powers of the Central Government of British India should be handed over . . . in the best interests of the people',[108] Mountbatten was appointed as a successor to Wavell from March 1947. Interestingly, before his departure for India, Mountbatten called on Churchill. He recounts this meeting and Churchill's parting advice to him: 'I'm sorry that you should perform this grievous duty . . . I'm not going to tell you how to do it, but I'll tell you one thing—whatever arrangements you may make, you must see that you don't harm a hair on the head of a single Muslim.' To this Mountbatten replied: 'I've no wish to harm the hair on anybody's head. The Muslims are very largely my army companions. Of course, I won't!' Churchill added: 'Yes, but they're the people who have been our friends, and they're the people the Hindus are now going to oppress, so you must take steps that they can't do it.'[109] This underscored the strategic importance that the Muslims had for the British, especially in their army and hence the counter to arm oneself and militarize the Hindus, as advocated by Savarkar and the Mahasabha, was all the more germane.

While this new deadline for transfer of power helped accelerate the political deadlock, it created an upheaval on the ground leading to another orgy of communal riots, this time in the Punjab and NWFP. As per official estimates, 2049 people were killed and over 1000 seriously injured in just a fortnight. Visiting Rawalpindi, Nehru reported: 'I have seen ghastly sights and I have heard of behaviour by human beings, which would degrade brutes.'[110] Mountbatten's Press attaché, visiting Rawalpindi, noted that the destruction of Hindu and Sikh quarters was 'as thorough as any produced by fire bomb raids in the war . . . the Muslims of the area were quite pleased with themselves'.[111] Some of the statements that Gandhi made during this time, as the country was ablaze in communal flame, annoyed several Hindu leaders including Savarkar. In a speech at a prayer meeting on 6 April 1947, Gandhi said:

> We should dispassionately think where we are drifting. Hindus should not harbour anger in their hearts against Muslims even if the latter wanted to destroy them. Even if the Muslims want to kill us all we should face death bravely. If they established their rule after killing Hindus we would be ushering in a new world by sacrificing our lives. None should fear death. Birth and death are inevitable for every human being. Why should we then rejoice or grieve? If we die with a smile we shall enter into a new life, we shall be ushering in a new India.[112]

Meanwhile, the Congress Working Committee in its resolution of 8 March 1947 recommended the division of Punjab into the Muslim and non-Muslim portions, given the horrific scenes of violence there. If violence were to be the criteria for division, the same formula would obviously be asked for resolving the issue in Bengal too.

The resolution was a clear precursor to what was to follow—a partition of India on communal grounds, which Mountbatten had to effect. Sardar Vallabhbhai Patel was convinced that Partition was now inevitable as 'whether we liked it or not, there were two nations in India . . . Hindus and Muslims could not be united into one nation . . . if two brothers cannot stay together, they divide . . . it was better to have one clean fight and then separate than have bickerings every day'[113]. Nehru came around to the same point of view too. Gandhi, while still making statements of Partition happening only over his dead body, quietly acquiesced and that alarmed many as to why he did not stick to his guns and force a fast unto death that he had earlier done for several smaller issues. Nehru himself admitted later that he and the Congress would have been adamant against Partition if Gandhi had strictly prevailed upon them.[114] As historian R.C. Majumdar rationalizes: 'Gandhi at last realized that he had been leaning throughout on the two broken reeds of Hindu-Muslim unity and mass non-violence—and that these were nothing but the will-o'-wasp which he had been pursuing throughout his political career.'[115] Elaborating on the inevitability of a vivisection, given the historical differences between the communities, the series of political developments related to communal politics and the flip-flop statements of the Congress leaders, in particular, Majumdar sums up:

This was emphasized by the separate electorate, originally devised by Minto, but later accepted by the Congress. Since then, the Congress had, in practice if not in theory, recognized the two-nation theory propounded by Syed Ahmed in the 19th Century and Jinnah in the 20th. As far back as 1934 the Congress pledged itself to reject any scheme of solving communal problem vis-à-vis Indian constitution, which was not agreed to by the Muslims. In 1942, Gandhi wrote in the *Harijan* that if the vast majority of Muslims want to partition India they must have the partition; and in 1944 he actually carried on negotiations with Jinnah on this basis. In 1945 the Congress Working Committee passed a resolution that it could not think 'of compelling the people in any territorial unit to remain in an Indian Union against their declared and establish will.' The eminent Hindu leader Rajagopalachari actually suggested the idea of

Pakistan as the only basis for a peaceful settlement of the Hindu-Muslim
problem and even Nehru conceded the possibility of Pakistan in January
1946. Early in March 1947, the Working Committee of the Congress
itself suggested the partition of the Panjab (and therefore also of)
Bengal, on communal basis.[116]

The arguments that Mountbatten put in favour of Partition were that the
alternative would be a weak Central government with Muslim-majority
provinces that could be up in rebellion and carnage ever so often, as was
witnessed. The option to give up some land on both sides of the country
and have the rest of India consolidate under a strong constitutional
framework and a Central government was infinitely more practical and
viable, according to him. This could possibly have been the dose of realism
that none could ignore. Mountbatten did have a tough time, like his
predecessors, convincing Jinnah for any rational agreement. In exasperation
he notes: 'I regard Jinnah as a psychopathic case; in fact until I had met
him I would not have thought it possible that a man with such a complete
lack of administrative knowledge or sense of responsibility could achieve or
hold down so powerful a position.'[117]

Savarkar who had been completely detached from the political
scenario—both by his own personal health being in shambles and the
increasing irrelevance of the Hindu Mahasabha after the post-war election
rout—did put out statements around this time denouncing the attempts to
partition India. But these were too little, too late and also held no practical
solutions to a problem that had now attained gangrenous proportions and
needed a surgery. Denouncement, without a solution, especially in the
wake of the communal carnages that India had witnessed in such a short
span of time, was well-intended bluster. However, a proposal with some
semblance of practical and actionable steps, was issued by him on 2 April
1947, when he announced:

To frustrate the vivisection of our Akhand Hindusthan, we must first
vivisect their Pakistan. To this end, three immediate steps are imperative.
The first, the creation of a Hindu province in West Bengal, the second
the expulsion of Moslem trespassers from Assam at any cost, so as to
sandwich and smother the Eastern Pakistan between the two Hindu
provinces, the third, the creation of a Hindu-Sikh Province in East Punjab
and to rejoin the contiguous Hindu districts in Sindh to the Bombay

Presidency. Thus about ten large Hindu provinces will get consolidated into a strongly centralized government of Akhand Hindusthan and will enable it all the more effectively to re-annex the revolting Pakistani areas too in near future. But all this or any other jugglery will pale to help Hindudom if we do not emphatically declare and manfully act up to the rule that the Moslem minority in Hindu provinces be given the same treatment as is meted out to the Hindu minority in Moslem provinces. The very fact that Jinnahji, Gandhiji and his Shahid Sahib are perceptibly irritated by these proposals does in itself prove that they are most likely to benefit Hindudom and undermine Moslem designs. Consequently intense agitation and action should be resorted to by us forthwith to effect it all.[118]

Savarkar feared that Assam, tagged so close to the eastern frontier of Pakistan, might fall prey to aggression. Towards end-April 1947, he wrote to the chief minister of Assam, Gopinath Bordolai, and Vishnudas, the revenue minister, to not surrender a single inch of land and eject every Muslim trespasser from the soil of Assam. Both of them acknowledged his telegram and assured him of appropriate action.

But with the rank and file of the Mahasabha in near disarray and disillusionment, and given their own track record of promising effective direct action and never living up to it, the call of Savarkar to 'intense agitation and action' too seemed a bleak possibility. Savarkar and several other Hindu political ideologues fancied the idea that Pakistan, even if created, would be such a weak state that it was just a matter of time before it could be re-annexed and made a part of united and undivided India. This idea comes through in Savarkar's telegram, dated 4 June 1947, to his loyalist L.B. Bhopatkar, who had taken over as the President of the Mahasabha, on the eve of the meetings of the Working Committee and All-India Committee that were to be held in New Delhi, on 6, 7 and 8 June 1947.

My personal view is that we must vigorously protest against the creation of a Moslem State independent of the Central Indian State. We will not sign willingly the death warrant of the integrity of Hindusthan. If Britain thrusts Pakistan on us per force, that is another matter. We will in spite of it continue our struggle to re-annex these revolting Moslem provinces. Secondly, to register our protest against Pakistan, a Black Day should be

observed throughout India on a convenient date. Thirdly, Pakistan or
no Pakistan, three Hindu Majority provinces must be framed in Bengal,
Punjab and Sind in the interest of Akhand Hindusthan itself. Like the
district of Sylhet, the four Hindu majority districts in Sind must be
allowed to decide their own separate voting to join Hindusthan. Fourthly,
the Congressite Ministry must be called upon not to accept Pakistan and
betray the Hindu electorate even if they cannot prevent Britain from
thrusting it per force on us. Long Live Akhand Hindusthan![119]

Interestingly, sections of the Congress too shared this view of a collapse
of Pakistan as being inevitable. Mountbatten had taken the proposals to
London and returned with what was called a 'June 3 plan' finalizing the
terms of the division of the subcontinent. Though, not veering towards
Savarkar's prophecy or desire of an armed re-annexation, sections in
the Congress believed that the economic and political unviability of the
Pakistan scheme would prove to be its eventual nemesis. The Congress
Working Committee resolution of 14–15 June 1947 conceded its failure to
maintain the unity of the country to achieve the goal of freedom. However,
Maulana Azad who seconded the resolution felt that 'the Partition
would be short-lived and the seceding parts of India, would in the very
near future, hurry back to the Indian Union'.[120] Tempers ran high and
several leaders castigated the leadership for an abject surrender to Jinnah's
whims. Several leaders especially from the Sind were angry about how the
leadership had literally thrown the Hindus of the region to the wolves
and no concrete thoughts had been spared on the plight or protection of
the religious minorities, the Hindus and Sikhs in the proposed Pakistan.
They were vaguely assuaged that 'the Hindus in Pakistan need have no
fear as there would be 45 millions of Muslims in India and if there was any
oppression of Hindus in Pakistan, the Muslims in India would have to bear
the consequences'.[121] These were empty promises in private to dissenting
intra-party voices. Finally, it was left to Gandhi to make a lengthy forty-
minute speech urging all dissenters to accept the Partition proposal as there
was no other feasible alternative.

The Hindu Mahasabha Working Committee resolved that India was
one and indivisible and that there 'will never be peace unless and until the
separated areas are brought back into the Indian Union and made integral
parts thereof'.[122] Savarkar gave a call for observing 3 July as a 'Black Day'
and a day of protest. In a message he asked the Hindus to not despair, as

'a glorious future awaits the Hindus—if only they do not betray themselves!'[123] To the Muslims who had voted for the new country of Pakistan, he held out 'the fate which overtook them when they had succeeded in converting the whole of Hindusthan into an actual and factual Pakistan led by the might of an Aurangzeb cannot but overwhelm the puny Pakistan of today led by Mr. Jinnah! If they still want to try again let them try to do their worst'.[124] But the die had been cast long ago for the situation to change at this point of time.

With much trepidation, Mountbatten also met Gandhi separately—as 'he never comes with the Congress leaders'. The viceroy was apprehensive that Gandhi was suddenly 'carrying out an intense propaganda against the new plan', though it was he who got 'Congress to turn down the Cabinet Mission plan on the country'. He notes that Gandhi 'may be a saint but he seems also to be a disciple of Trotsky. I gather that the meetings of the Congress Working Committee have been most acrimonious in consequence, and I believe the leaders were quite apprehensive of my seeing Gandhi . . . I certainly was. Judge then of my astonished delight on finding him enter my room with his finger to his lips to indicate it was his day of silence.'[125]

~

The Indian Independence Bill was introduced in the House of Commons on 4 July 1947, passed without amendments on 15 July and received royal assent on 18 July. Dominion status was to be granted to two independent units, India and Pakistan, from 15 August 1947. Sind, British Baluchistan, NWFP, West Punjab and East Bengal comprised the new unit called Pakistan. For each dominion, there was to be a Governor General who was to be appointed by the British emperor to govern the dominion. The legislatures of the dominions would have full powers to make laws for their respective units, the jurisdiction of the British Parliament would cease to exist and the Constituent Assembly in each unit would work towards making the statutes for themselves. Mountbatten became the first Governor General of the Indian unit and Jinnah of Pakistan. Mountbatten launched his 'Operation Princes' on 25 July 1947 to begin discussions with the multitude of Indian princes of the various princely states, with all their gigantic egos in tow, to convince them to integrate into the Indian Union and the terms for this merger. Here, Savarkar's ill-advised support to the dewan of Travancore, Sir C.P. Ramaswamy Iyer, who was planning to declare autonomy and independence of the Hindu princely state was unfortunate and detrimental to the integration process of the new Indian Union.

On 7 July, Savarkar sent a telegram to Ambedkar, Rajendra Prasad, Sardar Patel and N.B. Khare, expressing his views on how the flag of free India ought to be. 'The standard of Hindusthan must be,' he said 'Bhagwa—Ochre coloured. At any rate, no flag, which does not bear at least a stripe of Bhagwa colour can be recognized by the Hindus as a standard they can respect. The Charkha too must be replaced by a Chakra wheel or any other such symbol signifying progress and strength.'[126]

The Constituent Assembly was in fact deliberating among other things, the new flag of free India at that time. They had indeed reached a consensus to replace the spinning wheel of Gandhi with the Chakra, which was called as that of Emperor Ashoka. Savarkar clarified this too through a public statement on 29 July that the wheel was not a creation of Ashoka. According to him, it was a 'Dharma Chakra' that had been set in motion during Buddha's first sermon in Sarnath that later Ashoka adopted and it symbolized the valour of people like Chandragupta Maurya and Chanakya who drove foreign invaders away. But even after this, he struck an oddly strident and bitter note against the new tricolour:

> Having thus noted impartially the good points in the new Flag adopted for the Indian Union, which render it much less objectionable, I must emphatically state it can never be recognized as the National Flag of Hindusthan. Firstly, because the state of Indian Union and the so-called Constituent Assembly are the creation of the British will and not of the free choice of our people ascertained by a national plebiscite and their ultimate sanction even today is the British bayonet and not the national consent or national strength. Secondly, the very mention of the Indian Union reminds us of the break-up of the Unity of India as a nation and a state, the vivisection of our Motherland, and the treacherous Congressite abetment of that crime. How can a genuine nationalist salute such a Flag adopted by such a party with no mandate from the nation as a national flag. No! The authoritative Flag of Hindusthan, our Motherland and Holyland, undivided and indivisible from the Indus to the Seas, can be no other than the Bhagva with the Kundalini and the Kripan inscribed on it to deliver expressly the message of the very Being of our Race! It is not made to order but it is self-evolved with the evolution of our National Being. It mirrors the whole panorama of our Hindu History, is actually

worshipped by millions on millions of Hindus and is already flying from
the summits of the Himalayas to the Southern Seas. Other Party Flags
will be tolerated, some may even be respected in corresponding courtesy
but Hindudom at any rate can loyally salute no other Flag but this pan-
Hindu Dhwaja, this Bhagva flag as its national standard.[127]

Interestingly, Savarkar had company in his sense of disapproval of the new
national flag in his ideological opponent Gandhi. At a speech in a prayer
meeting on 19 July 1947, Gandhi felt it would be good to have the British
Union Jack too in a corner of the new Indian flag.

> If harm has been done to us by the British, it has not been done by their
> flag and we must also take note of the virtues of the British. They are
> voluntarily withdrawing from India, leaving power in our hands . . . we
> are having Lord Mountbatten as our chief gate-keeper. So long he has
> been the servant of the British king. Now he is to be our servant. If while
> we employed him as our servant we also had the Union Jack in a corner
> of our flag, there would be no betrayal of India in this . . . It pains me
> that the Congress leaders could not show this generosity. We would have
> thereby shown our friendship for the British. If I had the power that
> I once had I would have taken the people to task for it. After all, why
> should we give up our humanity.[128]

Gandhi was not too happy with the trademark charkha symbol being
removed from the flag. Talking to Congress workers in Lahore on 6
August 1947, he said:

> I must say that if the flag of the Indian Union will not contain the
> emblem of the charkha I will refuse to salute that flag. You know the
> National Flag of India was first thought of by me and I cannot conceive
> of India's National Flag without the emblem of the charkha. We have,
> however, been told by Pandit Nehru and others that the sign of wheel or
> the chakra in the new National Flag symbolizes the charkha also. Some
> describe the wheel-mark as Sudarshan Chakra.[129]

But he eventually made peace with it.

~

Savarkar visited Poona from 1 to 3 August to attend the Maharashtra Political Conference and demand for a united Maharashtra. From there he went to Delhi to attend the Working Committee meeting of the Hindu Mahasabha on 9 August where it was resolved that in the wake of the inhuman tortures and migration woes, murders, rapes and mayhem that the minorities, especially the Hindus, were facing in the new unit of Pakistan, the Mahasabha found it meaningless to participate in any celebratory events around independence on 15 August.

Speaking at the All-India Hindu Conference in Alwar on 9 August, Savarkar said:

> Pandit Nehru says that they accepted Pakistan to avoid bloodshed. But this is wrong. This will not help to avoid bloodshed. On the contrary, they will again use threats of bloodshed in order to press their additional demands. If you do not stop them, there would come about 14 Pakistans. They will demand Mayostan near Alwar, in the South they will demand Moplastan in Kerala and in Hyderabad they will demand Nizamistan. Their demands will have to be crushed by the policy of reciprocity. For that purpose, the Hindus irrespective of political party must unite and consolidate their strength.[130]

Meanwhile, the red-letter day in the annals of Indian history finally arrived when, on the night of 14 August, the Constituent Assembly, presided over by Rajendra Prasad, met and India obtained her Dominion status starting 15 August, after British subjugation for nearly two centuries. Mountbatten was sworn in as the new Governor General and administered oath to the new prime minister, Jawaharlal Nehru, and his Cabinet. It was a freedom that was born amidst untold human sufferings, strife, anarchy and cold-blooded murders, especially on the frontier provinces on the west and east bordering Pakistan.

Despite his earlier dissonant view on the tricolour, Savarkar decided to acknowledge and respect the national flag once it was adopted formally. Quite ironically, despite his contribution to the freedom movement since his revolutionary days, Savarkar was not even invited to the independence-day celebrations, either in Delhi or in Bombay. In Bombay, the flag was being officially hoisted within half a kilometer of his house. Undeterred, he decided to commemorate the occasion himself. Hence on 15 August atop his house in Bombay, he hoisted both the new national tricolour, as also the bhagwa flag that represented the unfinished Hindu dream of a unified and undivided India. This caused a lot of discontent among several of his adherents in the Hindu Sangathan movement who found him to be wavering from the cause. Their apprehensions were further raised when Savarkar gave his consent to his erstwhile protégé Syama Prasad Mookerjee to join the Nehru government as a nominee from Bengal. The government was a provisional government principally tasked with the creation of a Constitution, leading up to the first general election towards a popular franchise. It had to be comprised of diverse viewpoints and political opinions. Given Mookerjee's standing as a legislator and administrator par excellence in his stint in the Bengal government, and his affability with the Congress, he was the natural choice to represent a Hindu Mahasabha opinion within the government and the Constituent Assembly. Mookerjee was to become the industry and supply minister in the new government. In the spirit of cooperation with the Central government, Savarkar gave his blessings to Mookerjee to join the Cabinet.

As the celebrations gradually subsided and the actual work of drawing borders with the Border Commission got under way under the chairmanship Sir Cyril Radcliffe, notifying the Partition of Bengal and Punjab and the separation of Sylhet from Assam, bedlam broke out. Communal frenzy gripped people on both sides of the border as an unplanned population migration was set in motion. Both India and Pakistan did sign a declaration on 20 July on Mountbatten's behest that the rights of minorities would be respected. But the haste with which the entire transfer of power and the mass migration of people across borders was executed unleashed a mayhem of communal violence and murders. '6,00,000 dead, 14,000,000 driven from their homes, 1,00,000 young girls kidnapped by both sides, forcibly converted or sold on the auction block,' said an official report of the times.[131] Inconsolable refugees, persecuted minorities from Pakistan, thronged most frontier provinces and the capital city of Delhi, crying for help and rehabilitation.

Standing up for the rights of the Hindu–Sikh community, Savarkar issued a statement on 25 September 1947 denouncing the Nehru government for its inability to protect their lives and property. He questioned Nehru's diktat that the people should not take law into their hands, at a time when thousands and thousands of Hindus and Sikhs were 'faced by an imminent danger of being massacred in cold blood, looted, burnt alive, forcibly converted, in short, of being exterminated as a racial and National

Being by the most barbarous attacks of an organized, dangerously armed and fanatically hostile foe'.[132] Defending themselves, their lives, property and faith became more important for the refugees, especially when the state and its police and armed forces were nowhere in sight to stand up for them or protect them. He warned the Indian government against the slogans that were being raised such as '*Haske liya hai Pakistan, Maarke lenge Hindustan*'[133] (We have effortlessly taken Pakistan, we will kill and usurp India) and urged the government to wake up to the danger that was real and staring them in the face. When Hindu Sangathanist forces had warned of these dangers that lay ahead and contended that it was no time for celebration as we were 'stranded on the top of a volcano already in eruption',[134] they were denounced as anti-nationals and traitors. But now these very prophecies were coming true, he rued. Savarkar opined that this was a civilizational and cultural war to alter the core of Hindustan by a determined and aggressive force and warned of repeated and concerted attacks for which the new state of Pakistan was readying itself by militarily arming itself. Muslim-majority states within India, be they Hyderabad, Kashmir, Junagarh, etc., would rise in open revolt against the Indian state, in aid of the invading armies were it to so happen, he feared. To ensure the safety, life and property of the Hindu–Sikh and other minorities in Pakistan, the Government of India must make it very clear that Muslims in India 'shall receive the same treatment for better or for worse in kind and in scale that the Hindu-Sikh minority receives at the hands of the Moslem Government, in all respects such as representation, services and even rights of citizenship'.[135]

Savarkar took on Nehru's repeated attacks on the Hindu Sangathanist leadership. Reacting to one of Nehru's assertion that any attempt by Hindu Sangathanist leaders to establish a Hindu Rashtra in India would meet the same fate that Hitler and Mussolini met in Europe, Savarkar denounced his threats through a statement on 22 October 1947.

As if the mere demand for a Hindu Raj constitutes a danger to his Government so much more imminent, impending, incalculably disastrous as to call for his immediate attention than the already established Moslem Raj in Pakistan where fanatical atrocities, arson, bloodshed and butchery have been the order of the day . . . Pusillanimous enough to tolerate these diabolical actions and threats on the part of the Moslems against his 'Indian Union' Pandit Nehru and his pseudo-nationalistic section in the

Congress are delivering mock heroics against the Hindus and swearing that they will fight tooth and nail against those who demand a Hindu Raj.[136]

He bitterly questioned the anathema that the Congress, and in particular Nehru, had with any reference to the 'Hindu-ness' of India or it being called Hindustan too, but willingly accepted, recognized and saluted a Pakistan that was explicitly theocratic even as many non-Muslim minorities tried to live within that country. Was it not the League of Nations prescription that all states and nations were to be called after the predominant majority community that lived there, he asked. 'How is it then,' questioned Savarkar, 'that the very mention of the name Hindustan or the Hindu State alone takes your breath away as if you were smitten by a snake bite?'[137] According to him, the choice for the country and especially its Hindu population was 'not between two sets of personalities, but between two ideologies, not Indian Raj or Hindu Raj but Moslem Raj or Hindu Raj; Akhand Hindustan or Akhand Pakistan.'[138]

Quite coincidentally, on the very day that Savarkar issued this statement, Pakistani tribesmen began their invasion of Kashmir to merge the state into their country. The Indian government and its leaders, Nehru and Patel in particular, decided to withhold the payment of Rs 550 million to Pakistan that was decided as per the Partition agreement, as a condition for withdrawal from Kashmir and also not to use this money to buy arms against India in this skirmish. While Mountbatten termed this as a dishonourable act of the Indian Union, Gandhi began a fast unto death to coerce the government to stick to its commitments to Pakistan. In deference to his wishes, realpolitik was given a go-by and Pakistan was paid the promised amount, as also pledges made to the Muslim minorities in India, particularly in Delhi.

Even as 1947, the most momentous and at the same time a bloody year in the annals of India's history drew to a close, the new year was to usher in more tumult and strife. And it was to change Savarkar's life and legacy too, almost forever.

9

Murder, Mayhem, Madness

30 January 1948, Birla House, New Delhi

There were two pressing concerns on Gandhi's mind on the morning of 30 January 1948. He had just succeeded in convincing Nehru's government to make good its promise of transferring Rs 55 crore to Pakistan, irrespective of whether that country was engineering armed incursions into India's northern-most province of Kashmir. On 12 January, Gandhi had taken recourse to the route that he knew would almost never fail, even with the inimical colonial government, what to speak of one led by his own trusted acolyte—that of a fast unto death. The results were predictably successful. A veneer of Hindu–Muslim unity and a temporary extinguishing of the communal fires that had set the capital city ablaze had been achieved. With 'Mission Delhi' accomplished, Gandhi was now readying to move to other parts of India and possibly even Pakistan to quell the horrendous fires that the bloody Partition had brought in its wake.

However, there were tasks that he had left undone. One of them was the status of the party that he had led and also held complete control over in the long road to freedom—the Indian National Congress. The political skirmishes and the power struggles within the organization, in the run-up to government formation had given an impression that the entire struggle for seeking freedom was motivated by the spoils of victory, of personal gains and the greed for power. To remove such apprehensions from the minds of people, Gandhi was to deliberate that day on his plan to disband the party altogether, which according to him had outlived its purpose. He wanted the Congress to withdraw from active politics and allow itself to metamorphose into a voluntary non-governmental organization that served the people.

The other pressing concern was the growing feud between his two trusted lieutenants who held the top two positions in the nascent government—Prime Minister Nehru and Deputy Prime Minister and Home Minister Sardar Vallabhbhai Patel. In the wake of growing differences between the two men, Patel had volunteered to relieve himself from the duties of government rather than play second fiddle to a man he did not agree with on several issues of national concern. There were rumours that the Mahakaushal Provincial Hindu Sabha was making overtures to Patel through Ravishankar Shukla, the first chief minister of Central Provinces and his home minister Dwarka Prasad Mishra. In a letter dated 12 January 1948, Ramakrishna Pandey of the Mahakaushal Provincial Hindu Sabha informed Savarkar of his meeting Shukla and Mishra at Sagar two days ago and their earnest desire to convene a meeting between Savarkar and Patel to chalk out "future course of action of the Hindu Mahasabha.[1]" There was obviously some simmering tension in the central government that had made Patel so restive. He had expressed his desire to quit the Government to Gandhi, who had called him over for a meeting with him on the afternoon of 30 January, just before his evening public prayers. Patel came in at 4 p.m. with his daughter Maniben and stayed closeted with the Mahatma for about an hour. Patel was told that he was indispensable to the government and it was not possible to pull on without either of them—Nehru and him. Gandhi had assured him of resolving the issue the following day and having a tripartite meet to sort out matters further.

A little before 5 p.m., Gandhi's two teenaged grandnieces, Manu and Abha, came in to remind him about the prayer meet. They had unsuccessfully tried to catch his attention by noisily arranging his evening meals of cooked vegetables, twelve ounces of goat's milk, carrot juice and a decoction of ginger, lime and aloe. But the political discussion was too intense to disturb the men. Finally, Abha mustered the courage to interrupt them and lead her granduncle to his daily prayers, which he would be deeply angry with himself if he skipped or got late for. Always a stickler for time and discipline, Gandhi consulted the big watch that dangled from his waist, bid Patel farewell and got ready to leave. Manu carried his spittoon and rosary. Resting himself lightly on their shoulders, Gandhi steadily made way to the open lawns by about ten past five, where nearly 200 to 300 people had gathered, as always, for the evening prayers. These usually included recitations from the holy books of all religions, sometimes a short speech by Gandhi and concluded with his favourite bhajans or devotional songs. Walking briskly across the lawn, Gandhi climbed the five shallow semicircular steps that led to the raised portion of the lawn where the audience waited for him anxiously and greeted him enthusiastically on catching sight of his visage.[2] He folded his hands and greeted them with a wide, toothy smile.

Three men among the crowd waited for Gandhi's arrival much more anxiously than any of the others who had gathered there. One of them wore a grey militia-cloth shirt that had deep pockets and shoulder flaps and a khaki forage cap, quite like what a foot soldier of some military regiment of the times might have dressed up as. He kept checking on the prized possession in his shirt pocket and exchanged glances at the two other men who stood at a close distance from him, swathed in grey shawls. The young man in the militia shirt moved forward and came directly in Gandhi's path with a reverential salute saying 'Namaste!' to him. Manu tried to fob him off as Gandhi was already late for the prayers and if he got into lengthy conversations with visitors, as he normally did, it would delay him further. But even before she could complete, the young man pushed her aside, causing her to slip and tumble, and the spittoon and rosary that she carried fell on the ground. Even as Manu barely gathered herself to get up, she saw the man whip out a snub-nosed automatic pistol that he had concealed in his pocket and shot at Gandhi at point-blank range repeatedly. Gurbachan Singh, a Sikh businessman and a Gandhi devotee, who was a few steps behind him, recollected that Gandhi fell to the ground with the words 'Hey Ram!' The young man and his associates however recalled later in court that Gandhi gasped an 'Aaah!' and fell. The assassin held on to his weapon tightly and yelled, 'Police! Police.' He did not want anyone to think this was anything other than a deliberate and premeditated exercise, not one that was acted upon in a fit of passion and that he had no intention of running away or giving up his pistol. For a minute and a half or so, the entire crowd had gone comatose and was shocked out of its wits to say or do anything. A man in an air force uniform then sprung on him, caught his wrist and made him release his weapon. When asked his name, he announced nonchalantly: 'Nathuram Vinayak Godse!'

The Conspirators

Nathuram, the young man who brought Gandhi down on that fateful evening in January 1948, was born in a small village in Maharashtra called Uksan in an orthodox Brahmin family on 19 May 1910. His father Vinayak Godse was a junior employee in the postal department. His wife and he had a string of male children who died in infancy, even as their only daughter miraculously survived. This made them believe in an inexplicable curse that sons born in the family faced. To hoodwink the curse and its progenitor, they came up with an ingenious method. When they had their next son, they decided to bring him up in stealth, almost like a girl. This, they believed, would save his life. So the little boy named Ramchandra, had his nose pierced with a ring or *nath* as it was called in Marathi, earning him the sobriquet of 'Nathuram' from family and friends. That name stuck. Crossing this 'Rubicon' with the curse proved propitious for the Godse family. Three sons who followed Nathuram and another daughter survived—making it a large family of six children. As a child, Nathuram was believed to have miraculous psychic powers of channelling the energies of his family goddess and solving problems or answering existential questions of near and dear ones. He grew up to be a young lad who was fond of physical exercise and swimming, and was the characteristic do-gooder of the neighbourhood. But being rather dull in academics and particularly weak in English, he failed to pass the matriculation examinations. Taken in, ironically, by Gandhi's call for non-cooperation with the Raj, the idea of joining a government service, even at the junior levels, was anathema to him. So he toyed along with odd jobs of carpentry, tailoring and selling fruits to assist his impoverished father support their large family.

But his life and its course were to change forever when as a nineteen-year-old he visited Ratnagiri, in 1929. The family was making a visit to the sleepy coastal town and decided to also take a darshan of the great revolutionary leader who had been lodged there in conditional captivity, Veer Savarkar. The little time he spent with the man was enough for Nathuram to come completely under Savarkar's spell. His joy knew no bounds when after a few months Savarkar asked him to serve him as a secretary. From then on, his mentor and his political philosophy meant everything for Nathuram. Under Savarkar's tutelage, he learnt English and the craft of writing well, particularly political commentaries. Nathuram became an enthusiastic participant in all of Savarkar's political and social projects be it social reforms, untouchability eradication, inter-caste dining, Hindu Sangathan and shuddhi movements. Leading a completely Spartan life, Nathuram pronounced his intention to remain unmarried all his life. He neither smoked nor drank, wore the simplest of clothes, but read voraciously on subjects related to religion, politics and history, presumably under Savarkar's strong influence and guidance. Pledging himself to strict celibacy, he literally shunned the very sight and company of women and strove to keep himself away from the 'temptations' of life.

Once Savarkar took to active politics, Nathuram became a natural trusted lieutenant. As mentioned earlier, he played a lead role in the Hyderabad agitation of 1938, for which he also faced imprisonment of an entire year. After being released, he returned to Poona to resume work at the Hindu Mahasabha office.

This was where he first met a young and dynamic man, in 1941, who had worked for the party in Ahmednagar, a cantonment town that was about 115 km away from Poona. He was Narayan Dattaray Apte, who was just a year younger than him and someone who was to become his closest friend and ally over the next few years. Apte was born to a historian and Sanskrit scholar and his family lived in Poona's Budhwar Peth in a building named 'Anandashram'. He had gone on to graduate in science from the Bombay University in 1932. With no job openings, he managed to find himself a teaching job in the American Mission High School in Ahmednagar. He had an early marriage with a girl named Champa who bore him a son, who unfortunately turned out to be mentally challenged. Apte was an assiduous worker, besides being lively, quick-witted and garrulous—quite the antithesis of his friend Godse. Inspired by the philosophy of the Mahasabha, he considered opening a rifle club in Ahmednagar in 1938, to train young men in the use of firearms. He had written letters to Savarkar requesting his intervention to secure a licence for the rifle club from the Central Provinces government through its premier N.B. Khare or through K.M. Munshi.[3] By October 1938, he did manage to procure the licence from the collector to use four rifles (miniature 22 bore) on certain conditions.[4] Correspondences followed between him and Savarkar on the issue of the rifle club, how to raise more funds for it, popularize it and expand the activity to other towns.

The following year, Apte formally joined the Mahasabha branch in the town, though he was not very keen on a political career. It was here that he came in contact with the leading light of the Mahasabha in Ahmednagar, Vishnu Ramkrishna Karkare, who initially viewed him with suspicion as he worked in a school run by Christian missionary.

When Savarkar toyed the idea of establishing the Hindu Rashtra Dal, as the Mahasabha's own youth corps militia distinct from the RSS, Godse roped in Apte too as one of its office-bearers. However, in early 1943, taking advantage of the increased openings for Indians in the army, Apte applied for the post of recruiting officer in the Royal Indian Air Force and was hired as an assistant technical officer. He was posted in Poona as a flight lieutenant. Though a temporary job that lasted only till the duration of the war, it gave him an opportunity to run away from Ahmednagar and the depressing domestic scenario that he faced. His students were heartbroken at their favourite teacher who was departing from their midst. A seventeen-year-old student Manorama Salvi, born in an Indian Christian family, shed copious tears at the farewell. She had lost her heart to this charming teacher of hers and the fire had been ignited on both ends. The clandestine affair and heady romance between the two went on unabated despite the vicissitudes of domestic life that Apte faced with his wife Champa and their only son. They spent nights together in several hotels across various cities, bravely signing in as 'Mr and Mrs Apte'.

The stint in the air force did not interest Apte for too long and he soon rejected a permanent commission. Even as he was at the crossroads of his career, his friend Nathuram sought his support in starting a newspaper to propagate the ideals of Hindu Sangathan. Nathuram had sought his mentor Savarkar's help and the latter lent him Rs 15,000 as seed capital. Titled *Agrani*, or Forerunner, it began its publication on 28 March 1944 with Nathuram as is editor and Apte as a manager. Its masthead bore Savarkar's portrait and carried his famous quotation: '*Varam jana hitam dhyeyam kevalam na janastuti*' (I strive for public good and not for public praise). The newspaper had begun its operations under difficult times when the country was in the grip of the war and political uncertainty, struggling to keep itself afloat. The Congress government of Bombay too tried its best to muzzle any publications of rival political ideologies and either put the newspaper under surveillance or dry up its advertising sponsors. When Savarkar was requested by the duo to contribute regular articles to bolster its reach, subscription and popularity, he flatly refused. He seemed to however be sympathetic to their cause and helped them raise funds for it on and off. The police dossier later revealed how on several occasions Nathuram wrote to Savarkar informing him of donations from a certain patron or the other who had contributed on Savarkar's request. For instance, a letter from him to Savarkar, dated 30 October 1946, mentioned businessman Jugal Kishore Birla's donation of Rs 1000. Details of the cheque number, the receipt sent back to Birla's office and sundry details too were dutifully noted and informed to Savarkar by Nathuram.[5] Despite the help, running the newspaper was a tall order and the two young men struggled hard to keep the press going against all odds. They set up a small office at 495, Shaniwar Peth in Poona.

The one time that the *Agrani* shot to some fame was when Apte dared to lead an agitation against Gandhi when the latter was released from jail in 1944 and had begun preparing for his marathon discussions with Jinnah regarding Partition. Apte had led a batch of young workers when Gandhi came to the hill resort of Panchgani near Poona, waved black flags at him for encouraging Partition. As nearly 400 people began to gather in the protests, the police caught hold of all of them including Apte for questioning and later let them off. The *Times of India* of 23 July 1944 carried the headline of 'Mr. Gandhi heckled' by a Poona journalist. The *Agrani* itself carried a full-page article on this incident, along with photographs of Gandhi and Apte with the former saying: 'Yes, I have consented to [give] Pakistan' and the latter's audacious reply to it: 'And therefore I denounce you a hundred times!'[6] In the article, Apte explained how he had several questions shouted at Gandhi amidst 'sky-rending shouts of Akhand Hindustan' by the gathered crowds. He wrote: 'Replying to one question, Gandhiji said: "We will speak later privately." But I at once replied, I don't want your private interview. I want your confession in public about the consent to Pakistan. I want to hear once for all and publicly the execution of your thoughts in favour of Pakistan so that nobody may remain in illusion.'[7]

However, *Agrani*'s open and daring coverage of communal riots and the sufferings of Hindus in particular was detested by the Congress government, which invoked the Press Act against it that necessitated blacking out communally sensitive news. A fine of Rs 6000 was imposed on the newspaper too, leading to its folding up, only to resurface the very next morning under a new name, *Hindu Rashtra*. But its daring coverage won it sympathizers from affluent Hindu businessmen and landlords who were willing to sponsor the activities of the Poona duo.

The third principal player in the conspiracy was Vishnu Ramkrishna Karkare, the man who had spearheaded the Mahasabha in Ahmednagar. Born in a Brahmin family (sometime in 1910) he had been orphaned early in life and grew up at the Nortcote Orphanage in Bombay. As a boy of ten, he started his own tea shop in the lanes of Bombay and transported this 'business' to Ahmednagar about fifteen years later. It became a huge success there and his ingenious brain managed to diversify the business into a hotel of sorts too called the Deccan Guest House. Having faced a traumatic and tough childhood, Karkare's heart always beat for those in misery and suffering and made good some part of his income on regular charity and social work. In fact, during the post-Partition refugee crisis, Karkare organized relief in Ahmednagar on a war footing. Borrowing tents from the army, he had them set up for the refugees and for more than a month at the Visapur refugee camp made nearly 25,000–30,000 free meals available for them from his hotel.

Karkare had a softer side to him with an interest in theatre and had put together an amateur drama company as well. Being quite inspired by the Hindu Sangathan philosophy, he gravitated towards the work of the Mahasabha in Ahmednagar. His dream came true when the president of the party and icon for Hindu political workers, Savarkar, came calling to Ahmednagar. Karkare beseeched him to pay a brief visit to his theatre. Savarkar was extremely busy but seeing the man's earnestness agreed to spare just fifteen minutes at the theatre. But so mesmerized was he by the performance that he sat through the entire show for three full hours and warmly congratulated Karkare for his efforts. By 1942, Karkare stood for municipal elections and won unopposed, given his track record as a good Samaritan. He began to be known as 'Seth', a businessman— something that he had literally toiled single-handedly to build, despite his childhood troubles.

When communal riots and carnage broke out in Noakhali in Bengal, Karkare and six other Hindu Mahasabha workers set off to that town across the country to offer relief and succour to the suffering Hindu brethren. To ward off attacks, they wore chain-mail jackets under their shirts that were provided by an acquaintance of Karkare in Poona named Digambar Ramachandra Badge. The scenes at Noakhali and the destruction horrified the young Mahasabha men. They toured hamlet to hamlet and opened relief centres in the name of 'Veer Savarkar'. Seeing the sufferings first-hand made them hold Gandhi responsible for the plight of the Hindus. They blamed the situation on Gandhi's pusillanimity and non-violent philosophy, in addition to his eventual capitulation to the Partition demand. Karkare wanted to have all that he saw in these riots published in newspapers so that the rest of India could know what horrors the Hindus of the country had faced. And that was when he remembered his old associate, Apte, from Ahmednagar and through him, made acquaintance with Nathuram to narrate his travelogue. Karkare even nudged a friend of his in Poona, B.D. Kher, to assist in the running of the newspaper and the latter agreed. Whenever Karkare came to Poona to meet Nathuram and Apte, he normally stayed at Kher's residence at No. 2, Narayan Peth. Kher incidentally lived in the same residential complex as that of the senior police officer of the city, Deputy Superintendent N.Y. Deulkar, who had questioned Apte in Panchgani.

Hearing the horror tales of genocide from Karkare and publishing it in their newspaper infuriated the three men. They were inspired by bravado to do something to avenge these acts. But with shocking naivety their plans of retaliation included destruction of the entire Pakistan Constituent Assembly when its leaders were gathered inside and carrying out a midnight raid on a busy octroi post on the Hyderabad side of the border, kill the Nizam's officials and loot their treasury. The latter plan was of course inspired by the separate tales of horror that had been emerging from Hyderabad where a fanatic militia that called itself 'Razakars' or volunteers had unleashed a reign of terror and murder on the Hindu population of the state, under the militant leadership of Kassim Rizvi. The intention was to proclaim independence for Hyderabad and not allow its integration with India. Known for his bluster and complete lack of discretion, Apte went around making tall claims on these matters quite openly with his close circle. None of the plotters had any knowledge or experience of carrying out operations such as these, nor did they even know how to operate the hand grenades and pistols and other weapons that might be required. Yet, they were fully convinced of their own heroism and ability to execute the plans with perfection and avenge the wrongs. In this process, they came in touch with a wide melange of diverse characters, many of whom got co-opted into the larger plot that eventually materialized.

One of them was Dada Maharaj, a forty-two-year-old saintly figure of a sect of Hindus known as the Pushtimarg Vaishnavas. He lived in Bombay along with his younger brother Dixitji Maharaj. Dada also secretly collected arms and explosives that he freely distributed to Hindus for self-defence, especially in the Nizam's territory. He also had an impressive corpus of funds for such outrageous acts and a ready retinue of arms suppliers. Apte, Nathuram and Karkare paid several visits to Dada Maharaj's palatial temple-turned-residence in the precincts of Bombay's Bhuleshwar temple from July 1947. With his gift of the gab and hyperbole and with the airs of a former army officer, Apte floored the 'saint'. Dada was willing to fund all their attempts and help purchase two mortars to blow up the Pakistan

Assembly. None of them obviously worked out the simpler finer details of how to actually operate mortars or even how to get to Pakistan with all this ammunition and blow the entire leadership up in the air. These 'finer details' could always be worked out—the bigger picture was of course retribution. They also planned to amass some Sten guns to execute some of the other plans they had.

Dada's prime contact was an ace weapons dealer in Poona, Digambar Ramachandra Badge, who ran a proprietary firm known as 'Shastra Bhandar' or armoury. Badge was the same man who had also supplied chain-mail jackets to Karkare and his team on their Noakhali trip. A short-statured man with one eye smaller than the other, Badge excelled over Apte when it came to the swagger of talking big and dropping names. Given that he dealt with arms and was constantly under police vigil, he had also mastered the art of garish disguise with a plethora of garbs. He proudly showed off an entire album of photographs of the various roles he had donned and gave lengthy explanations of which of them was necessitated during which police raid.

The most tragic element of the entire plot was Badge's unlettered servant Shankar Kistayya. A man who did not even know who Gandhi was or why he needed to be killed or what he was to do, Shankar got pulled into a lethal chain of events of his master's making. Shankar was born in Sholapur, knew no Marathi or Hindi and spoke only Telugu. He lived with his widowed mother and eked out a living as an apprentice carpenter. Badge was looking for an assistant and the offer of a salary of Rs 20 a month along with food and clothes was too enticing to let go of. Shankar prepared handles for Badge's daggers or ferried the weapons and basically did everything that he was asked to do by his master. The duties did not end here but went on to the domestic sphere too where he washed his master's clothes, massaged him when he felt tired, cooked, ran errands, bought groceries, swept and mopped the house and again, did anything that his master asked him to do. In addition, he also worked gratis for Badge's sister who lived next door and inundated him daily with a barrage of the choicest abuses. Despite working so hard, Badge hardly paid Shankar his entire salary. Shankar's mother too visited from Sholapur pleading for settlement of salary arrears but was shooed away. By mid-1946, when Shankar realized that there was almost a six-month arrears that were due to him, he was incensed and ran away. But Badge was too clever to be outsmarted. He filed a complaint with the police that his servant had fled stealing him of Rs 200. Shankar was arrested from Sholapur and brought in chains and whacked black and blue in the police station. He pleaded with his master to have mercy on him. Badge magnanimously conceded, dropped the case but in the process eighteen-year-old Shankar realized that for good or bad, he was to be a bonded labourer to this evil man whom he served.

The penultimate cog in this wheel of amateur crime aspirants was twenty-year-old Madanlal Kashmirilal Pahwa, a Punjabi refugee who came from the town of Pakpattan, which became part of Pakistan. Karkare discovered him in a refugee camp in Chembur in Bombay as someone who made hand grenades. Karkare was trying to stock ammunition for the planned loot of the Nizam's treasures. Madanlal had passed his matriculation examination and served in the Royal Indian Navy as a wireless operator. Since he had spent time in Bombay during his navy stint, it became the natural place of refuge for him after the borders got drawn and his family forced out of their ancestral home. In search of a livelihood in Bombay, he was led to Jagdish Chandra Jain, a thirty-nine-year-old professor of Hindi at the Ramnarain Ruia College in Matunga. Jain engaged the muscular young man as a salesman of his books and offered a 25 per cent commission on the sales he made. The books hardly sold, though Madanlal kept up his efforts. Alongside this, he even found employment in a small fire-crackers factory, Vassen Puspasen. The firm was also surreptitiously making hand grenades and crude bombs and that was what interested Madanlal more. They used his services to also ferry the explosives to their end-customers and Madanlal used Jain's books as a nice cover for the actual operations. During the sale of a book to Dixitji Maharaj, Madanlal managed to establish an excellent rapport with him as well. Karkare met him and was impressed by his skills and offered him employment under him in Ahmednagar. Madanlal was deeply inspired by all that Karkare had done for refugees like him. He readily agreed and left Bombay with Karkare, carrying along a steel trunk filled with bombs that the former had made along with some slabs of explosive and fuse wire. Before departing from Bombay Madanlal however informed his initial benefactor Professor Jain, whom he considered as his father. Jain was told that a businessman from Ahmednagar 'Karkara Seth' had offered him an opportunity to open a fruit stall and that he was going there to chart out a new life. He had yet to settle financial accounts with Jain, which he promised to do at a later date.

After all the bombast and the loans taken from Dada Maharaj, Apte and Godse had realized that their Pakistan plan was going nowhere. Dada too was getting restive and kept demanding status update. He had also provided a car to the duo when they asked for it to ferry explosives. But Apte had used it largely to drive around with his lady-love Manorama. Apte's personal life was tumultuous. Manorama had just confessed to him that she was pregnant with his child and that her religious Christian parents would hack her to death for such heresy. Back home, he was forced to put his son into an asylum as he was getting violent and this caused lot of upheaval between him and his wife Champa. And with all of this, Apte was also making these grand retribution plans for the cause of the motherland.

As inquiries from Dada got more intense, they decided to finalize their plans. But most of the Muslim League leaders including Jinnah had already left India right from July–August 1947 and it was next to impossible to try this misadventure in another country. Hence it was decided to concentrate on the Nizam plan instead and the three men, along with the new entrant Madanlal, sat huddled in the *Hindu Rashtra* office in December 1947 sketching plans to execute this.

Meanwhile in Ahmednagar, there was a sudden spike in cases where bombs went off on Muslim religious processions and the like. The police did not realize that these were being sold from Karkare's hotel to miscreants. Though some clues did emerge in investigation about Karkare's possible association, the police simply looked the other way. They also knew that his new assistant was a troublemaker. On 5 January 1948, Madanlal had jumped on to the podium when Congress leader Raosaheb Patwardhan came there to preach communal harmony to the masses. He was heckled and the microphone was snatched away from Patwardhan even as Madanlal berated him and the Congress for doing nothing for refugees like him. He was promptly arrested but later released. The police was told to keep a close watch on him and his master, Karkare. But with some tip-off from someone in the police department, the duo got wind of this and possible detention and fled from Ahmednagar on 9 January. Their stock of hoarded explosives too was confiscated by the police. Interestingly, Madanlal decided to go to Delhi where his family had lined up prospective brides for marriage. So even in the midst of such ghastly plans of loot and murder, he quite nonchalantly was planning on meeting girls, as though his life would remain the same once he committed such acts. He even left behind a wailing, love-sick girlfriend called Shevanta back in Bombay.

Before heading to Delhi, the duo reached Poona and met Badge to stock more explosives as they had lost everything they had to the police. Madanlal testified the quality of the explosives, guncotton slabs, cartridges, hand grenades, fuse wires and pistols that Badge showed them. They met Apte and Nathuram too to appraise them of the ammunition they had found, though they also wanted to have a look at alternatives in Bombay the following day. In Bombay, Madanlal met his old benefactor Professor J. C. Jain and his textile broker Angad Singh who had come to visit him. He talked big about how they had made up their mind to teach the Muslims a lesson and that a wealthy man of Ahmednagar named Karkara Seth was spearheading this entire project. He also exaggerated his own exploits of shouting down the Congress leader that had brought him coverage in the local press. Jain was more interested in the money that Madanlal owed him from the sales of his books, which the latter promised he would clear soon.

The entire plan of this motley gang was to change all of a sudden on 12 January when Apte and Nathuram received news of the fast that Gandhi was planning to undertake. They found Gandhi's stand of fasting for the cause of money to be paid to the enemy state of Pakistan as little short of treason and decided on an impulse that they had finally found the target for the retribution that they so earnestly sought. Gandhi had to be killed if the Hindus and India had to be saved, they surmised. Again, the finer details, the logistics, the weapons, the finance, the protagonists and other action items would be decided in due course. But the target was now fixed and they were resolute on what they needed to do now.

This new plan brought into the portrait the last of the plotters, Gopal Godse, the younger brother of Nathuram who was twenty-seven years old then. A quiet, self-effacing man who was more concerned with bringing up his family, Gopal too had joined the Military Ordnance Service as a civilian clerk. During the war, he volunteered for overseas service and was sent off with the British column named PAIFORCE to Iran and Iraq in 1941. He returned to India in 1944 and worked ever since as an assistant storekeeper in the ordnance depot at Kirkee, near Poona. He had two daughters then, one aged two years and another four months. Gopal's involvement in the plot that had now zeroed in specifically on murdering Gandhi was important as he had brought back to India after his tenure at PAIFORCE a service revolver without the knowledge of the authorities. He had buried it in the backyard of his village house. His elder brother now wanted him to retrieve this weapon as a possible tool in the planned murder, in addition to the other ammunition that they would try to procure from Badge. In any case, by 13 January, Apte and Nathuram decided to also buy all the explosives that Badge had showed Karkare and Madanlal and that they would take delivery for them and pay for them in Bombay where they would raise some funds for it. All of them decided to meet in Bombay at the Hindu Mahasabha office the following evening.

Badge and Shankar left for Bombay too by the Deccan Express that left Poona on 14 January at 3.30 p.m. Badge had disguised himself in the most outlandish manner as a sadhu, dressed in shocking saffron clothes, wore several garlands around his neck and smeared sacred ash all over himself. In the same train's second-class compartment Nathuram and Apte sat too, facing each other by the window seats. As the train was to start, they saw a pretty woman who was pacing up and down, desperately trying to find a window seat. She was a famed Marathi actress of the time, Shanta Modak, whose screen name was Bimba. Ever on the prowl when it came to matters of beauty, Apte readily got up and offered her his seat by the window. He began with how much he admired her acting in the film *Chul and Mul*.[8] In the course of the four hours from Poona to Bombay the two of them hit it off, even as Nathuram perhaps sat squirming in his seat. As the train neared Dadar, Bimba offered to drop the two of them as her brother Irumbak was coming to pick her up at the station. Her house was in Shivaji Park, almost next to Savarkar Sadan, the residence of Veer Savarkar. Nathuram and Apte had to go to the Hindu Mahasabha office, which was about half a mile away from Savarkar's house. But the lure of spending more time with her made Apte coax Nathuram to tag along. She dropped them off at the gate of Savarkar's house, though did not see them going inside it. Bimba's testimony later was to add to Savarkar's woes that the future assassins of Gandhi were dropped by her on that fateful evening at his doorstep.

The Conspiracy

Apte and Nathuram met Badge and Shankar, as planned, at the Hindu Mahasabha office in Bombay on the night of 14 January. The main hall in the ground floor of the three-storeyed building was normally used by several visitors to rest, read newspapers or spend the night. Badge and Shankar decided to remain there while Nathuram and Apte checked into the Sea Green Hotel (South) on Marine Drive. They had booked air tickets to Delhi for the noon flight by Tata Airlines on 17 January under the pseudonyms of D.N. Karmarkar (Apte) and S. Marathe (Nathuram). Incidentally, Madanlal too was among the many people who were spending that night at the Mahasabha shelter. Along with Karkare all the conspirators met at Dada Maharaj's house to flesh out the plans of assassinating Gandhi. Badge volunteered to join them in their Delhi sojourn and assist in the execution of the plans. This also meant his helpless servant Shankar too got tagged along.

Before leaving Bombay, on the evening of 15 January, Madanlal went to his benefactor Professor Jain's house and as was his nature went on a bragging spree. He revealed the plans that his party was making to assassinate Gandhi in Delhi. Not taking it too seriously, Jain admonished him and dissuaded him from attempting such foolhardy acts. He however did not think it prudent to alert the police about whatever he heard, for reasons best known to him. Jain also discussed all that he heard with his family friend Angad Singh, who too dismissed these as tall claims of a disgruntled refugee.

Nathuram meanwhile made a quick dash to Poona to meet Gopal and also get hold of another pistol or revolver. He managed to buy a .22 bore magazine pistol, which he later discovered was unsatisfactory. He took Badge's help to get this exchanged for a revolver from a man called S.D. Sharma. The revolver was of .32 bore, but the cartridges that Sharma gave ended up being of a slightly smaller bore though they fit well into its chamber. It was not till the morning of the plot that the protagonists were going to discover this major goof-up.

Just before leaving Bombay for Delhi on 17 January, Nathuram, Apte and Badge crisscrossed through the city. They made a vain attempt with Dixitji Maharaj to part with one of the pistols. From there, they went all the way to Sea Green Hotel (South) where Manorama had been staying with Apte and had cried her heart out on realizing that her paramour was heading for such a dangerous mission. In this crowded itinerary and with their flight scheduled to depart at 2 p.m. Badge was to claim later under police custody that they all went in the opposite direction, back to Dadar again, to visit Savarkar's house and take his blessings before heading to the airport. The trio had engaged a taxi since 7 a.m. The meter had clocked Rs 55-10-00 and its driver Aitappa Kotian had been screamed at to drive fast to the airport as they were running terribly late. Nathuram and Apte reached Delhi by 8.30 p.m. that evening and stayed at

Hotel Marina in Connaught Place, calling themselves as 'M. Deshpande' and 'S. Deshpande'. Badge stayed on in Bombay at Hotel Asra in Dadar, run by his friend, and came to Delhi later.

Meanwhile, Karkare and Madanlal reached Delhi and checked into Hotel Sharif in Chandni Chowk, after they found no vacant rooms available at the Hindu Mahasabha Bhawan. It was only later with a letter of introduction to the Mahasabha secretary Ashutosh Lahiri from Nathuram who was an influential party worker, that Karkare was allotted Room No. 3 in the Mahasabha Bhawan from 18 January. In the interim however, unwittingly and true to his good Samaritan nature, Karkare had befriended a refugee in the train named Angchekar and since the latter had no place to go, he was also very generously brought along to the Hotel Sharif. He stayed with them till the time Gopal reached Delhi to join them, after which he was summarily dismissed, perhaps with the afterthought of having let in a complete stranger in their midst while they were embarking on such a dangerous mission. But such were the lapses of rookie criminals, something that was to cost them dearly as they were to discover later. As Manohar Malgonkar notes in his book:

> Just as Apte had made sure that he would be identified by the taxi driver Kotian, Karkare had made sure that Angchekar would remember him and Madanlal. Both would pay dearly for these indiscretions . . . the cases against Apte and Karkare might not have been so convincingly established if both had not been so prodigal in leaving clues behind and gone repeatedly out of their way to impress their identity on total strangers, transforming bystanders into material witnesses.[9]

The Delhi that the conspirators arrived at was abuzz with political activity and tension. Gandhi's fast was into its fifth day and the government had gone into an overdrive to accede to all his demands, justified or unjustified. Important members of the Cabinet kept making visits, pleas and entreaties to their messiah to give up his fast, but he was obdurate. Finally, the government capitulated and agreed to pay up the promised reserves to Pakistan by the very third day of his fast, on 15 January. But this was not all. Gandhi also wanted to ensure that the communal riots in Delhi were quelled and the Muslims there made to feel safe and secure. He wanted specific concessions made to them by the Hindus and Sikhs, and for them to abide by this in letter and spirit. Rajendra Prasad drafted a peace formula for this, most of the terms of which were contingent on the Hindu and Sikh leaders and community members. The broad elements of the plan were a pledge assuring Gandhi that:

(i) The annual fair at Khawaja Qutabuddin's mausoleum at Mehrauli will be held as usual;

(ii) Muslims will be able to move about in Delhi;

(iii) Mosques left by the Muslims and taken possession of by Hindus and Sikhs will be vacated, Muslim areas will not be forcibly occupied, and;

(iv) Hindus will not object to the return of Muslims who had migrated.[10]

A lot of Gandhi's actions of this time and the moral coercion he put on the Hindu and Sikh community angered particularly the refugees who had come in droves to take shelter in Delhi. They had been persecuted by Muslims back in their hometown and literally hounded out to India to save their lives. To witness Gandhi staking his own life for the protection of the same community that they desperately wanted to take revenge against and also getting the government to part with money to that country incensed the refugees. Several of them gathered in droves outside Birla House shouting loud, angry slogans against Gandhi, wishing him death and seeking revenge for blood with blood. Cries of '*Marta hai toh marne do!*' (Let Gandhi die if he so wishes) rent the air around Birla House. The police would lathi-charge and disperse them, but a new batch would gather soon enough.

On the morning of 19 January, Apte and Nathuram sought time to meet Ashutosh Lahiri in his office at the Hindu Mahasabha Bhawan. Lahiri was busy. He was releasing a press statement on behalf of the Mahasabha rubbishing the Congress and the government's claim that his party too had endorsed the peace plan to end Gandhi's fast. Lahiri was angry that the Mahasabha was made to appear as being unconcerned about the plight of the Hindu and Sikh refugees though they valued Gandhi's life and did not want him to undertake such a fast. He was deliberating with others when Apte and Nathuram came to his room. All of them were given advance copies of his press statement that he intended to release later in the day. Around that very time a trunk call was booked to Bombay from Lahiri's phone at 9.20 a.m. It was to Savarkar's residence. The caller had left a message with the operator that they wished to speak to Gajanan Damle, Savarkar's secretary, or his bodyguard Appa Kasar. It was impossible that a call of this nature and on the day as politically volatile for the Mahasabha as that could be done from Lahiri's phone without his knowledge. And the reason too was justified that he possibly wanted to take Savarkar's advice before releasing the statement to the press. Significantly, they were unable to reach Damle or Kasar and the call got cancelled by 11.30 a.m. Much later, the police investigation team was to deduce that this call was actually made by Apte and Nathuram to give updates to Savarkar on the conspiracy.

Badge, Shankar and Gopal were yet to arrive and this had caused much flutter among the key conspirators since they carried the weapons. However, by the evening of 19 January all the characters managed to reach Delhi, a day before the D-Day planned for the murder, i.e., 20 January 1948. They now had Gopal's .38 revolver, Badge's .32 revolver, 'five 36 hand grenades fitted with seven-second fuses; and two one-pound slabs of gun-cotton with ninety-second fuses. They had, or at least Madanlal had, handled explosives before, but none of them had fired a revolver or thrown a 36 grenade and they had very little idea of the capabilities or limitations of either weapon.'[11] That was not all. With less than twenty-four hours to go for the execution of their designs, they still did not know the exact details of how to go about it, who would do what, nor had they tested their armoury or their skills at using it. These minor distractions were left for the late morning–early afternoon of the 20 January, just hours before they planned to storm into Gandhi's prayer meeting at Birla House and bump him off. On 19 January, at 4 p.m. and later at 10 p.m. some of them visited Birla House to survey the prayer grounds and confabulate on the course of action for the following evening. Incredibly, Nathuram and Apte had given their clothes to be washed by the hotel's laundry the next morning, quite confident that after committing such a big crime they would be able to easily head back to their hotel room and collect their laundry too.

The next morning, Apte, Badge and Shankar did a recce of Birla House. Nathuram was down with migraine and was resting. The plan drawn seemed foolproof to the gang. Badge was to enter Room No. 3 of the servants' quarters there that belonged to the Birla family's chauffeur Chhotu Ram on the pretext of wanting to photograph Gandhi from within the grilled window. The window gave a direct view of Gandhi as he sat for the evening prayers. There were twenty-six holes in the intricate trellis work that the window had. Madanalal was to throw a hand grenade on the gathering causing chaos and confusion, not to speak of several innocent lives that might also be lost. At that very moment, taking advantage of the unrest among the crowd, Badge was to point Gopal's revolver from within one of those grills and shoot Gandhi down. Shankar was to get as close to Gandhi as possible and pump the bullets from Badge's revolver at point-blank range into Gandhi to ensure fully that the man was done with. Interestingly, the lead actors—Apte, Nathuram and Karkare—were mere bystanders and had no major role to play in such a major operation. The next task was to practise a bit with the weapons for which the gang dispersed into the woods behind the Hindu Mahasabha Bhawan. To their dismay, they discovered that Gopal's .38, by virtue of being buried for so long, had been encrusted with mud and rust. When Badge's .32 revolver was tested, they realized the discrepancy with the cartridges that Sharma had given them. It was veritably a dead end and that too within a few hours of execution of the grand plan. With coconut oil they then began scraping off the rust from Gopal's revolver that seemed any day more reliable than Badge's worthless device. It was barely a few hours before the evening that Gopal finally managed to get the revolver in action and they tested it in the room, causing a stir there, as black smoke filled the room.

By late afternoon, they engaged Surjit Singh, a young Sikh refugee from Pakistan who was running his cab to take them to Birla House, stay there for half an hour and bring them back. Apte, Gopal, Badge and Shankar travelled in this cab, while Nathuram, Madanlal and Karkare had already reached Birla House. Everything seemed to be going as per plan. Just as Badge was to enter the room of Chhotu Ram to take his position, he saw a one-eyed man sitting near the door. He was overcome with terrible fright that this was a bad omen and that their operation would be a colossal failure. Without bothering to let his accomplices know, he made up his mind in an instant to drop the idea of shooting at Gandhi. His dutiful servant Shankar had no option but to follow suit. The two quickly rushed back to the taxi and hid the weapon there and with strange and inexplicable duplicity Badge sauntered back pretending the weapon was still safe in his pocket. He even signalled to Apte that he was ready to strike once Madanlal threw the grenade.

The prayer meeting began. A little over 200 people had gathered. Gandhi had come in on time, as always, and the chant of sonorous hymns had begun. At the other end, unmindful of Badge's treachery, Madanlal was readying his ammunition from the side of Room No. 9 of the servants' quarters. As luck would have had it, that evening, Sulochana, the wife of one of the servants, Nanak Chand, saw Madanlal placing a bomb and lighting a matchstick. She ran away in horror to save her child who was playing close by. The bomb was thrown by Madanlal and the explosion was loud enough to be heard even from a distance. To the horror of Apte and Nathuram, instead of taking to their positions and pumping Gandhi with bullets, both Badge and Shankar were seen taking to their heels. Madanlal, it so happened, had never been on the recce to Birla House and had no clue about the exit routes. As he tried to run, the police apprehended him and right in front was Sulochana who identified him as the man who was lighting the bomb a few minutes ago. His game was over. Madanlal was immediately arrested by the Delhi Police. Even as he was being dragged away by the police, Madanlal triumphantly declared, '*Phir Aayega!*' (We will come back again), suggesting that this was not a plan they intended to abandon so soon.

On his part, Gandhi remained unruffled by the pandemonium and the noise. The prayers continued and the meeting ended peacefully with his favourite bhajans. When he heard about Madanlal later, Gandhi praised the young boy's courage and also requested the police not to be very harsh with him.

Amidst the melee, Gopal decided to be the brave man who saves the situation for his gang. He went to the taxi, reclaimed the pistols that Badge and Shankar had hid there and got back to Room No. 3 of Chhotu Ram, shutting the door behind him. He then took out the .38 revolver. He was a short-statured man and the window was way above his height on the wall. He however jumped, grabbed hold of the ledge and tried to heave himself up. Keeping balance with one hand and with the revolver in the second, he struggled to both keep himself stable, as also aim at his target. Expectedly, it was an impossible task and he gave up and ran for his life. He joined Nathuram, Apte and Karkare and sped off in the taxi. Karkare was especially crestfallen that his protégé Madanlal was literally fed to the wolves by the machinations of Badge and was now in police custody. He wanted to stay back in Delhi for a day to arrange any legal help for him, while the rest made plans to leave the city. Karkare and Gopal checked out of the Hindu Mahasabha Bhawan and found another cheap hotel in Old Delhi near the railway station, named Frontier Hindu Hotel. They checked in as 'Rajagopalan' (Gopal) and 'G.M. Joshi' (Karkare).

After their cowardly exit from Birla House, Badge and Shankar went to their room at Hindu Mahasabha Bhawan, packed up to leave and decided to bury their two cloth bags full of grenades and explosives in the woods behind the Bhawan. Apte and Nathuram came in around this time and a verbal spat ensued between them all. But that was the last they would see of Badge in the operation as he abused the duo and left. Nathuram and Apte checked out of Marina Hotel, though they completely forgot to collect their laundry that they had given that morning. To avoid leading a trail, they decided to take a circuitous route to Bombay by taking a train to Kanpur. From there they boarded the Lucknow–Jhansi Mail, and at Jhansi took the Punjab Mail to reach Bombay by the noon of 23 January. During this long train journey, the two of them seemed terribly disillusioned by their plans having gone awry. They had initially thought of going back, regrouping, hiring a professional killer and executing the plan later on. In the course of the journey, however, Nathuram announced his decision to Apte that he would take up the responsibility on himself and that no third person was needed to be hired. So resolute was his decision that Apte found it difficult to sway him. The duo checked in to Apte's favourite hideout with Manorama, the Arya Pathikashram on Sandhurst Road, whose manager Gaya Pershad Dube was a friend. Simultaneously they booked another room at the Elphinstone Annexe in Carnac Road, checking in as 'N. Vinayakrao and friend.' Nathuram stayed at the second hotel while Apte brought in Manorama to the Pathikashram as always and she stayed with him throughout 24 and 25 January. On 25 January, the two lovers checked out and moved in to the Annexe where they spent the next two days with each other, even as Nathuram went out to the city to see movies and distract his mind, leaving the lovers to themselves. While leaving for Delhi, Apte told Manorama that if anything untoward happened to his friend Nathuram he would send her a telegram for further action that would read as 'arriving Delhi arrange for Godse's defence'.

~

Back in Delhi, despite Gandhi's appeal, the police went ahead with extreme third-degree torture to extract information from Madanlal who was proving to be a very tough cookie. He hid the identities of his colleagues and revealed the bare minimum with the ruse that he understood no Marathi in which they all spoke. He was taken to the Marina Hotel handcuffed and face covered to lead them to the room where his associates stayed. There a search was conducted in Room No. 40 and in the drawer of a table the police saw a typewritten sheet. This was the press statement of Ashutosh Lahiri who was declaring the other day that the Hindu Mahasabha was not part of the peace pledge. He had distributed it to all the people in his room and quite unwittingly, Nathuram and Apte had left behind their copy in the hotel itself, leading to a link with the Mahasabha. Madanlal was then led to the Old Delhi railway station to identify his associates among any of the travellers there. Incidentally, Gopal and Karkare were there at the tea room at the same time and watched nervously as the police led him everywhere to identify his accomplices. Though he saw both of them, Madanlal stared through them and shook his head to the police saying none of them were his friends there. Gopal and Karkare heaved a huge sigh of relief, though they felt immensely bad for Madanlal and also grateful to him for saving them despite being in such a difficult situation.

The news of Madanlal's attempt and his subsequent arrest reached Bombay. His former patron Jain was petrified. Given that he had prior information about such a plan, which he had laughed away as a refugee's bravado, Jain decided to now discharge his duties as a good citizen and share information about what he knew. In his confession as Witness no. 9 to the police on 26 February 1948, Jain stated that he knew of Madanlal and also of someone called Karkare in Ahmedabad:

> Madanlal said that a group had been formed at Ahmednagar and that Karkare was financing the group. Madanlal stated that the party to which he belonged had plotted to do away with some great leader. Madanlal mentioned the name of Mahatma Gandhi . . . I will be able to identify Madanlal. I think I shall be able to identify Karkare also.[12]

Nowhere in his initial statement as witness did Jain bring up Savarkar's name, as he began to at a later point of time.

Interestingly, after the news of the bomb blast at Birla House, instead of going to the police, Jain sought interviews with Deputy Prime Minister Sardar Patel (who was in Bombay then) and the chief minister of Bombay, B.G. Kher. The former naturally did not materialize. The interview with Kher too was not fixed till 4 p.m. on 21 January. But Kher was in a tearing hurry and assigned the professor to Home Minister Morarji Desai and left. Morarji gave him a patient hearing and the only names that he got from

Jain were that of Madanlal and his fellow conspirator, a certain businessman from Ahmednagar named 'Karkara Seth'. Jain left by 5 p.m. after narrating all that he knew, and Desai, who also had the Bombay Police under him, summoned Jamshed Dorab Nagarvala, the deputy commissioner in charge of the Intelligence Branch. The affable Parsi, 'Jimmy' to his friends, was busy and met the minister only at 8.30 p.m. at the Bombay Central railway station when he was leaving for Gujarat.

And this is where the noose began to tighten on Savarkar. Jain, who changed his statements several times in the course of the investigation that was to follow, initially had mentioned only Madanlal and Karkare to Desai, but had later added, in a subsequent interrogation, that Madanlal had been taken by Karkare to meet Savarkar who heard all of his exploits for two hours and patted him on his back with his wishes saying, 'Carry on!' Whether this step was taken by Desai to settle scores with a political opponent would not be known but that definitely brought Savarkar under Nagarvala's scanner. Boasting that 'we already had a dossier on Savarkar'[13], Nagarvala decided to organize an unobtrusive, round-the-clock surveillance of Savarkar's house. Even after Savarkar's clearance from the case, and his own elevation to the position of inspector general of police, Nagarvala was sure of Savarkar's complicity. He had told Manohar Malgonkar in the course of the research for his book, 'To my dying day I shall believe that Savarkar was the man who organized Gandhi's murder.'[14] What facts predicated this strong belief are unknown, just as Nagarvala's other fantastic theory—till the very end, he believed that there was no plot to murder Gandhi, but to kidnap him and seek assurances as ransom from the Government of India. He held on to this belief till the day Gandhi was murdered and as a consequence the police force too was led in the same direction. A huge botch-up in the course of investigation by the police forces of Delhi and Bombay was to follow but for which Gandhi's life might well have been saved.

T.G. Sanjevi, the chief of Delhi Police, amped up the security at Birla House from five men to twenty-six, of whom seven were to be in plain clothes to keep a watch. But intriguingly, despite the innocuous link they found to the Mahasabha through the recovery of Ashutosh Lahiri's statement in the conspirators' room in the Marina, the Delhi Police did not deem it fit to even seek any clarifications from Lahiri. In the course of his torturous interrogation, Madanlal had merely stated that there was some editor who was being spoken about and who was involved with a newspaper called the *Hindu Rashtra*. Despite this information, the Delhi

Police did not pass this on to their counterparts in Bombay or find out what could have been easily accessible information on who the editor was. The newspaper was anyway always in police records and under scrutiny for its numerous violations of the Press Act for publishing communally sensitive information. In addition, the laundry from Marina with the initials 'NVG' was also recovered by the Delhi Police. This, along with the fact that it belonged to an editor, would have been sufficient enough to discover the identity of 'Nathuram Vinayak Godse'. But that was not to be and this vital piece of information was not given any importance.

To complicate the bureaucratic lethargy, there was also the inherent rivalry between Delhi Police and Bombay Police. On the morning of 21 January, two officers of the Delhi Police, Deputy Superintendent Jaswant Singh and Inspector Balkishen were sent to Bombay to meet Nagarvala and then proceed to Poona to meet Raosaheb Gurtu, the deputy inspector general of police, Crime Investigation Department (CID). They also carried a copy of Madanlal's statement to them, which was written in Urdu script and undecipherable to any of the officials in Bombay. According to the two Delhi policemen, they were cold-shouldered by Nagarvala, whom they met thrice between 22 and 23 January. They were rudely told not to come wearing uniforms as that undermined the prestige of the Bombay Police and its dependency on Delhi for information in their territory. Nagarvala asked them to return immediately without carrying out their original orders to go to Poona and meet Gurtu. Gurtu would have had the names and addresses of the *Hindu Rashtra* editor and manager on his official records and that could have nabbed the culprits. On their return, they bitterly complained to Sanjevi that they were ill-treated by Nagarvala and were put under some kind of *nazar qaid* or house arrest.

Instead of confronting or picking issue with the Bombay Police, Sanjevi sent for U.G. Rana, the Deputy Inspector-General of Bombay CID who was in Delhi then for some routine work. On 25 January, he gave Madanlal's statement to Rana and asked him to specifically get the Bombay Police acting on nabbing the larger conspiracy plotters. If they were serious, Rana would have been put on a flight to Bombay the same day. Instead he took the longest train route back, going via Allahabad where he alighted to take a holy dip in the Sangam and leisurely reached Bombay by the afternoon of 27 January. He saw Nagarvala that very day, gave him Madanlal's statement and the connecting links to Hindu Rashtra. Rana, Nagarvala and Sanjevi got on a call where these dots to be connected were discussed and Nagarvala was to send a report within a day to Sanjevi. However, that report from Nagarvala, who was still adamant about his kidnap theory, reached Sanjevi only on the morning of 30 January, a few hours before the murder. The report anyway did not have any relevant details of the potential assassins.

The conspirators meanwhile seemed more efficient than the police force of the two major Indian metropolises. They had dispersed all over the country and now needed to regroup. Nathuram and Apte, as mentioned, were ensconced in Bombay. Gopal had reached Poona and hidden his .38 along with the spare cartridges with a friend Pandurang Godbole who lived in Sadashiv Peth. He held on to the other .32 that had been exchanged from a certain Sharma who lived in Poona. Karkare arranged for an advocate, Puran Chand Mehta, for Madanlal and left Delhi on 23 January, reaching Thana on the third day. He sent a telegram to Apte's residence at Anandashram with a code name Vyas, and a terse message 'Come Immediately' that his wife Champa Apte received on the same day. She sent it to Gopal who was thrilled to know that the plan and the plotters were still active and needed to regroup in Bombay.

Nathuram and Apte reached the house of a wealthy businessman and a partner in the Silver Bank Company, Paranjpe, who was sympathetic to the Hindu cause and sought a loan for their newspaper. Paranjpe promised them Rs 10,000 to be collected the following day from his office. They booked their air tickets to Delhi for 27 January by Air India as 'D. Narayan Rao' (Apte) and 'N. Vinayaka Rao' (Nathuram) and gave their address as Sea Green Hotel, though they were staying at the Elphinstone Annexe. On 26 January, they met Dada Maharaj to seek his help, but the latter was extremely angry with their inaction for so long and refused to cooperate. Given the bad track record of their earlier weapons, Nathuram wanted to procure a new and foolproof one this time. It was decided that from Delhi, the duo would go to Gwalior where there was someone who might be better placed than Dada Maharaj to help them with this. Gopal and Karkare were to join them in Delhi by 29 January.

From the Delhi airport, Nathuram and Apte left for Gwalior by train to meet Dattatreya Sadashiv Parchure, a forty-seven-year-old medical practitioner and a controversial Mahasabha leader who had built up the party there. He had built his own militant boy scouts wing named 'Hindu Rashtra Sena' as a counterpart of the Dal that Nathuram and others were part of. They were hence known to each other intimately. The Sena claimed a strength of nearly 3000 and was hoping to merge with Nathuram's Dal.

With the relinquishing of power by the maharaja of Gwalior, Jayajirao Scindia, there was to be a means to elicit public opinion as to who would take on the reins of power. The Mahasabha was strong in Gwalior and hoped to assume charge with Parchure, possibly as the chief minister. Even the maharaja was sympathetic to the Mahasabha and preferred them to succeed him. But through its political shenanigans from Delhi, the Congress managed to wrest power claiming that only they represented the true public opinion of the people of the princely state of Gwalior. On 24 January, a Congress ministry thus got installed in Gwalior causing a lot of angst to the people at large, and the Mahasabha and Parchure in particular who were waiting for revenge. Parchure welcomed Nathuram and Apte to his house late at night, heard their plans out and offered help. He sent his son Nilkanth and bodyguard Roopa to fetch a man named G.S. Dandavate who had a country-made revolver. Nathuram and Apte approved of the weapon, an automatic 9 mm Beretta (bearing No. 606824)[15] in excellent working condition. The pistol had travelled the world literally before its final infamous use at the Birla House on 30 January. It was manufactured in Italy in 1934, was taken to Abyssinia by one of Mussolini's officers and then brought back by an officer of the 4th Gwalior Infantry who was in Abyssinia during the war, after the surrender of the Italians. They paid Dandavate Rs 300 for it and promised to pay the balance Rs 200 later. On the night of 28 January, Nathuram and Apte left for Delhi from Gwalior by train, to reach the capital for their final operation, in the wee hours of the following morning.

Delhi was then reeling under the impact of a horrific news that was coming from across the border. Gandhi's fast was intended to be a soothing balm to communities on both sides of the newly vivisected country. While at least an outward appearance of camaraderie and restraint was on display on this side of the border, no such compunctions existed in Pakistan. On the night of 22 January, the Parachinar tragedy had struck there where more than 130 non-Muslims were butchered, thirty wounded and fifty abducted. The honour of women was violated in the most grotesque manner. Even as news of this began trickling in to India, the tenuous nature of the much-touted peace pledge began to have an automatic meltdown, with calls for retribution growing stronger.

Nathuram and Apte decided to check in into the retiring room in the Old Delhi railway station. The clerk on duty then, Sundarilal, allotted Room No. 6 where Nathuram signed in as 'N. Venaik Rao'. They soon united with Karkare at the station. Taking a stroll in the busy bazars of Chandni Chowk, Nathuram got his photographs taken in a studio there.

The fated morning of 30 January finally arrived. After a breakfast at the railway station restaurant, Nathuram sat down to write some letters even as his accomplices watched silently. 'We felt already separated from him,' reminisced Karkare later, 'and ashamed of ourselves that we could not do more for him. All that we could do was to stay with him, till the end, to show him that he was not alone, that I and Apte [sic] were with him.'[16] These letters were intended by him to serve as alibis that would protect Karkare and Apte from prosecution and were dated 30 January. They were in Marathi and two were addressed to Apte at his residential and office addresses in Poona and another to Karkare at Ahmedabad. They were attached with a photograph each of Nathuram that he had clicked at the Chandni Chowk studio the previous evening. Among other things it said:

> My mental condition is inflamed in the extreme, so that it has become impossible to find out any reliable way out of the political atmosphere. I have therefore decided for myself to adopt a last and extreme step. You will of course know it in a day or two. I do not think that the peaceful demonstrations like those we formerly staged at Panchgani and Delhi will serve no [sic] useful purpose in the present circumstances. I have therefore decided to do what I want to do, without depending on any one else. The photo enclosed herewith should be carefully preserved.[17]

By noon, they went to the woods behind the Birla temple. Here, according to Karkare:

> We selected a tree roughly as broad as a man's trunk. On it we drew circles to indicate the head, the chest and stomach. Nathuram stood about 20 to 25 feet away and began firing. He was able to get his bullets into the circles. After that he fired more shots from varying distances, from fifteen feet, then ten, and in the end five. He was fully satisfied with the performance of the Beretta. He put on the safety catch and slipped the automatic in his pocket.[18]

Tense and emotional moments preceded the final departure to Birla House. Given Gandhi's strict orders to the police not to subject visitors to frisking and checking, the three entered unhindered. The same evening, a little over fifteen minutes after 5 p.m., the Beretta from Nathuram's hand pumped its bullets into an unsuspecting Gandhi, who fell instantly to his assassin. Karkare and Apte stood beside Nathuram, swathed in their blankets, ostensibly to save themselves from the bitter winter cold of Delhi. That evening, an era in the annals of Indian history came to a rude end.

The Aftermath

In the wake of Gandhi's murder, the violent repercussions were felt by organizations such as the Hindu Mahasabha and the RSS and particularly the Brahmin community of Maharashtra. Within a few hours of the assassination, the details of the murderer and his caste too miraculously trickled down to different parts of the country. While the press in India did not divulge too many details about the wave of communal violence that erupted the very night of the murder, the *New York Times* of 31 January 1948 reported through its journalist Robert Trumbull that 'communal riots quickly swept Bombay when news of Mr. Gandhi's death was received. The Associated Press reported that fifteen persons were killed and more than fifty injured before an uneasy peace was established'.[19] The death toll in the hometown of Nathuram and Apte, Poona, stood at around fifty.[20] The office of the *Hindu Rashtra* was obviously set on fire. Advocate P.L. Inamdar notes about the Brahmin persecution that followed the murder, only because the assassin belonged to that community:

> There also came the news of the manhunt of Maharashtrian Brahmins, irrespective of their party allegiance by non-Brahmins in Poona and other districts of Maharashtra. Some of my close relatives living in southern districts of Maharashtra were being made the victims of this manhunt only because they were Maharashtrian Brahmins. They escaped being lynched only by the sheer chance of not being found in their houses at the time of the raids. Gwalior also did not lag behind. Apart from the mass arrests of persons belonging to the Hindu Mahasabha or the R.S.S. the Maharashtrian Brahmins were generally looked down upon. Even in the Bar Room of Gwalior, we were insulted as Godsewallas! Leaders and

workers of the Gwalior Hindu Mahasabha, prominent or otherwise, were arrested en bloc . . .[21]

Scholar Maureen L.P. Patterson who was researching on the aftermath of Gandhi's murder on the Maharashtrian Brahmins, especially the Chitpawans to which sub-caste Nathuram and even Savarkar belonged, notes that she was refused access to relevant police files when she began her research in the 1950s. 'Even today,' she says, 'scholars cannot get access to Maharashtra's archival material for period since independence. So, the definitive study is yet to come.' Consequently, the exact numbers of the Brahmin casualties might have been lost in history forever. She estimates the total damage by action in the range of Rs 6,00,00,000 to Rs 10,00,00,000, basing it on 'fragmentary reports in newspapers and unofficial publications' and terming it as being quite underestimating of the actual extent of damage.[22] Patterson mentions that after the spurt of riots and killings in Bombay, Poona and Nagpur, the violence magnified and spread to the 'extreme southwest of the Deccan plateau—the *Desh*—of the Marathi linguistic region' that included Satara, Belgaum and Kolhapur.[23] Beginning initially with just the Chitpawans and those with surname as Godse, the ire spread to other Brahmin sub-castes and surnames. The violence and atrocities were driven by two factors, caste and politics.

In several parts of Maharashtra where the Chitpawans had held sway over a lot of political power, land and monetary heft since the days of the Peshwas and even under the British, the fervent anti-Chitpawan anger by the non-Brahmin communities spilt over. Dwarka Prasad Mishra, a senior Congress leader who was the home minister of the Central Provinces then, reminisces in his memoirs:

Although hardly half a dozen Maharashtrian Brahmans were involved in Godse's crime, a very large number of them had to pay for it. The murder of the Father of the Nation provided non-Brahmans with an opportunity to vent their wrath upon the Brahmans, who, though a mere four per cent of the population, had come to dominate every sphere of life in Maharashtra. No sooner the news of the Mahatma's murder was flashed than they protested that the murderer, Godse, should have been described as a 'Maharashtrian' [which in those days meant a Brahman only] and not a 'Maratha', a word exclusively used for the numerically largest section of the non-Brahman community, which claims a Kshatriya origin and into which Shivaji had been born.[24]

In fact, the *Kesari* printed a detailed apology on 14 February 1948 regretting its usage of the term 'Maratha Hindu' to describe Godse in its 31 January edition, terming it as a 'translation lapse'.[25]

Starting 2 February, violence rocked the city of Nagpur. The Samyukta (United) Maharashtra spokesperson G.T. Madkholkar 'lost his house and the premises of his newspaper together with an associated publishing concern'.[26] There was resentment against merger with the Bombay province, which was dominated by Gujarati and Parsi capitalists. Madkholkar had penned his angst in his memoirs, a Marathi book *Eka Nirvasitachi Kahani* (The Story of a Refugee). As Patterson surmises:

> By and large, in Nagpur, the 1948 disturbances were caused by a mix of anti-Hindu Sabha, anti-R.S.S. and anti-Samyukta Maharashtra feelings, but the common thread was anti-Maharashtrian Brahman [sic] hatred. While not all Brahmans [sic] were Chitpavan, a large number were, and the victims who were of other Brahman [sic] jatis were treated as though they were Chitpavans.[27]

The collector of Poona, in one of the very few official statements available, estimated the property damaged or destroyed at Rs 12,00,000 in the city and Rs 4,60,000 in the surrounding district.[28]

About Satara, which was the veritable seat of Chitpawan power, Patterson writes:

> Godse's act, which first set off anti-R.S.S. attacks, before long became the opportunity non-Brahmans [sic] had been waiting for to retaliate against Chitpavans for long years of real or imagined domination. Crowds in lorries reportedly owned by leading Maratha politicians and hundreds on foot surged through Brahman [sic] wards bent on revenge . . . In February 1948, one thousand of their houses were officially reported as having been burnt down, and an unspecified number were killed . . . one family named Godse was said to have lost three male members.[29]

In Kolhapur, apart from attacks on Hindu Mahasabha and RSS offices, the studio of film director Bhalji Pendharkar was gutted down for his alleged pro-Mahasabha stances. Kolhapur suffered the second highest amount of damages of property after Sangli. The maharaja of Kolhapur ordered an inquiry into the riots in June 1948 under Justice N.H.C. Coyajee of the Bombay High Court. Justice Coyajee brought out a detailed ninety-five-page report dwelling in depth about the intense anti-Brahmin feelings that existed. In his concluding remarks, he states:

> The anti-Brahmin feeling in the State, which existed for a long number of years was brought to a head in the speeches of Madhavrao Bagal[30] and the activities of his immediate followers . . . although it is on record that the initial outburst, in the sense that the first attack was made on the Hindu Mahasabha office and some members . . . of the R.S.S. were also objects of attacks, a scrutiny of the evidence . . . shows that this was only on a very small scale [and] that the opportunity was taken by the mobs for a concerted and general attack on the Brahmin community as a whole . . . the object was in fact to attack the community of Brahmins residing in the city of Kolhapur and in the State.[31]

Intense violence occurred in the seven Patwardhan princely states (Miraj Senior and Junior, Sangli, Tasgaon, Jamkhandi, Kurundvad Senior and Junior); factories, properties and homes of Brahmins were destroyed and their lives taken away. One of the great industrial successes from Sangli, Vishnu Ramachandra Velankar and his Sri Gajanan Weaving Mills bore the maximum brunt of destruction. Estimates of property damage in the Patwardhan princely states were put at about Rs 2,30,00,000, with the worst hit Sangli accounting for Rs 1,60,00,000.[32]

In the absence of documented or accessible records, fragments of this trauma exist in the works of several people—Vasanti Bhide Marathe's *1 February 1948: Turning Point*, Pratibha Ranade's *Smaranvela*, Vyankatesh Madgulkar's *Vavtal*, Priya Prabhu's *Gandhi Vadhotttar Jaalpol*, M.G. Patkar's *Gandhi Hatya: Itihaasaache hi Ek Paan*, Madhu Kulkarni's *Te Daha Divas* among many others.

Most villages in Maharashtra were thus ethnically cleansed of Brahmin households as majority of them deserted their lands, homes and property to safer hideouts in the cities of Bombay and Poona where they had to start life afresh. Patterson notes:

> Ever the adaptive Brahmans [sic], Chitpavans have deliberately moved into arenas where they are no longer vulnerable in a Maratha-dominated

state. They avoid local politics and administration, and aim at central government jobs; they enter the officer levels of the armed forces; and above all, pioneer once again, this time in new technologies and a variety of scientific endeavours . . . just as they parlayed the disaster of 1818 into success, so too Chitpavan Brahmans [sic] have turned the trauma of 1948 to their collective and individual advantage.[33]

The author's own small initiative to crowd-source oral history accounts, family anecdotes and first-person accounts of the few survivors through a post soliciting responses via social media opened a floodgate of information and angst. This was a story that had never been heard or told and the family and survivors were keen to share, many on strict conditions of anonymity, given the tenuous current socio-political situation in the country in general and Maharashtra in particular. However, a few of these accounts have been reproduced in the Appendix as the only possible link to those lost and unheard voices of the past.

The political angle to the riots was fanned, ironically by the Congress that had been fed on decades of Gandhian non-violent sermons. It saw this opportunity as the last nail in fixing the coffin of their political rivals in the Hindu Mahasabha. As Dwarka Prasad Mishra notes:

Besides attacking Brahman [sic] hearths and homes [in Nagpur], attempts had been made to set fire to the buildings housing Brahman [sic] educational institutions. When a municipal fire-brigade tried to save the Joshi High School it was forced to beat a retreat by the mob . . . in the rural areas orange trees in Brahman [sic] plantations were uprooted and their owners harassed . . . The Nagpur incidents were not isolated as more harrowing scenes of violence against Brahmans [sic] were enacted in many parts of Marathi-speaking areas, particularly in Southern Maharashtra. Those who indulged in these unlawful activities also included a large number of Congressmen belonging to non-Brahman [sic] communities. In fact, in Nagpur and Berar the troublemakers were mostly Congressmen, some being even office bearers of the various Congress Committees. Among those arrested by the police, there were more than a hundred Congressmen and I was immediately subjected to pressure for their release. In a meeting of prominent Congressmen of Nagpur, I had to face severe criticism. When they threatened to take their complaint to Home Minister Patel that I had to tell them to bring a directive for me from Delhi . . .[34]

Far from towing the line of the Congress leaders who hauled up Mishra, Patel was in fact unsatisfied with the action that the chief minister of Bombay, B.G. Kher, had taken. In a letter to him, dated 5 June 1948, he regretted that he was 'unconvinced that the action was wise and proper'. He added that the 'fear of further reprisals by perpetrators of evil and wrong-doers can hardly be a justification for treating such wrong-doers with leniency . . . such things are done under a spirit of mass hysteria, and leniency shown at one time is soon forgotten, more particularly it is ignored when the scene of another mass hysteria sets in.'[35]

The assassination and the aftermath also brought to fore the ugly intra-party conflicts, personal egos and caste clashes within the Congress. As Mishra was to discover through a Special Branch report that his Ministry was privy to, at a conference of Nagpur and Berar Congressmen held in Amravati, it was stated that 'the assassin of Gandhi was a Brahman and as such, no Brahman, be he a Maharashtrian, Gujrati, Marwari or from UP could be entrusted with the responsibility of governance' and that the 'CP was being governed by Brahman Ministers is a challenge of the purity of the Congress'.[36] Mishra explains in his memoirs that the barbs were aimed at him and R.S. Shukla as the UP 'Brahman' ministers, while the Gujrati stood for the state's finance minister D.K. Mehta. The episode also gave heft to the lobbies of Nehru versus Patel within the Congress and an attempt to besmirch the latter and his hold over law and order.

A hartal was meanwhile called in Bombay on 31 January, during which news spread of the fact that some Hindu Mahasabha workers had distributed sweets to celebrate Gandhi's death in Thakurdwar, Vitthalbhai Patel Road, Dadar and other areas.[37] Huge, irate mobs then attacked Hindu Mahasabha offices in Girgaum area. The offices of the Brahmin Sabha, the anti-Pakistan Front, the *Vividh Vritta* (Hindu Sabha weekly), and some houses and shops of prominent Mahasabha leaders was stormed and furniture burnt in massive bonfires. At Dadar, Phanshikar, a sweetmeat seller had to pay the penalty of his sweets being used for distribution with his entire shop smashed to pieces. Opposite the Brahmin Sahayak Mandal in Dadar, sugar had been distributed. Hence its office too was destroyed.[38] Hindu Sabha office in Parel and a shop called Hindu Sangathan Bhandar too met a similar fate.

Savarkar's house in Dadar became the next object of the mob's anger. A mob of 500–1000 people gathered outside his house, shouting slogans and throwing stones. As a news article notes, the streets had 'all the books, pictures and photos of Savarkar, which were then made into small bonfires by the people outside. At quite some places, before burning them up, people would first trample under foot Savarkar's photos that lay about'.[39]

Many of the mobsters slipped inside the house and to the ground floor that was occupied by Bhide Guruji, a former secretary of Savarkar and editor of an English weekly, *Free Hindusthan*. Savarkar was resting in his room on the first floor. The presence of mind of his associates Bal Savarkar and Bhaskar Shinde saved Savarkar's life, as also those of his wife Yamuna and son Vishwas who were with him. The previous night, ten persons of the household, including Savarkar's bodyguard Appa Kasar and his personal secretary Gajanan Damle, had been taken into custody by the Bombay Police. As Patterson notes: 'Congress supporters were incensed and swarmed around Veer Savarkar's house, but police intervention saved him from bodily harm. But police were not in time to prevent his brother, who lived nearby, from being hurt.'[40] Narayanrao Savarkar was dragged out and hit with stones and mortars till he fell down in a pool of blood. He suffered severe head injuries and was admitted to hospital, even as his family was shifted away in haste to a safe place.

By the noon of 31 January, a special team of the Central Intelligence Department from Delhi and the Special Branch of CID of Bombay Police raided Savarkar's house. Nagarvala too carried out a search along with his team and stated that 'Savarkar at the time looked frightened and full of anxiety. I did not find him ill at the time.'[41] The police witness mentions how in the first floor of Savarkar Sadan, there were 'glass panes broken and stones lying inside the house here and there'.[42] The team seized all his private papers—143 files and some 10,000 letters. The letters included correspondences that Savarkar had with Nathuram and a dozen or so from Apte, but none of the material was related to anything about the murder. There were also no letter exchanges between Savarkar and Karkare.[43] It was an indisputable fact that Nathuram and Apte knew Savarkar on intimate terms, that he had corresponded with them and also funded their newspaper. On their part they were staunchly devoted to him as the Savarkarite faction within the Mahasabha and shared his disdain for Gandhian and Congress ideology. Yet the police teams were bound to be disappointed with the material seized that had no prima facie linkages to a conspiracy to murder Gandhi that the group might have hatched with Savarkar.

Between 1 and 5 February, a nationwide mass detention of Hindu Mahasabha and RSS leaders was conducted. R.K. Tatnis, the famous editor of the Marathi weekly *Vividh Vritta*, Jamnadas Mehta, Anant Hari Gadre (president of Bombay Provincial Hindu Mahasabha), M.N. Talpade (vice-president of Bombay Provincial Hindu Mahasabha) and several prominent leaders of the Mahasabha were arrested. On 4 February, the RSS was declared an unlawful organization throughout India and about 160 members of the Sangh and Mahasabha were detained in Bombay alone.[44] Even women members of the RSS were not spared. Across India, the general figure in this massive and unprecedented round-up and arrests of leaders and workers of Hindu groups was said to have exceeded 25,000.[45] The ban on the RSS resulted in a whopping arrest of about 20,000 members of the organization on no charges and for the mere fact that they were associated with the body.[46] It was a matter of time before the police were to come for Savarkar too.

Savarkar had issued a statement on 31 January expressing deep shock on the tragic assassination of Gandhi and appealed to the people to stand by the Central government of free India to maintain order in the country.[47] He issued another statement on 4 February, the text of which is as follows:

The statement of the President [Hindu Mahasabha President L.B. Bhopatkar] and the joint statement of some members of the Working Committee of the Hindu Mahasabha at Delhi, have done well in expressing authoritatively the feelings and in clearing the position of the Hindu Mahasabha as a Democratic and Public Organization as regards the gruesome assassination of Mahatma Gandhiji. I too as one of the Vice Presidents of the Mahasabha subscribe to their feelings and condemn unequivocally such fratricidal crimes whether they are perpetrated by individual frenzy or mob fury. Let every patriotic citizen set to his heart the stern warning, which history utters that a successful national revolution and newly born national state can have no worse enemy than a fratricidal civil war, especially so when it is encompassed from outside by alien hostility.[48]

The Sarsanghchalak of the RSS, Golwalkar, too condemned the 'brutal assassination' and said:

A deed of exceptional brutality having been perpetrated in the inhuman assassination of the most revered and beloved personality of the times,

I feel it my duty to depart from our usual abstinence from making public statements and giving vent to the feelings of horror and grief, which the news has evoked in my mind. It is a tragedy of unparalleled magnitude— the more so, because the evil genius is a countryman and a Hindu. Every right-minded countryman will feel, on top of the inexpressible grief at this bereavement, a sense of shame in that this perverted being happens to be his countryman. Living in these critical times the country needs a great unifier and pacifier, that the great soul was, and encompassing his death is a deed of unpardonable national disservice. With outraged feelings, we mourn the loss and look to the future.[49]

Savarkar knew that the police were building a case against him. On the night of 4 February, Nagarvala knocked at his door. He had come with the police surgeon and doctor to examine Savarkar's medical condition. The next morning when the police once again knocked at his door he asked them: 'So you have come to arrest me for Gandhi's murder?' They nodded and said that in the absence of any evidence directly linking him to the murder, the police were arresting and booking him under a draconian colonial legislation, the Preventive Detention Act. Through its earlier versions such as the Defence of India Act or Rowlatt Act it empowered the government to detain anyone without trial, with no offence established or charges framed. Through Section (2) (1) (a) of the Bombay equivalent of the Act—Bombay Public Security Measures Act, 1947—Commissioner of Police Jehanger Sohrab Bharucha sent in his orders to detain Savarkar.[50] Savarkar ironically became the first victim of the Act exercised by the independent government of the country. Before entering the police van that had come to take him he asked them if he could use the toilet at home. The police were alerted and Savarkar is said to have smiled and told them: 'Do not be afraid. I am an old man now and you should not fear a repeat of Marseilles, nor is there any occasion for it.'[51]

Savarkar was taken away as a 'detenu' and lodged in the Arthur Road Jail. After building evidence against him, his detention would be converted into arrest with retrospective effect. Savarkar declined to avail of the facility and home food. His wife and son were allowed to meet him only one-and-a-half months after his arrest, on 24 March. No news about him trickled out of the prison, neither were any charges framed against him. On 18 February, he was served with another order of detention (Notice No. 1202) under Section 3 of the Bombay Public Security Measures Act, Act VI of

1947, by Commissioner Bharucha. This was on the charge of 'inciting Hindus against Mohammadans . . . to commit acts of violence against Muslims and persons, who are endeavouring to bring about unity between Hindoos and Muslims . . . therefore acting in a manner prejudicial to the public safety and peace of Greater Bombay'.[52]

Savarkar was not granted access to his legal adviser to draft a reply to this notice from Bharucha. He thereafter sent a lengthy letter, dated 22 February, addressing the charges that the commissioner had put on him for his detention:

> I never promoted hatred and incited Hindus to hate or to commit acts of violence against the Mohammadans as Mohammadans. I have been an advocate throughout my life of Genuine Indian Nationalism. I always emphasized that all citizens who owed loyalty to the Indian State must be loved as fellow citizens and treated with equality of rights and obligations to the state, irrespective of caste, creed, or religion, without the least distinction being made as Hindu or a Mohammadan or a Parsee or a Jew. 'One man, one vote' and 'Services to go by merit alone'—these two principles will be found endlessly repeated in all my writings and speeches made throughout my political career for some 50 years in the past. To substantiate these facts, I refer to my books like 'The History of 1857' written so early as in 1908 A.D. down to the six presidential speeches delivered by me from the platform of the Hindu Mahasabha itself. If required and given facilities, I will cite a number of passages from them to prove how I insisted on the foundation of a Secular State in India on the above principles and how I praised and loved those Mohammadans who fought in this genuinely national spirit for the Freedom of India in the past . . . but it is true that this very Genuine Indian Nationalism made me criticize and combat the anti-Hindu and anti-national demands of Muslim League. The Communal Award, the Muslim League demand for the vivisection of our common motherland, their repudiation of Indian Nationality, the horrible suffering of the Hindus, which followed the League's Direct Action movement, the Division of our integrated country and nation into two states brought about by the grant of Pakistan—are but a few leading events, which I cite to illustrate the reasons why I have been exhorting the Hindus to organize and militarize themselves so as to be able to defend their persons, hearths and houses against the attacks of fanatical Muslims—especially so when the then British Government

encouraged these fanatical and anti-national forces and failed to afford
any efficient State protection to the Hindus. But whenever I exhorted
the Hindus to defend themselves I never failed to point it out that their
self-defence must not trespass beyond the principles and the rights and
the scope of self-defence as defined in the Indian Penal Code itself. My
speeches referred to above and other writings will substantiate this fact . . .

Sardar Patel himself in replying [to] provoking speeches of some
Muslim leaders retorted 'Sword shall be met with Sword.' But that does
not surely mean that he hated all Muslims alike or incited violence. It is
quite to the point here to state that aggression on the part of Muslims alone
was not resisted by me to the best of my power through religious bigotry.
For I resisted oppressive and aggressive customs and action of Hindu
orthodoxy too against so-called untouchable Hindu castes. I led a vigorous
active campaign also for several years against the inequality and injustice
born of the caste-by-birth structure upheld by the Hindu orthodoxy.
But that could not mean that I promoted hatred against my orthodox
co-religionists . . . ever since our free India State came into existence I
have publicly emphasized the point that in this our own democratic state
all public activity must now be strictly limited to constitutional and legal
methods . . . on the 15th of August last I accepted and raised on my
house, our new National Flag even to the embarrassment of some of my
followers. I had already practically retired from public activity.[53]

On 11 March 1948, Savarkar was presented before the chief presidency
magistrate of Bombay. The same day he was deemed placed under arrest by
the Delhi Police (Tughlak Road Police Station). It was only on this day that
he was formally named as an accused in the conspiracy to murder Gandhi.

The magistrate granted police custody for fourteen days and Savarkar
was lodged in the same prison under a warrant from the Delhi presidency
magistrate. The efforts of a local advocate of Bombay, S.V. Deodhar,
enabled Savarkar to manage a meeting with his family and also execute a
general power of attorney in favour of his son Vishwas to facilitate funds
for the trial and for running the household.

The Investigation

From the scene of crime at Birla House, the Tughlak Road Police of Delhi
arrested Nathuram for questioning. He maintained that he alone was

responsible for the murder. But the police discovered a pocket diary from him where he had scrupulously noted down all the sums of money spent on every little expenditure including those paid to the taxi and tongas. He told the police that from 24 to 27 January he had stayed at the Elphinstone Hotel in Bombay. On 5 February the officers of Bombay CID went to the hotel to check the register at the hotel and quiz its manager Kashmiri Lal. Apte and Karkare were incidentally in the hotel then. They had been staying there since 3 February, but seeing the commotion and the inquiry happening, managed to slip away.

In other glaring examples of police inefficiency, Nagarvala had ordered the Poona Police to arrest Badge if found in the city, on 24 January. This was not based on the apprehension that he was part of the conspiracy. Badge was a frequent and habitual troublemaker and Madanlal's statement that people from Bombay and Poona were involved gave Nagarvala the idea to quiz the man in the province who knew all about explosives and their sales. Badge had rushed back from Delhi after the fiasco of 20 January and was very much at his residence. But possibly due to the differences between Bombay Police and Poona Police, it was not until 31 January, after the murder, that he was arrested. His arrest was a gold mine for the police as he began to sing like a canary under detention. Obviously, if the police had apprehended him six days prior to the murder, the plot would have been foiled and Gandhi's life saved.

Commenting on the police's questionable role in the whole case, Tushar Gandhi writes:

> One of the crucial factors in the success of the murder plot was that the police—who were hampered by Gandhi's decision not to allow additional security and frisking of his visitors—did not think of placing constables or inspectors from Bombay, Poona or Ahmednagar at Birla House, who would have been able to identify Godse, Apte and Karkare . . . The Congress Government and at least some of the members of the Cabinet were fed up of the interventions of the meddlesome old man. To them, a martyred Mahatma would be easier to live with . . . the way the investigation was carried out, and the lackadaisical approach of the police in trying to protect Gandhi's life, leads one to believe that the investigation was meant to hide more than it was meant to reveal. The measures taken by the police between 20th and 30th January 1948 were more to ensure the smooth progress of the murderers, than to try and prevent his murder.[54]

Badge was sent to Bombay for questioning by Nagarvala and to let him confront Madanlal who too was being brought there. Badge had broken up with his accomplices after his flight on 20 January and hence was unaware of what all transpired thereafter or how the Beretta was procured. But the plot prior to that and the names of everyone associated was sketched in detail by Badge. Shankar, who had gone to Sholapur to meet his mother, faced arrest after his return to Poona. Gopal Godse was also arrested and brought to Bombay.

After their flight from the Elphinstone Hotel, Apte and Karkare who were the only two conspirators still at large, tried in vain to find accommodation in their usual hideout Arya Pathikashram. They landed up at Karkare's friend G.M. Joshi's house in Navpada. The duo then took a train to Poona. The police apprehended that they might have slipped to the Portuguese territory of Goa or into Nizam's Hyderabad. It seemed their conscience did not let them remain in hiding for too long and they made up their mind to surrender, returning to Bombay on 11 February. They checked into Pykre's Apollo Hotel, behind Regal Cinema, on 13 February signing as 'N. Kashinath' (Apte) and 'R. Bishnu' (Karkare). Apte met his love Manorama that evening. The same night Inspector B.A. Haldipur came to the hotel and arrested them.

The name of Parchure and the Gwalior connection came out in the interrogation. Deputy Superintendent N.Y. Duelkar of the Bombay CID arrived in Gwalior on 14 February to secure the arrest of Parchure. But he realized that the man had already been arrested and held in the ancient fort of Gwalior where the erstwhile Mughal emperors incarcerated their most dreaded prisoners. His crime was that he had distributed sweets on hearing the news of Gandhi's murder and the newly established Congress government was determined to not let its main political rival alone for this indiscretion. Following communal disturbances in Gwalior after the murder, they locked Parchure and his associates in the local Hindu Mahasabha under the Maintenance of Public Order Ordinance.

Thus in a fortnight after the murder, all the conspirators, their alleged sponsors and suppliers were in police custody. Given the loose ends in the police investigation and multiple layers of command and control that had botched up the investigation till then, Sardar Patel decided to transfer the case entirely to Nagarvala. In a long letter dated 27 February 1948, addressed to Prime Minister Nehru, Patel, who had kept himself closely abreast of the investigations through daily evening briefings by Sanjevi, outlined the progress of the case and his own assessment of the suspects:

> All the main accused have given long and detailed statements of their activities. In one case, the statement extends to ninety typed pages. From the statements, it is quite clear that no part of the conspiracy took place in Delhi. The centres of activity were Poona, Bombay, Ahmednagar and Gwalior. Delhi was, of course, the terminating point of their activity, but by no means its centre; nor do they seem to have spent more than a day or two at a time, and that too only twice between 19 and 30 January. It also clearly emerges from these statements that the RSS was not involved in it at all. It was a fanatical wing of the Hindu Mahasabha directly under Savarkar that [hatched] the conspiracy and saw it through. It also appears that the conspiracy was limited to some ten men, of whom all except two have been got hold of. Every bit of these statements is being carefully checked up and verified and scrutinized, and where necessary, followed up ... every item of information that is being communicated to us through sources, known and unknown, real, anonymous or pseudonymous, is being investigated. More than 90 percent of these have been found to be just imagination. Most of these have been directed to the activities of RSS men in various centres. We have followed this up, and except vague allegations that sweets were distributed or joy was expressed, hardly anything of substance has been found in them . . . I have come to the conclusion that the conspiracy of Bapu's assassination was not so wide as is generally assumed, but was restricted to a handful of men who have been his enemies for a very considerable time—the antipathy can be traced to the time when Bapu went for his talks with Jinnah, when Godse and some others of the conspiracy went to Wardha to prevent him [Bapu] from going. Of course, his assassination was welcomed by those of the RSS and the Mahasabha who were strongly opposed to his way of thinking and to his policy. But beyond this, I do not think it is possible, on the evidence, which has come before us, to implicate any other members of the RSS or the Hindu Mahasabha. The RSS have undoubtedly other sins and crimes to answer for, but not for this one.[55]

On 17 February, Nagarvala was informed by the home ministry in Delhi that he had been appointed as the superintendent on special duty to conduct investigation into Gandhi's murder. With all the accused in his custody,

Nagarvala managed to compile a hefty dossier of evidence and traced the entire course of action of the plotters. Three men were still absconding: G.S. Dandavate, who had sold the Beretta to Nathuram in Gwalior; Gangadhar Jadhav, who was Parchure's lieutenant; and S.D. Sharma, who had given Badge the .32 revolver in exchange of Nathuram's .22 pistol. Confessions were extracted from all the accused, except Savarkar, and Nagarvala was adept at getting his prisoners to speak out 'Nagarvala had convinced himself,' as Malgonkar writes in his book, 'that Savarkar was the organizer of the plot to kill Gandhi and was desperate to be proved right. It is also possible that the entire police organization believed, rightly or wrongly, that "someone up there" would be highly gratified if Savarkar could be implicated.'[56] In Gopal Godse's memoirs, he mentions how not a part of his body was free of bruises from custodial torture by the police, as he tried to convince them in vain that he had not visited Savarkar on his way to Delhi, nor did he even know where his house was in Bombay.[57]

The one man who was most willing to comply was Badge who was turning out to be exceedingly useful and in due course was also to turn approver for the prosecution case. Extracting his confessions also meant getting those of Shankar too who would say nothing of his own accord but toe his master's voice. According to Gopal even Badge who held Savarkar in great veneration initially did hold fort but it was becoming increasingly difficult. 'The interrogators,' he reminisces, 'possessed the ability to make even a dumb man articulate.'[58] Badge finally capitulated and agreed to confess on oath that on 17 January, before leaving for Delhi, the three of them visited Savarkar's house to seek his blessings. His statement said that Shankar was asked to wait outside in the compound, while he himself was asked to sit in the waiting room of the ground floor. Nathuram and Apte went upstairs to seek their mentor's blessings and in 5–10 minutes, they came down. Savarkar himself came following them and while leaving blessed them cheerfully in Marathi, saying 'Yashaswi houn ya!' (Come back victorious!). He also confessed that when he asked Apte why they had all planned to go to Delhi in the first place, the latter told him that it was to carry out Savarkar's orders to finish off Gandhi, Nehru and Suhrawardy. With some more flourish, Badge added that he was told that Savarkar had wickedly prophesied that the hundred years of Gandhi were over now and his end was but a matter of time.

After he turned approver, Badge's prison woes miraculously ceased. He received meat, eggs, sweets, cigarettes and liquor and also got a stipend.[59] Shankar too came in for preferential treatment. He needed assiduous coaching to adhere to the tale that his master had put up and often got bashed up for his lapses and lack of intelligence. Shankar himself confessed that Nagarvala would meet Badge often and question him if Shankar has been sufficiently and suitably coached, even as the trial dates kept approaching.

In Morarji Desai's testimony on oath dated 23 August 1948, he mentioned about the meeting with Prof. Jain who shared details about his former help Madanlal who had bragged about a daring act that he was to commit in Delhi along with a businessman of Ahmednagar. Though Professor Jain's initial sworn statement had no such mention, Desai added: 'Madanlal had told him [Jain] that Karkare had taken him to Savarkar, that Savarkar had a talk with him for two hours and that Savarkar had praised him for what he had done, had patted him on his back and had asked him to carry on his work.'[60] He confirmed the orders that he gave Nagarvala to keep a strict surveillance over Savarkar's house from that very night, even as he kept the source of information anonymous, as desired by Jain.

The Gandhi murder investigation and trial became an opportunity and an excuse for the ruling establishment for witch-hunts to settle scores with political opponents. Not only Savarkar, but another important politician of the times, Narayan Bhaskar Khare, writes about this attempt to implicate him in the murder by the police investigation. Khare was a Congressman and had been chief minister of the Central Provinces and Berar from 1937 and later the prime minister of Alwar State (1947–48). He also served as a member of the Constituent Assembly in 1947. Khare had his huge ideological differences with Gandhi and Nehru even back in his political heydays. He mentions about how the police had arrested a staunch Hindu Mahasabha member Giridhar Sharma Siddh from Alwar and all possible methods of torture employed by the police to effect a confession against Khare were made. When none of this worked, he was put in a tiny cell and a tank dug out in the compound that faced his cell. This was filled with water and a whole swarm of mosquitoes were put in. This ensured that Siddh could not sleep for nights on end and was at his wits' end. Khare writes:

In this mental condition of Siddh caused by lack of sleep the Alwar Police threatened him with dire consequences and tried their special methods. Along with this they also tried to tempt him. The police said

'Siddhji, you are blameless. There is no accusation against you. Why are you unnecessarily undergoing all these tribulations? You listen to our advice a little and you will be benefitted for the whole of your life . . . we shall show you the photograph of Godse and you study its features carefully and remember them. After 4 or 5 days we will again show you the same photograph and ask you whether you had seen a man with such features in Alwar. You then say, "Yes, there was a man with such features in the bungalow of the Prime Minister, Dr. Khare. He was staying there as his guest. Dr. Khare took him to the Maharaja who gave him a pistol and that man was practicing shooting with that pistol in the compound of Dr. Khare." That is all. You say so and you will be benefited for the whole of your life.' While saying so, bundles of currency notes came out from the pockets of the police. It need not be mentioned that Godse had never come to Alwar. So all this was false. Mr. Siddh was a strong man. Therefore he told the police that he will never put innocent lives in jeopardy by making such false statements. He abused the police as dogs and said none of them were fit to speak to him.[61]

Savarkar was acutely aware of these attempts by the police to fix him. Hence in his affidavit before the chief presidency magistrate of Bombay, Oscar H. Brown, dated 18 May 1948, he narrated that a week earlier, on 11 May 1948, he was taken from the Arthur Road Jail to the CID Office by the Bombay Police officers. He was then made to sit in a chair and Nathuram and all the other suspects were made to sit by his side or stand behind him. They were then photographed together. 'That I apprehend,' stated Savarkar, 'that the same photograph may possibly be used to concoct evidence against me.'[62] Savarkar hence instructed his advocate Deodhar to plead before the magistrate that an order be issued to the police to deposit the positives and negatives of this photograph in court during the pendency of the trial as it might prejudice his defence.

Mindful of his former mentor's incarceration and possible implication in the conspiracy, minister of industry and supply Syama Prasad Mookerjee wrote to Sardar Patel on 4 May 1948:

I understand Savarkar's name is being mentioned in this connection. I do not know what evidence has been found against him. I have not the least doubt that you will satisfy yourself that nothing is done, which may give rise to the suggestion later on that he was being prosecuted on account of his political convictions. I hope the records will be placed before you before any decision is taken. His sacrifices and suffering in the past have been considerable and unless there is some positive proof against him, he should not, at this age, be subjected to a charge of conspiracy to commit murder. I leave the matter to your decision.[63]

Mookerjee also pleaded for a considerate view to be taken of the Mahasabha and the RSS and their reputations not besmirched by a wide brush of the pen painting all its workers or ideologues as murderers.

In his response two days later, on 6 May, Sardar Patel wrote to Mookerjee from Mussoorie:

As regards Savarkar, the Advocate-General of Bombay, who is in charge of the case, and other legal advisers and investigating officers met me at a conference in Delhi before I came here. I told them, quite clearly, that the question of inclusion of Savarkar must be approached purely from a legal and judicial standpoint and political considerations should not be imported into the matter. My instructions were quite definite and beyond doubt and I am sure they will be acted upon. I have also told them that, if they come to the view that Savarkar should be included, the papers should be placed before me before action is taken. This is, of course, in so far as the question of guilt is concerned from the point of view of law and justice. Morally, it is possible that one's conviction may be the other way about.

I quite agree with you that the Hindu Mahasabha as an organization, was not concerned in the conspiracy that led to Gandhiji's murder; but at the same time, we cannot shut our eyes to the fact that an appreciable number of the members of the Mahasabha gloated over the tragedy and distributed sweets. On this matter, reliable reports have come to us from all parts of the country. Further, militant communalism, which was preached until only a few months ago by many spokesmen of the Mahasabha, including men like Mahant Digbijoy Nath, Prof. Ram Singh and Deshpande, could not but be regarded as a danger to public security. The same would apply to the RSS, with the additional danger inherent in an organization run in secret on military or semi-military lines. Nevertheless, we have already decided upon a policy of gradual releases and more than 50 per cent of those originally detained have already been released in accordance with that policy.[64]

Patel's remarks in this letter to Mookerjee were quite the crux of what was to become of Savarkar's legacy. Even if he were to be acquitted from the point of view of 'law and justice', the belief of his complicity had got so enmeshed that the 'moral' culpability would be an albatross hanging around his neck all his life, and even thereafter.

10

The Red Fort Trial

Red Fort, New Delhi, 27 May 1948

The imposing imperial structure, the Red Fort in the Old Delhi area of the metropolis was commissioned by Mughal Emperor Shah Jahan in 1638 when he decided to shift his capital from Agra to Delhi. The fort was ready for occupation by 1648 and had been the seat of Mughal imperial power. In its long and momentous past other than the ups and downs of the Mughal dynasty, the Red Fort was also witness to some historic trials within its precincts. The first was that of Emperor Bahadur Shah Zafar after the First War of Indian Independence in 1857. The trial of the captured soldiers of the INA of Subhas Chandra Bose was also held here in 1945.

A couple of months after Gandhi's murder, a government notification (No. 54/1/48) dated 13 May 1948 declared the fort as the site for another momentous trial, that of Mahatma Gandhi's assassination. A building in a specially designated area in the Red Fort was declared as a prison where all the accused were to be housed in the barracks. There were nine accused who were to be tried on behalf of the Government of India under Sections 109, 114, 115, 120(B) and 302 of the Indian Penal Code; Sections 3, 4, 5 and 6 of the Explosive Substances Act of 1908 and Sections 19 (D) and 19 (F) of the Arms Act of 1878. The nine persons were: Nathuram Vinayak Godse (aged thirty-seven), Narayan Dattaray Apte (aged thirty-four), Vishnu Ramkrishna Karkare (aged thirty-seven), Digambar Ramachandra Badge (aged thirty-nine), Madanlal Kashmirilal Pahwa (aged twenty), Shankar Kistayya (aged twenty), Gopal Vinayak Godse (aged twenty-seven), Dattatreya Sadashiv Parchure (aged forty) and Vinayak Damodar Savarkar (aged sixty-five).

486

A spacious hall on the top floor of a twin wing in the fort, hitherto principal camp office of the British Military Police, was converted into a courtroom. It was completely barricaded and several layers of security for entry and exit built up. A raised wooden platform served as the seat of the judge and the reporter of the court, while wooden benches on the right side of the room was the dock for the accused. The witness was to stand on the left to testify. About 200 chairs were placed in the room to accommodate special visitors and the press to watch the proceedings of this high-profile case. A big hall on the ground floor was reserved for the Bombay Police to maintain all the documents to be produced during the trial. The district and circuit judge of Kanpur, Justice Atma Charan, ICS, was to hear the case. Chandra Kishan Daphtary, advocate general of Bombay Province, was to be the chief prosecutor (N.K. Pettigara, senior prosecutor officiating in his absence and J.C. Shah assisting him). L.B. Bhopatkar was to represent Savarkar as his lawyer. Jamnadas Mehta and Ganpat Rai were to assist. Later, P.R. Das, the barrister-at-law from Patna, was engaged by Savarkar to specifically counter the accusations of the approver Badge. The other lawyers for the accused included: V.V. Oak from Bombay (for Nathuram), K.H. Mengle and G.K. Dua (for Apte), Narhar Daji Dange and G.K. Dua (for Karkare), Purnachandra Bannerji (for Madanlal), Mohanlal Maniyar (for Gopal Godse), P.L. Inamdar (for Parchure) and Hansraj Mehta (for Shankar). Badge tuned government approver. The court itself was constituted by an order to exercise a special power that normal courts in Delhi did not hitherto have—tendering a full pardon to an accused in a murder case. All the accused were shifted to Delhi—Savarkar being brought in by a flight from Bombay on 25 May.

The case trial formally began on 27 May—ironically, a day before Savarkar turned 65 when he was to face one of the biggest challenges in his life. Excitement and tension were rife in the courtroom among everyone who had gathered in the sweltering summer heat of Delhi in end-May. Even as the proceedings began, Bhopatkar informed the court that given his client Savarkar's frail health he should be given a comfortable and cushioned chair and not made to sit on the wooden benches with the other accused. The judge immediately acceded to the request. Other than Savarkar and Nathuram who had sullen, sombre faces, all the other accused seemed to be happily smiling and joking with each other. Savarkar came to court in dhoti, shirt and an open collar coat, his high-walled black cap, his pince-nez and chappals. He sat pensive and silent throughout the proceedings, only occasionally exchanging a few words with his counsel Bhopatkar or Ganpat Rai. Parchure's lawyer, P.L. Inamdar, notes in his memoirs:

> During the whole trial, I never saw Savarkar turning his head towards even Nathuram, who used to sit by him, in fact next to him, much less speak with him. While the other accused freely talked to each other exchanging notes or banter, Savarkar sat there sphinx-like in silence, completely ignoring his co-accused in the dock, in an unerringly disciplined manner . . . he would look towards the Court, the witness in the witness box, the Counsels, even the spectators, but never towards the rest of the accused in the dock where he sat . . . he did not talk to me in Court during the whole of the trial, except once. He had, I thought, perhaps resolved to act in court, his defence against the charge of conspiracy with Nathuram or with any of the accused and, in fact, to perform his role demonstratively, even with respect to the counsels of the other accused![1]

The charge sheet was read out to all of them and preliminary formalities completed before adjourning the case to 3 June. During this brief hearing, Nathuram complained, speaking in fluent English, about being treated as C-class prisoners and being denied even water for washing for several days. His accomplices affirmed the charge, except Badge who seemed to have won himself favours and comforts by turning approver. On Badge's role and appearance in the court proceedings, P.L. Inamdar writes an interesting description:

> Badge was a short statured, bespectacled man with long hair and a beard . . . he had the smile of a wily man and the evasive gaze of a shifty creature in his eyes. He was quick witted and knew fairly well when to take shelter behind humour or ignorance. At the Red Fort Court, Badge exhibited, I think, all the mannerisms of a trained witness, like parrying a question with an irrelevant answer; seeking inspiration by looking at the ceiling; delaying his answer by wiping his mouth; glancing questioningly at the Prosecution; shifting his legs or moving the folds of his dress in apparently meaningless ways; but never failing to wear a confident smile and answering smartly and in an assertive tone when the question asked of him was an expected one. One of my colleagues asked Badge if the

person he was referring to, was a lean man or a plump man, Badge looked at the ceiling for a moment and then pat came the reply, 'A fat one . . . as fat as your goodself!' to the merriment of all of us but to the obvious discomfiture of the questioner. Unfortunately, Judge Atma Charan, with his insistence on only what was just 'sufficient and necessary' did not record anything to adequately describe the drama he was witnessing in the court.[2]

As Inamdar states, Badge was a 'lucky find' for the Bombay Police. With the fury of the anti-Brahmin riots and sentiments raging in Maharashtra, Badge 'the non-Brahmin, unearthing facts, witnesses and also material exhibits against the Brahmin accused' made him extra special. He enjoyed the police hospitality as much as he could 'to supply the links in the chain of the so-called evidence of conspiracy'.[3] On the very first day of the trial Madanlal expressed a desire to convey something in person to Judge Atma Charan. During the subsequent hearing on 22 June, it became known that he was complaining of the special and preferential treatment that Badge was receiving from the police in the prison, both in Bombay and in Delhi. Commenting on the primacy that Badge and his position meant for the case and the extent of police protection that he received, Inamdar states:

The whole edifice of the Mahatma Gandhi Murder case was erected on the statement of the Approver. Apart from the fact that the Approver happened to be a brother of an employee of the Police Department of the then State of Bombay, it is now (in 1976) being disclosed by the writers of Freedom at Midnight (page 368) that 'in seventeen years (prior to 1948) Badge (the Approver) had been arrested a record 37 times on such varied charges as bank robbery to murder, aggravated assault, and a dozen arms violations . . . But Badge had been convicted only in one case, viz. 'Cutting down trees in a protected forest in 1930 during one of Gandhi's civil disobedience campaigns. It had earned Badge a one month jail sentence.' Having read this the author [Inamdar] has rubbed his hands in acute frustration for not having known or been told any of these facts before 30 July 1948 on which day the author had cross-examined Badge in Red Fort Court. The whole edifice of the case was thus a sheaf of straws but for the steel helmeted protection given to Badge and other Prosecution Witnesses during the course of the trial, and the atmosphere of terror prevalent everywhere in those days of 1948.[4]

The actual trial began with the recording of evidence from 24 June 1948 and went on till 6 November. One hundred and forty-nine witnesses were examined (out of a listed 275) by the prosecution and their evidence ran into a whopping 720 pages. The prosecution brought on record 404 documentary and eighty material exhibits. Thereafter, all the accused were made to record their statements from 8 to 22 November. About 106 pages of recorded statements were filed and the written statements of all the accused, except Shankar, ran into 297 pages. The defence on their part brought in 119 documentary exhibits. The hearing of the defence arguments lasted from 1 to 30 December. This was the broad summary of the trial proceedings.

Even as the prosecution proceedings were under way, advocate Inamdar received a message through Bhopatkar in the second week of September that Savarkar wished to meet him. He had sought the court's permission to allow Inamdar to his 12 feet by 12 feet cell in the barracks. Inamdar accordingly went to meet the man who was hitherto a deeply venerated figure for Hindu Sangathanists across India, but now confined to this misery in a tiny cell. Looking around the cell, Inamdar saw a small cot and bed, a small table and chair, a pitcher of water and a glass, and some articles of daily use. The table was strewn with a pile of books and a large file of papers. He was sitting prepared for Inamdar's visit and all the relevant case-related papers had been laid out on the floor, on a durrie. In a low voice, Savarkar told him:

> Mr. Inamdar, I am glad to have you with me . . . I have very much liked
> your terse and correct expression. Your cross examination of witnesses is
> by far the best. Yes, all of you are working and doing your best. But you!
> I am really impressed by your work. I want your opinion and assistance.
> I hope you do not mind.[5]

For the next three hours, Savarkar took him through the minutest case details, the corroborating evidence and exhibits and sought Inamdar's approval and suggestions on what line of argument to make. Evidently and quite naturally, he was consumed by the worry of being drawn into the case and was restless about his acquittal. As Inamdar mentions:

> He repeatedly asked me if he would be acquitted and wanted me to assure
> him sincerely. What I noted was that he did not ask me a single question

about the case against my clients, Dr. Parchure and Gopal Godse or about any of the other accused including Nathuram, nor any question about me personally.[6]

Savarkar seemed to be deeply mindful of his words and actions with the co-accused and did not want any more suspicion drawn on him than what had already led him to this situation. In fact, Inamdar notes that Savarkar's complete lack of warmth and even recognition, 'his calculated, demonstrative, non-association with him either in court or in the Red Fort jail' deeply hurt Nathuram who 'yearned for a touch of Tatyarao's [Savarkar] hand, a word of sympathy, or at least a look of compassion in the secluded confines of the cells!'[7] But this was not to be! Nathuram simply did not exist in Savarkar's scheme of things where an honourable release was the only paramount concern. Nathuram even referred to his 'hurt feelings' during Inamdar's last meeting with him at the Simla High Court.

Nathuram Godse's Testimony

On 10 November, Nathuram began reading his written statement by about 10.15 a.m. The courtroom was presumably packed to capacity. His statement was a lengthy one, divided into five parts. The first dealt with the conspiracy and related matters and his answers to the charge sheet against him; the second was titled 'Gandhi's Politics X-rayed'; the third on Gandhi and independence; the fourth dealt with the frustration of an ideal and the last with the shattering of the dream of independence and a climax of anti-national appeasement. It was a masterful act by Nathuram, replete with high emotions and the attendant drama. So consumed was he by passion while reading it out that he felt giddy several times while making it and fell down and had to take some rest before resuming. His statement in court was banned by the Government of India for two decades thereafter and it was only in 1968 that the Bombay High Court allowed lifting the ban. It was then published by his brother Gopal Godse as a book *May It Please Your Honour*.

He detailed the entire career of Gandhi from the time he came back to India from South Africa and listed chapter and verse of those incidents that he considered were detrimental to the interests of the country, and particularly the Hindus. The Khilafat movement, Moplah carnage,

Afghan–Amir intrigue, the attack on Arya Samaj and the assassination of Swami Shraddhanand, the separation of Sindh, the capitulation to British demands in the Round Table Conference, the Communal Award, formation of governments with the British and resignations in a huff, accepting Cripps's Partition proposal, differential attitude towards Hindu and Muslim princes, capitulation to Jinnah's demands—all of these constituted the long litany of charges that he had against the Congress in general and Gandhi in particular. He considered Gandhi's silence against the inhuman crimes and tortures meted to the Hindus and Sikhs in the wake of Partition as his complicity in their misery. Families after families of pitiable refugees who were thronging Delhi and seeking shelter in mosques against the biting cold were asked by him to move away, he claimed.

He clarified that he was 'not an enemy of the Congress . . . always regarded that body as the premier institution which worked for the political uplift of the country.' He had and has differences with its leaders ideologically but there was no enmity between him and Gandhi on 'personal grounds'.

He said:

> I could foresee the result of my action against the life of Gandhiji and did very well realize that the moment the people came to know about it they would change their view about me in spite of the circumstances. My status and honour in the society and the sympathies, which the people entertained for me will be smashed completely. I fully realize that I would be looked upon as the most despicable fellow in the society.[8]

He continued:

> I am prepared to concede that Gandhiji did undergo sufferings for the sake of the nation. He did bring about an awakening in the minds of the people. He also did nothing for personal gain, but it pains me to say that he was not honest enough to acknowledge the defeat and failure of the principle of non-violence on all sides . . . to Gandhiji himself for the said service and before I fired the shots, I actually wished him and bowed to him in reverence. But I do maintain that even this servant of the country had no right to vivisect the country—the image of our worship—by deceiving the people . . . there was no legal machinery by which such an offender could be brought to book and it was therefore

that I resorted to the firing of shots at Gandhiji as that was the only thing for me to do.[9]

In the early part of his deposition, Nathuram dwelt on his association with Savarkar. He conceded to visiting Savarkar Sadan several times when he was in Bombay but hastened to add that these were limited to the Hindu Sangathan Office that was situated on the ground floor. Savarkar resided on the first floor of the building 'and very rarely that we could interview Veer Savarkar personally and that too by special appointment'.[10] Nathuram mentioned that in his own early years in politics Savarkar had been his mentor and ideal. Ever since his health plunged and Syama Prasad Mookerjee took over the reins of the Mahasabha, Nathuram mentioned that he and several others were increasingly disillusioned with their party toeing a line quite similar to that of the Congress. He decided then to 'organize a youthful band of Hindu Sangathanists and adopt a fighting program both against the Congress and the League without consulting any of those prominent but old leaders of the Mahasabha'.[11] He narrated instances where he felt disillusioned by Savarkar and the other old leaders of the Mahasabha. In 1946, after the blood-chilling incidents of the Noakhali carnage, Gandhi's prayer meetings in Delhi's Bhangi Colony had recitations from the Quran too. Could he dare read the Gita in a mosque in the 'teeth of Muslim opposition', questioned Nathuram. Apte and he therefore decided to disrupt many of these meetings with other refugees who were equally incensed. But when Savarkar heard about these disruptions, 'instead of appreciating our move, he called me and blamed me privately for such anarchical tactics, even though the demonstration was peaceful'.[12] Nathuram quoted Savarkar's admonishment:

Just as I condemn the Congressites for breaking up your party meetings and election booths by disorderly conduct, I ought to condemn any such undemocratic conduct on the part of Hindu Sangathanist also. If Gandhiji preached anti-Hindu teachings in his prayer meeting you should hold your party meetings and condemn his teachings. Amongst ourselves all different parties should conduct their propaganda on strictly constitutional lines.[13]

This does seem like Nathuram's over-zealousness and exaggeration, merely to protect his hero from any blemish as it is quite incredible that a retired

party president, a convalescing and reclusive one at that, would take the
trouble to call upon an ordinary party worker creating nuisance at a rival's
meeting and admonish or advise him, especially with his own claim of how
difficult and seldom it was that he gained Savarkar's personal audience.
This contradicts the claims by both him and Savarkar that theirs was
merely a casual and distant professional relationship, necessitated on and
off due to the *Agrani* or the Hindu Rashtra Dal, if the senior kept such a
close watch on the protégé's every action and sought to correct him as well.

Evidently Nathuram wanted to disassociate Savarkar from any blotch
by virtue of association with him. He claimed that after the tacit acceptance
of the Partition plan and the open call to support the new, independent
national government of free India by Savarkar and other leaders of the
Mahasabha, he and other Young Turks decided that 'the time had come
when we should bid good-bye to Veer Savarkar's lead and cease to consult
him in our future policy and program. Nor should we confide to him our
future plans.'[14] That the All-India Hindu Convention held during 9–10
August 1947 in Delhi and presided over by Savarkar rejected the resolutions
moved by him and Apte to appoint a council of action against Hyderabad
or boycott the Congress government that had vivisected the country added
to the sense of rage and disillusionment. The last straw was however
Savarkar's approval to Mookerjee to join the Nehru government as a
minister and his decision to go against the wishes of Hindu Sangathanists
to hoist the tricolour on his house on 15 August 1947. He said from then
on the Mahasabha and its policies came under attack by his newspaper too.
Nathuram claimed that he would not have gone into these details if the
prosecution had not averred that he was a mere pawn in Savarkar's hands,
devoid of a brain of his own, something that he considered as a 'deliberate
insult to my independence of judgment and action.' Laying to rest the
insinuations of his meeting Savarkar and the various confessions by Badge,
Nathuram said:

> I re-assert that it is not true that Veer Savarkar had any knowledge of my
> activities, which ultimately led me to fire shots at Gandhiji. I repeat that
> it is not true and it is totally false that either Mr. Apte in my presence or
> I myself told Badge that Veer Savarkar had given us an order to finish
> Gandhiji, Nehru and Suhrawardy as the approver is made to state falsely.
> It is not true that we ever took Badge to Veer Savarkar's house to take the
> last Darshan of Veer Savarkar in connection with any such plot or that

Veer Savarkar ever said to us: 'Yashaswi houn ya!' (Be successful and come back). Neither Mr. Apte in my presence nor I myself ever told Badge that Veer Savarkar told us that Gandhiji's hundred years were over and therefore we were bound to be successful. I was neither so superstitious as to crave for such blessings, not so childish as to believe in such fortune-telling.[15]

It took Nathuram a marathon five hours to finish his testimony. 'I have shown no mercy to the man I killed,' he said, 'I have no right to claim mercy from the Court—anyone—I do not want anyone to plead for mercy for me.'[16] He ended his speech saying: 'My confidence about the moral side of my action has not been shaken even by the criticism leveled against it on all sides. I have no doubt honest writers of history will weigh my act and find the true value thereof on some day in future.'[17] He signed off with cries of 'Akhanda Bharat Amar Rahe' and 'Vande Mataram'.

The entire court heard his speech with rapt attention. The judge, the advocate general and others listened, being visibly moved and in agonized silence. Many in the audience were moist-eyed and were seen wiping their tears. Savarkar however sat through this entire narration, unmoved 'in his chair, a sphinx sculpted in stone'.[18]

Despite the indifference shown demonstrably by Savarkar towards Nathuram and other accused so as to not jeopardize his own case, commentators inimical to him have alleged his hand even in this statement made by Nathuram in court. While there is no tangible supporting evidence for this, these insinuations however are repeated ever so often. As Tushar Gandhi alleges based entirely on conjectures:

> The language of the statement *leads one to the conclusion* that much of it either *flows directly from the pen* of the master orator and wizard wordsmith, V.D. Savarkar or *was definitely embellished* by him. Savarkar possessed a magical command over the spoken and written word. Even if not entirely written by Savarkar, the final drafted was *surely worked on by him* converting it into a highly emotionally charged document. Although he was known to be proficient in vitriolic writing, Nathuram was not known to possess the ability to sway people's emotions with words. His was a pen accustomed to spew abusive and vituperative language. It was *known that the accused were free to confer with each other* in prison and on several occasions, guards had been caught smuggling out messages from

the accused. There is *no reason to believe* that Nathuram was not able
to get his mentor and guru, V.D. Savarkar, to help him polish what is
today referred to by Nathuram's ideological offspring as his last will and
testament.[italicized emphasis mine][19]

On another occasion, Tushar Gandhi again states axiomatically that 'the
truth [emphasis mine] about his [Savarkar's] involvement in the plot
to murder Gandhi was buried in a pact of silence between him and his
protégés; Vinayak Damodar Savarkar, Nathuram Vinayak Godse and
Narayan Dattareya [sic]Apte knew the *truth* [emphasis mine] but they
never revealed it'.[20] While the emotions and the rhetoric from an aggrieved
descendant of the murdered is understandable, the 'truth' as he mentions
should have been made amply available by the prosecution while building
its case for the court too to take cognizance of and adjudicate accordingly.

Here, too, the insinuation is often made against Sardar Patel that
the home ministry, coming under his watch, wilfully botched up the
investigation and later even the prosecution's case to ensure freedom for
Savarkar and to win over the RSS and its mass base towards the Congress.
Patel's documented correspondences, some of which have been quoted
here, however show a completely different picture. But this has been an
old ploy to discredit Patel. The corrosive attacks took a terrible toll on his
health and political career even while he was alive. Questions were raised
against him even in the Parliament of India. The wedge between Prime
Minister Nehru and him was sought to be widened.

Savarkar's Testimony

After the depositions of the other accused, all of whom punctured holes
in the claims of the police approver Badge, it was Savarkar's turn on 20
November 1948. On his part, Daphtary tried his best to sound emphatic
and aggressive when it came to the prosecution's allegations against
Savarkar. As advocate Inamdar notes in his inimitable style:

> With regard to Savarkar, Daphtary [sic] argument sounded to me very
> hollow. I sensed that he could not do better because the evidence on record
> would not permit a more confident tone. When he tried to dramatize
> the evidence of the Approver Badge with regard to the part played
> by Savarkar, I could not but recall to my mind Aesop's picture of the

majestic king of the beasts being attempted to be disturbed in his sleep by the whining darts of a mosquito! The part shown to have been played by Badge *qua* Savarkar was nothing better than that! I could thus understand why Daphtary [sic] argument sounded so flat. I must say to the credit of Daphtary [sic] that he argued the Prosecution case against Savarkar not only without vehemence but also with demonstrative restraint, never ignoring Savarkar's presence, much less being disrespectful to him. But the nervous Savarkar had already insisted on engaging the biggest gun available to ward off the attacks of the mosquito of an approver. P.R. Das, Barrister-at-Law from Patna was reported to be arriving in Delhi to argue Savarkar's defence against Advocate General Daphtary [sic] and the Government.[21]

On the scheduled day, despite his fragile health, Savarkar read his lengthy fifty-seven-page long statement standing, and in a clear voice. It took him nearly two-and-a-half hours to finish reading his statement. He began with a narration of his own background of academic achievements, his literary and political career and the cause of Hindu Sangathan that he always strove for. He stressed on the Mahasabha's thrust under him for Hindu consolidation, even as it vouched for a secular state and constitution for all communities, after independence. He stated how he and leaders of his party were regular invitees by the erstwhile British government to the Round Table Conference discussions or to meetings with the viceroys and governors on the future course of the country and its polity. He stated that it was in the course of the work related to the Mahasabha that he was introduced to Nathuram Godse and to Apte who had stated his intent to start a rifle club in Nagar. Parchure was known to him as a leader of his party's Gwalior unit. He had heard of Karkare who had won the municipal elections on his party ticket. Savarkar mentioned that he had heard of Badge who had written to him stating that he was a Hindu Sangathanist and also sold arms for the defence of the community. He neither knew Shankar, Gopal and Madanlal, nor had he heard of them. As part of the organizational discipline of the party, leaders of different branches at district and provincial level were to send reports and updates to his office in the capacity of all-India president. Thus,he had received several letters from Poona, Gwalior, Ahmednagar and other places, some of which were those by the men who stood today as accused in this case, he stated. All the letters exchanged between him and Nathuram or Apte that the police had confiscated were hence totally linked with organizational matters and reports of the party. Hindu militarization was his pet project and that he had constantly even lobbied for this with the viceroy and the British government was an open secret. Thus, when local leaders conferred with him on this matter or sought his advice, he was always ready to guide them accordingly.

Even as he was eager to extricate himself from the case, the lengths to which Savarkar went to deny any close association with Nathuram were quite at tangent with the truth. Considering their closeness since the time they met in Ratnagiri in 1929 and Nathuram became his secretary and later went on to become a trusted lieutenant in the Mahasabha even in the intra-party factional jostles as a loyal acolyte, distancing Nathuram completely as just another acquaintance among the thousands of others Mahasabha workers was stretching it a bit too much. It was one thing to deny any involvement with the conspiracy to murder Gandhi and to highlight that the hitherto mentor–protégé relationship had soured in the recent years due to various reasons. But to term the overall association itself as anything but close or to call it a casual acquaintance, on par with the several others he had in the party, was being economical with the truth.

But like a practised lawyer, Savarkar thereafter went on to puncture the prosecution's arguments, layer by layer. To counter the prosecution's charge of his association with Nathuram and Apte through *Agrani,* Savarkar stated that like all other Hindu Sangathanist leaders in India, he too was trying to encourage and aid every effort to start new Mahasabha dailies in all provinces of the country. When the duo reached out to him with their desire to start one such in Marathi and when he was convinced of their ability shown through the securing of financial aid of other people, he decided to support the venture. He advanced a sum of Rs 15,000 on three conditions. First, it was to be a loan, a joint promissory note was to be passed on to him signed by Nathuram and Apte. Second, the concern had to be incorporated as early as possible as a limited liability company. Third, his loan should be converted into the share money of the said company. All the conditions were met by them and an incorporated company named Hindu Rashtra Prakashan was set up. Several well-known leaders and businessmen had contributed handsomely to this venture. Seth Gulabchand Hirachand, Shingre (ex-minister of the Bhor state), Vishnu Pant Velankar (mill-owner and millionaire of Sangli), Bhalji Pendharkar (cinema magnate of Kolhapur), Thopate (who was conferred the Nagar Bhushan title by the Raja of Bhor), Chandrashekhar Agashe, Rao Bahadur Shembekar of Baramati, Seth Jugal Kishore Birla and others had contributed to the share capital of this company. On his part, as the leader of the Mahasabha it was not just the *Agrani* that he patronized but other Hindu Sangathanist newspapers like *Vikram, Free Hindusthan* and others as well—both morally and financially. It was not, he claimed as the prosecution was making it out to be, that he helped the *Agrani* because of some special connection or fondness for its founding duo. Nathuram and Apte started the newspaper as their own concern and consequently the policy of the paper too was entirely under their control. To secure popularity and reach, they had pressed him to be associated with it either as chief editor or at least as a founder or patron, but he had not agreed to. He stated that it was communicated to them by him that he would remain only in the capacity of a well-wisher as he had been with other dailies and newspapers that propagated the Mahasabha ideology or 'Savarkar-vaad' (Savarkarism) as they called it.

Savarkar claimed that the duo had decided on their own accord to print his photo block on the front page of the issue and added that several other Hindu-minded papers in other provinces of India too had done so. Hence, he had not found anything objectionable in it. He added that in India it was very common for such photo blocks to appear on the front pages of newspapers and several of them carried Gandhiji's picture too—perhaps many that he had neither read nor heard of. The *Kesari* carried a photo block of the deceased Tilak. Would that mean that any court of law could indicate that the departed soul of Lokamanya Tilak should be still held accountable for whatever the *Kesari* publishes, he asked rhetorically. It was the editor of the newspaper alone who was responsible for the content of the newspaper.

After a year or so of starting the newspaper, the duo secured a press for the same. They then met Savarkar and insisted on their proposal to identify himself as a founder or patron. He once again refused and in fact sent them his views in writing as well, that he produced before the court:

The discussion had already taken place orally. Consequently I write about one point very clearly so that through any confusion in the oral talk it may not be lost sight of. It must appear in writing in the agreement that the policy of *Agrani* must remain exclusively and unconditionally in the hands of you two [Godse and Apte].[22]

Savarkar also stated that despite repeated requests from the two of them he did not write exclusive articles too for the *Agrani* as he felt it would be partial on his part to write only for them and not for the dozens of other Hindu Sangathanist papers. To write for all of them, his hectic political career did not permit. 'At times Apte and Godse were highly displeased on this account,' he admitted, 'but I could not make Agrani an exception.' They expressed their displeasure even in writing and he presented one such letter from Nathuram where he said:

> Gandhiji's *Harijan* has been re-started. At least ten volumes of writings in Gandhiji's own name and on a variety of topics appear in that paper. Unfortunately *Agrani* did not get even the slightest benefit (privilege) of your writing. *Kesari* had direct benefit of Tilak i.e. his writings. In *Harijan*, Gandhi is himself writing . . . as soon as your health improves than what it is, you please write at least one article every week and not only politics and Hinduism, but on revolution, mechanization, physics, intellectualism, literature, history, philosophy, poetry and such variety of subjects. This is my repeated prayer, which I offer with folded hands. It is not within propriety to speak in terms of money to you. If you begin to contribute articles to the *Agrani* regularly and on various topics, then with the intention that a part of the profit, which *Agrani* makes may be spent in your worship and out of devotion for you I shall send you Rs. 100 per month.[23]

Savarkar stated that 'inspite [sic] of the sincere but silly suggestion about paying'[24] money to him for his writings, he refused to write for them, nor did he advance a further Rs 10,000 as they had requested for.

Moving on to the prosecution's next allegation of Nathuram and/or Apte accompanying him on his political tours, Savarkar stated that it was common when he went on political tours and campaigns that several party members and office-bearers joined him from station to station. In the last eight years, he had undertaken no less than a hundred or so long-distance tours across the country. Among those, in about ten to twelve, the duo had indeed accompanied him. He also laboured the fact that the very letters that the prosecution presented amply demonstrated that in those cases too where he had accompanied him, Nathuram had pleaded several times with Savarkar's office for this. Many a time a regret too had been sent to him as other equally enthusiastic volunteers had to be accommodated as well. He quoted several letters including one by Nathuram in 1942: 'Please note that when you go to Delhi for the Working Committee meeting I wish to go to Delhi with your party. I am willing to travel on the servant's ticket even, with any second-class one your party has.' To this, Savarkar's secretary had written back: 'Thanks for your desire to go to Delhi with the President. But as it has been decided beforehand to take Mr. Bhagwat with us, we do not propose to trouble you this time.'[25] All this was to show the court that the duo had no special access or privilege accorded to them or to their journalistic work. 'How absurd, unfair and unjust would be,' opined Savarkar, 'any effort on the part of the Prosecution in alleging this legitimate association as an evidence against me in connection with a criminal case.'[26]

Savarkar then went on to demolish the testimony of the police approver Badge that had proved to be the most detrimental to his cause. He agreed with Badge's statement that in 1944–45, after attending a meeting at Gawalia Tank in Bombay, some thirty to forty people went to Savarkar Sadan to meet Savarkar. Badge was one of them. Here he was introduced as the proprietor of Shastra Bhandar and was asked to talk about his work, hearing which Savarkar had complimented him. Savarkar contended that there was nothing incriminating here as Badge was at that time (and till 1947) dealing with weapons that could be legally sold with a licence and given the Mahasabha's policy of militarization and a repeal of the Arms Act, anyone pursuing such a course would win his praise. He then referred to deposition of Badge relating to the night of 14 January 1948 that said: 'Apte, Godse and I proceeded to Savarkar Sadan. On reaching his house Apte took the bag from my hand and then Apte told me to wait outside. Apte and Godse went inside. They came back 5 or 10 minutes later. Apte had the bag with him, when he came out.'[27] Savarkar argued that nowhere did this indicate they went to meet him in person and even if true, it could be that the duo had gone inside to meet some friends in the Hindu Sangathan Office on the ground floor where normally a lot of party activists and workers routinely met and gathered. Referring to Badge's claim that Apte told him about Savarkar's orders to finish off Gandhi, Nehru and Suhrawardy, Savarkar debunked this as atrocious and as hearsay. Either of them could be merely inventing such wicked lies to exploit his moral influence on Hindu Sangathanists for their own purposes, he opined. He also brought to the attention of the court the emphatic denials of this claim by both Nathuram and Apte, made by Badge under possible police coercion and to save his own skin. 'An approver's statements,' he held, 'are not to be taken as reliable unless and until they are corroborated, in material particulars by independent and good evidence. But this part of Badge's evidence against me is not at all corroborated by any other independent and reliable evidence, which the prosecution could produce.'[28]

Debunking Badge's claim of having blessed Nathuram with his 'Yashaswi houn ya!' benediction and Apte thereafter claiming that he was told by his mentor that the hundred years of Gandhi were over, Savarkar emphatically denied this as well. By his own admission, since he was sitting in the room downstairs in the ground floor and if assumed to be true that Nathuram and Apte went upstairs and indeed managed to meet him, Savarkar argued that there was no way for Badge to then have known what the trio might have discussed at all. He said that despite the fact that gaining access to him was not that easy, if the duo had managed to meet him that evening, it was absurd to assume that they spoke only about some criminal conspiracy. He held that from the depositions of Nathuram and Apte, it was clear that on that day, 17 January, they had hired the same car and gone around Bombay on a flurry of errands. They had met one Afzulpurkar and he too had testified that they came to raise money for the Nizam Civil resistance movement from him that day. They met Patwardhan, Patankar, Kale and others to raise funds for their newspaper. So, he contended, that if at all they met him, they might have discussed these issues with him. And if at all he blessed them with those words, it could well have been for all these other projects of importance to the party and its ideology.

He then also referred to the deposition of the taxi driver Aitappa Kotian: 'At Shivaji Park I stopped with the taxi. The four passengers [Nathuram, Apte, Badge and Shankar] got down. So far as I could see they went up to the second house from the corner of the road on my right. They came back to the taxi in about five minutes time.'[29] Like a shrewd lawyer, Savarkar put up his case that Kotian's ambiguous statement of the location of the house they entered does not in any way corroborate the prosecution's claim that they all entered his house. He also drew the attention of the cross-examination done of Kotian where the latter stated that as a taxi driver running his meter, he had to be very clear about the time a passenger makes him wait as the billing would be determined by that. For Badge's account to be true that the four of them walked all the way up to his house, went upstairs, had a chat with Savarkar, came down with him and he blessed them and then they returned to the taxi, it would in all have taken about twenty to twenty-five minutes at the very least. He also asserted that in his testimony Shankar had inadvertently contradicted Badge's account where he said that he had stayed back in the taxi while the other three had gone somewhere that he did not know, the two pieces of evidence did not square up. Badge's assertion that he had decided to go along with the others to Delhi out of reverence for Savarkar and to carry out his commands too came under his attack. If he had such undying commitment towards him or the cause why did Badge run away on 20 January in the first bomb attack that got Madanlal into the net, Savarkar questioned.

Summing up all of Badge's evidences Savarkar opined that they were full of fabrications. Rationalizing his motive, Savarkar said:

He [Badge] saw that the police were working frantically on the basis of some shadowy suspicions they had to rope me in this case by hook or crook. Badge must have realized that the Police might be hoping that if they could implicate some outstanding public leading figure in this case, they could bank on sensational publicity and self-advertisement for themselves throughout the country, which otherwise was not likely to happen. In the depressing and harassing circumstances, which he himself was laboring under, as an accused on such serious charges, a man like Badge must have felt that the only way to save his skin was to turn approver and to render himself acceptable to the Police as an indispensable approver, the only implied condition was to bear false evidence against me. He fulfilled the condition and saved his skin. That Badge was both too shrewd and too unscrupulous is borne out by his character, which none else but himself made out throughout the evidence he has given before the court. Out of the several statements made in his deposition wherein he admits, even boastfully at times, that he spoke lies, made false pretensions and risked others' lives to save his own skin.[30]

Moving on to the deposition of Professor Jain and the appreciative statement that Savarkar allegedly made to Madanlal to carry on after hearing his exploits for two hours, Savarkar wholly denied this and claimed that he had absolutely no idea who Madanlal was.

If the versions of this story given particularly by Dr. Jain, relying on memory, slippery as an eel as human memory proverbially is, differ from

each other [sic]. Especially the present version of that part of it, which
refers to Madanlal's visit to me, and which is the only part that concerns
me, seems clearly 'cooked up to order'—under the pressure of the police.[31]

He asserted that Jain had made no such claim in his statement before the
magistrate in Bombay under Section 161 of the CrPC. He quoted Jain's
evidence testimony where he explicitly admitted: 'I also did not state before
the Magistrate that Madan Lal had told me that Veer Savarkar had sent
for him, had had a long talk with him for two hours, had patted him on his
back and had said "carry on".' It was only later under police coercion that
he added these elements to his original testimony, claimed Savarkar. He
hypothesized that after reading about the bomb explosion in Delhi on 20
January and Madanlal's name featuring in it, Jain got startled that he might
get implicated in some way given his proximity hitherto to Madanlal. It
was this that drove him to be better forearmed and hence decided not to
go to the police, but directly to the home minister of India and then of
Bombay state. Jain and his friend Angad Singh had repeatedly testified that
they thought Madanlal was a tall-talking young man given to parade his
own exploits with aplomb and hyperbole and seldom took him seriously.
How then did they come to believe what could have been Madanlal's brag
that the former president of the Hindu Mahasabha had called for him and
heard him out for two long hours, he quizzed. On similar lines, he went
on to dismiss the evidence provided by both Angad Singh (Jain's friend)
and Morarji Desai as 'being a hearsay and at that a third rate hearsay, it
is not admissible as evidence in law'[32] under Section 157. As a concocted
story passes from mouth to mouth, it gets increasingly fantastic and also
perverted, Savarkar claimed.

Taking a jibe at the prosecution that spent a lot of time in decoding
the case of the trunk call booked from the Hindu Mahasabha Delhi office
to Savarkar Sadan on 19 January morning, he said all it had found was
that somebody (who was never traced) made a call to Gajanan Damle and
Appa Kasar (which too was uncertain). Savarkar Sadan had a telephone
located in the reading room hall of the ground floor and was available for
use by secretaries and Mahasabha workers who visited the office and often
communicated with their counterparts from other cities, including Delhi.
It could well have been a personal call that someone from the Delhi office
might have made to Damle or Kasar, but the call did not go through. He
questioned the prosecution's intent and logic in linking this failed call to

assert that the conspirators had made that call to him to update him on the plot. Savarkar also distanced himself from the Hindu Rashtra Dal and said there were numerous such volunteer groups that helped the Mahasabha in its election campaigns, carrying out its propaganda and maintaining discipline. He had not even attended their yearly camps, causing them much irritation and displeasure at his indifference.

Savarkar claimed that the prosecution's claim at the beginning of the trial that there was an overwhelming documentary evidence to prove that Nathuram and Apte were unquestionably loyal and close to him and that they could not have committed the crime without his orders or consent was only to prejudice the court against him. Not a shred of incriminating evidence had been found among the 143 files containing about 10,000 letters confiscated from his residence office. The 120–125 letters exchanged between him and the duo too were purely of the nature he had discussed earlier. More so, he stated that in 1946, barring one letter there was no letter exchange between them and there was no correspondence in the years 1947 and 1948. The fact that after his resignation from the post of president of the Mahasabha and his subsequent ill health and withdrawal from public life, there was no letter communication proved that all of it was on purely party-related activity earlier, he asserted. Savarkar also highlighted the fact that since the time he and the top leadership of the Mahasabha began to take a conciliatory attitude towards the independent national government of India, many young Hindu Sangathanists, including Nathuram and Apte, saw it as a betrayal of the ideology. They openly began to oppose the leadership, which they saw as tilting in favour of the Congress and its stalwarts. They openly denounced Mahasabha resolutions and decisions. This was also one reason why the communication between the younger leaders and him dried up in the years leading up to independence and thereafter. The duo had, according to Savarkar, used their columns in *Agrani* for months for 'attacks on the failure of the Mahasabha under its old leaders to defend Hindudom and kept exhorting the Hindu youths to form an independent "Council of Action" wherein the "old lead" should have no hand whatsoever.'[33]

On the purported moral influence that he might have had, Savarkar took a swipe at his ideological bête noire, Gandhi:

Does it not often happen that some of the followers do actually try to exploit the moral influence of the leaders to further their activities, which the leader had never sanctioned? In 1942 in the 'Quit India' movement some leading workers who had been close associates of Gandhiji as Congressmen and respected him, resorted to underground violence. I am not concerned here with the question whether such an underground movement against a foreign domination was or was not justified. It is enough to say that Mahatma Gandhi condemned all underground violence. But masses resorted under the lead of these workers to arson, sabotage and bloodshed shouting all the while *'Mahatma Gandhiji ki Jai.'* But even the British Government did not put Gandhiji in the dock for their crime simply because the masses respected him and were doing these very criminal acts shouting *'Gandhiji ki Jai'* and therefore they must have consulted him.[34]

'The whole fabric of the prosecution evidence,' he emphasized, 'rests on but two sentences only: the first an hearsay; the second an inference.'[35] The first sentence was that he told Apte to finish off Gandhi, Nehru and Suhrawardy and the second was the blessing 'Be successful and come back'. To prove this, voluminous records were swollen up and manufactured, 'cartloads of correspondence, the searches, the numerous witnesses from the Minister down to the film-star and from the Maharaj down to the taxi driver . . . only to intensify the stage effect', and ended up being as ineffective as 'the trunk call on the telephone on the Mahasabha Bhawan'.[36]

Savarkar laboured then to show the court the numerous letters and public statements he had issued during his active tenure in politics, where despite an ideological opposition he had maintained camaraderie towards the Congress and League leadership. As evidence he exhibited the following—his press note of 6 November 1940 condemning Nehru's arrest; condemnation of the arrest of Gandhi, Nehru and other Congress leaders in August 1942; his note requesting Gandhi to end his fast in 1943; his letter to Jinnah and press note condemning the murderous attack on him in 1943; note on Kasturba Gandhi's death in 1944; his satisfaction and happiness on Gandhi's release from prison in 1944 and his statements of conciliation towards the new national government in 1947, among others. According to Savarkar this proved that though he might have been ideologically opposed to all these gentlemen, they were not his personal enemies whose deaths he wished for, and his past conduct vouched for this.

When he reached the end of his statement, touching upon aspects of India's independence and the vivisection of the country, Savarkar became emotional. His voice choked up and there were tears running down his cheeks. He could not speak for some time; he wiped his tears with a handkerchief and continued to read in a dignified manner.[37]

> I had been foremost in leading the movement against the vivisection of India. But in the year 1947 our Motherland was at last divided. However, although Pakistan came into existence, yet to counterbalance that loss, by far the larger part of Hindusthan succeeded in achieving its freedom from foreign domination. The fight for political independence in which as a soldier I too had fought, suffered and sacrificed for the last fifty years in no measure less than any other patriotic leader in my generation, had at least been won and a free and independent Indian State was born. I felt myself blessed to have survived to see my country free. No doubt a part of the mission remained unaccomplished, but we had not renounced our ambition to restore once more the integrity of our Motherland from the Indus to the Seas. For the realization of this ambition too it was imperative to consolidate that which we had already won. With this end in view I tried to impress upon the public mind that first of all the Central Government must be rendered strong, whatever party may happen to lead it. Any change in that lead however desirable should be effected by constitutional means alone. For, any act of violence or civil strife inside our camp was bound to endanger the State. Revolutionary mentality, which was inevitable and justifiable while we [were] struggling against an alien and armed oppression, must be instantly changed into a constitutional one if we wanted to save our State from party strifes and civil wars. With this motto I wished that the two leading organizations, the Congress and the Mahasabha, should form a common front and strengthen the hands of the Central Government of our State. To that end, I accepted the new National Flag.[38]

Savarkar ended his testimony with an emphatic denial of all the charges against him by the prosecution and pleaded his innocence, seeking an early and honourable acquittal from the court. Commenting on Savarkar's performance in court, advocate Inamdar writes:

> Savarkar had prepared a written statement in defence of his case replete with appendices of newspaper cuttings and he read out the statement in the Court with all the gimmicks of an orator bemoaning his fate of being charged with the murder of Mahatmaji by the independent Indian

Government, when he had admired and eulogized the personality of the Mahatmaji so sincerely and so often. Savarkar actually wiped his cheeks in court while reading this part of his oration. The Prosecution tried their level best to rope Savarkar into the conspiracy of murder, but all the evidence that the Prosecution could muster was the hearsay or vague evidence of the approver, the self-condemned cheat Badge, with no other corroboration than that of a Maharashtrian cine actress, who deposed, only that she had seen the two accused entering Savarkar's residence in Dadar, Bombay. There were such legal luminaries as P.R. Das, Barrister-at-Law from Patna, assisted by L.B. Bhopatkar, the famous criminal lawyer of Poona and Jamnadas Mehta, Barrister-at-Law from Bombay, who was a master artist of invective and incisive argument, to defend him. Savarkar claimed that he was wholly innocent of the crime! I am alive to the stage of his career at which Savarkar then was. But believe me, Savarkar was very nervous and was getting more and more agitated as the trial progressed.[39]

As mentioned above by Inamdar, Savarkar's defence was further buttressed by his advocate P.R. Das who argued his case vehemently on 20 December. Rubbishing the entire edifice of the prosecution's contentions against his client, he asked: 'Have the prosecution inadvertently omitted to produce any important evidence against Savarkar, when the Prosecution had cut down their original list of 275 witnesses to a mere total of 149 PWs only? For him I shall wait and I am prepared to come again before Your Honour if you do desire!'[40]

Making a scathing attack however on Savarkar and his line of defence during the trial, Gandhi's biographer Robert Payne notes:

He (Savarkar) went to extraordinary lengths to deny that he had anything to do with the conspiracy. He had never met the conspirators; if he did, then the meeting had nothing to do with the conspiracy; he never came down the stairs, if he did, and if he spoke the parting words: 'Be successful and come back!,' then it must be understood that he was talking about something entirely remote from the conspiracy such as the sale of shares of *Hindu Rashtra* or civil resistance to the Government of the Nizam of Hyderabad or any one of a hundred legitimate undertakings. So he went on, examining each word he was supposed to have said in purely legalistic terms, as though he were remote from the conflict. The circumstantial evidence was impressive; the story told by Badge was a convincing one.

Savarkar took each sentence out of its context and showed that it was devoid of any precise meaning. In this way he earned the intellectual admiration of the judge, who sat without a jury.[41]

. . . Savarkar was able to demonstrate that no one had seen him actively engaged in planning the assassination or in giving his blessings to the conspirators; he proclaimed his innocence by continual appeals to the laws of evidence. Sitting in the back row, resembling a death's head with the skin stretched tight over his brittle bones, his lips forming into a thin and contemptuous smile, his black-rimmed spectacles glinting, he professed his undying admiration of Gandhi and quoted the telegram he had sent to the Mahatma on the occasion of Kasturbhai's [sic] death. No one spoke of his moral responsibility for the crime; his earlier murders were forgotten; his defense was made all the easier by Nathuram Godse's determination to shoulder the entire responsibility. Yet to many who attended the trial he seemed more sinister than Nathuram Godse, who possessed many human qualities and showed no disposition to hide behind the letter of the law.[42]

That Savarkar had turned bitter and distrustful of everyone as the trial meandered along comes through in an anecdote narrated by advocate Inamdar. During one of the last days of the trial when everybody was seeking autographs from those whom they had been associated with during the trial, Inamdar approached Savarkar with a blank autograph book and requested him to oblige him with a signature on the very first page of the book. Given that Savarkar had personally called him a few months ago to his cell and conferred the case details with him made him feel confident enough that this was not too big a favour that the man would decline doing. But to his dismay, Savarkar said: 'Excuse me, Inamdar! If you want my autograph, you can buy if you like, one of my books, which have been signed by me, from the booksellers in Bombay. They are available in plenty.'[43] Is this the generosity one shows to someone who has assisted one during one's darkest hour, he wondered. 'I hung my head,' says Inamdar, 'and withdrew from him, wholly deflated.'[44]

The Judgment

The court was packed to full capacity on the morning of 10 February 1949. It was the day of judgment in the most high-profile case that free India had seen till then. There were mixed emotions of acute suspense, expectation and resignation among the accused, the advocates on both sides and the audience. At 11.30 a.m. sharp, Justice Atma Charan entered the courtroom wearing a black suit, with papers in his hand and a grim expression on his face. Nathuram and Apte were sentenced to be hanged. Karkare, Madanlal, Gopal, Shankar and Parchure were sentenced to transportation for life. Badge was given a pardon as he had turned approver. All the convicts shouted in one voice: 'Swatantrya Lakshmi ki Jai! Victory to Hindu Nation; Long live undivided India! Vande Mataram! Tod ke rahenge Pakistan.'[45] The only man to burst into violent sobs on hearing the judgment was Badge. All the accused were given fifteen days to file for appeals. They were to be packed off to the Central Jail in Ambala to serve their sentences.

In his judgment around the charges against Savarkar, Justice Atma Charan said:

> The approver in his evidence says that on 14.1.1948, Nathuram V. Godse and Narayan D. Apte took him from the Hindu Mahasabha Office at Dadar to the Savarkar Sadan saying that arrangements will have to made for keeping the 'stuff.' He had the bag containing the 'stuff' with him. Nathuram V. Godse and Narayan D. Apte then went inside leaving him standing outside the Savarkar Sadan. Nathuram V. Godse and Narayan D. Apte came back 5-10 minutes later with bag containing the 'stuff.' The approver then says that on 15.1.1948 in the compound of the temple of Dixitji Maharaj, Narayan D. Apte told him that Tatyarao Savarkar had decided that Gandhiji should be 'finished' and had entrusted that work to them. The approver then says that on 17.1.1948 Nathuram V. Godse suggested that they should all go and take the last 'darshan' of Tatyarao Savarkar. Then they proceeded to the Savarkar Sadan. Narayan D. Apte asked him to wait in the room on the ground floor. Nathuram V. Godse and Narayan D. Apte went up to the first floor and came down after 5-10 minutes. They were followed immediately by Tatyarao Savarkar. Tatyarao Savarkar addressed Nathuram V. Godse and Narayan D. Apte 'Yashaswi houn ya!'. Narayan D. Apte on their way back from Savarkar Sadan said that Tatyarao Savarkar had predicted: Gandhiji's hundred years were over—there was no doubt that their work would be successfully finished.
>
> The prosecution case against Vinayak D. Savarkar appears to rest just on the evidence of the approver and the approver alone. The contention

on behalf of prosecution is that part of the approver's story as against Vinayak D. Savarkar to certain extent stands corroborated to the evidence of Miss Shantabai B. Modak and Aitappa K. Kotian. No doubt there is the evidence of Miss Shantabai M. Modak that Nathuram V. Godse and Narayan D. Apte got down in front of Savarkar Sadan on 14.1.1948. The evidence to the effect, however, in no way goes to establish that Nathuram V. Godse and Narayan D. Apte had got down in front of Savarkar Sadan to visit Vinayak D. Savarkar. The evidence on record of the case goes to show that not only Vinayak D. Savarkar but A.S. Bhide and Gajanan Damle also reside in the Savarkar Sadan. No doubt there is also the evidence of Aitappa K.Kotian that Nathuram V. Godse and Narayan D. Apte and the approver got down at the Shivaji Park on 17.1.1948. The evidence to the effect however is no corroboration of the approver's story in regard to what the approver says he heard Vinayak D. Savarkar addressing Nathuram V. Godse and Narayan D. Apte. The approver in his evidence says that he had just heard Vinayak D. Savarkar addressing Nathuram V. Godse and Narayan D. Apte 'yashasvi houn ya!'

There is nothing on the record of the case to show as to what conversation had taken place just prior to that on the first floor between Nathuram V. Godse and Narayan D. Apte on the one hand and Vinayak D. Savarkar on the other. There is thus no reason to believe that the remarks said to have been addressed by Vinayak D. Savarkar to Nathuram V. Godse and Narayan D. Apte in the presence of the approver was in reference to the assassination plot against the life of Mahatma Gandhi. It would thus be unsafe to base any conclusions on the approver's story given above as against Vinayak D. Savarkar.

Vinayak D. Savarkar in his statement says that he had no hand in the 'conspiracy' if any, and had no control whatsoever over Nathuram V. Godse and Narayan D. Apte. It has been mentioned above that the prosecution case against Vinayak D. Savarkar rests just on the evidence of the approver and the approver alone . . . there is thus no reason to suppose that Vinayak D. Savarkar had any hand in what took place at Delhi on 20.1.1948 and 30.1.1948.[46]

Savarkar was 'found "not guilty" of the offences as specified in the charge and is acquitted thereunder. He is in custody and be released forthwith unless required otherwise.'[47] Castigating the police, Justice Atma Charan said:

I may bring to the notice of the Central Government the slackness of
the police in the investigation of the case during the period between
20-1-1948 and 30-1-1948. The Delhi Police had obtained a detailed
statement from Madanlal K. Pahwa soon after his arrest on 20-1-1948.
The Bombay Police had also been reported the statement of Dr. J.C. Jain
that he had made to the Honourable Morarji Desai on 21-1-1948. The
Delhi Police and the Bombay Police had contacted each other soon after
these statements had been made. Yet the Police miserably failed to drive
any advantage from these two statements. Had the slightest keenness
been shown in the investigation of the case at that stage the tragedy
probably could have been averted.[48]

Even as the sentenced were being taken away by the police to their
prisons, Savarkar and his counsel Bhopatkar were whisked away by a
large crowd that had gathered there, shouting slogans of 'Swatantrya Veer
Savarkar Zindabad!' Savarkar was to be honourably exonerated from all
the charges pressed against him in the murder. But in accordance with
the Punjab Public Security Act, the Delhi district magistrate ordered that
Savarkar leave the city immediately and be prohibited from entry for the
next three months.

The Appeal and Thereafter

Four days after the judgment, appeals were filed by the convicts in the
Punjab High Court against the judgment. Given the unprecedented
interest that the case had aroused, the Chief Justice of India decided
to constitute a three-judge bench to hear the appeals. The judges were
Justice G.D. Khosla, Justice A.N. Bhandari and Justice Acchuram. The
Punjab High Court was at that time located in Simla where this case
was heard. The entire procedure of the hearing of the appeal that began
on 23 May 1949 lasted for twenty-six sittings. Bannerjee, a senior
advocate from Calcutta, represented Apte and Madanlal, Dange for
Karkare, Mr Avasthi of the Punjab High Court was engaged at public
expense for Shankar, and Inamdar for Parchure and Gopal. Nathuram
declined to be represented by a lawyer and made a prayer that he should
be permitted to appear in person and argue his appeal himself. His
prayer had been granted. Writing about Nathuram's appearance in
court, Justice Khosla noted:

His small defiant figure with flashing eyes and close-cropped hair offered a remarkable and immediately noticeable contrast to the long row of placid and prosperous looking lawyers who represented his accomplices. The plea of poverty on which Godse had based his request to be present in person was only an excuse, and the real reason behind the manoeuvre was a morbid desire to watch the process of his disintegration at first hand and also to exhibit himself as a fearless patriot and a passionate protagonist of Hindu ideology. He had remained completely unrepentant of his atrocious crime, and whether out of a deep conviction in his beliefs or merely in order to make a last public apology, he had sought this opportunity of displaying his talents before he dissolved into oblivion.[49]

Like in the Delhi court, Nathuram made an impassioned and stirring speech highlighting the many lapses of Gandhi and the rationale behind his own trigger. As at the Red Fort, here too he managed to sway the audience with emotions. Justice Khosla reminisces this in his memoirs:

The audience was visibly and audibly moved. There was a deep silence when he ceased speaking. Many women were in tears and men were coughing and searching for their handkerchiefs. The silence was accentuated and made deeper by the sound of occasional subdued sniff or a muffed cough. It seemed to me that I was taking part in some kind of melodrama or in a scene out of a Hollywood feature film. Once or twice I had interrupted Godse and pointed out the irrelevance of what he was saying, but my colleagues seemed inclined to hear him and the audience most certainly thought that Godse's performance was the only worthwhile part of the lengthy proceedings. A writer's curiosity in watching the interplay of impact and response made me abstain from being too conscientious in the matter. Also I said to myself: 'The man is going to die soon. He is past doing any harm. He should be allowed to let off steam for the last time.' I have however no doubt that had the audience of that day been constituted into a jury and entrusted with the task of deciding Godse's appeal, they would have brought in a verdict of 'not guilty' by an overwhelming majority.[50]

The High Court delivered its verdict on 22 June 1949. Parchure and Shankar were both given the benefit of doubt and acquitted, but the sentences of all the others, including the execution of Nathuram and Apte, were upheld. The date for their hanging was decided: 15 November.

At dawn they came out of their cells wearing black and carrying in their hands a map of undivided India, the saffron flag of the Hindu Sanghatan movement and a copy of the Bhagavadgita. With the slogan of '*Akhand Bharat Amar Rahe!*' (Long Live Undivided India), Nathuram and Apte met their creator as the executioner pulled the noose. They were cremated with Hindu rites in the open ground outside the prison wall. To avoid any sort of monument coming up, the entire field there was ploughed and planted with grass. Their ashes were immersed in a nearby river, the Ghaggar, under a cloak of immense secrecy. With this, the curtains came down on one of the most poignant tragedies that free India had seen.

~

All through the long months of the trial, many dinner-table discussions and gossips in Delhi's power circles were centred around how Savarkar was being framed determinedly in the case. For his ardent followers, this was near axiomatic. However this theory got a boost decades later, when on 16 June 1983, the newspaper *Kal*, edited by S.R. Date, published a report on this matter. This was later reprinted in a volume published by the Savarkar Memorial Committee on 16 February 1989. This refers to a meeting that Savarkar's counsel Bhopatkar had with the then law minister of India, B.R. Ambedkar. Ambedkar had taken a keen interest in the case and had even attended the proceedings with his wife on 28 July 1948.[51] Bhopatkar had mentioned about this to his friends in Poona in 1949 after returning from the Red Fort trial.

> While in Delhi for the trial, Bhopatkar had been up in the Hindu Mahasabha office. Bhopatkar had found it a little puzzling that while specific charges had been made against all the accused, there was no specific charge against his client. He was pondering about his defence strategy when one morning he was told he was wanted on the telephone, so he went up to the room in which the telephone was kept, picked up the receiver and identified himself. His caller was Dr. Bhimrao Ambedkar, who merely said: 'Please meet me this evening at the sixth milestone on the Mathura Road' but before Bhopatkar could say anything more, put down the receiver.

That evening, Bhopatkar had himself driven to the place indicated. He found Ambedkar already waiting. He motioned Bhopatkar to get into his car, which he, Ambedkar himself, was driving. A few minutes later, he stopped the car and told Bhopatkar: There is no real charge against your client; quite worthless evidence has been concocted. Several members of the cabinet were strongly against it, but to no avail. Even Sardar Patel could not go against these orders. But take it from me, there just is no case. You will win.' Who . . . Jawaharlal Nehru? . . . But why?[52]

While the veracity of Bhopatkar's claim that was published in the newspaper is open for multiple interpretations, it reinforced the often-held belief that political differences and animosity were behind Savarkar's name being dragged into the murder case. It was not as if Sardar Patel had any soft corner for Savarkar, as is evidenced in his letters to Nehru and Syama Prasad Mookerjee. In such a case one wonders why Ambedkar would tell Bhopatkar that even Patel was forced to go down the path of implicating Savarkar. Of course, the fact that the case against him was flimsy and fell like a pack of cards is undeniable.

The judge might have acquitted him honourably, but the jury is still out in the public. Marathi poet Narayan Sadashiv Bapat, popularly known as Kavi Ulhas, had the opportunity of spending a lot of time with Savarkar during his internment at Ratnagiri. In his memoir, Bapat writes about one undated conversation he had with Savarkar:

I once asked Savarkar, 'What if someone kills Gandhi?' Immediately, he replied, 'No, he is one of our own people. He should not be killed.' On that I said, 'But suppose if his policies become too harmful for the nation?' He replied, 'If that happens then he should be kept in house arrest in some fort for some time.'[53]

This was quite in consonance with Savarkar's earlier stand too as an active revolutionary in the Abhinav Bharat where he considered killing of one's own countrymen as being wrong and the tool of political assassinations was to be used only against the colonial foreign power. When members of the Abhinav Bharat had planned to attack Gopal Krishna Gokhale, being incensed by his views, he had condemned their plans and disapproved of a resolution that sought death for Gokhale on the grounds that a revolutionary does not kill one's compatriots.[54]

Bapat mentions that he had been often telling many people about this conversation and even during the trial wanted to testify this in court. But both Savarkar and his counsel Bhopatkar rejected the idea. They contended that the government of the day was so full of prejudice against him that narrating this episode will lead them to draw the conclusion that Savarkar would often sit and talk about Gandhi's assassination with his associates. Bapat also reveals that in all their conversations Savarkar always addressed Gandhi reverentially as Mahatmaji and never by the first name, while Nehru was always addressed as Panditji. Savarkar's biographer Dhananjay Keer as well as his family doctor in his last few years, Dr Arvind Godbole[55] too mention the similar manner in which he addressed these national leaders in any conversation.

There was however the most curious case of Appa Ramachandra Kasar, Savarkar's bodyguard, and his secretary Gajanan Damle. They had been arrested by the Bombay Police from Savarkar Sadan, the day after Gandhi's murder. They recorded their statements to the Bombay Police on 4 March 1948 where they allegedly corroborated a lot of Badge's testimony, especially around Nathuram and Apte being regular visitors to the Sadan and having personal interviews with Savarkar often. They also allegedly confirmed the visit of Madanlal with Karkare to Savarkar Sadan and their meeting with him. Yet, given the prime importance of this evidence, the prosecution never brought Damle and Kasar to testify as witnesses in court, despite how indispensable such deposition would have otherwise been to clinch the case in their favour. It could well have been statements that were recorded from them under duress and police excesses in custody and would fall flat in court cross-examination. This could be the only reason why these two were not presented as witnesses, unless of course the prosecution itself was determined to let Savarkar off the hook, which however could not possibly be the case.

New evidence however came to light in May 2017 through the efforts of a researcher and admirer of Savarkar, Pankaj Phadnis that corroborates the contents of the Bhopatkar–Ambedkar meeting. This was a telegram sent by Howard Donovan, the American consul general to the US secretary of foreign affairs back in Washington, on 8 August 1948. He was sending regular dispatches to his home country right from the time of Gandhi's murder. Denovan states:

Mr. C.K. Daphtary, who is acting as special prosecutor in the trial of Gandhi's assassins, told me yesterday that he had 'a very thin case' against Savarkar and that he thought Savarkar would be acquitted. He said that in his judgment it was a mistake to try so many people and that the Government of India should have tried the men directly concerned with Gandhi's assassination and left Savarkar and the other conspirators alone.[56]

The suspicions of political fixing to ruin Savarkar's already flagging political career carried a lot of heft. It was an open secret that Nehru was fiercely opposed to the Mahasabha and the RSS. Even before Gandhi's murder, on 28 January 1948, he had written to his Cabinet colleague Syama Prasad Mookerjee that he 'was greatly distressed by the activities of the Hindu Mahasabha' as it was operating not only as 'the main opposition to the Government and to the Congress in India but as an organization continually inciting to violence'. He further wrote:

> The R.S.S. has behaved in an even worse way and we have collected a mass of information about its very objectionable activities and its close association with riots and disorder. Apart from what I have written above, what pains me the most is the extreme vulgarity and indecency of speeches being made from Hindu Mahasabha platforms. Gandhi Murdabad is one of their special slogans. Recently a prominent leader of the Hindu Mahasabha stated that an objective to be aimed at was the hanging of Nehru, Sardar Patel and Maulana Azad . . . I write to you specially because of your own close association with the Hindu Mahasabha. We are continually being asked in our party, in the Constituent Assembly as well as elsewhere as to your position in this matter. I should be grateful to you if you will let me know how you propose to deal with this situation, which must be as embarrassing to you as it is to me.[57]

Mookerjee had written back saying he himself was deeply worried about these tendencies within the Mahasabha and that he would look into the intra-party working. Then the tragedy of Gandhi's murder struck. Nehru was even more insistent now. In another letter he wrote to Mookerjee on 4 February 1948, he kept up his pressure. He wrote:

> In particular, it is difficult and embarrassing for all concerned for a Minister of the Central Government to be personally associated with a communal organization like a Hindu Mahasabha which, even on the

political plane is opposed to our general policy and to the Government as a whole. You must have given thought to these matters. It is a little difficult for me to advise you, but if I may do so, I think the time has come for you to raise your voice against communal organizations including the Mahasabha, and in any event, sever your connection with the Hindu Mahasabha. Any such action from you would be greatly appreciated by the party and, I think the country.[58]

Mookerjee was in quite an unenviable spot with repeated letters to this effect directed at him from both the prime minister and the home minister. The latter sent him a letter on 12 June 1948 conveying his displeasure when it came to be known that some members of the Mahasabha were raising a Defence Fund for the accused in the Gandhi murder trial.

Originally, it seems the idea was to do so for the defence of Savarkar, but now the objective has been widened in its scope . . . for the Mahasabha to associate itself with the defence would therefore be taken as an indication of that sympathy [for the accused]. I would therefore urge upon you, with all the earnestness at my command that you should try to dissociate the Mahasabha from this move.[59]

It was left to Mookerjee to constantly keep giving justifications on behalf of the Mahasabha to his Cabinet colleagues and his boss in government. He contacted Bhopatkar who was the president of the Mahasabha and also Savarkar's counsel in the case and the latter gave him an elaborate reply too dated 29 August 1948:

The Hindu Mahasabha has not as such opened any defence fund or appointed any defence committee. Not a penny from the funds of the Hindu Mahasabha has been utilized for the purpose of the trial. Some of the rooms in the Hindu Mahasabha Bhavan occupied by defence counsel are given on monthly rent. As I explained to you personally, the Defence Committee is an entirely separate body and it is raising its fund separately. The Defence Committee was appointed for giving legal aid to all such workers of the Hindu Mahasabha as required or called for it. When Mr. Savarkar was implicated in Mahatma Gandhi's murder case, there was naturally a demand from various parts of India, particularly Maharashtra, for giving him necessary legal aid, as a vast number of people generally felt that he could not be connected with such a crime . . . even now I would like to repeat what I told you earlier that had Mr. Savarkar not been implicated in the case, none of us connected with the Hindu Mahasabha would have come forward to conduct or participate in the defence.[60]

Patel remained unconvinced though. The pinpricks and the pressure were too much to bear and in due course, Mookerjee was to leave the Mahasabha in December 1948 and later float a political party of his own, the Bharatiya Jana Sangh in October 1951.

~

After the harrowing time for close to a year in Delhi, Savarkar returned to Bombay in February 1949. He wanted a complete dissociation with all aspects related to the case or his indictment in it, as also eschew every possible conflict with the new government of India. On 14 February 1949, he wrote to Bhopatkar:

> Owing to the shattered condition of my health, physical and mental, I have decided to retire from public life. But I was surprised to read this morning a U. P. Agency news that the President of the Hindu Mahasabha had called upon the Mahasabhaites to demand a governmental inquiry into the question as to who were responsible; in sanctioning my prosecution in the Gandhi Murder trial and to demand that those found responsible should be brought to book by the Government. If this be true, I regret that such a hasty step should have been taken without consulting or even informing me beforehand. I hold that there could not have been any individually vindictive motive that actuated the Government in sanctioning the prosecution. The legal advice given to the government might have been hasty, misleading, even panicky under the shock of the great tragedy, which we all deplore, but it could not have been intentionally malicious. I think it is better in public interest that so far as I am concerned we should all let the curtain fall on the tragedy now that I have secured such a fair and honourable acquittal to which you have contributed more than anyone else. Will you therefore cancel your circular by issuing a second confidential circular to the Mahasabhaites and spare me from figuring as a central figure in such an uncalled-for public controversy once again.

I hope you will excuse me for the request. More when we meet. I am dropping a note to the Home Minister Bombay too.[61]

A few years after the trial, advocate Inamdar visited Bombay and he thought it his duty to pay his respects to Savarkar at his residence. This was May 1951. Yamunabai, Savarkar's wife, received him and he expressed his desire to meet the great man. She went upstairs and returned after about ten minutes to tell him that Savarkar was really very unwell and would be unable to see him. The entire episode of the murder case had made Savarkar more of a social recluse who shunned public contact, especially with those associated with either the plot or the trial. Inamdar felt deflated a second time, after the rude rebuff he had got on his request for an autograph. 'I returned from Savarkar Sadan,' he reminisces 'pondering over the susceptibility of even great men to human infirmities.'[62]

11

Twilight Tales

After the Red Fort Trial

Thoughout the year of his release from the Red Fort jail, Savarkar maintained a low profile and consciously avoided any confrontation with the government. In an effort to mend fences with his ideological cohort, the RSS, he also sent a telegram to Golwalkar extending his felicitations to him in July 1949 when the ban that the government had imposed on the organization following Gandhi's murder was lifted. 'Long live the Sangh as the valorous champion of Hindudom,'[1] he wrote after he had made those famous jibes about the alleged lack of any achievements in the life of an average Sangh volunteer. He also constantly sent conciliatory letters and telegrams to Sardar Patel or Morarji Desai, praising them for their work in government. He sent a telegram to the president of the Constituent Assembly on 5 August when it was deliberating the new Constitution of India to 'adopt Bharat as the name of our nation, Hindi as the national language and Nagari as the national script'.[2]

But during this time, apart from his own physical and emotional health that took a toll through those months of incarceration and trial, he was plagued by a personal tragedy as well. His younger brother Narayanrao, who had been grievously injured on his head in the riots following Gandhi's murder, had just not recovered after that. He had been convalescing but largely remained confined to bed. Eventually he died of a brain hemorrhage on 19 October 1949 after remaining unconscious for over a fortnight following a paralytic stroke. With Babarao too having gone a couple of years ago, Savarkar deeply rued the departure of both his siblings.

The Hindu Mahasabha meanwhile was trying to reinvent itself after all the negative reactions it drew in the aftermath of the murder and trial.

Syama Prasad Mookerjee's suggestion to convert it into a sociocultural organization from a fighting fit political party was rejected and in response, he quit the party for good. The Working Committee turned to Savarkar, requesting him to take over as the new president in that year's annual session that was to be held at Calcutta. He sent a polite refusal to Devendranath Mookerji, the general secretary of the Bengal Provincial Hindu Sabha on account of his 'rapidly declining health',[3] though he agreed to inaugurate the session. N.B. Khare, who joined the Mahasabha from the Congress, was then elected as the new president at the Calcutta session.

In his ninety-minute inaugural address Savarkar stressed that the political freedom of India was a victory for the nation and not a gift from the colonial masters. This was achieved not merely by only the Congress or the revolutionaries but was the culmination of the saga of struggles and sacrifices of several known and unknown Indians, in and outside the country, from 1857 to 1947. He advised the Mahasabha that it must continue its activity as a strong sentinel of Hindu interests and also be a bulwark against the Congress, which he claimed took actions only from the perspective of winning elections and not in the larger interests always of the nation or the people. Yet, he stressed that any opposition to the government or the ruling party could come only through constitutional and democratic means and not by taking law into one's own hands or by violence. He exhorted Hindu youth to join the Indian army, navy and air force in large numbers and advised a tit-for-tat policy for any misadventures that Pakistan might try with the country. If one was true to the resolve, he felt in about ten years all the lost territories to Pakistan could well be easily recovered.

Shortly thereafter, the birth of the new Indian republic was heralded on 26 January 1950 after the adoption of the new Constitution of India. On this occasion, Savarkar greeted the people with a message similar to his inaugural address at the Mahasabha session and added:

> Every citizen whose loyalty to our motherland is above suspicion, unconditional and whole-hearted cannot but join rejoicingly [sic] the national celebrations on that day to commemorate the emancipation of our motherland from the British bondage. Let us sink our petty squabbles over provincialities, personalities and party platforms on that day and presenting a trailed front on the only one and common platform—the platform of our motherland—proclaim our national victory to the world . . . But we must not forget that mere rejoicing

on the Inauguration day would but amount to vain-gloriousness and frivolity if we fail to realize the corresponding responsibility we incur to protect the republic from all external aggression as well as from internal anarchy. That can only be done by building up a powerful army, navy, and air force. Consequently I appeal to youths in particular to make a grim resolve on this day to join these national forces in their hundreds of thousands and thus to discharge the first and foremost patriotic duty they owe to their motherland.[4]

Around this time, letter exchanges with his old comrade and colleague from the revolution days, Sardar Singh Rana from Paris, brought cheer to Savarkar. During the First World War, he had been deported to the Martinique Island where he bore several hardships. In the Second World War, the Germans had captured and thrown him into concentration camps. It was only on the arrival of Subhas Bose to Germany that he was finally acquitted from the camp. Savarkar exhorted Rana as one of the oldest surviving members of the revolutionaries to pen down his memoirs, which would also bring to light the life and achievements of several others who worked tirelessly with him for the liberation of India, such as Madame Bhikaji Cama, Virendranath Chattopadhyay, Lala Hardayal and several others.

By March 1950, East Bengal once again burst into flames of communal violence with a sad repetition of the Noakhali tragedies. Strong public sentiment prevailed of the need for some drastic step to be taken by the government through the use of the armed forces to stop the carnage. Even as these tragedies were being quelled, Nehru invited his Pakistani counterpart Liaquat Ali Khan to Delhi to sign the Nehru–Liaquat Pact on 8 April 1950. The bilateral treaty was aimed at a safe return of refugees and a protection of the rights of minorities in both countries—something that Pakistan never followed up on, in letter or in spirit. Minority commissions were set up in both countries and more than a million refugees migrated from East Pakistan to West Bengal.

But in a completely unexpected and draconian move, the Nehru government swooped down on all its political opponents within the country, especially the Hindu Mahasabha, in a spate of nationwide arrests under the Preventive Detention Act of 1950. Even before the dawn of 4 April 1950 nearly 100 policemen of Bombay's CID divided themselves into different groups under 'Operation Hindu Mahasabha'. Orders had been received in the late hours of the previous night and the officers had burnt the midnight oil making frantic preparations to carry out the morning's lightning raids. Working on a clockwork schedule the officers carried out the raids on several leaders. An officer knocked on Savarkar's house too by daybreak and showed him a warrant of arrest. This, when Savarkar had not even made any anti-government or anti-Nehru statements. He was just given time to finish his morning ablutions and taken to a waiting police conveyance, driving off to the Arthur Road Jail.[5] Nearly a dozen other leaders of the Mahasabha such as B.N. Bhagvat, S.V. Deodhar, Bal Savarkar, R. Agarwal, S.S. Sapre, N.H. Halelkar, L.B. Bhopatkar, the editor of the *Kesari* G.V. Ketkar, the editor of the *Kal*, S.R. Date and others were rounded up in Bombay and Poona. Similar raids were carried out in other parts of India as well. The high-handed attitude of the government was squarely condemned by several people and the press. *The Free Press Journal*, not known to be sympathetic towards the Mahasabha, commented:

> The offensive against the Hindu Mahasabha and the R.S.S. leaders and workers has only one implication. That is that, Premier Nehru has elected to appease Pakistan and imperil the integrity and the independence of India. The offensive against the Hindu Mahasabha and the R.S.S. had a two-fold purpose; one is to divert India's attention from the policy of appeasement; the other is to create a panic that there is a Hindu conspiracy and rally the progressive elements in support of the policy of appeasement of Pakistan.[6]

On his part, Nehru took recourse to Section 3 of the Preventive Detention Act that mentions any affront made to a foreign power as being valid reason to detain a person. He noted that 'the speeches of the Hindu Mahasabha leaders demand the liquidation of Pakistan. I can imagine no greater offence to a foreign power than to make such a suggestion.'[7]

All the Mahasabha leaders made representations denying the charges that they were out to create ill will between Hindus and Muslims or were conspiring to end the lives of prominent national leaders. The charges had no substance or proof but were merely the paranoia of Nehru and his government. It was a clear attempt to completely eliminate political opposition especially in the wake of the upcoming first general elections that the country was to witness in 1951.

The habeas corpus that Savarkar's son Vishwas filed in the Bombay High Court came up for hearing before the division bench of the Bombay High Court on 12 July 1950. Before Chief Justice M.C. Chagla and Justice Gajendragadkar, C.K. Daphtary, the advocate general of Bombay, stated that the government was of the view that it was willing to release Savarkar if he undertook to retire from politics and stay confined to his house. Savarkar had had enough and eventually decided to retire completely from public life. He was given an option to be released from prison only if he abstained from politics for a year or till the first general elections or the third world war, whichever took place first. In view of such ridiculous conditions put on him, he stated: 'In view of the restrictions put on me by Government, which I mean to observe, preventing me from taking part in politics for a specific period, I must inevitably resign even the primary membership of the Hindu Mahasabha.'[8] He was released from prison only in June 1950 after this undertaking.

The end of the year saw the passing away of Sardar Patel. Thereafter, Syama Prasad Mookerjee, who had quit the Nehru Cabinet opposing the pact with Liaquat Ali Khan, was agitating in Kashmir against the special status accorded to the state under Article 370 of the Constitution. He was strongly opposed to the concept of two prime ministers, two flags and two Constitutions within one country. The government arrested him and he died in prison under mysterious circumstances. Issuing a statement of shock and concern on the sudden demise of his one-time protégé, Savarkar said on 23 June 1953:

> The news of the passing away of Dr. Mukherjee [sic] was so shocking and sudden that I could not believe it till thrice confirmed. In him Bharat has lost one of the foremost patriots, politicians and a born parliamentarian. May his martyrdom seal the cause of the inseparable and total integration of the whole of Kashmir, with Hindusthan Republic. *Ek Vidhan* (one constitution) *Ek Pradhan* (one Prime Minister) *Ek Nishan* (one Flag) was the motto for which he fought and laid down his life on the field. Let us take up the flag and carry on the fight to success. That alone can be the real monument to commemorate the great leader. All Bharat and Hindudom in particular can never be too grateful to his memory who has served them so much and so long. To me it is not only a national loss but a personal one of a respected comrade and a friend.[9]

Given the restrictions on political activities, Savarkar began to focus his attention towards his favourite issues of reforms in society, in script and also in the Hindu calendar. He began writing several articles in newspapers and delivered lectures on Indian history in different parts of Maharashtra. He wrote two articles in the *Kesari* in May 1951 on the need for a national calendar, distinct from the Christian calendar that was followed. He did acknowledge the fact that there were nearly twenty different calendars among various Hindu sects and groups across the country. Many of these, according to him were rooted either in deep theological constructs or sheer religious dogma. Choosing any one of them was obviously a tough task. But he urged Indians to take a leaf out of the book of the French revolutionaries who evolved a similar national calendar from amidst many.

> The days of the first eleven months will be 30 each, the twelfth month having 35 days and after every four years the twelfth month will be of 36 days. The French had adopted this system, which has proved very useful. The Parsi calendar also follows the same system. The days of the week will continue to be seven. Their names will be retained as they are, but unlike the Christian calendar, the period of 24 hours will be counted from sunrise to sunrise and not from midnight to midnight.[10]

He theorized that since India's history according to him went back to 5000 years, the current year could be adopted as 5001. His proposal did not find many takers. The Union government actually adopted the Saka era, which is seventy-eight years behind the Christian era. The Calendar Reform Committee appointed by the Government of India in 1952, submitted its report in 1955. The national calendar was adopted with effect from 22 March 1957, corresponding to 1 Chaitra 1879 Saka. The five months following Chaitra consists of thirty-one days each and the last six months are of thirty days' duration each. Chaitra has thirty days in common years and thirty-one in a leap year.

Savarkar of course was speaking on a host of issues, including some highly controversial and socially tumultuous ones. In the wake of a near-famine situation in India, he delivered a talk in February 1952 in which he blamed the Congress for not bringing in sweeping land reforms that could usher in higher agricultural produce and income. The controversial aspect came when he began to advise Brahmins, Buddhists, Jains, Lingayats, Vaishnavas and Varkaris to change their food habits and begin eating meat, so that the food problem of nearly 5 crore Indians could be solved. He went on:

> What man should eat and what man should drink is not for religion to decide. In this respect one should follow the diktats of medical science. Whatever food that conduces to the health, to the betterment of one's health, if one likes it and could digest it, one should safely eat. One need not forsake it simply because the commands of Dharmashastras are otherwise . . . We have vast seas around our country. There are enormous stores of fish of all kinds . . . why not change our food habits and eat fish? Rains or no rains, fish would go on multiplying. Take advantage of these natural resources. We are to blame ourselves for shortage of food and consequent lack of stamina of our people. Remember the fish and eggs have much life-giving qualities . . . even a tiny state like Israel has sensibly started developing fish fields and sand fruits and because of that they are able to meet the needs of the countless immigrants who would have otherwise half-starved. The Jews are a brave and intelligent people. And although their State looks like a child before our great state of Bharat, we must emulate its example : . . the Hindus should act according to the needs of the time.[11]

The country was at that time gearing up for its first mammoth democratic challenge—the general elections. In the course of the campaigning, N.B. Khare, the president of the Hindu Mahasabha, noted that Nehru repeatedly maligned the Mahasabha as being the murderer of Gandhi, despite the court acquittal of Savarkar and no specific leads implicating the organization as a whole in the ghastly episode. On 17 December 1951, he said at a public meeting in Nagpur's Kasturchand Park that the Hindu Mahasabha had a hand in Gandhi's assassination. He had made similar statements in election campaign speeches in Bhopal, Gwalior and other places, thereby prejudicing the public against his opposition party.[12] Other Congress campaigners took the clue and added more creative stories to their leader's narrative, some claiming that Khare himself was the principal conspirator and so on. The pitch was so feverish and dangerous that after Nehru's election speech, when Khare's party workers Shankarrao Bait went to Pipri village in Nagpur, the people were so incensed that they began to attack his vehicle with stones and lathis and also tore up the election posters and propaganda material.[13] Expectedly, the Mahasabha fared poorly and won just three seats in Parliament with Khare being one of them. Syama Prasad Mookerjee's Jana Sangh too got a mere three seats. The Congress romped home with 363 seats, while the socialists and communists bagged twelve and sixteen respectively.[14] In the states too, barring Madhya Pradesh where it saw a little success, the Mahasabha was no match for the Congress behemoth.

Meanwhile at the instance of Savarkar a committee was set up to hold a three-day celebration in Poona from 10 to 12 May 1952 to pay tributes to all the revolutionaries and martyrs of the freedom struggle from 1857 to 1947. Savarkar also wanted to use this occasion to announce the formal dissolution of the revolutionary group and India's first organized secret society that he had created in 1899—the Abhinav Bharat. Speaking during the occasion Savarkar said the specific objective of the society was attainment of freedom for India and given its achievement, there was no longer a need for such a body. There was however a greater need than ever before of the spirit of service and sacrifice, which was the soul of the revolutionary movement in India. He also stressed that there was no place for an armed insurrection in an independent and democratic India. He considered himself more fortunate than Shivaji and Tilak who fought for the country's liberation to be alive, unlike them, to see the dawn of independence. Senapati Bapat, his indefatigable comrade, shared stage with him.

The same evening, Savarkar addressed a large gathering at Poona's Krantismriti Nagar. A portrait of Subhas Chandra Bose overlooked the proceedings. Savarkar called for a frank admission of the indispensable role that the armed struggle had brought about and the name of Subhas need not bring the nervousness and inferiority complex that it did to most Congressmen. The heroic deeds of the Abhinav Bharat and Bengali revolutionaries brought the early awakening among the Indian masses. The Abhinav Bharat Society in London had given India her first national flag and also highlighted her plight in front of the whole world. Savarkar asserted that all the reforms that the British brought in over different periods of time were in response to the violent outbursts and activities of revolutionaries—right from Vasudev Balwant Phadke down to the Naval Mutiny of 1946. He warned that efforts would be made to suppress that part of our history but the truth has a way of resurfacing itself. Savarkar expressed satisfaction at the fact that three-fourths of the country was liberated but the Sindhu on whose banks the sacred works of this nation were written remains occupied. Without the Sindhu, there could not be the Hindu, he opined.

On the third day, a civic reception to Savarkar and some of his colleagues marked the end of the commemoration. Here he told the people that despite the shortcomings of the Congress government, to claim that British rule was better was nothing short of treachery and anarchy. Even as the government should give space to opposition parties and views, the opposition too should not simply oppose for the sake of it. Instead, it should also support and strengthen the hands of the government whenever beneficial legislations are passed. He exhorted the youth to not take this hard-won freedom for granted and instead make greater sacrifices and work harder for the next ten years with a plan and vision to make their country strong and invincible. The nation's defence had attracted no attention and this was not something to be proud of. Even Hitler, Tojo and Mussolini were defeated not by the power of peace and love or through chanting verses from the Bible or *Dhammapada* but by stronger nations that possessed superior arms, force and atom bombs, he said. After arming oneself sufficiently the country could choose to be non-aggressive and neutral, but doing so before that was foolish and suicidal. Preparing for world peace without military strength was pompous and useless according to Savarkar.

Over the next year, Savarkar delivered almost a hundred speeches across Bombay and other cities to also raise funds for a memorial at Nasik where the Abhinav Bharat had been set up. Purses amounting to almost Rs 13,000 were collected and the Society that was established purchased the building that originally housed the small room in the narrow lanes of Nasik where the Abhinav Bharat began its operations surreptitiously. A marble slab was installed as a memorial, stating: 'Hail to the Goddess of Liberty! In the war of independence with the British from 1857 to 1947 to those that engaged in armed conflict, all sons of Bharat who have departed, martyrs and heroes this faithful homage is dedicated.' It was a walk down memory lane for Savarkar as he strolled along this little building and met the locals of Nasik. He unveiled a statue of Shivaji Maharaj at the Jackson Garden, which he declared as 'Shivaji Garden' thereafter.

With the restrictions on his political activities ceasing, Savarkar began to be more vocal on various aspects of national and foreign policy and governance. He was particularly sceptical and critical of Nehru's policy towards China. On 29 April 1954, India signed the *Panchsheel* or the Five

Principles of Peaceful Coexistence with China. Four years earlier, China had invaded and occupied Tibet and India had remained silent. Writing about these in the *Kesari* on 26 January 1954, Savarkar said:

> When China, without even consulting India, invaded the buffer state of Tibet, India should at once have protested and demanded the fulfillment of rights and privileges as per her agreements and pacts entered into with Tibet. But our Indian Government was not able to do any such thing. We closed our eyes in the name of world peace and co-existence and did not even raise a finger against this invasion of Tibet. Neither did we help this buffer state of Tibet when her very existence was at stake. Why? The only reason that I visualize is our unpreparedness for such an eventuality and/or war . . . That is the reason why after swallowing the whole of Tibet the strong armies of China and Russia are now standing right on our borders in a state of complete preparedness and on the strength of the above, China is today openly playing the game of liquidating the remaining buffer states of Nepal and Bhutan . . . We have not been able to put before her an army which can match the strength of her armies on these borders of ours even today. This is precisely the reason why China dares come forward with such an unabashed claim on our territories . . . China completely overran Tibet and destroyed the only buffer state so as to strengthen her vast borders. By this act of hers, China had with one stroke come right on our borders by force and prepared the way for an open aggression against India whenever she felt like it.
>
> Britain, when she was ruling over India, had by careful planning, pacts, treaties and agreements created a chain of buffer states like Tibet, Nepal and Bhutan in order to strengthen the borders of India and to safeguard it from China and Russia. Afghanistan also acted like a buffer state on the other side. Britain had on behalf of the Government of India, directly or indirectly taken upon herself by various pacts, charters and agreements even the guarantee of continued existence of these buffer states. Immediately on attainment of independence all these rights were transferred to the independent sovereign Republic of India. But in the very six years that we criminally wasted, China has equipped her whole nation with most modern and up-to-date arms, and without in the least caring for the feelings and sentiments of India had completely overrun Tibet and destroyed the only buffer state so as to strengthen her vast borders.[15]

Savarkar asked India to emulate the example of Israel that came into existence in May 1948 after almost a two-thousand-year struggle by the Jews for a homeland of their own. Israel, he said, 'is besieged by their staunch enemies Arab nations. But this tiny nation has given military education to its men and women, procured weapons from Britain and U.S.A., established arm [sic] factories in their own nation, intelligently signed treaties and with foreign nations and raised its own strategic power to that extent that their enemy Arab nations would never dare to invade them.'[16] He claimed that it was still not too late for India to wake up from its slumber and similarly increase her military and strategic strength as the world recognizes only that.

The Chinese prime minister Zhou Enlai was accorded a warm welcome in New Delhi on 26 June 1954 and Nehru coined his favourite phrase 'Hindi Chini Bhai Bhai'. In an interview on this India–China diplomacy in the Kesari on 4 July 1954, Savarkar welcomed this bonhomie with a sense of cautious optimism. He said:

In politics the enemy of our enemy is our best friend. Enlightened self-interest is the only touchstone on which friendship in political dealings could be tested, since there is no such thing as real and selfless friendship in the political arena. If the meeting between Chou En-Lai and Nehru angered the U.S.A., Indians should not pay attention to it because the U.S.A. too did not care to pause and think about India's sensitivities if America entered into a military pact with Pakistan. All the policies of India must be dependent on what was good or bad for India herself. If it was advantageous to India she should not in the least worry or care whether anyone felt enraged, insulted or irritated . . . The general principles that are being propagated as fundamental in this visit are very good and sound, so far as their language is concerned. Nothing is lost in proclaiming wishes for world peace, prosperity and brotherhood. But so long as India does not have any effective practical remedy or measures to check the transgressions, such visits have no more than a formal status. While crying from the roof tops about these principles it was worth noting that China, by swallowing Tibet, had ruthlessly trampled those very principles of world peace, brotherhood and peaceful co-existence. That was the funniest part of the whole deal, and it at once raised doubts in Indian minds about the bona fides of China and Chou En-Lai. There was at that time a political party in Tibet aiming at independence.

It was curious and in a way most astonishing that after preying on and swallowing the mouse of Tibet the Chinese cat was talking of going on a pilgrimage. That was exactly the role that the Chinese Premier Chou En-Lai and President Mao Tse-tung were playing.[17]

In the same piece Savarkar also emphasized on the fundamental theory of foreign policy, which was permanent national interests and not merely high-sounding, one-sided moral principles. He hoped that the Panchsheel did not run this risk. He said:

China, Russia, Britain and even the recently established Pakistan all are talking of high-sounding principles, but they do so as a step towards diplomatic measures to achieve their own ends, and for the success of their own political objectives. In the present state of human relationship it should be just so; but of all the countries India alone has for long been in the habit of preaching sermons of high principles to others and unilaterally bringing them into practice, which ultimately proves disastrous to the interests of India. I only hope that this does not happen in this case of the *Panchsheel*. What I feel is that if at all China uses India as a springboard to push forward her own territorial aims and interests, India should also primarily safeguard her own interests and if these moves do not go against her interests then alone take part in it. So long as China is looking to further her interests alone, India should also follow the same and use the good wishes of China only in so far as they help to push the interests of India forward. We should believe in their good faith and good intentions as much as and as long as they believe in ours.

One fact must be made clear here and it is that [the] U.K., U.S.A., U.S.S.R. and China can force India to bring into practice all these principles because they hold the upper hand, being in possession of atomic and nuclear weapons of warfare. But can India do the same? Can India force these nations to see that they follow the principles that they profess to preach? This is the most important question. It is no use having political or diplomatic friendship alone with either China or Russia. We must immediately undertake to see that military potential and preparedness of the Indian armed forces with modern and most up-to-date weapons of warfare is not being neglected and that we too can produce atomic and nuclear weapons just as these nations can. If China can erect plants and factories for the manufacture of atomic weapons of warfare in Sinkiang and other places we should also be able to do so. There is nothing difficult in it. Our scientists and laboratories might be able to invent and manufacture such weapons in a year or two or they might invent even more destructive ones . . . But so long a weak and impotent Government at the Centre does not take even one step to achieve these objectives it is no use talking of high principles and running after the mirage of world peace, peaceful co-existence, world brotherhood and prosperity, and nothing good can come out of such so-called good-will visits. High principles must have a robust armed strength behind them to see that they are brought into practice by those who wax eloquent about it. Taking all these things into consideration I feel that the time has come now when the Central Government must immediately take steps to increase the armed might and the military potential of India.[18]

A lot of what Savarkar wrote about and cautioned was to turn prophetically true in the decades to come as far as India's strategic, military and foreign relations were concerned.

Along with foreign aggression, Savarkar was also always alert to the threats to internal security of the country and kept warning the government and Hindu Sangathanists about it. For instance, he issued several statements and warnings and also spoke about the rapid proselytization of the hill tribes and indigenous communities undertaken in the north-eastern states of India by foreign-aided missionaries. The alarming rise in their numbers and the possible threat to national security and integrity from this process was something that he always warned about. He also encouraged the patriots to fight for the liberation of Goa, Diu and Daman from foreign yoke. As future events were to bale out Savarkar's apprehensions, insurgency in some of the north-eastern states of India had a communal overtone to it caused by this demographic change.

The government constituted the Backward Classes Commission on 29 January 1953. One of its members, N.S. Kajrolkar, wrote to Savarkar to elicit his views, given his long social reforms work in Ratnagiri and thereafter. On untouchability, Savarkar said:

Abolition of untouchability should be enforced by a very ruthless law . . . to refuse to give treatment of equality to members of the Scheduled Castes should be declared by Parliament a cognizable offence. If they did so then all the states would be bound by it. The police would then

be authorized to take legal action against the offenders and bring them
to book. Police protection should be given to members of the Scheduled
Castes . . . the Scheduled Castes should abolish untouchability among
themselves, as between Mahars and Mangs and others . . . the backward
classes should be given assistance on the basis of their poverty and
illiteracy.[19]

He also held that reservations and special rights that were made available
for Scheduled Castes must not be extended to the converted Christians
and Muslims, as that would become an incentive for more conversions.
They 'had boasted that their communities did not observe untouchability
based on birth. By so declaring they had converted thousands of
scheduled caste Hindus. They therefore should be ashamed to ask for
such preferential treatment,'[20] he opined. Savarkar also reiterated his
stand on cow slaughter and called for a ban on it from the viewpoint
of culture and economy. Notably though and rather ironically, Savarkar
gave his own children, son Vishwas and daughter Prabhat, in marriage to
those of his own caste, Chitpawan Brahmins, and did not encourage an
inter-caste union.

He had always had differing opinions from majority Hindus on the
worship of the cow. But on its protection, he was quite stern. Sacrificing
the cow to spite the Hindus or to please the gods should not be allowed
was his measured opinion.

Savarkar strongly supported the movement for a united Maharashtra
on a linguistic basis. He had hoisted a black flag atop his house, on 10
January 1956, to register his protest against the government's opposition
to the demands made for unification of Marathi-speaking districts by the
Samyukta Maharashtra Samiti.

~

The year 1957 marked the centenary of the First War of Indian
Independence. A centenary celebrations committee was set up in Delhi
and Savarkar was invited to deliver a lecture on the occasion given his
seminal work on the subject. The Committee members called on Prime
Minister Nehru and requested him to preside over the event. The extent
of antipathy that Nehru had for Savarkar is exemplified in what he is
supposed to have told them:

Savarkar is a brave man, a hero, a great man. When I was a student in England we were inspired by his book on 1857. It is a great book, which has inspired many Indians. But it is hardly history. We have differed on several problems and it would be embarrassing to him if I speak in a different tone. I have great respect for Savarkar and I would have certainly liked to meet him. But speaking on the same platform would be unjust for both of us.[21]

A mammoth meeting was held in Delhi where Savarkar, along with revolutionaries Raja Mahendra Pratap, Ashutosh Lahiri, V.B. Gogate, Lala Hridayram of the Hardinge bomb case fame, Lala Hanumant Sahay, the mother of Bhagat Singh and the widow of Ajit Singh were given a grand reception and felicitated. Savarkar was feted during this Delhi visit by several organizations such as the Arya Samaj, that gave him the title of *Hindu Hriday Samrat*, and the Maharashtra Samaj of Delhi under the leadership of N.V. Gadgil. The 1857 celebrations continued for a large part of the year and even in Bombay the event was celebrated grandly. Savarkar was made the vice-president of the citizens' committee in Bombay to commemorate the occasion. Between 1957 and 1960 the universities of Poona and Bombay conferred honorary doctorates on Savarkar for his immense contribution to literature.

Savarkar's admirers celebrated his seventy-fifth birthday in 1958 with aplomb. More importantly, 24 December 1960 would mark the completion of the fifty years' transportation to life that he had been slapped with in 1910 in the Nasik Conspiracy case. The day was called 'Mrityunjay Divas' or the day of conquering death. Savarkar's health had rapidly declined by then and he was too weak to receive or meet people. He stood in the balcony of his house, Savarkar Sadan, and received the wishes of the vast crowds that had gathered outside singing his praise. In his message Rajagopalachari said on the occasion: 'Veer Savarkar is one of the heroes of India's struggle against British and he will be held in esteem and loved by us all, as an *abhiratha* in the long battle for freedom.'[22] The president of India, Rajendra Prasad, Vice-President S. Radhakrishnan, Yashwantrao Chavan, the chief minister of Maharashtra and several other leaders sent their good wishes and felicitations. No message of good will was to come from the office of the prime minister of India though. The celebrations culminated on 15 January 1961 in Poona. Speaking feebly on the occasion, Savarkar said that the achievement of freedom was the happiest moment of his life, something that was so satisfying that he wished neither a restoration of his confiscated property nor the showering of awards on him like the Bharat Ratna. He once again called for modernizing and strengthening India's military might and called upon the youth to join the National Cadet Corps (NCC). He also criticized the Nehru government for trusting China blindly and being oblivious of the strategic threats that country posed.

Savarkar's repeated warnings since 1954 turned out to be opportune and prophetic, even as India received a decisive drubbing in the India–China War of 1962. Nehru died a dejected man in 1964 after this fatal blow to his failed diplomacy and misplaced trust in China. Savarkar displayed his animosity, departing from his characteristic nature and maintaining a deafening silence, not sending any public statement condoning Nehru's death.

~

The series of lectures on Indian history that Savarkar had been giving since the time of the restrictions on his political activities was compiled together in the form of a book in April 1963, titled *Bharateeya Itihaasateel Saha Soneri Paane* or 'Six Golden Epochs of Indian History'. The English translation was done by S.T. Godbole who says in his preface that a 'book of this type had to be substantiated with proofs, especially when it was replete with thought-provoking—even at times shocking—statements and conclusions'.[23] Savarkar had not mentioned citations and references. Since he was nearing eighty years of age by then and too unwell for such assiduous academic work, Godbole assisted him in putting these together.

The six epochs that Savarkar defined were:

1) Chanakya and Chandragupta,
2) Pushyamitra Shunga, the Yavana destroyer,
3) Vikramaditya, the Shaka–Kushana menace,
4) Yashodharma, the conqueror of the Huns,
5) A long period of history of Islamic invasions and Arab conquests, Vijayanagara Empire, the rise of the Marathas under Shivaji and thereafter, Tipu Sultan and the Third Battle of Panipat.
6) India freed from British domination.

It was a masterful treatise, drawing from several sources, especially Sanskrit texts for the entire canvas of ancient Indian history that he painted.

Expectedly, the fifth chapter that dealt with medieval India was full of controversial claims and details.

Savarkar's aim in writing this book seems to be the same as it was when he wrote the 1857 book. Given the malleability of the discipline of history and how amenable it is to be rewritten, this book provides a uniquely native perspective to Indian historiography, which is not seen from the lens of colonial and imperialist biases. Was it a revivalist and jingoistic version of the country's past? It possibly was to some extent. But as history makes itself amenable to be retold from varied perspectives, especially those of the victor, Savarkar's attempt here was to establish that sense of pride in place of that of shame and apology about one's past. As he states:

> How the histories written not only by foreign historians or those who are avowedly inimical to us, but even by our own people, ignore the glorious episodes of exceptional valour and monumental successes of the Hindus and in their stead, catalogue only the calamities that befell them and present them as the only true history of the Hindus, because they were never fearlessly written from the pure and simple Hindu standpoint . . . Generally speaking in all histories, especially in the history text-books used in schools, the writers invariably jump from an account of the Hunnish onslaught to the first successful Muslim campaign on Sindh, without writing even a line or two about the intervening long period of these hundred years or so. Next follow in quick succession the detailed narration [sic] of Muslim invasions one after another, so that a common reader, especially a pupil, catches an impression, which is very often carried even in his later life, that the history of the Hindus is nothing but a doleful tale of foreign subjugation and national defeats. Our enemies have publicized these false impressions as established facts all over the world for the last two or three centuries. For instance, a man like the late Dr. Ambedkar, burning with hatred against Hinduism, writes: 'The Hindus, has been a life of a continuous defeat [sic]. It is a mode of survival of which every Hindu will feel ashamed.'[24]

He postulated in depth the details of the various Islamic invasions, atrocities, plunder of lives, properties, modesty of women and of places of worship, and chided Hindus for lack of unity, a 'perverted conception of virtues'[25] and practices like the caste system that furthered the divisions amongst them. On these 'perverted virtues', he elaborated:

Even while the Muslim demons were demolishing Hindu temples
and breaking to pieces their holiest of idols like Somnath, they never
wrecked their vengeance upon those wicked Muslims, even when they
had golden opportunities to do so, nor did they ever take out a single
brick from the walls of Masjids, because their religious teachers and
priests preached the virtue of not inflicting pain on the offender: 'Never
pay the tormentor in his own coin but bear the torments meekly and be
patient that God will punish him.' The vilest of vices recorded in the
catalogues of the religious texts could never have been more detrimental
to the welfare of mankind, more harmful to the national interests, and
so more detestable than such virtues as give rise to horrible atrocities
and the greatest of sins. Naturally whoever cultivates, and lives up to
such virtues thoughtlessly and foolishly and with slavish adherence
to the religious texts, and also with fanatic obstinacy, is bound to
perish individually and bring about disaster of the nation in which
he lives. These qualities are not virtues; they are virtues distorted in
the extreme. Whichever virtue is adopted thoughtlessly and without
regard to the time, place and person is corrupted and rotten, and, like
putrefied food, becomes poisonous. Every Hindu seems to have been
made to suck, along with his mother's milk, this Nectar-like advice
that religious tolerance is a virtue. But nobody ever explains to him
the essence of that precept. If that alien religion is also tolerant of
our own religion, our tolerance towards it can be a virtue. But the
Muslim and the Christian religions, which boldly proclaim it to be
their religious duty to destroy most cruelly the Hindu religion and to
eradicate from the face of this earth the *kafirs* and the heathens, can
never be described as tolerant of other religions. In respect of these
intolerant foreign religions the very extremely enraged intolerance,
which seeks to retaliate their atrocities with super-atrocious reprisals,
itself becomes a virtue.[26]

Savarkar spoke about how the Islamic invasions were accompanied with
large scale abduction, molestation and outraging of the modesty of Hindu
women as a 'religious duty.'[27] However Hindu rulers stood by their own
values of never touching the womenfolk of the captured, even if the
defeated were the same Islamic hordes who heaped ignominy on their
mothers, wives, sisters and daughters. This trait was also lauded as being
chivalrous. Giving an example, he said:

Even now we proudly refer to the noble acts of Chhatrapati Shivaji and Chimaji Appa, when they honourably sent back the daughter-in-law of the Muslim Governor of Kalyan and the wife of the Portuguese governor of Bassein respectively. But is it not strange that, when they did so, neither Shivaji Maharaj nor Chimaji Appa should ever remember, the atrocities and the rapes and the molestation, perpetrated by Mahmud of Ghazni, Muhammad Ghori, Alla-ud-din Khilji and others, on thousands of Hindu ladies and girls like the princesses of Dahir, Kamaldevi, the wife of Karnaraj of Karnawati and her extremely beautiful daughter, Devaldevi. Did not the plaintive screams and pitiful lamentations of the millions of molested Hindu women which reverberated throughout the length and breadth of the country, reach the ears of Shivaji Maharaj and Chimaji Appa? The souls of those millions of aggrieved women might have perhaps said, 'Do not forget, O, Your Majesty, Chhatrapati Shivaji Maharaj, and O! Your Excellency, Chimaji Appa, the unutterable atrocities and oppression and outrage committed on us by the Sultans and Muslim noblemen and thousands of others, big and small. Let those Sultans and their peers take a fright that in the event of a Hindu victory our molestation and detestable lot shall be avenged on the Muslim women. Once they are haunted with this dreadful apprehension, that the Muslim women, too, stand in the same predicament in case the Hindus win, the future Muslim conquerors will never dare to think of such molestation of Hindu women. But because of the then prevalent perverted religious ideas about chivalry to women, which ultimately proved highly detrimental to the Hindu community, neither Shivaji Maharaj nor Chimaji Appa could do such wrongs to the Muslim women. It was the suicidal Hindu idea of chivalry to women, which saved the Muslim women (simply because they were women) from the heavy punishments of committing indescribable sins and crimes against the Hindu women.[28]

The above controversial illustration is often held against Savarkar as him having advocated the rape and molestation of Muslim women in contemporary India. The context in which this has been stated, albeit uncomfortable in the way it has been presented, makes it clear that this was not a prescription for current action but a hypothesis on what could possibly have been a better fate for the Hindu women if their menfolk had instilled similar fright in their opponents about the fate of their womenfolk in the event of a defeat. The same is explained further by him:

Suppose, if from the earliest Muslim invasion of India, the Hindus also, whenever they were victors on the battlefields, had decided to pay the Muslim fair sex in the same coin or punished them in some other ways, *i.e.,* by conversion even with force, and then absorbed them in their fold, then? Then with this horrible apprehension at their heart they would have desisted from their evil designs against any Hindu lady. If they had taken such a fright in the first two or three centuries, millions and millions of luckless Hindu ladies would have been saved all their indignities, loss of their own religion, rapes, ravages and other unimaginable persecutions. Our woman-world would not have suffered such a tremendous numerical loss, which means their future progeny would not have been lost permanently to Hinduism and the Muslim population could not have thrived so audaciously. Without any increase in their womenfolk the Muslim population would have dwindled into a negligible minority. But haunted with the fantastic idea of chivalry to enemy-women and a blind eye to time, place or person, the Hindus of that period, never tried to chastise the Muslim women-folk for their wrongs to Hindu women, even when the former were many a time completely at their mercy.

Well, did this misplaced chivalrous idea of the Hindus have any salutary effect on their Muslim foes? Were the latter ever ashamed of their sin of molesting a Hindu woman in view of this Hindu religious generosity and high-mindedness? Did the Muslims ever sincerely feel thankful to the Hindus for the safe return of thousands of Muslim women to their own kith and kin? Never! On the contrary they again and again reciprocated Hindu chivalrous behaviour with the same old treachery and atrocity, and thus held it to ridicule and scorn. On the contrary the Muslims were puffed up, perhaps, with the thought that if at all the Hindus were to show chivalry to anybody, it should have been to their own Hindu women! It was they who had the first right to such a chivalrous treatment! But if the Hindus could not rescue thousands of their own women who were being abducted, polluted, and forced into Islamic religion, in their very presence, through centuries, why should the Muslims not ridicule the Hindu chivalrous idea of civility to women, even enemy women? On the contrary they perhaps thought that the Hindus dared not think of violating or even insulting the Muslim women for fear of horrible reprisals. Thus they were more likely to misconstrue the Hindu idea of chivalry, than interpret it in the right sense, as to have been born of cowardice than of strength and bravery.[29]

Savarkar claimed that Hindus in the pre-Islamic era did not consider such chivalry as a virtue. The manner in which Rama or Krishna attacked and killed female demons was an example, according to him. The post-Puranic era kings too married the princesses of defeated Yavana, Shaka or Hun commandants and got their women into their harem. Tit for tat and pay the enemy in the same coin remained the strain of Savarkar's hypothesis for medieval India when the country fell to the scourge of repeated Islamic invasions. Countless examples are weaved into the narrative to emphasize this theory. He deftly brought in the genesis of most of the social evils that he had been fighting against—the seven fetters that held Hindu society captive according to him—and made out a case for inter-caste marriage, inter-caste dining, reconversions to the Hindu fold and crossing the seas without loss of caste.

Savarkar also dwelt at length on the religious conversions and persecutions that the missionaries embarked on, especially in Goa under the Portuguese rule from the fifteenth and sixteenth centuries. He quoted from several sources about the horrendous atrocities of St. Xavier and several other missionary heads against the local Hindus of Gomantak.

He rued the same lack of will of the Maratha forces who were part of the alliance that vanquished the despotic Tipu Sultan of Mysore who had wrecked havoc on people of other faiths. Though they had captured his kingdom and killed him, they made no attempts to reconvert those whom Tipu had forcibly converted or reclaim what had been lost during his tyrannical rule. When Tipu's two sons were taken hostage by Lord Cornwallis, the Maratha general Haripant Phadke spoke of how kindly he had the two of them fed when they claimed they were hungry. This, according to Savarkar, was the eternal foolishness of the Hindus, who treated even their enemy who never had similar civility towards them, with the utmost concern due to their own misplaced virtue system. On these one-sided war ethics of the Hindus, Savarkar writes:

> The ethics of war, which demanded that a charioteer must fight with another charioteer only, the sword should meet another sword alone, that the armed warrior ought not to fight with an unarmed one, till he has been armed equally, that a fallen, senseless warrior was never to be attacked till he had regained consciousness etc. etc., was perhaps quite suitable for the ancient times before Mahabharat. For both the contending parties obeyed the same set of rules: both worshipped the same ethics of war.

The Pandavas themselves had violated, at the instance of Lord Krishna, many of these chivalrous rules of war! But the Hindus of these middle ages forgot the lesson taught by the Bhagwat Geeta [sic], of giving due consideration to the time, place and person or persons concerned while obeying these rules of war. They on their own part kept on fighting the diabolic Muslim ways of war with the same old—originally sane and civilized but now outmoded and so highly suicidal tactics in war.[30]

In a lyrical and historical sweep, Savarkar then paints a panoramic portrait of all the dynasties that ruled India across the centuries—from the Khiljis, Lodhis, Tughlaks and Mughals to the Rashtrakutas, Cholas, the Vijayanagara Empire and the Maratha Empire under and after Chhatrapati Shivaji Maharaj. The story concludes with the attainment of Indian independence in the modern times, which Savarkar credits as much to the armed revolution right from 1857 onwards, as to the Congress movement for freedom. The prose was merciless and blunt, and received a mixed response from a shocked readership.

~

Savarkar's eightieth birthday was commemorated by his admirers all through 1963. Savarkar himself was reclusive and refused to meet anyone who wished to greet him. Curiously enough, when General K.M. Cariappa, the celebrated first Indian commander-in-chief of the Indian Army who had led the Indian forces in the western front during the war with Pakistan in 1947, tried to meet Savarkar while in Bombay, he was refused as well. Cariappa even wrote a couple of letters to Savarkar, which too were ignored.

Even as these celebrations were under way, Savarkar suffered a bad fall and broke his left thigh bone. He underwent a surgery at Dr Talwalkar's clinic in Dadar. He was bedridden for nearly three months. As the date of returning home came near, it was known that he was to be discharged on a new moon day, generally considered inauspicious by the orthodox and the astrologically inclined. Savarkar rebuffed these beliefs as irrational and ridiculous and insisted on being discharged that very day, on 24 June 1963.

Even as Savarkar slowly recovered, his wife Yamunabai was taken seriously ill and in October of that year was moved to the same clinic. The doctors had indicated that she might not live for too long. Yamuna too longed to go back home and die in peace by the side of her husband. But Savarkar remained adamant and refused this as well. He had started taking small steps after the surgery, with the help of a walking stick, and promised to visit her at the clinic. But he never kept that word as well. Eventually, Yamuna passed away on 8 November 1963. Savarkar's rationalism kicked in here too. He told the family not to bring the body home and instead take it directly to the Chandanwadi electric crematorium without any show of public sorrow. Quite unemotionally he added that there was not much reason to lament over a dead body and that Yamuna had led a complete, successful life, enjoyed marital bliss after his release from the Cellular Jail and had fondled her grandchildren. Her life, according to him, was literally therefore turned to gold and hence should only be celebrated and not mourned. Pushing his rationalism further, Savarkar refused to perform any obsequies and the Hindu rituals related to oblations to the departed soul through a feeding of the crows and so on. Many of his supporters and family members pleaded with him and insisted that he give up this obstinacy and instead follow whatever was prescribed in the scriptures as the last rites of passage for the soul. When a poor widow of the family intervened, she was gently told that if scriptures had to be so followed, ideally she should have shaved her head off. Since she had done away with that tradition, he too was dispensing with the superstitions of feeding crows. His son Vishwas however disregarded his father's commands and quietly performed all the prescribed rituals for his deceased mother. Savarkar possibly got to know of this but did not object, saying it was his individual choice and that he had no right to prevent his son from exercising it. This was the extreme rationalism that Savarkar practised, which many in his inner circle complained had robbed him of all his softer instincts.

But Yamuna's death possibly brought in his mind thoughts of his own departure from the world. He began talking about it increasingly with many people, including self-immolation and surrendering oneself to death wilfully. He had even asked his personal secretary Bal Savarkar whether he could help him go deep into the sea and cast a longing glance at the sea in Bombay.[31] In August 1964, he made his will and bequeathed a major part of his property to his daughter Prabhat and the rest to his son Vishwas. Bal Savarkar, who had served him devotedly for over fifteen years, was given the rights of publications of all his books and written material.

~

With Lal Bahadur Shastri becoming the prime minister after Nehru's death, the thaw in Savarkar's relationship with the Central government slowly eased. After repeated refusals of the previous government, Shastri's government decided to grant him a monthly aid from October 1964 as a veteran freedom fighter and as a token of his patriotic services for the nation. The blanket ban that existed on his name, in an unwritten code, was slowly being lifted. After the Gandhi murder case, Savarkar had become a veritable persona non grata and association with him began to cost people dearly. The famous music composer Hridaynath Mangeshkar for instance worked with All India Radio (AIR) and the entire family was extremely close to Savarkar. When the fifteen-year-old precocious composer approached Savarkar in 1955 seeking the latter's permission to set to music any of his poems, Savarkar had jokingly asked the young lad if he wished to go to prison by doing such a blasphemous task. When he insisted, Savarkar permitted him to use his poem '*Sagara Prana taLamaLalaa*' that he had written on the Brighton seaside in 1909 with his friend Niranjan Pal by his side. Hridaynath set this to music and got it recorded. But his bosses at AIR were livid. He was issued a show-cause notice seeking an explanation as to why he had chosen Savarkar's composition. Hridaynath gave a simple reply: 'Excellent poem, excellent poet.' He was summarily sacked from AIR.[32] Such was the 'untouchability' that was perpetrated ironically on a man who strove all his life to eradicate that very scourge.

But the winds were changing now. His epic poem, '*Jayostute Sri MahanmangaLe Shivaaspade Shubhade*' or 'Hail to Thee the Goddess of Liberty' was included for broadcast on the radio.

Savarkar's health meanwhile was on a rapid decline. He had suffered from piles for a while but the condition worsened from August 1965 with a prolapse of the rectum and severe swelling of the stomach. He was advised liquid diet for two weeks and endured unbearable pain. Savarkar kept appealing to his doctors to not treat him but let him die instead. His doctors refused to listen to him.

Amidst the gloom came the sweet news of India's decisive victory in the war against Pakistan in 1965. Savarkar was deeply overjoyed and sent his congratulatory messages to Prime Minister Shastri and Defence Minister Yashwantrao Chavan. When Shastri was leaving for Tashkent for peace negotiations with Pakistan, Savarkar publicly shared his apprehensions on Pakistan's untrustworthiness. Quite prophetically, Shastri died in

Tashkent under extremely mysterious circumstances on 11 January 1966, shortly after valorously leading the nation to a great victory.

~

Among the last interviews that Savarkar gave was the one to Shridhar Telkar for the RSS magazine *Organiser*, for its Diwali edition of 1965. The complete transcript of this delightful interview, which is a 'first-person' looking back of the entire stormy life that Savarkar led, is as under:[33]

Q: Looking back, what are the most thrilling memories, which you still cherish?

A: Of course, memories of old keep haunting me. I treasure these thrilling memories. They are now a part of me and will remain with me till the end of my life. The first thrilling event, which I still vividly remember was my dramatic escape from the steamer. It all happened like this: it was Sunday March 13 1910. I arrived in London from Paris. I was immediately arrested at the Victoria Terminus by the London Police. The arrest was made under a telegraphic warrant from the Bombay Government. I was held under the Fugitive and Offenders Act of 1881. The charges against me were: 1) Waging war or abetting the waging of war against His Majesty, the King Emperor of India; 2) Conspiring to deprive His Majesty the King of the Sovereignty of British India or a part of it; 3) Procuring and distributing arms, and abetting the murder of Jackson, the then Collector of Nasik; 4) Procuring and distributing arms in London and waging war from London; 5) Delivering seditious speeches in India from January 1906 onwards and in London from 1908 and 1909.

I was put on the steamer S.S. 'Morea' bound for Aden. I was a prisoner of the British in the steamer. And I realized what my fate would be once I reached homeland. So, I decided to escape from the jaws of death. Luckily for me, the steamer anchored at Marseilles for repairs. I now made a dramatic decision, to escape somehow from the steamer. So I went to the bathroom and bolted the door from inside. My guard waited outside. I jumped from the porthole into the sea and started swimming towards the harbor. The guards opened fire. And bullets whizzed by. I dodged them by diving, and cheated death. At last, I reached the harbor, and climbed the quay. I was happy that at last I was on the soil of France—a free man. But fate was cruel and unkind. The British guards pursued me and dragged me back to the steamer—clearly a breach of International law—for I had been arrested on a foreign land. Madam Cama and Ayyar who had planned to rescue me arrived in Marseilles by car late by a few minutes. They must have cursed themselves when they heard that I was captured after my dramatic escape.

The second episode, which lingers in my mind is when I was sentenced on two occasions for transportation for life. This meant that altogether I had to remain in the Andaman's Cellular Jail for fifty years. If I had served my full term of imprisonment, I would have been released on December 24, 1960. But I was sent to Hindustan after 14 years in the Andamans to be interned for 13 years in Ratnagiri. Altogether, I remained a prisoner of the British for nearly 27 years.

The third event, which I shall always cherish, was when I met my young patriotic brother and my noble wife in cellular jail for the first time in 8 years. The Government had permitted them to see me in the Andaman Jail. How can I express in cold words what I felt then? Anyhow, I was supremely happy to see and talk to my wife, who shared with me the sorrows and agonies of a revolutionary's life.

Q. You have been a great revolutionary in your time and a great fighter for India's freedom. Tell me, how and why you became a revolutionary?

A: It happened like this. Somewhere round about 1897, the country was in the grip of famine and plague. The people suffered much during this critical period. The soul of the people was in agony. The Government did little to alleviate the sufferings of the people. Death and disease took a heavy toll of life. The excesses committed by the soldiers and the antics of the bullying incompetent, tyrant Rand, the Plague Commissioner, infuriated the Chaphekar [sic] brothers of Poona. They shot dead Rand and another Englishman. The Chaphekar [sic] brothers were tried and hanged. The terrible news of their hanging stirred me. I was hardly 16 then. My enquiring mind became restless. I realized, even at that young age, the significance of the act of the Chaphekar [sic] brothers. I decided to take a vow—a pledge to fight and die, if need be, for the freedom and liberty of my country. So, at the dead of the night, I sat alone at the feet of our family deity—the Armed Goddess Durga—and invoked the blessings of the Great Mother, the source of Divine inspiration and strength. I took a solemn vow before Goddess Durga to do my duty towards my country and to fulfill the noble mission of the martyred Chaphekar [sic] brothers. I also took a vow to drive out the Britishers from my beloved motherland and make my country free and great once again—the glory that was Hind. This, then, is how and why I became a revolutionary.

Q. When you were a political prisoner in the Andaman Island, you were cut off from the main currents of Indian life and soil. How then, did your mind function, and what were your dominant thoughts?

A: Although I was far away from home, I was not really cut off from the life and thought of our people. We were operating a strange kind of a news agency—something like a Bush Wireless in the jail. News filtered through many channels. Once I received a letter from a prisoner in the Punjab. He had written on the back of a ticket of a convict who delivered it safely to me. I used to pick up old newspapers from the water closets of the British officers and old soiled wrapping papers. From these, I learnt a lot about what was happening in the world outside. Many prisoners lost their privileges of working outside the jail for bringing in pieces of newspapers. But the news agency worked continuously because of these daring messengers who knew the art of hoodwinking the jail warders and guards. Also, a system was devised by which messages were transmitted by political prisoners through peculiar sounds of the chain. My thoughts in the Andamans naturally turned to the revolutionary struggle that was being waged in India and by Indians abroad.

I was given a very hard job in the Cellular Jail. I was yoked to an oil-mill like a bullock. But I knew that each drop of oil that fell in the bucket would set aflame the hearts of all revolutionaries. It was this thought that helped and inspired me in the dark, difficult, agonizing solitary life in the cellular jail.

You have asked me, how my mind functioned in jail? Well, it required terrific willpower, grim determination and a passionate devotion to the cause to be able to face the deadly and maddening solitude of a solitary cell in Devil's Island. When I was given the work of chopping the barks of coconuts with a wooden mallet, my hands bled and swelled. But I endured. When I was yoked to the oil-mill—the most horrible, painful and demoralizing job given to me—I did not complain. I suffered in silence. The idea of committing suicide came once. But reason prevailed. For I wanted to die a hero in freedom's battle and not by committing suicide. So, you see, how the mind functioned during the grim battle, within and without.

Q: How would you compare Indian Revolutionaries with Revolutionaries in Russia and China?

A: Indian Revolutionaries had a tougher fight than the Revolutionaries in Russia or China. In Russia, they revolted against the Russian Czarist regime and in China against the Chinese Manchu Dynasty. But in India, we had to fight against foreign rulers whose way of life, culture, religion and philosophy had nothing in common with the Hindus of Hindusthan. In a way, our revolutionaries have been better than these revolutionaries of Russia and China.

Q: Do you think that the '1857 Mutiny' was India's first organized revolt against the British for the freedom of the country as a whole? Some historians say that the '1857 Revolt' was organized by half a dozen disgruntled but daring leaders who banded together for the maintenance of their respective privileges and status. What do you think?

A: I have written a book on 1857. I have done a great deal of research in the matter. I read original letters, numerous documents and hundreds of books both at the India House and in the British Museum. I have affirmed that the 1857 memorable event was not just a mutiny. Indeed, it was India's First War of Independence. Those historians who deny this basic fact of history are fooling themselves and also fooling others. They have yet to learn the real history.

Q: What are the factors, which contributed to the liberation of our country?

A: There are many factors, which contributed to the freedom of Bharat. It is wrong to imagine that Congress alone won Independence for Hindusthan. It is equally absurd to think that non-cooperation, Charkha and the 1942 'Quit India Movement' were sorely responsible for the withdrawal of the British power from our country. There were other dynamic and compelling forces, which finally determined the issue of freedom. *First*, Indian politics was carried to the Army, on whom the British depended entirely to hold down Hindusthan; *Second*, there was a revolt of the Royal Indian Navy and a threat by the Air Force; *third*, the valiant role of Netaji Subhas Bose and the I.N.A.; *four*, the War of Independence in 1857, which shook the British; Five, the terrific sacrifices made by thousands of revolutionaries and patriots in the ranks of the Congress, other groups and parties. So, freedom came with blood, sweat and tears of countless men and women of Hindusthan.

Q: Did Gandhiji and other Congress leaders persuade you at any time to join the Congress? If they did, why did you not join the Congress?

A: I have never believed in Gandhiji's doctrine of Non-Violence. Absolute non-violence is not only sinful but immoral. This doctrine of non-violence benumbed the revolutionary fervor, softened the limbs and hearts of the Hindus, and stiffened the bones of enemies. The lambs resolved to lead a vegetarian life but the wolves were not concerned with their pious resolution. Revolt, bloodshed and revenge have often been instruments created by nature to root out injustice. I felt I could not join the Congress because of my fundamental differences with the Congress on their methods, policies and programme.

The Hindu Mahasabha would have joined the Congress in the 1942 movement if the Congress had solemnly guaranteed that it would irrevocably stand by the unity and integrity of India and that the Congress would not make any pact with the anti-national Muslim League. The people now know that our dream of a free, independent, Akhand Hindusthan was systematically sabotaged by Congress leadership.

Q: Assuming you had joined the Congress years ago, don't you think you would have served your country and your ideology in a positive way?

A: I don't think so. It is wrong to assume a thing, which has no basis for assumption. Anyway, if I had, by magic, persuaded myself to join the Congress, I would have been a fish out of water—a complete misfit in the company of lambs dedicated to win freedom by spinning Charkha and shouting non-violence slogans. I would have been driven out of Congress like Subhas Bose, who tried to reorientate [sic] Congress policy and programme. I would have been a traitor to my conscience, to the ideal of Hindutva and the Hindu Nation, if I had served the Congress for a mess of pottage. I am indeed happy and proud that I am not a party to the partition of Hindusthan. Many generations yet unborn may well say that I served my country and my people with devotion and a passionate faith.

Q: What is the India of your dreams?

A: My India would be a democratic State in which people belonging to different religions, sects or races would be treated with perfect equality. None would be allowed to dominate others. None would be deprived of his just and equal rights of free citizenship, so long as everyone discharged the common obligation, which he owed to the State as a whole. Hindusthan, the motherland and the holy land of the Hindus, from the Indus to the Seas would be an organic, undivided State. The Hindus would be a casteless society, a consolidated and a modern nation. Science and technology would be encouraged. There would be a total liquidation of landlordism. All the land would belong to the State eventually. All key industries would be nationalized. India would be self-sufficient in respect of food, clothes, shelter and defence. The India of my dreams would have unbounded faith in a world commonwealth. Because the earth is the common motherland of all. But India would not go down under the evolution of this world commonwealth. The foreign policy of a militarily strong Akhand Hindusthan would be a policy of neutrality and peace. And a powerful centralized State of Hindusthan would contribute effectively towards an enduring peace and prosperity in the world.

Q: Some think that you believe in a Hindu Nation because you are a fanatic communalist. What have you to say about it?

A: Let us get this thing straight. People have a wrong notion of a Hindu Nation and about communalism. A Hindu means a person who regards this land of Bharatvarsha from the Indus to the Seas as his fatherland and holy land—the land of origin of his religion and the cradle of his faith. Therefore, the followers of Vedism [sic], Jainism, Buddhism, Sikhism and all hill tribes are Hindus. The Parsees, amongst the other minorities, are by race, religion, language and culture, almost akin to the Hindus. The Christians and Jews could be politically assimilated with the Hindus. Around this life-centre moves Hindutva—not a religious dogma or creed but the thoughts and activities of the whole being of the Hindu race. The problem of the minority is that of only one minority—

the Muslim minority. A Hindu nation, therefore, is a group of people bound together by ties of common religion and culture, common history and traditions, common literature, occupying a territory of geographical unity and aspiring to form a political unit. Therefore, in Hindusthan, the Hindus are a nation.

Those who think I am a fanatic Hindu and a communalist, are suffering from a strange malady—hallucination. I am neither a fanatic Hindu nor a communalist. I cannot make donkeys think like horses.

Q: What are your views on the present state of affairs in India?

A: After freedom, people hoped that they would have a little peace, a little comfort, a little happiness after all that happened during the regime of the British. Their hopes have been dashed. After 18 years of independence, we find people unhappy, miserable, demoralized and frustrated. Big projects and schemes have not yet touched the common man who is desperately fighting for his daily bread—fighting for his very existence. The Congress party and Government are filled with dead wood, old and tired men who have outlived their political usefulness to the country. They remain in power and prevent the training of young men for the tasks of tomorrow.

Q: What of the future?

A: It is sheer madness to imagine for a moment that the country will go to pieces. A country that has produced eminent statesmen like Chandragupta, Vikramaditya, Shalivahan, Chanakya, and Shivaji can never be a politically bankrupt nation. Hindusthan has a tradition of thousands of years of great men presiding over the destiny of Bharatvarsha in times of crisis. As in the past, so in the future, men of destiny will always be there to guide, to serve, and to die for the motherland.

Q: Do you think in an atomic age, militarization of the country is essential?

A: Yes, I have always maintained two things: Hinduize politics and militarize the nation. If you are strong, you can even show the shoe as Khrushchev did at the United Nations Assembly. But if you are weak, your fate will be in the hands of a powerful aggressor.

Q: Assuming that Congress disintegrates, do you foresee a contest for political power between a form of Hindu fascism and communism?

A: A Hindu of my conception is not a fascist, but a real democrat in the true sense of the word. He is also a communist in a way. If all the Hindus who believe in the fundamentals of Hindutva unite, then the question of a contest for a political power does not arise.

Q: And finally, is our revolution complete? Or are we still in the midst of it?

A: The end of our revolution has come with the attainment of our freedom. Those of us who fought for the country's liberty are naturally very happy to see it free and independent. The days of the bomb, the pistol, and the gun are over. We have now to devote ourselves to the consolidation of our hard-won freedom. But our aim of achieving Akhand Hindusthan with its natural boundaries still remains to be fulfilled. I am old now, and the time has come for me to say goodbye to all that! I have served the cause of my country in accordance with the dictates of my conscience. I am glad that I have lived to see my country free from bondage. As long as the world lasts, this, our ancient land—this, our great Bharatvarsha, will live in all its glory!

As the year 1965 was drawing to a close, Savarkar's health condition worsened. He had given up food and medicine given the digestive trouble he faced. He could not get up without support. What Savarkar had in mind of the course that his life must take was made clear by him in an article he wrote a Marathi monthly *Sahyadri*, in July 1964. It was titled '*Aatma Hatya aaNi Aatmaarpan*' (Suicide and Self-sacrifice), the full text of which is listed in the Appendix. He began the article with a Sanskrit verse: 'Blessed am I, blessed am I, I know of no duty now; Blessed am I, blessed am I, I have fulfilled what I wished to achieve.' He argued passionately of how several saints and scholars of the past had wilfully given up their body when they realized that they had fulfilled their earthly duties to the best of their ability. He referenced Kumarila Bhatta, the celebrated philosopher and champion of Vedic ritualism, who, after a successful life 'pledged to reduce his body to ashes by offering himself to the holy fire rather than await a natural demise. Accordingly, he lit a pyre and entered it. His body was reduced to ashes in the leaping flames. But this glorious act of martyrdom has not been described as "suicide"; rather it has been glowingly referred to in history as *agnidivya* (penance by fire) or *atmarpan* (self-sacrifice).'[34] Even Adi Shankaracharya had said: 'Renounce the world as soon as you feel detached, be it at home or in the forest.' After completing all the Maha Bhashyas or commentaries that he had compiled, in addition to numerous other achievements at a young age, Shankaracharya had gone into a cave, assumed a yogic posture, asked his disciples to shut the mouth of the cave with a boulder and left his mortal coil while in penance. Savarkar cited similar instances with saints like Chaitanya Mahaprabhu in Bengal and Dnyaneshwar, Eknath, Tukaram and Samartha Ramdas in Maharashtra who took wilful samadhi to leave their bodies behind. He hypothesized that from all these examples it was clear that all cases of wilful surrender of one's body were not derided as suicide or as a crime. He added:

> Those who end their lives in a spirit of frustration, dissatisfaction or discontentment and cannot live happily even though they so wish are said to have committed 'suicide'. But those who happily end their lives with the blessed sense of having fulfilled their life-mission or objective are said to have committed self-sacrifice. Though this changing and evolving earthly world can never be said to have achieved perfection, blessed souls voluntarily end their lives with the realization that they have nothing left to achieve or fulfill. They merge their mortal life into the immortal Universal Life. As the Yoga Vasishta says: 'An empty pot is in reality filled with the sky, a pot immersed in the sea has sea both within and without; it is hence full within and without.' With a feeling of self-satisfaction at having largely perfected their life-mission and rather than let their body become a burden to self and society, such souls renounce their bodies by entering a cave or fasting unto death or entering fire or water or enter a state of samadhi. Though their act may be grossly referred to as 'willful termination of life', it is only fitting that it should be referred glowingly as 'self-sacrifice'.[35]

From the beginning of February 1966, Savarkar gave up even his tea when he realized that his family and the doctors had started mixing it with vitamin tablets. Leaders and commoners from all over the country sent their inquiries and wishes even as the news of his fast began to gather momentum. Savarkar summarily refused meeting anyone, be it ministers or commoners. The entire battery of doctors—Arvind Godbole, Subhash

Purandare, Vasantrao Kale, Shrikhande, Avinash Godbole, R.V. Sathe and Sharad Marathe—were told not to meddle with him or attempt to revive him. Slowly his condition got so bad that he could not swallow water as well. He however allowed his barber Sadashiv Pawar to meet him on 23 February to give him a final shave. Bal Savarkar too was bid farewell with the lines of Tukaram that he feebly mumbled: 'We are going to our native Home; accept out goodbye; Now there can be no give and take, the speech itself is stopped.'[36]

The doctors' bulletin of 24 February said: 'The condition of Veer Savarkar is grave. There is a painful swelling on the right side of his face. He has extreme difficulty in talking. A panel of doctors is attending on him right round the clock.'[37] He had survived for almost twenty-two days by then with little or no medicine, and taking just a few spoonfuls of water daily and remaining alert and conscious till the very end.

As the morning of 26 February dawned, he came down with a very high fever when he woke up at 8.30 a.m. His entire family—son Vishwas and daughter Prabhat, their respective kids Vidula and Madhuri, his daughter-in-law Sunder and son-in-law Madhavrao Chiplunkar—gathered around him grief-stricken. Savarkar's breathing began to become increasingly shallow, his blood pressure dipped and the pulse worsened. The doctors tried artificial respiration and cardiac massage to try and revive him. But by 11.10 a.m. his body finally gave up. 'Swatantryaveer' Vinayak Damodar Savarkar's soul finally merged with its Maker, at the ripe age of eighty-three.

Savarkar had clearly stated in his will that upon his death there should be no mourning and inconvenience caused to the people at large with hartals and processions. He had also willed that he must be cremated in an electric crematorium and not on a pyre of wood, and with no religious rituals and ceremonies. At best, Vedic hymns could be chanted, even as the high voltage would incarcerate the body into an embrace of fire. He had to be carried to the crematorium in a mechanized transport and not on human shoulders or animal-drawn vehicles. No shraddha ceremonies or obsequies were to be performed for him.

His mortal remains were kept at the ground floor of Savarkar Sadan from 4.30 p.m. on 26 February to 3.30 p.m. on the following day. More than two lakh people thronged the building to catch a final glimpse of the leader they adored. The Hindu Mahasabha leaders requested the government to provide a gun carriage for the funeral. But such was the antipathy towards Savarkar that this request was denied. When 'Acharya' Atre came to know about this, he contacted V. Shantaram, the veteran Hindi film producer and director for help. Shantaram got a replica of a gun carriage from his studio, which was eventually used for the funeral procession.[38]

The final procession started on 27 February, lasting for six hours through the streets of Bombay, with almost 50,000 to a lakh people joining in at various points, with slogans of '*Swatantryaveer Savarkar Amar Rahe*' and '*Hindu Rashtra ki Jai*'. Devotional songs or abhangs were sung by Snehal Bhatkal and poems of Dnyaneshwar by Sudhir Phadke and Sopandeo Chaudhari. The body, with its head raised, was placed on the raised bier of the truck with Savarkar adorning his characteristic black cap. Finally, as willed by him, his mortal remains were consigned to the electric flames of the crematorium at Chandanwadi.

According to his will, his obsequies were not performed. His ashes were immersed in the sea at Dadar Chowpatty by his son Vishwas and they were not given to anybody for public immersion or deification.

~

Tributes poured in from all quarters on the passing away, not just of an individual but an era in the annals of Indian history. S. Radhakrishnan said: 'A steady and sturdy worker for the independence of our country, his career was for many youngsters a legendary one.'[39] Paying her glowing tributes, Prime Minister Indira Gandhi said that his death 'removes a great figure of contemporary India', that his name was a 'by-word for daring and patriotism', and that 'he was cast in the mould of a classic revolutionary and countless people drew inspiration from him'.[40] The chairman of the Communist Party of India, S.A. Dange said: 'The death of Veer Savarkar removes from the scene of Indian history one of the great anti-imperialist revolutionaries.'[41] Newspaper tributes and obituary columns were aplenty. *The Times of India* for instance wrote in its editorial:

Vinayak Damodar Savarkar was a rebel and a revolutionary till his last breath. He relished controversy, which he enlivened with his glowing patriotism and sense of dedication. History will salute him as a remarkable Indian, a man whose faith in the destiny of his country remained undiminished till the end despite so many vicissitudes. His

life reads like a legend. He matched his words with deeds. That is why
the British Raj never took to him kindly . . . he insistently raised his
voice in favour of strong Central Government, which would be able to
keep divisive tendencies under check and implement national policies
and programmes vigorously. Savarkar's most noteworthy contribution to
Indian political thinking was his emphasis on the defence of the country's
frontiers. Though the term he used 'militarization' was not a happy
one, his main concern was that India should guard against internal and
external weakening. His dauntless spirit will stir generations to come.[42]

Meanwhile, the crows that had perched on the window-sill of Savarkar
Sadan, waited patiently for long for their morsel, and then flew away,
hungry and dejected.

12

Contentious Legacy

A little over a year before Savarkar's death, on 12 October 1964, the accused in the Gandhi murder trial—Gopal Godse, Vishnu Karkare and Madanlal Pahwa—were released from prison after serving a life sentence (usually a period of about fourteen years or so amounts to a life sentence). Back in their hometown Poona, Gopal and Karkare were shockingly welcomed as heroes by their well-wishers and a felicitation was planned in their honour. A Satya Vinayak Puja was organized on 12 November 1964 at the Udyan Mangal Karyalaya in Poona's Shaniwar Peth and invitations were sent out in the name of one M.G. Ghasias. In the invite, Nathuram Godse was described as a *Deshbhakt* or patriot. The event was presided by G.V. Ketkar, the grandson of Tilak and the former editor of *Kesari*. In his exuberance Ketkar mentioned in his public address about having had prior knowledge of Nathuram's plans to murder Gandhi. He referred to Nathuram's outbursts when he was told of Gandhi's desire to live for 125 years saying 'Who will allow you to live till then?' Ketkar claimed that he and another veteran named Balukaka Kanitkar heard this outburst, were deeply perturbed by it and tried to dissuade Nathuram from undertaking any untoward step. Ketkar got so carried away by the moment that despite Gopal trying to gently interrupt him in his speech by warning him to be careful about what he was speaking, he went on to say that he had even advised Kanitkar to write to the government and warn them. Ketkar went on that he met Badge in Poona after the aborted murder attempt of 20 January 1948 and the latter had confirmed to him that Nathuram and Apte were determined to carry out their plan to fulfilment. Ketkar's bravado and loose talk got all of them into serious trouble, and resultantly he, Gopal and Ghasias were arrested. Expectedly, his explosive statements made it to the headlines of all newspapers, both nationally and in Maharashtra causing a huge upheaval. *The Indian Express,* Bombay noted:

> Mr. Ketkar presided over the function, which was held in Udyan Mangal Karyalaya. It was attended by about 100 men and women. Mr. Ketkar disclosed that for about three months prior to Gandhiji's murder, Nathuram 'used to discuss with me the pros and cons' of his idea to kill Gandhiji. He was opposed to the idea and 'used to tell Nathuram to consider the consequences, both social and political'. Mr. Ketkar said that after the first incident (Madan Lal had exploded a bomb at Gandhiji's prayer meeting a few days before the murder), Badge (who turned approver) had come to Poona and told him (Mr. Ketkar) of 'their future plans'. Mr. Ketkar added that he thus knew that they were going to kill Gandhiji. As Mr. Ketkar said these things, Mr. Gopal Godse asked him not to speak 'more about it'. But Mr. Ketkar said that 'they will not arrest me now for that'.[1]

Parliament and the Maharashtra Legislative Assembly were expectedly rocked by the storm that this caused. The Central government bowed to the immense and legitimate pressure from all quarters and a Commission of Enquiry was set up on 22 March 1965 to relook at the various angles behind the assassination of Gandhi, seventeen years after the dastardly crime and sixteen years after the Red Fort trial verdict. The Commission was headed by Member of Parliament Gopal Swarup Pathak initially. After he became a minister, Justice Jivan Lal Kapur, a retired judge of the Supreme Court of India replaced him on 21 November 1966.

The terms of reference of the Commission were as under:

a) Whether any persons, in particular Shri Gajanan Viswanath Ketkar, of Poona, had prior information of the conspiracy of Nathuram Vinayak Godse and others to assassinate Mahatma Gandhi.

b) Whether any of such persons had communicated the said information to any authorities of the Government of Bombay or to the Government of India; in particular whether the aforesaid Shri Ketkar had conveyed the said information to the late Bal Gangadhar Kher, the then Premier of Bombay, through the late Balukaka Kanitkar.

c) If so, what action was taken by the Government of Bombay, in particular by the late Bal Gangadhar Kher, and the Government of India on the basis of the said information.

Clause (c) was later amended by a notification dated 28 October 1968 to read: If so, what action was taken by the Government of Bombay, in particular by the late Bal Gangadhar Kher, and the Government of India, *and by the officers of the said Governments*, on the basis of the said information.[2]

Thus, what was a sad and closed chapter in the annals of free India was reopened for scrutiny. In the process, the legacy of the departed Savarkar and his alleged involvement in the conspiracy too was now reopened for public debate.

About the status of the Commission and its mandate, Justice Kapur himself states in his report:

This Commission is not sitting as a Court of Appeal against the High Court nor it is open to it to find fault with the findings of the High Court, still less to re-adjudicate on matters already dealt with by it. But this principle applies to matters, which deal with the guilt or innocence of the accused or matters so connected with the decision of that question as to be part of it, but not to matters wholly subsidiary, which do not affect the merits of the case. E.g.: the commission of the offence and those who committed it. Therefore, it is open to the sovereign or the State to find out through the agency of a Commission whether its protective and investigational machinery was properly geared to the protection of the Mahatma.[3]

The Kapur Commission examined 101 witnesses and 407 documents were produced by both the governments. The examination of witnesses took 162 days and were held at various places—Bombay, New Delhi, Dharwar, Nagpur, Poona, Baroda and Chandigarh. It came out with a six-volume exhaustive report. The evidence recorded by the Commission was contained in five volumes and the documents produced before it contained in another five. The record of the proceedings before Judge Atma Charan, the case diaries of the Delhi Police investigation into the bomb case and the murder case, the crime report of the Bombay Police, files produced by the Government of India, director of Intelligence Bureau and the inspector general of Delhi Police were all made parts of the record. The then director of intelligence, Sanjevi, blamed the Bombay Police and Nagarvala for paying scant regard to the warnings sent from Delhi after the 20 January 1948 episode, along with two policemen, who also carried Madanlal's confessional statement that had important clues to the culprits' identity. Much of the Commission's sphere of enquiry became the enormous bungling and lack of communication between the police forces of the two cities. The role or the alleged lack of sufficient proactive action on the part of the home minister of Bombay, Morarji Desai, also came under the scanner. The details of all the witness depositions and the reopened trail of the murder investigation are beyond the scope of this volume.

The Commission in its enquiry however rejected the veracity of claims made about repeated attempts on Gandhi's life, right from the Panchgani episode of 1944 where Apte had heckled him. There was a tale doing the rounds of how Godse had rushed towards Gandhi during this meeting with a knife and was overpowered by Gandhi's associates. The Commission held that if an incident as dramatic as this had indeed happened, it could not have remained suppressed or unknown as such a story 'would have been quite hot and certainly sensational in which the whole of India and many people outside' would have been aroused, 'and no newsmen who are watching for news like this would have dared not to report it' given the global figure that Gandhi was.[4] Justice Kapur held:

> Although on this evidence the alleged incident of the attack and its alleged details cannot be held to be proved, the important fact which emerges is that there was in existence an organization, which was extremely anti-Gandhi and its members persisted in pursuing Mahatma Gandhi by creating disturbances at his meetings and their attitude was not non-violent.[5]

It also similarly dismissed the incident at Wardha in 1944 where Gandhi was prevented from leaving for Bombay for talks with Jinnah or the plans to derail a train that was carrying Gandhi from Bombay to Poona on 30 June 1946 as being baseless and without any proof.[6]

On the basis of the examination of R.N. Bannerjee, ICS, who was the home secretary of the Central government during the time of the murder, and of Morarji Desai, the Commission also drew its inferences on the RSS and its alleged role in the episode.

The evidence of Mr. R.N. Bannerjee is that the R.S.S. as a body were not responsible for the bomb throwing or for the murder of Mahatma Gandhi nor were the conspirators acting in their capacity as members of the organization. As a matter of fact, the principal accused who have been shown to be members of the Hindu Mahasabha belonged to the Rashtra Dal organization, which was a distinct Savarkarite organization. It has not been proved that they were members of the R.S.S., which shows that they were believers in a more violent form of activities than mere parades, rallies, physical exercises and even shooting practices. There is no proof that any of the Ministers or any of the officers of the Government were patronizing or attending R.S.S. rallies and this charge made against them, on the evidence, which has been put before the Commission, is not established.[7]

Witness No. 39 of the Commission was Sarla Barve, the wife of the district magistrate of Poona. She accused the authorities of not taking proper notice of the threat to Gandhi's life despite her husband's repeated warnings that he had made to Morarji Desai over several telephonic conversations. The report reveals:

> She stated that two or three days before the murder of Mahatma Gandhi a man called Sathe came to their house but as her husband was not present he told her that some Poona people had gone to Delhi to take the life of Mahatma Gandhi and that she repeated the story to her husband and that Baburao Sanas and Vasantrao Deshmukh, other Maratha goondas, had made preparations to burn down houses of Brahmins who were vitally afraid of Maratha goondas. She asked Sathe where he lived and he said, 'Sadashiv Peth' and that he was a retired school teacher.[8]

Barve was the one responsible for suitably containing the anti-Brahmin riots in Poona through his proactive actions of calling for the army on time and imposing curfew for almost a fortnight.

Witnesses, including K.M. Munshi, also spoke about a 'Savarkarite' faction within the Mahasabha that believed in an extreme violent ideology of tit-for-tat and revenge, and 'that persons who were potentially dangerous were those who were Savarkarites'.[9] The Commission took note of the Hindu Rashtra Dal that was formed in Poona on 15 May 1942 by Mahasabha leaders such as S.R. Date, V.V. Gogate, Narayan Apte and Nathuram Godse. It said:

> On May 29 1943, V.D. Savarkar held private discussions with the Hindu Rashtra Dal in Anandashram, Poona. He required the volunteers to owe an implicit allegiance to him irrespective of who the President of the Hindu Mahasabha was. Dal was to remain a distinct body, its primary duty being to protect Hindudom and render help to every Hindu institution in their attempt to oppose encroachment on their rights and religion. Savarkar ideology was attainment of Hindudom, opposition to Pakistan and indivisibility of India.[10]

It held the Dal members as those associated with the conspiracy, rather than the entire Hindu Mahasabha as an organization. The Dal, after its initial flurry of activity, was either hibernating or remained underground to find any significant mention in police records. The Commission noted that the next significant reference to the Dal was a meeting held during 9–10 May 1947 presided over by Savarkar and attended, among others, by Apte. This fully contradicted Savarkar's defense in court that he had become a recluse from political activities or was distant from the Dal and it's members. Yet, there were no evidences of speeches or correspondence about plans to murder Gandhi and the activities were more on the lines of protecting Hindu lives in the wake of the horrific Partition and its aftermath. This meeting was held in the backdrop of the colossal human tragedies that were unfolding in the wake of Partition and the inhuman tragedies that the Hindu and Sikh refugees from East and West Pakistan were bringing to light. The report states that in this meeting Savarkar—

> . . . advocated a spirit of aggression to protect themselves (the Hindus) against Muslim atrocities. He also said that the Dal had a distinct identity, and that if the Hindu Mahasabha were to separate from the Dal its volunteers should oppose it. He advocated retaliation for everything that the Muslims did and stood for 'tooth for a tooth and an eye for an eye'. This shows that the Hindu Mahasabha was distinct from the Dal and the ideology of the one was quite different from that of the other. It may be that the Dal members were members of the Hindu Mahasabha but their methods were different.[11]

However, the Commission did not find any links between alleged conspiracies in and by Hindu princes in princely states such as Alwar or Gwalior, in conjunction with the Mahasabha or with Savarkar as a common link to perpetrate the crime. It did mention an atmosphere of strong resentment against the Congress and Gandhi for a host of reasons. As Justice Kapur states about Alwar, where the Congress had tried to implicate N.B. Khare as a conspirator too: 'An atmosphere had been created in Alwar State, which was anti-Congress and also anti-Gandhi . . . even though it may not have been an encouragement to the persons who wanted to murder Mahatma Gandhi.'[12] Regarding Gwalior Justice Kapur states that, 'the Maratha princes had no hand in the assassination and no connection with the Maratha conspirators'.[13]

The broad summary of the findings of the Justice Kapur Commission, submitted on 30 September 1969, on the terms of references that the government had set out for it to enquire were as follows:

a)   Mr. G.V. Ketkar did have prior information about danger to the life of Mahatma Gandhi in October or November 1947. He did have information of the conspiracy of Nathuram Godse, which he learnt from his talk with D.R. Badge on or about January 23 1948. Up to the time he met Badge, he did not know that Apte and Badge were in the conspiracy to murder Mahatma Gandhi; but he must have known about Nathuram Godse's complicity as Nathuram had told him in October or November of his intention or plan to assassinate the Mahatma.[14]

b)   Mr. G.V. Ketkar did not communicate any information to the Government of Bombay or the Government of India or any of its authorities. In particular, Mr. Ketkar did not get any information conveyed to the late Mr. B.G. Kher through the late Balukaka Kanitkar. The claim made by him is not established. Balukaka Kanitkar conveyed the information, the information of danger to the life of Mahatma Gandhi and other top leaders of the Congress, on his own and out of his own volition.[15]

c)   On the basis of the information conveyed to the Government of Bombay, and in particular to Mr. B.G. Kher, no action to try and get the information checked is proved to have been taken by the Government of Bombay or Mr. B.G. Kher, or by any authority under that Government. The information, in the opinion of the

Commission, was vague, misty, nebulous and obscure but the matter should have been referred to the Police C.I.D. and got properly vetted and confirmed. It must be added that it will be highly speculative and conjectural on the part of the Commission to say what the result of this investigation would have been. It might well have been as unproductive, sterile and fruitless as was the result of investigation following definite information given by Professor Jain or the confessional police statement of Madanlal. There is no evidence from Delhi Secretariat or official records or from evidence of Delhi witnesses to show that the information given by Balukaka Kanitkar to Mr. B.G. Kher was conveyed to Government of India, i.e. Sardar Patel. Mr. Balukaka Kanitkar in a subsequent letter . . . did say that Mr. B.G. Kher told him that he had conveyed the information to the Sardar. But there is no corroboration of this bald statement either in the evidence of Sardar's Private Secretary Mr. V. Shankar or of Mr. R.N. Bannerjee or Miss Maniben Patel [Sardar Patel's daughter]. Mr. Morarji Desai has stated that he informed the Sardar of this danger but he has also stated that Sardar already knew about it from his own sources. The information of Balukaka Kanitkar was neither conveyed to any officer of the Government of Bombay nor to any officer of the Government of India.[16]

On the different police forces and their role, the Commission said:

The investigation of the Delhi Police after the arrest of Madanlal was not of a high professional order and it lacked investigational skill and drive, which one should have expected from a trained police force and particularly in the case of threat to the life of a person of the eminence of Mahatma Gandhi taking into consideration the knowledge of the factum of a conspiracy to murder Mahatma Gandhi, which information Madanlal after his arrest gave to the Delhi Police.

The D.I.G., C.I.D., Poona, Mr. U.H. Rana seems to have ignored the importance and utility of Madanlal's fuller statement, wherein the mention of the proprietor of the 'Hindu Rashtriya' [sic] was a very valuable clue, which if pursued would have disclosed the identity of Apte and with a little more diligence also of Godse. Whether they could have arrested them or not would still be speculative.

It is unfortunate that Mr. Nagarvala was not allowed an opportunity
to read and study Madanlal's statement . . . and it is surprising why he did
not evince any interest in that statement and insist of reading it through
to find out what Madanlal had disclosed. This action is quite at variance
with his later action after the murder, when he got Madanlal over to
Bombay and interrogated him at great length . . .

In considering the measures taken by the authorities this crucial fact has
to be kept in view that the Congress Governments had just come into power
after several years of struggle by the Congress and its helpers against the
British Government, in which the strictness of police interference with the
liberty of the subject played a very important part. The Congress Government
could not suddenly adopt or allow the adoption of strict measures by the
police, a tail put on by them on and keeping, as it were, under surveillance
citizens of India even if they happened to be rather bad citizens.[17]

Evidently, it seemed like a colossal exercise in futility as the Commission
did not make any pointed references or castigate the people who had been
named as part of the enquiry in the terms of reference. What it however
ended up doing was to drag the name of the deceased Savarkar yet again
into the realm of culpability. All through Justice Kapur's report, he uses
the term 'Savarkarites' to mean a caucus within the Hindu Mahasabha
that was possibly inspired by Savarkar's ideology and believed in a militant
approach, as being the prime culprits in the murder. In a sweeping
statement describing Poona Savarkarites as a 'combination of disgruntled
Punjabis and angry Maharashtrians', the report very casually comes up with
the following assertion, not as an essential finding, but as an innocuous
insertion that is so easy to miss, in the middle of a chapter:

All these facts taken together were destructive of any theory other than
the conspiracy to murder by Savarkar and his group, and in the opinion
of the Commission, Mr. Nagarvala tripped because he was badly served
by informants and contacts on whom he had every right to rely or there
was some erroneous conclusion.[18]

In fact, just two pages prior to this statement, the report states:

The bundle of facts, which were given to Mr. Nagarvala were destructive
of any theory, but the theory of conspiracy to murder Mahatma Gandhi

by Savarkarites and if there were any circumstances which lent support to the theory of conspiracy to kidnap, they were far outweighed by the facts, which pointed to the conspiracy to murder by a set of Poona Savarkarites rather than a mixed group of Savarkarites and General Mohan Singh's Punjabi discontents.[19]

Yet, two pages thereafter the needle of suspicion moves from 'Savarkarites' to 'Savarkar' himself.

From a reference all through to an almost monolithic group (Savarkarites) that apparently thought and acted alike and on the diktats of a supreme dictator, the conclusion is drawn without any supporting evidence that the plot to murder itself was primarily hatched by Savarkar. Unlike the Red Fort trial, there was no assessment of the letter correspondences between Savarkar and the plotters, the detailed investigation of the approver Badge or even Savarkar's own testimony in court. Testimonies of Savarkar's aides Gajanan Damle and Appa Kasar before the Bombay Police in March 1948 where they allegedly admitted of regular meetings between Savarkar, Nathuram and Apte are referenced. The report states:

> Even the statement of A.R. Kasar, Savarkar's bodyguard puts the visit of Apte and Godse on or about 23rd or 24th January, which was when they returned from Delhi after the bomb incident and not on the eve of their departure, which if proved might have been an important link in the conspiracy case. G.V. Damle, Savarkar's Secretary deposed that Godse and Apte saw Savarkar in the middle of January and sat with him (Savarkar) in his garden.[20]

Yet among the long and exhaustive list of 101 witnesses, as during the trial, Damle and Kasar were never summoned or questioned. This casual insertion amidst reams of text whereby he names Savarkar as the prime suspect, goes contrary to Justice Kapur's own admission on the locus standi of the Commission, its mandate and jurisdiction, as also the terms of reference that the government had set for it. The Kapur Commission Report died a natural death with no clear Action Taken Report or the like filed by the Central government that had set it up in the first place. But since the time the report became public, it became a convenient handle to quote that one sentence from the report that alleges Savarkar as the chief conspirator in the murder.

An ardent admirer of Savarkar, Pankaj Phadnis, public interest litigation (PIL No. 30) in the Bombay High Court in 2016 seeking redemption for the name of Savarkar from the taint of the Kapur Commission. The petition was rejected. He then approached the Supreme Court. The Supreme Court basically had two questions to investigate on the basis of Phadnis's petition:

- How true is the claim that some unknown person also fired one shot at Gandhi along with three bullets of Nathuram Godse?
- Considering all things together in the Gandhi assassination case and the conclusions of the Kapur Commission, saying that Savarkar and his followers were behind the conspiracy of assassination of Gandhi is wrong. It strongly hurts the sentiments of Savarkar's followers. Hence, Commission should reconsider its conclusion or set up a new Commission to investigate this case.[21]

The second contention of Phadnis's petition is being taken up for discussion here as it relates to Savarkar. The petition came up for hearing at the Supreme Court of India in August 2017. The bench did not take favourably the petitioner's move on the first point of his plea, as it had been more than six decades since the murder and also the execution of the assassins. Even on relooking at the Kapur Commission findings, the bench held it to be inappropriate. But on Phadnis's insistence, it appointed Amarinder Sharan as amicus curiae to go through all the case files, documents and Commission reports meticulously before submitting his report. Finally, on 28 March 2018, the bench of Justice Sharad Bobde and Justice L. Nageshwar Rao gave its judgment. The portion relevant to Savarkar is as below:

The Learned Amicus Curiae submitted that this finding was rendered after the demise of Shri Savarkar and no opportunity was given to Shri Savarkar or any of his representatives. He submitted that the finding is unfair since Shri Savarkar had been acquitted at the trial. There is no doubt that this finding does not in any way interfere with the acquittal and is a general observation probably made since Godse and others were found to have been associated with Shri Savarkar. It cannot have the effect of overturning of the finding of the criminal court, which acquitted Shri Savarkar. Constitution bench of this Court in *Ram Kishan*

Dalmia v. *Justice S.R.Tendolkar* considered the effect of the findings of a Commission as follows:

> 'The Commission has no power of adjudication in the sense of passing an order which can be enforced *proprio vigore*.'[22]

Further, the Constitution bench declined to act on the findings in the report of Commission of Inquiry:

> But seeing that the Commission of Inquiry has no judicial powers and its report will purely be recommendatory and not effective *proprio vigore* and the statement made by any person before the Commission of Inquiry is, under s.6 of the Act, wholly inadmissible in evidence in any future proceedings, civil or criminal, there can be no point in the Commission of Inquiry making recommendations for taking action 'as and by way of securing redress or punishment' which, in agreement with the High Court, we think, refers, in the context, to wrongs already done or committed, for redress or punishment for such wrongs, if any, has to be imposed by a court of law properly constituted exercising its own discretion on the facts and circumstances of the case and without being in any way influenced by the view of any person or body, howsoever august or high powered it may be.
>
> The submission of the petitioner that Shri Savarkar has been held guilty for the murder of Gandhiji is misplaced.[23]

In Conclusion

While one hopes that the legal question of Savarkar's involvement in the murder finally got laid to rest by this recent judgment, the sordid political drama around his name that has become a football between political parties continues till date. His name gets invoked in election rallies, in manifestos of political parties, remains a hot and contentious topic of many raucous news debates on Indian national television, and claims and counterclaims on whether he should be posthumously awarded India's highest civilian award, the Bharat Ratna, continue unabated.

Savarkar's name continued to attract attention and controversy even after his death. Eight years after his passing on, in 1974, Marathi writer Vidyadhar Pundalik wrote a short story for the *Satyakatha* magazine. Titled 'Sati', it claimed to be a fictitious story of the vicissitudes of life of the wife

of a revolutionary who was jailed in the Andamans, the subtle tensions in
the married life of the two and how all her aspirations and desires were
crushed by him even after his return from prison.[24] It was obvious as broad
daylight to everyone that the story was about Savarkar and his wife Yamuna
and brought back to discussion, after both their deaths, a sensitive issue
that had hitherto been confined to the realm of gossips: Was Savarkar an
insensitive husband who trampled on his wife's feelings and dreams? The
publication created a stir and several Savarkar supporters had marched
to Pundalik's house in Poona demanding an apology that was never to
come through.

A few years later, on 8 May 1980, Pandit Bakhle of the Swatantryaveer
Savarkar Rashtriya Smarak in Bombay wrote to Prime Minister Indira
Gandhi regarding the upcoming centenary celebrations of Savarkar. In her
reply dated 20 May 1980, Indira Gandhi wrote: 'Veer Savarkar's daring
defiance of the British Government has its own importance in the annals
of our freedom movement. I wish success to the plans to celebrate the
birth centenary of the remarkable son of India.'[25] She even made a private
donation of Rs 11,000 to a memorial fund in his name. In 1970, Indira
Gandhi's government had released a postage stamp too in Savarkar's
honour on his birth anniversary on 28 May 1970. The stamp had the
portrait of Savarkar with a picture of the Cellular Jail in the background.
On Indira Gandhi's instructions, the Films Division that came under the
Union Ministry of Information and Broadcasting produced a documentary
on him. However, the political climate in India since the late 1990s
pre-empts any such generosity and accommodation to opposing and
alternative viewpoints and ideologies.

And each time these debates about his legacy erupt, Savarkar is pitted
against his life-long ideological opponent, Gandhi. Just as their portraits
hang diametrically opposite to each other in the Indian Parliament's
Central Hall, Gandhi and Savarkar remain the perfectly irreconcilable
polar opposites that would never meet and whose ideologies shaped the
two distinct 'Ideas of India'. The contrasts and similarities between the
two men are fascinatingly striking. Both spent significant times outside
mainland India; Gandhi in South Africa, Savarkar in London first and
then over a decade in the dreaded Cellular Jail in the Andamans. They were
both interestingly self-conscious Hindus, though their approach differed.
Both advocated Hindi as a lingua franca of a linguistically divided India.
Both wrote books in the same year 1909 that were banned by the British—

Gandhi's *Hind Swaraj* and Savarkar's *First War of Indian Independence* on the 1857 uprising. They were not only political rivals, but intellectual opponents too. There is an allusion that Gandhi had Savarkar in mind while writing *Hind Swaraj,* while Savarkar's 1923 treatise *Essentials of Hindutva* was undoubtedly his first major salvo against Gandhi whose pacifist philosophy he was totally opposed to. Though swaraj was the goal of both their works of 1909, for Gandhi, the means was intrinsically linked with the ends and non-violence was the guiding mantra. Savarkar however believed in self-assertion of the nation, which many a times could have no other outlet than a violent, armed one. He derided the pusillanimity of ahimsa and all his life believed that militarization was a prerequisite for a strong country. As the first leader to vociferously demand nothing short of complete freedom at a time the Congress was still petitioning the British for concessions, Savarkar articulated his vision of a grand constitutional republic for India, way back in 1908. It was to be a bicameral Parliament akin to Britain with native princes who helped the freedom struggle as members of the upper house and directly elected representatives to the lower house.

When Savarkar was unfairly tried and condemned to the dark dungeons of Kala Pani for two life terms equalling fifty long years. Gandhi was nowhere on the national scene. But by the time he was repatriated to an Indian jail in 1921, Savarkar had to contend a Gandhi who had not only returned to India but also managed to take complete control of the Congress and the nationalist struggle, especially after the death of Bal Gangadhar Tilak in 1920.

In terms of contrasts, while Savarkar stood for modernity and science, separation of ritualistic religion from politics, militarization and dismantling the caste system, Gandhi spoke in terms of faith, religion and ahimsa, approved of the caste system in principle, and had not much time or appetite for science. With economic liberalization, the Pokhran nuclear tests, our space conquests and rapid urbanization instead of gram swaraj—not to speak of course of the ascendant political right in India today that claims its ideological lineage from him—it is perhaps Savarkar's vision of India that is fructifying and not Gandhi's. Yet, he is the one icon and the tragic anti-hero of Indian history who shall not be named or credited for any of those, even by his political proponents.

All his life Savarkar romanticized the idea of dying a martyr. But even in death Gandhi stole a march and ended up becoming the martyred

'Father of the Nation' and Savarkar on the other hand, always insinuated as his murderer by implication. Sociologist and scholar Ashis Nandy terms him as the 'disowned father of the nation in India'.[26] Nandy writes:

> Probably more than any other Indian leader of his time, he was in awe of Europe's achievements in the area of nation building and state-formation. And such was the wide acceptance of these achievements in urban, middle-class India that few noticed that the basic categories of Savarkar's political ideology—nation, national state, nationality and nationalism—always remained aggressively European. It was his misfortune that, in his lifetime, this middle class was not a sizeable part of the country and he never emerged as a popular leader with a large mass base, not even as a leader of the Hindus. That position was occupied by Mohandas Karamchand Gandhi, much younger than Savarkar in Indian politics even if older in age, much less erudite, unimpressed by the full-blooded social evolutionism of the likes of Herbert Spencer, and full of strange, hare-brained ideas of politics such as nonviolence, fasting and Satyagraha—all of which, Savarkar felt, could only hobble the future of the Indian state.[27]

~

On being handcuffed and confined in the little chamber of the SS *Morea*, after his capture following the daring escape at Marseilles in 1910, Savarkar composed a poem in Marathi *'Anadi Mi, Anant Mi'* that possibly best describes his unenviable position in Indian political, academic and cultural discourse of today:

> Without beginning or end am I, inviolable am I.
> Vanquish me?
> In this world no such enemy is born!
> Resolutely, as the Upholder of Dharma,
> Challenging very Death, into the battlefield charge I.
> A sword cannot slice me nor can fire burn me,
> Craven Death itself shall flee in fear of me, aye!
> And yet, O Foolish Foe,
> By fear of Death you dare to scare me!
> Pushed into the cage of a ferocious lion

Reduce him to a cowering servility, I will!
Flung into the blaze of a roaring inferno
Reduce it to a gentle halo of brilliance, I will!
Bring on your mighty, skilled armed Legion,
Your weapons and missiles that deadly fire spill!
Ha! Like Lord Shiva consuming the poison *Halahal*,
Gulp down and digest all, I will![28]

Appendix 1

Recollections from survivors or descendants of the 1948 Anti–Maharashtrian Brahmin Genocide in the wake of Gandhi's assassination:

A social media request by the author to crowdsource information related to the completely forgotten episode of the genocide and attacks on the Maharashtrian Brahmins led to a deluge of information from several individuals who were keen to share their angst and the painful memories of their family histories. Some of them were willing to be interviewed too. Worldwide, history offers a space for wounds of the past to be healed, reconciled and to move on. Unfortunately, in India, such episodes are not only forgotten but their very occurrence is denied, thereby adding insult to the injury of the victims. While many people shared their grievous stories, many were extremely wary of it being published or their names being made known. The perpetrators of the crimes of 1948 have ascended positions of power in Maharashtra and outside, and the fear about retaliation still looms large. Hence, many of the below accounts have been stated as 'Anonymous.' A few brave-hearts were willing to be named and their request has been adhered to. The author is deeply grateful to all the respondents and offers sincere condolences to the trauma that they and their ancestors faced for no fault of theirs, other than belonging to a particular caste or bearing a certain surname.

1) Excerpts from author's interview with Gopal Waman Kulkarni, aged eighty-nine years, formerly of Udtare Village (Wai Taluka, Satara District, Maharashtra), now a resident of Mumbai and an eyewitness and survivor of the 1948 genocide:

We lived in Udtare village in Satara district. My father was actively involved in the freedom struggle, was allied to Tilak and in the Udtare Riots case he was given the harshest punishment of two years rigorous imprisonment in 1918. Slowly his interests gravitated towards the Hindu Mahasabha and Savarkar. I have even seen Savarkar in a public rally as a child of five. When Gandhiji was murdered, I was fifteen years old. Within a day of the event, a huge mob came in. Seven Brahmin houses were burnt down and ours was the first. By 5.30 p.m., the burning and arson began with a huge mob that came from outside of 200–300 people. Inside our house there were some 20–25 people. The front door was closed and from the rear door several ladies of the house tried to escape. Some of them were caught by the mob and beaten badly. Some of the members of the house used ladders to jump out and escape from the house. My father, mother, grandmother, sister and her fourteen-day old kid were all inside the house. My sister and her kid managed to somehow escape, but my grandmother unfortunately could not. A lot of such cases of rioting were heard from Satara, Sangli and Kolhapur. In Kaner, we heard of a case of a primary school teacher whose surname was Godse and who lived in abject poverty. The teacher, his father and grandfather were sleeping outside. Since their surname was Godse, they were attacked, tied to their cots and burnt alive! Government or police was not doing a thing as the word was that there were orders from 'above' to let things go on and not stop the killings. Trains were stopped, Brahmins identified, pulled out and hacked or attacked. The Press remained silent and seldom covered any news of this pogrom. The police too did not register FIRs or complaints; it was as if this episode never happened at all. Instead, they would recklessly arrest several of the victims themselves if they were even remotely associated with the RSS or Hindu Mahasabha. My elder sister used to head the women's wing in the RSS and was arrested for being complicit in Gandhi's murder! Funnily, her husband who had nothing to do with the RSS was also arrested, only because his spouse belonged to the RSS. With no specific charges, they spent 4–5 months in jail and were then let off. We suffered all this despite our entire family having participated in the freedom struggle and having been fiercely anti-British. Many politicians were actively involved in leading these mobs. They later went on to flourish in their political career and occupied the senior-most positions as well. Obviously, with no complaint registered and the very occurrence of the pogrom denied, and with the tacit blessings for it from the powers that be, expecting any justice would have been a foolish thing. We somehow struggled to rebuild our lives after 1948.

2) Several anecdotes to share from 1948 when Marathi Brahmins were targeted in the aftermath of Gandhi's murder by Godse. My family and other Marathi people living in Naya Bazar area of Old Delhi were targeted by Congress mobs . . . They came with rods and bamboos to beat up people, a lot of families used red chilli powder to throw in their eyes. My great-grandfather, who was a rich man and had good relations with Bania people of Tis Hazari, got a lot of personal guards from the Banias to protect Naya Bazar houses of Marathi people. Maharashtra Bhawan in Pahadganj was also attacked and Akka Mahajani, the caretaker there, threatened the mob with boiling oil. My grandfather and his brother had gone in the procession of the final rites of Gandhi's body and as they were talking in Marathi, some people attacked them and beat them up; after that, my grandfather kept a knife with him for several days while going out. In Nagpur, the office of a prominent daily *Tarun Bharat*, run by the Hindu Mahasabha, was burned down by Maratha mobs.

My name is Siddharth Deshmukh and you can also share my grandfather's name—Satyapal Patait—ex-editor (1956 to 1984) of RSS-owned Hindi daily *Yugdharma* in Nagpur, the sister concern of RSS-owned Marathi daily *Tarun Bharat*. Please note that since 1990, *Yugdharma* was no longer the sister concern of *Tarun Bharat* as RSS had sold it . . . The above stories are as narrated by my grandfather to me. He lived in Delhi since his birth in 1931 to 1949, and then from 1949 until his death in 2019, he lived in Nagpur and Pune. He was also a close aide of RSS chief Guruji Golwalkar and Balasaheb Deoras and Rajju Bhaiya. You can also share my great-grandfather's name K.S. Patait, a rich business-owner in pre-Partition Delhi. You can get more references like this from Brihan Maharashtra Bhavan Pahadganj in Delhi of which many families like mine are members since 1920s; many such families were affected in 1948 by the anti-Marathi Brahmin mobs.

3) Nilesh Nilakanth Oak

My father who passed away in 2013 told me this story many times. He was about fifteen years old at that time and was a responsible adult at that young age. He started working at seventeen. Many houses of Brahmin families were burnt. In most cases, the family members were asked to come out of their houses before the mob burnt their houses. The Taluka/tehsil for my village is Chiplun (in Ratnagiri district) which had a decent, prosperous and active marketplace for a long time . . . at least going back to

Raja Shivaji's time (Shivaji had visited this place). Chiplun-based Brahmin homes were saved and this is due to one brave Brahmin businessman who was in the business of oil—kerosene, other oils and also petrol. Only petrol pump in that area (old style) in 1950s. He dared/threatened that if even a single Brahmin house in Chiplun area is affected, he will burn the entire marketplace using his store of oil/kerosene/petrol. The threat worked.

4) Mangesh Kashinath Tambulwadkar:
My paternal grandfather had to flee with family from Belgaon to a safer place—Kolhapur—in 1948. My father, now seventy-three, was youngest of the six children then, aged six months that time. Since then, our family has been in Kolhapur. We are Gaud Saraswat Brahmins of Goa. Had known of big *waada* (house) and land owned by joint family, which is still there. My grandfather's name is Sambaji Bhikaji Tambulwadkar Deshpande; father's name is Kashinath Sambaji Tambulwadkar. Post migration we dropped Deshpande from our surname. Goan Gaud Saraswat Brahmins have two last names . . . one of which is called 'vangad'. Our vangad is Deshpande.

5) Anonymous:
I've heard about the Brahmin genocide in Maharashtra from my grandfather and his brothers and sisters. We, Palsule-Desai, belonged to the Ichalkaranji area and had two *waadas* (houses) where there were cows, and our business was to do with textile. Pre-genocide was a very flourishing time for the family back then, but the aftermath was very painful. There are some yesteryear generational copper and other vessels that the family could run away with after the waadas were literally burnt down. After everything was lost my grandfather came to erstwhile Bombay. I want go back and do some research on it.

6) Anonymous:
My paternal grandmother, who had lost her father, lived with her mother and two younger brothers, in the house of her elder cousin in Kanpur since years. She used to tell us that when Gandhiji was killed, many areas of Brahmins, especially Maharashtrian Brahmins, were attacked. Male members of family were forced to hide themselves and their identity or go underground or they would be brutally attacked.

7) Ajinkya Apte:
We had started a sugar factory in Phalton called Phalton Sugar Works in 1932. In addition, we had also started an oil mill in Sangli Sangalwadi around 1947–48. The idea was to expand it, to include a vegetable ghee plant and that of tobacco. Specifically about the issues:

1) In Phalton, we had a civil overseer called Sadubhau Deshpande. Post Gandhi's murder, a truckload of mob came from Phalton to his home and beheaded him in front of his wife.
2) 75 acres of surgarcane of the factory was burned down.
3) We also ran a train that took sugarcane from the farmers straight to our factory—it was destroyed too. The mob managed to destroy fifteen transport bogies.
4) In Sangalwadi our entire oil mill was burned down by the mob.
5) At the same Sangalwadi location, we had equipment for starting a vegetable ghee plant. The mob hammered the equipment and completely destroyed it.

   Our family had insurance from fire but not arson. So the loss was huge. My aunt Tejaswini Apte-Rahm recently released a book mainly for our family members called: *Tatyasaheb: The Story of a Bombay Entrepreneur*. All these details have been cited in her book.

8) Anonymous:
I remember a story my mother used to tell. My mother's maternal grandfather was in the police in Wai, Satara district. People came to burn down his house and he stood outside ready to fight. They spared his house due to his posture.

9) Anonymous:
There was a prominent lady living in Bombay called Tai Patwardhan. She was born in 1916. In anti-Brahmin riots, her husband was murdered by the mob; 80–90 kg of gold was stolen from the house. She became mentally ill after this episode. Then, she was married to another person; he was alcoholic. After few years, she regained her mind and taught her children (from her previous husband and the existing one). She was a brave lady who could swim, ride horses, etc. I heard this story from her grandson who is now around 55–56 years old. They have written a book on her, which is not yet published.

10) Anonymous (responded in Kannada):
My grandfather Govind Shankar Patil was the village head (Kulkarni) of
Hidkal in Belagavi's Hukkeri taluk. When Gandhiji was murdered, my
grandfather was not in town. In the middle of the night, some miscreants
attacked our house to set fire to it. My grandmother was alone at home
then and she managed to flee with her three-year-old child and three other
children to a sugarcane farm nearby where they spent the night in the
cold to save their lives. The ancestral house was burnt to ashes. The next
morning when grandfather came, he was shocked to see the house, the
jewels and everything else reduced to rubble, but was overjoyed that his
wife and children were at least saved. Our family deity Goddess Tulaja
Bhawani's idol however remained untouched by the fire. Even now, we
worship the idol in our house. In Hidkal, among 200 families, there were
only three Brahmin families, of which ours was one. They burnt down
only our house first. When they realized there were two more Brahmin
households in the village, they returned the next day and attacked them
too— these belonged to Gopalrao Kulkarni and Narayanrao Kulkarni. The
mobs kept chanting 'Gandhiji ki Jai' as they burnt down all our houses.
These mobs were all mobilized from outside and not from within Hidkal.

11) Anonymous
My grandmother told me her story. She used to live in a big house. A mob
came to burn the house. Everyone in the family fled from the house, except
her uncle. Her uncle had a pistol; he fired a few rounds in the air and told
the mob that he wouldn't move. The mob would have to burn him along
with the house. The mob did just that . . . burnt him along with the house!
This happened in Solapur; with waada, jewelry, money gone, the family
fled with nothing and came to Bombay . . . They went from being well-off
to very poor. My late grandmother's surname was Gore.

12) Anonymous
Thanks for crowdsourcing these experiences! I have heard several times
from my Mom that the multistoried building (waada) that she grew up
in, in the heart of Pune city, was burnt down by Congress mercenaries
in broad daylight post Gandhi-assassination. She along with her entire
joint family had to literally run away taking whatever belongings they
could in a day's notice . . . The building was called 'Bhonde Waada', as
her maiden name is Bhonde. One of the hypotheses is that in addition to

being Brahmin, one of Mom's uncles was a Hindu Mahasabha member in pre-independence times. You will hear several such accounts from Marathi Brahmins spread out in erstwhile Bombay state, part of Maharashtra. Not so much in Vidarbha or perhaps, even the Marathwada part didn't see such large-scale rioting against Brahmins.

13) Anonymous:

My own grandfather, owner of two villages and most kindhearted person, had to leave everything in the middle of the night with his family from a place called Igatpuri near Nasik where we lived; we had to change our surname from Bhat to another name. The entire land was taken over by people working in the lands, great-grandfather and grandfather started all over again from scratch. There is today, no Brahmin family in the village, and also in many nearby villages. My grandfather was part of Abhinav Bharat organization later, when it was established in Tilbhandeshwar Mandir of Nasik by Savarkarji, which on paper was called 'Gavkari' in Nasik. Never was I able to discuss much about it; heard all this from my father. Village name: Belgaon Tarhale, and Taked in Igatpuri district, our name was on land records until the last decade and 7/12 was changed by locals.

14) Anonymous:

After the assassination of Gandhiji, there were riots in Sangli too; we had our waada on the main road in Sangli; a huge mob had come outside the door to decimate it, but my great-grandfather Anna Shripad Bhave, stood at the door, and because of the respect for his sheer courage, they went away. He saved almost fifty people that day just by standing at the door. Ukidave waada was saved because of one man. Or else, I would not have been alive to send you a message.

15) Anonymous:

Our waada in Kodoli near Kolhapur was burnt down and my grandfather's generation was forced to leave. They then came to Mumbai and stayed in a chawl for many years until they bought two homes in Kurla and Mulund. Though everyone in their generation did not pass on the horror to the next generation, but we can understand what pain they had gone through when the house was burnt and they were forced to leave the village because of their caste.

16) Anonymous:

1948 genocide victim: My family. We were landlord of Sangli surroundings. During genocide my grandparents lived in a crematorium fifteen days to save themselves, their three daughters (9 months, 9 years, 18 years old) and a son (my dad) sixteen years of age. My grandmother prepared food on the funeral pyres. We had lost everything. Dad joined the army, neither he nor we saw ancestral area till now. A Congress leader who later became chief minister of Maharashtra was leading from the front to finish off the Brahmins. He attacked us, threw us away and grabbed the property. Later Grandpa lost his mental health and died. Grandma stayed their lifetime, worked as a maid to earn living, and till her last breath (1981) fought against system. Post retirement, my father settled down in Belagavi. Now I am in Goa, far away from my ancestors' place.

Appendix 2

Aatmahatya Aani Aatmaarpan
(Suicide and Self-Sacrifice)
~ Vinayak Damodar Savarkar

Dhanyoham Dhanyoham, Kartavyam me na Vidyate Kinchit
Dhanyoham Dhanyoham, Praaptavyam Sarvamadhya Sampannam.
(Blessed am I, blessed am I, I know of no duty now,
Blessed am I, blessed am I, I have fulfilled what I wished to achieve)

Those who bring about their own death because they are fed up with life for some reason and whose death does not result from illness, accident or some such unavoidable circumstance are said to have committed suicide. In several societies, this is counted as a punishable offence. Without going into the theoretical distinction between 'soul' and 'life', in practice the act of taking one's own life is counted as suicide. However, in some instances, the voluntary act of taking one's own life which would otherwise qualify as 'suicide' is not considered as such; it is variously described by Sanskrit words such as *atmarpan* (self-sacrifice), *atmavisarjan* (self-immersion) and has been spoken of glowingly since ancient times. How has this distinction come about? Why has human society not considered certain types of suicide as punishable offences, has instead looked upon them as hallowed and glorious? The reason for this should be clear from some examples that I have given below. It is possible that in giving these examples, there are some deficiencies in my arguments in the present circumstances. Old age and illness have confined me to bed. As such, I have neither strength nor desire nor do I feel the need to look up the relevant reference books while giving these examples. I have relied solely on my memory while giving them. I am certain that minor deficiencies such as may exist shall not detract from the final conclusion that I seek to draw from these examples.

Some prominent examples are as follows:

1. Let us first consider the case of Kumārila Bhatta, the celebrated *Mimansak* and confirmed champion of Vedic ritualism. In order to refute Buddhist philosophy by logic and argument, he first made a deep study of the *Tripitaka* and other Buddhist scriptures, adopted Buddhist practices and lived the life of a Buddhist. He then embarked on his life mission of demonstrating the folly of these teachings. He participated in debate and discourse and re-established the primacy of Vedic *Mimansa* throughout Bharat. When he finally felt that he had successfully fulfilled his life mission. He decided to seek penance for reading and abiding by non-Vedic and profane Buddhist scriptures, albeit done to secure victory for the Vedic religion. Hence, he pledged to reduce his body to ashes by offering himself to the holy fire rather than await a natural demise. Accordingly, he lit a pyre and entered it. His body was reduced to ashes in the leaping flames. But this glorious act of martyrdom has not been described as 'suicide'; rather it has been glowingly referred to in history as *agnidivya* (penance by fire) or *atmarpan* (self-sacrifice).

    One can likewise give the example of Jagadguru Sri Adi Sankaracharya. In the course of his victorious nationwide march for the spread of *Advaita* philosophy, he reached Kamrup or present-day Assam, he successfully debated with proponents of the *Shakta* school of philosophy. Unable to digest his victory, some hotheads of the *Shakta* school tried to poison him. This adversely impacted his health. Nonetheless, he continued his victorious march to Kashmir, successfully concluding it. In Kashmir he established his fourth principal seat. His great mission of establishing seats of Advaita philosophy in four corners viz. Sringeri, Dwarka, Puri and Kashmir was thus complete. It is well-known that Sri Sankaracharya was in the prime of his youth at that time. Nonetheless, his ingrained renunciant [sic] bent of mind, best expressed by his aphorism: "*Yadahareva Virajyet, Tadahareva Pravrajet | Gruhaat vaa, vanaat Vaa*" (Renounce the world as soon as you feel detached, be it at home or in the forest), coupled with his poor health, the immense satisfaction gained from the writing of the *Mahabhasya* and other books, and the founding of aforementioned four seats, led him to be overcome with the desire to end his earthly life and become one with the Supreme Brahman in a spirit of total self-satisfaction.

Hence, in keeping with the tradition of past *yogis*, he decided to enter a cave. Inside the cave, he assumed a *yogic* posture and had his disciples roll a huge boulder to close its mouth. Jagadguru Sankaracharya thus ended his own life in a spirit of supreme satisfaction. While there is something common in what is called willful ending of one's life or the offence of suicide and this type of *yogic* self-sacrifice, Jagadguru Sankaracharya's entry into the cave of death is rightly referred to in history not as 'suicide' but as 'self-sacrifice'. Our ancient history is replete with such examples of great *yogis* entering the cave of death. Let us now turn to similar examples of self-sacrifice from relatively recent chapters of our history.

2. A similar tale is narrated in relation to the well-known Vaishnava *acharya* from Bengal, Chaitanya Mahaprabhu or Gaurang Prabhu as he is endearingly called. Spreading the message of total devotion to Sri Krishna, he would wend his way through various towns leading huge multitudes of devotees engrossed in the collective singing of *bhajans*. Chaitanya Mahaprabhu would dance away totally immersed in the spirit of bhakti. Having thus flooded the whole of Bengal with bhakti, he finally made his way to Jagannath Puri. While leading a throng of devotees on the seashore, he saw the blue ocean and overcome by sublime devotion took it to be the manifestation of the dark blue Sri Krishna. An irresistible urge to become one with his Lord prompted him to leap into the vast ocean all the while chanting "O Krishna! O Shyam! O Shyam!!" He thus committed self-sacrifice. This act has been termed in history as 'jalasamadhi' (water immersion) or *atmarpan* (self-sacrifice) and not as 'suicide'.

3. The tale of Dnyaneshwar is well-known in Maharashtra. While still in his youth, this genius wrote Dnyaneshwari and Amrutanubhav, two books that can be called the pinnacle of the temple of philosophy. With a feeling of deep contentment of having thus completed his life mission, he ended his earthly journey when he was not yet thirty years old. A state of samadhi may not be final and irreversible in yogis who can enter that state. A yogi who has

entered a state of samadhi is capable of reversing it as well. He can re-enter the material world after a short period. But Dnyaneshwar did not choose to enter a state of temporary samadhi; rather he decided to enter such a state permanently. His elder brother and guru Nivruttinath gave his consent to Dnyaneshwar's decision. Accompanied by the singing of bhajans by scores of saints, Dnyaneshwar voluntarily entered his final resting place, which he had himself built and assumed a yogic posture. Nivruttinath himself sealed the final abode. Dnyaneshwar thus entered final samadhi. Though the acts of deliberately taking away one's own life and entering a state of samadhi are outwardly similar, saints and commoners unanimously pronounce that Dnyaneshwar entered samadhi or that he did self-sacrifice, not that he committed suicide.

4. Similar is the case of Samartha Ramdas' self-sacrifice. Samartha Ramdas took upon the rooting out of foreign invasion as his life mission. He kindled the fire of *dharmayuddha* (righteous war) in the Hindus of Maharashtra and built a formidable organization by dint of his penance. Imbued with the same zeal, Chhatrapati Shivaji rattled the thrones of various Moslem chiefs and emperors. When Shivaji thumbed Aurangzeb himself and established a sovereign Hindu State, Hindu Flag and Hindu Throne at Raigad, Samartha Ramdas was beside himself with joy at this glorious Hindu victory. Having thus experienced the unimaginable success of his pledge, the 80-year-old Samartha Ramdas felt that his life mission was now complete. Just then, the terrible news of Shivaji's passing away reached him. "Our king has left us" he exclaimed sorrowfully. Soon thereafter, Sambhaji Raja impulsively arrested several prominent lieutenants of Chhatrapati Shivaji and put many of them to death. Brothers became enemies in *swarajya*. Sambhaji himself sat at the foot of Sajjangad (Ramdas's abode) and insisted on meeting him. Sensing that Sambhaji who had harmed his father's trusted lieutenants could very well harm his mentor, Samartha Ramdas declined to come down the fort on health grounds and instead sent a letter as a gesture of blessing. In this famous letter, Samartha Ramdas appealed to Sambhaji to remember Shivaji's personality, valour and perspicacity; stake his life to strike the *mlecchas* and maintain and expand the Maratha Empire. Aurangzeb who was incensed at the news of a sovereign Hindu Empire was planning to personally attack the Marathas.

Hearing this ominous news, Samartha Ramdas felt that his old and frail body was now incapable of meeting this new challenge. Thinking that the Almighty had desired to bless him with the founding of an independent Hindu state and that the new generation ought to rely on their own valour and the grace of Almighty to solve their problems, Samartha Ramdas resolved to end his earthly life by fasting unto death. He called his disciples and expressed his resolve to renounce his body as it had fulfilled its mission. Consoling his grieving disciples that he would forever live with them and guide them through his *Dasbodh* (his famous literary work), he seated himself and accompanied by *Ramdhun*, gave up food and water. Legend has it that at the conclusion of the *Ramdhun*, Samartha Ramdas was blessed by the *darshan* of Sri Rama himself and he surrendered his frail body at the lotus feet of the Lord.

The willful termination of a life that has fulfilled its mission and is now a mere burden to self and society is the common factor in 'suicide' and '*atmarpan*' (self-sacrifice). Yet, no one says that "Samartha Ramdas committed suicide". "Samartha fasted unto death; he did self-sacrifice" has been the verdict of history.

5. Similar are the legends associated with Eknath and Tukaram. Eknath's health deteriorated after a lifetime spent in writing several excellent books and spreading *Haribhakti*. He started feeling that the Lord probably did not desire any further service from him. Despite a transient flicker of recovery in his sick body, he resolved to end a burdensome existence. With immense satisfaction, he performed a ritual bath in the river Godavari in Paithan and entered the waters. His act of entering the water has not been vilified as 'suicide'; rather it has been glorified to the extent that the site of his self-immersion is considered sacred.

Later, Sant Tukaram visited this sacred site in Paithan. Sant Tukaram was well aware of the legend of Eknath's self-immersion. Having completed his life mission of spreading *bhakti* by his mid-life, Tukaram intensely desired to meet his Lord. Having resolved to end his earthly life, he visited the residents of his Dehu town one by one and bid farewell. Singing his valedictory *abhang*, he told those assembled that he was going to his native village and this was thus their last meeting. He went to the bank of the river Indrayani and felt that the Lord had come in his aerial vehicle to take him away. One version has it that like Eknath before him, Tukaram too, entered he waters of the Indrayani in a state of pure bliss. Others say that he physically sat in the Lord's airplane and went to heaven.

The inference from both versions is that Tukaram felt that his earthly life had been blessed and that he renounced this world to become one with the Lord in a spirit of deep contentment. Hence, Tukaram's renouncing of his material existence has not been termed as 'suicide' but has been glowingly referred to as 'self-sacrifice'.

From the few examples given above, one may conclude that not all acts of willful termination of one's life are condemned as 'suicides'. Those who end their lives in a spirit of frustration, dissatisfaction or discontentment and cannot live happily even though they so wish are said to have committed 'suicide'. But those who happily end their lives with the blessed sense of having fulfilled their life mission or objective are said to have committed self-sacrifice. Though this changing and evolving earthly world can never be said to have achieved perfection, blessed souls voluntarily end their lives with the realization that they have nothing left to achieve or fulfill. They merge their mortal life into the immortal Universal Life. As the *Yogvasishtha* says:

Antarrikto Bahirrikto, Rikta Kumbharivaambare |
Antah Poorno, Bahihi Poorno, Poorne Kumbharivaarnave ||
(An empty pot is in reality filled with the sky, a pot immersed in the sea has sea both within and without; it is hence full within and without)
With a feeling of self-satisfaction at having largely perfected their life mission and rather than let their body become a burden to self and society, such souls renounce their bodies by entering a cave or fasting unto death or entering fire or water or enter a state of samadhi. Though their act may be grossly referred to as 'willful termination of life', it is only fitting that it should be referred glowingly as 'self-sacrifice'.

Dhanyoham Dhanyoham, Kartavyam me na Vidyate Kinchit
Dhanyoham Dhanyoham, Praaptavyam Sarvamadhya Sampannam.
(Blessed am I, blessed am I, I know of no duty now,
Blessed am I, blessed am I, I have fulfilled what I wished to achieve)

Notes

Chapter 1: Rising from the Ashes

1. Savarkar too attests to this fact in a speech that he made on 10 May 1952, where he mentions that the British were very particular that no one should utter the name of any revolutionary with respect. Doing so or having their photographs, invited strong penalties since they considered the revolutionaries to be the most dangerous people in the country. Balarao Savarkar, *Krantighosh, Speeches of V.D. Savarkar*, 1st ed., Bombay: Manorama Prakashan, 1994, pp. 77–78.
2. Home-Political NA_1924 F-8, National Archives of India, New Delhi.
3. 60-D (e)/1923-24, Home (Special). Maharashtra State Archives, Mumbai.
4. 60-D (e)/1923-24, Home (Special). Maharashtra State Archives, Mumbai.
5. Home-Political NA_1924 F-8, National Archives of India, New Delhi.
6. Reference to Montagu-Chelmsford Reforms, 1919.
7. V.D. Savarkar, *My Transportation for Life*, 2nd ed., Bombay: Veer Savarkar Prakashan, 1984, pp. 380-381.
8. V.D. Savarkar, *An Echo from Andamans*, Poona: Venus Book Stall, 1947, pp. 88–93.
9. Home-Political NA_1924 F-8, National Archives of India, New Delhi.
10. V.S. Joshi, *Jhunjh Savarkarancha*, Bombay: Manorama Prakashan, n.d. p. 10.
11. Balarao Savarkar, *Ratnagiri Parva*, 1st ed., Bombay: Veer Savarkar Prakashan, 1972.
12. Joshi, *Jhunjh Savarkaraancha*.
13. Savarkar, *Ratnagiri Parva*, 1st ed.
14. P.B. Bhave, *Pratham Purush Ek Vachani*, Nagpur: Lakhe Publication, 2017.
15. Incident narrated to Subodh Naik (interviewed by author) by Arvind Vitthal Kulkarni, private secretary of Velankar and former editor of *Mid-Day*, and also by Velankar's daughter Veena Godbole, in Dadar, Mumbai.
16. Keer, *Veer Savarkar*, p. 167.

17. *Savarkar, Ratnagiri Parva*, p. 18.

18. Joshi, *Jhunjh Savarkarancha*, n.d. p. 11.

19. Home Department, Special File #60 (D)(9) (Secret), p. 147, Maharashtra State Archives, Mumbai.

20. Home Dept. No. 724-II-C, Microfilm Roll No. 22, Savarkar Private Papers, Nehru Memorial Museum and Library (NMML), New Delhi.

21. Savarkar, *Ratnagiri Parva*, p. 49.

22. Ibid., p. 50.

23. Joshi, *Jhunjh Savarkarancha*, pp. 15–16.

24. *Savarkar, Ratnagiri Parva*, p. 52.

25. *Savarkar, Ratnagiri Parva*, p. 54. One is not certain of the veracity of the numbers quoted by Savarkar in his speech. This is just an extract from the speech as published in the *Ratnagiri Parva*.

26. *Savarkar, Ratnagiri Parva*, pp. 56–57.

27. *Samata*, 21 September 1928.

28. Ibid., p. 153.

29. *Savarkar, Ratnagiri Parva*, p. 62.

30. Jayawant Joglekar, *Veer Savarkar: Father of Hindu Nationalism*, n.p. n.d. p. 104.

31. Ibid.

32. Joshi, *Jhunjh Savarkarancha*, p. 26.

33. Savarkar, *Ratnagiri Parva*, 2nd ed., p. 70.

34. Keer, *Veer Savarkari*, pp. 169–70.

35. Home Department. Microfilm Roll No. 22, Savarkar Private Papers, Nehru Memorial Museum and Library (NMML), New Delhi.

36. Vide letter dated 6 October 1924 by Montgomerie, Microfilm Roll No. 22, Savarkar Private Papers, NMML, New Delhi.

37. Savarkar, *Ratnagiri Parva*, p. 74.

38. Y. D. Phadke, *Senapati Bapat*, New Delhi: National Book Trust, 1993, pp. 32–42.

39. Y. D. Phadke, *Shodh Savarkarancha*, Bombay: Shrividya Prakashan, 1984, pp. 76–77.

40. Ibid.

41. Joglekar, *Veer Savarkar*, p. 105.

42. Savarkar, *Ratnagiri Parva*, p. 73.

43. Ibid., p. 170.

44. Savarkar gave these cuttings and his comments to his private secretary Balarao Savarkar, who gave them to the Kesari Maratha Trust of Pune.

45. Joshi, *Jhunjh Savarkarancha*, p. 40.

46. Ibid., pp. 39–40.

47. Ibid.

48. V.D. Savarkar, *Savarkar Samagra*, New Delhi: Prabhat Prakashan, 2000, Vol. 7, pp. 316–24. Translation by author.

49. Microfilm Roll No. 22, Savarkar Private Papers, NMML, New Delhi.

50. Y. D. Phadke, *Shodh Savarkarancha*. Bombay: Shrividya Prakashan, 1984: pp. 76–77.

51. Joshi, *Jhunjh Savarkarancha*, pp. 43–44.

52. Ibid., p. 44.

53. Microfilm Roll No. 22, Savarkar Private Papers, NMML, New Delhi.

54. Ibid.

55. P.C.I. No. 278 of 1925; From P.B. Malabari Esq., Barrister-at-Law, Prothonotary and Registrar of His Majesty's High Court, Bombay; Microfilm Roll No. 22, Savarkar Private Papers, NMML, New Delhi.

56. Joshi, *Jhunjh Savarkarancha*, p. 44.

57. Quoted in Sir Sankaran Nair, *Gandhi and Anarchy*, Indore: Holkar State (Electric) Printing Press, n.d., Appendix, p. iii.

58. Letter from Sir Henry Wheeler to Lord Irwin, Halifax Collection, MSS Eur C 152, Vol. 20, India Office Library, London.

59. Richard Lambert, 'Hindu Communal Groups in Indian Politics,' in Richard L. Park and Irene Tinker (eds.), *Leadership and Political Institutions in India*, Princeton: Princeton University Press, 1959, p. 214.

60. Wilfred Cantwell Smith, *Modern Islam in India*, London: Victor Gollancz Ltd., 1946, p. 172.

61. Majumdar, *History of the Freedom Movement in India*, Vol. 3, p. 278.

62. Letter from Viceroy Lord Reading to the Secretary of State for India, MSS EUR E 238, Vol. 6, India Office Library, London.

63. Indian Annual Register (IAR), 1924, II, 25–6.

64. Ambedkar, *Pakistan or the Partition of India*, p. 185.

65. Savarkar, *Ratnagiri Parva*.

66. Correspondence and reports enclosed in GI, Political, 249/VIII-KW, 1924.

67. Ibid.

68. Olivier to Reading, 15 October 1924, Reading MSS, Eur E 238, Vol. 7, British Library, London.

69. Home-Political-1924, F. No 249/XIII, Telegram correspondences between Gandhi and the Viceroy's Office, National Archives of India, New Delhi.

70. Home-Political, 1925, F-No. 31/III, Telegram No 383-C dated and received on 12 February 1925 from NWF, Peshawar to Foreign Office, Delhi. National Archives of India, New Delhi.

71. Ambedkar, *Pakistan or the Partition of India*, p. 185.

72. M.K. Gandhi, *The Collected Works of Mahatma Gandhi*, Ahmedabad, 1967, Vol. 29, pp. 210–11.

73. Ambedkar, *Pakistan or the Partition of India*, p. 183.

74. Majumdar, *History of the Freedom Movement in India*, Vol. 3, p. 283.

75. Ibid., p. 285.

76. Statutory Commission's Report, Vol. IV, Part I, p. 106 and Indian Annual Register.

77. Majumdar, *History of the Freedom Movement in India*, pp. 285–86.

78. Savarkar, *Ratnagiri Parva*.

79. A danger, a peril.

80. Savarkar, *Ratnagiri Parva*.

81. V.S. Godbole, *Rationalism of Veer Savarkar*, Thane: Itihas Patrika Prakashan, 2004, p. 321.

82. Letter from D. O'Flynn, Esq., Acting Deputy Secretary to Government of Bombay, Home Department, No. 724/3266. Microfilm Roll No. 22, Savarkar Private Papers, NMML, New Delhi.

83. W. Kenneth Jones, 'Politicised Hinduism: The Ideology and Programme of the Hindu Mahasabha' in Robert D. Baird (ed.) *Religion in Modern India*, New Delhi: Manohar Publications, 1981, p. 449.

84. *Memorandum on the Census of British India of 1871-72*, quoted in Ibid., pp. 15–16.

85. Ibid., p. 16.

86. Ibid.

87. Ibid., p. 17

88. Jones, 'Politicised Hinduism', p. 450.

89. B.R. Purohit, *Hindu Revivalism and Indian Nationalism*, Sagar (MP): Sathi Prakashan, 1965.

90. *Maharashatra Hindu Sabhechya?*; Indra Prakash, *Hindu Mahasabha: Its Contribution to Indian Politics*, New Delhi: Akhil Bharat Hindu Mahasabha, 1966, p. 9.

91. Jones, 'Politicised Hinduism', p. 450.

92. Ibid., p. 452.

93. Ibid., p. 454.

94. Dr Kurtkoti, Presidential Address at the All-India Shuddhi Conference, Poona, 1935.

95. Christophe Jaffrelot, *The Hindu Nationalist Movement in India 1925-1990*, Delhi: Viking/Penguin India, 1996, p. 24.

96. *Maharashtra Hindu Sabhechya?* p. 43.

97. Jaffrelot, *The Hindu Nationalist Movement*, p. 24.

98. Prakash Pawar, 'Akhil Bharatiya Maratha Mahasangha: Ek Chikitsak Abhyaas', Unpublished MPhil Dissertation, University of Poona, Pune, 1996, pp. 7–13.

99. V.D. Savarkar, *Sphuta Lekh*, Bombay: Veer Savarkar Prakashan, 1982, p. 8.

100. Y.D. Phadke, *Visawya Shatakatil Maharashtra*, Pune: Shrividya Prakashan, 1991, p. 164.

101. D.N. Gokhale, *Krantiveer Babarao Savarkar*, 1979, pp. 271–72.

102. The Abhinav Bharat was virtually dead and disbanded especially after the arrest of the Savarkar brothers. Many of its erstwhile members now joined the Tarun Hindu Sabha, being inspired by their former mentors.

103. Gokhale, *Krantiveer Babarao Savarkar*, pp. 168, 271-72.

104. Presidential address of N.C. Kelkar, The Dacca Provincial Hindu Conference, 27 August 1929, Indian Quarterly Register, July–December 1929, pp. 3–4.

105. Ibid., p. 336.

106. S.T. Naigaonkar, 'N.C. Kelkar: A Political Study', Unpublished PhD Thesis, University of Poona, Pune, March 1979.

107. Presidential address of Kelkar, pp. 5–7.

108. G.R. Thursby, *Hindu-Muslim Relations in British India: A Study of Controversy, Conflict and Communal Movements in Northern India, 1923-1928*, Leiden, 1975. pp. 164–5.

Chapter 2: Caste in Stone

1. *Ratnagiri Hindu Sabeche Pahilya Paanch Varshaanche Prativrutta*, Part I: 23 January 1924 to 31 December 1928. Published by M.G. Shinde, Vice President of Ratnagiri Hindu Sabha and printed by G.V. Patwardhan, Balwant Mudranalaya, Ratnagiri, November 1929.

2. Ibid., p. 5.

3. Ibid.

4. For details, please see Chapter 12 of Volume 1 of this series.

5. *Ratnagiri Hindu Sabeche Pahilya Paanch Varshaanche Prativrutta*, 1929.

6. Keer, *Veer Savarkar*, p. 173.

7. *Ratnagiri Hindu Sabeche Pahilya Paanch Varshaanche Prativrutta*, pp. 115, 135–169.

8. V.D. Savarkar, *Samagra Savarkar Vangmaya*, Poona: Maharashtra Prantik, Vol. 3, 1963, pp. 592–603.

9. Savarkar, *Ratnagiri Parva*, pp. 255–56.

10. Ibid., p. 273.

11. *Ratnagiri Hindu Sabeche Pahilya Paanch*, p. 150.

12. Leaves of the Apta tree whose scientific name is Bauhinia Racemosa are given as a sign of goodwill during festivals, especially Dussehra. It is akin to giving gold leaves (*sona patta*) to someone.

13. Savarkar, *Ratnagiri Parva*, pp. 78–80.

14. Ibid., p. 98.

15. *Ratnagiri Hindu Sabeche Pahilya Paanch Varshaanche Prativrutta*, p. 5.
16. Savarkar, *Ratnagiri Parva*, p. 142.
17. Ibid., p. 173, 179.
18. Keer, *Veer Savarkar*, p. 182.
19. Ibid., p. 192; see also *Ratnagiri Hindu Sabeche Pahilya Paanch*, p. 19.
20. Keer, *Veer Savarkar*, p. 183.
21. Ibid., pp. 204–05.
22. Savarkar, *Ratnagiri Parva*, p. 179.
23. Shabnum Tejani, 'From Untouchable to Hindu: Gandhi, Ambedkar and Depressed Class Question 1932', *Indian Secularism: A Social and Intellectual History, 1890-1950*, Bloomington, Indiana: Indiana University Press, 2008, pp. 205–10.
24. Phadke, *Visawya Shatakatil Maharashtra*, Vol. 3, pp. 256–61.
25. *Maharashtra Hindu Sabhecha?* p. 61.
26. Dhananjay Keer, *Savarkar and His Times*, Bombay: Popular Prakashan, 1988, p. 182.
27. Balarao Savarkar, *Ratnagiri Parva*, Chapter 5.
28. V.D. Savarkar, *Samagra Savarkar Vangmaya*, Vol. 3, p. 485.
29. Y.D. Phadke, *Shodh Savarkarancha*, Bombay: Shrividya Prakashan, 1984, p. 266.
30. Translation courtesy Anurupa Cinar; http://anurupacinar.net/wp-content/uploads/2013/09/Mala-Devache-Darshan-Gheudya-Translation.pdf
31. Keer, *Veer Savarkar*, p. 184.
32. Savarkar, *Samagra Savarkar Vangmaya*, pp. 514–15.
33. Savarkar, *Ratnagiri Parva*, p. 234.
34. V.S. Godbole, *Rationalism of Veer Savarkar*, Thane: Itihas Patrika Prakashan, 2004, p. 281.
35. Savarkar, *Ratnagiri Parva*, pp. 305–06.
36. V.D. Savarkar, *Samagra Savarkar Vangmaya*, Vol. 3, p. 80.
37. Ibid., p. 301.
38. Keer, *Veer Savarkar*, p. 186.
39. Ibid.
40. Balarao Savarkar, *Ratnagiri Parva*, p. 229.
41. V.D. Savarkar, *Samagra Savarkar Vangmaya*, Vol. 3, p. 638.
42. Ibid., p. 419.
43. Ibid., pp. 632–33.
44. Savarkar, *Ratnagiri Parva*, pp. 287–88.
45. Ibid., p. 288.
46. Ibid., p. 306.
47. Ibid., pp. 632–33.
48. Savarkar, *Ratnagiri Parva*, pp. 351–52.

49. Ibid., pp., 361–62.
50. Ibid., p. 224.
51. Ibid., pp. 235–37.
52. Ibid., pp. 269–70.
53. Ibid., p. 332.
54. *Janata*, 9 March 1931.
55. Savarkar, *Ratnagiri Parva*, pp. 276–77.
56. Interestingly, Patwardhan was a staunch Gandhian and when he asked Mahatma Gandhi's permission to work with Vinayak, he was told that while he had no objection, Patwardhan better be cautious as Savarkar is a shrewd man ('*Aa unda maanas chhe*' in Gujarati)—as mentioned in Gandhi's letter to Patwardhan. See Patwardhan's autobiography, *Maajhi Jeevan Yatra*.
57. Joshi, *Jhunjh Savarkarancha*, n.d., p. 50.
58. Balarao Savarkar, *Ratnagiri Parva*, pp. 261–62.
59. V.D. Savarkar, *Samagra Savarkar Vangmaya*, Vol. 3, pp. 592–603.
60. Writing in 1936. See V.D. Savarkar, *Savarkar Samagra*, Vol. 4, p. 638.
61. Speech in village Shirode in 1937. Balarao Savarkar, *Ratnagiri Parva*, p. 372.
62. Speech at a sahabhojan organized on 1 July 1937. Balarao Savarkar, *Hindu Mahasabha Parva*, Bombay: Veer Savarkar Prakashan, 1972, p. 31.
63. The four varna system that categorized Hindus into Brahmins, Kshatriyas, Vaishyas and Shudras.
64. Keer, *Veer Savarkar*, p. 190.
65. V.D. Savarkar, *Savarkar Samagra*, pp. 575–77.
66. Ibid.
67. B.R. Ambedkar, 'Gandhism: The Doom of the Untouchables', *What Congress and Gandhi Have Done to the Untouchables*, New Delhi: Samyak Prakashan, 2012, Chapter XI. (The extracts are taken by Ambedkar from an article by Gandhi on the subject and is reproduced in the *Varna Vyavastha*—a book which contains Gandhi's writings in original Gujarati.)
68. Ibid.
69. Gandhi. *The Collected Works*, Vol. 58, p. 488. Also see https://www.gandhiashramsevagram.org/gandhiliterature/mahatma-gandhi-collected-works-volume-58.pdf
70. V.D. Savarkar, *Savarkar Samagra*, Vol. 7, pp. 25–46. These are compilations of the articles Savarkar wrote for the *Kesari* on dismantling caste.
71. Ambedkar, *What Congress and Gandhi Have Done to the Untouchables*, Chapter XI.
72. Statement of Ambedkar, 7 February 1933, in Gandhi, *The Collected Works*, Vol. 59, p. 227. Also see https://www.gandhiashramsevagram.org/gandhi-literature/mahatmagandhi-collected-works-volume-59.pdf

73. Ambedkar, *What Congress and Gandhi Have Done to the Untouchables*, Chapter XI.

74. Excerpt from his famous speech 'Annihilation of Caste' that was written but not delivered; later published as a book. See Narendra Jadhav (ed.), *Ambedkar Speaks*, Vol. 1, New Delhi: Konark Publishers Pvt. Ltd., 2013, p. 144.

75. *Harijan*, 11 February 1933 in Gandhi, *The Collected Works*, Vol. 59, pp. 228–29.

76. *Young India*, 27 April 1921.

77. Ambedkar, *What Congress and Gandhi Have Done to the Untouchables*, Chapter XI.

78. *Young India*, 5 February 1925.

79. Ibid.

80. Ambedkar, *What Congress and Gandhi Have Done to the Untouchables*.

81. V.D. Savarkar, *Samagra Savarkar Vangmaya*, Vol. 3, pp. 483–85.

82. Ibid., Vol. 7, pp. 161–65.

83. Balarao Savarkar, *Ratnagiri Parva*, p. 351.

84. V.D. Savarkar, *Samagra Savarkar Vangmaya*, Vol. 3, p. 573. Also translated & cited in V. S. Godbole, *Rationalism of Veer Savarkar*, Thane: Itihas Patrika Prakashan, 2004, p. 265.

85. Ibid., Vol 4, pp. 694–96. Also translated & cited by Godbole, pp. 266–67.

Chapter 3: Communal Cauldron

1. *Hindi Navjian*, 6 January 1927, excerpted from Gandhi, *The Collected Works*, Vol. 37, pp. 434–37. See also https://www.gandhiashramsevagram.org/gandhi-literature/mahatmagandhi-collected-works-volume-37.pdf

2. Gandhi, *The Collected Works*, Vol. 37, pp. 442–45. Also see https://www.gandhiashramsevagram.org/gandhi-literature/mahatma-gandhi-collected-works-volume-37.pdf

3. *Young India*, excerpted from Gandhi, *The Collected Works*, Vol. 37, p. 457.

4. The following paragraphs related to the essay are translated by author from V.D. Savarkar, *Savarkar Samagra*, Vol. 4, pp. 648–50.

5. Ibid., p. 650.

6. Quoted from Ambedkar, *Pakistan or the Partition of India*, p. 177.

7. Ibid., p. 177.

8. Ibid., p. 179.

9. Ibid., p. 181. Quote from Swami Shraddhanand's statement in the *Liberator* dated 31 August 1926.

10. Ambedkar, *Pakistan or the Partition of India*, p. 176.

11. Swami Shraddhanand, *Inside Congress*, Bombay: Phoenix Publications, 1946, pp. 179–80.

12. For more, see Chapter 10 of the volume 1 of this series; *Savarkar: Echoes from a Forgotten Past*, New Delhi: Penguin Viking, 2019.

13. The article has been translated by author from V. D. Savarkar, *Savarkar Samagra*, Vol. 4, pp. 709–14.

14. V.D. Savarkar, *A Hot Spicy Medley*, Bombay: Swatantryaveer Savarkar Rashtriya Smarak Trust, n.d., p. 54.

15. Balarao Savarkar, *Ratnagiri Parva.*

16. V.D. Savarkar, *Savarkar Samagra*, Vol. 4, pp. 48–49.

17. Ibid. p. 124.

18. Savarkar Private Papers: Microfilm Roll 22, Nehru Memorial Museum and Library (NMML), New Delhi.

19. Ibid.

20. Jaywant D. Joglekar, *Veer Savarkar: Father of Hindu Nationalism*, n.p., n.d. p. 113.

21. Letter from I.H. Thurnton Esquire, Acting Secretary to the Government of Bombay, dated 9 September 1926, No. 724/111 of 1926. Savarkar Private Papers: Microfilm Roll 22, Nehru Memorial Museum and Library (NMML), New Delhi.

22. References in this paragraph from letter sent by I.H. Thurnton of the Home Department, No. 724/111, dated 21 September 1926. Savarkar Private Papers: Microfilm Roll 22, Nehru Memorial Museum and Library (NMML), New Delhi.

23. Letter from the Head of the Police Office in Bombay, dated 14 October 1926. Savarkar Private Papers: Microfilm Roll 22, Nehru Memorial Museum and Library (NMML), New Delhi.

24. References from letter sent by C.G. Adam Esquire, CSI, Secretary to Government of Bombay, No. 724-III, dated 11 May 1926. Savarkar Private Papers: Microfilm Roll 22, Nehru Memorial Museum and Library (NMML), New Delhi.

25. Letter from D.J. McDonnell, Assistant Secretary to the Government of Bombay, who writes to the general secretary of the Hindu Depressed Classes Mission, Naya Bazar, Delhi, on 25 October 1927, regarding the latter's request to allow Vinayak Damodar Savarkar to preside over their conference. Savarkar Private Papers': Microfilm Roll 22, Nehru Memorial Museum and Library (NMML), New Delhi.

26. *Young India,* 20 January 1927, from Gandhi, *The Collected Works*, Vol. 38, pp. 85–88.

27. Ibid., p. 86.

28. References for all the quotes in Gandhi's reply. Ibid., p. 87.

29. Savarkar, *Savarkar Samagra*, Vol. 4, pp. 651–53.

30. Ibid., pp. 652–53.

31. *Young India*, 17 March 1927, excerpted from Gandhi, *The Collected Works*, Vol. 38, pp. 179–80.

32. Ibid., p. 180.

33. Ibid., p. 176.

34. Ibid., p. 179.

35. Keer, *Veer Savarkar*, p. 219.

36. Jaywant D. Joglekar, *Veer Savarkar: Father of Hindu Nationalism*, n.p., n.d. pp. 110–11.
    See also A.G. Salvi, *Swatantryaveer Savarkaranchya Sahawasat*, Part 1, p. 5.

37. Keer, *Veer Savarkar*, p. 219.

38. Ibid.

39. V.D. Savarkar, *Samagra Savarkar Vangmaya*, Vol. 3, pp. 25–29.

40. Ibid.

41. Balarao Savarkar, *Ratnagiri Parva*, pp. 138–39.

42. Ibid., p. 154.

43. Ibid., pp. 161–62.

44. Possible allusion to those who were involved in prostitution or whose modesty had been unfortunately violated.

45. Balarao Savarkar, *Ratnagiri Parva*, p. 113.

46. Ibid., p. 121.

47. Ibid., pp. 156–57.

48. V.D. Savarkar, *Samagra Savarkar Vangmaya*, Vol. 4, pp. 22–23.

49. Shriranga Godbole, *Govyatil Margadarshak Shuddhikarya*, Pune: Sanskrutik Vartapatra, 2010, p. 112.

50. Balarao Savarkar, *Ratnagiri Parva*, p. 178.

51. Ibid., pp. 97–98.

52. Ibid., p. 142.

53. Jaywant D. Joglekar, *Veer Savarkar: Father of Hindu Nationalism*, n.p., n.d., p. 110.

54. Savarkar Private Papers, Microfilm 22, NMML, New Delhi.

55. Home Political NA_1929 F.36-ii. Resolution dated 2 September 1929. National Archives of India, New Delhi.

56. Letter from H.F. Knight Esquire to District Magistrate of Ratnagiri, No. S.D. 1644, Home Political NA_1929 F.36-ii. National Archives of India, New Delhi.

57. Y.D. Phadke, *Shodh Savarkarancha*, Bombay, 1984, 1st Edition. pp. 111–113.

58. Ibid.

59. *Shraddhanand*, 16 February 1928.

60. Ibid.

61. Ibid.

62. V.D. Savarkar, *Hindu Pad Padashahi* Madras: B.G. Paul & Co., 1925 pp. vi-c. – vi-d.
63. Ibid., p. vii.
64. Ibid., pp. x–xiii.
65. Y.D. Phadke (ed.), *Mahatma Phule Samagra Vangmay*, Bombay: Maharashtra Rajya Sahitya ani Sanskriti Mandal, 1991, p. 43.
66. Ibid., p. 471.
67. For a description of Shivaji, please see: Grant Duff, *A History of the Mahrattas*, London: Longman, Rees, Orme, Brown, and Green, 1826.
68. M.G. Ranade, *Rise of the Maratha Power*, New Delhi: Publications Division, Government of India, 1974, p. 5.
69. K.T. Telang, 'Gleanings from Maratha Chronicles', paper read before the Deccan College Union on 17 September 1892. It appears as an appendix in ibid., pp. 124–25.
70. D.K. Bedekar, 'Review of Interpretations on Shivaji's Achievements', *Science and Human Progress: Essays in Humanities, Indology, Science, Mathematics and Personal Tributes to late Prof. Damodar Dharmanand Kosambi*, Bombay: Popular Prakashan, 1974, pp. 79–80.
71. Balarao Savarkar, *Ratnagiri Parva*, p. 44.
72. V. D. Savarkar, *Hindu-Pad Padashahi or a Review of the Hindu Empire of Maharashtra*, Madras: B.G. Paul & Co., 1925, p. 6.

Chapter 4: Making the Deaf Hear

1. Subhas Chandra Bose, *The Indian Struggle 1920-1934*, London: Wishart & Company Ltd., 1935. pp. 181–82.
2. Shiv Verma (ed.), *Bhagat Singh on the Path of Liberation*, Chennai: Bharathi Pusthakalaya, 2007, p. 196.
3. Ibid., p. 39.
4. Malwinderjit Singh Waraich and Gurudev Singh Sidhu (eds.), *The Hanging of Bhagat Singh: Confessions, Statements and Other Documents*, Chandigarh: Unistar, 2007, Vol. 3, p. 271.
5. V.D. Savarkar, *Savarkar Samagra*, Vol. 4, pp. 593–94.
6. Bhawan Singh Rana, *Bhagat Singh*, New Delhi: Diamond Pocket Books, 2005, p. 36.
7. Centre of Asian Studies, Cambridge, Oral History Collection (available online at http://www.s-asian.cam.ac.uk/audio.html), L.F. Chand interview by Uma Shanker, 5 September 1970, Interview No. 205, p. 44.
8. Malwinderjit Singh Waraich and Gurudev Singh Sidhu (eds.), *The Hanging of Bhagat Singh: Confessions, Statements and Other Documents*, Chandigarh: Unistar, 2007, Vol. 3, p. 77.

9.   Nehru Memorial Museum and Library (NMML) Oral History Transcripts,
     New Delhi, Jaidev Kapoor interview by S.L. Manchanda, 3 October 1974,
     Acc. No. 431, p. 112.
10. Bose, *The Indian Struggle*, p. 187.
11. Ibid.
12. Ibid. p. 188.
13. V.D. Savarkar, *Savarkar Samagra*, Vol. 4, pp. 661–64.
14. Bose, *The Indian Struggle*, p. 187.
15. Gandhi, *The Collected Works*, Vol. 47, pp. 264–65.
16. One of the dailies published from Ahmedabad and edited by Gandhi.
17. Gandhi, *The Collected Works*, Vol 47, pp. 353–54.
18. V.D. Savarkar, *Savarkar Samagra*, Vol. 4, pp. 665–70.
19. Bose, *The Indian Struggle*, pp. 193–94.
20. Ibid., p. 195.
21. Gandhi, *The Collected Works*, Vol, 48, p. 271.
22. Ibid., p. 363.
23. Gandhi, *The Collected Works*, Vol. 48, p. 367.
24. Jawaharlal Nehru, *Nehru on Gandhi* (*Selections from Writings and Speeches*),
     New York: John Day Company, p. 55.
25. Bose, *The Indian Struggle*, p. 211.
26. V.D. Savarkar, *Savarkar Samagra*, Vol. 4, pp. 657–60.
27. V.D. Savarkar, *A Hot Spicy Medley*, Bombay: Swatantryaveer Savarkar
     Rashtriya Smarak Trust, n.d., p. 32.
28. Ibid., pp. 32–34.
29. V.D. Savarkar, *Savarkar Samagra*, Vol. 4, pp. 654–66.
30. Sir Reginald Coupland, *The Constitutional Problem in India-I*, Oxford,
     n.p. 1945, p. 121.
31. Ibid.
32. Bose, *The Indian Struggle*, p. 224.
33. Quoted in ibid., p. 225.
34. Subhas Bose's recollections in ibid., p. 228.
35. Nehru, *Nehru on Gandhi* (*Selections from Writings and Speeches*), New York:
     John Day Company. p. 68.
36. Ibid., pp. 68–69.
37. Bose, *The Indian Struggle*, p. 232.
38. Courtesy Ranjit Savarkar & Swatantryaveer Savarkar Rashtriya Smarak,
     Mumbai.
39. Y.D. Phadke, *Shodh Savarkarancha*, Pune: Srividya Prakashan, 1984,
     pp. 123–31.
40. Balarao Savarkar, *Ratnagiri Parva*, Pg 7 of Appendix.
41. Bose, *The Indian Struggle*, pp. 242–44.

42. Majumdar, *History of Freedom Movement in India*, p. 390.
43. Bose, *The Indian Struggle*, pp. 259–60.
44. Excerpts from Gogate's interview; https://www.s-asian.cam.ac.uk/archive/audio/collection/v-b-gogate/
45. Ibid., p. 5.
46. G.M. Joshi, 'The Story of This History', in V.D. Savarkar, *The Indian War of Independence*, 1857, Bombay: Phoenix Publications, 1947, p. xvi.
47. Hamsaraja Rahabara, *Bhagat Singh and His Thought*, Delhi: Manak Publications, 1990, p. 90.
48. Recorded in the Oral Archives Interview Transcripts at the Nehru Memorial Museum and Library (NMML), New Delhi.
49. Bhagat Singh, Malwinder Singh Jit Waraich (ed.), *Jail Notebook of Shaheed Bhagat Singh*, Mohali: Unistar Books, 2016, p. 300.
50. Satyam (ed.), *Bhagat Singh aur unke saathiyon ke sampoorn upalabdh dastaavez*, Lucknow: Rahul Foundation, 2006. p. 93.
51. Ibid., pp. 166–68.
52. Ibid., pp. 243–48.
53. Ibid., pp. 443–52.
54. V. S. Joshi. *Mrityunjayacha Aatmayagnya*, n.p., 3rd Edition. 1981, pp. 367-368.
55. Author's interview with Ranjit Savarkar, grandnephew of Veer Savarkar.
56. Prithvi Singh 'Azad', *Baba Prithvi Singh Azad—The Legendary Crusader An Autobiography* 1st Edition, Bombay: Bhartiya Vidya Bhavan, 1987, pp. 121–122.
57. Note on Terrorism, 1932, IOR/L/PJ/12/404; 106. Also see, Maclean, Kama. 'Imagining the Indian Nationalist Movement: Revolutionary Metaphors in Imagery of the Freedom Struggle.' *Journal of Material Culture*. 19.1 (2014).
58. This incident was narrated by the priest himself to Babarao's biographer D.N. Gokhale. D. N. Gokhale, *Krantiveer Babarao Savarkar*, Srividya Prakashan Vol. 2. Poona, 1979, pp. 108 (pp. 108 of the English biography).
59. V. S. Joshi, *Mrityunjayacha Aatmayagnya*, n.p., 3rd Edition. 1981, pp. 367–368.
60. D. N. Gokhale. *Krantiveer Babarao Savarkar*, Srividya Prakashan, Vol. 2. Poona, 1979. p. 109.
61. Letter dated 4 November 1934. Savarkar Private Papers, Microfilm Roll 22, NMML, New Delhi.
62. Y. D. Phadke, *Lokmanya Tilak ani Krantikarak*, Bombay: Srividya Prakashan, n.d. pp. 40–51.
63. V.D. Savarkar, *Savarkar Samagra*, Vol. 9. pp. 543–45.
64. Ibid., pp. 549–51.
65. V.D. Savarkar, *Savarkar Samagra*, Vol. 9, pp. 511–12.
66. Ibid., pp. 552–56.
67. Ibid., p. 559.

68. Ibid., pp. 586–91.

69. Balarao Savarkar, *Ratnagiri Parva*, p. 246. See also, V.D. Savarkar, *Savarkar Samagra*, Vol. 9, pp. 503–04.

70. Correspondences with All-India Gurkha League, Savarkar Private Papers, Microfilm Roll 22, NMML, New Delhi.

71. Ibid., Letters dated 15 June 1926 and 13 September 1926.

72. Ibid.

73. Ibid., Letter dated 28 July 1931.

74. Ibid., Letter dated 31 August 1931.

75. Ibid., Letter dated 5 February 1932.

76. Correspondences with All-India Gurkha League, Savarkar Private Papers, Microfilm Roll 22, NMML, New Delhi.

77. Ibid., Letter dated 16 March 1937.

78. Joglekar, p. 114.

79. Savarkar, *Ratnagiri Parva*, pp. 72–73.

80. Balshastree Hardas, *Dharmaveer Do Balkrishna Shivaram Munje yanche Charitra*, 2nd edition, Nagpur: Lakhe Prakashan, 2013, p. 119.

81. Balarao Savarkar, *Ratnagiri Parva*, Bombay: Veer Savarkar Prakashan, 1972, pp. 93–94.

82. V.D. Savarkar, *Savarkar Samagra*, Vol. 4, Vol. 10, p. 530.

83. Ibid., p. 532.

84. Ibid., p. 533.

85. Ibid., pp. 636–56.

86. For details, see ibid., Vol. 9, pp. 627–22.

87. Bose, *The Indian Struggle*, p. 361.

88. Ibid., p. 279.

89. Jawaharlal Nehru *Nehru on Gandhi* (*Selections from Writings and Speeches*), New York, John Day Company, pp. 72–73.

90. Pattabhi Sitaramayya, *History of Congress-I*, New Delhi: S Chand and Company, 1988, pp. 538–39.

91. Bose, *The Indian Struggle*, p. 297.

92. Ibid.

93. Ibid.

94. Ibid.

95. Bose, *The Indian Struggle*, p. 9.

96. Microfilm No. 22, Savarkar Private Papers, NMML, New Delhi, No C/4.

97. Ibid., No. S.D-1079.

98. Ibid., No. S.D. 3963.

99. Ibid., No. S.D. 1251.

100. Ibid., No. S.D. 1251.

101. Ibid., No. S.D. 1251.

Chapter 5: The Hindu Mahasabha Years

1. Balarao Savarkar, *Hindu Mahasabha Parva*, p. 3.
2. Ibid., p. 7.
3. Ibid., p. 8.
4. Ibid., p. 10.
5. *Prabhat*, 26 June 1937.
6. Keer, *Veer Savarkar*, p. 224.
7. Digitized Private Papers of Sardar Patel, 'Nariman Parakarna', No. 1-9-1-121 (1937), 'Letters and Newspaper Articles', National Archives of India, New Delhi.
8. Balarao Savarkar, *Hindu Mahasabha Parva*, p. 22.
9. Ibid.
10. Ibid., pp. 22–23.
11. Ibid., p. 23.
12. *Bombay Chronicle, July, 1927.*
13 Ibid., p. 23.
14. *Dai Ajia Shugi*, March 1939 Issue, Asiatic Society Tokyo Publication. Source: Savarkar Rashtriya Smarak, Mumbai.
15. Balarao Savarkar, *Hindu Mahasabha Parva*, p. 27.
16. Ibid., pp. 28–29.
17. *Bombay Chronicle*, 12 May 1937.
18. Balarao Savarkar, *Hindu Mahasabha Parva*, pp. 41–42.
19. Ibid., pp. 42–43.
20. Keer, *Veer Savarkar*, p. 225.
21. Home-Political-NA-1937-F-18-8, 'Fortnightly Reports on the Political Situation in India'. Month of August 1937. National Archives of India, New Delhi.
22. Ibid.
23. Extract from the Bombay Presidency Weekly Letter No. 32 dated 14 August 1937, 800 (75)-II-1937, Maharashtra State Archives, Mumbai.
24. Extract from the Bombay Presidency Weekly Letter No. 31 dated 7 August 1937, 800 (75)-II-1937, Maharashtra State Archives, Mumbai.
25. Balarao Savarkar, *Hindu Mahasabha Parva*, p. 44.
26. Keer, *Veer Savarkar*, p. 228.
27. Ibid., pp. 228.
28. Balarao Savarkar, *Hindu Mahasabha Parva*, p. 49.
29. Ibid., pp. 50–51.
30. Extract from the Weekly Confidential Report of the District Magistrate of Poona, dated 5 November 1937 and 6 November 1937, 800 (75)-II-1937, Maharashtra State Archives, Mumbai.

31. Extract from the Bombay Presidency Weekly Letter No. 31 dated 27 November 1937, 800 (75)- II-1937, Maharashtra State Archives, Mumbai.

32. For good source material on Rash Behari Bose, see Elizabeth Eston and Lexi Kawabe, *Rash Behari Bose: The Father of the Indian National Army*, Vols. 1 and 2, Tenraidou, April 2019.

33. Balarao Savarkar, *Hindu Mahasabha Parva*, p. 53.

34. Ibid., p. 60.

35. Richard Gordon, 'The Hindu Mahasabha and the Indian National Congress, 1915 to 1926' in *Modern Asian Studies*, 9.2 (1975): 145-203.

36. References from V D Savarkar, *Hindu Rashtra Darshan* Poona: Maharashtra Prantik Hindu Sabha, n.d.

37. V. D. Savarkar, *Hindu Rashtra Darshan*, n.d., p. 4.

38. Ibid., p. 6.

39. Ibid., p. 8.

40. Ibid., p. 10.

41. Ibid., p. 8.

42. Ibid., p. 10.

43. Ibid., p. 11

44. Ibid., pp. 12–13.

45. Ibid., p. 13.

46. Ibid., p. 14.

47. Ibid.

48. Ibid.

49. Extract from the Bombay Province Weekly Letter No. 9 dated 5 March 1938, 800 (75)-II-1937, Maharashtra State Archives, Mumbai.

50. Balarao Savarkar, *Hindu Mahasabha Parva*, p. 86.

51. Balarao Savarkar, *Ratnagiri Parva*.

52. Keer, *Veer Savarkar*, p. 233.

53. Letter from Tulzaphurkar to Jayakar, dated 10 February 1938. Roll_00013_ File No 80-P.A. Microfilm, 'Digitized Private Papers of M.R. Jayakar', 1938, National Archives of India, New Delhi.

54. V.D. Savarkar, *Samagra Savarkar Vangmaya*, Vol. 4, pp. 449–68.

55. Ibid.

56. Ibid.

57. Keer, *Veer Savarkar*, p. 235.

58. Balarao Savarkar, *Hindu Mahasabha Parva*, p. 111.

59. Quoted in the *Mahratta*, 20 May 1938.

60. Ibid.

61. Keer, *Veer Savarkar*, p. 239.

62. Balarao Savarkar, *Hindu Mahasabha Parva*, p. 125.

63. Ibid., p. 208.

64. 987-A-1938, Maharashtra State Archives, Mumbai.

65. S.R. Date, *Bhagnagar Struggle: A Brief History of the Movement led by Hindu Mahasabha in Hyderabad State in 1938-39,* Poona: Lokasangraha Press, n.d., p. 16.

66. Ibid., p. 29.

67. Ibid., p. 39.

68. Ibid., p. 48.

69. Ibid., pp. 55–56.

70. Ibid., pp. 67–68.

71. B.P.P.A.I. (Secret) November 19 and 26, 1938. Paras 980 & No 7. This is a government document.

72. 'Congress Activities in Hyderabad State'. Intelligence Bureau, Home Department (Secret) Political Department Papers IOR R/1/1/3173.

73. *Bhagnagar Struggle,* n.d., p. 87.

74. Ibid., p. 88.

75. Ibid., pp. 88–90.

76. Balarao Savarkar, *Hindu Mahasabha Parva,* pp. 147–48.

77. *Bhagnagar Struggle,* n.d., p. 96.

78. Ibid., pp. 97–98.

79. Ibid., p. 102.

80. Ibid., p. 105.

81. Ibid., p. 110.

82. *Bhagnagar Struggle,* n.d., p. 129.

83. V.D. Savarkar, *Hindu Rashtra Darshan,* n.d., p. 17.

84. Ibid., p. 18.

85. Ibid., p. 24.

86. Ibid.

87. Ibid., pp. 27–28.

88. Ibid., p. 30.

89. Ibid., p. 31.

90. Ibid., p. 31.

91. Ibid.

92. Ibid.

93. Ibid., p. 34.

94. Ibid.

95. *Bhagnagar Struggle,* n.d., p. 130.

96. Ibid., pp. 132–33.

97. Ibid., p. 140.

98. Ibid. p. 146.

99. Ibid., p. 148.

100. Ibid., pp. 148–49.

101. Ibid., pp. 151–52.
102. Ibid., p. 178.
103. Ibid., pp. 181–83.
104. Ibid., p. 186.
105. Ibid., p. 188.
106. Ibid.
107. Hindu Mahasabha Papers, C-21-22, NMML, New Delhi.
108. Balarao Savarkar, *Hindu Mahasabha Parva*, p. 186.
109. Ibid., p. 190.
110. Ibid., pp. 199–200.
111. Ibid., pp. 257–259.
112. Letter from Savarkar to Ganpat Rai, dated 11 July 1939, Hindu Mahasabha Papers, C-21-22, NMML, New Delhi.
113. L/P-J/8/683- IOR, British Library, London.
114. No. 1-F, L/P-J/8/683-IOR, British Library, London.
115. Ibid. Report of Sir Francis Wylie on the Hindu Mahasabha.
116. Hindu Mahasabha Papers, NMML, New Delhi.
117. *Dai Ajia Shugi*, March 1939 issue, Asiatic Society Tokyo Publication. Source: Savarkar Rashtriya Smarak, Mumbai.
118. Balarao Savarkar, *Hindu Mahasabha Parva*, p. 269.
119. Moonje Papers, Letter of Savarkar to Rash Behari Bose, NMML, New Delhi.
120. *Dai Ajia Shugi*, April 1939 issue, Asiatic Society Tokyo Publication. Source: Savarkar Rashtriya Smarak, Mumbai.
121. Reported in the Sholapur newspaper *Syadvada Kesara*, dated 28 September 1927, File No. 436, Jayakar Papers, National Archives of India, New Delhi.
122. Ambedkar, *Pakistan or the Partition of India*, p. 99.
123. Ibid., pp. 99–100.
124. Ibid., p. 108.
125. Ibid., p. 109.
126. Ibid., pp. 112–13.
127. Ibid., p. 114.
128. Ibid.
129. Ibid., p. 108.
130. Moonje Papers, Microfilm Roll No. 1, NMML, New Delhi.
131. Ibid. Meeting between Moonje, Hedgewar and Laloo Gokhale on 31 March 1934.
132. Home/Political/National Archives of India, 88/33, 1933.
133. Moonje Papers, N24, 1932-1936, NMML, New Delhi.
134. Medha M. Kudaisya, *The Life and Times of G.D. Birla*, New Delhi: Oxford University Press, 2003.

135. *Bombay Chronicle*, 23 March 1936, quoting from file No. 53 (Vol. 2), Moonje Papers, NMML, New Delhi.

136. Quoted in Marzia Casolari, 'Hindutva's Foreign Tie-Up in the 1930s: Archival Evidence', *Economic and Political Weekly*, Vol. 35, No. 4, 22–28 January 2000, pp. 218–28.
The declaration is attributed to the Auswartiges Amt-Polischen Archiv, Bonn/Pol VII and quoted in Milan Hauner, *India in Axis Strategy: Germany, Japan and Indian Nationalists in the Second World War*, Stuttgart: Klett-Cotta, 1981, p. 67.

137. 'Surveys on the Activities of Foreigners in India', Home/Political/EW/1940_NA_F-59-2, National Archives of India, New Delhi.

138. 'Question of giving publicity to the note prepared in the DIB on Japanese intrigues in India dropped', Home/Pol/EW/1939/NA-F-115, National Archives of India, New Delhi.

139. Moonje Papers, Letter from Savarkar to Birla, dated 2 November 1938, NMML, New Delhi.

140. Marzia Casolari, 'Hindutva's Foreign Tie-Up in the 1930s'.

141. List No. ii, List of Germans who are objects of particular suspicion, HOM/POL/EW/1939/NA-F-93 KW, National Archives of India, New Delhi.

142. For a detailed account of her life, see her biography: Nocholas Goodrick-Clarke, *Hitler's Priestess: Savitri Devi, the Hindu-Aryan Myth, and Neo-Nazism*, New York & London: New York University Press, 1998.

143. Savitri Devi, *A Warning to the Hindus*, Calcutta: A.K. Mukkherji, 1939, pp. 10-11.

144. These letters are with the Swatantryaveer Savarkar Rashtriya Smarak, Mumbai.

145. Letter dated 21 November 1941, Savitri Devi to Ganesh Damodar Savarkar.

146. Ibid.

147. Savitri Devi, *Defiance*. Calcutta: A.K. Mukherji, 1950, p. 342.

148. 'The Rashtriya Swayamsevak Sangh-II: Who represents the Hindus?', *Economic and Political Weekly*, Vol. 7, No. 12, 18 March 1972, pp. 633–40.

149. Moonje Papers, No. 3, 1939, pp. 98–99, NMML, New Delhi.

150. Ibid. No. 30, Statements, 21 October 1939.

151. Ibid.

152. Ibid., Moonje to the editor, *Times of India*, 26 September 1940.

153. Letter from Lumlev to Linlithgow, January 15, 1942. Linlithgow Collection IOR MSS Eur F 125/56, British Library, London.

154. Linlithgow to Zetland, Linlithgow Papers, MSS Eur F 125/8 1939, IOR, British Library, London.

155. John Glendevon, *The Viceroy at Bay: Lord Linlithgow in India, 1936-1943*, Collins, 1971, p. 153.

156. 'Statement to the Press', Gandhi, *The Collected Works*, Vol. 76, pp. 311–12.

157. Majumdar, *History of Freedom Movement in India*, Vol. 3, p. 598.

158. Cited in V.P. Menon, *Transfer of Power*, Calcutta: Orient Longman, 1957, pp. 59–60.

159. Ahmad, *Speeches and Writings of Mr. Jinnah*, Vol. 2, Lahore: n.p., 1947, 6th edition, 1964, p. 245.

160. Political Department Collections L/P&J/8/506, November 1939, pp. 113–14, IOR, British Library, London.

161. *Hindustan Times*, 3 December 1939.

162. V.D. Savarkar, *Hindu Rashtra Darshan*, n.d., p. 57.

163. Ibid., p. 62.

164. Ibid.

165. Ibid., p. 65.

166. Hindu Rashtra Darshan, p. 53.

167. Quoted in *Mahratta*, 5 January 1940.

Chapter 6: Tumultuous Times

1.   Ambedkar, *Pakistan or the Partition of India*, p. 36.

2.   Menon, *Transfer of Power*, p. 55.

3.   C. Khaliquzzaman, *Pathway to Pakistan*, Lahore, n.p. 1961, pp. 160–61.

4.   For an excellent analysis on the mobilization of the Muslim *Qaum*, especially in UP, see Venkat Dhulipala, 'Rallying the Qaum: The Muslim League in the United Provinces, 1937-1939', *Modern Asian Studies*, Cambridge University Press, Vol. 44, No. 3, May 2010, pp. 603–40.

5.   Mahomed Ali Jinnah, Jamil-ud-Din Ahmad (ed.), *Speeches and Writings of Jinnah*, 'Lucknow Session of the League, 1937', Lahore: Shaikh Muhammad Ashraf, 1964.
      Also see Deepak Pandey, 'Congress-Muslim League Relations 1937-39: The Parting of Ways', *Modern Asian Studies*, Vol. 12, No. 4, 1978, pp. 629–654.

6.   *Madina*, 21 January 1938.

7.   This has been dealt in detail in Volume 1 of this book, Chapter 11.

8.   V.D. Savarkar, *Hindu Rashtra Darshan*, n.d., pp. 57–58.

9.   Ambedkar, *Pakistan or the Partition of India*. http://www.columbia.edu/itc/mealac/pritchett/00ambedkar/ambedkar_partition/412d.html. Chapter titled 'National Frustration'. (Interestingly, several portions of his original text have been edited for these comments in subsequent print editions!)

10.   Ibid.

11. Ambedkar, *Pakistan or the Partition of India*, p. 322.
12. Ibid., pp. 161–62.
13. Ibid., p. 162
14. Ibid.
15. Ibid.
16. Ibid., pp. 162–64
17. Ibid., p. 164.
18. Balarao Savarkar, *Hindu Mahasabha Parva*, pp. 316–17.
19. Bose, *The Indian Struggle*, p. 34.
20. Ibid.
21. Ibid., p. 34.
22. Balarao Savarkar, *Hindu Mahasabha Parva*, p. 348.
23. Georges Ohsawa, *The Two Great Indians in Japan: Sri Rash Behari Bose and Subhas Chandra Bose*, Kusa Publications, 1954, p. 95.
24. Keer, *Veer Savarkar*, p. 260.
25. L\P&J\8\683-IOR-British Library, London.
26. The British Government's Offer of 8 August 1940, Gwyer & Appadorai. Documents, ii. 504-505, IOR, BL, London.
27. Ibid.
28. L\P&J\8\683-IOR-British Library, London.
29. Ibid.
30. Bose, *The Indian Struggle*, p. 37.
31. Statement of Accused No. 7: Savarkar: Mahatma Gandhi Murder Case Trial, p. 53, National Archives of India, New Delhi.
32. V.D. Savarkar, *Veer Savarkar's "Whirl-wind Propaganda.": Statements, Messages & Extracts from the President's Diary of His Propagandistic Tours, Interviews from December 1937 to October 1941*, Anant Sadashiv Bhide (Ed.), n.p. 1941, pp. 262–66.
33. V.D. Savarkar, *Hindu Rashtra Darshan* Poona, n.d., p. 80.
34. Ibid., p. 81.
35. Ibid., p. 82.
36. Ibid.
37. Ibid., p. 84.
38. Ibid., p. 85.
39. Ibid., p. 87
40. Ibid.
41. Ibid.
42. Ibid., p. 90.
43. Ibid., p. 91.
44. Ibid., p. 67.
45. Ibid., p. 75.

46. Ibid., p. 93.
47. 'Resolution of the Hindu Mahasabha 1940 Madura Session', HOME_ POLITICAL_I_1941_NA_F-138_41, National Archives of India, New Delhi.
48. Ibid.
49. Ibid.
50. Ibid.
51. Ibid.
52. L\P&J\8\683, IOR, British Library, London.
53. Ibid.
54. Ibid.
55. Ibid.
56. 'Statement on Correspondence between President of Hindu Mahasabha and Viceroy with specific demands of HMS & replies of the Viceroy', Statement dated 22 April 1941, Roll No. 10, Savarkar Private Papers, NMML, New Delhi.
57. Ibid.
58. *The Mahratta*, 2 May 1941.
59. Source: Census Data of Government of India. https://censusindia.gov.in/ DigitalLibrary/browseyearwise.aspx
60. Ibid.
61. 'SPM Diary note of 6 December 1945'; Roy, *The Life and Times of Dr. Syama Prasad Mookerjee*, p. 92.
62. Ibid.
63. *Evolution of Muslim Political Thought in India, Vol. 5, The Demand for Pakistan*, A.M. Zaidi (ed.), New Delhi: S. Chand & Company, 1978, p. 290.
64. https://sites.google.com/site/cabinetmissionplan/speeches-and-statementsby-jinnah-1941-1942
65. Keer, *Veer Savarkar*, p. 294.
66. Ibid., p. 295.
67. 'Savarkar to Viceroy on the Working Committee of AIHMS', L\P&J\8\683-IOR, British Library, London.
68. Ibid.
69. Ibid.
70. 'Fortnightly Report of the Political Situation in India for the month of April 1941', HOME_POLITICAL_1_1941_NA_F_18-4-41, National Archives of India, New Delhi.
71. 'Viceroy to Secretary of State on 16 April 1941', L\P&J\8\683-IOR, British Library, London.
72. Ibid.

73. Ibid.
74. 'Secretary of State to Viceroy regarding Savarkar's Letter on the Riots in Dacca: 18 April 1941', L\P&J\8\683-IOR, British Library, London.
75. 'Reply from Viceroy to the Secretary of State, 20 April 1941', L\P&J\8\683-IOR, British Library, London.
76. 'Intercepted Letter of Rao Bahadur Bole to N.C. Chaterji, 16 May 1941', L\P&J\8\683-IOR, British Library, London.
77. Ibid.
78. V.D. Savarkar, *Historic Statements*.
79. Viceroy to Secretary of State, dated 17 June 1941, L\P&J\8\683-IOR, British Library, London.
80. 'Statement of VD Savarkar regarding Direct Action of Hindu Mahasabha': HOME_POLITICAL_I_1941_NA_F-214_41, National Archives of India, New Delhi.
81. Ibid.
82. Ibid.
83. Ibid.
84. Ibid.
85. Roy, *The Life and Times of Dr. Syama Prasad Mookerjee*, p. 89.
86. Keer, *Veer Savarkar*, p. 297.
87. Guy Winant to Secretary of State, Cordell Hull, 4 November 1941, Foreign Relations to the United States: Diplomatic Papers, USA 1941, iii, 181–82.
88. R. J. Moore, *Churchill, Cripps and India, 1939-1945*. Clarendon Press, Oxford, 1979.
89. Ibid.
90. Guy Winant to Secretary of State, Cordell Hull, 4 November 1941, Foreign Relations to the United States: Diplomatic Papers, 1941, iii, 181-182.
91. L\P&J\8\683-IOR, British Library, London.
92. Keer, *Veer Savarkar*, p. 298.
93. *Bombay Chronicle*, 24 August 1941.
94. V.D. Savarkar, *Veer Savarkar's "Whirl-wind Propaganda"*, pp. 461–62.
95. V.D. Savarkar, *Historic Statements*, p. 32.
96. Moonje to Viceroy: L\P&J\8\683-IOR, British Library, London.
97. Ibid.
98. Ibid.
99. Ibid.
100. Viceroy to Secretary of State regarding AIHMS, 14 October 1941, L\P&J\8\683-IOR, British Library, London.
101. 'Miscellaneous Reports on Hindu Mahasabha: Statement by V.D. Savarkar dated 7 October 1941' HOME_POLITICAL_1_1941_NA_F_243-41, National Archives of India, New Delhi.

102. 'Circular Memorandum by VD Savarkar regarding Hindu Militarization Boards, dated 27-8-1941', HOME_POLITICAL_I_1941_NA_F-200_41, National Archives of India, New Delhi.

103. 'Extracts from DCIO Assam's Report on Political Situation in India: Reports from Central Intelligence on Political Situation in India', dated 3 December 1941, HOME_POLITICAL_1-1941_NA_F-241-41, National Archives of India, New Delhi.

104. Pattabhi Sitaramayya, *History of the Indian National Congress,* New Delhi: S Chand, 1988, Vol. 3, pp. 541–43.

105. Ibid., p. 529.

106. Ibid., p. 542.

107. V.D. Savarkar, *Hindu Rashtra Darshan* Poona, pp. 111–12.

108. *Forward*, Vol. III, No. 7, 9 March 1940, p. 10.

109. *Hindusthan Standard*, 19 April 1940.

110. *Forward*, Vol. III, No. 13, 20 April 1940.

111. *The History of the Bhagalpur Struggle: The 23rd Session of the A.I.H. Mahasabha,* Bhagalpur: Madhukari Bookseller, Publishers & General Order Supplier, 1942, p. 18.

112. Ibid., p. 19.

113. Ibid., p. 24.

114. Ibid., p. 43.

115. Ibid., pp. 48–50.

116. Ibid., p. 82.

117. Ibid., p. 80.

118. Ibid., p. 85.

119. Ibid., p. 86.

120. Ibid., pp. 86–87.

121. Ibid., pp. 90–91.

122. *Bombay Chronicle*, 29 December 1941.

123. *History of Bhagalpur Struggle*, p. 96.

124. Ibid., p. 98.

125. Ibid., pp. 101–02.

126. Ibid., p. 103.

127. Ibid., p. 99.

128. Ibid., pp. 94–95.

Chapter 7: 'Leaning on a Broken Reed'

1. Kanji Dwarkadas, *Ten Years of Freedom*, Bombay: Popular Prakashan, 1968, p. 62.

2. Ibid.

3. *Foreign Relations of the Unites States, Diplomatic Papers*, 1942, Vol. 1, pp. 605–06.
4. N. Mansergh and E.W.R. Lumby (ed.), *Constitutional Relations between Britain and India: The Transfer of Power 1942-7. Volume 1:* "The Cripps Mission" London, 1970. Exhibit No. 6.
5. Ibid., No. 23.
6. Ibid., No. 43.
7. Kanji Dwarkadas, *Ten Years of Freedom*, Bombay: Popular Prakashan, 1968, p. 63.
8. Ibid.
9. Ibid.
10. Mansergh and Lumby (ed.), *Constitutional Relations between Britain and India.*
11. Ibid., No. 265.
12. 'Telegram from Governor-General to Secretary of State, File No 40-D/42, 4 March 1942: Miscellaneous Reports of Hindu Mahasabha, 1942, HOME_POLITICAL_I_1942_NA_F-222, National Archives of India, New Delhi.
13. Majumdar, *History of Freedom Movement in India*, p. 615.
14. Ibid.
15. 'Reactions to Cripps Mission': HOME_POLITICAL_I_1942_NA_F-221, National Archives of India, New Delhi.
16. Keer, *Veer Savarkar*, p. 304.
17. Ibid.
18. Anthony Read and David Fischer, *The Proudest Day: India's Long Road to Independence*, London: Random House UK, 1997, p. 317.
19. 'Telegram from Governor General to Secretary of State, dated 12 March 1942: Reactions to Cripps Mission': HOME_POLITICAL_I_1942_NA_F-221, National Archives of India, New Delhi.
20. Keer, *Veer Savarkar*, p. 304.
21. *New York Times*, 29 March 1942.
22. Quoted in *The Mahratta*, 28 August 1942.
23. N. Mansergh and E.W.R. Lumby (eds.), *Constitutional Relations between Britain and India: The Transfer of Power 1942-7, Volume 1:* "The Cripps Mission", London, 1970, Linlithgow to Amery, 7 April 1942, Exhibit No. 559.
24. *The Scotsman*, 10 April 1942, British Newspaper Archives (BNA), British Library, London.
25. Jawaharlal Nehru, *The Discovery of India*, New Delhi: Jawaharlal Nehru Memorial Fund and Oxford University Press, 1981, p. 463.
26. Louis, Fischer, *The Life of Mahatma Gandhi*. HarperCollins: London, 1982, p. 448.

27. Sir Reginald Coupland, *The Indian Problem, Pt. II, Indian Politics, 1936–1942*. Oxford University Press, 1943, p. 193.

28. Ibid.

29. *Foreign Relations of the Unites States, Diplomatic Papers*, 1942, Vol. 1, pp. 630–34.

30. 'Secret Report Dated 2-4-1942': Miscellaneous Reports of Hindu Mahasabha: 1942: HOME_POLITICAL_I_1942_NA_F-222, National Archives of India, New Delhi.

31. Ibid.

32. Ibid.

33. Ibid.

34. *Lincolnshire Echo*, 6 April 1942, British Newspaper Archive (BNA), British Library, London.

35. Ibid.

36. 'Telegram from Governor General to Secretary of State': No. 63-D, New Delhi, dated 10 April 1942. Miscellaneous Reports of Hindu Mahasabha: 1942: HOME_POLITICAL_I_1942_NA_F-222, National Archives of India, New Delhi.

37. Keer, *Veer Savarkar*, pp. 309–10.

38. 'Congress Affairs 40-42: Digitized Private Papers of Sardar Patel', PP_000000005413, National Archives of India, New Delhi.

39. Keer, *Veer Savarkar*, p. 314.

40. V.D. Savarkar, *Historic Statements*, p. 21.

41. Ibid., pp. 15–16.

42. Tom Treanor, *One Damn Thing After Another: The Adventures of an Innocent Man Trapped between Public Relations and the Axis*, New York: Doubleday, Doran & Company, Inc., 1944. p. 84.

43. Ibid., p. 85.

44. Ibid.

45. Ibid., p. 84.

46. Ibid.

47. Ibid., p. 84.

48. Ibid., p. 85.

49. Ibid., p. 86.

50. Ibid., pp. 84–86.

51. V.D. Savarkar, *Historic Statements*, p. 29.

52. Ibid., p. 28.

53. Ibid., p. 29.

54. Ibid.

55. Ibid., p. 22.

56. Ibid.

57. Miscellaneous Reports of Hindu Mahasabha: 1942: HOME_
    POLITICAL_I_1942_NA_F-222, National Archives of India, New Delhi.
58. Ibid.
59. Ibid.
60. V P Menon, *The Transfer of Power in India*. Longman, 1957., p. 140.
61. Ibid.
62. Gandhi, *The Collected Works*, Vol. 78, p. 178.
    Also see https://www.gandhiashramsevagram.org/gandhi-literature/
    mahatma-gandhi-collected-works-volume-78.pdf.
63. Dhanajay Keer, *Mahatma Gandhi*, Bombay: Popular Prakashan, 1973, p. 682.
64. Gandhi, *The Collected Works*, Vol. 78, p. 415.
65. Pattabhi Sitaramayya, *History of the Indian National Congress*, Vol. II, New
    Delhi: S Chand, 1988, p. 635.
66. Ibid.
67. Gandhi, *The Collected Works*, Vol. 82, p. 295.
    Also see https://www.gandhiashramsevagram.org/gandhi-literature/
    mahatma-gandhi-collected-works-volume-82.pdf.
68. Narendra Singh Sarila, *The Shadow of the Great Game: The Untold Story of
    India's Partition*, New Delhi: HarperCollins, 2005, p. 141.
69. Keer, *Veer Savarkar*, p. 308.
70. Ibid., p. 306.
71. Nazir Yar Jung (ed.), *The Pakistan Issue*, Lahore: Sh. Muhammad Ashraf,
    1943, pp. 116–19.
72. 'Reactions to Cripps Mission': HOME_POLITICAL_I_1942_NA_F-
    221, National Archives of India, New Delhi.
73. Sir Reginald Coupland, *The Indian Problem, Pt. II, Indian Politics,
    1936-1942*. Oxford University Press, 1943, p. 290.
74. Statement published by the Government of India on the Congress party's
    responsibility for the disturbances in India, 1942-43. *Parliamentary Report,
    Accounts and Papers, 1942-43*, Volume IX. Also reproduced in Indian Annual
    Register, 1942, pp. 237–54.
75. 'Telegram of Governor-General to Secretary of State, dated 30 May
    1942.' External Affairs Department Periodical Appreciations Information
    & Broadcasting; HOME_POLITICAL_I_1942_NA_F-97, National
    Archives of India, New Delhi
76. Maulana Abul Kalam Azad, *India Wins Freedom: An Autobiographical
    Account*, Hyderabad: Orient Longman Limited, 1959, pp. 73–77.
77. 'Telegram of Governor-General to Secretary of State, dated 14 July
    1942.' External Affairs Department Periodical Appreciations Information
    & Broadcasting; HOME_POLITICAL_I_1942_NA_F-97, National
    Archives of India, New Delhi.

78. Pattabhi Sitaramayya, *History of Congress*, Vol. 2, New Delhi: S. Chand, 1988, pp. 340–42.

79. Keer, *Mahatma Gandhi*. Bombay: Popular Prakashan, 1973, p. 701.

80. Maulana Abul Kalam Azad, *India Wins Freedom: An Autobiographical Account*, Hyderabad: Orient Longman Limited, 1959, p. 81.

81. Nehru, *The Discovery of India*, p. 427.

82. Statement of Accused No. 7: Savarkar: Mahatma Gandhi Murder Case Trial, p. 53, National Archives of India, New Delhi.

83. Nehru, *The Discovery of India*, p. 419.

84. Sir Reginald Coupland, *The Indian Problem, Pt. II, Indian Politics, 1936-1942*, Oxford University Press, 1943, p. 303.

85. Nehru, *The Discovery of India*, p. 429.

86. 'Telegram #6925 of Governor-General to Secretary of State, dated 1 September 1942', External Affairs Department Periodical Appreciations Information and Broadcasting, HOME_POLITICAL_I_1942_NA_F-97, National Archives of India, New Delhi.

87. Azad, *India Wins Freedom*, p. 91.

88. V.P. Menon, *The Transfer of Power in India*, Longman, 1957, p. 141.

89. Sir Reginald Coupland, *The Indian Problem, Pt. II, Indian Politics, 1936-1942*, Oxford University Press, 1943, p. 299.

90. C. Khaliquzzaman, *Pathway to Pakistan*. Lahore, 1961., pp. 282–23. See also, Majumdar, *History of Freedom Movement in India*, Book 4, Chapter 9.

91. Ibid. p. 142.

92. N. Mansergh and E.W.R. Lumby (Ed.) *Constitutional Relations between Britain and India: The Transfer of Power 1942-7. Volume 2*, London, 1970. Exhibit No. 2169-S.

93. Majumdar, *History of Freedom Movement in India*, p. 689.

94. M.R. Masani, *The Communist Party of India*, n.p. London, 1954, p. 84; Majumdar, *History of Freedom Movement in India*, Book 4, Chapter 9, p. 138.

95. Gene D. Overstreet and Marshall Windmiller, *Communism in India*, Berkeley and Los Angeles: University of California Press, 1959, p. 219. R. C. Majumdar states: 'The authenticity of the letter is denied by the CPI, and there is no positive evidence of its existence. Batlivala challenged the CPI to publish the correspondence, but the challenge was not accepted.' In Majumdar, *History of Freedom Movement in India*, Vol. 3, p. 851.

96. 'Hindu Mahasabha, Resolution Registration Regarding Enquiry Committee and Collective Fines', HOME_POLITICAL_I_1942_NA_F-3-53, National Archives of India, New Delhi.

97. *Yorkshire Evening Post*, 3 August 1942, British Newspaper Archive (BNA), London.

98. Keer, *Veer Savarkar*, p. 325.
99. 'Hindu Mahasabha, Resolution Registration Regarding Enquiry Committee and Collective Fines', HOME_POLITICAL_I_1942_NA_F-3-53, National Archives of India, New Delhi.
100. Transcribed Tape Recording of S.R. Date, S 32, Centre of South Asian Studies Archive Collection, Cambridge.
101. Anil Chandra Banerjee, *A Phase in the Life of Dr. Syama Prasad Mookerjee*, 1937–46, Kolkata: Ashutosh Mookerjee Memorial Institute, 2000, pp. 102–20.
102. 'Hindu Mahasabha, Resolution Registration Regarding Enquiry Committee and Collective Fines', HOME_POLITICAL_I_1942_NA_F-3-53, National Archives of India, New Delhi.
103. Ibid.
104. 'Intercepted letter of N.C. Chatterjee to B.S. Moonje, dated 14 August 1942', R/3/2/33, IOR, British Library, London.
105. 'Hindu Mahasabha, Resolution Registration Regarding Enquiry Committee and Collective Fines'- HOME_POLITICAL_I_1942_NA_F-3-53, National Archives of India, New Delhi.
106. Ibid.
107. *Kaal*, 19 August 1943.
108. Arun (compiled and edited), *Testament of Subhas Bose, 1942-1945*, Delhi: Rajkamal Publication, 1946. p. 24.
109. Radhanath Rath and Sabitri Prasanna Chatterjee (eds.), *Rash Behari Basu: His Struggle for India's Independence*, Calcutta: Biplabi Mahanayak Rash Behari Basu Smarak Samiti, 1959, pp. 171–174.
110. Linlithgow Papers, India Office Library and Records, London.
111. Keer, *Veer Savarkar*, pp. 325–26.
112. Ibid., p. 326.
113. Ibid.
114. 'Letter from S.P. Mookerjee to Laithwaite, dated 2 September 1942', L/P&J/8/683, British Library, London.
115. Ibid.
116. 'Telegram of The Marquess of Linlithgow to Viscount Halifax, dated 22 September 1942', MSS. EUR. F. 125/130, British Library, London.
117. *Lincolnshire Echo*, 12 September 1942, British Newspaper Archive (BNA), British Library, London.
118. V.D. Savarkar, *Historic Statements*, p. 62.
119. 'Hindu Mahasabha, Resolution Registration Regarding Enquiry Committee and Collective Fines', HOME_POLITICAL_I_1942_NA_F-3-53, National Archives of India, New Delhi.
120. 'Telegram of Dr. Savarkar to Churchill, dated 9 October 1942': L/P&J/8/510: ff 176-177; British Library, London.

121. V.D. Savarkar, *Historic Statements*, p. 62.
122. Ibid., p. 59.
123. 'Telegram #7356 of Governor-General to Secretary of State, dated 16 September 1942'. External Affairs Department Periodical Appreciations Information and Broadcasting; HOME_POLITICAL_I_1942_NA_F-97, National Archives of India, New Delhi.
124. 'Telegram #8352 of Governor-General to Secretary of State, dated 21 October 1942'. External Affairs Department Periodical Appreciations Information and Broadcasting; HOME_POLITICAL_I_1942_NA_F-97, National Archives of India, New Delhi.
125. M.S.M. Sharma had worked with the Associated Press and *The Hindu* and was thereafter the editor of Bihar's leading daily, *The Searchlight*.
126. M.S.M. Sharma, *Peeps into Pakistan*, Patna: Pustak Bhandar, 1954, p. 110.
127. Ibid.
128. Ibid., p. 111.
129. Statement of Accused No. 7: Savarkar: Mahatma Gandhi Murder Case Trial, pp. 55–56, National Archives of India, New Delhi.
130. HOME_POLITICAL_I_1942_NA_F-169, National Archives of India, New Delhi.
131. Ibid.
132. Ibid.
133. Linlithgow Papers, MSS EUR.F. 125/124; India Office Library and Records, British Library, London.
134. Letter # 11201-G/42; HOME_POLITICAL_I_1942_NA_F-169, National Archives of India, New Delhi.
135. 'Telegram # 8623 of Governor-General to Secretary of State, dated 30 October 1942', External Affairs Department Periodical Appreciations Information and Broadcasting; HOME_POLITICAL_I_1942_NA_F-97, National Archives of India, New Delhi.
136. Ibid.
137. Ibid.
138. Ibid.
139. Enclosed in letter of 1 December 1942 from Private Secretary to Viceroy to Private Secretary to Secretary of State for India, MSS EUR F.125/137, British Library, London.
140. 'Telegram of Governor-General to Secretary of State, dated 11 December 1942'. External Affairs Department Periodical Appreciations Information and Broadcasting; HOME_POLITICAL_I_1942_NA_F-97, National Archives of India, New Delhi.
141. V.D. Savarkar, *Hindu Rashtra Darshan*, n.d., pp. 109–10.
142. Ibid., p. 110.

143. Ibid. p. 111.
144. Ibid., p. 118.
145. Ibid., p. 119.
146. Ibid.
147. Ibid., pp. 119–20.
148. Ibid., p. 123.
149. Fortnightly Report for the Month of January 1943, HOME_ POLITICAL_I_1943_NA_F-18-1, National Archives of India, New Delhi.
150. Ibid.
151. Ibid.
152. Ibid.
153. Ibid.
154. Ibid.
155. V.D. Savarkar, *Historic Statements*, pp. 57–58.
156. Savarkar's own statement to this effect dated 31 July 1943, in V.D. Savarkar, *Hindu Rashtra Darshan*, n.d. p.128.
157. Balraj Madhok, *Portrait of a Martyr*, Bombay: Jaico Publishing House, 1973, p. 26.
158. Letter from S.P. Mookerjee to M.D. Seth, 23 November 1942. India Office Records R/3/2/41, British Library, London.
159. S.P. Mookerjee Papers, File 207, Nehru Memorial Museum and Library (NMML), New Delhi.
160. Indian Annual Register, July-December, 1942 Vol. II, p. 30.
161. 'Note on the Organization, Aims etc. of the Rashtriya Swayam Sewak Sangh', HOME_POLITICAL_I_1942_NA_F-28-8, National Archives of India, New Delhi.
162. Namrata Ganneri, 'Whither Hindu Unity? Unravelling the RSS-Hindu Mahasabha Relationship: Perspectives from Maharashtra', in *Proceedings of the Indian History Congress*, 2015, Vol. 76, 2015, p. 468.
163. 'Note on the Organization, Aims etc. of the Rashtriya Swayam Sewak Sangh', HOME_POLITICAL_I_1942_NA_F-28-8, National Archives of India, New Delhi.
164. *Times of India*, p. 10, 10 October 1935.
165. D.N. Gokhale, *Krantiveer Babarao Savarkar*, Srividya Prakashan, Poona, 1979, pp. 93–94.
166. 'Note on the Organization, Aims etc. of the Rashtriya Swayam Sewak Sangh', HOME_POLITICAL_I_1942_NA_F-28-8, National Archives of India, New Delhi.
167. 'Activities of Hindu Rashtra Dal', File No. 382, Home Department (Special) 1943-45, Maharashtra State Archives, Mumbai.

168. Walter Andersen and Shridhar Damle. *The Brotherhood in Saffron*, Boulder: Westview Press, 1987, p. 63.

169. N.B. Khare, *My Political Memoirs or Autobiography*, Nagpur: S.R. Joshi, 1959.

170. 'Note on the Organization, Aims etc. of the Rashtriya Swayam Sewak Sangh', HOME_POLITICAL_I_1942_NA_F-28-8, National Archives of India, New Delhi.

171. Ibid.

172. Ibid.

173. '"Hindusthan for Hindus" Challenge to Congress', *Times of India*, 2 May 1938.

174. Walter Andersen and Shridhar Damle. *The Brotherhood in Saffron*, Boulder: Westview Press, 1987, p. 40.

175. S.R. Deshpande and Ramaswamy, *Dr. Hedgewar, The Epoch Maker: A Biography*, Sahitya Sindhu, 1981, p. 167.

176. T. Basu, et al., *Khaki Shorts and Saffron Flags: A Critique of the Hindu Right*, New Delhi: Orient BlackSwan, 1993, p. 23.

177. Walter Andersen, 'The Rashtriya Swayamsevak Sangh: Who Represents the Hindus?', *Economic and Political Weekly*, Vol. 7, No. 12, 18 March 1972, p. 636.

178. Ibid.

179. 'Note on the Organization, Aims etc. of the Rashtriya Swayam Sewak Sangh', HOME_POLITICAL_I_1942_NA_F-28-8, National Archives of India, New Delhi.

180. Ibid.

181. Ibid.

182. Note dated 30 November 1943; HOME_POLITICAL_I_1943_NA_F-28-3, National Archives of India, New Delhi.

183. Ibid.

184. Ibid.

185. 'Note on the Organization, Aims etc. of the Rashtriya Swayam Sewak Sangh', HOME_POLITICAL_I_1942_NA_F-28-8, National Archives of India, New Delhi.

186. 'Note on the Organization, Aims etc. of the Rashtriya Swayam Sewak Sangh', HOME_POLITICAL_I_1942_NA_F-28-8, National Archives of India, New Delhi.

187. Note dated 30 November 1943; HOME_POLITICAL_I_1943_NA_F-28-3, National Archives of India, New Delhi.

188. Note dated 30 November 1943; HOME_POLITICAL_I_1943_NA_F-28-3, National Archives of India, New Delhi.

189. Namrata Ganneri, 'Whither Hindu Unity? Unravelling the RSS-Hindu Mahasabha Relationship: Perspectives from Maharashtra' in *Proceedings of the Indian History Congress*, 2015, Vol. 76, 2015, p. 473.

190. Official Note dated 22 December 1943, Intelligence Bureau's note, Home Department File# 28/3/43-Home Poll (I), National Archives of India, New Delhi.

191. HOME_POLITICAL_I_1943_NA_F-28-3, National Archives of India, New Delhi.

192. 'Savarkar's statement on India's unity' in Partha Sarathy Gupta (ed.), *Towards Freedom: Documents on the Movement for Independence in India, 1943-44*, New Delhi: Oxford University Press, 1998, op. cit. p. 2976.

193. K.R. Malkani, *The RSS Story*, New Delhi: Impex India, 1980, p. 115.

194. *Maharashtra Hindusabhecha Karyacha Itihas*, Pune: Kesari, 1975, p. 2; Also see, 'Hindu Militia-Ram Sena Rules', File no. C-190, 1947, All India Hindu Mahasabha Papers, NMML, New Delhi.

195. 'Extract from Secret Abstract No. 21, dated 23 May 1942, Hindu Mahasabha, in 'Activities of Hindu Rashtra Dal', File no 382, Home Department, National Archives of India, New Delhi.

196. Allama Inayatullah Khan Mashriqi was an Islamic scholar and theorist who founded the Khaksar movement of violent and tribal Islamic armed militia and corps in Lahore, Punjab, in 1931.

197. Secret Note dated 13 December 1943; HOME_POLITICAL_I_1943_NA_F-28-3, National Archives of India, New Delhi.

198. 'Report for the Rashtriya Swayam Sewak Sangh', HOME_POLITICAL_I_1943_NA_F-28-3, National Archives of India, New Delhi.

199. Namrata Ganneri, 'Whither Hindu Unity? Unravelling the RSS-Hindu Mahasabha Relationship: Perspectives from Maharashtra', in *Proceedings of the Indian History Congress*, 2015, Vol. 76, 2015, p. 475.

200. S.R. Date, *Maharashtra Hindusabhecha Karyacha Itihas*, Pune: Kesari, 1975, p. 422.

Chapter 8: Hurtling Towards Disasters

1. Statement of Accused No. 7: Savarkar: Mahatma Gandhi Murder Case Trial, pp. 52–53, National Archives of India, New Delhi.

2. Fortnightly Reports for the Month of February 1943, HOME_POLITICAL_1_1943_NA_F_18-2-43. National Archives of India, New Delhi.

3. Sir R. Lumley to the Marquess of Linlithgow, M.S.S. EUR. F. 125/57 dated 12 March 1943, British Library, London.

4. The Marquess of Linlithgow to Mr. Amery, 13 March 1943, M.S.S. EUR.F. 125/24, British Library, London.

5.   Ibid.
6.   'An Authentic Account of Leaders' Conference', Digitized Private Papers of
     M.R. Jayakar, Microfilm Roll_00130_File_No_741A, National Archives of
     India, New Delhi.
7.   Ibid.
8.   Sir R. Lumley to the Marquess of Linlithgow, M.S.S. EUR. F. 125/57
     dated 12 March 1943, British Library, London.
9.   *Proceedings of the Sind Legislative Assembly,* Official Report, Vol. xvii, No. 6,
     3 March 1943, pp. 17–43.
10. Ibid.
11. V.D. Savarkar, *Historic Statements,* p. 65.
12. Ibid.
13. Letter dated 14 January 1944, Intercepts by the DIB, HOME_
     POLITICAL_I_1944_NA_F-51-4, National Archives of India, New Delhi.
14. 'Fortnightly Reports for May 1943'; Home_Political_1_1943_NA_F-18-5-
     43, National Archives of India, New Delhi.
15. V.D. Savarkar, *Historic Statements*, pp. 68–69.
16. 'Copy of Proceedings of the Working Committee of the All-India Hindu
     Mahasabha held on 7-8 August 1943 at Bombay', NA_1_1943_NA_F-9-5,
     National Archives of India, New Delhi.
17. Fortnightly Reports for May 1943, HOME__POLITICAL_1_1943_
     NA_18-5-43, National Archives of India, New Delhi.
18. Keer, *Veer Savarkar*, pp. 350–51.
19. Fortnightly Reports for May 1943, HOME__POLITICAL_1_1943_
     NA_18-5-43, National Archives of India, New Delhi.
20. Ibid.
21. Ibid.
22. V.D. Savarkar, *Historic Statements,* p. 66.
23. 'Letter from Field Marshal Viscount Wavell to Mr. Amery', dated 29
     November 1944; L/PO/10/21, British Library, London.
24. Shashi Tharoor, *An Era of Darkness: The British Empire in India*, New Delhi:
     Aleph, 2016, pp. 187–88.
25. Ibid.
26. V.D. Savarkar, *Historic Statements,* pp. 60–61.
27. File No. 87/43-Poll (I), PR_000005014536, National Archives of India,
     New Delhi.
28. Ibid.
29. Ibid.
30. J.S. Bright, *The Woman Behind Gandhi*, Lahore: Paramount Publications,
     n.d., p. 107.
31. V.D. Savarkar, *Historic Statements*, p. 70.

32. Ibid.
33. Ibid., p. 73.
34. Confidential Letter released by Chicago-based researcher Shridhar Damle and quoted in http://savarkar.org/en/encyc/2018/3/23/Download-section.html
35. V.D. Savarkar, *Historic Statements*, p. 74.
36. 'Intercepted Letter dated 18 June 1944, from V.G. Deshpande, Secretary AIHMS, New Delhi, to Pandit Sukhdeo Behari Misra, General Secretary, Oudh Province HMS, Lucknow', HOME_POLITICAL_I_1944_NA_F-9-1, National Archives of India, New Delhi.
37. *The Constitution of the Hindusthan Free State*, Printed by V.G. Ketkar, Poona: Loksangraha Press, pp. ii–iii.
38. Ibid., p. v.
39. Ibid., p. 1.
40. Ibid., pp. 4–5.
41. Ibid., pp. 5–7.
42. Ibid., p. 9.
43. https://www.constitutionofindia.net/constitution_assembly_debates/volume/11/1949-11-18
44. Statement of Accused No. 7: Savarkar: Mahatma Gandhi Murder Case Trial, p. 57, National Archives of India, New Delhi.
45. *St. Petersburg Times*, 13 July 1944, British Newspaper Archive (BNA), British Library, London.
46. V.P. Menon, *The Transfer of Power in India*. Longman, 1957, p. 160.
47. Ibid., pp. 160-61.
48. Ibid., p. 161.
49. V.D. Savarkar, *Historic Statements*, p. 77.
50. Ibid.
51. Ibid., p. 78.
52. Minuted in the file by Gibson, that he did not consider it necessary to acknowledge this telegram.
53. Telegram of Savarkar to Amery: L/P&J/8/683: ff. 56–57.
54. 'News from India: Dated 1 September 1944' HOME_POLITICAL_I_1944_NA_F-51-8_KW_PART-2; National Archives of India, New Delhi.
55. Ibid., dated 26 August 1944.
56. Ibid.
57. Ibid.
58. Ibid.
59. Fortnightly Report for the month of August 1944: HOME_POLITICAL_I_1944_NA_F-18-8, National Archives of India, New Delhi.
60. 'News from India: Dated 1 September 1944', HOME_POLITICAL_I_1944_NA_F-51-8_KW_PART-2; National Archives of India, New Delhi.

61. Ibid.
62. Fortnightly Report for the month of August 1944: HOME_
     POLITICAL_I_1944_NA_F-18-8, National Archives of India, New
     Delhi.
63. Ibid.
64. V.P. Menon, *The Transfer of Power in India*. Longman, 1957., p. 163.
65. RCM #154 (Ibid., p. 163).
66. Menon, *Transfer of Power*, p. 163.
67. V.D. Savarkar, *Historic Statements*, p. 87.
68. V.D. Savarkar, *Hindu Rashtra Darshan*, n.d., p. 130.
69. Keer, *Veer Savarkar*, p. 360.
70. V.D. Savarkar, *Historic Statements*, pp. 86–87.
71. Ibid., p. 93.
72. D.N. Gokhale, *Krantiveer Babarao Savarkar*, Poona: Srividya Prakashan,
     1979., pp. 114–15.
73. Ibid. p. 116.
74. Ibid., pp. 118–20.
75. Gandhi, *The Collected Works*, p. 86.
     Also see: https://www.gandhiashramsevagram.org/gandhiliterature/mahatma-
     gandhi-collected-works-volume-86.pdf
76. V.D. Savarkar, *Historic Statements*, p. 96.
77. Ibid., p. 97.
78. Ibid., p. 98.
79. Press Report: Wavell Papers, Political Series, April 1944–July 1945, Pt. 1,
     pp. 244–45; #510 in Transfer of Power, Volume 5.
80. 'Letter from Field Marshal Viscount Wavell to Mr. Amery', dated 1 July
     1945; L/PO/10/21, British Library, London.
81. Telegram #237, dated 9 January 1945: Governor General to Secretary
     of State, I&B Department Weekly Appreciation Reports, HOME_
     POLITICAL_I_1945_NA_F-51-3, National Archives of India, New
     Delhi.
82. Keer, *Veer Savarkar*, p. 366.
83. V.D. Savarkar, *Historic Statements*, p. 103.
84. Fortnightly Report of May 1945, HOME_POLITICAL_I_1945_NA_F-
     18-5, National Archives of India, New Delhi.
85. Keer, *Veer Savarkar*, p. 371.
86. Ibid.
87. Ibid., p. 372.
88. Ibid., p. 371.
89. Leonard Mosley, *Last Days of the British Raj*. Harcourt, Brace & World,
     Inc.1962 p. 12.

90. V.D. Savarkar, *Historic Statements*, p. 130.

91. L/WS/1/1577:ff:142-7, "India and Burma Committee Paper (IB)(45) 16. Memorandum by Secretary of State for India & Burma," Annexure 1; British Library, London.

92. Letter from Field Marshall Viscount Wavell to Lord Pethick-Lawrence, dated 31 October 1945; L/WS/1/1577: ff:96-100, British Library, London.

93. Quoted in *Indian Independence League*'s publication and in Keer, *Veer Savarkar*, p. 350.

94. This was published in Himani Savarkar, *Tejasvi Taare* (in *Samagra Savarkar* Vol. 5), Mumbai: Savarkar Smárak, n.d., p. 397.

95. Keer, *Veer Savarkar*, pp. 349–50.

96. Arun (compiled and edited), *Testament of Subhas Bose, 1942-1945*, Delhi: Rajkamal Publication, 1946, p. 24.

97. Letter courtesy Prof. Kapil Kumar.

98. Interview with author.

99. N.B. Khare, *My Political Memoirs or Autobiography*, Nagpur: J.R. Joshi, n.d., p. 64.

100. Ibid. p. 63.

101. Menon, *Transfer of Power*, pp. 240-41.

102. Majumdar, *History of Freedom Movement in India*, pp. 769–70.

103. Leonard Mosley, *Last Days of the British Raj*. Harcourt, Brace & World, Inc. 1962, p. 27.

104. Ibid., p. 11.

105. Menon, *Transfer of Power*, p. 319.

106. Ibid., p. 323.

107. Majumdar, *History of Freedom Movement in India*, p. 791.

108. Ibid.

109. Larry Collins and Dominique Lapierre, *Mountbatten and the Partition of India*, New Delhi: Wide Canvas, 1982, p. 27.

110. Majumdar, *History of Freedom Movement in India*, p. 793.

111. Ibid.

112. Gandhi, *The Collected Works*, pp. 248–49.

113. Majumdar, *History of Freedom Movement in India*, Vols 1–3, p. 796.

114. Ibid., p. 800.

115. Ibid.

116. Ibid., p. 801.

117. Collins and Lapiere, *Mountbatten and the Partition*, p. 125.

118. V.D. Savarkar, *Historic Statements*, p. 131.

119. Ibid., p. 135.

120. Majumdar, *History of Freedom Movement in India*, Vol. 3, p. 810.

121. Maulana Abul Kalam Azad, *India Wins Freedom: An Autobiographical Account*, Hyderabad: Orient Longman Limited, 1959, p. 198.
122. Majumdar, *History of Freedom Movement in India, Vol. 3*, p. 813.
123. V.D. Savarkar, *Historic Statements*, p. 136.
124. Ibid., p. 137.
125. Collins and Lapiere, *Mountbatten and the Partition*, p. 144.
126. V.D. Savarkar, *Historic Statements*, p. 138.
127. Ibid., pp. 139–40.
128. Gandhi, *The Collected Works*, pp. 86–87.
129. Ibid., p. 196.
130. Jaywant D. Joglekar, *Veer Savarkar: Father of Hindu Nationalism*, n.p. n.d. p. 158.
131. Majumdar, *History of Freedom Movement in India*, Vol. 3, p. 820.
132. V.D. Savarkar, *Historic Statements*, p. 142.
133. Ibid.
134. Ibid.
135. Ibid., p. 144.
136. Ibid.
137. Ibid., p. 145.
138. Ibid., p. 146.

Chapter 9: Murder, Mayhem, Madness

1. Letter courtesy Savarkar Rashtriya Smarak, obtained from National Archives of India, New Delhi # D/83
2. For more details see Malgonkar, Manohar. *The Men Who Killed Gandhi*. New Delhi: Roli Books, 2008.
3. Ex. D/22. Letter from Apte to Savarkar, dated 13 February 1938, Mahatma Gandhi Murder Case trial, Volume V, pp. 3–4, National Archives of India, New Delhi.
4. Ex. D/23. Letter from Apte to Savarkar, dated 29 October 1938, Mahatma Gandhi Murder Case trial, Volume V, pp. 3–4, National Archives of India, New Delhi.
5. Ex. D/29, Letter from Nathuram Godse to Savarkar, dated 30 October 1946, Mahatma Gandhi Murder Case Trial, Vol. V, p. 16. National Archives of India, New Delhi.
6. Ex. D/15, Mahatma Gandhi Murder Case Trial, Vol. V, p. 4, National Archives of India, New Delhi.
7. Ibid.
8. Ex. D/19, Statement of Witness No. 5 for the prosecution dated 24 February 1948, Mahatma Gandhi Murder Case Trial, Vol. V, p. 8. National Archives of India, New Delhi.

9.   Manohar Malgonkar, *The Men Who Killed Gandhi*, New Delhi: Roli Books, 2008, p. 150.
10.   Jeevan Lal Kapur Commission Report, 1969, p. 15.
11.   Malgonkar, *The Men Who Killed Gandhi*, p. 176.
12.   Ex. D/11. Mahatma Gandhi Murder Case Trial, Volume V, pp. 3–4, National Archives of India, New Delhi.
13.   Malgonkar, *The Men Who Killed Gandhi*, p. 199.
14.   Ibid.
15.   Ex. D/3, Mahatma Gandhi Murder Case Trial, Volume V, p. 1. National Archives of India, New Delhi.
16.   Malgonkar, *The Men Who Killed Gandhi*, p. 236.
17.   Ex. D/115, Mahatma Gandhi Murder Case Trial, Volume V, p. 50, National Archives of India, New Delhi.
18.   Ibid., p. 239.
19.   *New York Times*, 31 January 1948, pp. 1–2, NYT Web Archive.
20.   Koenraad Elst, *Gandhi and Godse: A Review and a Critique*, New Delhi: Voice of India, 2001, p. 12.
21.   P.L. Inamdar, *The Story of the Red Fort Trial 1948-1949*, Bombay: Popular Prakashan, 1979, p. 4.
22.   Maureen L.P. Patterson, 'The Shifting Fortunes of Chitpavan Brahmins: The Focus on 1948', in *City, Countryside and Society in Maharashtra*, D.W. Atwood et al. (eds.), University of Toronto, Centre for South Asian Studies, 1998, pp. 36, 54.
23.   Ibid. p. 37.
24.   Dwarka Prasad Mishra, *Living an Era*, New Delhi: Har Anand Publications, 2001, p. 72.
25.   *Kesari*, 14 February 1948, Kesari Archives, Pune.
26.   Maureen L.P. Patterson, 'The Shifting Fortunes of Chitpavan Brahmins: The Focus on 1948', in *City, Countryside and Society in Maharashtra*, in D.W. Atwood et al. (eds.), University of Toronto, Centre for South Asian Studies, 1998, p. 38.
27.   Ibid., p. 39.
28.   *Kesari*, 23 April 1948.
29.   Maureen L.P. Patterson, 'The Shifting Fortunes of Chitpavan Brahmins: The Focus on 1948', in D.W. Atwood et al. (eds.). *City, Countryside and Society in Maharashtra*, pp. 39–40.
30.   Madhavrao Bagal was a noted artist, writer, journalist and orator.
31.   Stated by Patterson, pp. 43–44 'The Shifting Fortunes of Chitpavan Brahmins: The Focus on 1948', in D.W. Atwood et al. (eds.), *City, Countryside and Society in Maharashtra*, and quoted from 'Kolhapur State, *Report of the Commission of Enquiry appointed by H.H. the Chhatrapati Maharajasaheb of*

Kolhapur and presided over by the Hon'ble Justice N.H.C. Coyajee, Kolhapur
Government Press, 9 October 1948'.

32. Maureen L.P. Patterson, 'The Shifting Fortunes of Chitpavan Brahmins:
     The Focus on 1948,' in D.W. Atwood et al. (eds.), *City, Countryside and
     Society in Maharashtra*, University of Toronto, Centre for South Asian
     Studies, 1998, p. 47.

33. Ibid. p. 52.

34. Dwarka Prasad Mishra, *Living an Era*, New Delhi: Har Anand Publications,
     2001, p. 73.

35. Ibid., p. 74.

36. Ibid.

37. 'Digitized Private Papers of Sardar Patel: Letters and Newspaper Articles',
     PP_000000005710, National Archives of India, New Delhi.

38. Ibid.

39. Ibid.

40. Maureen L.P. Patterson, 'The Shifting Fortunes of Chitpavan Brahmins:
     The Focus on 1948', in D.W. Atwood et al. (eds.), *City, Countryside and
     Society in Maharashtra*, p. 37.

41. Testimony of Jamshed Dorab Nagarvala, Deposition of Witnesses in the
     Mahatma Gandhi Murder Case Trial, Volume III. National Archives of
     India, New Delhi.

42. Testimony of Police Inspector Anandarao Raghunathrao Pradhan who
     looked into and serialized the 143 files recovered from Savarkar Sadan,
     Deposition of Witnesses in the Mahatma Gandhi Murder Case Trial,
     Volume III. National Archives of India, New Delhi. He states that there
     were in all seventeen files relating to 1943 and ten of 1944. None of these
     were from Gandhi to Savarkar. Some 101 letters were from Nathuram to
     Savarkar.

43. Testimony of Gajjanan Balakrishna Kowlankar, Deposition of Witnesses in
     the Mahatma Gandhi Murder Case Trial, Volume III. National Archives of
     India, New Delhi.

44. 'Digitized Private Papers of Sardar Patel: Letters and Newspaper Articles',
     PP_000000005710, National Archives of India, New Delhi.

45. Keer, *Veer Savarkar*, p. 404.

46. Dwarka Prasad Mishra, *Living an Era*, New Delhi: Har Anand Publications,
     2001, p. 75.

47. Keer, *Veer Savarkar*, p. 403.

48. Statement of Accused No. 7: Savarkar: Mahatma Gandhi Murder Case
     Trial, pp. 61, National Archives of India, New Delhi.

49. 'Digitized Private Papers of Sardar Patel: Letters and Newspaper Articles',
     PP_000000005710, National Archives of India, New Delhi.

50. Ex. D/102. Mahatma Gandhi Murder Case Trial, Volume V, p. 46, National Archives of India, New Delhi.
51. Keer, *Veer Savarkar*, p. 404.
52. Ex. D/103. Mahatma Gandhi Murder Case Trial, Volume V, pp. 46–47, National Archives of India, New Delhi.
53. Ex. D/104. Mahatma Gandhi Murder Case Trial, Volume V. pp. 47–49, National Archives of India, New Delhi.
54. Tushar Gandhi, *Let's Kill Gandhi*, New Delhi: Rupa Publications, 2007, pp. xvii–xviii.
55. Durga Das (ed.), *Sardar Patel's Correspondence 1945-50*, Volume VI, Ahmedabad: Navjivan Publishing House, 1973, pp. 56–57.
56. Manohar Malgonkar, *The Men Who Killed Gandhi*, New Delhi: Roli Books, 2008, p. 332.
57. Ibid.
58. Ibid., p. 333.
59. Ibid., p. 334.
60. Deposition of Witnesses in the Mahatma Gandhi Murder Case Trial, Volume III, National Archives of India, New Delhi.
61. N.B. Khare, *My Political Memoirs or Autobiography*, Nagpur: Shri J.R. Joshi, n.d., pp. 368–69.
62. Ex. D/18, Affidavit of Mr. Vinayak Damodar Savarkar, Mahatma Gandhi Murder Case Trial, Volume V, p. 7, National Archives of India, New Delhi.
63. Durga Das (ed.), *Sardar Patel's Correspondence 1945-50*, Volume VI, Ahmedabad: Navjivan Publishing House, 1973, p. 63.
64. Ibid. p. 65.

Chapter 10: The Red Fort Trial

1. P.L. Inamdar, *The Story of the Red Fort Trial 1948-1949*, Bombay: Popular Prakashan, 1979, p. 141.
2. Ibid., p. 74.
3. Ibid., p. 76.
4. Ibid., p. 79.
5. Ibid., p. 143.
6. Ibid.
7. Ibid., p. 141.
8. Statement of Accused: Nathuram Godse, Mahatma Gandhi Murder Case Trial, Volume IV, p. 99, National Archives of India, New Delhi.
9. Ibid., pp. 108–09.
10. Ibid., p. 31.
11. Ibid., p. 32.

12. Ibid., p. 33.

13. Ibid.

14. Ibid., p. 34.

15. Ibid., pp. 36–37.

16. P.L. Inamdar, *The Story of the Red Fort Trial 1948-1949*, Bombay: Popular Prakashan, 1979, p. 94.

17. Statement of Accused: Nathuram Godse; Mahatma Gandhi Murder Case Trial, Volume IV, p. 112, National Archives of India, New Delhi.

18. Inamdar, *Story of the Red Fort Trial*, p. 142.

19. Tushar Gandhi, *Let's Kill Gandhi*, New Delhi: Rupa Publications, 2007, p. 607.

20. Ibid., p. 636.

21. Inamdar, *Story of the Red Fort Trial*, pp. 91–92.

22. Statement of Accused No. 7: Savarkar; Mahatma Gandhi Murder Case Trial, pp. 10–11, National Archives of India, New Delhi.

23. Ibid., pp. 12–13.

24. Ibid.

25. Ex. P/286 and Ex. P/299; Ibid., p. 15.

26. Ibid., p. 18.

27. Ibid., p. 21.

28. Ibid., p. 23.

29. Ibid., p. 26.

30. Ibid., pp. 29–30.

31. Ibid., p. 35.

32. Ibid., p. 39.

33. Ibid., p. 60.

34. Ibid., p. 48.

35. Ibid., p. 49.

36. Ibid., pp. 49–50.

37. Gandhi, *Let's Kill Gandhi*, p. 636.

38. Statement of Accused No. 7: Savarkar; Mahatma Gandhi Murder Case Trial, pp. 57-58, National Archives of India, New Delhi.

39. Inamdar, *Story of the Red Fort Trial*, p. 142.

40. Ibid., p. 98.

41. Robert Payne, *The Life and Death of Mahatma Gandhi*, New Delhi: Rupa Publications, 1969, pp. 618–19.

42. Ibid., p. 642.

43. Inamdar, *Story of the Red Fort Trial*, p. 144.

44. Ibid.

45. Gopal Godse, *Why I Assassinated Gandhi*, Delhi: Farsight Publisher and Distributors, 2017, p. 130.

See also, *Hindustan Times*, 10 February 1948, quoted in Volume 3 of the Mahatma Gandhi Murder Case Trial, National Archives of India, New Delhi.

46. Judgment in the Mahatma Gandhi Murder Case Trial, National Archives of India, New Delhi.

47. Ibid.

48. Ibid.

49. G.D. Khosla, *The Murder of the Mahatma and Other Cases from a Judge's Notebook*, Bombay: Jaico Press Pvt. Ltd, 1977, p. 19.

50. Ibid, pp. 47-48.

51. Gandhi, *Let's Kill Gandhi*, p. 573.

52. Quoted in Manohar Malgonkar, *The Men Who Killed Gandhi*, New Delhi: Roli Books, 2008, p. 284.

53. Narayan Sadashiv Bapat, *Smruti Pushpe*, Charuchandra Publication, 1984, pp. 60–61.

54. S. L. Karandikar, *Savarkar Charitra Kathan*, Pune: Modern Book Depot, Prakashan, 1947, p. 445.

55. Arvind Godbole, *Mala Umajlele Swatyatraveer Savarkar*, Pune: Bharatiya Vichar Sadhana Publication, 2011, p. 167.

56. *Mumbai Tarun Bharat*, 28 May 2017.

57. Jawaharlal Nehru, *Selected Works of Jawaharlal Nehru*, Series 2, Vol. 5 (January–April 1948), Delhi: B.R. Publishing Corporation, 1988, pp. 30–31.

58. Ibid., pp. 46–47.

59. *Sardar Patel's Correspondence 1945-50*, Durgadas (ed.), Ahmedabad: Navjivan Publishing House, 1973, Vol. VI, p. 81.

60. Ibid., p. 86.

61. V.D. Savarkar, *Historic Statements*, p. 137.

62. Inamdar, *Story of the Red Fort Trial*, p. 145.

Chapter 11: Twilight Tales

1. V.D. Savarkar, *Historic Statements*, p. 140.

2. Ibid.

3. Ibid., p. 141.

4. Ibid., pp. 141–42.

5. *Bombay Chronicle*, 5 April 1950, Digitized Private Papers of Sardar Patel, PP000000005203, National Archives of India, New Delhi.

6. *The Free Press Journal*, 5 April 1950.

7. Jawaharlal Nehru, *Selected Works of Jawaharlal Nehru*, Series 2, Vol. 15 (Part 1), New Delhi: Jawaharlal Nehru Memorial Fund, 1993. pp. 159–60.

8. V.D. Savarkar, *Historic Statements*, p. 146.

9. Ibid., p. 149.

10. Keer, *Veer Savarkar*, p. 438.

11. Ibid., pp. 443–44.

12. N.B. Khare, *My Political Memoirs or Autobiography*, Nagpur: J.R. Joshi, 1959, p. 450.

13. Ibid.

14. Keer, *Veer Savarkar*, p. 442.

15. *Kesari*, 26 January 1954.

16. Ibid.

17. Ibid., 4 July 1954.

18. Ibid.

19. Keer, *Veer Savarkar*, pp. 492–93.

20. Ibid., p. 493.

21. Account given by Prof. V.G. Deshpande, quoted in ibid., p. 500.

22. Ibid., p. 520.

23. V.D. Savarkar, *Six Golden Epochs of Indian History*, translated and edited by S.T. Godbole, Bombay: Bal Savarkar, Savarkar Sadan, 1971.

24. Ibid., p. 131.

25. Ibid., p. 167.

26. Ibid., p. 169.

27. Ibid., p. 175.

28. Ibid., p. 179.

29. Ibid., pp. 180–81.

30. Ibid., p. 237.

31. Keer, *Veer Savarkar*, p. 532.

32. Interview of Hridaynath Mangeshkar to a Marathi news channel, ABP Majha, 13 January 2018.

33. *Organiser*, Diwali 1965 (Original Copy Courtesy Akshay Jog).

34. *Sahyadri*, July 1964.

35. Ibid.

36. Keer, *Veer Savarkar*, p. 543.

37. Ibid.

38. Reference from: Vishwas Savarkar, *Aathavani Angaarachya*, Pune: Snehal Prakashan, 2001, pp. 24–25.

39. Keer, *Veer Savarkar*, p. 548.

40. Ibid.

41. Ibid.

42. Ibid., pp. 547-48

Chapter 12: Contentious Legacy

1. J.L. Kapur Commission Report, Vol. 1, p. 61.

2.   Ibid., p. 3.
3.   Ibid., p. 92.
4.   Ibid., p. 124.
5.   Ibid.
6.   Ibid., pp. 125–28.
7.   Ibid., p. 165.
8.   Ibid., Vol. 3, p. 301.
9.   Ibid., Vol. 4, p. 53.
10. Ibid., p. 67.
11. Ibid., p. 53.
12. Ibid., Vol. 2, p. 246.
13. Ibid., p. 250.
14. Ibid., Vol. 4, p. 358.
15. Ibid.
16. Ibid., p. 359.
17. Ibid., pp. 360–62.
18. Ibid., p. 303.
19. Ibid., p. 301.
20. Ibid., p. 300.
21. Special Leave Petition (Civil) 8293 of 2018 [Arising out of D. No. 15103/2017], p. 3.
22. Ibid., pp. 3–4. Also available at: https://sci.gov.in/supremecourt/2017/15103/15103_2017_Judgement_28-Mar- 2018.pdf
23. Ibid., pp. 3–4. Also available at: https://sci.gov.in/supremecourt/2017/15103/15103_2017_Judgement_28-Mar- 2018.pdf
24. Vidyadhar Pundalik, 'Sati', in *Devchaafa* (A Short Story Collection), Bombay: Mauj Prakashan, 2010, pp. 24–57.
25. Letter Courtesy Swatantryaveer Savarkar Rashtriya Smarak, Mumbai.
26. Ashis Nandy, 'A disowned father of the nation in India: Vinayak Damodar Savarkar and the demonic and the seductive in Indian nationalism', *Inter-Asia Cultural Studies*, Vol. 15, No. 1, pp. 91–112, 2014
27. Ibid., p. 91.
28. Translation by Anurupa Cinar, http://anurupacinar.com/wp-content/uploads/2013/09/Atmabal-Translation.pdf

Bibliography

1) Unpublished Government Records

National Archives of India (NAI), New Delhi
Home (Public) Proceedings (These include files from the Ecclesiastical, Educational, Judicial, and Police Departments)
Home (Political) Proceedings including Fortnightly Reports, 'A' and 'B' files

Mahatma Gandhi Murder Trial Papers, NAI, New Delhi:

Sl. No.	Exhibit No.	Subject	No. of Pages	Remarks
1	P-8, P-9, 10	Payment of Bills Reg:	206	
		a) Rent for one day		
		b) Food etc.		
2	P-257, 257A	Horoscope by Shankar Das Jyotishi	322	
3	P-72	Entry Register of a Hotel	64	
4	P-135	One Diary Register-Addl. District Magistrate, Poona		
5	P-185-C	Special Branch CID, Bombay, Criminal Reports 20.1.1948 and 30.1.1948	283	Crime Report from 1 to 91 along with history of Hindu Mahasabha
6	P-14	Visitor Index book—Hotel Marina	56	

Sl. No.	Exhibit No.	Subject	No. of Pages	Remarks
7	P-367-A	The Gwalior Quarterly Civil List	202	
8	P-170 & 171	Single ticket Entry Book— Railways from 24.1.48 to 3.2.48	70	
9	P-4, P-5, P-6, P-7	Register showing the particulars of customers Detailed book	121	
10	P-270, 271	Register Deccan College Students	149	
11	P-267-268	Delhi—Air India Booklet No. 565—Passenger Ticket (Internal: Bombay-Delhi-Bombay)	106	
12	P-39	Receipt book (hotel) Payment for daily routine	103	
13	D-20	Passenger Ticket (Internal) Air India	103	
14	P-106 & 106	Receipt book (hotel) Payment for daily routine	102	
15	P-366A	The Gwalior Quarterly Civil List XLIV	202	
16	P-363A	Civil List of the Gwalior State	84	
17	P-364A	Civil List of the Gwalior State	102	
18	P-362	Civil List of the Gwalior State - Quarterly List	37	
19	P-362A TO P-362	The Quarterly Civil List for the Gwalior State No X since March 1910	78	
20	-	Yearly report	21	
21	-	Register Dabike and Co.	443	
22	-	Book—'Hindustani Dawakhana'	153	
23	-	Statement of Accused in original	236	
24	-	Important Papers Vol. V1	124	

Sl. No.	Exhibit No.	Subject	No. of Pages	Remarks
25	-	Printed Record Mahatma Gandhi Murder Case- Vol. 11	234	
26	-	FIR No. 68, Dated 30 January 1948—Vol. 11, Original Appeal Nos 66, 67, 68, 70, 71 & 72 of 1949, in the High Court of Judicature for the Province of East Punjab and Simla	161	
27	-	-do- Vol. 1	209	
28	-	Original Vol. 11, Deposition of witnesses, PW1 to PW77	186	
29	-	FIR No 40 dated 30 January 1948, Vol. 1	326	
30	-	Original Vol.1 Important Papers	274	
31	-	Vol.11- Judgement of the Special Judge, Red Fort, Delhi	73	
32	-	Original Volume 7- c	356	
33	-	Unimportant papers	151	
34	-	Vol. VII, Typed record of Documents in Marathi- Important papers	100	
35	-	Vol. 7(A) unimportant papers	99	
36	-	Original Vol 7-B unimportant papers	346	
37	P-348	Attendance Register- NWR	395	
38	P-348	-Do-	21	
39	P-349	Attendance Register, Telegraph Peon Delhi	44	
40	P-346	One NWR Register	183	
41	-	Original Statement of Accused	284	
42	-	Vol IV	136	
43	P-20	Credit Note	107	
44	P-187 P19	Credit Voucher- Hotel Marina	113	

Sl. No.	Exhibit No.	Subject	No. of Pages	Remarks
45	P-73	Credit Voucher- NWR	54	
46	P-61	NWR- Credit Voucher- Retiring Room	53	
47	P-377	One horoscope in Sanskrit		
48	-	Statement of Accused- Shankar, Vinayak Damodar Savarkar and Madan Lal before Deputy Commissioner of Police, Special Branch, CID Bombay	88	
49	P-13	One register including names	55	
50	P-323, 324, 338, 378	One envelope containing Diary	30	
51	-	Deposition of Witnesses- Vol. 3	244	
52	-	Judgment of the Full Bench	301	
53	-	The Jayaji Pratap, Weekly	349	
54	P-1	Register- Sharif Hotel Delhi	49	
55	-		74	
56	-	Original Judgment	211	
57	P-368	The Half Yearly Gwalior Army List	92	
58	P-36, 38	One form of register under Section 8 of the Serais Act	194	
59	P-167 17	Hotel Marina Bill Register	104	
60	P-347	Duty Register of Hotel	80	
61	P-233 TO P-344	Register Containing Panchnama (Vol. 5-C)	372	
62	P-345 TO P-404	Original Misc. Documents (Vol. 5-D)	254	
63	-	Prosecution Exhibits (Vol. IV)	156	
64	D1 TO D119	Newspaper Cuttings (Vol. 5E)	303	
65	-	Printed Records (Vol. V)	72	

Sl. No.	Exhibit No.	Subject	No. of Pages	Remarks
66	P-132 TO 230	Specimen handwriting of Nathuram Godse and others (Vol. 5B)	345	
67	–	Judgment in Mahatma Gandhi Murder Case	207	
68		Criminal Appeal Judgment	55 (14)	
		Total No of Pages	11,186	

Maharashtra State Archives, Bombay
Fortnightly Reports
Home Department (Political) Records
Home Department (Public) Records
Judicial Department Records
Revenue Department Records
Police Department Records
Plague Compilation

Deputy Inspector General's Office, Bombay
Secret Abstract of Police Intelligence for the Bombay Presidency

Oriental and India Office Collections, London
Bombay (Home) Confidential Proceedings
Bombay Judicial Proceedings
Bombay Political Proceedings
EPP/1/3 (Proscribed Publications in non-European Languages)
Legal Adviser's Records: L/L Series
Military Department: L/MIL/7 Series
Public and Judicial Records L/P&J/6 Series
Political and Secret Department: L/PS/8 Series
Political Department: Indian States: R/R Series
Private Manuscripts: MSS EUR Series

National Archives of UK (Kew), London
Colonial Office (CO)
Foreign Office (FO)
Home Office (HO)
Metropolitan Police (MEPO)

2) Private Papers

Oriental and India Office Collections, London
Dow Papers, Mss. Eur. E 372
Hirtzel Diaries. Mss. Eur. D 1090
Lamington Papers, Mss. Eur. B 159
Montague Papers, Mss. Eur. D 523
Morley Papers, Mss. Eur. D 573
Northbrook Papers
Reading Papers, Mss. Eur. E 238
Willingdon Papers, Mss. Eur. F 93
Memoirs of Sir Maurice Henry Weston Hayward, ICS Bombay, 1889-1926, Mss. Eur. D 839
Linlithgow Collection, Mss. Eur. 125

National Archives of India, New Delhi
N.C. Kelkar Papers
Sardar Patel Papers
M.R. Jayakar Papers

ILI, New Delhi

Justice Jeevan Lal Kapur Commission Report, Vol. 1-4

Nehru Memorial Museum and Library, New Delhi
Ambedkar Papers
Mohamed Ali Papers
All-India Congress Committee Papers
All-India Hindu Mahasabha Papers
Savarkar Papers.
Syama Prasad Mookerjee Papers
B.S. Moonje Papers
Oral Archives—Transcripts of Interviews—Senapati Bapat, Prithvi Singh Azad and Durgadas Khanna.

Kesari Office, Pune
Tilak Papers
Press cuttings

3) Published Government Sources

Administration Report of the Government of Bombay
Bombay Legislative Council Debates
Bombay Gazette
Gazetteer of the Bombay Presidency (all vols.)
Indian Annual Register (I.A.R.)
Indian Quarterly Register
Indian Law Reports, Bombay Series
Source Material For A History of the Freedom Movement In India. Bombay, Bombay
    State Publication, 1957
Terrorism in India: 1917-1936; Compiled in the Intelligence Bureau, Home
    Department, Government of India, 1937

4) Other Published Sources

Ambedkar, B. R. *Dr. Babasaheb Ambedkar, Writings and Speeches.* Bombay,
    Government of Maharashtra, 1979.
Gandhi, M.K. *The Collected Works of Mahatma Gandhi.* Ahmedabad, 1967.
Indian National Congress Presidential Addresses, 1881–1924.
Foreign Relations of the Unites States, Diplomatic Papers, 1942, Vol. 1.
The History of the Bhagalpur Struggle: The 23rd Session of the A.I.H. Mahasabha,
    Limited publication by Madhukari Bookseller, Publishers & General Order
    Supplier, Bhagalpur City, 1942.
Ratnagiri Hindu Sabeche Pahilya Paanch Varshaanche Prativrutta, Part I: 23
    January 1924 to 31 December 1928. Published by M.G. Shinde, Vice
    President of Ratnagiri Hindu Sabha & Printed by G.V. Patwardhan, Balwant
    Mudranalaya, Ratnagiri, November 1929.
N. Mansergh and E.W.R. Lumby (eds.). *Constitutional Relations between Britain
    and India: The Transfer of Power 1942-7.* Volumes 1-12. London, 1970.
'Arun' (compiled and edited). *Testament of Subhas Bose, 1942-1945.* Delhi:
    Rajkamal Prakashan, 1946.
Durga Das (ed.), *Sardar Patel's Correspondence 1945-50,* Navjivan Publishing
    House, Ahmedabad, 1973.
Selected Works of Jawaharlal Nehru. New Delhi: B.R. Publishing Corporation,
    1988.
Jamil-Ud-Din, *Speeches of Jinnah,* Lucknow Session of the League, 1937.
The Constitution of the Hindusthan Free State, Printed by V.G. Ketkar, Poona:
    Loksangraha Press, 1945.

5) Works of Vinayak Damodar Savarkar

Samagra Savarkar Vangmaya. 8 Vols. Poona: Maharshtra Prantik, 1963.

Savarkar Samagra, 10 Vols. New Delhi: Prabhat Prakashan, 2000.

The Indian War of Independence of 1857, London: n.p. 1909.

Londonchi Baatmipatre (Newsletters from London), 1940.

An Echo from Andamans, Poona: Venus Book Stall, 1947. (eds.) *Historic Statements.* Bombay: Popular Prakashan, 1967.

My Transportation for Life, Bombay: Veer Savarkar Prakashan, 1984.

Inside the Enemy Camp (Shatruchya Shibiraat)

Josepha Majhini: Atmacharitra ani RaajakaaraNa

Hindutva: Who Is a Hindu? Bombay: Swatantryaveer Savarkar Rashtriya Smarak, 1999 (7th ed.).

Six Golden Epochs of Indian History. Translated and edited by S.T. Godbole. Published by Bal Savarkar, Savarkar Sadan, Bombay, 1971.

Historic Statements by Savarkar, Edited by S.S. Savarkar and G.M. Joshi. Bombay: Popular Prakashan, 1967.

Veer Savarkar's "Whirl-wind Propaganda.": Statements, Messages & Extracts from the President's Diary of His Propagandistic Tours, Interviews from December 1937 to October 1941, n.p. 1941.

A Hot Spicy Medley, Bombay: Swatantryaveer Savarkar Rashtriya Smarak Trust, n.d. *Hindu Rashtra Darshan.* Poona: Maharashtra Prantik Hindu Sabha, n.d.

Krantighosh: Speeches of V.D. Savarkar by Balarao Savarkar, Manorama Prakashan, 1st ed., 1994.

Sputha Lekh, Bombay: Veer Savarkar Prakashan, 1982.

Hindu-Pada Padashahi or a Review of the Hindu Empire of Maharashtra. Madras: B.G. Paul & Co., 1925.

Veer Savarkar Prakashan, Bombay. 1972 compilations by Balarao Savarkar:
- *Hindu Samaj Samrakshak Swatantryaveer V.D. Savarkar*
- *Ratnagiri Parva*
- *Hindu Mahasabha Parva*
- *Akhand Hindustan Ladha Parva*

6) Newspapers

Amrita Bazar Patrika
Bande Mataram
Bombay Chronice
Comrade
Dai Ajia Shugi

Dnyan Prakash
Forward
Harijan
Hindustan Standard
Hindustan Times
HT Mint
Indian Express
Indian Mirror
Indu Prakash
Kaal
Kesari
Kirloskar Magazine
Madina
Mahratta
Mumbai Tarun Bharat
Navjivan
New York Times
Organiser
Prabhat
Quarterly Journal of the Poona Sarvajanik Sabha
Sahyadri
Sakal
Samata
Shraddhanand
Sudharak
The Free Press Journal
The Pioneer
The Search Light
The Hindu
The Justice
Times of India
Young India

British Newspaper Archive (BNA)
Aberdeen Press
Bellin
Chronicle
Daily Dispatch
Daily Express
Daily News
Daily Press

Daily Telegraph
Daily Gazette
Der Wanderer
Echo
Evening Telegraph
Evening News
Globe
La Society Nouvelle
L'Humanite
L'Eclaire
Le Matin
L'Monde
Le Temps
Manchester Guardian
Mercury
National Review
New Age
New York Times
Petit Provincial
Sunday Chronicle
The Standard
The Scotsman
The Homeward Mail from India, China and The East
The (London) Times
The Morning Post
The Yorkshire Evening Post

7) Unpublished Dissertations

Brückenhaus, Daniel. "The Transnational Surveillance of Anti-Colonialist Movements in Western Europe, 1905-1945." Yale: Yale University, 2011.

Deshpande, Prachi. "Narratives of Pride: History and Regional Identity in Mahrashtra, India c. 1870-1960." Tufts University, 2002.

Fatima Ilahi, Shereen. "The Empire of Violence: Strategies of British Rule in India and Ireland in the Aftermath of the Great War". Texas: University of Texas and Austin, 2008.

Jasper, Daniel Alan. "Commemorating Shivaji: Regional and Religious Identity in Maharashtra, India." New School University, 2002

Naigaonkar, S.T. "N.C. Kelkar: A Political Study" (Unpublished PhD Thesis), University of Poona, Pune. March 1979.

Pawar, Prakash. "Akhil Bharatiya Maratha Mahasangha: Ek Chikitsak Abhyaas" (Unpublished MPhil Dissertation), University of Poona, Pune, 1996.

Mengel Jr., William H. "Guerilla Diplomacy: Germany and Unconventional Warfare, 1884-1945." Princeton University, 2007.

Navalgundkar, S .N. "The Social and Political Thought of Vinayak Damodar Savarkar." University of Poona, Pune, 1974.

Sen, Satadru. "Punishment and Society in Colonial India: The Penal Settlement in the Andaman Islands, 1858-1898". Washington: University of Washington, 1998.

Tejani, Shabnum. "A Pre-history of Indian Secularism: Categories of Nationalism and Communalism in Emerging Definitions of India, Bombay Presidency c. 1893-1932." Columbia: Columbia University, 2002.

Trivedi, Shefali. "Caste and Contentious Politics: State-Society Interactions and non-Brahman Movements in the Madras and Bombay Presidencies, 1880-1940." Columbia: Columbia University, 2003.

8) Published Books and Journal Articles (Bengali, English, Gujarati, Hindi, Kannada and Marathi)

Acharya, M.P.T. *Reminiscences of an Indian Revolutionary.* (Edited by B. D. Yadav). New Delhi: Anmol Publications, 1991.

Acworth, Harry Arbuthnot. *Powadas or Historical Ballads of the Marathas.* Bombay: Nimayasagar Press, 1891.

Agarwala, B.R. *Trials of Independence, 1858-1946.* New Delhi: National Book Trust, 1991.

Aggarwal, Som Nath. *The Heroes of Cellular Jail.* 1st ed. Patiala: Publication Bureau, Punjabi University, 1995.

Ahmad. *Speeches and Writings of Mr. Jinnah, 6th Ed.* Lahore: 1947, 1964.

Ahluwalia, B. K., and Shashi Ahluwalia. *Shivaji and Indian Nationalism.* New Delhi: Central Pub. House, 1984.

Ahmed, Rafiuddin, *The Bengal Muslims, 1871-1906 - A Quest for Identity.* New Delhi, 1981.

Aldred, Guy Alfred. *Rex v. Aldred, London Trial, 1909, Indian Sedition; Glasgow Sedition Trial, 1921.* Glasgow: Strickland Press, 1948.

Ambedkar, B.R. *Dr. Babasaheb Ambedkar, Writings and Speeches, Vols. 1-8.* Bombay, 1989.

----. *What Congress and Gandhi Have Done to the Untouchables,* New Delhi: Samyak Prakashan, 2012.

----. *Pakistan or the Partition of India.* New Delhi: Samyak Prakashan, 2013.

Anand, Vidya Sagar. *Savarkar: A Study in the Evolution of Indian Nationalism.* London: Cecil & Amelia Woolf, 1967.

Andersen, Walter K., and Shridhar D. Damle. *The Brotherhood in Saffron: The Rashtriya Swayamsevak Sangh and Hindu Revivalism.* Boulder: Westview Press, 1987.

Andersen, Walter. "The Rashtriya Swayamsevak Sangh I: Early Concerns". *Economic and Political Weekly*, 7. 11 (11 March 1972): 589-597.

----."The Rashtriya Swayamsevak Sangh: II: Who Represents the Hindus?" *Economic and Political Weekly*, 7.12 (Mar. 18, 1972): 633–640.

----. "The Rashtriya Swayamsevak Sangh: III: Participation in Politics ." *Economic and Political Weekly*, 7.13 (Mar. 25, 1972), 673–682.

Anderson, Benedict. *Imagined Communities: Reflections on the Origin and Spread of Nationalism.* 2nd ed. London: Verso, 1991.

----. *Under Three Flags: Anarchism and the Anti-Colonial Imagination.* London: Verso, 2005.

Anderson, David M. and David Killingray (eds.) *Policing and Decolonisation: Politics, Nationalism and the Police, 1917-65.* Manchester: Manchester University Press, 1992.

Apte, Dattatraya Vishnu. *Aitihasika Dantakatha Va Goshti.* Pune: Chitrashala Press, 1925.

Apte, M.L. "Lokahitavadi and V.K. Chiplunkar: Spokesmen of Change in Nineteenth-Century Maharashtra." *Modern Asian Studies 2.2* (1973): 193–208.

Agarwala, B.R. *Trials of Independence, 1858-1946.* Delhi: National Book Trust, 1991.

Arnold, David. "Touching the Body: Perspectives on the Indian Plague, 1896-1900." *Subaltern Studies 5.* Ranajit Guha (Ed.) New Delhi: Oxford University Press, 1987.

----. *Colonizing the Body: State Medicine and Epidemic Disease in Nineteenth Century India.* Berkeley: University of California Press, 1993.

----. "The Colonial Prison: Power. Knowledge and Penology in Nineteenth-Century India," in. *Subaltern Studies 7.* Arnold and Harden (eds.). Oxford, 1994.

Arnold, David and Stuart H. Blackburn. (eds.) *Telling Lives in India: Biography, Autobiography and Life History.* Bloomington, 2004.

Argov Daniel. *Moderates And Extremists In Indian Nationalist Movement: 1883-1920.* Bombay: Asia Publishing House, 1967.

Arya, Rakesh Kumar. *Gandhi aur Savarkar.* New Delhi: Diamond Books, 2017.

Athalye, D.V. *The Life of Lokamanya Tilak.* Poona, 1921.

Atindranath. *A History of Anarchism.* Calcutta: World Press, 1967.

Azad, Maulana Abul Kalam. *India Wins Freedom: An Autobiographical Account.* Hyderabad: Orient Longman Limited, 1959.

'Azad', Prithvi Singh. *Baba Prithvi Singh Azad—The Legendary Crusader: An Autobiography.* 1ˢᵗ ed. Bombay: Bhartiya Vidya Bhavan, 1987.

Baiq, M.R.A. *The Muslims' Dilemma in India.* Vikas, 1947.

Bakhle, Janaki. "Country First? Vinayak Damodar Savarkar (1883-1966) and the Writing of *Essentials of Hindutva.*" *Public Culture* 22.1(2010): 149-186.

----. "Savarkar (1883–1966), Sedition and Surveillance: The Rule of Law in a Colonial Situation." *Social History* 35.1 (2010): 51-75.

Ball, Charles. *The History of the Mutiny: Giving a Detailed Account of the Sepoy Insurrection in India and a Concise History of the Military Events which have tended to Consolidate British Empire in Hindostan.* 2 vols. Repr. New Delhi: Master Publications. 1981.

Ballard, Roger. "The South Asian Presence in Britain and its Transnational Connections". *Culture and Economy in the Indian Diaspora.* H. Singh and S. Vetovec. (eds.) London: Routledge, 2002.

Bamford P.C. *Histories of the Non-Cooperation and Khilafat Movement.* New Delhi: Deep Publication, 1974.

Banerjea, S.N. *The Nation in the Making: Being the Reminiscences of Fifty Years of Public Life.* London: Oxford University Press, 1925.

----.*Speeches of Surendra Nath Banerjea.* New Delhi: Indian Association, 1970.

Banerjee, Anil Chandra. *A Phase in the Life of Dr. Syama Prasad Mookerjee,* 1937-46. Kolkata: Ashutosh Mookerjee Memorial Institute, 2000.

Banerjee, Kalyan Kumar. *Indian Freedom Movement Revolutionaries in America.* Calcutta: J1JNASA, 1969.

Banerjee, Upendranath. *Nirvasiter Atmakatha.* N.p.

Bapat, G.P. *Govind Pandurang Bapat: Atmakatha.* Pune: Kal Prakashan, 1972.

Bapat, Narayan Sadashiv. *Smruti Pushpe.* Charuchandra Publication, 1984.

Barker, Col. F.A. *The Modern Prison System of India.* London: Macmillan and Co., 1944.

Barooah, Nirode K. *Chatto: The Life and Times of an Indian Anti-Imperialist in Europe.* Np.

----. *India and the Official Germany, 1886–1914.* Frankfurt: Peter Lang, 1977.

Barrier, N. Gerald. *Banned: Controversial Literature and Political Control in British India, 1907-1947.* Columbia: University of Missouri Press, 1974.

Basu, T et.al. *Khaki Shorts and Saffron Flags: A Critique of the Hindu Right.* New Delhi: Orient BlackSwan, 1993.

Basu, Tapan, Pradip Datta, Sumit Sarkar, Tanika Sarkar, and Sambuddha Sen. *Khaki Shorts and Saffron Flags: A Critique of the Hindu right.* New Delhi: Orient Longman, 1993.

Bayly, C. A. *Indian Society and the Making of the British Empire.* Cambridge, Cambridge University Press, 1987.

----. *Empire and Information: Intelligence Gathering and Social Communication in India*. Cambridge: Cambridge University Press, 1996.

Bashford, Alison & Carolyn Strange. *Isolation: Places and Practices of Exclusion*. Taylor & Francis, 2004.

Beck, Sanderson. *World Peace Efforts Since Gandhi*. World Peace Communications, 2006.

Bemtsen, E. Z. a. M. (ed.) *The Experience of Hinduism: Essays on Religion in Maharashtra*. Albany: State University of New York Press, 1988.

Bedekar, D.K. "Review of Interpretations on Shivaji's Achievements." *Science and Human Progress: Essays in Humanities, Indology, Science, Mathematics and Personal Tributes to late Prof. Damodar Dharmanand Kosambi*. Bombay: Popular Prakashan, 1974.

Besant, Annie Wood. *The Future of Indian Politics: A Contribution to the Understanding of Present Day Problems*. Theosophical Publishing House, 1922.

Bhalerao Sudhakar. *Swatantryaveer Savarkar Vicharmanthan*. Nagpur: Swatantryaveer Savarkar Putala Smarak Samiti, 1984.

Bhat, Bhaskar Vaman. *Maharashtra Dharma Arthat Marathyanchya Itihasache Atmik Swaroop*. Dhule: Satkaryottejaka Sabha, 1925.

Bhat, V.M. *Abhinav Bharat athava Savarkaranchi Krantikari Gupta Sanstha*. Mumbai: G.P. Parchure Prakashan Mandir, 1950.

Bhave, P.B. *Savarkar Navaachi Jyot*. Nagpur: Lakhe Prakashan, n.d.

----. *Pratham Purush Ek Vachani*. Nagpur: Lakhe Prakashan, 2017.

Bhave, Vasudev Krishna. *Peshwekalina Maharashtra*. New Delhi: Bharatiya Itihasa Anusandhana Parishad, 1976.

Blunt, W.S. *Secret History of the English Occupation of Egypt*. London, 1907.

----. *My Diaries, Being a Personal Narrative of Events, 1884-1914*, 2 Vols. New York: Knopf, 1921.

Brown D.M. *Nationalist Movement: Indian Political Thought From Ranade To Bhave*. Berkeley, University of California Press, 1964.

Bose, A.C. *Indian Revolutionaries Abroad: 1905-1927. Select Documents*. New Delhi: Northern Book Centre, 2002.

Bose, Nemai Sadhan. *The Indian Awakening and Bengal*. Calcutta: Sri Gouranga Press, 1969.

Bose, Subhash Chandra. *The Indian Struggle 1920-1934*, London: Wishart & Company Ltd., 1935.

----. *The Indian Struggle 1935-1942*, Calcutta: Chuckervertty, Chatterjee & Company Ltd. 1952.

Bose, Sugata. *The Nation as Mother and other Visions of Nationhood*. New Delhi: Penguin Random House India, 2017.

Bright, J.S. *The Woman Behind Gandhi*. Lahore: Paramount Publications, n.d.

Brown, F.H. "Sir William-Lee Warner (1846-1914)." *Oxford Dictionary of National Biography*, Brian Harrison, H.C.G. Matthew and Lawrence Goldman (eds.) Oxford: Oxford University Press, 2004.

Brown, Judith. *Gandhi: Prisoner of Hope*. New Haven: Yale University Press, 1989.

----. "Gandhi and Nehru: Frustrated Visionaries." *History Today*. 47 (1997): 22-27.

Brown, Judith, and Martin Prozesky (eds.) *Gandhi and South Africa: Principles and Politics*. New York: St. Martin's Press, 1996.

Brown, Mark. "The Politics of Penal Excess and the Echo of Colonial Penalty". *Punishment and Society* 4.4 (2002): 403–423.

Burman, J.J. Roy. "Shivaji's Myth and Maharashtra's Syncretic Traditions." *Economic and Political Weekly*, April 14–20 2001.

Burton, Antoinette. *At the Heart of Empire: Indians and the Colonial Encounter in Late-Victorian Britain*. Berkeley: University of California Press, 1998.

Candana, Amarajita. *Indians in Britain*. New Delhi: Sterling Publishers, 1986.

Cannadine, David. *Ornamentalism: How the British Saw their Empire*. Oxford: Oxford University Press, 2001.

Carter, Anthony T. *Elite Politics in Rural India: Political Stratification and Political Alliances in Western Maharashtra*. London. New York: Cambridge University Press, 1974.

Cashman. R. I. *Myth of the Lokamanya: Tilak and Mass Politics in Maharashtra*. Berkeley, University of California Press, 1975.

Casolari, Marzia. "Hindutva's Foreign Tie-Up in the 1930s: Archival Evidence". *Economic and Political Weekly*, 35. 4 (Jan 22–28, 2000): 218–228.

Catanach, I.J. "Poona Politicians and the Plague." South Asia: *Journal of South Asian Studies*, 7:2 (1984): 1–18.

Chandavarkar. R. *The Origins of Industrial Capitalism in India: Business Strategies and the Working Classes in Bombay: 1900-1940*. New York: Cambridge University Press, 1994.

Chand, Feroz. *Lajpat Rai: Life and Works*. New Delhi: Publication Division, Government of India, 1978.

Chakraberty, Chanda. *New India: Its Growth and Problems*. Vijayakrishna Brothers, n.d.

Chakravarty, Debdutta. *Muslim Separatism and the Partition of India*. New Delhi: Atlantic Publishers and Distributors, 2003.

Chakravarty, Gautam. *The Indian Mutiny and the British Imagination*. Cambridge: Cambridge University Press, 2005.

Chakravarty, Suhash. *The Raj Syndrome: A Study in Imperial Perceptions*. Delhi: Chanakya Publications, 1989.

Chatterjee, Choi. "Imperial Incarcerations: Ekaterina Breshko-Breshkovskaia, Vinayak Savarkar, and the Original Sins of Modernity." *Slavic Review* 74. 4 (2015): 850–872.

Chatterjee, Partha. *Nationalist Thought and the Colonial World: A Derivative Discourse?* London: Zed, 1986.

Chaturvedi, Vinayak. "A Revolutionary's Biography: The Case of V.D. Savarkar." *Postcolonial Studies* 16.2 (2013): 124–139.

Chaudhary, S.K. *Great Political Thinker: Vinayak Damodar Savarkar.* New Delhi: Sonali Publications, 2008.

Cinar, Anurupa. *Burning for Freedom.* Trafford Publishing, 2012.

Chirol, Valentine. *Indian Unrest.* London, 1910.

Chitragupta. *Life of Barrister Savarkar.* Madras, 1926.

Chopra, Prabha & P.N. Chopra. *Secret British Intelligence Report: Indian Freedom Fighters Abroad.* New Delhi: Criterion Publications, 1988.

Choudhury, D. K. Lahiri. "Sinews of Panic and the Nerves of Empire." *Modern Asian Studies* 38.4 (2004): 965–1002.

Chushichi, Tauzuhi. *H.N. Hyndman and British Socialism.* London, 1961.

Cohen, Stephen. P. "Subhas Chandra Bose and the Indian National Army". *Pacific Affairs*, 36. 4 (Winter, 1963-1964): 411–429.

Collet, Nigel. *The Butcher of Amritsar: General Reginald Dyer.* London: Hambledon and London, 2005.

Collier, Richard. *The Indian Mutiny.* London: Collins, 1966.

Collins, Larry and Dominique Lapierre. *Freedom at Midnight.* Noida: Vikas Publishing House, 2016.

----. *Mountbatten and the Partition of India.* New Delhi: Wide Canvas, 1982.

Coupland, Sir Reginald. *The Constitutional Problem in India- I.* Oxford, n. p. 1945.

----. *The Indian Problem, Pt. II, Indian Politics, 1936-1942.* Oxford University Press, 1943.

Cox, Edmund. *Police and Crime in India.* London, 1911.

Craton, Michael. *Sinews of Empire: A Short History of British Slavery.* Garden City, N.Y.: Anchor, 1974.

Craddock, Sir R. *The Dilemma in India.* London, 1929.

Crawford, Arthur. *Our Troubles in Poona and the Deccan.* Westminster, 1897.

Curran Jr, J.A. *Militant Hinduism in Indian Politics: A Study of the RSS.* New York: Institute of Pacific Relations, 1951.

Daly, F.C. *First Rebels: Strictly Confidential Note on the Growth of the Revolutionary Movement in Bengal.* Government of India, Home (Political) Department, 1911, Sankar Ghosh (Ed.). Calcutta, 1981.

Date, S. R. *Bharatiya Swatantryache Ranazhunzhaar: Abhinava Bharat.* Pune: Smarak Chitraprabodhini, 1970.

----. *Maharashatra Hindusabhechya Karyacha Itihaas.* Pune: Kal Prakashan, 1975.

----. *Bhagnagar Struggle: A Brief History of the Movement led by Hindu Mahasabha in Hyderabad State in 1938-39,* Poona: Lokasangraha Press, n.d.

Datta, P.K. *Carving Blocs: Communal Ideology in Early Twentieth Century Bengal.* New Delhi: Oxford University Press, 1999.

Datta, V.N. *Jallianwala Bagh.* Ludhiana: Lyall Book Depot, 1969.

----. *Madan Lal Dhingra and the Revolutionary Movement.* New Delhi: Vikas Publishing House, 1978.

----. "The Cripps Mission, Its Failure and Significance." *Indian History Congress.* 63 (2002): 644–652.

Datta, V.N. and S.C. Mittal. (eds.) *The Sources of National Movement, I, January 1919 to September 1920: Protests, Disturbances and Defiance.* New Delhi: Allied Publishers, 1985.

Desai, Sudha V. *Social Life in Maharashtra under the Peshwas.* Bombay: Popular Prakashan, 1980.

Deshpande, A.M., Shrikant Paranjpe, Raja Dixit, and C. R Das. *Western India: History, Society, and Culture.* Kolhapur: Itihas Shikshak Mahamandal Maharashtra, 1997.

Deshpande, Prachi. "Caste as Maratha: Social categories, colonial policy and identity in early twentieth-century Maharashtra." *Indian Economic & Social History Review* 41.1(2004): 7–32.

Deshpande, S.R. and Ramaswamy. *Dr. Hedgewar—The Epoch Maker: A Biography.* Sahitya Sindhu, 1981.

Deshpande, Satish. "Hegemonic Spatial Strategies: The Nation-Space and Hindu Communalism in Twentieth-Century India." *Public Culture* 10.2 (1998): 249–283.

Devi, Savitri. *A Warning to the Hindus*, Calcutta: A.K. Mukherji, 1939.

----. *Defiance.* Calcutta: A.K. Mukherji, 1950.

Dhulipala, Venkat. "Rallying the Qaum: The Muslim League in the United Provinces, 1937-1939." *Modern Asia Studies*, Cambridge University Press, 44.3 (May 2010).

Devanesan, D.S. *The Making of the Mahatma.* Madras: Orient Longman, 1969.

Dharmavir. *Bhai Paramanand aur Unka Yug.* New Delhi: Bhai Paramanand Smarak Samiti, 1981.

Dignan, Don. *The Indian Revolutionary Problem in British Diplomacy, 1914-1919.* New Delhi: Allied Publishers, 1983.

Divekar, V.D. *Lokmanya Tilak in England, 1918-19: Diary and Documents.* Pune: Tilak Smarak Trust, 1997.

Dixon, William Macneile. *Summary of Constitutional Reforms for India: Being Proposals of Secretary of State Montagu and the Viceroy, Lord Chelmsford.* New York; G.G. Woodwark, n.d.

Doshi, Saryu (Ed.) *Shivaji and Facets of Maratha Culture.* Bombay: Marg Publications, 1982.

Dublish, Kaushalya Devi. *Revolutionaries and Their Activities in Northern India.* New Delhi: B. R. Publishing Corporation, 1982.

Duff, James Grant. *History of the Mahrattas.* Indian (Reprint ed.) Bombay: Printed at the "Exchange Press" Fort, 1863.

Durrani, F.K. Khan. *The Meaning of Pakistan.* Lahore: Sh. Muhammad Ashraf, 1943.

Dwarkadas, Kanji. *Ten Years of Freedom.* Bombay: Popular Prakashan, 1968.

Elst, Koenraad. *Gandhi and Godse: A Review and a Critique.* New Delhi: Voice of India, 2001.

Eston, Elizabeth and Lexi Kawabe. *Rash Behari Bose: The Father of the Indian National Army Vols. 1 and 2.* Tenraidou, 2019.

Fasana, Enrico. *Deshabhakta:* "The Leaders of the Italian Independence Movement in the Eyes of Marathi Nationalists." *Writers, Editors, and Reformers: Social and Political Transformations of Maharashtra, 1830-1930,* N.K. Wagle (Ed.) New Delhi: Manohar, 1991.

Fay, Gaston. "How Lamirande was Caught". *The Galaxy* 5.3 (1868): 355–364.

Fischer, Louis. *The Life of Mahatma Gandhi.* HarperCollins: London, 1982.

Gandhi, Mohandas Karamchand. *Young India: 1919-1922.* B. R. Prasad. (Ed.) 2nd ed. Madras: S. Ganeshan, 1924.

----. *An Autobiography or the Story of My Experiments with Truth.* Ahmedabad: Navjivan Publishing House, 1996.

Gandhi, Tushar. A. *Let's Kill Gandhi.* New Delhi: Rupa Publications, 2007.

Ganneri, Namrata. "Whither Hindu Unity? Unraveling the RSS-Hindu Mahasabha Relationship: Perspectives from Maharashtra". *Indian History Congress,* 76 (2015).

Gawade P.L. *Vinayak Damodar Savarkar: Ek Chikitsak Abhyas.* Pune: Swadhyay Mahavidyalaya Prakashan, 1970.

Ghapure, K.V. *Svatantryavira Savarkar.* Nagpur: Savarkara Tatvajnana Prasara Kendra, 1965.

Ghodke, H. M. *Revolutionary Nationalism in Western India.* New Delhi: Classical Pub. Co., 1990.

Ghose, Barindra Kumar. *The Truth of Life.* Madras: S. Ganesan, 1922.

----. *The Tale of My Exile,* Pondicherry: Arya Office, 1922.

Ghose, Sankar. (Ed.) First Rebels, A Strictly Confidential Report.

Glendevon, John. *The Viceroy at Bay, Lord Linlithgow in India, 1936-1943.* Collins, 1971.

Godbole, Dr. Arvind. *Mala Umajlele Swatyatraveer Savarkar.* Pune: Bharatiya Vichar Sadhana Publication, 2011.

Godbole, Shriranga. *Govyatil Margadarshak Shuddhikarya.* Pune: Sanskrutik Vartapatra, 2010.

Godbole, V.S. *Rationalism of Veer Savarkar.* Thane: Itihas Patrika Prakashan, 2004.

Godse, Gopal. *Why I Assassinated Gandhi*. New Delhi: Farsight Publisher and Distributors, 2017.

Goel, Sita Ram. *Muslim Separatism: Causes and Consequences*. New Delhi: Voice of India, 2002.

Gokhale, B.G. "Shivram Mahadeo Paranjpe: Nationalism and the Uses of the Past". *Journal of Indian History*, 48. 143 (1970): 259–274.

Gokhale D.N. *Krantiveer Babarao Savarkar*, Srividya Prakashan Vol. 2. Poona, 1979.

----. *Swatantryaveer Savarkar: Ek Rahasya*. Mumbai: Mauj Prakashan Gruha, 1989.

Gokhale, Gopal Krishna. *Speeches of Gopal Krishna Gokhale*. Madras: G.A. Natesan (Ed.), 1920.

Gondhalekar, Nandini and Sanjoy Bhattacharya. "The All India Hindu Mahasabha and the End of British Rule in India, 1939–1947." *Social Scientist*, 27. 7/8 (July–August, 1999): 48–74.

Goodrick-Clarke, Nicholas. *Hitler's Priestess: Savitri Devi, the Hindu–Aryan Myth, and Neo-Nazism*, New York & London: New York University Press, 1998.

Gopal, Ram. *Indian Muslims: A Political History (1858-1947)*. Bombay: Asia Pub. House, 1964.

Gordon, Leonard. A. *Bengal: The Nationalist Movement 1876-1940*. New Delhi: Manohar Book Service, 1974.

Gordon, Richard. "The Hindu Mahasabha and the Indian National Congress, 1915 to 1926". *Modern Asian Studies*, 9.2 (1975): 145–203.

Gordon, Stewart. *The Marathas, 1600-1818*. New York: Cambridge University Press, 1993.

Gokhale, Jayashree. "The Mahratta and Nationalism in Maharashtra." *Indian Political Science Review* 9. 1 (1975): 1–26.

Goyal, D.R. *Rashtriya Swayamsewak Sangh*, New Delhi: Radha Krishna Prakashan, 1979.

Gould, Harold. *Sikhs, Swamis, Students, and Spies: The India Lobby in the United States, 1900-1946*. New Delhi: Sage Publications, 2006.

Great Britain, Foreign Office. *Savarkar arbitration*. London: Harrison and Sons, 1911.

Green, L.C. "The Indian National Army Trials". Wiley: *Modern Law Review* 11.1. (Jan. 1948): 47–69

Grover, Verinder. *Political Thinkers of Modern India, Vol. 14, V.D. Savarkar*. New Delhi: Deep & Deep Publications, 1992.

Griffiths, Sir Percival. *The British Impact on India*. London: Macdonald, 1952.

Gruhenheck Taponier, Susan and James A. Cohen (eds.) *Globalization of Surveillance: The Origins of the Securitarian Order*. Cambridge: Polity Press, 2010.

Guha, A.C. *First Spark of Revolution: The Early Phase of India's Struggle for Independence, 1900-1920*. Bombay: Orient Longman, 1971.

Guha, Sumit. *The Agrarian Economy of the Bombay Deccan, 1818–1941*. New Delhi: Oxford University Press, 1985.

----. "Speaking Historically: The Changing Voice of Historical Narration in Western India, 1400-1900." *American Historical Review* 109. 4 (2004): 1084–1103.

Gupta, H.P. and P. K. Sarkar. *Law relating to Press and Sedition in India*. Bombay, 2002.

Gupta, Jugal Kishore. "Myths and Realities of the Quit India Movement." *Indian History Congress*, 46 (1985): 569–583.

Gupta, Partha Sarathy (Ed.). *Towards Freedom: Documents on the Movement for Independence in India, 1943-44*. New Delhi: Oxford University Press, 1998.

Gupta, Manmathanath. *Bharatiya Krantikari Andolan ka Itihas*. New Delhi, Atmaram and Sons, 1966.

Hale, H.W. *Political Trouble in India: 1917-1937*. Allahabad: Chugh Publications, 1974.

Hall, Catherine. (Ed.) *Cultures of Empire: Colonizers in Britain and the Empire in the Nineteenth and Twentieth Centuries: A Reader*. New York: Routledge, 2000.

Hamsaraja Rahabara. *Bhagat Singh and His Thought*. New Delhi: Manak Publications, 1990.

Hardas, Balshastri. *Armed Struggle For Freedom: Ninety Years War of Independence, 1857-1947*. Pune: Kal Prakashan, 1959.

----. *Dharmaveer Do Balkrishna Shivaram Munje yanche Charitra*, 2nd Ed. Lakhe Prakashan, 2013.

Hasan, Mushirul. *Mahomed Ali: Ideology and Politics*. New Delhi, 1981.

Hay, Stephen. *Sources of Indian Tradition*. Columbia University Press, 1958.

Heehs, Peter. *The Bomb in Bengal: The Rise of Revolutionary Terrorism in India, 1900-1910*. Delhi; New York: Oxford University Press, 1993.

----. "Foreign Influences on Bengali Terrorism, 1902-1908." *Modern Asian Studies* 28.3 (1994): 533–556.

----. *Nationalism, Terrorism, Communalism: Essays in Modern Indian History*. Delhi; New York: Oxford University Press, 1998.

Hopkirk, Peter. *On Secret Service East of Constantinople*. London, 1994.

----. *Like Hidden Fire: The Plot to Bring Down the British Empire*, New York: Kodansha, 1994.

Hunt, James. D. *Gandhi in London*. New Delhi: Promilla and Company Publishers, 1978.

Hyndman, H.M. *The Bankruptcy of India: An Enquiry into the Administration of India Under the Crown*. London: Swan Sonnenshein, Lowery and Co., 1886.

----. *The Growing Catastrophe in India*. London: Twentieth Century Press, 1897.

----. *The Awakening of Asia*. London: Cassell and Company, 1919.

Ikram, S.M. *Indian Muslims and Partition of India*. Atlantic Publishers and Distributors, 1995.

Inamdar, P.L. *The Story of the Red Fort Trial 1948-1949*. Bombay: Popular Prakashan, 1979.

Islam, Shamsul. *Hindutva: Savarkar Unmasked*. New Delhi: Media House, 2016.

Israel, Milton and N. K. Wagle. *Religion and Society in Maharashtra*. Toronto, Ont.: University of Toronto, Centre for Asian Studies, 1987.

Jadhav, Narendra (Ed.) *Ambedkar Speaks*, Vol. 1–3. New Delhi: Konark Publishers Pvt. Ltd. 2013.

Jaffrelot, Christophe. *The Hindu Nationalist Movement in India 1925-1990*. New York: Columbia University Press, 1995.

James, Lawrence. *Raj: The Making and Unmaking of British India*. New York: St. Martin's Press, 1998.

Jayakar, M.R. *The Story of My Life*. Bombay, 1958.

Jinnah, Mahomed Ali, Jamil-ud-Din Ahmad (Ed.), *Speeches and Writings of Jinnah*, Lahore: Shaikh Muhammad Ashraf, 1964.

Joglekar, Jaywant D. *Dnyanayukta Krantiyoddha*. Bombay: Manorama Prakashan, 2002.

----. *Veer Savarkar: Father of Hindu Nationalism*. n.p., 2006.

Johnson, G. *Provincial Politics and Indian Nationalism: Bombay and the Indian National Congress*. Cambridge: Cambridge University Press, 1973.

Jones, Kenneth W. *Arya Dharm*. Berkeley: University of California Press, 1976.

----. "The Arya Samaj in British India, 1875–1947." *Religion in Modern India*. Robert Baird. (Ed.) New Delhi: Manohar, 1976.

----. *Socio-religious Reform Movements in British India*. New York: Cambridge University Press, 1989.

----. *"Politicised Hinduism: The Ideology and Programme of the Hindu Mahasabha"*, in Robert D. Baird (ed.) *Religion in Modem India*. New Delhi: Manohar Publications, 1981.

Jordens, J.T.F. *Dayananda Sarasvati: His Life and Ideas*. Delhi: Oxford University Press, 1978.

----. *Swami Shraddhananda: His Life and Causes*. Delhi: Oxford University Press, 1981.

Josh, Sohan Singh. *Hindustan Ghadr Party: A Short History*. New Delhi: People's Publishing House, 1977.

Joshi, G.M. *V. D. Savarkar, The Indian War of Independence, 1857*. Bombay: Phoenix Publications, 1947.

Joshi, P.M. *Students' Revolts in India*. Bombay: Sirur Printing Press, 1972.

Joshi, V.S. *Kranti Kallol*. Bombay: Manorama Prakashan, 1985.

----. *Jhunjh Savarkarancha*, Bombay: Manorama Prakashan, n.d.

----. *Mrityunjayacha Aatmayagnya*, n.p., 3rd Edition. 1981.

Karandikar, S.L. *Savarkar Charitra Kathan*. Pune: Modern Book Depot Prakashan, 1947.

Keer, Dhananjay. *Veer Savarkar*. Bombay: Popular Prakashan, 1950.

----. *Mahatma Gandhi*. Bombay: Popular Prakashan, 1973.

Kelkar, B.K. *Savarkar Darshan: Vyakti Ani Vichar*. Bombay, G.P. Parchure Prakashan, 1952.

Kerr, James Campbell. *Political Trouble in India: 1907-1917*. New Delhi: Orient Longman, 1973.

Khare, N.B. *My Political Memoirs or Autobiography*. Published by Shri J.R. Joshi, Nagpur, n.d.

Khaliquzzaman, C. *Pathway to Pakistan*. Lahore, n.p. 1961.

Khole, Vilas (Ed.). *Suryabimbacha Shodh*. Pune: Shodh Prakashan, n.d.

Khosla, G.D. *The Murder of the Mahatma and other cases from a Judge's Notebook*. Bombay: Jaico Press Pvt. Ltd, 1977.

Koss, Stephen E. *John Morley at the India Office, 1905-1910*. New Haven: Yale University Press, 1969.

Krishna, Gopal. "The Development of the Indian National Congress as a Mass Organization, 1918-1923." *The Journal of Asian Studies* 25.3 (1966): 413–30.

Krishnamurthy, Babu. *Madanlal Dhingra*. Translated by Wasant Kawali. Bangalore: Rashtrotthana Sahitya Trust, 1974.

Kudaisya, Medha M. *The Life and Times of G.D. Birla*. New Delhi: Oxford University Press, 2003.

Kulkarni, Mangesh (2014) "Memories of Maratha History and Regional Identity in Maharashtra, India." *India Review* 13.4 (2014): 358–371.

Kumar, Megha. "History and Gender in Savarkar's Nationalist Writings." *Social Scientist* 34. 11/12 (2006): 33–50.

Kumar, Ravinder. Western India in the Nineteenth Century: A Study in the Social History of Maharashtra. London, Routledge. 1968.

----. (Ed.) *Essays on Gandhian Politics: The Rowlatt Satyagraha of 1919*. Oxford: Clarendon Press, 1971.

Lahiri, Shompa. *Indians in Britain: Anglo-Indian Encounters, Race and Identity, 1880-1930*. London; Portland, OR: Frank Cass, 2000.

----. *Indian Mobilities in the West, 1900-1947: Gender, Performance, Embodiment*. New York: Palgrave MacMillian, 2010.

----. "South Asian Resistances in Britain 1858–1947, Immigrants & Minorities." 32.1 (2013): 129–132.

Lajpat Rai, Lala. *Young India: An Interpretation and A History of the Nationalist Movement from Within*. Lahore: Servants of People Society, 1927 (Fourth Reprint).

Llewellyn, J.E. *The Arya Samaj as a Fundamentalist Movement: A Study in Comparative Fundamentalism*. New Delhi: Manohar, 1993.

Lal, Bahadur. *The Muslim League: Its History, Activities and Achievements*. Lahore: Book Traders, 1979.

Lambert, David, and Alan Lester. *Colonial Lives across the British Empire: Imperial Careering in the Long Nineteenth Century*. Cambridge, UK; New York: Cambridge University Press, 2006.

Lambert, Richard. "Hindu Communal Groups in Indian Politics." *Leadership and Political Institutions in India* (Eds. Richard L. Park and Irene Tinker). Princeton: Princeton University Press, 1959.

Lobban, Michael. "From Seditious Libel to Unlawful Assembly: Peterloo and the Changing Face of Political Crime c.1770-1820." *Oxford Journal of Legal Studies* 10.3 (1990): 307–52.

MacDonald, James Ramsay. *The Awakening of India*. London: Hodder and Stoughton, 1910.

Maclean, Kama. "Imagining the Indian Nationalist Movement: Revolutionary Metaphors in Imagery of the Freedom Struggle." *Journal of Material Culture* 19.1 (2014): 7–34.

Madhok, Balraj. *Portrait of a Martyr*. Bombay: Jaico Publishing House, 1973.

Majumdar, Bimanbehari. *Militant Nationalism in India: And its Socio-Religious Background (1897-1917)*. Calcutta: General Printers & Publishers, 1966.

Majumdar, R.C. *History of Freedom Movement in India, Vols 1-3*. Calcutta: Firma, K.L. Mukhopadhyay, 1962.

Malgonkar, Manohar. *The Men Who Killed Gandhi*. New Delhi: Roli Books, 2008.

Malkani, K.R. *The RSS Story*. New Delhi: Impex India, 1980.

Malshe, S.G. (Ed.). *Savarkarancha Aprasiddha Kavita*. Bombay: Marathi Samshodhan Mandal, 1969.

Mandlik, V. N. "Preliminary Observations on a Document giving an Account of the Establishment of a New Village named Muruda, in Southern Konkana". *Journal of the Bombay Branch of the Royal Asiatic Society 8.3* (1864–66).

Masani, M.R. *The Communist Party of India*. n.p.: London, 1954.

Masselos, Jim. *Indian Nationalism: A History*. Elgin, IL: New Dawn Press, 2005.

Mayadeo V.S. (Ed.). *Savarkaranchi Kavita*. Bombay: Karnatak Prakashan Samstha, 1967.

McAlpin, M. B. *Subject to Famine: Food Crises and Economic Change in Western India. 1860-1920*. Princeton: Princeton University Press, 1983.

McLane, John R. *Indian Nationalism and the Early Congress*. Princeton, N.J.: Princeton University Press, 1977.

Menon, V.P. *The Transfer of Power in India*. Longman, 1957.

Metcalf, Thomas R. *Ideologies of the Raj*. Cambridge: Cambridge University Press, 1994.

Misra, Amalendu. "Savarkar and the Discourse on Islam in Pre-Independent India." *Journal of Asian History*, 33.2 (1999): 142–184.

Misra, Salil. "Muslim League in U.P in 1937: Understanding Muslim Communalism." *Indian History Congress.* 60 (1999): 765–773.

Mishra, Anil Kumar. *Hindu Mahasabha: Ek Adhyayan, 1906-1947.* New Delhi: n.p. 1988.

Mishra, Dwarka Prasad. *Living an Era.* New Delhi: Har Anand Publications, 2001.

More, Sheshrao. *Savarkarancha Buddhivad: Ek Chikitsak Abhyaas.* Nanded: Nirmal Prakashan, 1988.

Mookerjee, Syama Prasad. *Leaves From a Diary.* Calcutta: n.p. 1993.

Moon, Penderel (Ed.). *Lord Wavell, The Viceroy's Journal.* London 1973.

Moore, R.J. *Churchill, Cripps and India, 1939-1945.* Oxford: Clarendon Press, 1979.

Morton, Stephen. "Fictions of Sedition and the Framing of Indian Revolutionaries in Colonial India." *The Journal of Commonwealth Literature* 47.2 (2012): 175–189.

Mosley, Leonard. *Last Days of the British Raj.* Harcourt, Brace & World, Inc. 1962.

Mukherjee Uma. *Two Great Indian Revolutionaries: Ras Behari Bose And Jyotindranath Mukherjee.* Calcutta: Firma, K.L. Mukhopadhyay, 1966.

Muralidharan, Sukumar. "Patriotism without People: Milestones in the Evolution of the Hindu Nationalist Ideology." *Social Scientist* 22.5/6 (1994): 3–38.

Nair, C. Sankaran. *Gandhi and Anarchy.* Madras: Tagore Press, 1923.

Nanda, B.R. *The Nehrus: Motilal and Jawaharlal,* Allen & Unwin, 1962.

----. *Gokhale: The Indian Moderates and the British Raj.* New Delhi, 1977.

----. *The Collected Works of Lala Lajpat Rai. Vol 1-2.* New Delhi: Manohar Publications, 2008.

Nandy, Ashis. "The Demonic and the Seductive in Religious Nationalism: Vinayak Damodar Savarkar and the Rites of Exorcism in Secularizing South Asia." *Heidelberg Papers in South Asian and Comparative Politics* 44 (February 2009).

----. "A Disowned Father of the Nation in India: Vinayak Damodar Savarkar and the Demonic and the Seductive in Indian Nationalism". *Inter-Asia Cultural Studies.* 15.1 (2014): 91–112.

Nath, Shaileshwar. *Terrorism in India.* New Delhi: National Publishing House, 1980.

Navalgundkar, S.N. *Swatantryaveer Savarkar Vicharvishwa.* Pune: Anmol Prakashan, 1999.

Navare, Shripad Shankar. *Senapati.* Bombay: Mauj Prakashan, 1976.

Nehru, Jawaharlal. *Nehru on Gandhi: Selections from Writings and Speeches.* New York: The John Day Company, 1948.

----. *Towards Freedom: The Autobiography of Jawaharlal Nehru.* New York: The John Day Company, 1958.

----. *The Discovery of India*. New Delhi: Jawaharlal Nehru Memorial Fund and Oxford University Press, 1981.

----. *A Bunch of Old Letters*. Asia, 1958.

----. *Selected Works of Jawaharlal Nehru*, Series 2, Vol. 5 (January–April 1948), Delhi: B.R. Publishing Corporation, 1988.

Noorani, A.G. *Indian Political Trials: 1775–1947*. New Delhi, 1976.

----. *Savarkar and Hindutva: The Godse Connection*. New Delhi: Leftword Books, 2002.

Ohsawa, Georges. *The Two Great Indians in Japan: Sri Rash Behari Bose and Subhas Chandra Bose*. Kusa Publications, 1954.

Overstreet, Gene D & Marshall Windmiller. *Communism in India*. Berkeley and Los Angeles: University of California Press, 1959.

Owen, Nicholas. *The British Left and India: Metropolitan Anti-Imperialism, 1885–1947*. Oxford, 2007.

----. "The Cripps Mission." *The Journal of Imperial and Commonwealth History*, 30.1(January 2002): 61–89.

Pal, Bipin Chandra, *The Soul of India: A Constructive Study of Indian Thoughts and Ideals*. Calcutta, 1911.

----. *Nationality and Empire: A Running Study of some Current Indian Problems*. Thacker and Spink, Calcutta, 1916.

Padmanabhan, R. A. *V. V. S. Aiyar*. New Delhi, 1980.

Pandey, Deepak. "Congress-Muslim League Relations 1937-39: The Parting of Ways" *Modern Asian Studies* 12.4 (1978).

Pandey, Gyanendra. *Routine Violence: Nation, Fragments, History*. California: Stanford University Press, 2006.

Paranjpe, S., R. Dixit, and C.R. Das. (eds.) *Western India: History, Society, and Culture*. Kolhapur: Itihas Shikshak Mahamandal, 1997.

Paranjpe, Waman Krishna. *Kal Karte Shivaram Panth Paranjpe Jeevan*. Published by R.S. Deshpande, 1st ed. 1945.

Parel, Anthony. (Ed.) *Hind Swaraj*. Cambridge: Cambridge University Press, 1997.

Patterson, Maureen L.P. "The Shifting Fortunes of Chitpavan Brahmins: The Focus on 1948". *City, Countryside and Society in Maharashtra*, D.W. Atwood et.al (eds.) University of Toronto, Centre for South Asian Studies, 1998.

Phadke, Y.D. *Shodh Savarkarancha*. Bombay, 1984.

----. *Tatwadnya Savarkar*. Pune: Maharashtra Tatvadnyan Maha Mandal and Continental, 1988.

----. *Visaya Shatakatil Maharashtra*, Vol. 1, Pune: Srividya Prakashan, 1989.

----. *Lokmanya Tilak aani Krantikarak*. Bombay: Srividya Prakashan, n.d.

----. *Mahatma Phule Samagra Vangmay*. Mumbai: Maharashtra Rajya Sahitya ani Sanskriti Mandal, 1991.

----. *Senapati Bapat*. New Delhi: National Book Trust, 1993.

Pattanaik, D. D. *Hindu nationalism in India, 4* Vols. New Delhi: Deep & Deep Publications, 1998.

Payne, Robert. *The Life and Death of Mahatma Gandhi.* New Delhi: Rupa Publications, 1969.

Philips, Cyril H. *The Evolution of India and Pakistan 1858-1947.* London, 1962.

Pinney, Christopher. *'Photos of the Gods': The Printed Image and Political Struggle in India* London: Reaktion Books, 2004.

Pradhan, R.G. *India's Struggle for Swaraj.* Madras: J.A. Natesan & Co., 1930.

Prakash, Indra. *Hindu Mahasabha Its Contribution to Indian Politics.* New Delhi: Akhil Bharat Hindu Mahasabha, 1966.

Prasad, Rajendra. *India Divided.* New Delhi: Penguin, 2017.

Pundalik, Vidyadhar. "Sati" in *Devchaafa.* Mauj Prakashan, 2010.

Purohit B.R. *Hindu Revivalism and Indian Nationalism.* Sagar: Sathi Prakashan, 1965.

Raghavan, T.C.A. "Origins And Development Of Hindu Mahasabha Ideology: The Call of V.D. Savarkar and Bhai Paramananda". *Economic And Political Weekly* 10.15(1983): 595–600.

Rahabara, Hamsaraja. *Bhagat Singh and His Thought,* Delhi: Manak Publications, 1990.

Rana, Bhawan Singh. *Bharat ke Amar Krantikari.* New Delhi: Diamond Publications, 2007.

----. *Bhagat Singh.* New Delhi: Diamond Pocket Books, 2005.

Ranade, Mahadev Govind Rao Bahadur. *The Miscellaneous Writings of the Late Hon'ble Mr. Justice M. G. Ranade.* Bombay: Manoranjan Press, 1915.

----. *Rise of the Maratha Power.* New Delhi: Publications Division, Government of India, 1974.

Rath, Radhanath & Sabitri Prasanna Chatterjee, (eds.) *Rash Behari Basu: His Struggle for India's Independence.* Kolkata: Biplabi Mahanayak Rash Behari Basu Smarak Samiti, 1959.

Read, Anthony & David Fischer, *The Proudest Day: India's Long Road to Independence.* London: Random House UK, 1997.

Rege, Sharmila. 2002. "Conceptualizing Popular Culture: Lavani and Powada in Maharashtra." *Economic and Political Weekly* 37.11(2002).

Renavikara, R.L. *Savarkaryancya athavani.* Pune: Adhikari Prakashana, 1962.

Rosalind, O. H. "Maratha History as Polemic: Low Caste Ideology and Political Debate in late Nineteenth Century Western India." *Modern Asian Studies* 17.1(1983): 1–33.

Roy, Tathagata. *The Life and Times of Dr. Syama Prasad Mookerjee.* New Delhi: Prabhat Prakashan, 2008.

Ryland, Shane. (2011) "Edwin Montagu in India: Politics of the Montagu Chelmsford Report." South Asia: *Journal of Asian Studies* 2011: 79–92.

Saha, Panchanan. *Madam Cama (Bhikaji Rustom K.R.), Mother of Indian Revolution, International Women's Year Series;* No. 1. Calcutta: Manisha Granthalaya, 1975.

Sahasrabuddhe, Uttara. *Bharatiya Swatantryaladhyatil Streeya*. Mehta Publishing House, n.d.

Sandhu, Sohan Singh and Kaur, Sukhjeet. *The Fight for Freedom the Story of Shaheed Madan Lal Dhingra*. Lalkar: Indian Workers Association (UK), 1998.

Sanyal, Sachindranath. *Bandi Jeevan*. New Delhi: Atma Ram & Sons, 1963.

Sarkar, Sumit. *Swadeshi Movement in Bengal, 1903–1908*. New Delhi, 1973.

----. "Indian Nationalism and the Politics of Hindutva." *Contesting the Nation: Religion, Community, and the Politics of Democracy in India*. David Ludden (Ed.) Philadelphia: University of Pennsylvania Press, 1996.

----. *Beyond Nationalist Frames: Postmodernism, Hindu Fundamentalism, History*. Bloomington, Ind.: Indiana University Press, 2002.

Sareen T. N. *Japan and The Indian National Army*. New Delhi: Agam Publication, 1986.

Sareen, T. R. *Indian Revolutionary Movement Abroad*. New Delhi, 1979.

Sarila, Narendra Singh. *The Shadow of the Great Game: The Untold Story of India's Partition*. New Delhi: HarperCollins, 2005.

Satyam (Ed.). *Bhagat Singh aur Unke Saathiyon ke Sampoorn Upalabdh Dastaavez*. Lucknow: Rahul Foundation, 2006.

Savarkar, Himani. *Tejasvi Taare*. Mumbai: Savarkar Smarak, n.d.

----. *Ranashingha*. Mumbai: Savarkar Smarak, n.d.

Savarkar, Vishwas Vinayak. *Athavani Angarachya*. Pune: Snehal Prakashan 3rd ed. 2001.

Sen, Amiya. *Hindu Revivalism in Bengal, 1872-1905*. New Delhi: Oxford University Press, 1993.

Sen, N.B. (Ed.) *Punjab's Eminent Hindus*. Lahore: New Book Society, 1953.

Sen, Sachin. *The Birth of Pakistan*. Calcutta: General Printers & Publishers, 1955.

Sethna, Khorshed Ali. *Madam Bhikaji Rustom Cama*. New Delhi: Publication Division, Government of India, 1987.

Schnokel, Wolfe W. *Dream of Empire: German Colonialism, 1919-1945*. New Haven: Yale University Press, 1964.

Schneer, Jonathan. *London 1900: The Imperial Metropolis*. New Haven: Yale University Press, 2001.

Shah, A. M. "The Indian Sociologist, 1905-14, 1920-22." *Economic and Political Weekly* 41.31 (2006): 3435–39.

Sharma, Jai Narain. *Encyclopedia of Eminent Thinkers, Vol. 12: The Political Thought of Veer Savarkar*. New Delhi: Concept Publishing Company, 2008.

Sharma, Jyotirmaya. "History as Revenge and Retaliation: Rereading Savarkar's 'the War of Independence of 1857". *Economic and Political Weekly* 42. 19 (2007): 1717–19.

Sharma, Mallikarjuna. *Role of Revolutionaries in the Freedom Struggle*. Hyderabad: Marxist Study Forum, 1987.

Sharma, M.S.M. *Peeps into Pakistan*. Patna: Pustak Bhandar, 1954.

Shay, Theodore L. *The Legacy of the Lokamanya: The Political Philosophy of Bal Gangadhar Tilak*. Bombay, 1956.

Setlur, S.S. and K.G. Deshpande. A *Full and Authentic Report of the Trial of the Hon'ble Mr. Bal Gangadhar Tilak, B.A., LL.B. at the Fourth Criminal Sessions 1897*. Byculla: The Education Society's Press, 1897.

Shraddhanand, Swami. *Inside Congress*. Phoenix Publications, Bombay, 1946.

Singh, Gulab. Under the Shadow of Gallows: A Story of a Revolutionary. New Delhi: Rup Chand, 1964.

Singh, Hari. *Gandhi, Rowlatt Satyagraha, and British Imperialism: Emergence of Mass Movements in Punjab and Delhi*. Delhi: Indian Bibliographies Bureau, 1990.

Singh, K.V. *Our National Flag*. Publications Division, Government of India, 1991.

Singh, Pardaman, *Lord Minto and Indian Nationalism (1905-1910)*. Allahabad, 1976.

Singh, Purnima. *Indian Cultural Nationalism*. New Delhi: India First Foundation, 2004.

Singha, Radhika. "Settle, Mobilize, Verify: Identification Practices in Colonial India". *Studies in History* 16.2 (2000): 151–98.

Singh, Ujjwal Kumar. *Political Prisoners in India*. Oxford University Press, 1998.

Sinha, Bejoy Kumar. *In Andamans: The Indian Bastille*, 2nd Rev. Ed. New Delhi: People's Publishing House, 1988.

Silvestri, Michael. "The Sinn Féin of India: Irish Nationalism and the Policing of Revolutionary Terrorism in Bengal." *Journal of British Studies* 39 (2002): 454–486.

Sitaramayya, Pattabhi. *History of the Indian National Congress (1885-1947)*. New Delhi: S. Chand, 1988.

Smith, Wilfred Cantwell. *Modern Islam in India*. London: Victor Gollancz Ltd., 1946

Sonpatki, Mukund. *Daryapar*. Pune: Purandare Prakashan, 1980.

Srivastav, Geeta. *Mazzini And His Impact on the Indian National Movement*. Allahabad: Chugh Publication, 1982.

Srivastav, Harindra. *Five Stormy Years: Savarkar in London*. New Delhi, Allied Publishers, 1983.

Sullivan, O'Noel (ed.) *Terrorism, Ideology and Revolution*. Sussex: The Harvester Press Publishing Group, 1986.

Sulibele, Chakravarthy. *Apratima Deshabhakta, Swatantryaveera Savarkar*. Bangalore: Rashtrotthana Sahitya, 2004.

Tahmankar, D.V. *Lokmanya Tilak, Father of Indian Unrest and Maker of Modern India*. London: John Murray, 1956.

Taunk, B.B.M. *Non-Cooperation Movement in Indian Politics, 1919-1924*. New Delhi: Sandeep Prakashan, 1978.

Tejani, Shabnum. "Music, Mosques and Custom: Local Conflict and 'Communalism' in a Maharashtrian Weaving Town, 1893–1894". South Asia: *Journal of South Asian Studies*, 30.2 (2007): 223–240.

----. "From Untouchable to Hindu: Gandhi, Ambedkar and Depressed class question 1932". *Indian Secularism: A Social and Intellectual History, 1890-1950*. Bloomington: Indian University Press, 2008.

Telang, K.T. "Gleanings from Maratha Chronicles", paper read before the Deccan College Union on 17 September 1892.

Thakar, Sharad. *Sinhapurush: Navalkatha*. Ahmedabad: Parshwa Publication, 2008.

Tharoor, Shashi. *An Era of Darkness: The British Empire in India*. New Delhi: Aleph Book Company, 2016.

Thursby, G.R. *Hindu-Muslim Relations in British India: A Study of Controversy, Conflict and Communal Movements in Northern India, 1923-1928*. Leiden, 1975.

Tilak, B.G. *Bal Gangadhar Tilak: His Writings and Speeches* (with an appreciation by Aurobindo Ghose). Madras: Ganesh and Co., 1922.

Treanor, Tom. *One Damn Thing After Another: The Adventures of an Innocent Man Trapped between Public Relations and the Axis*. New York: Doubleday, Doran & Company, Inc., 1944.

Trehan, Jyoti. *Veer Savarkar: Thought and Action of Vinayak Damodar Savarkar*. New Delhi: Deep & Deep Publications, 1991.

Tribhuvan Nath (ed.) *Freedom to Breathe: The Revolutionaries' Legacy to India*. Rajpura: Sarvodaya News Service, 1983.

Tripathi, Amles. *The Extremist Challenge: India between 1890 and 1910*. Calcutta, 1967.

Vaidya, Prem. *Savarkar, A Lifelong Crusader*. New Delhi: New Age International (P) Ltd, 1996.

Vajpeyi, J.N. *The Extremist Movement in India*. Allahabad: Chugh Publications, 1974.

Varma, Vishwanath Prasad. *The Life and Philosophy of Lokmanya Tilak*. Agra: Lakshmi Narain Agarwal, n.d.

Vartak, Shridhar Raghunath. *Swatantryaveer Savarkaranchi Prabhaval*. Nasik, S.R.Vartak, 1972.

----. *Bhaartiya Swatantryache Ranazunzar*, n.d.

Veer, Peter van der. *Religious Nationalism: Hindus and Muslims in India*. Berkeley, CA: University of California Press, 1994.

Verma, Shiv (ed.). *Bhagat Singh on the Path of Liberation*. Chennai: Bharathi Puthakalaya. 2007.

Vidwans, M.D. (Ed.). *Letters of Lokmanya Tilak*. Poona: Kesari Prakashan, 1966.

Virmani, Arundhati. *A National Flag for India: Rituals, Nationalism and the Politics of Sentiment*. Ranikhet: Permanent Black, 2008.

Visram, Rozina. *Asians in Britain: 400 Years of History*. London; Sterling, Va.: Pluto Press, 2002.

Wagle, N.K. (Ed.) *Writers, Editors, Reformers: Social and Political Transformations of Maharashtra 1830-1930*. New Delhi: Manohar, 1999.

Waraich, Malwinderjit Singh and Gurudev Singh Sidhu (eds.) *The Hanging of Bhagat Singh, Vol 3: Confessions, Statements and Other Documents*. Chandigarh: Unistar, 2007.

----. *Jail Note Book of Shaheed Bhagat Singh*. Unistar Books, 2016.

Ward, Alan. J. *The Easter Rising: Revolution and Irish Nationalism*, Wheeling, IL: Harlan Davidson, 1980.

Wardlaw, Grant. *Political Terrorism: Theory, Tactics and Counter-Measures*. Cambridge: Cambridge University Press, 1982.

Wasti, Syed Razi. *Lord Minto and the Indian Nationalist Movement, 1905 to 1910*. Lahore: People's Pub. House, 1976.

Wedderburn, William Bart. *Allan Octavian Hume, C.B.: Father of the Indian National Congress, 1829 to 1912*. London, 1913.

Wilkinson, Paul. *Political Terrorism*. New York: Macmillan, 1976.

Wilson, J. *Indian Caste Vol. II*. Bombay; Edinburgh and London, 1877.

Woods, Philip. "The Montagu-Chelmsford Reforms (1919): A Re-Assessment." South Asia: *Journal of Asian Studies* 25–42.

Wolpert, Stanley. *Tilak and Gokhale: Revolution and Reform in the Making of Modern India*. Berkeley: University of California Press, 1961.

----. *Gandhi's Passion: The Life & Legacy of Mahatma Gandhi*. Oxford University Press, 2001.

----. *Jinnah of Pakistan*. Oxford University Press, 1984.

Yar Jung, Nazir (ed.). *The Pakistan Issue*. Lahore: Sh. Muhammad Ashraf, 1943.

Zaidi, A.M. (ed.), The Demand for Pakistan. *Evolution of Muslim Political Thought in India*, Vol.5, New Delhi: S. Chand Company, 1978.

Zavos, John. *The Emergence of Hindu Nationalism in India*. New Delhi; New York: Oxford University Press, 2000.

Zavos, John, Andrew Wyatt, and Vernon Marston Hewitt. *The Politics of Cultural Mobilization in India*. New Delhi: Oxford University Press, 2004.

Index

(Sampath, Vikram. Savarkar: A CONTESTED LEGACY 1924–1966.
Gurugram: 2021/22052021)

Batlivala, S.S. 343
Battle of Panipat 100, 536
Bedi, Baba Gurubaksh Singh 35
Behere 202
Belgaum 23, 155, 468
Bengal Hindu Mahasabha 275
Bengal Provincial Hindu Sabha 112,
    345, 522
Bengal relief programme 389
Beretta 465–67, 479, 481
Bhabha, Covesji Hormusji 426
Bhagalpur 28, 305–14, 322, 361, 415
Bhagalpur Affair 305–15
Bhagnagar (Hyderabad) 207–15,
    415
Bhagur 11–13, 185
Bhagwat, B.N. 289, 501, 524
Bhandari, A.N. 53
Bhandaris 49, 53, 272, 512
Bharat Dharma Mahamandal 32
Bharucha 476
Bhatkal, Snehal 555
Bhat, R.M. 5
Bhatta, Kumarila 552
Bhatt, A.R. 147
Bhave, P.B. 7
Bhide, A.S. 178, 386
Bhide, Madhavrao 377, 386, 473
Bhonsle, Raje Laxmanrao 38
Bhopal State Hindusabha 275
Bhopatkar, Bhaskar Balwant 40, 58,
    61, 186, 515–16
Bhopatkar, L.B. 187, 189, 193, 199,
    213, 223, 226–27, 277, 300, 346,
    370, 394, 404, 406, 431, 474, 487,
    490, 508, 514–16, 519, 524
'bhrashtikaran' 30; *see also*
    'shuddhikaran'
Bhuskute, Vinayakrao 58
Bible 84, 127, 329, 529
Bicameral legislatures 140, 172

Bihar Hindu Mahasabha 231, 305,
    308–9, 312, 315, 373
Bijapur prison 1
Birkenhead, Lord 133
Birla, G.D. 240, 380
Birla House 440, 456–62, 465, 467,
    477–78
Birla, J.K. 241, 373–74, 445, 499
Birze, Vasudeorao, writings of 37
Bismil, Ramprasad 126
Bobde, Sharad 567
Boer War 136–37
Bole, C.K. 56, 62
Bole, Rao 289
Bole, S.K. 288
Bombay 15–17, 99, 101, 112, 114,
    153–55, 157–58, 175–76, 180–82,
    184–85, 189–90, 201–2, 240–41,
    311, 355–56, 409, 421–22, 436,
    445–46, 450–52, 454–56, 460,
    464, 474–75, 478–81, 483–84,
    508–9, 535, 559–60, 563–65;
    cycle procession in 332
Bombay High Court 24–25, 55, 470,
    525, 567
Bombay Pradesh Congress Committee
    182
Bombay Provincial Hindu Mahasabha
    347, 474
Bombay Public Security Measures Act
    1947 475
Bombay University 444; withdrawing
    BA degree of Savarkar 6
Border Commission 437
Bordolai, Gopinath 431
Bose-League Pact 305
Bose, Rash Behari 158, 191–92,
    200, 235–36, 241, 265–66, 348,
    418–19, 422
Bose, Sarat Chandra 296, 302,
    426